ECONOMICS

Paul R. Gregory
University of Houston

Roy J. Ruffin
University of Houston

 HarperCollins*CollegePublishers*

To Elizabeth Gregory and Blanche Ruffin

Senior Acquisitions Editor: Bruce Kaplan
Project Coordination and Text Design: York Production Services
Cover Design: Ed Smith Design
Production Manager: Kewal Sharma
Compositor: York Production Services
Printer and Binder: R. R. Donnelley and Sons Company
Cover Printer: Lehigh Press

Economics

Library of Congress Cataloging-in-Publication Data

Gregory, Paul R.
    Economics / Paul R. Gregory, Roy J. Ruffin.
        p.   cm.
    Includes indexes.
    ISBN 0-673-99395-7
    ISBN 0-673-99041-9 (PBK.)
    1. Economics.   I. Ruffin, Roy.   II. Title.
HB171.5.G8245   1993
330—dc20   93-37143
                                                       CIP

9   8   7   6   5   4   3   2   1

CONTENTS IN BRIEF

Part and Chapter Title	Part and Chapter Number in		
	Economics	**Macro-economics**	**Micro-economics**
THE BUILDING BLOCKS OF ECONOMICS	**One**	**One**	**One**
What Is Economics?	1	1	1
The Price System	2	2	2
Supply and Demand	3	3	3
Government and the Economy	4	4	4
MACROECONOMICS: THE ECONOMY AS A WHOLE	**Two**	**Two**	
Unemployment, Inflation, and the Business Cycle	5	5	
Measuring Gross Domestic Product	6	6	
Aggregate Demand and Supply	7	7	
The Keynesian Income-Expenditure Model	8	8	
MACROECONOMICS PROBLEMS AND POLICIES	**Three**	**Three**	
Fiscal Policy and National Debt	9	9	
Money and Prices	10	10	
Commercial Banking and the Federal Reserve	11	11	
Monetary Policy	12	12	
Inflation, Unemployment, and Stagflation	13	13	
Stabilization Policy	14	14	
THE GLOBAL ECONOMY	**Four**	**Four**	
Productivity, Growth, and Development	15	15	
International Trade and Protection	16	16	20
The International Monetary System	17	17	

Part and Chapter Title	Part and Chapter Number in		
	Economics	**Macro-economics**	**Micro-economics**
MICROECONOMICS AND THE PRODUCT MARKETS	**Five**		**Two**
Elasticity of Demand and Supply	18		5
Demand and Utility	19		6
Business Firms, Information, and Contracts	20		7
Costs and Productivity	21		8
Perfect Competition	22		9
Monopoly	23		10
Oligopoly and Monopolistic Competition	24		11
Regulation, Deregulation, and Antitrust	25		12
The Economics of Agriculture	26		13
FACTOR MARKETS	**Six**		**Three**
Factor Markets	27		14
Labor Markets	28		15
Labor Unions	29		16
Interest, Rent, and Profit	30		17
Income Distribution and Poverty	31		18
ISSUES IN ECONOMICS	**Seven**	**Four**	**Four**
Environmental Economics and Market Failure	32		19
Capitalism and Socialism	33	18	

CONTENTS

PART ONE

THE BUILDING BLOCKS OF ECONOMICS 1

CHAPTER 1   What Is Economics?   2

Scarcity and Choice   3
  The Law of Scarcity ▪ Scarcity and Allocation

Economic Systems   4

Opportunity Costs   5

Resources   6

Definition of Economics   7

The Production-Possibilities Frontier   7
  The Law of Increasing Costs ▪ Efficiency ▪ The *Ceteris Paribus* or "Other Things Equal" Assumption

Microeconomics and Macroeconomics   11
  Microeconomics ▪ Macroeconomics

Positive and Normative Economics   12
  Positive Economics ▪ Normative Economics

Policy Focus   14

Gallery of Economists   15

Chapter Summary   15

EXAMPLE 1   Opportunity Cost and Orbital Slots in Outer Space   5
EXAMPLE 2   Hawaiian Pineapples and the Production-Possibilities
            Frontier   9

APPENDIX 1   Reading Graphs   18

The Value of Graphs   19
    Positive and Negative Relationships   ▪   Graphs Show Relationships and Display
    Data Efficiently   ▪   Shifts in Graphs

Understanding Slope   21
    Straight Lines   ▪   Curvilinear Relationships   ▪   Scatter Diagrams

Areas of Rectangles   27

Appendix Summary   27

CHAPTER 2   The Price System   29

The Circular Flow of Economic Activity   30

The Economic Problem   30
    What?   ▪   How?   ▪   For Whom?

Relative Prices and Money Prices   32
    Prices in the Land of Markkas

Calculating Relative Prices   33

The Principle of Substitution   34

Property Rights   34

The Price System as a Coordinating Mechanism   35
    The Invisible Hand   ▪   Equilibrium

How the Price System Decides What, How, and For Whom   36

Specialization   37
    Specialization and Exchange   ▪   Specialization and Productivity   ▪
    Specialization and Money

Transaction Costs and Information Costs   41

Policy Focus   43

Chapter Summary   44

EXAMPLE 1   The Decline of IBM and the Principle of Substitution   35
EXAMPLE 2   The Invisible Hand: The Paradox of Progress   38
EXAMPLE 3   How Transaction Costs Limit Exchange: Return Airline
            Tickets   42

GALLERY OF ECONOMISTS   Adam Smith (1723–1790)   32

━━━

C H A P T E R 3   Supply and Demand   46

Markets   47
    Types of Markets ▪ Perfectly Competitive Markets

Demand   49
    The Law of Demand ▪ The Demand Curve ▪ Factors That Cause the Demand
    Curve to Shift

Supply   54
    The Supply Curve ▪ Factors That Cause the Supply Curve to Shift

Equilibrium of Supply and Demand   58
    What the Market Accomplishes

Changes in the Equilibrium Price   60
    Change in Demand (or Supply) Versus Change in Quantity Demanded (or
    Supplied) ▪ The Effects of Changes in Supply and Demand ▪ ·Simultaneous
    Changes in Supply and Demand

Unconventional Use of Supply and Demand   63

Policy Focus   66

Chapter Summary   67

EXAMPLE 1   M&Ms and the Law of Demand   50
EXAMPLE 2   Shifts in Demand: Wine, Health, and Recession   53

GALLERY OF ECONOMISTS   Alfred Marshall (1842–1924)   48

━━━

C H A P T E R 4   Government and the Economy   70

Government Spending   71
    Types of Government Spending ▪ Size of Government ▪ Shares of Federal,
    State, and Local Governments

Taxes   74
    Efficiency, Fairness, and Social Goals ▪ Principles of Fairness ▪ Incidence of
    Taxation: Who Actually Pays? ▪ Progressive and Regressive Taxes

Government Surpluses and Deficits   78

Reasons for Government Action   81
    Monopoly ▪ Externalities ▪ Public Goods ▪ Inequality ▪ Macroeconomic
    Instability

Evaluating Government Resource Allocation   83
    The Market Test ▪ The Rationality of Public Choices

Policy Focus   86

Chapter Summary   86

EXAMPLE 1   The U.S. Income Tax: A Brief History   80
EXAMPLE 2   Sugar: Special Interests and Logrolling   85

GALLERY OF ECONOMISTS   James Buchanan (1919–   )   72

PART TWO

MACROECONOMICS: THE ECONOMY AS A WHOLE 89

CHAPTER 5 Unemployment, Inflation, and the Business Cycle 90

Macroeconomic Issues 91

Unemployment 91
Three Labor Market Classifications ▪ The Unemployment Rate ▪ Types of Unemployment ▪ Labor Market Search ▪ Full Employment ▪ Trends in Unemployment

Inflation 96
Measuring Inflation ▪ Trends in Inflation ▪ Two Types of Inflation ▪ Why People Fear Inflation

Stagflation 102

Business Cycles 105
The Four Phases of the Business Cycle ▪ Business Cycles and the World Economy

Chapter Summary 108

Policy Focus 109

EXAMPLE 1 How Inflation Redistributes Income: Wages and Inflation 103
EXAMPLE 2 Stop-and-Go Policies: The Dance Between Inflation and Unemployment 105

GALLERY OF ECONOMISTS John Maynard Keynes (1883–1946) 92

CHAPTER 6 Measuring Gross Domestic Product 111

National-Income Accounting 112
The Circular Flow ▪ A Simple Example ▪ Gross Domestic Product: Definition

Gross Domestic Product: The Sum of Output or Income 115
The Sum of Final Expenditures ▪ GDP as the Sum of Incomes

Real GDP 120

From GDP to Disposable Income 120

Saving Equals Investment 123

Omissions from GDP 124
Nonmarketed Goods and Services ▪ Illegal Activities ▪ The Value of Leisure ▪ Economic "Bads" and Measures of Economic Welfare

Policy Focus   128

Chapter Summary   128

EXAMPLE 1   How the Commerce Department Ensures the Security and Neutrality of
            GDP Estimates   116
EXAMPLE 2   Foreign Saving as a Source of Investment Finance   125
EXAMPLE 3   GDP in International Perspective   127

GALLERY OF ECONOMISTS   Simon Kuznets (1901–1985)   113

CHAPTER 7   Aggregate Demand and Supply   131

Aggregate Demand   132
    The Slope of the Aggregate Demand Curve ▪ The Conditions of Aggregate
    Demand

Aggregate Supply   136
    Wage Rigidities ▪ Aggregate Supply in the Short Run

Short-Run Equilibrium   138

Changes in Equilibrium Output and Prices   138
    Supply Shocks ▪ Shifts in Aggregate Demand

Inflationary and Deflationary Gaps   140

Long-Run Equilibrium: The Self-Correcting Mechanism   143
    The Automatic Removal of a Deflationary Gap ▪ The Automatic Removal of an
    Inflationary Gap

Policy Focus   145

Chapter Summary   146

EXAMPLE 1   Is Wage Flexibility Increasing?   137
EXAMPLE 2   Supply Shocks: The Energy Crisis   141
EXAMPLE 3   Inflationary and Deflationary Gaps   143

GALLERY OF ECONOMISTS   John R. Hicks (1904–1989)   134

CHAPTER 8   The Keynesian Income-Expenditure Model   149

Two Views of Macroeconomics   150

Classical Macroeconomics   150
    Say's Law ▪ *Laissez Faire* Policy

The Transition to Keynesian Macroeconomics   153
    The Great Depression ▪ Fixed Prices in the Keynesian Model

The Income-Expenditure Approach   155
    Consumption, Income, and Saving ▪ The Marginal Propensities ▪ Other
    Factors That Affect Consumption

Equilibrium Expenditures   160
    Desired Aggregate Expenditures ▪ Realization of Desired Aggregate
    Expenditures ▪ Saving and Investment ▪ Two Definitions of Equilibrium Are
    One

Multipliers 165

Policy Focus 168

Chapter Summary 168

EXAMPLE 1   Images from the Great Depression 154
EXAMPLE 2   The Classical and Keynesian Models and the Great Depression 156

GALLERY OF ECONOMISTS   James Tobin (1918–   ) 152

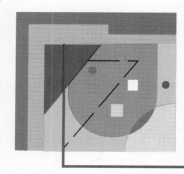

PART THREE

MACROECONOMIC PROBLEMS AND POLICIES 173

CHAPTER 9   Fiscal Policy and National Debt 174

Policy Goals 175

Automatic Stabilizers Versus Discretionary Policy 175
   Automatic Stabilizers ▪ Discretionary Fiscal Policy

Fiscal Policy and Deficits 178
   Facts and Trends

The Full-Employment Deficit 181

The Effectiveness of Fiscal Policy 183
   Lags in Fiscal Policy ▪ Permanent Income ▪ Crowding Out ▪ National Debt

Internal Versus External Debt 187
   Deficits, Inflation, and Interest Rates ▪ Problems of Deficit Reduction

Policy Focus 192

Chapter Summary 193

EXAMPLE 1   Supply-Side Economics 185
EXAMPLE 2   The Burden of the Debt on Different Generations 188

GALLERY OF ECONOMISTS   Franco Modigliani (1919–   ) 176

CHAPTER 10   Money and Prices 195

The Functions of Money 196
   Money as a Medium of Exchange ▪ Money as a Unit of Value ▪ Money as a Store of Value

The Supply of Money 199
   Types of Money ▪ Definitions of Money Supply

The Relationship Between Money and Prices   203

The Classical Quantity Theory of Money ▪ Velocity of Circulation ▪ The Equation of Exchange ▪ Changes in Money Supply and Prices ▪ The Money Sector and the Real Sector ▪ Aggregate Supply and Aggregate Demand in the Quantity Theory

Policy Focus   207

Chapter Summary   208

EXAMPLE 1   The Stone Money of the Island of Yap   198
EXAMPLE 2   Does Anything Back the Dollar?   201

GALLERY OF ECONOMISTS   Irving Fisher (1867–1947)   197

CHAPTER 11   Commercial Banking and the Federal Reserve   210

Financial Intermediation   211

Commercial Banks   211
How Commercial Banks Make Profits ▪ Balance Sheets

The Federal Reserve System   214
Functions of the Fed ▪ The Structure of the Federal Reserve System ▪ Bank Regulation ▪ Reserve Requirements ▪ Borrowing from the Fed ▪ The Federal Open Market Committee ▪ The Monetary Base

How Banks Create Money   218
Money and Debt ▪ Multiple-Deposit Creation ▪ The Deposit Multiplier ▪ Money-Supply Expansion in the Real World ▪ The Money Multiplier

Federal Reserve Policy   224
Open-Market Operations ▪ Changes in Reserve Requirements ▪ Changes in the Discount Rate

Policy Focus   227

Chapter Summary   227

EXAMPLE 1   The Problem of Bank Failures   216
EXAMPLE 2   Stock Market Crashes and the Money Supply: Where Did All the Money Go?   223

GALLERY OF ECONOMISTS   Knut Wicksell (1851–1926)   212

CHAPTER 12   Monetary Policy   230

Instruments of Monetary Policy   231
Open-Market Operations ▪ The Discount Rate ▪ Reserve-Requirement Policy

Keynesian Monetary Policy   233
Bond Prices and Interest Rates ▪ Money and Interest Rates ▪ How Money Affects Aggregate Demand

Monetary Policy and Deflationary and Inflationary Gaps   236

The Complexities of Monetary Policy   238
Target Interest Rates or the Money Supply? ▪ Interest-Rate Targeting ▪ Money-Supply Targeting: 1979–1982 ▪ Recent Fed Policy

Problems of Monetary Policy 240
    Problems of Controlling the Money Supply ▪ Knowing the Money Multiplier ▪
    The Problem of Lags

The Independence of the Fed 243

Policy Focus 244

Chapter Summary 244

EXAMPLE 1   The Policy Directive of the FOMC 241
EXAMPLE 2   Money and Unintended Consequences 242

GALLERY OF ECONOMISTS   Milton Friedman (1912–   ) 232

CHAPTER 1 3   Inflation, Unemployment, and
                Stagflation 247

Inflation 248
    Demand-Side and Supply-Side Inflation ▪ Monetary Growth and Sustained
    Inflation ▪ Cases of Supply-Side Inflation ▪ Inflation and Interest Rates ▪
    How Inflationary Expectations Are Formed ▪ The Wage/Price Spiral

Unemployment 255
    Matching People to Jobs ▪ The Long-Run Rise in Unemployment

Stagflation 257
    The Phillips Curve ▪ The Breakdown of the Phillips Curve ▪ The New Phillips
    Curve ▪ Upward Shifts of Short-Run Phillips Curves ▪ Understanding the
    Swirls

Policy Choices 261
    Lowering Inflationary Expectations ▪ The Unemployment Costs of Lowering
    Inflation ▪ Gradualism ▪ Human-Resource Policies

Policy Focus 265

Chapter Summary 265

EXAMPLE 1   Inflation, Death, and Taxes 252
EXAMPLE 2   The Nixon Wage/Price Controls 263

GALLERY OF ECONOMISTS   A. W. Phillips (1914–1975) 250

CHAPTER 1 4   Stabilization Policy 268

The Policy Options 269
    Activism ▪ Nonactivism ▪ Self-Correction Versus Demand Management

Policy Instruments and Activism 271
    Monetary Policy ▪ Fiscal Policy ▪ Matching Policies to Macroeconomic Goals

The Case for Activism 274
    The Costs of Lost Output ▪ Activism Versus Nonactivism

The Case for Nonactivism 277
    The Difficulty of Devising Activist Policy ▪ The Counterproductive Effects of
    Activism ▪ Rational Expectations Theory and Activist Policy

A Reduction in Differences? 280

Activism as the Choice of U.S. Policymakers 281

Policy Focus 282

Chapter Summary 282

EXAMPLE 1   Economic Policymaking 273
EXAMPLE 2   The Policy Blunders of the 1930s 279

GALLERY OF ECONOMISTS   Robert Lucas (1937–   ) 270

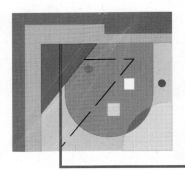

PART FOUR

THE GLOBAL ECONOMY 285

CHAPTER 15   Productivity, Growth, and Development 286

Economic Growth 287

The Haves and the Have Nots 289

Economic Growth of the Haves 290
    Extensive and Intensive Growth ▪ The Role of Productivity ▪ Labor Productivity

Why the LDCs Are Poor 295
    The Classical Growth Model ▪ The Sources of LDC Poverty ▪ Signs of
    Progress? ▪ Trade Policies ▪ External Assistance

Policy Focus 302

Chapter Summary 303

EXAMPLE 1   Are Economic Growth Rates Increasing? 288
EXAMPLE 2   Productivity as a Source of Growth: World Experience 294

GALLERY OF ECONOMISTS   Thomas R. Malthus (1766–1834) 287

CHAPTER 16   International Trade and Protection 305

The Reasons for International Trade 306

The United States in World Trade 306
    The Volume of U.S. Trade ▪ U.S. Exports and Imports

The Law of Comparative Advantage 307
    The Case of Self-Sufficiency ▪ The Case of International Trade

The Gains from Trade 313

Protectionism 314

Trade Barriers 315

Tariffs ▪ Import Quotas ▪ Voluntary Export Restraints ▪ Other Nontariff
Barriers

The Case Against Protection 318
Measuring Benefits and Costs ▪ Why Tariffs Impose Net Costs ▪ The
Explanation for Tariffs

U.S. Trade Policies 321
The Trade-Agreements Program and GATT

Policy Focus 323

Chapter Summary 324

EXAMPLE 1 U.S. Comparative Advantage 315
EXAMPLE 2 Measuring the Costs of Protection 321

GALLERY OF ECONOMISTS David Ricardo (1772–1823) 307

CHAPTER 17 The International Monetary System 326

International Monetary Mechanisms 327
The Foreign-Exchange Market ▪ Floating Exchange Rates ▪ Market Forces
Affecting the Exchange Rate ▪ Fixed Exchange Rates and the Gold Standard

The Balance of Payments and International Capital Movements 333
The Balance of Payments ▪ International Capital Movements ▪ The U.S.
Trade Deficit

The Evolution of the International Monetary System 336
The Breakdown of the Gold Standard ▪ The Bretton Woods System ▪ The
Fall of Bretton Woods ▪ The Current International Monetary System

Policy Focus 340

Chapter Summary 341

EXAMPLE 1 Competitiveness 337
EXAMPLE 2 The European Monetary System 339

GALLERY OF ECONOMISTS Harry G. Johnson (1923–1977) 328

PART FIVE

MICROECONOMICS AND THE PRODUCT MARKETS 343

CHAPTER 18 Elasticity of Demand and Supply 344

The Price Elasticity of Demand 345
Calculating Price Elasticity of Demand ▪ Elastic and Inelastic

Demand ▪ Elasticity and Slope ▪ Perfectly Elastic or Perfectly Inelastic Demand Curves ▪ Determinants of Price Elasticity of Demand

The Income Elasticity of Demand 352

The Cross-Price Elasticity of Demand 353

The Price Elasticity of Supply 353
Perfectly Elastic and Perfectly Inelastic Supply Curves ▪ Elasticity of Supply in Three Time Periods

Chapter Summary 357

Policy Focus 358

EXAMPLE 1 Vanity Plates and College Tuition: When Do Higher Prices Yield More Revenue? 349
EXAMPLE 2 Elasticities: Theory and Practice 356

GALLERY OF ECONOMISTS Paul A. Samuelson (1915–   ) 346

CHAPTER 19 Demand and Utility 362

Rational Consumer Behavior 363

Consumer Preferences 363
Marginal Utility ▪ The Law of Diminishing Marginal Utility

Marginal Utility and the Law of Demand 365
The Law of Demand ▪ Income and Substitution Effects

Market Demand 371

Chapter Summary 373

Policy Focus 372

EXAMPLE 1 Why Diamonds Cost More Than Water 366
EXAMPLE 2 Marginal Utility, "All You Can Eat for $10," and the Daily Newspaper 370

GALLERY OF ECONOMISTS Walter Stanley Jevons (1835–1882) 364

APPENDIX 19 Indifference Curves and Demand 376

Consumer Preferences 377
The Law of the Diminishing Marginal Rate of Substitution ▪ The Budget Line

Consumer Equilibrium 380

The Effect of an Income Change 382

The Effect of a Price Change 382

Appendix Summary 385

CHAPTER 20 Business Firms, Information, and Contracts 387

Business Firms and Their Goals 388

Forms of Business Organization   389
   Sole Proprietorships ▪ Partnerships ▪ Corporations

Principals and Agents   394
   Contracts and Information Costs ▪ Opportunistic Behavior

Intermediaries and the Information Business   398
   The Role of Intermediaries ▪ The Value of Intermediaries

Policy Focus   399

Chapter Summary   400

EXAMPLE 1   Unlimited Liability and Lloyds of London   394
EXAMPLE 2   Carl Icahn, Texaco, and the Principal/Agent Problem   397
EXAMPLE 3   Moral Hazard and Contracts   398

GALLERY OF ECONOMISTS   Adolf A. Berle (1895–1971)   389

APPENDIX 20   Corporate Finance and Financial Markets   403

How Corporations Raise Capital   404
   Present Value ▪ Bond Prices ▪ Stock Issues ▪ Stock Markets ▪ The Efficient Stock Market Hypothesis ▪ Stock Prices and Resource Allocation

Appendix Summary   411

CHAPTER 21   Costs and Productivity   413

Opportunity Costs   414
   Explicit and Implicit Costs ▪ Opportunity Costs as the Sum of Explicit and Implicit Costs ▪ Economic Profits ▪ Average/Marginal Rules

Cost Curves in the Short Run   417
   Short Run and Long Run ▪ Fixed and Variable Costs ▪ The Law of Diminishing Returns ▪ Marginal and Average Costs ▪ The Cost Curves

Long-Run Costs   426
   Shifts in Cost Curves ▪ The Long-Run Cost Curve ▪ Economies and Diseconomies of Scale

Chapter Summary   429

Policy Focus   430

EXAMPLE 1   Air Force Pilots, Commercial Pilots, and Opportunity Costs   416
EXAMPLE 2   Why Economic Decisions Are Based on Marginal Costs   423
EXAMPLE 3   The Do-It-Yourself Car: Economies of Scale   429

GALLERY OF ECONOMISTS   Johann Heinrich von Thunen (1783–1850)   415

CHAPTER 22   Perfect Competition   433

The Four Market Models   434

Characteristics of Perfect Competition   434
   The Conditions for Perfect Competition ▪ The Firm and the Industry

The Short-Run Supply Curve   437
    Selecting Output to Maximize Profit ▪ Three Cases ▪ The Industry Supply
    Curve ▪ Short-Run Equilibrium

Long-Run Supply   446
    Economic Profit Attracts Resources ▪ Entry and Exit ▪ Characteristics of
    Long-Run Equilibrium ▪ The Long-Run Industry Supply Curve

Chapter Summary   451

Policy Focus   452

EXAMPLE 1   Competition and World Trade   436
EXAMPLE 2   Competition, Freedom of Entry, and One-Hour Photo Processing   451

GALLERY OF ECONOMISTS   Leon Walras (1834–1910)   435

CHAPTER 23   Monopoly   455

Characteristics of Monopoly   456
    Definition of Monopoly ▪ Limitations on Monopoly Power ▪ Barriers to Entry

How Monopolists Maximize Profits   458
    Price and Marginal Revenue ▪ Monopoly Equilibrium in the Short Run ▪ The
    Loss-Minimizing Monopolist ▪ Monopoly Profits in the Long Run ▪ Price
    Discrimination

Monopoly and Efficiency   466
    The Case of Perfect Competition ▪ Monopoly and Contrived Scarcity ▪
    Monopoly-Profit-Seeking Behavior ▪ Monopoly and Innovation

Policy Focus   470

Chapter Summary   471

EXAMPLE 1   What Price for a Cancer Cure?   461
EXAMPLE 2   Intel's Microprocessor Monopoly   465
EXAMPLE 3   Price Discrimination: Manufacturer's Coupons   466

GALLERY OF ECONOMISTS   Joan Robinson (1903–1983)   457

CHAPTER 24   Oligopoly and Monopolistic
                       Competition   473

Monopolistic Competition   474
    Characteristics of Monopolistic Competition ▪ Profit Maximization in the Short
    Run ▪ Monopolistic Competition in the Long Run ▪ Advertising, Brand
    Names, and Product Differentiation

Oligopoly   478

Determinants of Concentration   479
    Barriers to Entry Revisited ▪ Measuring Concentration

Oligopoly Theory   481
    Mutual Interdependence ▪ The Prisoners' Dilemma ▪ The Oligopolist's
    Dilemma ▪ Kinked Demand ▪ Oligopoly Coordination ▪ Obstacles to
    Collusion

Oligopoly and Efficiency   489

Policy Focus   490

Chapter Summary   491

EXAMPLE 1   Tit-for-Tat and the Prisoners' Dilemma   482
EXAMPLE 2   Yakutia Diamonds Threaten the DeBeers Cartel   487

GALLERY OF ECONOMISTS   Edward Hastings Chamberlin (1899–1967)   475

CHAPTER 25   Regulation, Deregulation, and Antitrust   493

Regulation   494
   The Scope of Regulation ▪ Regulation of Prices ▪ Regulatory Lag ▪ The
   Effects of Regulation

Deregulation   498
   Deregulation Legislation ▪ The Results of Deregulation

Antitrust Law   501
   The Sherman Act of 1890 ▪ The Clayton Act and the Federal Trade Commission
   Act, 1914 ▪ Other Antitrust Legislation ▪ Interpretation of the Sherman Act

Mergers   504

Do We Need Antitrust Laws?   506

Policy Focus   507

Chapter Summary   508

EXAMPLE 1   Who Should Pay the Cost of Nuclear Power?   497
EXAMPLE 2   Does Regulation Protect the Consumer or the Regulated Company?   499
EXAMPLE 3   Coke, Pepsi, Dr. Pepper, and Seven-Up   505

GALLERY OF ECONOMISTS   George J. Stigler (1911–1992)   495

CHAPTER 26   The Economics of Agriculture   510

The Business of Farming   511
   Facts and Figures ▪ Farming and Competition

Trends in Farm Prices and Farm Incomes   512
   Farm Prices Fluctuate More Than Other Prices ▪ Declining Relative Prices

The Declining Share of Agriculture   516

The Agricultural Crisis of the 1980s   517

Speculation and Futures Markets   519

Government Farm Programs   520
   Price Supports ▪ Direct Payments to Farmers ▪ Supply Control Programs

Policy Focus   522

Chapter Summary   523

EXAMPLE 1   Price Elasticities of Demand in Agriculture   513
EXAMPLE 2   How Productive Are American Farms?   517

GALLERY OF ECONOMISTS   Ernst Engel (1821–1896)   512

PART SIX

FACTOR MARKETS 525

CHAPTER 27   Factor Markets 526

The Circular Flow Diagram 527

The Two Faces of the Firm 527
Price Making and Price Taking in the Factor Market ▪ Marginal Factor Cost

The Firm's Demand for Factors of Production 532
Derived Demand ▪ Joint Determination of Factor Demand ▪ Marginal Revenue Product

Profit Maximization 535
The $MRP = MFC$ Rule ▪ The Demand Curve for a Factor

Cost Minimization 537

The Marginal-Productivity Theory of Income Distribution 537
Marginal Productivity and Factor Incomes

Policy Focus 540

Chapter Summary 541

EXAMPLE 1   Derived Demand: Air Travel, and Aircraft Leases 533
EXAMPLE 2   Paying for Merchandise 538

GALLERY OF ECONOMISTS   John Bates Clark (1847–1938) 528

CHAPTER 28   Labor Markets 543

How Labor Differs From Other Factors 544

Wages and Incentive Payments 544

The Demand for Labor 546
The Firm's Demand for Labor ▪ The Market Demand for Labor

The Labor Supply Curve 549

Labor-Market Equilibrium 549
Shifts in Labor Supply and Demand ▪ Factors Causing Shifts in Labor Demand and Supply Curves

Wage Structure 553
Compensating Wage Differentials ▪ Noncompeting Groups

Leisure and Household Production 555
Backward-Bending Labor Supply ▪ Opportunity Costs and Household Production

Policy Focus   557

Chapter Summary   558

EXAMPLE 1   First-Class Fares for Coach: The Principal/Agent Problem   546
EXAMPLE 2   Compensating Wage Differentials: Land Mine Disposal in
Kuwait   555

GALLERY OF ECONOMISTS   Gary Becker (1930–   )   545

CHAPTER 29   Labor Unions   561

What Is a Union?   562

Decline of Unionism   563

History of Unionism   564

Union Legislation   567

Union Objectives   568
How Unions Deal with the Tradeoff   ▪   Limitations of Labor Supply   ▪   Collective
Bargaining   ▪   Collective Bargaining with Monopsony
The Effect of Unions on Wages   574
Effect on Union Wages   ▪   Effect on Nonunion Wages

Policy Focus   575

Chapter Summary   577

EXAMPLE 1   Labor Unions in International Perspective   566
EXAMPLE 2   The Wage/Employment Tradeoff: A Union Strikes for Lower
Wages!   570

GALLERY OF ECONOMISTS   H. Gregg Lewis (1914–1992)   563

CHAPTER 30   Interest, Rent, and Profit   579

Capital and Interest   580
Capital and Saving   ▪   Credit Markets   ▪   The Rate of Interest   ▪   Interest-Rate
Determination   ▪   The Structure of Interest Rates

Rent   585
Pure Economic Rent   ▪   Economic Rent and Other Factors of Production

Profits   588
Sources of Economic Profits

Policy Focus   590

Chapter Summary   591

EXAMPLE 1   Interest Rates, Present Value, and Insulation   582
EXAMPLE 2   Babe Ruth and Economic Rents   588

GALLERY OF ECONOMISTS   Frank Knight (1885–1972)   581

CHAPTER 31   Income Distribution and Poverty   593

Measuring Income Inequality   594

Sources of Inequality   595
   Differences in People and in Jobs ▪ Chance and Inheritance ▪ Discrimination

Distributive Justice   601
   Natural Law ▪ Utilitarianism ▪ Rawlsian Equality

Government Policy and Income Distribution   604

Poverty   605
   Trends in Poverty ▪ Who Are the Poor?

Policy Focus   607

Chapter Summary   609

EXAMPLE 1   International Comparisons of Income Distributions   597
EXAMPLE 2   Chance, Luck, and Earnings: The Vietnam Draft Lottery   599
EXAMPLE 3   Christy Turlington: Fashion Model at $1.75 Million per Year   603

GALLERY OF ECONOMISTS   John Stuart Mill (1806–1873)   595

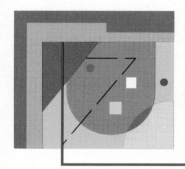

PART SEVEN

ISSUES IN ECONOMICS   613

CHAPTER 32   Environmental Economics and Market
             Failure   614

Externalities and Market Failure   615
   Redefining Property Rights ▪ Voluntary Agreements

Internalizing Externalities   618
   Government Action

Public Goods   620
   Nonrivalry ▪ Nonexclusion ▪ Free Riders

Externalities and Environment   622
   Optimal Abatement

Policy Focus   625

Chapter Summary   626

EXAMPLE 1   Classifying Selected Goods as Private Goods or Public Goods   623
EXAMPLE 2   Trading Pollution Rights   626

GALLERY OF ECONOMISTS   Ronald Harry Coase (1910–   )   616

CHAPTER 33   Capitalism and Socialism   629

Economic Systems   630
Property Rights ▪ Allocation Arrangements ▪ Incentive Systems

The Rise and Fall of Communist Socialism   633

Reasons for Failure   634
Incentives and Information ▪ Transition to a Market Economy

Policy Focus   637

Chapter Summary   638

EXAMPLE 1   Soviet Productivity and the Origins of Perestroika   635

GALLERY OF ECONOMISTS   Ludwig von Mises (1881–1973) and Karl Marx (1818–1883)   631

Glossary   641
Photo Credits   652
Index   653

Economics reflects our conviction that principles of economics texts have become too long and encyclopedic. *Economics* is meant to teach students the most important economic principles—not *every* principle and its qualifications—and how these concepts can be applied to the real world in which we live. We have sought to provide a nontechnical, modern, policy-oriented text that can be covered in the normal-length course.

Economics meets three basic needs of first-time students of economics. First, it teaches the core theory of economics in an up-to-date format. Second, it addresses the key economic policy issues of the day, from growth and deficits to unemployment and international competition. Third, it teaches students to apply economics to the real world. Each chapter contains two or more real-world applications of theory to practice.

The emphasis on policy is achieved through a structural innovation. Each chapter begins with a "policy focus" to illustrate the policy issues that the chapter addresses. Each chapter ends with a "policy example" that applies the material of the chapter to a selected policy issue. This structure reinforces the importance of policy. This strengthens the student's interest in such policy issues as health-care reform, the independence of the Fed, balanced-budget amendments, and assistance to the former Soviet Union.

The "Doing Economics" sections at the end of each chapter, written by Jeffrey Parker of Reed College, challenge students to apply what they have learned in the chapter to a small project. The assignment poses an economic question and tells the student how and where to gather the information necessary to complete the assignment. In this way, students can test concepts they have learned and round out their understanding.

In recent years, many instructors have expressed a desire to teach macroeconomics using the tools of aggregate demand and supply entirely in place of the income-expenditure and multiplier approach of Keynes. *Economics* allows the instructor to follow either approach. The aggregate demand and aggregate supply chapter is placed before the Keynesian model. This placement allows the instructor either to go directly from aggregate demand and supply to the remaining macro chapters or to the Keynesian income-expenditure model.

ORGANIZATION

Economics is organized into seven parts. Part One (Chapters 1–4) introduces the building blocks of economics that should be learned before proceeding to the study of either macroeconomics or microeconomics. These chapters discuss scarcity, opportunity costs, the production-possibilities frontier, the law of comparative advantage, the price system, the laws of supply and demand, and the role of government. An appendix to Chapter 1 explains how to read graphs. From Part One, the instructor can move either to macroeconomics (Chapters 5–17) or to microeconomics (Chapters 18–33).

The development of macroeconomic theory begins in Part Two with an outline of the basic concepts of unemployment and inflation (Chapter 5) and the basic principles of national-income accounting (Chapter 6). Chapter 7 covers the core of macroeconomic theory by introducing aggregate demand and aggregate supply. Chapter 8 covers Keynes's income-expenditure model and multipliers.

Part Three is devoted to problems and policies in macroeconomics, beginning with fiscal policy and national debt (Chapter 9), the monetary sector (Chapters 10–12), and ending with a discussion of the problems of stagflation and stabilization (Chapters 13–14).

Part Four examines the global economy by first examining the determinants of economic growth (Chapter 15) and then moving to the discussion of international economics in Chapters 16 and 17. Chapter 16 shows how the law of comparative advantage applies on an international scale and gives an analysis of protectionism. Chapter 17 studies the foreign exchange market, the balance of payments, and the problems of international monetary coordination.

Part Five begins with a study of the product markets (Chapters 18–26). Chapter 18 teaches price elasticities of demand and supply as well as income and cross-price elasticities of demand. Chapter 19 presents demand and utility (with an appendix on indifference curves for instructors desiring to give a more rigorous treatment). Business firms are studied in Chapter 20. Chapter 21 explains how costs and productivity are related. The standard market models—perfect competition, monopoly, oligopoly, and monopolist competition—are covered in Chapters 22–24. The problems of antitrust and agriculture conclude Part Five.

Factor markets are taught as a five-chapter unit in Part Six (Chapters 27–31). Chapter 27 presents a theoretical overview of the workings of factor markets, and Chapters 28–30 focus on particular markets. Chapter 31 considers the determinants of income distribution.

Part Seven is a two-chapter unit dealing with the broad issues of environmental economics (Chapter 32) and capitalism and socialism (Chapter 33).

SUGGESTIONS FOR COURSE PLANNING

This book is intended for the two-semester sequence in macroeconomics and microeconomics that is traditionally taught as a first- or second-year college course. The book is available in both single hardbound volume and macro/micro split softbound volumes. The single volume has only 33 chapters and can be adapted to an intensive one-semester or one-quarter course by selecting core chapters, as listed below. (Chapters with an asterisk can be included in a one-quarter course.) Because the book was written with the macro/micro splits in mind, the instructor who is using the single volume can teach either macro or micro first.

Introduction

  *1. What Is Economics?
  *2. The Price System

★3. Supply and Demand
　　　★4. Government and the Economy

Macroeconomics

　　　★5. Unemployment, Inflation, and the Business Cycle
　　　★6. Measuring Gross Domestic Product
　　　★7. Aggregate Demand and Aggregate Supply
　　　★8. The Keynesian Income-Expenditure Model
　　　★9. Fiscal Policy and National Debt
　　★10. Money and Prices
　　★11. Commercial Banking and the Federal Reserve
　　★12. Monetary Policy
　　★13. Inflation, Unemployment, and Stagflation
　　★14. Stabilization Policy
　　　16. International Trade and Protection
　　　17. The International Monetary System
　　　　　 Instructors who wish to eliminate the Keynesian model can do so by
　　　　　 dropping Chapter 8 and making proper adjustments in the chapter on
　　　　　 fiscal policy.

Microeconomics

　　★18. Elasticity of Demand and Supply
　　★19. Demand and Utility
　　★21. Costs and Productivity
　　★22. Perfect Competition
　　★23. Monopoly
　　　24. Oligopoly and Monopolistic Competition
　　★27. Factor Markets
　　★28. Labor Markets
　　　31. Income Distribution and Poverty
　　　32. Environmental Economics and Market Failure

SUPPLEMENTS

This book's supplements include an *Instructor's Manual, Study Guide,* and *Test Bank* (available in both print and computer form for the IBM-PC and compatibles).

　　The *Instructor's Manual,* prepared by Henry Thompson of Auburn University, is a valuable teaching aid because it supplies the instructor with examples and real-world illustrations in addition to those in the text. A chapter outline gives a brief overview of the material; it assists the instructor in preparing lecture outlines and in seeing the logical development of the chapter. Each chapter contains teaching hints designed to bring economic concepts to the student level, key points, examples, short-answer questions and problems, and answers to questions and problems in the text.

　　The *Study Guide,* prepared by Jeffrey Parker of Reed College, contains an extensive review section for each chapter/appendix. The "Key Graphs" subsection features important in-text graphs, along with a detailed explanation of the meaning of each. "Key Equations" takes important in-text equations and links the symbolic representation to the verbal explanation. "Preparing Yourself for This Chapter" informs students of prior theories or chapters that should be reviewed to better understand the chapter at hand. "Foundations for Future Chapters" indicates what material in the present chapter will be built upon in future chapters. Multiple-choice problems, true/false questions, essay questions, and more advanced challenge problems all teach as well as test. Full solutions are available.

The *Test Bank* contains 2,200 questions, mainly multiple choice, and some short-answer questions.

ACKNOWLEDGMENTS

We are deeply indebted to our colleagues at the University of Houston who had to bear with us in the writing of this book. Joel Sailors helped us with a number of the examples. John Antel, Richard Bean, Thomas Mayor, Irwin Collier, Janet Kohlhase, and David Papell gave us valuable advice on many pedagogical points. To Gary Smith of Pomona College, Calvin Siebert of the University of Iowa, and Allan Meltzer of Carnegie-Mellon University we are particularly grateful for sharing with us their vast knowledge of macroeconomic issues.

The following people from across the country reviewed the manuscript in various stages of preparation. To them it is impossible to express the depth of our appreciation for their suggestions and contributions.

Wesley F. Booth	San Antonio College
Gary Burbridge	Grand Rapids Junior College
Louis P. Cain	Loyola University, Chicago
John F. Dahlquist	College of Alameda
Jan L. Dauve	University of Missouri-Columbia
Bernard Davis	Morehead State University
Gregg E. Davis	Marshall University
Donald H. Farness	Oregon State University
Martin G. Giesbrecht	Economics Associates
Robert Charles Graham	The University of North Carolina, Charlotte
Cole Gustafson	North Dakota State University
Judy Hoagland	Roane State Community College
Keith R. Leeseberg	Manatee Community College
George A. Loughran, Jr.	San Jacinto College North
Robert Metts	University of Nevada, Reno
Michael S. Miller	DePaul University
Ravindra Parashar	Saint Mary's College
Timothy Payne	Shoreline Community College
Doug Pressel	Cochise College
Ronald Schuelke	Santa Rosa Junior College
B. Ted Stecker	North Hennepin Community College
Robert W. Thomas	Iowa State University

Paul R. Gregory
Roy J. Ruffin

Many students find economics a difficult subject because economics cannot be mastered through memorization. Economics relies on economic theories to explain real-world occurrences—such as why people buy less when prices rise or why increased government taxation may increase unemployment. An economic theory is simply a logical explanation of how the facts fit together in a particular way. If the theory were not logical, or if the theory failed to be confirmed by real-world facts, it would be readily discarded by economists.

The successful student will be the one who learns that economics is built upon a number of fairly simple and easy-to-understand propositions. These propositions and assumptions—that businesses seek to maximize profits or that consumers base their expenditure decisions on disposable income—form the building blocks upon which economics is based. These propositions are typically little more than common sense. If a major building block is missing, however, the whole structure can fall apart. To prevent the student from overlooking or forgetting a critical building block, we frequently engage in pedagogical review. In other words, when a new proposition is added to a theoretical structure, the underlying propositions are briefly reviewed.

Economics—like other academic disciplines—has its own vocabulary. Unlike the physical sciences, however, where the student is encountering terms for the first time, much of the vocabulary of economics—terms such as *efficiency, capital, stock, labor*—has a common usage that is already familiar to the student. Economists, however, use the vocabulary of economics in a very exact way, and often the common usage of a term is not the same as the economic usage. In this book, each key term appears in boldface type where it is first discussed in text. Immediately following the paragraph where the term first appears in boldface type, the formal, economic definition of the term is set off in color. At the end of each chapter is a list of all the key terms that have been boldfaced and given formal definitions in that chapter; a glossary at the end of the book contains all the definitions of key terms and gives the chapter number in which the term was defined.

Economics attempts to explain in a logical manner how the facts bind together. Modern developments have occurred because established theories were not doing a good job of explaining the world around us. Fortunately, the major building blocks of modern theory—that people attempt to anticipate the future, that rising prices motivate wealth holders to spend less, that people and businesses gather information and make decisions in a rational manner—rely on commonsense logic.

Economics is valuable only if it explains the real world. Economics should be able to answer very specific questions like: Why are there three major domestic producers of automobiles and hundreds or even thousands of producers of textiles? Why is there a positive association between the growth of the money supply and inflation? Why does the United States export computers and corn to the rest of the world? Why do restaurants rope off space during less busy hours? If Iowa corn land is the best land for growing corn, why is corn also grown in Texas while some land stands idle in Iowa? Why do interest rates rise when people expect the inflation rate to increase? What is the impact of the well-publicized government deficit? The successful student will be able to apply the knowledge he or she gains of real-world economic behavior to explain any number of events that have already occurred or are yet to occur.

In writing this book, we have made a conscious effort to present arguments and evidence on both sides of every economic controversy. We attempt to make a case for each distinct viewpoint, even if it would be more interesting and less complicated to come out strongly in one camp. We believe it is best to allow the student to keep an open mind at this very early stage in the study of economics.

This book contains a number of important learning aids.

1. The *Learning Objectives* that precede each chapter provide a brief overview of the important points to be learned in that chapter.
2. *Definitions* are set off in color following the paragraphs in which key terms are introduced in context.
3. *Key Ideas*—important economic principles or conclusions—appear in the margins.
4. *Boxed Examples* allow the student to appreciate how economic concepts apply in real-world settings, without disrupting the flow of the text, and supplement the numerous examples already found in the text discussions.
5. A *Chapter Summary* of the main points of each chapter is found at the end of each chapter.
6. *Key Terms* that were defined in color in the chapter are listed at the end of each chapter.
7. *Questions and Problems* that test the reader's understanding of the chapter following each chapter.
8. A *Glossary*—containing definitions of all key terms defined in color in chapters and listed in chapter "Key Terms" sections—appears at the end of the book. Each entry contains the complete economic definition as well as the number of the chapter where the term was first defined.
9. A thorough *Index* catalogs the names, concepts, terms, and topics covered in the book.
10. The *Doing Economics* sections are end-of-chapter assignments and projects concerning the theoretical material in that chapter.

The Building Blocks of Economics

P A R T   O N E

CHAPTER 1

What Is Economics?

APPENDIX 1

Reading Graphs

CHAPTER 2

The Price System

CHAPTER 3

Supply and Demand

CHAPTER 4

Government and the Economy

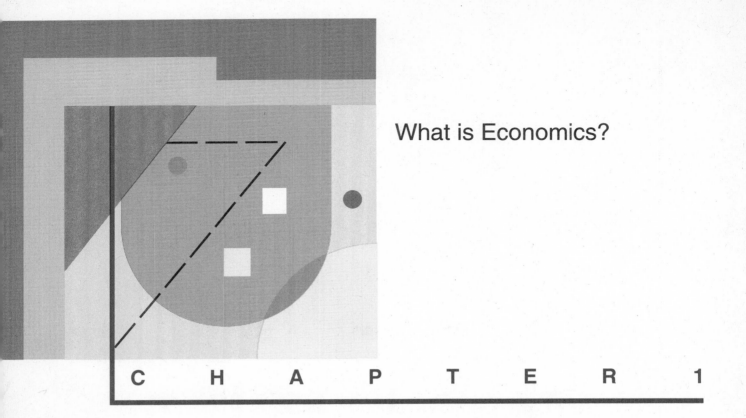

What is Economics?

CHAPTER FOCUS

Common expressions often reveal important truths. The expression, "There's no such thing as a free lunch," reveals a fundamental truth about economics. People are constantly being told there is indeed such a thing as a "free lunch." Unscrupulous companies promise unsuspecting small investors a "guaranteed" doubling of their money in one year. Tourists in vacation spots are promised a "free dinner and show" by peddlers of local condominium projects. Politicians promise unwitting voters that they can build new superhighways and have the best public health system in the world without an increase in taxes.

Everyone yearns for a "free lunch," but economics explains it doesn't exist. Goods are scarce; resources are scarce. If we want more of one thing, we must give up something of another. If the government wishes to enact one spending program, society must sacrifice something else. If we want the "free lunch and show" from the condominium salesperson, we must sit through irritating sales pitches and be pestered by annoying telephone calls for the next month. Small investors who expect a guaranteed doubling of their money find either that the investment is a fraud or that the chance of the money doubling is remote.

This chapter is about scarcity and choice, and why scarcity rules out free lunches. An understanding that there are no free lunches, and why, provides an important guide to policy. Later in this chapter, we apply the principles of scarcity and choice to explain why providing good medical care for all citizens, despite the claims of politicians and various interest groups, cannot be done on a "free lunch" basis. Each public policy must be examined in terms of its costs and benefits.

After studying this chapter, you will be able to:

- Define scarcity and how scarcity dictates hard choices.
- Understand the definition of economics as the study of how scarce resources are allocated among competing ends.
- Explain opportunity costs and how are they measured.
- Understand the shape of the production-possibilities frontier and how it can be used to show efficiency.
- Understand the use of the *ceteris paribus* assumption.
- Clearly differentiate between microeconomics and macroeconomics.
- See why most disagreements are in the area of normative economics and not positive economics.
- Understand the principle of unintended consequences.

SCARCITY AND CHOICE

The Law of Scarcity

Scarcity is the most important fact of economics. If there were no scarcity, there would be no need to study economics. As Nobel Laureate George Stigler notes: "Scarcity is the economist's equivalent of the law of conservation of matter." There is scarcity because society's virtually unlimited wants exceed the economy's ability to meet these wants.

> Scarcity exists when the goods and services that people want exceed the ability of the economy to produce those goods and services.

If we were to add up everyone's wants, it quickly would be apparent that not all wants could be met. One person's list of wants might include a different luxury car for each day of the week, a 10-bedroom and 7-bath home in the best part of town, a 15-room ski lodge, a full household staff, a private jet, several ounces of the best Russian caviar per week, a glass of the best champagne at every meal, a 20-carat diamond ring—the list could go on and on for pages. The only limits are time, imagination, and appetite. If we added together everyone's wish lists, the total number of luxury cars desired might equal 100 million per year; the total weight of Russian caviar might be 10 tons per week; the total number of household workers desired might be 50 million; people might want 100 million ski lodges. Wants are for all practical purpose unlimited.

The economy could not conceivably produce enough goods and services to meet all these wants. There is not enough land for 100 million ski lodges; virtually the entire adult population would have to become household workers; there are not enough skilled engineers and craftspersons to build the millions of luxury autos; the Caspian Sea would not yield the desired tonnage of Russian caviar per week.

The imbalance between wants and ability to meet wants is present at all times and in all places. This imbalance is such an important fact of economic life that we call it the **law of scarcity**.

> The **law of scarcity** states that the wants of every society exceed its ability to satisfy those wants.

It is impossible to escape the law of scarcity. A rich country like the United States faces scarcity just as a poor country like India does. The difference between the United States and India is in the urgency of their economic problem: Indians face so much scarcity that starvation is commonplace; most Americans face far less scarcity.

Scarcity and Allocation

We all have to make tough economic choices. Some are monumental; some are trivial. What kind of education is best for us and our children? How much should we save for retirement? Should we invest our money in stocks, bonds, real estate, or precious metals? What kind of jobs do we want? What should we do when we lose our jobs? Should we look for new jobs or should we wait to be recalled to our old jobs? Should we buy an expensive sports car and have less money for other things? Should we rent or buy a house? Should we go to a movie or eat at a restaurant?

The law of scarcity says that there will never be enough to meet everyone's wants. This means that someone or something must decide who is to get society's scarce goods. The task of allocating the goods and services that could be produced with society's resources among all the people who want them is not easy. Some wants could be met, but an even larger number would have to be denied.

There are different ways of deciding who gets what. Each of these ways is a possible means of allocating resources. One allocation system would be a lottery where only the lucky lottery winner would get the scarce good, such as a luxury car. Another allocation system would give luxury cars only to those who offer something in return—such as home repair or money. A third allocation system would be to let public officials decide who is to get luxury cars. (See Example 1.)

ECONOMIC SYSTEMS

The **economic system** is responsible for managing the allocation problem. Societies need an orderly system of allocating resources. The alternative is a breakdown in the social order as people fight among themselves for scarce goods.

> An **economic system** is the set of arrangements that a society uses to allocate scarce goods.

The two major alternative economic systems are **capitalism** and **socialism.** This book is primarily about capitalist or market economies. The next chapter explains how market economies use prices to deal with scarcity and choice. A later chapter discusses how planned socialist economies deal with scarcity and choice.

> **Capitalism** is an economic system in which the factors of production are privately owned and resource allocation decisions are made by private markets.

EXAMPLE 1

Opportunity Cost and Orbital Slots in Outer Space

Most people think of outer space as a limitless frontier. It would seem that there would be plenty of outer space in which to place the communications satellites that circle the globe. In fact, orbital slots for communications satellites are a scarce resource. The best place to put communications satellites is in a ring 22,300 miles above the equator. Satellites in this ring remain fixed relative to the point directly below on earth and are able to provide relay communications 24 hours per day.

Only a limited number of satellites can be placed in this ring at any point in time. If satellites get too close, they interfere with each other's signals, and their communications capabilities are diminished. Many communications firms would like to place their satellites in this ring, but all the slots are taken. Orbital slots are a scarce resource because the number communications firms want far exceeds the number available. Each satellite has an opportunity cost. Its presence means that another satellite cannot occupy its orbital slot.

Later chapters will show that scarce goods usually command a positive price. One economist estimates that communications companies might be willing to pay one billion dollars per year for a satellite in a prime orbital slot.

SOURCE: Timothy Tregarthen, "Outer Space: The Scarce Frontier," *The Margin*, Volume 3, No. 1 (September 1987), pp. 8–9.

Socialism is an economic system in which land and capital are owned by the state and the use of these resources is determined by the state.

The most important examples of socialism have been the former Union of Soviet Socialist Republics (USSR) and the People's Republic of China. Socialist leaders promised that their system would outlast capitalism. But the opposite has occurred. Socialism worked so poorly in the USSR that in 1991 the Soviet Union dramatically broke up into numerous separate republics, such as Russia, Latvia, and many others. All of the republics now have the goal of converting from socialism to capitalism; they are currently in the process of making this difficult transition. Socialism ran into similar difficulties in the People's Republic of China, but instead of a dramatic revolution, as in the USSR, the Chinese economy has been slowly converting from socialism to capitalism since 1979.

Unlike the examples of socialism, the laboratories of capitalism have flourished. The developing Asian countries of Hong Kong, Singapore, South Korea, and Taiwan—called the "four tigers" by some—have followed highly capitalistic policies. These countries have been so successful that other developing countries around the world are trying to use them as role models.

OPPORTUNITY COSTS

Scarcity requires that choices be made because not all wishes can be met. Scarcity means that when one person obtains more of a commodity, someone else will get less of it. Scarcity also means that when I buy one good, I cannot buy as much of other goods. Choice means that some alternatives must be forgone.

A sacrificed opportunity is called an **opportunity cost** because the economic cost of any choice is that which must be sacrificed in order to make that choice.

> The **opportunity cost** of a particular action is the value of the next best alternative.

If a person buys a new stereo, the next best alternative (its opportunity cost) might be new clothes, a television, or a video recorder. Because the person chose the car, he or she sacrificed these other things. The loss of the next best alternative is the true cost of the car. If the government increases defense spending, the opportunity cost is the next best government program that had to be sacrificed to make the funds available. If a business uses its fleet of trucks to deliver its own goods, it passes up the opportunity to rent these trucks to other businesses. If I study an extra three hours for tomorrow's exam, the opportunity cost is the next best use of that study time.

The law of scarcity implies that our economic choices involve sacrifices—opportunity costs cannot be avoided.

Every choice involving the allocation of scarce resources involves opportunity costs. Economic actions (decisions on what to buy, how to produce, what to sell at what price) are based on their opportunity cost. As we shall see, opportunity costs are a cornerstone of economic analysis.

RESOURCES

Economies face the law of scarcity because resources are limited compared to wants. The limitation of *resources* is the fundamental source of scarcity.

Resources are the natural resources (land, mineral deposits, oxygen), the capital equipment (plants, machinery, inventories), and the human resources (workers with different skills, qualifications, ambitions, managerial talents) that are used as *inputs* to produce scarce goods and services. Productive resources are also called **factors of production**. These resources determine how much output a society can produce. Because the factors of production are limited, society's ability to produce output is limited. The limitation of resources is the fundamental source of scarcity.

> The **factors of production** are the **resources** used to produce goods and services. They can be divided into three categories—land, labor, and capital.

When economists speak of capital, they mean physical capital goods—buildings, computers, trucks, plants. This concept is distinct from *financial capital.* Physical capital and financial capital are related. Financial capital is needed to purchase physical capital; financial capital represents the ownership's claims to physical capital. The owner of 1,000 shares of General Motors (GM) owns financial capital. But GM owns many automobile manufacturing plants and has a huge inventory of cars and trucks in various stages of completion. The owner of the financial shares indirectly owns GM's physical capital.

Aside from physical capital, which results from investing in machines, there is also *human capital,* which results from people making investments in themselves. People go to school to become lawyers, engineers, doctors, mechanics, and plumbers; they learn on the job to become even better at their chosen occupation. Through education and on-the-job training, the productive capacity of individuals is increased.

DEFINITION OF ECONOMICS

There are a number of definitions of economics. Despite differences, they all focus on the basic ingredients of economics—scarcity, choice, allocation, and resources. **Economics** studies how society allocates its scarce resources among all of the competing uses for those resources. It recognizes that different societies use different economic systems to allocate scarce resources, but it emphasizes that all societies—be they capitalist or communist—must grapple with the same problem.

> **Economics** is the study of how *scarce resources* are *allocated* among *competing ends.*

The following chapters will explain how land, labor, and capital resources are directed by market prices to produce the goods and services desired by consumers. We shall consider how resources are allocated, the purposes to which they are put, and how effectively this is done by market economies.

THE PRODUCTION-POSSIBILITIES FRONTIER

Economists use models to explain the economy. A *model* shows how different factors or variables fit together. These models portray the world in a simplified fashion, yet they illustrate and explain economic principles powerfully. The **production-possibilities factor** *(PPF)* is a useful analytical model for illustrating scarcity, choice, and opportunity costs.

> The **production-possibilities frontier** *(PPF)* shows the alternative combinations of different goods and services that a society can produce given its available resources and its technical know-how.

Suppose an economy produces only two types of goods: cars and space shuttles. The table in Exhibit 1 shows the number of space shuttles and cars that this hypothetical economy can produce with its limited supply of factors of production and its acquired technical knowledge. The graph gives a pictorial representation of the accompanying table.

What do these numbers mean? Think of the economy as having resources that can be used for either space shuttles or cars. If our hypothetical economy chose to be at point *a*, it would be producing no cars and a *maximum* of 18 space shuttles from the factors of production available. At point *f* the economy would be producing no space shuttles and a *maximum* of 5,000 cars. Point *c* shows that if 2,000 cars are produced, the maximum number of space shuttles that can be produced is 15. Each intermediate point on the *PPF* between *a* and *f* represents a different combination of space shuttles and cars that could be produced using the same resources and technology.

Our hypothetical economy is capable of producing output combinations *a* through *f*. The economy is unable to produce output combination *g* (17 space shuttles and 3,000 cars) because *g* requires more resources than the economy has available. Point *h* is an attainable combination because it lies inside the frontier. The economy can produce any combination of outputs on or inside the *PPF*. (See Example 2.)

EXHIBIT 1   The Production-Possibilities Frontier (PPF)

a. PPF Graph

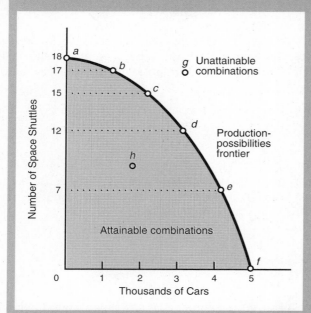

b. Production-Possibilities Schedule

Combination	Cars (thousands)	Space Shuttles	Opportunity Cost of Cars (number of space shuttles)
a	0	18	0
b	1	17	1
c	2	15	2
d	3	12	3
e	4	7	5
f	5	0	7

The *PPF* shows the combination of outputs of two goods that can be produced from society's resources when these resources are utilized to their maximum potential. Point *a* shows that if 18 space shuttles are produced, no car production is possible. Point *f* shows that if no space shuttles are produced, a maximum of 5,000 cars can be produced. Point *d* shows that if 3,000 cars are produced, a maximum of 12 space shuttles can be produced. Point *g* is above society's *PPF*. With its available resources, the economy cannot produce 17 space shuttles and 3,000 cars. Points like *h* inside the *PPF* represent an inefficient use of the society's resources.

The Law of Increasing Costs

The production-possibilities frontier is curved like a bow; it is not a straight line. Why? The economic cost of any action is the loss of the next best opportunity. In our example, the economy produces only two goods. The opportunity cost of increasing the production of one good is the amount of the other good that must be sacrificed. In this case, the opportunity cost of cars is simply the space shuttle production that must be sacrificed.

At *a* the economy is producing 18 space shuttles and no cars. The opportunity cost of increasing the production of cars from zero to 1,000 is the 1 space shuttle that must be sacrificed in the move from *a* to *b*. The opportunity cost of 1,000 more cars (moving from *b* to *c*) is 2 space shuttles. The opportunity cost of the fifth thousand of cars (moving from *e* to *f*) is much higher, 7 space shuttles. The number of space shuttles that must be given up at each level to increase car production is given in the last column of the table in Exhibit 1. The opportunity cost per thousand of car production rises with the production of cars, which is consistent with the **law of increasing costs.**

> The **law of increasing costs** states that as more of a particular commodity is produced, its opportunity cost per unit will increase.

EXAMPLE 2

Hawaiian Pineapples and the Production-Possibilities Frontier

In our daily lives, we rarely see that the economy must sacrifice some of one good to produce more of another. On a two-dimensional diagram in which the economy produces only two goods, this is obvious. In real life, where we encounter millions of distinct goods, it is rarely apparent that the economy must trade off goods because resources are limited.

The small Hawaiian island of Lanai provides a rare direct insight into the principle of the production-possibilities frontier. As a small island economy. Lanai cannot produce everything. Its land mass is limited; its population is limited.

Until 1992, Lanai was renowned as the home of Dole Pineapple. The moist, fertile, volcanic soil of Lanai had proven ideal for pineapple production for more than a century, and Lanai Dole pineapples were known throughout the world. Yet, as the tourism industry spread from Oahu and Maui to Lanai, more money was to be made by building hotels and condominiums than by growing pineapples. Lanai could not produce more tourism services without producing fewer pineapples. As tourism expanded, workers were drawn from the Dole fields and plants into hotel and restaurant services. Land was switched from plantations to golf courses. Resources shifted from the declining industry to the rising industry, and Dole closed its historic pineapple operations in 1992.

The law of increasing costs is responsible for the bowed-out shape of the *PPF*. Suppose our hypothetical economy produced only cars. Its arch-rival plans to land a person on Mars by the end of the century. To respond to this challenge, our hypothetical economy must suddenly increase its production of space shuttles. The amount of resources available to the economy is not altered by the declaration of a space race, so the increased space shuttle production must be at the expense of cars. The economy must move along its *PPF* in the direction of more shuttle production.

At low levels of shuttle production, the opportunity cost of a unit of shuttle production will be relatively low. Some factors of production will be suited to producing both space shuttles and cars; they can be shifted from cars to space shuttles without raising opportunity cost. As space shuttle production increases further, resources suited to car production but not to space shuttle production (some assembly line workers, perhaps) must be diverted into shuttle production. As resources are increasingly used that are poorly suited for shuttle production, the extra shuttle output gained from shifting these resources falls. The opportunity cost of a space shuttle (the number of cars sacrificed) will rise, as the law of increasing costs would require.

Efficiency

The *PPF* shows the combination of goods an economy is capable of producing when its limited resources are utilized to their maximum potential. Whether an economy actually operates on its production-possibilities frontier depends on whether the economy utilizes its resources with maximum **efficiency**.

In Exhibit 1, if the economy produces output combinations that lie on the

PPF, the economy is said to be *efficient.* When an economy is operating on its *PPF,* it cannot increase the production of one good without reducing the production of another good. If the economy operates at points inside the *PPF,* such as *h,* it is *inefficient* because more space shuttles could be produced without cutting back on the other good.

> **Efficiency** results when no resources are unemployed and when no resources are misallocated.

The production-possibilities frontier shows the limits of what an economy can produce or consume without additional resources or new technology.

If workers are unemployed or if productive machines stand idle, the economy is not operating on its *PPF* because some resources are not being employed. If these idle resources were used, more of one good could be produced without reducing the production of other goods. *Misallocated resources* are resources that are used but not to their best advantage. For example, if a surgeon works as a ditchdigger, if cotton is planted on Iowa corn land, or if bananas are grown in Alaska, resources are misallocated. Again, if resource misallocations are removed, more of one good could be produced without sacrificing the production of other goods.

The Ceteris Paribus or "Other Things Equal" Assumption

The *PPF* illustrates the choice of outputs open to an economy operating with a *given supply of resources and a fixed technology.* The *PPF* in Exhibit 1 is drawn for a given amount of resources and a given technology. The *PPF* in effect asks the question: If the economy produces more space shuttles, how many cars would have to be sacrificed *if this were the only thing that changed in the economy?* The practice of asking what would happen if one thing changed and all other things remained the same is the ***ceteris paribus*** assumption.

> The ***ceteris paribus*** assumption (meaning "all other things equal") considers the effects of a change in one factor assuming that all other relevant factors remain the same.

The *ceteris paribus* conditions for the *PPF* are that technology and the quantities of the various resources are constant at every point along the curve. Holding these factors constant means that any change in auto production must be at the expense of space shuttle production. However, it may be possible to produce more of both cars and space shuttles if more resources become available or if an improved technology allows the economy to produce more cars or space shuttles from the same resources. In Exhibit 2, the *PPF* of Exhibit 1 is labeled as *XX.* It shows the trade-off between cars and space shuttles *with given resources and given technology.*

As time passes, however, resources grow and technology improves. With more resources and better technology, the economy is capable of producing more cars along with the same number of space shuttles (or more space shuttles along with the same number of cars). The change in resources and technology has caused the production-possibilities frontier to shift out to the right (from *XX* to *YY*). The outward shift of the *PPF* illustrates the process of economic growth, studied in a later chapter.

Ceteris paribus is a tool used frequently in economic analysis. It allows us to concentrate attention on one single factor at a time and hence to make sense of complicated processes.

EXHIBIT 2   Shifts in the *PPF* and the *Ceteris Paribus* Assumption

The production-possibilities frontier labeled *XX* is for the amount of resources and technology given in Exhibit 1. Movements along this *PPF* show what happens if more of one good is produced and there is no change in resources or technology. The *PPF* labeled *YY* shows that the *PPF* shifts to the right when resources increase and technology improves.

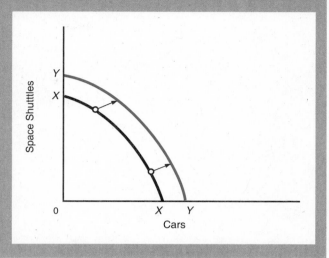

MICROECONOMICS AND MACROECONOMICS

Economics is divided into two main branches, *microeconomics* and *macroeconomics*. Microeconomics and macroeconomics deal with the economy from different vantage points.

Microeconomics

Microeconomics focuses on the individual participants in the economy: the producers, workers, employers, and consumers. In everyday economic life, things are bought and sold, people decide where and how many hours to work. Business managers decide what to produce and how to organize this production. These activities result in transactions that take place in markets where buyers and sellers come together.

> **Microeconomics** studies the economic decision-making of firms and individuals in markets; it is the study of the economy in the small.

Because it deals with economic decisions made in a market setting, microeconomics studies how all the buyers and sellers in particular markets (such as the market for wheat, or the market for cars, or the market for local residential real estate) come together to make transactions. Microeconomics studies how business firms operate under different competitive conditions in different types of markets and how the combined actions of buyers and sellers determine prices in specific markets. Microeconomics studies households as earners of wages, interest, rent, and profit and, accordingly, studies the distribution of income. Microeconomics studies all kinds of transactions.

Macroeconomics

Instead of analyzing prices, outputs, and transactions in individual markets, **macroeconomics** studies the production of the entire economy. Macroeconomics studies the *general* price level (rather than individual prices), the national employment rate, government spending, the federal deficit, interest rates, and the nation's money supply.

> **Macroeconomics** is the study of the economy in the large. Rather than dealing with individual markets and individual consumers and producers, macroeconomics examines the economy as a whole.

Because macroeconomics studies the economy as a whole, measures of total economic activity are required. Macroeconomic *aggregates,* such as gross domestic product, the consumer price index, the unemployment rate, and the government surplus and deficit, are used to determine macroeconomic outcomes. These measures are called *aggregates* because they add together (or aggregate) individual microeconomic components.

Just as microeconomics studies the relationships between individual participants in the economy, macroeconomics studies relationships between aggregate measures. What are the determinants of inflation? What is the relationship between inflation and interest rates? What are the effects of government deficits on prices and interest rates? What is the relationship between the money supply and inflation?

Microeconomics and macroeconomics share common ground. Macroeconomists study the behavior of persons and individual businesses to shed light on a number of key macroeconomic issues. How does inflation affect the output decisions of businesses and the job searches of unemployed individuals? How are individual saving decisions affected by government debt? How do individuals and businesses form expectations of inflation, and how are interest rates and inflation affected when these expectations change?

POSITIVE AND NORMATIVE ECONOMICS

Economists have the unfair reputation of being unable to agree on anything. People joke about getting "six different answers from five economists." While those in other sciences disagree, their disagreements are less visible. Theoretical physicists have long disagreed about the physical nature of the universe, but this scientific controversy is little understood by the public. Economic disputes, however, quickly receive public attention. Everyone is interested in economic questions: Will inflation accelerate? Will I lose my job? Will interest rates fall?

The amount of disagreement among economists differs depending on whether issues of *positive economics* or *normative economics* are involved.

Positive Economics

Positive economics studies how the economy works. It avoids the question of how the economy *should* work.

> Positive economics is the study of *what is* in the economy.

Economists generally agree on matters of positive economics. They agree that rising prices reduce consumption (*ceteris paribus*), that rising income will have predictable effects on consumer purchases, that wage and price controls cause shortages, that tariffs and quotas raise prices to consumers, and that minimum-wage laws increase unemployment among youth and unskilled workers. The easiest matters on which to achieve agreement involve the microeconomic relationships that actually prevail in an economy.

The areas of disagreement in positive economics tend to be concentrated in macroeconomics. Economists disagree on the causes of inflation and unemployment, on the relationship between deficits and unemployment, and on the role of government in fighting inflation and unemployment. It is not surprising that economics has not resolved these issues. The economy is a complex organism, comprised of millions of individuals, hundreds of thousands of business firms, and thousands of local, state, and federal government offices. Collective economic actions are difficult to analyze. Emotions are volatile; expectations can change overnight; relationships held last year no longer hold today; it is costly and difficult to collect up-to-date economic facts. Many economic events are random and unpredictable. Economists are not to be blamed for the complexity of these problems.

Normative Economics

Economists do disagree—often strongly—about **normative economics.**

> **Normative economics** is the study of *what ought to be* in the economy.

Economists disagree on whether we should have more unemployment or more inflation; over whether income taxes should be lowered for the middle class, the rich, or the poor; over job programs; over government-subsidized health programs. These disagreements are only partly over "what is"; opponents in a debate may agree on what will happen if Program A is chosen over Program B, but they may disagree sharply over their personal evaluation of the desirability of those consequences. Disputes over "what ought to be" are often the foundation for why economists disagree.

Normative economics always involves some concern over an economic problem—perhaps people think that there is too much inflation, too much poverty, too much unemployment, or inadequate medical care. In democracies, there is usually some pressure to pass a piece of legislation designed to correct the problem, but economic problems are not easy to solve. Normative economists must pay attention to the **principle of unintended consequences,** according to which the ultimate effects of economic or social policies may be different from the apparent or intended effects. Indeed, the "cure" can sometimes be worse than the "disease."

> The **principle of unintended consequences** holds that policies may have ultimate or actual effects that differ from the intended or apparent effects.

Numerous economic policies have unintended consequences. Rent control can cause housing shortages; unemployment benefits can increase unemployment; raises in the minimum wage can hurt the poor by eliminating jobs; welfare checks given to poor mothers can break up families; free housing for the homeless can hurt other poor people; taxing the goods rich people buy also taxes those who serve the

Why There Is No Free Lunch in Medical Care

Everyone agrees that people should have good medical care. It is not fair that some people get better medical care than others. This complaint is particularly prominent during political campaigns when the different candidates and parties try to persuade voters that their plan is better than others. Most often it is "fee-for-service" medicine that is criticized. If people have to pay to get medical service, those who can't afford it will be excluded.

If everyone agrees that everyone should have access to good medical care, why can't we simply do it?

Let's consider the options. One option would be for medical services to be free of charge. The government simply pays through tax dollars. Anyone who wants medical care can have it. In effect, medical care appears to be a "free lunch" in this situation. Although people typically do not relish going to doctors or to hospitals, the amount of medical care that people would want if it were free would far exceed the limited numbers of doctors, nurses, and medications available. Medical resources are scarce. As long as people want more than is available, someone must do without. Either those willing to stand in line the longest get the service or those with special connections get the service. The government may wish to set rules and standards (such as excluding the elderly or terminally ill) to limit the number of people receiving free medical care.

Another option might be for the government to mandate compulsory health insurance so that the insurance company pays health expenses. Even more appealing: Why don't we let the employer "pay" by requiring all businesses to pay for employee health insurance?

The appearance of the free lunch is deceiving. If the employer has to pay the employee's health insurance, hiring becomes more expensive, and the employer would cut back on the payroll. Many small businesses would not be started. People would be thrown out of work, and wages would fall. What appears to be a "free lunch" has been paid for by employees in the form of fewer jobs and lower wages. Moreover, if people knew that the insurance company had to pay the medical bill, they again would demand more medical resources than are available, and the insurance company, not the government, would have to establish rules concerning what kinds of medical treatments are insured and which are not. All of these reactions are examples of the law of unintended consequences explained in this chapter.

Why is it important to understand the principle that "there is no such thing as a free lunch"? In our everyday lives, we must carefully analyze what things really cost, either directly or indirectly. In our political lives, we must be wary of the promises of politicians that they can give us something for nothing. All private and public policies must be examined in terms of their true costs and benefits.

rich; equal pay for men and women can result in fewer jobs for women; bank deposit insurance to protect consumers can encourage bankers to act irresponsibly; medical insurance for some can lead to an explosion of medical costs for everyone; safety legislation for workers can lower their wages; and making cigarette advertising illegal can raise the profits of cigarette producers.

Economists can make important contributions to sound economic policy. It is one thing to identify a problem. The principle of unintended consequences tells us that the development of a sound economic policy requires creating private incentives that are consistent with the ultimate goal. For example, economists have suggested that we deal with pollution by setting up a market for pollution rights, or that we address the failure of public schools by giving students vouchers that can be used to purchase education from any private or public school.

Each of the following chapters contains a biographical sketch of one of the great economists of the past. Economists are a varied lot. Most are professors, but some have been stockbrokers, preachers, or journalists. They are interesting because their ideas affect the way we live. John Maynard Keynes, a great economist and one of economics' most fascinating personalities, once explained how the ideas of economists become widely applied.

". . . the ideas of economists . . . , both when they are right and when they are wrong, are more powerful than is commonly understood. Indeed the world is ruled by little else. Practical men, who believe themselves to be quite exempt from any intellectual influences, are usually the slaves of some defunct economist. Madmen in authority, who hear voices in the air, are distilling their frenzy from some academic scribbler of a few years back. I am sure that the power of vested interests is vastly exaggerated compared with the gradual encroachment of ideas. Not, indeed, immediately, but after a certain interval; for in the field of economic . . . philosophy there are not many who are influenced by new theories after they are twenty-five or thirty years of age, so that the ideas which civil servants and politicians and even agitators apply to current events are not likely to be the newest. But soon or late, it is ideas, not vested interests, which are dangerous for good or evil."

SOURCE: John Maynard Keynes, *The General Theory of Employment, Interest, and Money* (New York: Harcourt Brace and Jovanovich, 1936), pp. 383–84.

How the price system allocates scarce resources and the workings of a market economy will be discussed in the next chapter.

Chapter Summary

The most important point to learn from this chapter is: The law of scarcity means that people's wants cannot be fully satisfied from limited resources and that any choice of any scarce good involves sacrificed opportunities. That is, there is no free lunch.

1. Wants are unlimited; there will never be enough resources to meet unlimited wants. Scarcity dictates that choices be made among alternatives. The economic system allocates scarce resources.

2. Economics is the study of how scarce resources are allocated among competing ends. The ultimate source of scarcity is the limited supply of resources. The factors of production are land, labor, and capital.

3. The opportunity cost of any choice is the next best alternative that was sacrificed to make the choice.

4. The production-possibilities frontier *(PPF)* shows the maximum combinations of goods that an economy is able to produce from its limited resources when these resources are utilized to their maximum potential and for a given state of technical knowledge. If societies are efficient, they will operate on the production-possibilities frontier. The law of increasing costs says that as more of one commodity is produced at the expense of others, its opportunity cost will increase. The two sources of economic inefficiency are unemployed resources and misallocated resources.

5. Economists study how one factor affects another by considering what would happen if all other things remained the same. This is the *ceteris paribus* assumption.

6. Microeconomics studies the economy in the small. Macroeconomics studies the economy in the large.

7. Most disputes in economics are about normative economics (what ought to be) rather than about positive economics (what is). Policies often have unintended consequences because they create private incentives inconsistent with the ultimate goal.

Key Terms

scarcity (p. 3)
law of scarcity (p. 3)
economic system (p. 4)
opportunity cost (p. 5)
capitalism (p. 4)
socialism (p. 4)
factors of production (p. 6)
economics (p. 7)
production-possibilities frontier *(PPF)* (p. 7)

law of increasing costs (p. 8)
efficiency (p. 9)
ceteris paribus (p. 10)
microeconomics (p. 11)
macroeconomics (p. 12)
positive economics (p. 12)
normative economics (p. 13)
principle of unintended consequences (p. 13)

Questions and Problems

1. "The fundamental nature of economics has changed. Today, we worry about buying VCRs or compact disks; yesterday we worried about where our next meal was coming from." Evaluate.

2. This chapter argues that scarcity results from the fact that resources are limited. Does it follow that scarcity will be eliminated as resources increase?

3. Henry spends all of his extra money on compact disks. They cost $15 each. If Henry must spend $45 for a new tire, what is his opportunity cost measured in terms of sacrificed compact disks?

4. Because I bought a new stereo today, I am no longer able to buy a new TV set. Is the TV set my opportunity cost?

5. If higher TV prices mean that people will want to buy fewer TV sets, explain how the *ceteris paribus* assumption might be used to clarify this statement.

6. What are *ceteris paribus* conditions that apply to the production-possibility frontier?

7. Consider the data in Table A on a hypothetical economy's production-possibilities frontier *(PPF)*.
   a. Graph the *PPF*.
   b. Does the *PPF* have the expected shape?
   c. Calculate the opportunity cost of cars in terms of space shuttles. Calculate the opportunity cost of space shuttles in terms of cars. Do your results illustrate the law of increasing costs?
   d. If this economy produced 700 cars and 3 space shuttles, what would you conclude about how this economy is solving the *how* problem?

e. If this economy at some later date produced 700 cars and 12 space shuttles, what would you conclude?

TABLE A

Number of Cars	Number of Space Shuttles
800	0
700	4
500	10
300	14
100	16
0	16.25

8. In a hypothetical economy that produces only two goods, how would opportunity costs be defined? In a real-world economy that produces millions of goods and services, how would the opportunity cost of buying one good be defined?

9. One economist believes that higher interest rates lead to higher inflation. Another believes that inflation can be reduced by raising interest rates. Is this a disagreement over normative or positive economics? Why or why not?

10. Which of the following topics would fall under macroeconomics? Which under microeconomics? Explain why in each case.
   a. The price of fish.
   b. The effect of the stock market on the economy.
   c. Employment in the computer industry.
   d. The general price level.

e. The national unemployment rate.
f. The price of cars.
g. The number of new plants built in the United States.

11. Economists would be more likely to agree on the answers to which of the following questions? Why?
   a. Should tax rates be lowered for the rich?
   b. What would be the effects on economic output of a lowering of tax rates for the rich?

c. What would be the effects of an increase in the price of VCRs on purchases of VCRs?
d. Should government expenditures on defense be reduced?
e. What would be the effects of an increase in military spending on employment?

12. Why are economic policies difficult to design?

Doing Economics

Suppose that you have an economics test and a test in another subject next Monday. What would it mean for your study time to be scarce in this context? Suppose that your study time is, in fact, scarce. How could you represent the tradeoff between studying for economics and studying for the other subject on a production-possibilities frontier? (Hint: Make sure that you draw the frontier in terms of the outputs of your studying, not the input of time.) What shape would this *PPF* have? Why?

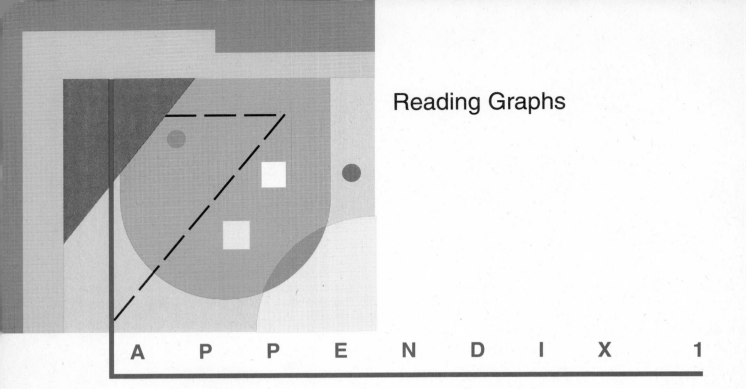

Reading Graphs

APPENDIX FOCUS Graphs are an important tool in learning economics. In this appendix you will learn how to work with graphs. Topics covered are graph construction, positive and negative relationships, dependent and independent variables, and the concept of slope for both linear and curvilinear relationships. This appendix shows how slopes are used to find the maximum and minimum values, and it explains how to calculate the areas of rectangles. The use of scatter diagrams to view positive and negative relationships in real data is also discussed.

After studying this appendix, you will be able to:

- Understand positive and negative relationships.
- Determine the slopes of linear and curvilinear relationships.
- Understand how to read scatter diagrams.
- Know how to calculate the areas of rectangles.

THE VALUE OF GRAPHS

Economics makes extensive use of graphs. A graph is simply a visual scheme for picturing the quantitative relationship between two different variables. Not only can a graph display a great deal of data, a graph can efficiently describe the quantitative relationship that exists between the variables. As the Chinese proverb says, "a picture is worth a thousand words."

Positive and Negative Relationships

Graphs can show whether there is a **positive** (or **direct**) **relationship** or a **negative** (or **inverse**) **relationship** between two variables.

> A **positive** (or **direct**) **relationship** exists between two variables if an increase in the value of one variable is associated with an *increase* in the value of the other variable.

When two variables are positively related the graph of the relationship is an upward-sloping curve.

For example, an increase in the *horsepower* of a car's engine will increase the *maximum speed* of the automobile (holding other factors, such as the weight of the car, constant). Panel (a) of Exhibit 1 depicts this relationship in a graph. The *vertical axis* measures the maximum speed of the car from the 0 point (called the *origin*); the *horizontal axis* measures the horsepower of the engine. When horsepower is 0 (the engine is broken down), the maximum speed the car can attain is obviously 0; when horsepower is 300, the maximum speed is 100 miles per hour. Intermediate values of horsepower (between 0 and 300) can be graphed. When a line is drawn through all these points, the resulting curved line describes the effect of horsepower on maximum speed. Since the picture is a line that goes from low to high speeds as horsepower increases, it is an example of an *upward-sloping curve*.

> A **negative** (or **inverse**) **relationship** exists between two variables if an increase in the value of one variable is associated with a *reduction* in the value of the other variable.

When two variables are negatively related the graph of the relationship is a downward-sloping curve.

For example, as the *horsepower* of that automobile increases, the *gas mileage* (for given driving conditions) will fall (again, other things equal). In panel (b), horsepower is still measured on the horizontal axis, but now gas mileage is measured on the vertical axis. Since the picture is a curve going from high to low values of gas mileage as horsepower increases, it is an example of a *downward-sloping curve*.

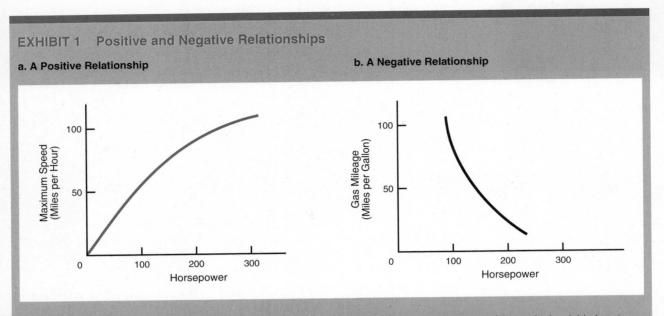

EXHIBIT 1   Positive and Negative Relationships

a. A Positive Relationship

b. A Negative Relationship

Panel (a) shows a positive relationship. As the horizontal variable (horsepower) increases, the value of the vertical variable (maximum speed) increases. The curve rises from left to right. Panel (b) shows a negative relationship. As the horizontal variable (horsepower) increases, the vertical variable (mileage) decreases. The curve falls from left to right.

Graphs Show Relationships and Display Data Efficiently

Panel (a) of Exhibit 2 shows a graph drawn from data shown in panel (b). The numbers in the table describe the quantitative relationship between *minutes of typing* and *number of pages typed*. The quantitative relationship between minutes and pages is that every 5 minutes of typing will produce 1 page of manuscript. Thus, 5 minutes produces 1 page, 15 minutes produces 3 pages, and so on. Zero minutes will, of course, produce 0 pages.

Each pair of numbers is plotted at the intersection of the vertical line that corresponds to that value of X and the horizontal line that corresponds to that value of Y. Point a shows that 5 minutes of typing produces 1 page. Point c shows that 15 minutes of typing produces 3 pages, and so on. Points a, b, c, d, and e completely describe the data in the table.

The first advantage of graphs over tables is that it is easier to see the relationship between two variables in a graph than in a table. Graphs provide an immediate visual understanding of the quantitative relationship between the two variables just by observing the plot of points. Since the points in this case move upward from left to right, we know that there is a *positive relationship* between the variables. This may not seem to be a great advantage for this simple and obvious case. However, if the data in the table had not been arranged in ascending order, it would have taken a while to figure out that the relationship was positive.

The second advantage of graphs over tables is that large quantities of data can be represented more efficiently in a graph. Suppose that in addition to the table, we had data for the number of pages that could be typed at all kinds of intermediate values of typing time: 6 minutes, 13 minutes, 24 minutes and 25 seconds. A large table would be required to report all these numbers. In a graph, however, the intermediate values can be represented simply by connecting points a, b, c, d, and e with a line.

EXHIBIT 2 Advantages of Graphs over Tables

a. Graph of Pages Typed per Minute

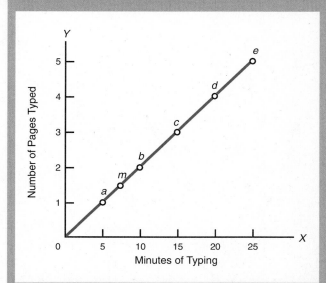

b. Table of Pages Typed per Minute

	Minutes of Typing (X axis)	Number of Pages Typed (Y axis)
	0	0
a	5	1
b	10	2
c	15	3
d	20	4
e	25	5

The graph reproduces the data in the table. Point a shows that 5 minutes of typing produces 1 typed page, b shows that 10 minutes of typing produces 2 typed pages, and so on. Graphs have two advantages over tables. First, the upward-sloping line drawn through a, b, c, d, and e shows clearly that the relationship between minutes of typing and number of pages typed is positive. Second, graphs suggest intermediate values. The points between a, b, c, d, and e (such as m) suggest the number of pages typed for amounts of typing time between the 5-minute intervals.

Shifts in Graphs

The relationship between minutes of typing and number of pages typed is graphed in Exhibit 2. The relationship can change, however, if other factors that affect typing speed change. Assume that Exhibit 2 shows minutes and pages typed on a manual typewriter. If the typist works with a high-speed electric typewriter, a different relationship will emerge. With the electric typewriter, the typist can type 2 pages every 5 minutes instead of one. Both relationships are graphed in Exhibit 3, which shows that if factors that affect speed of typing change (the quality of the typewriter), the relationship between minutes and pages can shift. Economists work frequently with relationships that shift, so it is important to understand shifts in graphs.

UNDERSTANDING SLOPE

The relationship between two variables is represented by a curve's **slope**. Many central concepts of economics require an understanding of slope.

Straight Lines

The slope reflects the response of one variable to changes in another. Consider the typing example. Every 5 minutes of typing on a manual typewriter produces 1

EXHIBIT 3   Shifts in Relationships

The curve *abcde* shows the relationship between minutes of typing and pages typed using a manual typewriter. The new (higher) curve *fghij* shows the relationship between minutes of typing and pages typed with an electric typewriter. As a consequence of the change from a manual to an electric typewriter, the relationship has shifted upward.

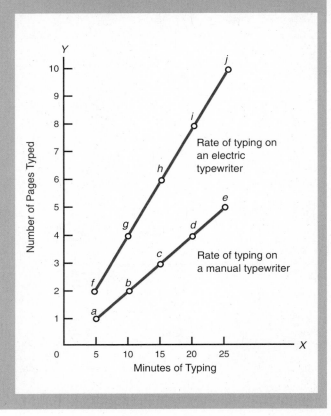

page; equivalently, every minute of typing produces 1/5th of a page. As we shall demonstrate below, the slope of the line *abcde* is 1/5th of a page of typing per minute.

> The **slope** of a straight line is the ratio of the rise (or fall) in *Y* (measured on the vertical axis) over the run in *X* (measured on the horizontal axis).

A positive value of the slope signifies a positive relationship between the two variables. *A negative value of the slope signifies a negative relationship* between the two variables.

To understand slope more precisely, consider in panel (a) of Exhibit 4 the straight-line relationship between the two variables X and Y. When $X = 5$, $Y = 3$; when $X = 7$, $Y = 6$. Suppose now that variable X is allowed to *run* (to change horizontally) from 5 units to 7 units. When this happens variable Y *rises* (increases vertically) from 3 units to 6 units.

The slope of the line in panel (a) is:

$$\frac{\text{Rise in } Y}{\text{Run in } X} = \frac{3}{2} = 1.5.$$

This formula works for negative relationships as well. In panel (b) of Exhibit 4, when X runs from 5 to 7, Y *falls* 4 units to 1 unit, or rises by −3 units. Thus, the slope is:

EXHIBIT 4   Positive and Negative Slope

a. Positive Slope

Slope = $\dfrac{\text{rise}}{\text{run}}$ = $\dfrac{3}{2}$ = 1.5

Rise in Y

Run in X

b. Negative Slope

Slope = $\dfrac{\text{fall}}{\text{run}}$ = $\dfrac{-3}{2}$ = 1.5

Run in X

Fall in Y

Positive slope is measured by the ratio of the rise in Y over the run in X. In panel (a), Y rises by 3 and X runs by 2, and the slope is 1.5. Negative slope is measured by the ratio of the fall in Y over the run in X. In panel (b), the fall in Y is –3, in the run in X is 2, and the slope is –1.5.

$$\frac{\text{Rise in } Y}{\text{Run in } X} = \frac{-3}{2} = 1.5.$$

If ΔY (delta Y) stands for the change in the value of Y and ΔX (delta X) stands for the change in the value of X,

$$\text{Slope} = \frac{\Delta Y}{\Delta X}.$$

This formula holds for positive or negative relationships.

Let us return to the typing example. What slope expresses the relationship between minutes of typing and number of pages? When minutes increase by 5 units ($\Delta X = 5$), pages increase by one unit ($\Delta Y = 1$). The slope is therefore $\Delta Y/\Delta X = 1/5$.

In Exhibits 2, 3, and 4, the points are connected by straight lines. Such relationships are called *linear relationships*. The inquisitive reader will wonder how slope is measured when the relationship between X and Y is *curvilinear*.

Curvilinear Relationships

A curvilinear example is given in Exhibit 5. When X runs from 2 units to 4 units ($\Delta X = 2$), Y rises by 2 units ($\Delta Y = 2$); thus, between a and b the slope is $2/2 = 1$. Between a and c, however, X runs from 2 to 6 ($\Delta X = 4$), Y rises by 3 units ($\Delta Y = 3$), and the slope is 3/4. In the curvilinear case, the value of the slope depends on how far X is allowed to run. Between b and c, the slope is 1/2. The slope changes

EXHIBIT 5 Tangents and Slopes of Curvilinear Relationships

The ratio of the rise over the run yields a slope of 1 from *a* to *b* but a slope of 3/4 from *a* to *c*. From *b* to *c*, the slope is 1/2. To compute the slope at point *a*, the slope of the tangent to *a* is calculated. The value of the slope of the tangent is 3/2.

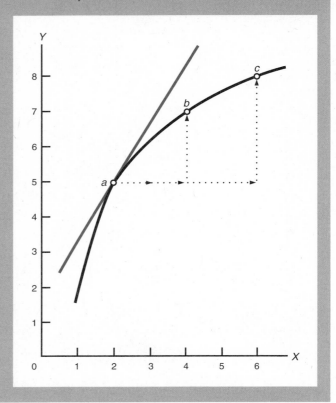

as one moves along a curvilinear relationship. In the linear case, the value of the slope will *not* depend on how far X runs because the slope is constant and does not change as one moves from point to point.

There is no single slope of a curvilinear relationship and no single method of measuring slopes. The slope can be measured between two points (say, between *a* and *b* or between *b* and *c*) or at a particular point (say, at point *a*). Insofar as the measurement of the slope between points depends on the length of the run, a uniform standard must be adopted to avoid confusion. This standard is the use of *tangents* to determine the slope at a point on a curvilinear relationship.

To calculate the slope at *a*, let the run of X be "infinitesimally small," rather than a discrete number of units such as 1/2, 2, 4, or whatever. An infinitesimally small change is difficult to conceive, but the graphic result of such a change can be captured simply by drawing a **tangent** to point *a*.

> A **tangent** is a straight line that touches the curve at only one point.

The **slope** of a curvilinear relationship at a particular point is the slope of the straight line tangent to the curve at that point.

If the curve is really curved at *a*, there is only one straight line that just barely touches *a* and only *a*. Any other line (a magnifying glass may be required to verify this) will cut the curve at two points or none. The tangent to *a* is drawn as a straight line in Exhibit 5.

The slope of the tangent at *a* is measured by dividing the rise by the run.

EXHIBIT 6   Maximum and Minimum Points

a. Y Is Maximized When Slope Is Zero

b. Y Is Minimized When Slope Is Zero

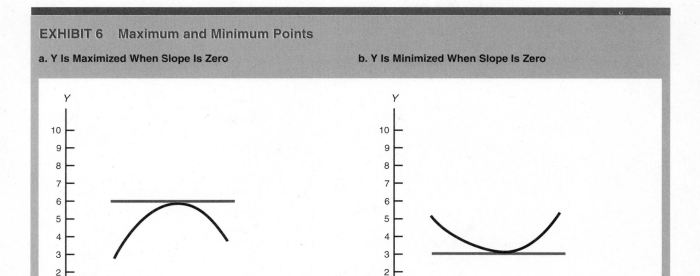

Some curvilinear relationships change directions. Notice that in panel (a), when the curve changes direction at $X = 6$, the corresponding value of Y is maximized. In panel (b), when $X = 6$, Y is minimized. In either case, the slope equals zero at the maximum or minimum value.

Because the tangent is a straight line, the length of the run does not matter. For a run from 2 to 4 ($\Delta X = 2$), the rise (ΔY) equals 3 (from 5 to 8). Thus, the slope of the tangent is 3/2 or 1.5.

Exhibit 6 shows two curvilinear relationships that have distinct high points or low points. In panel (a), the relationship between X and Y is positive for values of X less than 6 units and negative for values of X more than 6 units. The exact opposite holds for panel (b). The relationship is negative for values of X less than 6 and positive for X greater than 6. Notice that at the point where the slope changes from positive to negative (or vice versa), the slope of the curve will be exactly 0; the tangent at point $X = 6$ for both curves is a horizontal straight line that neither rises nor falls as X changes.

When a curvilinear relationship has a zero slope, the value of Y reaches either a high point, as in panel (a), or a low point, as in panel (b), at the X value where slope is zero.

Maximum and minimum values of relationships—as when a firm maximizes profits or minimizes costs—are of great importance in economics. Suppose, for example, that X in panel (a) represents the 1993 production of automobiles by General Motors (in units of 1 million) and that the variable Y represents GM's profits from automobile production (in billions of dollars). According to this diagram, GM should settle on $X = 6$ million units of automobile production because GM's profits would be higher at $X = 6$ than at any other production level.

Suppose that in panel (b), Y measures GM's costs of producing an automobile while X still measures automobile production. Production costs per automobile are at a minimum at $X = 6$. In other words, GM will produce cars at the lowest cost per car if GM produces 6 million cars.

Scatter Diagrams

The **scatter diagram** is a statistical tool frequently used to examine whether a positive or negative relationship exists between two variables. Statisticians have more powerful and exact tools to measure relationships, but the scatter diagram shown in Exhibit 7 is a simple analytical instrument.

> A scatter diagram consists of a number of separate points, each of which plots the value of one variable (measured along the horizontal axis) against a value of another variable (measured along the vertical axis) for a specific time interval.

In Exhibit 7, mortgage interest rates are measured along the horizontal axis, and new housing starts (the number of new homes on which construction has started) are measured along the vertical axis. Each dot on the scatter diagram shows the combination of mortgage rate and number of housing starts for a particular year. Because mortgage rates are plotted against housing starts for the years 1970 to 1986, there are 17 dots on this particular scatter diagram (each labeled by year). The pattern of dots on a scatter diagram provides convenient visual information about the relationship between the two variables. If the dots tend to concentrate in a pattern where low mortgage rates accompany high housing starts and high mortgage rates accompany low housing starts, then the scatter diagram suggests a *negative relationship* between mortgage rates and housing starts. A negative relationship is indicated by a generally declining pattern of dots from left to right. If the relationship were positive, there would be a generally rising pattern of dots from left to right. If there were no relationship, the dots would be distributed randomly on the scatter diagram.

EXHIBIT 7   A Scatter Diagram: Mortgage Rates and Housing Starts

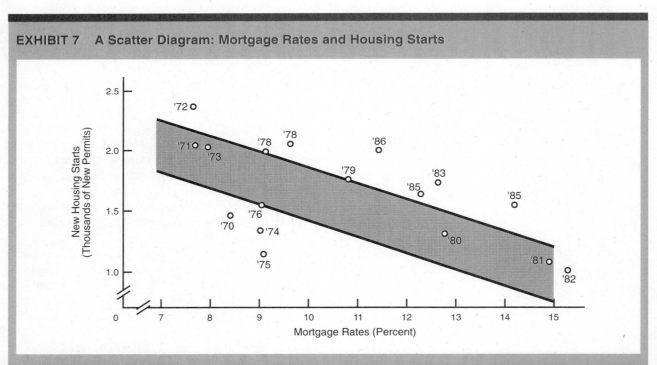

The generally falling pattern of dots suggests that there is a negative relationship between these two variables. The fact that not all dots lie on a single line suggests that other factors besides the independent variable (mortgage rates) affect the dependent variable (housing starts).

SOURCE: *Economic Report of the President*

EXHIBIT 8   Areas of Rectangles

The area of the rectangle *abcd* is calculated by multiplying its height (*ad*, or equivalently, *bc*) by its width (*ab*, or equivalently, *dc*). The height equals $4 and the width equals 8 units; therefore, the area of the rectangle equals $32. As the text explains, $32 is the amount of this firm's profits.

Exhibit 7 shows what appears to be a negative relationship between mortgage rates and housing starts. We have inserted a broad, negatively sloped band that traces out the general pattern of declining dots. This negative pattern indicated by the scatter diagram is not surprising. Most people would expect the number of houses being built to drop when the cost of borrowing to buy a home rises. The fact that all the dots do not lie neatly on a single negatively sloped line suggests that factors other than mortgage rates also affect housing starts.

AREAS OF RECTANGLES

In economics, it is important to understand areas of rectangles. Exhibit 8 shows how to calculate the area of a rectangle using a common economic example. It shows a firm selling 8 units of its product for a price of $10 while it costs $6 per unit to produce the product. How much profit is the firm earning? The firm's profit is the area of the rectangle *abcd*. To calculate the area of a rectangle, the height of the rectangle (*ad* or *bc*, or $10 − $6 = $4 per unit) must be multiplied by the width of the rectangle (*ab* or *dc*, or 8 units). Multiplication shows that the area of the rectangle is $4 per unit times 8 units equals $32 of total profit. If the good sells for $10 and costs $6 per unit, profit per unit is $4. The firm sells 8 units for a total profit of $32.

Appendix Summary

1. Graphs effectively present positive and negative relationships between two variables. A positive relationship exists between two variables if an increase in one

is associated with an *increase* in the other; a negative relationship exists between two variables if an increase in one is associated with a *decrease* in the other.

2. Graphs have two advantages over tables: the relationship between the variables is easier to see, and graphs can accommodate large amounts of data more efficiently.

3. For a straight-line curve, the slope of the curve is the ratio of the rise in *Y* over the run in *X*. The slope of a curvilinear relationship at a particular point is the slope of the straight line tangent to the curve at that point. When a curve changes slope from positive to negative as the *X* values increase, the value of *Y* reaches a *maximum* when the slope of the curve is zero; when a curve changes slope from negative to positive as the *X* values increase, the value of *Y* reaches a *minimum* when the slope of the curve is zero. Scatter diagrams are useful tools for examining data for positive or negative relationships between two variables.

4. The area of a rectangle is calculated by multiplying its height by its width.

Key Terms

positive (or direct) relationship (p. 19)
negative (or inverse) relationship (p. 19)
slope (p. 21)

tangent (p. 24)
scatter diagram (p. 26)

Questions and Problems

1. Graph the following data:
   X: 0 1 2 3
   Y: 10 20 30 40
   a. What is the slope?
   b. Is the slope in going from 0 to 1 different from the slope going from 2 to 3?
   c. Is this a linear or curvilinear relationship?

2. As income falls, people spend less on cars. Is the graph of this relationship positively or negatively sloped?

3. As the price of a good falls, people buy more of it. Is the graph of the relationship positively or negatively sloped?

FIGURE A

4. Answer the following questions using Figure A.
   a. What is the slope?
   b. What is area A (shaded area)?

5. Prepare two scatter diagrams relating the inflation rate to each of the other two variables from the data in Table A. In your opinion, do these diagrams reveal any positive or negative relationships?

TABLE A

	Inflation Rate	Unemployment Rate	Interest Rate
1980	9.5	7.0	11.5
1981	10.0	7.5	14.0
1982	6.2	9.5	10.7
1983	4.1	9.5	8.6
1984	4.4	7.4	9.6
1985	3.7	7.1	7.5
1986	2.6	6.9	6.0
1987	3.2	6.1	5.8
1988	3.9	5.4	6.7
1989	4.3	5.2	8.1
1990	4.2	5.4	7.5

SOURCE: *Economic Report of the President*

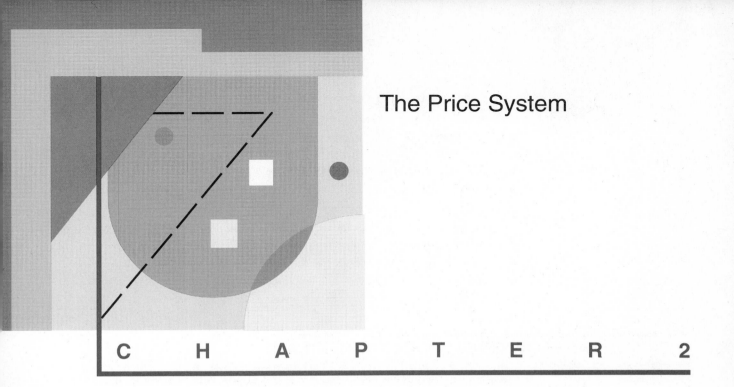

The Price System

CHAPTER FOCUS

We experience a daily wonder that has become so routine as to go unnoticed. The things that we wish to buy are waiting for us in stores, shops, and supermarkets. Residents of cities that manufacture only automobiles or power tools find that their stores are amply stocked not only with cars and power tools but also with products of every description. These things happen without direction from officials or bureaucrats. Adam Smith, the father of modern economics, described this phenomenon as *the invisible hand*.

Although the workings of the price system are routine to us, the leaderships of the newly emerging capitalist countries in the former Soviet Union remain skeptical. After decades of decision-making from above, they do not know if the price system can be trusted to coordinate economic decisions. Does not someone "upstairs" really have to decide? How can the price system ensure that people will have fuel to heat their homes and drive their cars, computers for their homes and offices, and even pencils for lecture notes and messages?

The price system coordinates the decisions of millions of consumers and producers without direction from above. Producers need not know much about their buyers. Buyers need not know how producers make the product. Moreover, producers themselves need not even understand the extraordinary chain of events required to make their product. The common wooden pencil requires the felling of trees, their milling by specialized equipment in faraway lands, the mining of graphite in Sri Lanka for the lead, and the production of rapeseed oil in the Dutch West Indies for the eraser. No single person in this chain need understand the entire chain. The decisions of all the people involved from the felling of the trees to the packaging of the pencils are coordinated by the price system.

After studying this chapter, you will be able to:

- See how the economy is a circular flow of goods and money from consumers to firms.
- Understand how solving the economic problem for any economy involves answering three questions: What? How? and For Whom?
- Know the difference between relative prices and money prices.
- Appreciate how relative prices guide decisions through the principle of substitution.
- See the importance of property rights in solving the economic problem.
- Understand how the price system coordinates economic activity and solves the economic problem.
- Explain the determinants of specialization and the role of money.
- Understand how transaction and information costs affect specialization and exchange.

THE CIRCULAR FLOW OF ECONOMIC ACTIVITY

Economic activity is circular. Consumers buy goods with the incomes they earn by furnishing labor, land, and capital to the business firms that produce the goods they buy. The dollars that households spend come back to them in the form of income from selling the services of their factors of production. A starting point for understanding how the price system works is to examine a **circular-flow diagram** of economic activity.

> The circular-flow diagram summarizes the flows of goods and services from producers to households and the flows of the factors of production from households to business firms.

Exhibit 1 illustrates the circular flow of economic activity. The flows from households to firms and from firms to households are regulated by two markets: the market for goods and services and the market for the factors of production. The circular-flow diagram consists of two circles. The outer circle shows the *physical flows* of goods and services and of productive factors. The inner circle shows the *flows of money expenditures* on goods and services and on productive factors. The physical flows and the money flows go in opposite directions. When households buy goods and services, physical goods flow to the households, but the sales receipts flow to the business sector. When workers supply labor to business firms, productive factors flow to the business sector, but the wage income flows to the household sector.

There are two pairs of supply and demand transactions in the circular flow:

1. The supply and demand for consumer goods are mediated by the market for goods and services.
2. The supply and demand for factors of production are mediated by the market for the factors of production.

THE ECONOMIC PROBLEM

Every society faces the **economic problem** of how to allocate scarce resources among competing ends. Three questions must be answered: *What* products will be produced? *How* will they be produced? *For whom* will they be produced?

EXHIBIT 1 The Circular Flow of Economic Activity

Economic activity is circular. The outside circle describes the flow of physical goods and services and productive factors through the system: business furnishes goods to households, which furnish land, labor, and capital to business. The inside circle describes the flow of dollars: households provide dollar sales to business, whose costs become incomes to households. These two circles flow in opposite directions.

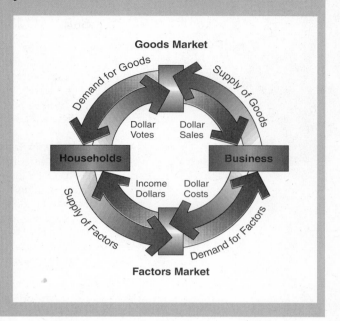

The **economic problem** is how to allocate scarce resources among competing ends.

What?

Should society devote its limited resources to producing civilian or military goods, luxuries or necessities, goods for immediate consumption or goods that increase the stock of capital (plant and equipment, housing, roads, and so forth)? Should small or large cars be produced, or should buses and subways be produced instead of cars? Should the military concentrate on strategic or conventional forces?

How?

Once the decision is made on what to produce, society must determine what combinations of the factors of production will be used. Will coal, petroleum, or nuclear power be used to produce electricity? Will bulldozers or workers with shovels dig dams? Should automobile tires be made from natural or synthetic rubber? Should tried-and-true production methods be replaced by new technology?

For Whom?

Will society's output be divided equally, or will claims to society's output be unequal? Will differences in wealth be allowed to pass from one generation to the next? What role will government play in determining *for whom?* Should government intercede to change the way the economy is distributing its output?

Adam Smith (1723–1790)

Adam Smith, the founder of modern economics, was born in Kirkaldy, Scotland, in 1723. He became Professor of Moral Philosophy at the University of Edinburgh in 1753. He was the prototype of the absent-minded professor, so engrossed in his thoughts that he sometimes forgot where he was. Smith lectured on ethics and published *The Theory of Moral Sentiments* in 1759—a book that brought him much fame but little fortune. The book argued that morals were the result of sympathy rather than self-interest.

At the time of Adam Smith, governments were active in granting monopolies and controlling foreign trade. In 1764, Smith had the good luck to have the time required to develop his thoughts on economics. Because of his reputation, he received an appointment as the tutor of a young Duke. He spent the next three years in France, where he discussed economic issues with leading French intellectuals and began a book on economics. Finally, in 1776, he published *An Inquiry into the Nature of Causes of the Wealth of Nations,* usually called *The Wealth of Nations.* One of the greatest books ever written, it brought Smith lasting fame.

Smith's great idea was that private greed may be a public virtue. He wrote:

> It is not from the benevolence of the butcher, the brewer, or the baker, that we expect our dinner, but from their regard to their own interest. We address ourselves, not to their humanity but to their self-love, and never talk to them of our own necessities but of their advantages

The self-interest of individuals leads them to specialize in those activities that maximize their own gain. In so doing, the nation as a whole experiences the greatest improvement in the productive powers of its labor force. The degree of specialization—or what Smith called the division of labor—is the consequence of the propensity of humans to engage in bargaining and exchange of one good or service for another. Smith has been regarded as the patron saint of capitalism. He argued that a system of free enterprise can solve the economic problems of society better than government monopolies and regulations.

RELATIVE PRICES AND MONEY PRICES

This chapter explains how a market economy, working through the price system, coordinates the millions of economic activities that enter the circular flow to solve the problems of what, how, and for whom. We begin our tour of the price system with the concept of relative prices.

Prices in the Land of Markkas

Suppose you find yourself in a strange land where the hospitable natives welcome you with a gift of local currency called the *markka.* Being in a hurry to eat breakfast, you locate a diner and order coffee, which costs 400 markkas. Is coffee cheap or expensive? Is the price high or low? You have no idea. Given the information you have at this point, the price of 400 markkas is meaningless.

How do you discover whether the price of coffee is high or low? You have to gather more information. The menu lists the price of a soft drink as 1,200 markkas, and another customer tells you that the typical worker earns something like 24,000 markkas per hour. Now you decide that coffee is cheap by reasoning: "Back home I pay $0.50 for a cup of coffee and $0.50 for a soft drink, and I earn $10.00 an hour. At home, an hour's work will purchase 20 soft drinks or 20 cups of coffee. But here an hour of work will purchase 20 soft drinks and 60 cups of coffee." This example delivers an important lesson: A money price in isolation from other money prices is meaningless. What is important is how a particular money price stands relative to other money prices.

CALCULATING RELATIVE PRICES

A **relative price** indicates how one price stands in relation to other prices. A relative price is quite different from a **money price**. In the above example, coffee sells for 400 markkas and soft drinks for 1,200 markkas. Three cups of coffee is the relative price of a soft drink, and one-third of a soft drink is the relative price of coffee. If coffee and soft drinks had both sold for 400 markkas, then the relative price of a soft drink would have been one cup of coffee.

A **relative price** is a price expressed in terms of other commodities.

A **money price** is a price expressed in monetary units (such as dollars, francs, etc.).

As these examples show, relative prices can be expressed in terms of anything. The relative price of a soft drink can be expressed in terms of cups of coffee, cups of tea, hours of work, number of T-shirts, or anything else that has a money price. If the price of apples is $0.50 per pound and the price of bananas is $0.25 per pound, the relative price of one pound of apples is two pounds of bananas. Conversely, one pound of bananas cost 0.5 pound of apples. If potatoes are $.10 per pound, the relative price of one pound of apples can also be expressed as five pounds of potatoes.

Money prices are meaningful when they are compared to prices of related goods. For example, as the price of electricity rises relative to the price of natural gas, it pays people to substitute gas heat for electrical heat. If pork prices rise relative to beef prices, it pays people to substitute beef for pork. If coffee prices rise relative to tea prices, people will substitute some tea consumption for coffee consumption.

As the relative price of a good falls, people tend to substitute that good for other goods.

Relative prices play a prominent role in answering the economic questions of *what, how,* and *for whom.* Money prices do not. Relative prices signal to buyers and sellers what goods are cheap or expensive. *Buying and selling decisions are made on the basis of relative prices.* If the relative price of one good rises, buyers substitute other goods whose relative prices are lower.

The emphasis on relative prices does not mean that money prices are unimportant. Money prices are important in macroeconomics. *Inflation* is defined as a general increase in money prices. Even in the case of inflation, money prices are not considered in isolation. Instead, the level of money prices today is compared to the level of money prices yesterday. Ultimately, this is also a form of relative price.

THE PRINCIPLE OF SUBSTITUTION

Relative prices are important because of the **principle of substitution**.

> The **principle of substitution** states that as the relative price of a product rises people will substitute another product to satisfy their demand.

Virtually no good is fully protected from the competition of substitutes. Aluminum competes with steel, coal with oil, electricity with natural gas, labor with machines, movies with TV, one brand of toothpaste with another, and so on. The only goods impervious to substitutes are such things as certain minimal quantities of water, salt, or food and certain life-saving medications, such as insulin.

To say that there is a substitute for every good does not mean that there is an *equally good* substitute for every good. One mouthwash is a close substitute for another mouthwash; a television show is a good substitute for a movie; apartments may be good substitutes for private homes. However, carrier pigeons are a poor substitute for telephone service. Costly insulation may be a poor substitute for fuel oil; public transportation may be a poor substitute for the private car in sprawling cities; steel is a poor substitute for aluminum in the production of jet aircraft.

Relative prices signal to consumers that substitutions are advantageous. If the price of one good rises relative to its substitutes, consumers will tend to switch to the relatively cheaper substitute. Substitutions are being made all around us. As the relative price of crude oil rises, utilities switch from oil to coal; retailers use fewer neon lights and hire more sales personnel. When the relative price of coffee increases, people consume more tea; when beef prices rise, the consumption of poultry and fish products increases. There is no single recipe for producing a cake, a bushel of wheat, a car, comfort, recreation, or happiness. (See Example 1.)

PROPERTY RIGHTS

Relative prices provide information to buyers and sellers on what goods are cheap and what goods are expensive. Substitutions depend on relative prices. The manner in which buyers and sellers act on relative-price information depends on **property rights**.

> **Property rights** are the rights of an owner to use and exchange property.

The individual owner of private property (whether it be land, a house, a horse, a truck, a wheat crop, or a can of peaches) has the legal freedom (the right) to sell that property at terms that are mutually agreed upon between the buyer and the seller. Normally, when property is sold, the buyer and the seller agree on a dollar price.

The legal system protects private-property rights. It protects private property from theft, damage, and unauthorized use and defines where property rights reside. An owner of private property usually has the right to use the property to the owner's best advantage and to sell the property at the best price possible. Most societies, however, place some restrictions on the use of private property. Deed restrictions, zoning, and licensing restrict the property owner's exercise of private property rights.

EXAMPLE 1

The Decline of IBM and the Principle of Substitution

This chapter teaches that when the price of one good rises, people substitute other goods that meet the same need. IBM, or "Big Blue," as it is called, has become an unexpected victim of the principle of substitution.

Since its rise to dominance of the computer industry in the late 1950s and early 1960s, IBM was the envy of all industry. Its markets grew every year; it employed the best salespersons who showed remarkable loyalty to the company. IBM stock became the favorite of Wall Street. No stock portfolio was complete without some shares of IBM. IBM's dominance of the computer industry became so strong that the Justice Department even charged it with monopolization of the computer industry in the 1970s.

As the 1990s progress, the luster appears to be wearing off IBM. IBM's share of the computer market is eroding. People are no longer rushing to buy IBM personal computers. Instead they are buying computers from companies with the unfamiliar names of Leading Edge, Eagle, Epson, and Macintosh. People are even buying "generic" IBM-compatible computers from companies that few have heard of.

Whereas in the 1970s and 1980s, people were reluctant to buy untested computers manufactured by unknown companies, in the 1990s people have come to realize that, with existing technology, a generic IBM-compatible computer can perform the same services as an IBM personal computer but at a lower price. Like wheat and corn, the personal computer market is becoming a generic market in which one computer brand is viewed as a good substitute for another, even if that other brand is made by IBM.

Owners of private property will be guided by relative prices in making decisions. The private owner of an oil refinery will use the relative prices of gasoline, fuel oils, and kerosene to determine how much of each petroleum product to refine and will look at the relative prices of imported and domestic crude oil to determine whether to use domestic or imported crude.

The private owner of labor (that is, the individual worker) will look at the relative wage rates in different occupations to determine where to seek employment. The private owner of farmland will look at the relative prices of agricultural products to determine what mix of crops to plant.

THE PRICE SYSTEM AS A COORDINATING MECHANISM

An economy consists of millions of consumers and hundreds of thousands of enterprises, and virtually every member of society owns some labor, land, or capital resources. Each participant makes economic decisions to promote his or her self-interest. What coordinates the decisions of all these people and businesses? What prevents the economy from collapsing when all these decisions clash? If all participants are looking out for themselves, will not the end result be chaos? Is it not necessary to have someone or something in charge?

The Invisible Hand

Adam Smith (see Gallery of Economists) described how the price system solves economic problems efficiently without conscious direction:

Every individual endeavors to employ his capital so that its produce may be of greatest value. He generally neither intends to promote the public interest, nor knows how much he is promoting it. He intends only his own security, only his own gain. And he is led by an invisible hand *to promote an end which was no part of his intention. By pursuing his own interest he frequently promotes that of society more effectively than when he really intends to promote it.*[1]

Smith's "invisible hand" works through the **price system**. A modern economy produces millions of commodities and services, each of which has a money price. These millions of money prices form millions of relative prices that inform buyers and sellers what goods are abundant and what goods are in short supply. If prices are set in free markets, the relative prices that emerge reflect the true economic scarcities of each good.

> The **price system** coordinates economic decisions by allowing people with property rights to resources to trade freely, buying and selling at whatever relative prices emerge in the marketplace.

Equilibrium

Each participant makes buying and selling decisions on the basis of relative prices. The family decides how to spend its income; the worker decides where and how much to work; the factory manager decides what inputs to use and what outputs to produce. Insofar as all these decisions on what to buy and sell are being made individually in isolation, what is to guarantee that there will be enough steel, bananas, foreign cars, janitorial services, steel workers, copper, and lumber for homes? What is to ensure that there will not be too much of one good and too little of another? Is Adam Smith's invisible hand powerful enough to prevent shortage and surplus?

Consider what would happen if U.S. automobile producers decide to produce more cars than buyers want to buy *at the price asked by the automobile producers.* The automobile manufacturers will be made aware of this fact, not by a directive from the government, but by the simple fact of too many unsold cars. Dealers must pay their bills and cannot live from unsold cars; therefore, they must sell the cars at lower prices. As the money price of cars falls, its relative price tends to fall, and customers begin to substitute automobiles for European vacations, home computers, or remodeled kitchens. The decline in the relative price of automobiles signals automobile manufacturers to produce fewer cars. Eventually, a balance between the number of cars people are prepared to buy (the demand) and the number offered for sale (the supply) will be struck, and the corresponding price is called an **equilibrium price**.

> The **equilibrium price** of a good or service is that price at which the amount of the good people are prepared to buy equals the amount offered for sale.

HOW THE PRICE SYSTEM DECIDES WHAT, HOW, AND FOR WHOM

The price system solves the *what, how,* and *for whom* problems without conscious direction. No single participant in the economy needs to see the big picture; each participant need only know the relative prices of the goods and services of

---

[1]Adam Smith, *The Wealth of Nations,* ed. Edwin Cannon (New York; Modern Library, 1937), p. 423.

immediate interest to that person. No single person or governmental organization is required to be concerned about the economy as a whole. No single person needs *all* the information available to the economy. The millions of individual economic decisions made daily are coordinated by the price system.

Consider an economy in which all property is privately owned and owners can freely use their property rights. Prices are set freely in markets. Each individual owns certain quantities of resources—land, labor, capital—that are sold or rented to business firms that produce the goods and services people want. Everything is sold at a price agreeable to the buyer and seller.

What the economy produces is determined by *dollar votes* cast by consumers for different goods and services and by the dollar costs of producing these goods and services. When consumers choose to buy a particular good or service, they are casting a dollar vote that communicates their demand for that good or service. Consumers, in casting their dollar votes, determine what will be produced. If no dollar votes are cast for a particular product, it will not be produced. If enough dollar votes are cast for a product relative to its cost of production, it will be produced. Just what quantities will be produced will be determined by prices. A higher price for any product signals to firms that greater profits can be made by increasing production. To illustrate, if consumers want more wheat, they will bid up wheat prices. In turn, the higher wheat prices will encourage farmers to grow more wheat.

How goods are produced is determined by business firms who seek to utilize their land, labor, and capital resources as economically as possible. Business firms produce those outputs that receive high dollar votes by combining resources in the least costly way. Business firms follow the principle of substitution. If the relative price of land is increased, farmers will use less land and more tractors and labor to work the land more intensively. If the relative price of farm labor increases, farmers will use less labor and more tractors and land. If the relative price of business travel rises, businesses will travel less and make more long-distance telephone calls. If the relative price of long-distance calls increases, businesses will telephone less and use more business travel. If business firms fail to reduce their costs through the use of the best available techniques and the best combination of the factors of production, the competition of other firms may drive them out of business.

The invisible hand that solves the what, how, and for whom questions works through the setting of free market prices.

For whom is determined by the dollar values the market assigns to resources owned by each separate household in the economy. The distribution of income between rich and poor reflects the prices paid for each resource and the distribution of ownership claims to scarce labor, land, and capital. People who own large quantities of land or capital will have a correspondingly large claim on the goods and services produced by the economy; those who are fortunate enough to provide high-priced labor services (doctors, lawyers, gifted athletes) will similarly receive a large share of the total output. At the other extreme, the poor are those who own few resources and furnish low-priced labor services to the market. (See Example 2.)

SPECIALIZATION

The price system automatically encourages the factors of production to specialize in those activities that they do better than others. Specialization raises efficiency and allows economies to produce ever larger output from their available inputs.

Specialization and Exchange

Suppose a single sailor were stranded on a remote island with no other human beings around—a modern Robinson Crusoe. While the sailor would have to

EXAMPLE 2

The Invisible Hand: The Paradox of Progress

As the U.S. economy entered the 1990s, Adam Smith's invisible hand brought about stunning downsizing in America's best-known companies. General Motors cut its labor force 74,000, Sears 83,000 employees, 25,000 at IBM, and 27,000 at Boeing. Such layoffs are big news and frightening to the average person.

But the invisible hand creates as well as destroys. While Sears downsized, Wal-Mart added 260,000 jobs; while IBM cut back, Microsoft, Intel, and Dell Computer expanded. General Motors shrank, but some 29,000 Americans were employed at new jobs with Honda, Toyota, Nissan, and other new Japanese plants built in the U.S.

Every day jobs are created and destroyed. In the short run, the process seems cruel. But in the long run, it is key to economic progress. In 1900, for example, 40 out of every 100 Americans worked in farms. Today, only 3 out of 100 need be farmworkers, while the remaining 97 out of 100 workers are involved in new homes, computers, pharmaceuticals, appliances, movies, video games, and many other goods and services.

Joseph Schumpeter called this process "creative destruction." In 1920, there were over 2 million railroad employees, now there are but 230,000. In 1900 only 51,000 workers repaired electronic equipment; today, 711,000 people do such work on much more advanced equipment. There are hardly any blacksmiths, boilermakers, or milliners today; but there are plenty of engineers, auto mechanics, and truck, bus, or taxi drivers.

The entire process is led by the invisible hand. Most people fear the process because it leads to lost jobs. Politicians sometimes want to freeze old jobs through government intervention. As pointed out in the 1992 annual report of the Federal Reserve Bank of Dallas: "History demonstrates the futility of saving jobs. For instance, it's hard to miss the absurdity of a well-intentioned program that 100 years ago might have aimed to keep blacksmiths and harness makers employed. As recently as 70 years ago, the United States had 10 million registered passenger cars but 20.5 million horses. Had our ancestors been able to freeze jobs, the United States would be stuck in the horse-and-buggy era."

SOURCE: "The Churn: The Paradox of Progress," Federal Reserve Bank of Dallas, 1992 Annual Report. Joseph Schumpter, *Capitalism, Socialism and Democracy,* 3d ed. New York: Harper and Brothers, 1950.

constantly make decisions about whether to make fish nets or fish hooks or whether to sleep or break coconuts, the economy of the desert island would lack many features of a modern economic system. The sailor would not be *specialized;* he would have to be a jack-of-all-trades. He would produce only those things that he wanted to consume, and he would not use *money.* He would still have to solve the problems of *what* and *how.* The *for whom* problem would be easy. Everything he produced would be for himself He could solve *what* and *how* without explicit relative prices, property rights, or markets.

In the modern economy, it is somewhat unsettling to think about the degree to which people are specialized. A typical household consumes thousands of articles; yet the principal breadwinner of the household may specialize in aligning suspension components on an automobile production line. In short, everyone in our economy (except hermits) is dependent on the efforts of others. We produce one or two things; we consume many things.

Specialization gives rise to exchange. Indeed, the exchange of one thing for another thing is the reverse side of the coin of specialization. If people consumed only those things they produced, there would be no trade and no need for money. Money, trade, exchange, and specialization are all characteristics of a complicated economy. Specialization means that people will produce more of particular goods than they consume and that these surpluses will be exchanged for other goods that they want.

Specialization and Productivity

Productivity increases when more output is produced from the same amount of productive resources. Specialization raises the productivity of the economy and raises incomes through economies of scale and by allowing resources to be used according to their comparative advantage.

Economies of Scale. Productivity can be raised by specialization to achieve **economies of scale**.

> Economies of scale are present when large volumes of output can be produced more cheaply than small volumes of output.

Economies of scale are achieved by concentrating certain resources in specific tasks. A worker spending all day typing and another worker spending all day sweeping floors can get more done than both spending half-days on each job. Individuals who focus on one task learn their jobs better and don't waste time switching from job to job. More cars can be produced by investing heavily in an elaborate assembly line that will produce millions of cars more cheaply than a few.

Comparative Advantage. Specialization allows resources, which have different characteristics, to be allocated to their best use, thereby raising their productivity and giving them higher income. People, land, and capital all come in different varieties. Some people are agile seven-footers; others are small and slow. Some people take easily to math and computers; others are frightened by numbers and technology. Some land is moist; other land is dry. Some land is hilly; other land is flat.

Because the factors of production have different characteristics and qualities, specialization offers opportunities for productivity advances. Economists refer to the best employment of a resource as its *comparative advantage*. The agile seven-footer has a comparative advantage in basketball; the fast-talker as a sales representative; the math whiz as a computer specialist. Land with high moisture content is best used in corn production; land with a relatively low moisture content is best used in wheat production.

Comparative advantage is not the same thing as an *absolute advantage*. It is possible that the agile seven-footer may also be the fastest typist. The math whiz may be the best salesperson. Particular farm acreage may be better suited to growing both wheat and corn than other farm acreage. Some people are poorly suited to just about everything in the sense that at every task they are less efficient than other people. How are comparative advantages determined in these more complicated cases?

In 1817, the English economist, David Ricardo, formulated the **law of comparative advantage**.

> The **law of comparative advantage** states that it is better for people to specialize in those activities in which their advantages over other people are greatest or in which their disadvantages compared to others are the smallest.

The easiest way to see this principle at work is to examine two extreme cases. Suppose that you can do any and every job better than anyone else. What would you, as such a superior person, do? You would not want to be a jack-of-all trades because it is likely that your *margin* of superiority will be greater in one occupation than in another. The job in which your margin of superiority over others is *the greatest* is the job you will do because it will give you the highest income.

Now examine the other extreme. Suppose there is no person in the community to whom you are superior *in any job;* you are less productive than any other person in the community in every occupation. What would you do in such an unfortunate situation? The job in which your disadvantage compared to others is the smallest would be the job that maximizes your income.

A mediocre computer programmer could possibly be the best clerk in the local supermarket. The clerks in the local supermarket may not be able to stock shelves and work a cash register as well as the computer programmer, but they have a *comparative advantage* in that occupation. An attorney may be the fastest typist in town, yet the attorney is better off preparing deeds than typing deeds. An engineering major may have verbal skills that exceed those of an English major, but his or her comparative advantage is in engineering.

The law of comparative advantage is nothing more than the principle that people should engage in those activities where their income is maximized. The price system encourages the factors of production to work according to their comparative advantage. For example, Sally can earn $1,000 a month as a bricklayer and $2,000 a month as a computer programmer. Joe can earn $500 a month as a bricklayer and $400 a month as a computer programmer. Sally is better than Joe at either bricklaying or programming. However, Sally should devote her time to computer programming and Joe to bricklaying. Each maximizes his or her income by devoting his or her energies to that task that maximizes income. Sally is 5 times better as a programmer, and only 2 times better as a bricklayer. Joe is disadvantaged at everything, but his least disadvantage is in bricklaying.

Everybody, from the best to the worst, has a comparative advantage in some job or line of work.

International Trade. The law of comparative advantage applies to people *and* countries. Both people and countries have one thing in common: Just as one person cannot transfer his or her talents to another, one country cannot transfer its people, climate, or natural resources to another country.

Each person has inborn "resources," such as intelligence, looks, manual dexterity, verbal skills, and mathematical skills. So do countries. The resource profile of the United States is quite different from that of South Korea. The United States is rich in capital and scientific personnel. South Korea has an industrious work force. A country's resources are best committed to those activities for which its advantages are the largest or its disadvantages are the smallest. America's largest advantages are in the production of high-technology goods, such as airplanes, and in agricultural products, such as wheat. South Korea's least disadvantages are in the production of such goods as TV sets and clothing. We say that South Korea has the "least disadvantage" because American workers produce TVs and clothing at higher levels of productivity than South Korean workers. The American productivity advantage is much higher in aircraft manufacturing and wheat farming than in TV and clothing manufacturing.

Just as people specialize in those activities in which they have a comparative advantage, so do countries specialize. Countries specialize and exchange, just as people specialize and exchange. The farmer exports wheat in return for manufactured goods. The United States exports aircraft and wheat in return for TV sets and clothing.

Specialization and Money

Money arises because people are specialized and do not produce everything they need. Money is useful because it reduces the cost of transacting with others. *Barter* is a system of exchange where products are traded for other products rather than for money. In barter, for example, it would be necessary for a barefoot baker to meet with a hungry shoemaker. In other words, a successful barter deal requires that the two traders have matching wants. In barter, successful trades require a double coincidence of wants.

Money is useful precisely because double coincidences of wants are rare. Money enables any person to trade with anyone else in a complicated economy. The form money takes differs from society to society. Money in a simple society will be quite different from money in a complicated society. In simple societies, things like fish hooks, sharks' teeth, beads, or cows have been used as money. In modern societies, money is issued and regulated by government, and money may (gold coins) or may not (paper money) have an intrinsic value of its own.

> **Money** is anything that is widely accepted in exchange for goods and services.

It is likely that if one form of money were abolished (by law), some other form would arise to serve as money. It is not necessary to pay the costs of barter.

TRANSACTION COSTS AND INFORMATION COSTS

People exchange goods and services because of specialization. One of the largest impediments to exchange is the existence of **transaction costs**. It is costly to bring buyers and sellers together. Some examples are the cost of transportation, the cost of negotiation, the cost of property-rights enforcement, government taxes and regulations, and the cost of acquiring information.

> **Transaction costs** are the costs associated with bringing buyers and sellers together and include the costs of negotiation, transportation, information, taxes, and government regulation.

A major part of the cost of making a transaction between a buyer and a seller is the **information costs** associated with searching for and acquiring economic information about prices and products. The buyer and seller must first find each other and then agree on the price and other terms of the contract. Knowledge of the existence and location of a willing buyer is valuable information to the seller, just as knowledge of a willing seller is valuable information to the buyer. Without this information, economic transactions cannot take place.

> **Information costs** are the costs of acquiring information on prices and products and include the costs of shopping, advertising, telephoning, and inspecting goods.

Buying and selling houses vividly illustrates the importance of transaction and information costs. Houses are not a homogeneous product, such as wheat or steel or sugar. Matching up buyers and sellers is a time-consuming process. Each buyer

How Transaction Costs Limit Exchange: Return Airline Tickets

The airlines often offer discounted round-trip fares that are cheaper than unrestricted one-way fares. Discounted round-trip fares have a number of restrictions (such as weekend travel or staying over a Saturday) that most passengers cannot meet. Because it is cheaper, many passengers buy round-trip tickets, fly one way, and let the return ticket go unused. Why don't ticket-holders simply sell their return tickets to people who can use them? There are any number of people who would welcome the opportunity to fly cheap from city A to city B.

High transaction costs explain why this opportunity for exchange is seldom utilized. Passengers with return tickets must use time and money resources to locate people willing to travel on the scheduled return date. If the return ticket is from Kansas City to St. Louis, the transaction costs of arranging a successful exchange would be too high relative to the benefits to the transacting parties. If the return ticket is from Honolulu to New York, the advantages of getting a cheap ticket may be high enough to outweigh the transaction costs.

In fact, Honolulu newspapers are full of personal advertisements offering to sell cheap return tickets to the mainland. The Kansas City newspapers, on the other hand, have virtually no ads offering cheap return tickets.

may have to inspect dozens of houses, and each seller may have to wait months or even years before finding a willing buyer. It is quite conceivable that for any given house, there are many people who would be more than willing to pay the seller's price. But finding them is another matter. It is so difficult that people often remain in an undesirable house for years. In a world of zero transaction costs, houses could presumably be sold instantly at the highest possible price! Obviously, it is the cost of transacting that makes the business of being a real estate agent a highly profitable occupation for those with a knack for matching potential buyers with potential sellers. (See Example 3.)

Because information is costly, each person specializes in certain types of information. Chemical engineers may know a great deal about producing plastics but may know little about building houses. The produce clerks know a great deal about displaying lettuce or apples but little about how they are grown. Homemakers know a great deal about the prices of groceries in their town but little about the prices of industrial machinery. Industrial-purchasing agents know more about machinery prices than about grocery prices. Some people—the industrial purchasing agent, the realtor, the stockmarket broker—make a profession of specializing in information, but their knowledge is limited to very specific areas. As the Chapter Focus explained, no one person knows how to make even a pencil from start to finish.

The role of scarce information in the economy is fundamental. Friedrich von Hayek, a Nobel laureate in economics, was one of the first to emphasize the way in which economies process and utilize information about prices and products. To Hayek, the principal problem of economics is "how to secure the best use of resources known to any member of society, for ends whose relative importance only those individuals know."[2]

---

[2]F. A. Hayek, "The Use of Knowledge in Society," *American Economic Review* 35 (1945): 510–30.

The Limits of the Invisible Hand

The same comment applies the invisible hand as to democracy: "Although democracy is a flawed system, mankind has yet to invent a superior system of government." Although there may be flaws in the workings of the price system, no one has yet to discover a superior means of allocating scarce resources. The collapse of the major alternative—the communist command economy—bears eloquent testimony to this point.

The fact that the invisible hand works well does not mean it works well in all cases. The most important policy issues in economics hinge on those instances when the invisible hand should not be used. Later chapters will show that, when the producer has a monopoly, the invisible hand may not provide the "best" result and that there are goods, called public goods, that private markets do not supply efficiently. The major policy question in macroeconomics is whether the invisible hand can provide an appropriate level of output and employment for the economy as a whole or whether some form of government guidance is required.

Societies are constantly exploring the limits to the invisible hand. Activities that had previously been the preserve of government allocation are no longer "off limits" for the invisible hand. The 1980s saw the advent of the private prison and the increasing use of private firms in garbage collection and waste disposal.

In the 1990s, private firms became involved in the business of managing welfare programs, an area that had been exclusively handled by government offices. Firms like MAXIMUS, Inc., America Works, and Lockheed IMS manage welfare training and disbursement programs in California, New York, and Colorado. Although private companies account for a small portion of the nation's massive $30 billion annual welfare bill, they promise to help more clients for less by using better computer programs, more flexible staff, and less bureaucracy. Some studies show that the use of private firms can cut welfare costs by half. Private firms are paid only if they are successful, while the government welfare bureaucracy must be paid no matter what.

Policy makers must choose what goods and services should be provided by the invisible hand and which by administrative and bureaucratic decisions. The choice between private or public provision of welfare administration is only one example. Others are the proposed "privatization" of public schools and the use of market principles to deal with pollution rights.

SOURCE: Jay Mathews, "Taking Welfare Private," *Newsweek,* June 29, 1992, p. 44.

How is the economy to utilize knowledge about product prices, qualities, and locations that is not available to any one person or institution in its entirety? Hayek's answer is that the price system allows specialization in information that is specific to each person's particular circumstances of time and place. People can acquire only the knowledge about those things that they need to know. By allowing people to be paid for their scarce information, the price system economizes on information costs. The auto mechanic does not have to learn nuclear physics, and the physicist does not have to know how to repair a car.

This chapter has described in general terms how scarce resources are allocated by the price system and has explained the organization of property rights. Equilibrium prices are like an invisible hand that coordinates the decisions of many different persons. The next chapter examines the detailed workings of supply and demand in an individual market and answers the questions: How is the equilibrium price set? What causes equilibrium prices to increase or decrease?

Chapter Summary

The most important point to learn from this chapter is: The price system can act like an invisible hand to guide people to do what is best for society even though people are looking out only for themselves.

1. The circular-flow diagram summarizes the flows of goods and services from producers to households and the flows of factors of production from households to producers.

2. Relative prices guide the economic decisions of individuals and businesses. They signal to buyers and sellers what substitutions to make.

3. The principle of substitution states that no single good is irreplaceable. Users substitute one good for another in response to changes in relative prices.

4. Property can be owned by private persons, by the state, or by combinations of the two.

5. The "invisible hand" analogy, originated by Adam Smith in 1776, describes how a price system can allow individuals to pursue their self-interest and yet provide an orderly, efficient economic system that functions without centralized direction. If too much of a product is produced, its relative price will fall. If too little of a product is produced, its relative price will rise. The balance of supply and demand is called an equilibrium. The *what* problem is solved by dollar votes. Consumers determine what will be produced. The *how* problem is solved by individual producers. Competition among producers will encourage them to combine resource inputs efficiently. The solution of the *for whom* problem is determined by who owns productive resources and by the relative prices of resources.

6. Specialization is responsible for productivity improvements. Specialization occurs because of the differences among people, land, and capital and because of the economies of large-scale production. The law of comparative advantage states that the factors of production will specialize in those activities in which their advantages are greatest or in which their disadvantages are smallest.

7. Transaction costs make profitable exchanges more difficult. Information costs encourage people to specialize in information.

Policy Focus: Policy makers must choose what goods and services are to be produced by private markets or by government decisions.

Key Terms

circular-flow diagram (p. 30)
economic problem (p. 30)
relative price (p. 33)
money price (p. 33)
principle of substitution (p. 34)
property rights (p. 34)
price system (p. 36)

equilibrium price (p. 36)
economies of scale (p. 39)
law of comparative advantage (p. 39)
money (p. 41)
transaction cost (p. 41)
information cost (p. 41)

Questions and Problems

1.   In 1963, a typical car could be bought for about $2,000 and in 1994 a typical car sold for about $15,000. But on the average what cost $100 in 1963 costs about $500 in 1994. Did the relative price of a car increase or fall compared to most goods and services?

2.   In the circular-flow diagram, how are the dollar costs of business firms related to the incomes of households?

3.   If you own an automobile, what property rights do you

have? What restrictions are placed upon these property rights?

4. Explain why you can usually find the items you want at a grocery store without having ordered the goods in advance.

5. From the data in Table A, calculate the relative price of coffee. Explain your answer. (As an exercise in graphing, you may want to plot the various prices.)

TABLE A

	Price of Coffee (dollars per pound)	Price of Electricity (dollars per million BTUs)	Price of Tea (dollars per pound)
1970	0.535	5.83	0.390
1975	0.683	9.23	0.582
1980	1.70	14.09	0.858
1982	1.40	18.04	0.764

6. This chapter noted that not every product has a good substitute. Which of the following pairs of products are good substitutes? Which are poor substitutes? Explain the general principles you used to get your answers.
   a. Coffee and tea.
   b. Compact Chevrolets and compact Fords.
   c. Cars and city buses.
   d. Electricity and natural gas.
   e. Telephones and express mail.

7. Computer manufacturers want to sell more personal computers than customers want to buy at the going price. Explain why the equilibrium price could be higher or lower than the going price.

8. You own a 3-carat diamond ring which you no longer like. In fact, you would like to have a new color television set. How would you go about getting the television set in a barter economy? From this generalize about the efficiency of exchange in a barter economy versus a monetary economy.

9. "Specialization takes place only when people are different. If all people were identical, there would be no specialization." Evaluate this statement.

10. Assume that while shopping, you see long lines of people waiting to buy bread while fresh meat is spoiling in butcher shops. From these observations, what can you say about prevailing prices? What is your prediction about what will happen to the relative price of bread?

11. Bill can prepare 50 hamburgers per hour and wait on 25 tables per hours. Mike can prepare 20 hamburgers per hour and wait on 15 tables per hour. Hamburgers earn a profit of $0.60 each and tips are a dollar per table. If Bill and Mike were to open a hamburger stand, who should be the cook? Who the waiter? Would Bill do both?

12. In an hour's time, Jill can lay 100 tiles and can mortar 50 bricks. Tom can lay 10 tiles and 20 bricks in an hour's time. If every tile laid or every brick mortared pays $1, what would be the hourly earnings of Tom and Jill when they practice their comparative advantage?

13. Which of the following transactions would enter the circular flow and which would not?
   a. U.S. Steel sells steel to General Motors.
   b. General Motors sells a car to Jones.
   c. Jones takes a job from General Motors and receives $100 pay.
   d. Jones has his suit cleaned at the local dry cleaner and pays $5.
   e. Jones washes his dress shirt.

14. Why would an economy that used money be more efficient than the same economy that utilized only barter (where people exchanged their surplus goods for wanted goods)?

15. Unmarried males under 25 pay higher car insurance rates than married males. Yet, there are some unmarried males who are far safer drivers than the average married males. Why do these unmarried males still pay higher insurance rates?

Doing Economics

Interview two or more people who have been working for at least ten years. Inquire about how they chose their occupations. In particular, ask what alternative occupations they considered (or perhaps worked at for some time) and why they rejected these in favor of their current jobs. Find out what role (if any) the salary they expected to earn played in their decisions. What particular skills of each individual are utilized well in his or her current job? After completing the interviews, evaluate what role comparative advantage played in making the occupational decisions. How did the price system convey the information that the individuals needed to make the best occupational decision? Were any considerations other than comparative advantage important in occupational choice? How would these considerations affect the price system?

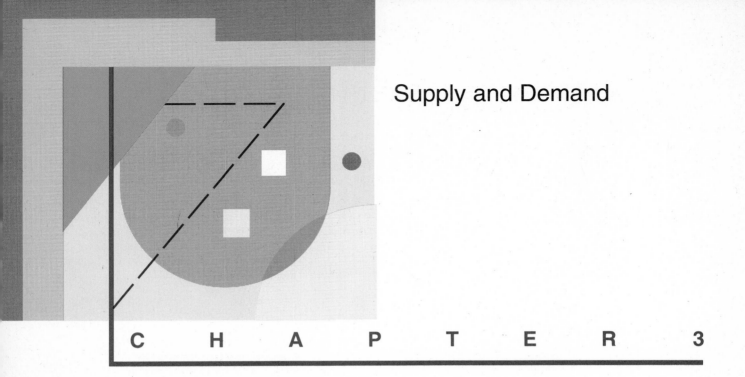

Supply and Demand

CHAPTER 3

CHAPTER FOCUS   Just as some people think that all doctors prescribe "two aspirin and call me in the morning" for all ailments, people think that economists only use supply and demand to deal with all economic problems. Supply and demand are indeed powerful tools in the hands of the experienced economist. They explain how the forces of supply and demand determine prices. The previous chapter explained how economic decision-making is based on the price system; therefore, it is important to know where prices come from.

When supply and demand work smoothly, the resulting market prices attract little attention. However, when there are disruptions—such as cutoffs of the Mideast oil supply or panic purchases before and after massive hurricanes—there is a cry for intervention. Rather than letting supply and demand set prices, people then say, the government should intervene to hold prices down!

Sometimes it is easier to understand what supply and demand do during those very periods when prices are set by administrative means. This chapter shows that markets set equilibrium prices that strike balances between buyers and sellers. At any other prices, there will be imbalances. These imbalances, called shortages and surpluses, must be well understood by the public and policymakers alike to prevent poor public policy from being followed.

After studying this chapter you should be able to:

- Define perfect competition.
- State the law of demand.
- Understand the difference between changes in demand and changes in quantity demanded.
- See why the supply curve is usually upward sloping.
- Understand the difference between changes in supply and changes in quantity supplied.
- Appreciate the meaning of the equilibrium price.
- Understand the causes of shortages and surpluses.

MARKETS

People buy and sell goods through established channels and institutions. To understand the mechanics of supply and demand, we must narrow our vision to the study of the way a *single market* works. In each **market**, buyers and sellers are guided by price in their buying and selling decisions.

> A **market** is an established arrangement by which buyers and sellers come together to exchange particular goods or services.

Types of Markets

There are many types of markets. A retail store, a gas station, a farmer's market, real-estate markets, the New York Stock Exchange (where stocks are bought and sold), Chicago commodity markets (where livestock, grains, and metals are traded), auctions of works of art, gold markets in London, Frankfurt, and Zurich, labor exchanges, university placement offices, and hundreds of other specialized arrangements are all markets. A market brings together buyers and sellers of a particular good or service. The New York Stock Exchange brings together the buyers and sellers of corporate stock by means of modern telecommunications. Sotheby's auctions in London and New York bring together the sellers and buyers of rare works of art. The Rotterdam oil market brings together buyers and sellers of crude oil not under long-term contracts. The gas station brings together the buyers and sellers of gasoline.

In some markets, the buyers and sellers confront each other face-to-face (roadside farm markets). In other markets, the buyer never sees the seller (the Chicago commodity markets). Some markets are local (brining together local buyers and sellers); others are national (brining together buyers and sellers in all parts of the nation); others are international (bringing together buyers and sellers in all parts of the world). Real estate is traded in local markets; houses and buildings cannot be shipped from one place to another. College textbooks are usually exchanged in a national market. The New York Stock Exchange, the various gold exchanges, and the Chicago commodity exchanges bring together buyers and sellers from around the world.

Alfred Marshall (1842–1924)

Born in England in 1842, Alfred Marshall was to become Professor of Political Economy at Cambridge University. At the age of 75 he wrote:

> . . . the more I studied economic science, the smaller appeared the knowledge which I had of it, in proportion to the knowledge that I needed; and now, at the end of nearly half a century of almost exclusive study of it, I am conscious of more ignorance of it than I was at the beginning of the study.

Marshall developed many of his most important ideas while taking long walks in the high Alps. He would leave Cambridge in early June and return in October. According to Mary Marshall:

> He would walk with a knapsack on his back for two or three hours. He would then sit down, sometimes on a glacier, and have a long pull at some book. . . .

Marshall's masterpiece was his *Principles of Economics,* published in 1890. He combined simple graphical methods with wisdom and learning about the facts and circumstances of various industrious. Earlier economists emphasized the primacy of supply conditions in determining price. Marshall maintained that price was the outcome of both supply *and* demand forces, and used an analogy to make his point: "We might as reasonably dispute whether it is the upper or the under blade of a pair of scissors that cuts a piece of paper." Marshall was the first to use graphical methods in economics. The demand and supply curves in this book are drawn the way he drew them. We put price on the vertical axis and quantity on the horizontal axis because Marshall did it that way.

It is difficult to study economics without being Marshall's "student." His contributions grace microeconomics, macroecnomics, and the field of international trade.

Perfectly Competitive Markets

Markets exhibit different degrees of competition among the buyers and sellers. This chapter deals with a very special type of market called a **perfectly competitive market**.

A **perfectly competitive market** has the following characteristics:

1. The product's price is uniform throughout the market.
2. Buyers and sellers have perfect information about price and the product's quality.
3. There are a large number of buyers and sellers.
4. No single buyer or seller purchases or sells enough to change the price.

The principal characteristic of a perfectly competitive market is that buyers and sellers face so much competition that no person or group can control the price. The markets where most people buy and sell goods are not perfect. Buyers and sellers may not be perfectly informed about prices and qualities. Two homemakers pay different prices in nearby grocery stores for the same national brand of cookies. Chemically equivalent brand-name and generic drugs sell at different prices. AT&T, General Motors, and Saudi Arabia exercise some control over the prices they charge.

Many products, however, are exchanged in perfect markets. Stocks and bonds and commodities such as wheat, silver, copper, gold, foreign currencies, oats, pork bellies, soybeans, lumber, cotton, orange juice, cattle, cocoa, and platinum are bought and sold in perfectly competitive markets. Although markets like the local grocery store, the dry cleaner, the gas station, or the roadside stand are not perfectly competitive, they function in a way that *approximates* perfect competition. Perfectly competitive markets serve as a useful guide to the way many real-world markets function and are a valuable starting point for examining economic behavior.

DEMAND

As a consumer, you may want a good, but not buy it. You may want a Rolls-Royce, but it is unlikely that you can afford one. To *demand* a good or service a consumer must be willing and able to purchase it. The actual **quantity demanded** of a good depends on its price, holding all other factors constant.

> The **quantity demanded** is the amount of a good or service consumers are prepared to buy at a given price (during a specified time period), holding other factors constant.

The Law of Demand

People buy more of a good if its price falls; they buy less if the price rises, holding other factors constant. A fundamental law of economics is the **law of demand**.

> The **law of demand** states that as the price of a good falls the quantity demanded rises, holding other factors constant.

Chapter 2 studied the principle of substitution. As the price of any product goes up, people will tend to find substitutes for that product. If the price of gasoline rises, drivers will cut back on less essential driving, and more people will take the bus, or walk, or ride their bicycles to work. If the price of tea rises, more people will drink coffee, or cut back one or two cups a day, or buy a soft drink. If the price rises enough, some people will stop buying it entirely, and the number of users will fall. The universal and natural tendency is for people who consume or use the goods to *substitute other goods or services* when the price of a good goes up. Higher prices discourage consumption.

People also tend to buy less of a good as its price goes up because *they feel poorer*. If a person buys a new car every year for $5,000 (after trade-in), and the price rises to $9,000 (after trade-in), the person would need an extra $4,000 yearly income to maintain the old standard of living. The $4,000 increase in the price of the car is like a cut in income of $4,000. The rise in a price, especially of a good that is important in family budgets, reduces the amount of income left to purchase not only the good whose price has risen but also other goods. (See Example 1.)

The Demand Curve

The relationship between quantity demanded and price is called the **demand curve** or the **demand schedule**. The relationship is negative because of the law of

M&Ms and the Law of Demand

The law of demand states that the quantity demanded will increase as the price is lowered, as long as other factors that affect demand do not change. In the real world, factors that affect the demand for a particular product change frequently. Tastes change, income rises, and prices of substitutes and complements change. In 1984, the makers of M&M candy conducted an experiment that illustrates the law of demand. Over a 12-month test period, the price of M&Ms was held constant in 150 stores, and the content weight of the candy was increased. When the price is held constant and the weight increased, the price per ounce is lowered. In the stores where the price per ounce was dropped, sales rose by 20 to 30 percent almost overnight, according to the director of sales development for M&Ms. As predicted by the law of demand, a reduction in price causes the quantity demanded to rise, *ceteris paribus*.

SOURCE: "Why Do Hot Dogs Come in Packs of 10 and Buns in 8s and 12s?" *Wall Street Journal,*September 21, 1984.

demand; along a demand curve price and quantity go in opposite directions. To avoid confusion, we shall talk about the *demand schedule* when the relationship is in tabular form and about the *demand curve* when the relationship is in graphical form.

> The **demand curve** or **demand schedule** for a good shows the various quantities demanded at different prices over a specified time period, holding other factors constant.

Exhibit 1 shows a hypothetical demand curve for corn. Buyers in the marketplace will demand 20 million bushels of corn per month at the price of $5 per bushel (point *a*). It is important to state the units of the measurement for both the price and the quantity. In this example, price is in dollars per bushel, and quantity is in millions of bushels per month. Should the price of corn be lower—say, $4 per bushel—then the quantity demanded is higher. In this case, the quantity demanded at the lower price of $4 is 25 million bushels (point *b*). By continuing to decrease the price, it is possible to get buyers to purchase more and more corn. At the price of $1, quantity demanded will be 50 million bushels (point *e*).

The demand curve drawn through points *a* to *e* is labeled *D*. It has a negative slope. Since the relationship between price and quantity demanded is downward sloping, the law of demand is sometimes called the *law of downward sloping demand*.

Most of the demand curves used in this book are **market-demand curves**. A later chapter will discuss the demand curves of individuals and will show that market-demand curves are the sum of individual demand curves. The market-demand curve summarizes the actions of all the buyers in a particular market.

> The **market-demand curve** is the demand curve of all persons participating in the market for that particular product.

EXHIBIT 1   The Demand Curve for Corn

a. Graph of Demand Curve for Corn

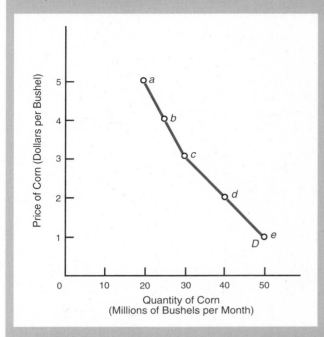

b. Demand Schedule for Corn

	Price (dollars per bushel)	Quantity Demanded (millions of bushels per month)
a	5	20
b	4	25
c	3	30
d	2	40
e	1	50

Panels (a) and (b) describe how the quantity of corn demanded responds to the prices of corn, holding all other factors constant. At *a*, when the price of corn is $5 per bushel, the quantity demanded is 20 million bushels per month. At *e*, when the price of corn is $1, the quantity demanded is 50 million bushels. The downward-sloping curve in panel (a) *(D)* is drawn through these points and is the demand curve for corn. Graphically, it shows the amounts of corn consumers would be willing to buy at different prices in the specified time period.

The demand curve shows the quantities people are prepared to buy at a different prices, *ceteris paribus.*

The *demand curve for corn* in Exhibit 1 refers to all buyers in the corn market. The corn market is an international market that brings together virtually all buyers of corn. The demand curve for Detroit real estate brings together all buyers of Detroit real estate. The demand curve for U.S. automobiles brings together the demand curves of all private, corporate, and governmental buyers of U.S. produced automobiles.

Factors That Cause the Demand Curve to Shift

The willingness of people to buy a good or service depends on a number of factors other than the price of the good or service itself. The demand curve for corn shows how corn purchases would change *if only the price of corn changed and all other factors remained the same.* Factors other than the price of corn can affect people's willingness to purchase corn. When those factors change, people may be willing to buy more (or less) corn at the same price as before. A change in one of the other factors would cause the demand curve to shift either to the right or to the left.

In the real world, other factors that affect demand are constantly changing; therefore, it is crucial to understand how changes in factors other than the good's own price affect the demand for a good. The main factors that can affect the demand for a good (in addition to its own price) are:

1. the prices of related goods,
2. consumer income,
3. consumer preferences,
4. the number of potential buyers, and
5. expectations.

The Prices of Related Goods.   Goods can be related to each other in two ways. Two goods are **substitutes** if the demand for one rises when the price of the other rises (or when the demand falls when the price of the other falls). Examples of substitutes are: coffee and tea, two brands of soft drinks, stocks and bonds, bacon and sausage, pork and beef, oats and corn, foreign and domestic cars, natural gas and electricity. Some goods are very close substitutes (two different brands of fluoride toothpaste), and others are very distant substitutes (Toyota cars and horsedrawn buggies).

> Two goods are substitutes if the demand for one rises when the price of the other rises (or if the demand for one falls when the price of the other falls).

Two goods are **complements** if increasing the price of one good lowers the demand for the other. Examples of complements are: automobiles and gasoline, food and drink, white dress shirts and neckties, skirts and blouses. When goods are complements there is a tendency for the two goods to be used jointly in order to achieve something more general (for example, automobiles plus gasoline equals transportation). An increase in the price of one of the goods effectively increases the price of the joint product of the two goods together. Thus, an increase in the price of one of the goods will reduce the demand for the other.

> Two goods are complements if the demand for one rises when the price of the other falls (or if the demand for one falls when the price of the other rises).

Income.   It is easy to understand how income influences demand. It is a fact of economic life that as incomes rise, people spend more on a great many **normal goods** and services. But as income increases, people also spend less on a few **inferior goods** and services.

> A normal good is one for which demand increases when income increases, holding all prices constant.

> An inferior good is one for which demand falls as income increases, holding all prices constant.

Lard, day-old bread, and second-hand clothing are examples of inferior goods for the market as a whole. For some people, inferior goods might be hamburgers, margarine, bus rides, or black-and-white TV sets. But most goods—from automobiles to water—are normal goods. All goods are normal at low enough levels of income.

Preferences.   To the economist, the word *preferences* means what people like and dislike without regard to budgetary considerations. One may *prefer* a 10-bedroom mansion but may only be able to afford a 3-bedroom bungalow. One may prefer a Mercedes-Benz but may drive a Volkswagen. One may prefer T-bone

Shifts in Demand: Wine, Health, and Recession

This chapter teaches that demand shifts as incomes and tastes change. Prices rise when demand increases and fall when demand falls.

The demand for wine, especially fine wines, is sensitive to income. When incomes are generally rising, the demand for wine rises, and there is upward pressure on wine prices. When incomes are generally falling the reverse happens. The prolonged U.S. business slump that began in 1990 caused the demand for wine to fall in the United States. Retail outlets had to discount the prices of their finer wines by 20 percent or more. The 1990s made wineries long for the booming 1980s—a period of rising incomes throughout the world.

All was not lost for wineries. The much-watched television show "60 Minutes" aired a segment in late 1991 which suggested that moderate wine consumption reduces the risk of heart attacks. After the original broadcast and its rebroadcast, sales of red wine shot up, reversing some of the decline caused by the slumping economy. People called the "60 Minutes" segment the 20 minutes that changed the industry.

When one winery ran an ad claiming that wine has therapeutic values as well as being recommended by the Bible, the government stepped in to ban this claim.

The public perception that wine is good for your health caused consumer preferences toward wine to improve, thereby increasing the demand for wine.

SOURCES: "Wineries and Government Clash Over Ads That Toast Health Benefits of Drinking," *Wall Street Journal,* October 19, 1992, p. B8. "Fine French Vintages Become a Hard Sell in Slumping Economy," *Wall Street Journal,* October 20, 1992, p. A1.

steaks but may eat hamburgers. Preferences plus budgetary considerations (price and income) determine demand. As preferences change, demand will change. If people learn that walking will increase their life span, the demand for walking shoes will increase. Business firms spend enormous sums trying to influence preferences by advertising on television, in newspapers, and in magazines. The goal of advertising is to shift the demand curve for the product to the right (See Example 2).

The Number of Potential Buyers. If more buyers enter a market, the demand will rise. The number of buyers in a market can increase for a number of reasons. Relaxed immigration barriers or a baby boom may lead to a larger population. The migration of people from one region to another changes the number of buyers in each region. The relaxation of trade barriers between two countries may increase the number of foreign buyers. If Japanese restrictions on imports of U.S. meat products were removed, the number of buyers of U.S. meat products would effectively increase. Lowering the legal age for alcoholic-beverage purchases will increase the number of buyers of beer.

Expectations. If people believe that the price of coffee over the next year will rise substantially (for whatever reason), they may decide to stock up on coffee. During inflationary times, when people find prices of goods rising rapidly, they often start buying durable goods, such as cars and refrigerators. The mere expectation of a good's price rising can induce people to buy more of it. Similarly, people can postpone the purchase of things that are expected to get cheaper. During the 1980s home computers grew cheaper and cheaper. Some buyers deliberately postponed purchasing home computers expecting that the good could

When the demand curve shifts to the left, *people want to buy smaller quantities of the good at each price.* A leftward shift of the demand curve indicates a *decrease in demand.* When the demand curve shifts to the right, *people want to buy larger quantities of the good at each price.* A rightward shift of the demand curve indicates an *increase in demand.*

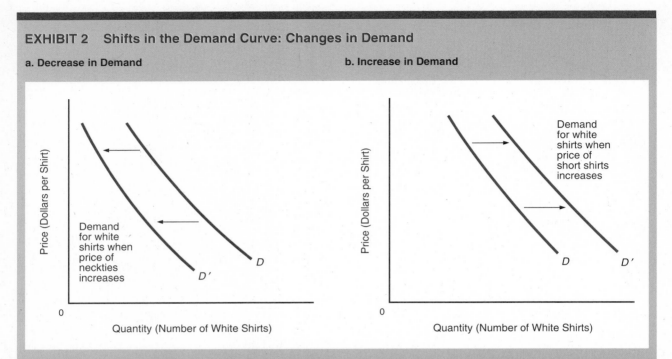

EXHIBIT 2   Shifts in the Demand Curve: Changes in Demand

a. Decrease in Demand

b. Increase in Demand

Panel (a) shows a decrease in the demand for white dress shirts. Initially, the demand curve is *D*. If income decreases or if the price of some substitute falls or if tastes turn against white dress shirts, then at each price for white dress shirts the demand falls. The demand curve shifts to the left from *D* to *D'*. Panel (b) shows an increase in demand for white dress shirts. If income increases or if the price of some substitute increases or if tastes shift in favor of white dress shirts, then at each price demand increases. The demand curve will shift rightward from *D* to *D"*. A rightward shift reflects an increase in demand, and a leftward shift reflects a decrease in demand.

be purchased for less in the future. Finally, expecting income increases may dramatically affect consumer purchases in general.

Changes in any of the above five factors will *shift the entire demand curve* for the good. Exhibit 2 shows the demand curve for white dress shirts. This curve, *D*, holds constant such factors as the prices of complements and substitutes, income, preferences, and the number of buyers.

Demand curves shift to the right or left when factors other than the good's own price change. If consumer income increases, and if white dress shirts are a normal good, demand will increase (*D* will shift to the right). If preferences change and white dress shirts fall out of fashion, demand will decrease (*D* will shift to the left). If buyers expect prices of white dress shirts to rise substantially in the future, demand will increase.

> A change in a factor other than the good's own price that affects demand (such as prices of substitutes and complements, income, preferences, expectations, or the number of buyers) will cause the entire demand curve to shift.

SUPPLY

The **quantity supplied** of a particular good and service depends very much on the price of the product, holding other factors constant.

> The **quantity supplied** of a good or service is the amount of the good or service offered for sale at a given price, holding other factors constant.

The quantity supplied of a good should change when its price changes. As a general rule, the higher the price, the greater is the quantity supplied. A higher price for corn, for example, will induce farmers to cultivate fewer soybeans and plant more corn. A higher price for corn will cause farmers to ensure that corn is not wasted during harvesting or harmed by the weather or pests. A higher price for oil makes it more profitable for oil companies to take more risks when searching for new oil or when drilling for oil (for example, drilling deeper or through rock). In most cases, the higher the price of a good, the greater the quantity supplied.

The Supply Curve

The **supply curve** or **supply schedule** shows the different quantities supplied at different prices. Consider now the typical case of a positive relationship between price and quantity supplied. Panel (a) of Exhibit 3 shows a hypothetical curve for corn (drawn from the accompanying supply schedule panel (b)). When the price of corn is $5 per bushel, farmers are prepared to supply 40 million bushels per month (point *a*). As the price falls to $4, the quantity supplied falls to 35 million bushels (point *b*). Finally, when the price is $1 farmers are prepared to sell only 10 million bushels (point *e*).

EXHIBIT 3   The Supply Curve for Corn

a. Graph of Supply Curve for Corn

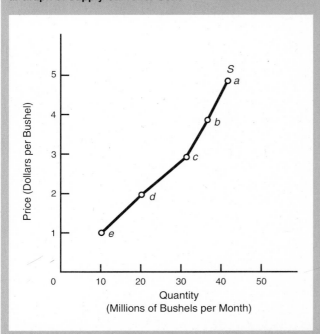

b. Supply Schedule for Corn

	Price (dollars per bushel)	Quantity Supplied (millions of bushels per month)
a	5	40
b	4	35
c	3	30
d	2	20
e	1	10

Panel (a) shows how the quantity of corn supplied responds to the price of corn. In situation *a*, when the price of corn is $5 per bushel, the quantity supplied by farmers is 40 million bushels per month. In the last situation, *e*, when the price is $1 per bushel, the quantity supplied is only 10 million bushels per month. The upward-sloping curve *(S)* drawn through these points is the supply curve of corn.

> The **supply curve** or **supply schedule** of a particular good or service shows the various quantities supplied at different prices, holding other factors constant, during a particular time period.

The curve drawn through points *a* through *e*, labeled *S*, is the supply curve. *It shows how much farmers are prepared to offer for sale at each price.* Along the supply curve, the price of corn and the supply of corn are positively related: in order to induce farmers to offer a large quantity of corn on the market, a higher price is required.

Factors That Cause the Supply Curve to Shift

Factors that shift the supply curve are changes in prices, resource prices, technology, number of sellers, and expectations.

Just as factors other than the good's own price can change the relationship between price and quantity demanded, other factors can change the relationship between price and quantity supplied, causing the supply curve to shift. The principal factors that can cause the supply curve to shift are:

1. the prices of other goods,
2. the prices of relevant resources,
3. technology,
4. the number of sellers, and
5. expectations.

The Prices of Other Goods. The resources that are used to produce any particular good can almost always be used elsewhere in the economy. Farmland can be used for corn or soybeans; engineers can work on cars or trucks; unskilled workers can pick strawberries or cotton; trains can be used to move coal or cars. As the price of a good rises, resources are naturally attracted away from other goods that use those resources. Hence, the supply of corn will fall if the price of soybeans rises; if the price of cotton rises the supply of strawberries may fall. If the price of trucks rises, the supply of cars may fall. If the price of fuel oil rises, less kerosene may be produced.

The Prices of Relevant Resources. The production and provision of goods and services requires certain resources that must be purchased in resource markets. As these resource prices change, the supply conditions for the goods being produced change. An increase in the price of coffee beans will increase the costs of producing coffee and decrease the amount of coffee that coffee companies are prepared to sell at each price; an increase in the price of corn land, tractors, harvesters, or irrigation will tend to reduce the supply of corn; an increase in the price of cotton will tend to decrease the supply of cotton dresses; an increase in the price of jet fuel will decrease the supply of commercial aviation at each price.

Technology. *Technology* is the knowledge that people have about how different things can be produced. If technology improves, more goods can be produced from the same resources. For example, if lobster farmers in Maine learn how to feed lobsters more cheaply with a new and cheaper combination of nutritious food, the quantity of lobsters supplied at each price will tend to increase. If a firm finds that the assembly line can be speeded up by merely rearranging the order of assembly, the supply of the good will tend to increase. If new oil-recovery procedures are discovered, the supply of oil will increase.

The Number of Sellers. If more sellers produce a particular good (perhaps because of high profits or in anticipation of high profits), the supply of the good

When the supply curve shifts to the left, *producers are prepared to sell smaller quantities at each price.* A leftward shift indicates a *decrease in supply.* When the supply curve shifts to the right, *producers are prepared to sell larger quantities at each price.* This rightward shift indicates an *increase in supply.*

will increase. The lowering of trade barriers (such as dropping cumbersome licensing requirements for foreign firms) may allow foreign sellers to enter the market, increasing the number of sellers.

Expectations.   It takes a long time to produce many goods and services. When a farmer plants corn or wheat or soybeans, the prices that are expected to prevail at harvest time are actually more important than the current price. A college student who reads that there are likely to be too few engineers four years hence may decide to major in engineering in expectation of a high income. When a business firm decides to establish a plant that may take five years to build, expectations of future business conditions in that industry are crucial to that investment decision.

Changes in each of the above factors *will shift the entire supply curve.* Exhibit 4 shows the supply curve, *S*, for corn. The supply curve is based on a $10-per-bushel price of soybeans and a $2,000 yearly rental on an acre of corn land. If the price of soybeans rises to, say, $15 a bushel, then the supply curve for corn will shift leftward to *S'* in panel (a) because some land used for corn will be shifted to soybeans. If the rental price of an acre of corn land goes down from $2,000 a year per acre to $1,000 a year, the supply curve will shift to the right—to, say, *S"* in panel (b). The reduction in the land rental price lowers the costs of producing a bushel of corn and makes the corn producer willing to supply more corn at the same price as before.

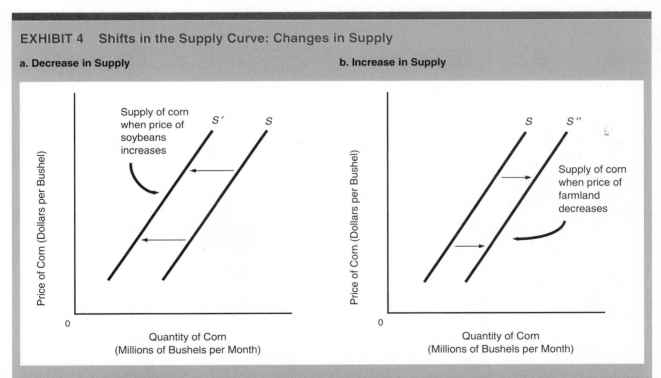

EXHIBIT 4   Shifts in the Supply Curve: Changes in Supply

a. Decrease in Supply

b. Increase in Supply

The supply curve of corn depends on the price of soybeans and on the price of farmland. When farmland is $2,000 an acre per year and soybeans are $10 per bushel, *S* might be the supply curve for corn. Panel (a) shows that if farmland stays at $2,000 per acre per year but soybeans fetch $15 instead of $10, profit-seeking farmers will switch farmland from corn to soybeans and cause the supply curve for corn to shift to the left fron *S* to *S'* (a decrease in supply). On the other hand, panel (b) shows that if soybeans remain at $10 per bushel and farmland falls from $2,000 to $1,000 per acre, the supply curve for corn will shift to the right from *S* to *S"* (an increase in supply).

EQUILIBRIUM OF SUPPLY AND DEMAND

Along a given demand curve, such as the one in Exhibit 1, there are many price/quantity combinations from which to choose. Along a given supply curve, there are similarly many different price/quantity combinations. Neither the demand curve nor the supply curve is sufficient by itself to determine the *market* price/quantity combination.

Exhibit 5 puts the demand curve of Exhibit 1 and the supply curve of Exhibit 3 together on the same diagram. Remember that the demand curve indicates what consumers are prepared to buy at different prices; the supply curve indicates what producers are prepared to sell at different prices. These groups of economic decision makers are (for the most part) entirely different. How much will be produced? How much will be consumed? How are the decisions of consumers and producers coordinated?

Suppose that the price of corn happened to be $2 per bushel. Exhibit 5 tells us the same thing that Exhibits 1 and 3 tell us separately: at a $2 price, consumers will want to buy 40 million bushels and producers will want to sell only 20 million bushels. This discrepancy means that at $2 there is a **shortage** of 20 million bushels.

> A **shortage** results if at the current price the quantity demanded exceeds the quantity supplied; the price is too low to equate the quantity demanded with the quantity supplied.

At a $2-per-bushel price, some people who are willing to buy corn cannot find a willing seller. The demand curve shows that a number of consumers are willing to pay more than $2 per bushel. Such buyers will try to outbid each other for the available supply. With free competition, the price of corn will be bid up if there is a shortage of corn.

The increase in the price of corn in response to the shortage will have two main effects. On the one hand, the higher price will discourage consumption. On the other hand, the higher price will encourage production. Thus, the increase in the price of corn, through the action of independent buyers and sellers, will lead both buyers and sellers in the marketplace to make decisions that will reduce the shortage of corn.

According to the demand and supply curves portrayed in Exhibit 5, when the price of corn reaches $3 per bushel, the shortage of corn disappears completely. At this **equilibrium** (or **market-clearing**) **price**, consumers want to buy 30 million bushels and producers want to sell 30 million bushels.

The equilibrium price equates the quantity demanded with the quantity supplied. If the price is not at equilibrium there will be a surplus or shortage.

> The **equilibrium (market-clearing) price** is the price at which the quantity demanded by consumers equals the quantity supplied by producers.

What would happen if the price rose above the equilibrium price of $3 per bushel? At the price of $4 per bushel, consumers want to buy 25 million bushels and producers want to sell 35 million bushels. Thus, at $4 there is a **surplus** of 10 million bushels on the market.

> A **surplus** results if at the current price the quantity supplied exceeds the quantity demanded; the price is too high to equate the quantity demanded with quantity supplied.

EXHIBIT 5   Market Equilibrium

This figure shows how market equilibrium is reached. On the same diagram are drawn both the demand curve for corn (from Exhibit 1) and the supply curve for corn (from Exhibit 3). When the price of corn is $2, the quantity demanded is 40 million bushels, but the quantity supplied is only 20 million bushels. The result is a shortage of 20 million bushels of corn. Unsatisfied buyers will bid the price up.

Raising the price will reduce the shortage. When the price of corn is raised to $4 per bushel, the quantity demanded is 25 million bushels while the quantity supplied is 35 million bushels. The result is a surplus of 10 million bushels of corn. This surplus will cause the price of corn to fall as unsatisfied sellers bid the price down to get rid of excess inventories of corn. As the price falls the surplus will diminish. The equilibrium price is $3 because the quantity demanded equals the quantity supplied at that price. The equilibrium quantity is 30 million bushels.

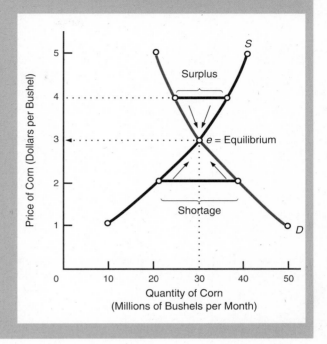

When there is a surplus some sellers will be disappointed as corn inventories pile up. Willing sellers of corn will not be able to find willing buyers. The competition among sellers will lead them to cut the price.

This fall in the price of corn will simultaneously encourage consumption and discourage production. Through the automatic fall in the price of corn, *the surplus of corn will therefore disappear.*

Again we find that the price will tend toward $3 and the quantity will tend toward 30 million bushels. This equilibrium point is where the demand and supply curves intersect. In Exhibit 5, there is no other price/quantity combination at which quantity demanded equals quantity supplied; any other price brings about a shortage of corn or a surplus of corn. The arrows in Exhibit 5 indicate the pressures on prices above or below $3 and how the amount of shortage or surplus—the size of the brackets—gets smaller as the price adjusts.

The equilibrium of supply and demand is stationary in the sense that once the equilibrium price is reached, it tends to remain the same. Movements away from the equilibrium price will be restored by the bidding of frustrated buyers or frustrated sellers in the marketplace. The equilibrium price is like a rocking chair in the rest position; give it a gentle push and the original position will be restored.

What the Market Accomplishes

The equilibrium price is discovered in the marketplace. The market coordinates the actions of a large number of independent suppliers and demanders. Their actions are brought together by the pricing of the good in a free market.

An equilibrium price accomplishes two basic goals. First, it *rations* the scarce supply of the commodity or service among all the people who would like to have it if it were given away free. Some people must be left out if the good is scarce. The price, by discouraging or restraining consumption, rations the good out to the various claimants of the good.

Second, the system of equilibrium prices *economizes on the information required* by individuals and firms. Buyers do not need to know how to produce the good, and sellers do not need to know why people use the good. Buyers and sellers need only be concerned with small bits of information, such as price, or small portions of the technological methods of production. The market can accomplish its actions without any one participant knowing all the details. Recall the pencil example discussed in Chapter 2: pencils are produced even though no single individual knows *all* the details for producing a pencil (from making the saw to felling the trees to making the rubber eraser).

The same is true of the corn-market example. Sellers of corn do not need to know anything about the buyers of corn, and vice versa. The price buyers pay tells sellers all they need to know, and the price sellers ask tells buyers all they need to know. When the price settles at equilibrium, the actions of buyers and sellers are harmonized.

CHANGES IN THE EQUILIBRIUM PRICE

Prices change. Sometimes prices go up, and sometimes they go down—and in relative-price terms, prices go down as often as they go up. Why do prices change? Equilibrium prices are determined by the intersection of the demand and supply curves. The only way for the price to change is for the demand or supply curves themselves to shift. The supply and demand curves can shift only if one or more of the factors *besides the good's own price* changes.

Change in Demand (or Supply) Versus Change in Quantity Demanded (or Supplied)

We make a careful distinction between movements along a demand curve and shifts in the entire curve. A change in the price of a good—as from p_2 to p_1 in panel (a) of Exhibit 6—causes a movement along the demand curve and is referred to as a **change in quantity demanded**. When a change in a factor other than the good's own price shifts the entire curve to the left or to the right, we call that a **change in demand**.

> A change (increase or decrease) **in quantity demanded** is a movement along the demand curve because of a change in the good's price. (See Exhibit 6).

> A change (increase or decrease) **in demand** is a shift in the entire demand curve because of a change in a factor other than the good's own price.

Similarly, panel (a) of Exhibit 7 shows that a rise in the price of a good (from p_1 to p_2) **changes the quantity supplied** but does not change the location of the supply curve. A **change in supply** occurs when a factor other than the good's own price changes, shifting the entire supply curve to the left or to the right.

> A change (increase or decrease) **in quantity supplied** is a movement along the supply curve because of a change in the good's price (see Exhibit 7).

EXHIBIT 6   Change in Demand Versus Change in Quantity Demanded

a. Change in Quantity Demanded

b. Change in Demand

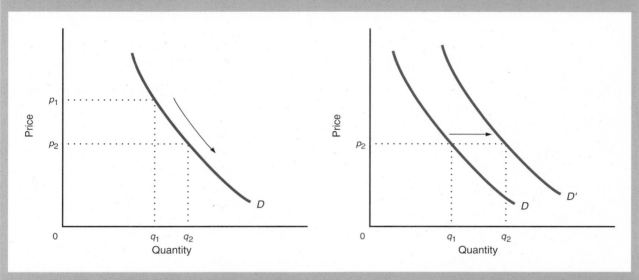

In panel (a), the increase in quantity demand (from q_1 to q_2) is due to the drop in price (from p_1 to p_2). The change in price causes the movement along the demand curve *(D)*. In panel (b), the increase in quantity (from q_1 to q_2) is due to a shift in the demand curve (an increase in demand) to D', holding price constant. When demand increases, the whole demand curve shifts due to some change that leads consumers to buy more of the product at each price.

EXHIBIT 7   Change in Supply Versus Change in Quantity Supplied

a. Change in Quantity Supplied

b. Change in Supply

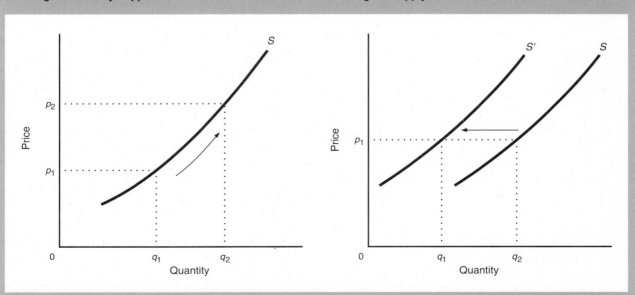

In panel (a), the increase in quantity supplied (from q_1 to q_2) is due to a rise in price (from p_1 to p_2). The change in price causes a movement along the supply curve S. In panel (b), the decrease in supply (from q_2 to q_1) is due to the shift in the supply curve (decrease in supply) from S to S', holding price constant. Firms wish to sell less at the same price.

The Effects of Change in Supply and Demand

Changes in supply or demand factors can change the equilibrium price and quantity in any given market. Consider first the effects of a change in supply.

Suppose a sudden and severe drought in America's breadbasket causes a substantial portion of the wheat crop to be lost. Exhibit 8 (a) illustrates the effect of the drought on the wheat market. The demand curve, *D*, and the supply curve, *S*, are based on conditions *before* the drought. The drought ruins about one half of the potential wheat crop. Now, at a price of $5 per bushel, instead of 50 million bushels being offered, only 25 million bushels are offered by farmers. Similarly, at all other prices smaller quantities of wheat are offered on the market. The supply curve for wheat has shifted to the left to *S'* (the supply of wheat has decreased). How will this supply reduction affect the demand curve?

When the supply curve for a single good, like wheat or corn, changes, the demand curve normally does not change. The factors influencing the supply of wheat *other than the price of wheat* have little or no influence on the demand for wheat. The severe drought will not shift the demand curve. In the analysis of a single market we can usually assume that the demand and supply curves are independent.

A decrease in supply causes the price to rise and the quantity demanded to fall. An increase in supply causes the price to fall and the quantity demanded to rise.

The supply curve has shifted to the left (supply has decreased); the demand curve remains unchanged. What will happen to the equilibrium price? Exhibit 8(a) shows that after the reduction in supply, the quantity supplied is less than the quantity demanded at the original equilibrium price. At the original price, there is a shortage of wheat. Therefore, the price of wheat will be bid up until a new higher equilibrium price is attained, at which quantity demanded and quantity supplied are equal. As the price rises, there is a movement up the new supply curve *(S')* as higher prices coax more wheat out of drought-ridden farmers.

A change in demand is illustrated in Exhibit 8(b). The initial situation is depicted by the demand curve for wheat, *D,* and the supply curve of wheat, *S.* The equilibrium price is $5 and the equilibrium quantity is 50 million bushels. Medical evidence is now uncovered showing that eating bread increases one's life span. This news would shift the demand curve for wheat to the right (from *D* to *D'*). People now want to buy more wheat than before at the same prices. The medical evidence, however, would not affect the supply of wheat. Because of the increase in demand, people want to buy more wheat at the original price of $5 than farmers are willing to supply. There is a shortage of wheat, and the price of wheat would rise until a higher price is established that equates quantity demanded and quantity supplied.

The rise in price causes a movement up the new demand curve, as higher prices cause people to cut back their purchases. *There has been no increase in supply, only an increase in quantity supplied* in response to the higher price.

An increase in demand causes the price to rise and the quantity supplied to rise. A decrease in demand causes the price to fall and the quantity supplied to fall.

Notice again that when the demand curve shifts due to some change in demand factors other than the good's price, there is no shift in the supply curve: the supply curve remains the same. The supply curve and the demand curve should be considered to be independent of one another at this level of analysis. In our example, the change in preferences should not affect the willingness of farmers to supply wheat at different prices during any given time period.

Exhibit 9 reviews the factors that cause shifts in supply and demand curves and shows how they affect equilibrium prices and quantities.

EXHIBIT 8   The Effects of Changes in Supply and Demand on the Price

a. Decrease in Supply   **b. Increase in Demand**

In panel (a), the natural disaster shifts the supply curve of wheat from *S* to *S'*. This decrease in supply raises the equilibrium price from $5 to $10. The movement from *e* to *e'* is a movement along the demand curve. Although the demand curve does not change, there is a decrease in quantity demanded from 50 million to 30 million bushels as the price rises from $5 to $10 per bushel. Panel (b) shows an increase in the demand for wheat because of, say, increased tastes for bread. The shift in the demand curve from *D* to *D'* depicts an increase in demand. This increase in demand drives up the equilibrium price from $5 per bushel to $13 per bushel. As price rises from $5 to $13, there is an increase in quantity supplied from 50 million to 58 million bushels that results from the movement along the supply curve, *S*.

Simultaneous Changes in Supply and Demand

In many instances, demand and supply can change at the same time. There can be nine combinations of supply and demand shifts (shown in Exhibit 10). Each combination yields different price/quantity outcomes. In some cases, the effects on price and quantity are known. In other cases, the effects are indeterminate. For example, as in Exhibit 10(e), a simultaneous increase in both supply and demand may raise or lower price. The price will rise if the demand shift exceeds the supply shift, as illustrated.

UNCONVENTIONAL USE OF SUPPLY AND DEMAND

The concepts of supply, demand, and the equilibrium price apply to a wide range of exchanges, even exchanges that appear to lie outside the traditional realm of economics. Anything that admits to being priced and exchanged freely can be analyzed by the tools of this chapter. In fact, the 1992 Nobel laureate in economics, Gary Becker, earned the award for his application of supply and demand to issues of marriage, crime, divorce, and discrimination. Economists now speak of "markets" for marriage and for crime. They note that in some traditional societies,

EXHIBIT 9   Shifts in Demand and Supply Curves: Effects on Prices and Quantities

Shifts in Demand Curves

Factor	Example	Result
Price of substitutes	Increase in price of coffee shifts demand curve for tea to right	Price of tea rises, quantity of tea rises
Price of complements	Increase in price of coffee shifts demand curve for cream to the left	Price of coffee falls, quantity of cream falls
Income	Increase in income shifts demand curve for automobiles to the right	Price of autos rises, quantity rises
Preference	Judgment that cigarettes are hazardous shifts demand curve for cigarettes to left	Price of cigarettes falls, quantity falls
Number of buyers	Trade agreement with Japan increases number of buyers of farm products and shifts demand curve to the right	Prices of farm products rise, quantity rises
Expectations of future prices	Expectation that PC prices will fall in future	Prices of PCs fall, quantity falls

Shifts in Supply Curves

Factor	Example	Result
Price of another good	Increase in price of corn shifts supply curve of wheat to left	Price of wheat rises, quantity falls
Price of resource	Decrease in wage rate of autoworkers shifts supply curve of autos to right	Price of autos falls, quantity rises
Technology	Higher corn yields due to genetic engineering shift supply curve of corn to right	Price of corn falls, quantity rises
Number of sellers	Trade agreement with USSR opens U.S. market to Soviet steel producers	Price of steel falls, quantity rises
Expectations	Expectation of higher ball bearing prices in the future causes more investment, shifting supply curve to right	Price of ball bearings rises, quantity rises

marriage proceeds as does any other market—the groom may pay a bride's price or the bride's family might provide a dowry. In modern societies there is less explicit use of prices, but marriages are formed and dissolved in a manner that resembles market transactions.

In the "market" for crime, the price of crime might be the amount that thieves can earn per day of mugging, robbing, or burglarizing. Even gambling appears to use prices to govern exchanges. The sports pages contain interesting market information every weekend during the National Football League season. Each game has a certain point spread, where one team is given an advantage over the other. The purpose of the point spread is to bring about equilibrium in the market for betting so that, for example, the number of people betting on favored team A equals the number of people betting on the underdog team B.

The extension of supply-and-demand analysis into non-economic areas such

EXHIBIT 10   Summary of Effects of Supply-Curve and Demand-Curve Shifts

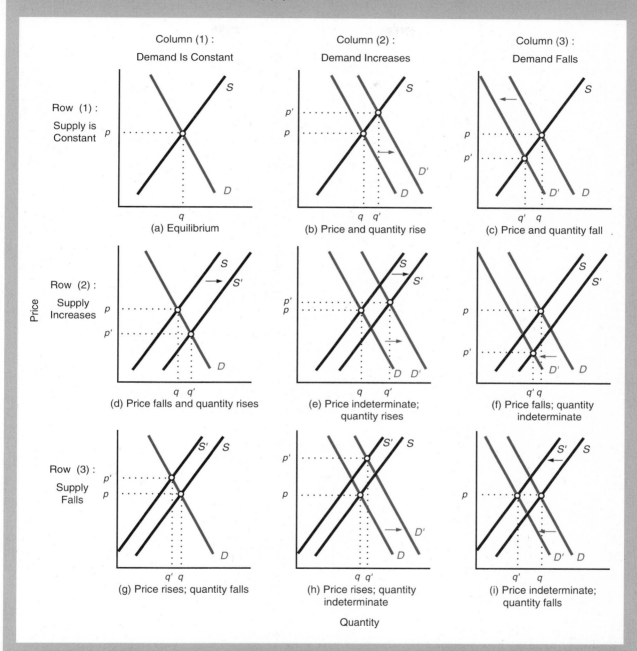

Column (1): Demand Is Constant

Column (2): Demand Increases

Column (3): Demand Falls

Row (1): Supply is Constant

(a) Equilibrium

(b) Price and quantity rise

(c) Price and quantity fall

Row (2): Supply Increases

(d) Price falls and quantity rises

(e) Price indeterminate; quantity rises

(f) Price falls; quantity indeterminate

Row (3): Supply Falls

(g) Price rises; quantity falls

(h) Price rises; quantity indeterminate

(i) Price indeterminate; quantity falls

Price

Quantity

This figure shows the effects of all possible combinations of shifts in supply curves and demand curves. As panels (e), (f), (h), and (i) demonstrate, the effects of simultaneous changes in supply and demand are sometimes indeterminate. If supply increases (shifts right) and demand decreases (shifts left), the price will fall. If supply decreases and demand increases, the price will rise. If, however, both the demand and supply curves move in the same direction (if both increase or if both decrease), the price effect depends on which movement dominates.

Interfering with Supply and Demand; The 1974 Energy Crisis

Dramatic shifts in supply or demand can prompt a public outcry for the government to set prices in place of the market. After natural disasters, for example, the government penalizes merchants who raise prices (price gouging). When the Arab oil embargo threatened world gasoline supplies in 1974, the federal government was determined not to let gas prices rise through the roof. Prior to the embargo, gas was selling at 40 cents per gallon. With supplies cut off, the forces of supply and demand threatened to push the price toward $1—a price rise that was regarded as unacceptable at the time. To prevent such unconscionable price increases, the federal government began to allocate gas supplies to the various states and to set ceiling prices for gasoline.

The diagram shows the consequences of setting price ceilings during a period of dramatically reduced supply. With a price ceiling of 50 cents per gallon, the quantity demanded fell far short of the quantity supplied.

The American public will not soon forget the energy crisis of 1974. The government allocated ample supplies to some states. Other states received little gas, and gas shortages were severe. People had to get up early in the morning and wait in line for gas. A number of fatal shootings occurred at gas stations as impatient customers tried to cut in line. Gas station attendants were threatened at gunpoint by irate customers when they tried to shut the station in the evening.

The policy implication of the 1974 experience is that there are severe and unexpected costs when government allocation and price ceilings replace allocation by supply and demand. Although it is appealing to think of the government as holding prices to a reasonable level and preventing evil speculators from getting rich, the price of government intervention can be severe. The oil embargo is only one example. When rents threaten to rise in major cities, the public clamors for rent controls, which ultimately create housing shortages. When interest rates rise, there is

The Effect of Price Ceilings on the Market for Gasoline

a public outcry for interest rate ceilings. Those least able to obtain credit (the poor), accordingly, are shut out of credit markets.

It is noteworthy that the European countries did not experience the lines and panics that characterized the U.S. gasoline market. Most of the European countries simply let the price of gas rise to its market level. People paid higher prices but lines and shootings were avoided.

as sociology, law, international relations, and anthropology has caused economics to be called the "imperialist" discipline of social science.

The first three chapters have focused on the way market economies use the price system to solve the economic problem. The next chapter looks at the way governments allocate resources.

Chapter Summary

The most important point to learn from this chapter is: In a perfectly competitive market, there is always an equilibrium price that coordinates the independent actions of firms that supply goods to the market and of consumers who demand goods from the market.

1. A perfectly competitive market consists of many buyers and sellers in which each buyer or seller accepts the market price as given.

2. The law of demand states that as price goes up the quantity demanded falls, and vice versa; the demand curve is a graphical representation of the relationship between price and quantity demanded—other things being equal. The demand curve is downward sloping.

3. As price goes up the quantity supplied usually rises; the supply curve is a graphical representation of the relationship between price and quantity supplied. The supply curve tends to be upward sloping because of the law of diminishing returns.

4. The equilibrium price/quantity combination occurs where the demand curve intersects the supply curve, or where quantity demanded equals quantity supplied at the market-clearing price. Competitive pricing rations scarce economic goods and economizes on the information necessary to coordinate supply/demand decisions. A shortage results if the price is too low for equilibrium; a surplus results if the price is too high for equilibrium.

5. A change in quantity demanded means a *movement along* a given demand curve; a change in demand means the entire demand curve shifts. A change in quantity supplied means a *movement along* a given supply curve; a change in supply means the entire supply curve shifts. Supply-and-demand analysis allows one to predict what will happen to prices and quantities when supply or demand schedules shift.

6. The concepts of supply, demand, and the equilibrium price can be applied to a wide range of exchanges.

Policy Focus: **It may be appealing for the government to interfere with the forces of supply and demand by setting price ceilings. The public must recognize that such actions create shortages and require government rationing if chaos is to be prevented.**

Key Terms

market (p. 47)
perfectly competitive market (p. 48)
law of demand (p. 49)
quantity demanded (p. 49)
demand curve or schedule (p. 49)
market-demand curve (p. 50)
substitutes (p. 52)
complements (p. 52)
normal goods (p. 52)
inferior goods (p. 52)

quantity supplied (p. 54)
supply curve or schedule (p. 55)
shortage (p. 58)
equilibrium (market-clearing) price (p. 58)
surplus (p. 58)
change in quantity demanded (p. 60)
change in demand (p. 60)
change in quantity supplied (p. 60)
change in supply (p. 60)

Questions and Problems

1. List the four characteristics of a perfectly competitive market. Explain why if any of the four conditions are not met, the principal characteristic of a perfectly competitive market (no person or group can control price) may not be met.

2. Suppose you live in a very cold climate and pay on the average 25 percent of your income for fuel. If the price of fuel rises by 15 percent, and there are no good substitutes for fuel, why would you cut back on fuel consumption?

3. Plot the supply and demand schedules for the hypothetical product in Table A as supply and demand curves.
   a. What equilibrium price would this market establish?
   b. If the state were to pass a law that the price could not be more than $2, how would you describe the market response?
   c. If the state were to pass a law that the price could not be less than $8 how would you describe the market response?
   d. If preferences changed and people wanted to buy twice as much as before at each price, what will the equilibrium price be?
   e. If, in addition to the above change in preferences, there is an improvement in technology that allows firms to produce this product at lower cost than before, what will happen to the equilibrium price?

TABLE A

Price (dollars)	Quantity Demanded (units)	Quantity Supplied (units)
10	5	25
8	10	20
6	15	15
2	20	10
0	25	5

4. American baseball bats do not sell well in Japan because they do not meet the specifications of Japanese baseball officials. If the Japanese change their specifications to accommodate American-made bats, what will happen to the price of American bats?

5. "The poor are the ones who suffer from high gas and electricity bills. We should pass a law that gas and electricity rates cannot increase by more than 1 percent annually." Evaluate this statement in terms of supply-and-demand analysis, assuming that equilibrium prices rise faster than 1 percent annually.

6. Much of the automobile-rental business in the United States is done at airports. What would be the predicted effect of a reduction in airfares on automobile-rental rates?

7. If both the supply and demand for coffee increase, what would happen to coffee prices? If the supply increased and the demand fell, what would happen to coffee prices?

8. Which of the following statements uses incorrect terminology? Explain.
   a. The recent fare war among the major airlines has increased the demand for air travel."
   b. "The recession of 90–91 has caused the demand for air travel to fall."

9. What are the factors held constant along the demand curve? Explain how each can shift the demand curve to the right. Explain how each can shift the demand curve to the left.

10. What are the factors held constant along the supply curve? Explain how each factor can shift the supply curve to the right. Explain how each factor can shift the supply curve to the left.

11. Why is the demand curve downward sloping?

12. Why is the supply curve normally upward sloping? Can you think of any exceptions?

13. What is the effect of each of the following events on the equilibrium price and quantity of hamburgers?

a. An increase in the price of steak (a substitute for hamburgers).
b. An increase in the price of french fries (a complement).
c. A given population becomes older.
d. The government requires that all the ingredients of hamburgers be absolutely fresh (that is, nothing can be frozen).
e. Beef becomes more expensive.
f. More firms enter the hamburger business.

14. "As a general rule, if *both* supply and demand increase or decrease, the change in price will be indeterminate." Is this statement true or false? Illustrate with a diagram.

15. "As a general rule, if demand increases and supply decreases, or vice versa, the change in quantity will be indeterminate." Is this statement true or false? Illustrate with a diagram.

Doing Economics

Think about the market for gasoline in the United States. Based on your experience, should the demand for gasoline vary over the seasons of the year? What about the supply? Now go to the Government Documents section of your school's library and find recent issues of *Monthly Energy Review,* a publication of the U.S. Department of Energy. In this publication, you should be able to find monthly data on retail gasoline prices and quantities sold. List the prices and quantities for unleaded gasoline month by month for a period of at least two years. Are there any major shifts in price? Thinking about the dates on which they occurred, what do you think caused them? Ignoring these major shifts, what pattern do you notice in the movements of prices over the seasons of the year? What is the pattern in quantity sold? Based on these observations, is this seasonal pattern likely to be explained by seasonal fluctuations in demand or supply? Does your evidence correspond to your intuitive prediction about seasonal movements in demand and supply?

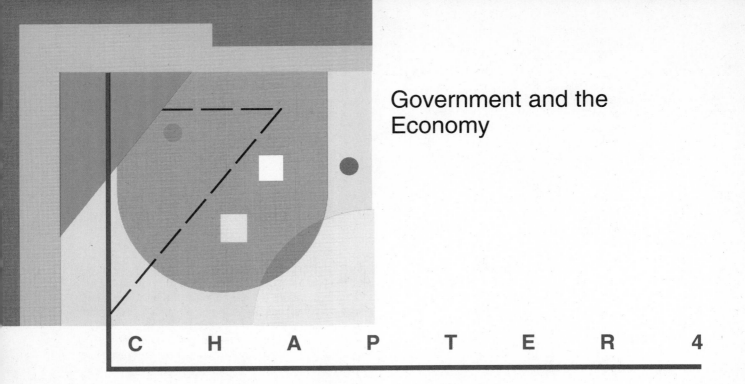

Government and the Economy

C H A P T E R   4

CHAPTER FOCUS   This chapter addresses two fundamental policy issues: How should
government raise the funds it needs to conduct its business in a fair and
rational manner? What procedures and safeguards should democratic
societies use to make sure that public funds are spent in the public interest?

The first question has been on the public mind since governments began
taxing their citizens. Given that governments have to raise money to support
government activities, what is the best and fairest way of sharing the burden?
Social thinkers have given us two approaches. One is that those who benefit
from the government service should pay for it. The other is that those who are
better off should pay.

Economists can say a great deal about the consequences of different tax
regimens; they cannot decide which type of tax system is the most fair. We
shall return to the issue of fairness of the tax system in a later chapter.

How governments can ensure that public funds are spent efficiently and in
the public interest is a question of more recent vintage. Early philosophers
thought that democratically elected officials would automatically act in the
interests of the majority. Centuries of logrolling and vote trading, however,
have shown that majority rule can produce spending programs that favor
special interests over the interests of the majority.

After studying this chapter, you will be able to:

- Explain why the relative size of government in the economy has grown.
- Define the ability-to-pay and benefit principles of taxation.
- Tell the difference between progressive and regressive taxes.
- Tell how the incidence of taxes can be changed by tax shifting.
- Define the types of government spending that actually use scarce resources.
- Understand how majority rule can result in inefficient government spending policies.
- Tell the reasons for government action.

GOVERNMENT SPENDING

Government operates businesses (for example, the government printing office, and weapons arsenals). Government provides for the national defense, education, police protection, streets and highways, public parks, and even garbage collection. The government pays for most of its spending by collecting taxes. People pay all kinds of taxes: income taxes, sales taxes, excise taxes, property taxes, and taxes on imported goods, called tariffs.

Types of Government Spending

Governments make two types of expenditures: **exhaustive expenditures** and **transfer payments.**

> **Exhaustive expenditures** are government purchases of goods and services that divert economic resources from the private sector, making them no longer available for private use.

> **Transfer payments** are simply transfers of income from one individual or organization to another by a combination of taxes and subsidies.

When the government buys a fleet of cars or hires a statistician, these are exhaustive payments because the fleet of cars and services of the statistician are no longer available to the private sector. Government transfer payments do not raise the amount of economic resources that the government consumes. Social Security transfers income from currently employed workers to retired or disabled workers. The federal government transfers funds to state and local governments through its various grants programs. Transfer payments affect the distribution of income among families but do not change the amount of goods and services exhausted (consumed) by government. Transfer payments may indirectly affect economic activity by affecting economic incentives: if Peter is taxed to pay Paul, both may work less.

Exhibit 1 shows that exhaustive government expenditures account for 19 percent of all goods and services produced by the economy. But exhaustive expenditures account for only 57 percent of government spending. Exhaustive government expenditures and transfer payments add up to 33 percent of the value of all goods and services produced by the economy.

James Buchanan (1919–)

James Buchanan founded public-choice economics—the branch of economics that studies political economic decision-making. Buchanan started the Public Choice Society and promoted a new journal, *Public Choice*. He was born in 1919 in Tennessee, where his grandfather had been governor from 1891 to 1893. Buchanan received his Ph.D. in 1948 from the University of Chicago and taught at the University of Virginia and George Mason University. In 1986, he received the Nobel Prize in economics for his contributions to the study of government and the economy.

Prior to Buchanan, economists assumed that government functions were carried out efficiently. Monopoly, externalities, and macroeconomic instability were reasons given for government action. Yet few economists had considered *how well* government itself would perform its resource-allocation functions in place of private markets. It was simply assumed that government action would be better than private action. Buchanan raised the fundamental issue of how well democratic societies, operating under majority rule, allocate resources. Buchanan pointed out that when politicians seek to maximize their reelection chances they engage in logrolling and vote trading. Unwise public expenditures are the likely outcome. Buchanan predicted the difficulties of balancing federal budgets in majority-rule societies where government expenditures are popular and taxes unpopular. He also pointed out that majority-vote elections can reject public expenditures that are in the economic interests of the voters. Buchanan's main contribution has been to expand economics to include self-interested politicians and bureaucrats, who join Adam Smith's self-interested producers and consumers in pursuing their own self-interest.

Buchanan argues that constitutional constraints must be placed on democratic governments. Without such constraints he believes that attempts to, say, reduce the federal deficit must fail. He argues that the potential gains from reducing government expenditures and raising taxes would be dissipated by enormous lobbying efforts on behalf of special-interest groups.

Size of Government

Government revenues and expenditures have been increasing at a rapid pace. In 1929, receipts of local, state, and federal government were $11 billion and expenditures were $10 billion. In 1992, government receipts and expenditures were nearly $2 trillion each. Dollar figures such as these give an exaggerated view of the growth of government because of rising prices and growing output. The most relevant yardstick of the economic role of government is the share of total government spending of total economic output, or GDP. Exhibit 2 shows that government expenditures accounted for a small 6.5 percent of the value of all goods and services produced at the turn of the century. By 1950, government spending was 20 percent in the United States, and by 1992, this percentage had risen to 33 percent. Government economic activity has been increasing in the United States even after adjustment for growth distortion and inflation distortion.

Exhibit 2 shows the rise of government has been an international phenomenon. Government spending has risen as a percentage of economic activity in all the industrialized countries.

The rising share of government economic activity in the United States can be explained by a number of factors.

Government	Purchase of Goods and Services, Including Interest Payments (billions of dollars)	Purchase as Percent of Gross Domestic Product	Transfer Payments (billions of dollars)*	Total Expenditures for Goods and Services and Transfers (billions of dollars)	Total Expenditure as Percent of GDP
Federal	445	7.8	754	1,199	21.0
State and local	644	11.3	64	708	12.4
Total	1,089	19.1	818	1,907	33.4

*Federal transfers exclude grants to state and local governments.

SOURCE: *Economic Report of the President.*

EXHIBIT 2   Total Government Spending as a Percentage of GDP, U.S., and Other Countries,1890–1991

The ratio of total government expenditures to total economic activity (or GDP) is a better measure of the changing role of government than measures of government spending alone. This exhibit shows the general increase in government spending as a percentage of total economic activity

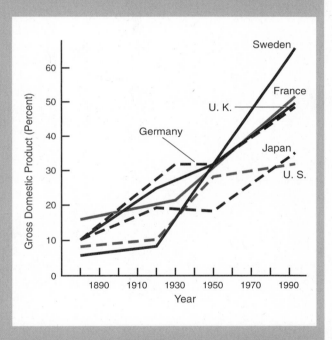

SOURCE: *World Development Report 1991* (Oxford: Oxford University Press, 1991), p. 139. Figures updated by authors.

1. Two world wars and the Cold War caused military spending to increase. The United States, as a military superpower, devoted an increasing share of its economic resources to national defense. On the eve of World War II, national defense accounted for 1.3 percent of total spending. At the peak of the Vietnam conflict, national defense accounted for almost 9 percent. The end of the Cold War should cause defense spending to drop as a percentage of total spending.

2. Government has increasingly taken responsibility for health, education, and income security. Prior to the Great Depression of the 1930s, it was primarily the responsibility of the individual to provide for family health, income security, and retirement needs. In 1929 government social-welfare programs cost a minute fraction of 1 percent of total economic activity, whereas today they account for more than 10 percent.

3. Modern urban societies require more government services—sanitation, traffic control, water supplies. Congested areas require more police protection than low-density farming communities. Modern industrial societies require a more complex legal system to carry out complex business contracts.

4. Democratic political processes increase government spending. Democratic politics can lead to logrolling, vote trading, and special interest legislation. Government spending decisions are determined by what benefits specific individuals and specific groups. Such actions cause the costs of government actions to be underestimated and government spending to rise.

Shares of Federal, State, and Local Governments

Each society must determine at what level of government public services are to be provided. Should roads be built by federal, state, or local government? Should the municipalities, the states, or the federal government provide public education? There has been intense debate over these issues since the founding of this country. Some citizens fear a powerful federal government. Others consider the federal government to be more efficient and the best enforcer of national standards and legislation.

The federal government accounted for 61 percent of all government expenditures in 1991, while state and local governments accounted for 39 percent. Exhibit 3 shows that the larger share of federal spending dates from the post-World War II era.

The government's share of economic activity has been rising over the long run.

TAXES

Most government spending is financed by taxes. In the early 1990s, personal income taxes amounted to 15 percent of personal income. The inclusion of sales, excise, and Social Security taxes raise the average tax burden to about 36 percent of personal income.

Exhibit 4 shows the relative importance of the various sources of government revenue to the federal government and to state and local governments. Note the importance of individual income taxes to the federal government. State and local governments depend on sales taxes, federal government revenue-sharing, and various fees and charges.

Efficiency, Fairness, and Social Goals

How governments tax is important for a number of reasons.

First, taxes affect economic behavior. People can typically alter their tax obligations by modifying their economic behavior. They pay lower sales taxes if they buy less; they pay lower income taxes if they earn less; they pay no property taxes if they own no property. Any tax that causes people to reduce their work effort, to be less innovative, or to take fewer business risks causes less output to be produced. With less output, there is less to go around for all.

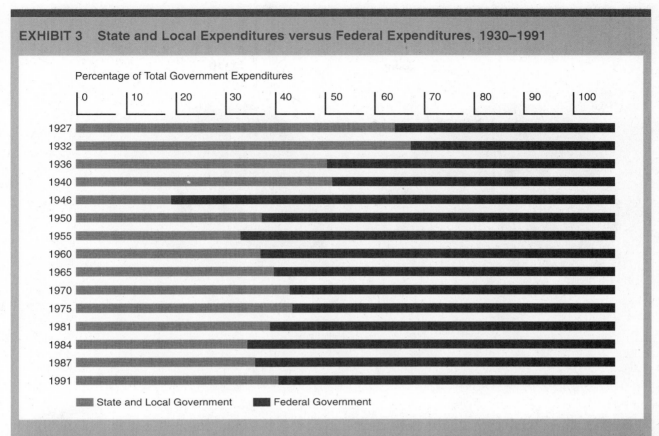

EXHIBIT 3   State and Local Expenditures versus Federal Expenditures, 1930–1991

Percentage of Total Government Expenditures

| | 0 | 10 | 20 | 30 | 40 | 50 | 60 | 70 | 80 | 90 | 100 |

1927
1932
1936
1940
1946
1950
1955
1960
1965
1970
1975
1981
1984
1987
1991

■ State and Local Government   ■ Federal Government

This graph shows that the dominance of federal over state and local spending is a fairly recent phenomenon. *Note:* Federal expenditures do not include grants in aid to state and local governments.

SOURCE: *Survey of Current Business; Historical Statistics of the United States*, vol. 2, pp. 1124–29.

Second, people should feel that taxes are fair. Poor people might think rich people are not paying their fair share. Rich people might think they are taxed too much. If people are convinced that the tax system is unfair, they try to evade taxes. Taxes are hard to collect when people consider the tax system unfair.

Third, taxes can be used to promote social goals. Taxpayers alter their economic behavior in response to taxes. The negative side is that people may reduce their work effort to reduce their taxes. The positive side is that the taxes can be used to encourage desirable activities or discourage undesirable activities. A high sales tax on cigarettes, for example, discourages smoking. Tax exemptions for military personnel encourages enlistment in the armed forces.

Principles of Fairness

The two principles of taxation are the benefit principle and the ability-to-pay principle.

Two principles of fairness underlie most taxes. The first is that the tax burden should be distributed according to benefits received. The second principle is that the tax burden should be distributed according to the ability to pay.

The Benefit Principle.   The *benefit principle* states that those who benefit from a public expenditure should pay the tax that finances it. The persons who benefit

EXHIBIT 4   Sources of Government Revenue, 1992

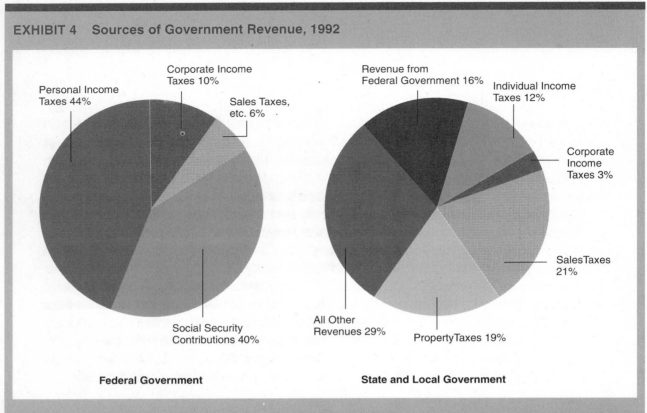

Personal Income Taxes 44%

Corporate Income Taxes 10%

Sales Taxes, etc. 6%

Social Security Contributions 40%

Federal Government

Revenue from Federal Government 16%

Individual Income Taxes 12%

Corporate Income Taxes 3%

Sales Taxes 21%

Property Taxes 19%

All Other Revenues 29%

State and Local Government

This exhibit shows that taxes are the major source of government revenues at all levels of government.

SOURCE: *Economic Report of the President*

from a new state highway, a new airport, or a flood-control project should pay. A prominent example of a benefit tax is the tax on gasoline that finances highway construction. In many communities, special taxes are assessed for road repairs, street lighting, and sidewalks. In these cases, the people who benefit pay for the government services from which they benefit.

If community members won't pay for a public project—if citizens vote against a flood-control project in their community—their votes show that they do not consider the project's benefits to outweigh its costs. If all taxes were levied on the principle that the beneficiaries bear the full burden of the tax (and if the beneficiaries were given the opportunity to vote on each public expenditure), taxpayers would only approve projects whose benefits equal or exceed their costs.

It is often difficult to determine exactly who benefits from different government expenditures. While it is obvious that automobile drivers benefit from public highways and that residents of New York City benefit from public expenditures on the New York subway system, other cases are less certain. Who benefits from national defense? Who benefits from police protection and from the legal system? Do the poor benefit more than the rich? In order to apply the benefit principle, one must first know who is the beneficiary.

Even if the beneficiaries could be identified, there is the question of whether they should pay. Many public expenditures are designed for the very purpose of benefiting the less able. It makes no sense to make the beneficiaries of welfare programs or job training programs pay because these programs' aim to raise the incomes of those least able to pay.

The Ability-to-Pay Principle.   The second approach to fairness is the *ability-to-pay principle*. This principle maintains that those better able to pay should bear the greater burden of taxes, whether or not they benefit more. The rich benefit less from public education and from public hospitals because they use private hospitals and send their children to private schools, but because they are better able to pay, they should bear a heavier tax burden.

Like the benefit principle, the ability-to-pay principle has disadvantages. If those who benefit from a tax do not have to pay, public programs whose costs outweigh their benefits may be approved. If one group benefits from a flood-control project that is paid for by another group (and the first group has more votes), flood-control projects will be approved that yield only minimal benefits.

Incidence of Taxation: Who Actually Pays?

Surprisingly, the individual or company that is being taxed does not necessarily "pay" the tax. In many cases, the tax can be shifted to someone else. The **incidence of the tax** can fall on someone other than the designated payer of the tax.

> The **incidence of a tax** is the actual burden after considering the effect of the tax on actual prices paid or received.

When a $1 tax is placed on each carton of cigarettes, cigarette manufacturers may reduce the supply of cigarettes. The previous chapter showed that a reduction in supply will raise price. When the price of cigarettes rises, the manufacturer has *shifted the tax forward* to the consumer. The consumer ends up paying at least part of the tax in the form of a higher price. If the $1 tax pushes up the price by $0.80, then 80 percent of the tax has been shifted to the consumer. Most of the tax burden is borne not by the manufacturer but by the consumer.

A tax is shifted forward when the buyer of the product subject to a tax pays a portion of the tax by paying a higher price.

Virtually any tax—an income tax, a sales tax, an inheritance tax, or a tariff on foreign goods—can be shifted. Some taxes can be shifted almost entirely to others; other taxes must be completely paid by the individual or organization that nominally pays the tax.

Progressive and Regressive Taxes

With a progressive tax, the share of income paid as taxes rises with income. With a regressive tax system, the share falls as income rises.

Taxes can redistribute income. If Jones pays 50 percent of her income and Smith pays 10 percent of his income, the distribution of after-tax income has been altered in favor of Smith. Taxes can redistribute income in favor of poor people or rich people. If higher income people pay proportionately higher taxes, after-tax income will be redistributed in favor of poor people. A tax can be either **proportional, progressive, or regressive.**

> A **proportional tax** is one where taxpayers pay the same percentage of income as taxes irrespective of their income.

> A **progressive tax** is one where the higher the income, the larger is the percentage of income paid as taxes.

> A **regressive tax** is one where the higher the income, the smaller is the percentage of income paid as taxes.

The federal income tax is a progressive tax. For example, income tax rates in effect in the early 1990s started at 15 percent for moderate income families and rose to 34 percent for high income families. The higher the family income, the larger the percentage of income paid in taxes.

A sales tax varies proportionally with purchases with a 5 percent sales tax, a sales tax of $0.50 is paid for every $10 of purchases. Sales taxes are regressive because the wealthy spend a smaller portion of their income than the poor. Suppose the family with a $40,000 income spends $20,000 and saves the rest, while the family with $10,000 income spends every dime. Each pays a 5 percent sales tax; the higher income family pay sales tax of $1,000, or 1/40th of its income, while the poor family pays sales taxes of $500, or 1/20th of its income. Although the poor family spends fewer dollars on the sales tax, it spends a larger-percentage of its income.

What type of tax system is "best" is an issue of normative economics. Those who favor a progressive tax system believe that those with a greater ability to pay should bear a proportionally larger burden. They believe that those fortunate to be at the top of the income ladder should be willing to transfer income to those at the bottom. Those who favor proportional taxes (few favor regressive taxes) argue that progressive taxes depress initiative and risk-taking and divert efforts away from productive economic activities to tax avoidance.

The "best" tax is an issue of normative economics.

The U.S. tax system is a combination of progressive taxes (the personal income tax and corporate income tax) and regressive taxes (sales taxes). As Exhibit 5 shows, there is disagreement over how progressive the U.S. tax system is. (See Example 1 on the U.S. income tax.)

GOVERNMENT SURPLUSES AND DEFICITS

Government operates like a household or business firm. If its revenues (its income) exceed its outlays, it saves, or runs a **government surplus.** If, on the other hand, its outlays exceed its revenues, it is dissaving, or running a **government deficit.** The relationship between government revenue and outlays is shown by the government budget.

> A **government surplus** is an excess of government revenues over government outlays.

> A **government deficit** is an excess of government outlays over government revenues.

If households or firms spend more than they take in, they must finance the difference by borrowing. A government unit (be it a state, local, or federal government) that runs a deficit must borrow the difference as well. Governments borrow by selling IOUs (in the form of bonds and notes) both at home and abroad. Government borrowing accumulates as a **government debt.**

Government debt rises when government runs a deficit.

EXHIBIT 5 Two Views of the Tax Burden

a. Pechman, 1980

b. Browning-Johnson, 1976

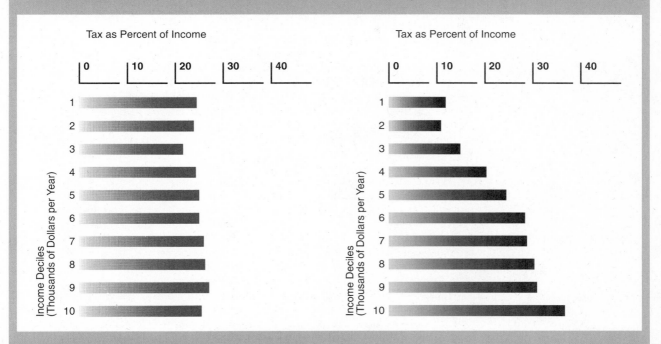

SOURCES: Joseph Pechman, *Who Paid the Taxes, 1966–85* (Washington, D.C.: The Brookings Institution, 1985). Edgar K. Browning and William R. Johnson, *The Distribution of the Tax Burden* (Washington, D.C.: American Enterprise Institute, 1979).

The U.S. tax system consists of different taxes at the local, state, and federal levels. When all taxes are combined, is the overall U.S. tax system regressive, proportional, or progressive?

The above chart shows that economists disagree on the answer. In a study conducted in 1985, Joseph Pechman concluded that the U.S. tax system is proportional over most income ranges. Only the very poor (those in the bottom 5 percent) and the very rich (those in the top 5 percent) pay a higher proportion of their income in taxes than other families.

A 1979 study by Edgar Browning and William Johnson found that the overall tax system was, as of 1976, highly progressive.

Why do economists come to different conclusions.[2] Taxes can be shifted forward to the consumer. It is difficult to determine whether taxes (such as sales taxes) are shifted forward to rich or to poor families. It is difficult to determine tax rates actually paid by the rich and the poor. The rich have been able to reduce their tax burden by investing in real estate and selling stocks and other assets at a profit. Poor families who received transfer payments have paid no income taxes and no social security taxes on this income.

> The **government debt** is the cumulated sum of outstanding IOUs that government owes its creditors.

A government debt can be reduced by running a surplus. If the government debt were $100 billion and government ran a $10 billion surplus, the government debt would be reduced by approximately $10 billion.

Exhibit 6 shows government budgets, surpluses, deficits, and debt in the United States. It shows that in total, government spent almost $2 trillion in 1991, or almost $200 billion more than it took in. The federal government ran a deficit, while state and local governments ran a surplus.

EXAMPLE 1

The U.S. Income Tax: A Brief History

In 1913, the Sixteenth Amendment to the U.S. Constitution authorized the federal government to levy a personal income tax. Prior to World War II, the personal income tax was not a major source of federal government revenue. In the 1930s, it accounted for only about 14 percent of federal revenues. Tax rates were low. In the 1920s and 1930s, the tax rate on the lowest income bracket ranged from 1 to 4 percent and the tax rate on an income of $100,000 (the equivalent of more than $1 million in the early 1990s) was 55 percent in 1935. It was during World War II that the federal personal income tax became the federal government's most important revenue source. Tax rates on the bottom and top income brackets were raised (to over 20 percent for the bottom income bracket and to a high of 92 percent for the top income bracket). By the end of the war, the 1948 personal income tax accounted for 40 percent of all federal revenue.

The United States entered the postwar era with high personal tax rates. In 1951, for example, the tax rate on the top income bracket ($200,000 and above) was 91 percent. Tax rates of this magnitude were clearly unacceptable; therefore, various tax reforms altered the personal income tax system in three directions between 1951 and 1986. First, tax rates were reduced. By 1970, the tax rate on the lowest income bracket was 20 percent, and the tax rate on the top income bracket was 75 percent. The tax reform of 1981 lowered rates to a range of 11 to 50 percent and indexed tax rates to prevent them from being pushed up by inflation.

The second direction was to allow numerous deductions and exemptions from taxable income. Over the years, interest earned on bonds of state and local government (so-called *tax-exempt bonds*), contributions to retirement programs (such as Keogh accounts), taxes paid to state and local governments, medical expenditures, charitable contributions, fire and theft losses, and child-care costs for working mothers have been deductible. Capital gains were taxed at a lower rate than other forms of income.

The third direction of tax change was to use the personal income tax to promote economic or social goals. Tax credits for investments in equipment (the investment tax credit) were used to encourage capital formation. The deduction of certain forms of savings (such as in retirement accounts) from taxable income encouraged increased savings. Mortgage-interest deductions encouraged home ownership.

All these changes had made the federal income tax extremely complex. The system's critics felt it gave too many tax loopholes to the rich and that its high marginal tax rates discouraged hard work and risk takings.

In September 1986, Congress passed, and President Reagan signed, the Tax Reform Act of 1986. The number of tax rates was reduced from the previous fourteen (ranging from 11 percent to 50 percent) to three (15 percent, 28 percent, and 34 percent). The top rate on taxable income was lowered from 50 percent to 34 percent. Tax rates were adjusted for inflation by indexing tax-rate brackets, personal exemptions, and standard deductions to inflation. Many low-income families were removed from the tax rolls.

Deductions, exemptions, and exclusions from income were dramatically restricted to make up for the loss of tax revenue due to lower tax rates. Special tax treatment of certain industries such as oil drilling, cattle raising, and apartment construction was terminated. Capital gains income was no longer taxed at lower rates than ordinary income. Corporate income taxes were raised.

The 1992 presidential campaign focused on how to change the income tax system. The challenger, Bill Clinton, proposed to raise the top marginal tax rate to 36 percent, while President George Bush proposed to hold the line on tax rates. Both candidates proposed measures to encourage investment and saving.

EXHIBIT 6 Government Budgets and Debt, 1991

	Receipts (billions of dollars)	Expenditures (billions of dollars)	Surplus or Deficit (billions of dollars)	Total Debt (billions of dollars)	Total Debt as Percent of GDP
Total government	1,738	1,909	−171	3,860	68
Federal government	1,119	1,320	−201	3,618	64
State and local governments	771	741	30	242	4

SOURCES: *Statistical Abstract of the United States; Economic Report of the President*

People fear that expanding deficits depress saving, worsen trade balances, burden future generations, and raise interest rates. The validity of these fears will be explored in depth in later chapters.

REASONS FOR GOVERNMENT ACTION

If the private sector could deal with all resource-allocation decisions efficiently and fairly, there would be little need for government action. There are five economic problems that the market may not solve efficiently or fairly on its own.

Monopoly

Private markets may not work well when there is a single supplier of a commodity. If a monopoly firm controlled the nation's telephone system, steel production, or its airlines, that *monopolist* could restrict supply and drive up the price. The monopolist would earn monopoly profits, and consumers would pay in the form of higher prices. Income would be redistributed from the consumers to the owners of the monopoly. Monopoly cannot be avoided when for technological reasons the market has room for only one producer. When private markets are needlessly monopolized, laws against monopoly may be required. The threat of monopoly is one rationale for government action. Government action to control monopoly can take a variety of forms. A later chapter explains how governments can control monopoly.

Externalities

Private markets tend to work well when all participants bear the full costs and enjoy the full benefits of their actions. Private markets do not work well when private parties bear only a part of the costs and enjoy only a part of the benefits of their actions. **Externalities** cause private parties to make socially incorrect resource-allocation decisions.

> Externalities are present when private parties do not bear the full costs (or enjoy the full benefits) of their actions. A part of the costs (or benefits) is borne by third parties.

It is thought that private markets do not deal well with externalities. The firm that imposes costs on third parties will not automatically consider the *external* third-party costs in deciding how much output to produce. Instead, it bases its production decisions exclusively on its private costs.

Consider a chemicals firm that must dispose of 10 tons of waste by-products daily. Its cheapest method of waste disposal would be to burn them at a private cost of $1,000 per day. If the firm chooses to burn its waste by-products, however, it damages the health of residents living nearby, and it lowers the value of their property. The costs that the firm imposes on nearby residents amount to $100,000 per day. As long as the chemicals firm does not bear any of these third-party costs, private calculations would cause it to produce a large daily output of chemicals and to dispose of its waste products by burning. If, on the other hand, it had to pay the third-party costs along with its private costs, its costs of production would be raised, and it would produce less output. (In fact, the daily $100,000 cost may force it to close its doors.)

When external costs are present, the invisible hand of markets induces firms (who consider only their private costs) to produce "too much" output. The "correct" amount of output would be that output that the firm would voluntarily choose to produce if it bore both the private and the external costs of its activities. Later chapters will discuss remedies to the problem of externalities and the role of government in these remedies.

Public Goods

The private sector cannot supply **public goods**—goods that are publicly useful but not privately profitable. Public goods differ from private goods in two important respects:

> **Public goods** have two properties:
> 1. no one can be excluded from using the good once it is provided; and
> 2. the use of the good by one person does not detract from the use by another person

The best example of public goods is national defense. Consider the differences between national defense and private goods. In the case of private goods, consumers are rivals. If I buy the car, only I can benefit from it. If I buy a loaf of bread and eat it, you cannot. Public goods, such as national defense, do not involve this rivalry. My being protected by national defense does not detract from your being protected by national defense. In this case, consumers are not rivals.

In the case of private goods, it is quite easy to prevent nonpayers from enjoying the benefits. I can prevent you from using my car by locking the door. I can prevent you from enjoying my loaf of bread by eating it. Public goods are different. If I were to pay for national defense and you did not pay, there is no way I could prevent you from receiving the benefits of national-defense protection. Payers and nonpayers would have to be treated the same.

In private markets, if nonpayers enjoy the same benefits as payers, most people would not pay. Most people would want a *free ride*—letting someone else pay. If the number of free riders is substantial, private markets would not be able to provide the good. If few are willing to pay, why should a private firm produce the good?

Public goods are paid for by tax dollars and are provided by the government because of free riding and because consumers are not rivals. The price system, therefore, breaks down in failing to provide public goods. Yet society must have public goods to survive.

Government intervention may be required because of monopoly, externalities, public goods, inequality, and macroeconomic instability.

Inequality

There is no guarantee that private markets will solve the *for whom* problem to satisfy the ethical norms of society. If society, through its elected officials, decides that the income distribution generated by private markets is unfair, government can redistribute income. Governments redistribute income by taxing those who have "too much" more heavily than those who have "too little." Government can transfer income to those who have too little either by giving them transfer payments or by giving them goods and services (like free lunches, free medical care, and the like). The political process yields social judgments about the distribution of income in the form of income-tax legislation and antipoverty legislation.

Macroeconomic Instability

In solving the economic problem, the private sector may not provide a stable level of economic activity. It is a historical fact that market economies have been subject to fluctuations in output, employment, and prices—called *business cycles*. During booms, output grows rapidly, unemployment falls, and optimism prevails. Busts follow booms with declining output, rising unemployment, and falling stock markets.

The study of the instability of capitalism was pioneered by John Maynard Keynes during the Great Depression of the 1930s, and this theme remains a principal concern of macroeconomics. The major debate in modern macroeconomics is over the role of government in stabilizing the economy. Should the government attempt to stabilize the economy, or should the economy be left to recover from the business cycle on its own?

EVALUATING GOVERNMENT RESOURCE ALLOCATION

The Market Test

The private sector bases its decisions on the costs and benefits of alternative actions. Private economic decisions are affected by incentives (that is, the "carrots" and "sticks") that people face. The carrots are the benefits from engaging in an economic activity; the sticks are the costs of the activity. If a firm produces a product, its benefit is the revenue it earns from selling the product. Its cost is the opportunity cost of the resources used to make the product. If an individual buys a product, the benefit is the enjoyment from consuming the product; the cost is the opportunity cost of sacrificed alternatives.

In making decisions, the private sector weighs costs and benefits at the margin. Economists use **marginal analysis** to study private-sector decision-making.

> Marginal analysis examines the consequences of making relatively small changes from the current state of affairs.

The following chapters discuss marginal analysis as used in the private sector. In this chapter, it is important to understand only its basic principles. Marginal analysis teaches that private parties undertake an economic action *only if the marginal benefits of the action are greater than (or equal to) its marginal costs.* Consider the decision of Burger Bonanza about whether to expand its current hours of operation (11 A.M. to midnight) by opening for breakfast. Burger Bonanza would calculate how much extra revenue would be gained and the extra costs of opening earlier. If the extra (marginal) benefits exceed the extra (marginal) costs, Burger Bonanza would decide to open for breakfast. If the extra benefits fell short of the extra costs, Burger Bonanza would not change its hours of operation.

As long as private economic decisions follow the marginal rule that the marginal benefits must exceed or equal marginal costs, the private sector will produce goods and services that pass a **market test**.

If only those activities are undertaken whose marginal benefits exceed their marginal cost, no activity will be selected that yields benefits less than costs. The market prevents costs from exceeding benefits. If private firms produce a product whose benefit to society is less than its cost, the firm will either go out of business or switch to producing other products. Goods and services produced by the private sector must pass the market test.

The Rationality of Public Choices

When the ballot-box is used instead of private economic decisions, majority-rule voting can result in public expenditures whose costs outweigh their benefits. Politicians, who are concerned about getting reelected, can have strong reasons for supporting programs whose costs exceed their benefits. Although voters can always vote out of office politicians who support unwise expenditures, voters typically do not vote on single issues. The senator who has supported a pork barrel spending program may have an excellent record on other issues. Voters must judge politicians on a wide range of issues.

Interest groups engage in vote trading and logrolling that cause public programs to be adopted that cost more than the benefits they bring in. Politicians representing one interest group trade votes with other politicians representing another interest group. They agree to pass spending programs that benefit both interest groups at considerable cost to the majority of taxpayers. Politician A tells politician B, "you vote for my project and I'll vote for yours," and both pay more attention to special interests than to the benefits of the majority. Politicians trade votes and logroll not out of greed or malice but because they want to be reelected. Special-interest groups that favor special-interest legislation contribute heavily to reelection campaigns. (See Example 2.)

Vote trading and logrolling typically do not cost politicians the votes of the majority who must bear the costs. Voters lack sufficient information on complex government programs to make well-informed choices. The benefits of special-interest legislation are concentrated on a few who well understand its implications. The costs of special-interest legislation are spread broadly, often among millions of voters, who stand to lose a few cents or a few dollars. The costs of each special-interest program are so small to the average voter that it would be irrational to gather information about the program.

Public choice economics explains why it is virtually impossible to balance the federal budget despite the best intentions. Politicians know it is in their interests to vote for public spending programs and against tax increases. Spending programs that benefit constituencies are popular. Tax increases are unpopular. As a consequence, insufficient revenue is raised to cover government spending. Balancing the budget would be easy if everybody knew what politicians were doing and what other people were receiving from government programs. (See Exhibit 7.)

Government services do not have to pass a market test.

Vote trading and logrolling can result in programs whose costs exceed benefits.

EXAMPLE 2

Sugar: Special Interests and Logrolling

American sugar refiners, who refine imported sugar and then re-export it, can claim refunds for import duties paid on imported sugar. Current law allows them to claim refunds for duties paid up to five years from the date of the exports. In late 1987, a special-interest bill passed the Senate by a close vote to extend refunds for duties paid more than a decade ago.

Estimates of the costs of this program to taxpayers range from $65 to $200 million per year. The bulk of these payments would go to three large sugar refiners located in New York, Georgia, and Texas. One refiner alone would get at least $35 million per year. One opponent of the bill declared it "a government handout of the most outrageous kind."

The sugar bill illustrates the classic ingredient of special interest legislation. First, the legislation benefits a few people at lot. Major sugar refiners stand to gain millions of dollars per year in government payments. This prospect provides the incentive to contribute heavily to key elected political officials. Second, the sugar refiners and their political supporters can engage in vote trading and logrolling. In this case, sugar refiners received support from a diverse group of backers including the International Longshoremen's Association. They also arranged an agreement with the Sugarbeet Growers Association that senators from the sugarbeet growing states would not oppose the refund bill. Third, the costs of the sugar bill to the average taxpayer would be between $0.65 and $2.00 per year. Senators voting against the bill would save each of their taxpaying constituents only a little money. Voters, who stand to lose a little money, have less incentive to learn about the costs and benefits of the sugar bill. Most voters will remain "rationally ignorant"—they will not even know that such a bill has been enacted.

SOURCE: "Protecting Friends: Trade Bill is Full of Import Curbs Aiding Local Interests, and Major Fight Is Looming," *The Wall Street Journal,* November 12, 1987.

EXHIBIT 7   Majority Rule and Public Choice

Even without logrolling, vote trading, and imperfect information, majority-rule voting can lead to the approval of public-expenditure projects whose costs exceed their benefits. It can also cause projects to be rejected whose benefits exceed their costs. The accompanying table illustrates how this can happen.

Majority Rule and Public Goods

	Bridge A			Bridge B		
	Taxes	Benefit	Vote	Taxes	Benefit	Vote
Betty	$10	$2	Against	$10	$2	Against
Mary	10	11	For	10	8	Against
Harry	10	12	For	10	30	For
Totals	$30	$25	Wins	$30	$40	Loses

Suppose Betty, Mary, and Harry are the sole residents of a mini-community that is considering building a publicly financed bridge. The cost of bridge A is $30 and is to be divided equally among the three people. Each person will vote for the project only if their benefit exceeds their $10 tax share. If the project is worth $2 to Betty, $11 to Mary, and $12 to Harry, the bridge would be built because the majority (Mary and Harry) would vote for it. The total worth of the bridge to the community—$25 ($2 + $11 + $12)—is less than its $30 cost, and the bridge should not be built. But under majority-rule voting the bridge will be built.

On the other hand, majority rule may reject projects whose benefits exceed their cost. Suppose bridge B costs $30 as well, but Betty's benefits are $2, Mary's $8, and Harry's $30. The total benefit of the bridge is $40 (= $2 + $8 + $30), but since the taxes to finance the bridge are $10 each, only Harry would vote for the project. The bridge would not receive a majority of the votes, even though its benefits exceed its costs.

The Causes and Possible Cures of Special Interest Legislation

A key plank in independent presidential candidate Ross Perot's 1992 campaign was the urgent need to eliminate special-interest legislation. Perot presented himself as the only candidate unbeholden to special interests. He eloquently pointed out the dangers of continuing the present system of special-interest legislation, which he claimed was the prime cause of the burgeoning national debt.

Perot's comments are not new. The informed public is well aware of public harm caused by logrolling and vote trading. Examples abound: The U.S. dairy industry receives price support payments under a program passed by Congress and signed by the president which artificially raises milk costs to the consumer by $10 per year, while benefiting a few large dairy producers. The U.S. automobile industry receives protection from foreign imports that raises the average price of U.S.-produced automobiles by several hundred dollars per year. U.S. taxpayers pay up to $200 million per year to a few large sugar producers. (See Example 2.) These examples are routinely repeated at the state and local level.

In all cases, the ingredients are the same: A few people are helped a lot, while the majority must foot the bill. Votes are traded among special-interest groups. Spending bills are passed that clearly hurt the majority while helping a small minority. The general public, which loses in the form of higher prices, is only vaguely aware of what is happening. The pork barrel politician does not have to fear voter retaliation. Special-interest contributions supply an ample war chest and the voting public is confused by the vast array of issues on which to judge the incumbent.

Can a public policy be devised that will correct the abuses of special-interest legislation? A number of approaches have been suggested. First, strict limits should be placed on the campaign contributions of special-interest groups (typically called Political Action Committees, or PACs). If PACs cannot reward politicians for their votes, politicians will not support special-interest legislation. Second, term limits on politicians might be used to discourage "professional politicians." If elected officials knew in advance that their terms are limited, they would worry less about reelection war chests and more about the majority. Third, Congress may need to pass a balanced budget amendment. If the federal government is required to balance its budget on an annual basis, Congress would have to limit the amount of pork barrel legislation. Fourth, more political decisions should be made at the local level. The closer the link between the spending decision and the voting community, the less likely is the passage of special-interest legislation. If a local community votes on a local spending project for which it must pay, the wishes of the majority are more likely to be heard.

Special-interest legislation has been around for more than a century despite repeated efforts to correct obvious abuses. Its continuation suggests that it is not easy to devise public policy that deals effectively with this issue.

Chapter Summary

The most important point to learn from this chapter is: Politicians—like other economic actors—are motivated by self-interest. They want to be reelected or to increase their political power. As a consequence, public decisions to spend or tax may not be efficient even under majority rule.

1. Exhaustive government expenditures divert resources to the public sector. Transfer payments transfer resources from one group to another. Total government

expenditures are about one-third of total economic activity, and the government share of economic activity has been increasing over the years.

2. There are two competing principles of fairness in taxation. One is that taxes should be levied according to the benefits received; the other is that taxes should be allocated on the basis of ability to pay. Regressive taxes fall more heavily on poor people, progressive taxes fall more heavily on rich people, and proportional taxes are strictly proportional to income.

3. There is a government deficit if the government spends more than it takes in in taxes; the deficit is financed by selling government bonds. The government debt increases or decreases as the government runs a deficit or a surplus.

4. Cost/benefit analysis applied to government spending suggests that government activities should occur only when social benefits equal or exceed social costs. Cost/benefit analysis serves as a substitute for the market test that private goods must pass.

5. Government action may be justified to control private monopolies, correct externalities, provide public goods, achieve an equal distribution of income, and stabilize the private economy.

6. Majority rule may not select government projects where the benefits exceed the costs and may select projects where the benefits fall short of the costs. Vote trading and logrolling by politicians and the lack of information of voters explain such public-choice patterns.

> *Policy Focus:* **Society can devise policies, such as limitations on special-interest contributions, term limits, balanced-budget amendments, and more local spending decisions to limit the abuses of special-interest legislation.**

Key Terms

exhaustive expenditures (p. 71)
transfer payments (p. 71)
incidence of a tax (p. 77)
proportional tax (p. 77)
progressive tax (p. 77)
regressive tax (p. 77)
government surplus (p. 78)

government deficit (p. 78)
government debt (p. 78)
externalities (p. 81)
public goods (p. 81)
marginal analysis (p. 83)
market test (p. 84)

Questions and Problems

1. Explain how the market test for private spending balances costs and benefits and how cost/benefit analysis may substitute for the market test in the case of public spending.

2. Explain the different principles of fairness in taxation. Why can't the benefit principle simply be applied to all taxes?

3. Mr. Jones has a taxable income of $25,000. He pays a tax of $5,000. Ms. Smith has a taxable income of $50,000. How much tax would Smith have to pay for the tax system to be:
   a. proportional
   b. progressive
   c. regressive

4. A tax on shoe sales that requires the dealer to pay a $2 tax on every pair of shoes sold should not concern consumers because the dealer has to pay the tax. Evaluate this statement.

5. The state of Michigan hires an assistant professor to teach at one of its state universities. The state of Michigan pays an unemployed automobile worker $500 in unemployment compensation out of state funds. Which transaction is an exhaustive expenditure? How will the two transactions differ in their effect on resource allocation?

6. Explain how U.S. government expenditures as a proportion of GDP can be 35 percent while the government only uses 20 percent of U.S. resources.

7. Which of the following taxes satisfies the benefit principle? Which satisfies the ability-to-pay principle?
   a. A gasoline tax
   b. A progressive income tax
   c. A general sales tax
   d. A special levy on a community to build a dam

8. Professor Sailors grows roses; his neighbors benefit by his horticultural skills. Does the private market value Professor Sailors' roses appropriately?

9. A small town is bothered by mosquitoes. A private company will spray the town for $20,000. Is mosquito spraying a private or public good? Would the decision be a public or private one?

10. Explain why voters do not vigorously oppose tariffs on imported goods that raise prices to them while benefiting special interest groups?

11. Give at least three reasons for government intervention in private markets.

Doing Economics

Obtain a copy of your local city's annual budget. (Check with local public libraries or with city officials if you have trouble locating a copy.) What are the major categories of revenues and expenditure for your local government? How do they differ from those of the federal government? How do you think they differ from those of other cities that are larger or smaller? For each of the major revenue categories, evaluate who is likely to end up paying the tax and whether the tax is proportional, progressive, or regressive. For each category of expenditure, consider whether it can be justified based on one or more of the reasons for government action discussed in the text.

Macroeconomics: The Economy as a Whole

P A R T   T W O

CHAPTER 5

Unemployment, Inflation, and the
Business Cycle

CHAPTER 6

Measuring Gross National Product

CHAPTER 7

Aggregate Demand and Supply

CHAPTER 8

The Keynesian Income–Expenditure
Model

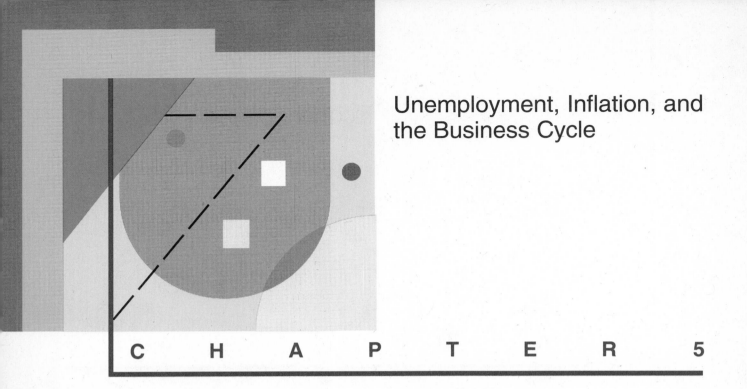

Unemployment, Inflation, and the Business Cycle

C H A P T E R 5

CHAPTER FOCUS   Macroeconomics studies unemployment, inflation, and the business cycle. People's lives are affected by unemployment and inflation. Some are hurt by inflation; others benefit. People must consider inflation in making home purchases, in negotiating wage increases, or in putting funds aside for retirement. Job security depends on the state of the economy. When business activity is down, more people lose their jobs through layoffs or firings. When business activity is expanding, job opportunities are plentiful. Because private lives are affected by inflation and unemployment, people are naturally interested in macroeconomic issues. They worry about a business downturn, about growing inflation, and about job security. They are concerned about budget deficits, trade deficits, stock market drops, the declining dollar, and rising interest rates. People are confused by these things, but they understand that they are important to their material well-being.

Economists disagree most often on macroeconomic matters. They disagree on the causes and cures of unemployment and inflation. They disagree on the effects of budget deficits on inflation and interest rates. They offer different explanations of high interest rates. Most of all, they disagree on the appropriate policy responses to macroeconomic problems. Should the government actively deal with inflation and unemployment or should the government adopt a hands-off policy? Macroeconomics is a relatively young branch of economic science. It is in a state of flux. This makes macroeconomics exciting. Macroeconomics is a field in search of answers.

After studying this chapter, you will be able to:

- Explain the three conditions required for a person to be counted as unemployed.
- Understand the definition of the labor force and the unemployment rate.
- Identify and explain the three types of unemployment.
- Describe how to measure inflation.
- Identify the two types of inflation.
- Explain why people fear inflation.
- Give the four phases of the business cycle.

MACROECONOMIC ISSUES

In an ideal economic world, prices would be stable, unemployment low, and there would be no business cycle.

If we had our choice, we would prefer a world in which all able-bodied persons wishing to work had satisfactory jobs. Prices would be stable, and living standards would rise steadily. This ideal world would not be subject to sudden external shocks, such as worldwide crop failures or unexpected movements in energy or raw-material prices. Businesses and consumers could be confident of a bright and predictable future.

The real world is far from this ideal. The pace of economic expansion is not steady. During one period, economic activity is expanding; in the following period, economic activity contracts. During the boom period, jobs are easy to find, but prices are rising. During the bust period, jobs are scarce, but prices are stable or even falling. The unemployed suffer from the loss of income, and society loses the output they would have produced. In some countries, there have been times of price increases so rapid that the economy as a whole has been paralyzed. Germany experienced a period such as this, called *hyperinflation,* between 1920 and 1923.

The task of macroeconomics is to explain rising or falling unemployment, rising or falling prices, and movements in the level of business activity both at home and throughout the world's economies. The problem of unemployment and inflation are the central issues of macroeconomics. We begin with unemployment.

UNEMPLOYMENT

The federal government is committed by the Employment Act of 1946 to create and maintain "useful employment opportunities . . . for those able, willing, and seeking to work." To meet its obligations, the federal government must know how many willing and able persons there are seeking work but unable to find jobs.

Three Labor Market Classifications

The Bureau of Labor Statistics classifies each person 16 years or older into one of three labor market categories:

1. employed
2. unemployed, or
3. not in the labor force.

John Maynard Keynes (1883–1946)

John Maynard Keynes was one of the great intellectual innovators of the twentieth century. Keynes was born in Cambridge, England, the son of the prominent economist, John Neville Keynes. Keynes attended Eton and later studied mathematics and economics at Cambridge. Keynes taught at Cambridge before leaving to work for the Treasury at the outbreak of the First World War. His exceptional ability in international finance led to his serving as the principal Treasury representative at the Versailles Peace Conference. Keynes resigned from the Treasury in protest over the economic clauses of the peace treaty, and his *Economic Consequences of the Peace,* published in 1919, warned against the economic ruin of Germany and made him an international figure overnight. He resigned his position at Cambridge and earned his living from writing and stock market speculation. His articles were syndicated in newspapers throughout the world, and his stock market speculation made him wealthy.

Keynes was a prominent member of London's literary Bloomsbury Circle, which included England's major literary figures. He divided his time between London and Cambridge, spending long weekends in Cambridge to deal with academic and university business matters. On Mondays, he gave an informal course on monetary economics attended by students and faculty alike and would then preside in the evening over his famous Political Economy Club. In 1925, he married a famous Russian ballerina.

The Great Depression prompted Keynes to write his most famous work, *The General Theory of Employment, Interest, and Money,* published in 1936. In this work, Keynes gave the reasons for the Great Depression and argued that it is the government's responsibility to use discretionary monetary and fiscal policy to pull economies out of depressions and recessions. Keynes is regarded as the father of macroeconomics. Prior to Keynes, economists looked at the economy in a microeconomic framework. The equilibrium forces of individual product and factor markets were supposed to prevent severe and sustained economic downturns. Keynes, on the other hand, emphasized aggregate consumption and investment to explain the business cycle. Keynes taught that budget deficits would have to be used to extricate an economy from depression.

The *General Theory* established Keynes as the preeminent economist of his day. Written in a complex style, it remained for later interpreters to explain Keynes' ideas. By the early 1960s, Keynes' policies of deficit finance were widely accepted in the United States and Western Europe.

A person is employed if he or she currently has a job. Persons who want to have full-time jobs but are able to find only part-time work are counted as employed. Employment is an either/or state; either you have a job or you don't, even if it is a part-time position.

A person is classified as *unemployed* if he or she (1) did not work at all during the preceding week, (2) actively looked for work during the previous four weeks, and (3) is currently available for work. "Actively looking for work" means registering at an employment office, being on a union or professional job register, answering help-wanted ads, or asking friends and relatives about job openings. Persons laid off from jobs or waiting to report to a new job within 30 days are also classified as unemployed.

Persons without jobs who do not meet the three conditions of unemployment are classified as *not in the labor force.* A person is not in the labor force either through choice or because he or she is discouraged. Examples of people who

To be counted as unemployed, a person must be without a job, actively looking for work, and available for work.

choose *voluntarily* to stay out of labor force are some women with young children, students, persons disabled or suffering prolonged ill health, or retired persons. A *discouraged worker* is one who stops seeking work in the belief that no suitable job is available in his or her line of work. Discouraged workers in some sense do not choose to be out of the labor force. They have concluded that jobs are not available for them. Despite the "involuntary" nature of their unemployment, discouraged workers are counted as "not in the labor force." They are, however, placed in a separate category of those not in the labor force.

The Unemployment Rate

All persons 16 and over are placed into one of three labor-market classifications: employed, unemployed, or not in the labor force. The **labor force** consists of all persons either currently working or unemployed.

> The **labor force** equals the number employed plus the number unemployed.

The number of persons unemployed does not show the relative magnitude of unemployment. The **unemployment rate** relates the number unemployed to the size of the labor force.

> The **unemployment rate** is the number unemployed divided by the number in the labor force.

The unemployment rate relates the number unemployed to the size of the labor force.

For example, in 1992, 117.6 million persons were employed, and 9.4 million were unemployed, for a labor force total of 127 million. The unemployment rate was the number unemployed divided by the labor force or 7.4 percent.

Types of Unemployment

Unemployment is a complex phenomenon. Those people without jobs who do not want to hold jobs are simply not in the labor force. Of those who meet the three conditions of unemployment, there are different degrees of *voluntariness* to their unemployment. The unemployed family head—the sole income earner in the family—who is prepared to accept virtually any job is clearly involuntarily unemployed. The unemployed person who narrows his or her job search to a difficult-to-find job (such as professional acting on Broadway) has a strong element of voluntary unemployment. Until that specific job comes along, the person remains unemployed. The majority of the unemployed fall between these two extremes.

There are both voluntary and involuntary elements to unemployment. It is difficult to establish the degree of involuntariness.

People have job preferences; they have regional preferences; they have been trained for jobs in specific fields. If they find themselves unemployed, they will not be prepared to accept any job that is available. The trained engineer would prefer to wait for a job in engineering rather than to accept work as a janitor or fast-food manager. The textile worker whose mill has closed down in New England may not want to relocate to the South where mill jobs are available. The fired corporation president, not wishing to return to the ranks of middle management, is prepared to wait for a corporation presidency.

For the unemployed person who passes up suitable jobs given that person's skill, training, and regional preferences, there is a stronger voluntary element than for the unemployed person who is willing to accept virtually any reasonable job offer.

There are no accepted ground rules for differentiating unemployment that is less voluntary from unemployment that is more voluntary. Economists identify three types of unemployment—*frictional unemployment, cyclical unemployment,* and *structural unemployment*—that differ in their degree of voluntariness.

Frictional Unemployment.   Employment opportunities are being created in one business, region, or industry at the same time that they are being lost in others. Employed workers are usually on the lookout for better jobs; employers are usually on the lookout for better workers. The information about job opportunities that one worker possesses is incomplete. The information potential employers have about prospective employees is incomplete as well.

The labor market is like a revolving door. At any point in time, some workers will be changing from one job to another. Some will be entering the labor force for the first time or reentering after an absence; others will be leaving the labor force. The labor force is in a constant state of flux, and the result is **frictional unemployment.**

> **Frictional unemployment** is the unemployment associated with the time required to change jobs in a dynamic or ever-changing economy.

Frictional unemployment is of less concern than other types of unemployment, and in some ways it is even necessary for economic efficiency. If the frictionally unemployed are moving into better jobs, then they (and society) are benefiting. Frictional unemployment would disappear only if people were frozen into their current jobs by a static economy in which opportunities for job advancement had disappeared.

Frictional unemployment is unavoidable and even necessary in a dynamic economy.

Cyclical Unemployment.   Unlike frictional unemployment, **cyclical unemployment** does nothing to improve private or social well-being.

> **Cyclical unemployment** is unemployment associated with general downturns in the economy.

During business downturns, fewer goods and services are purchased, employers cut back on jobs, and employees are let go. Workers in basic industrial employment (steel, autos, farm equipment) are unemployed, and return to their jobs only when the economy improves. Unlike frictional unemployment, the job changes associated with cyclical unemployment are involuntary. People become unemployed because their jobs evaporate in a generally declining economy.

Structural Unemployment.   In a changing economy, some industries, companies, and regions experience a general increase in their economic fortunes at the same time that others experience a long-term decline. In declining industries— particularly those concentrated in specific regions of the country—employees suffer **structural unemployment.**

> **Structural unemployment** results from the long-run decline of certain industries due to rising costs, changes in consumer preferences, or technological change.

Long-term structural unemployment is especially prominent when it is concentrated in a specific region of the country. An example would be the high unemployment in the oil industry in the mid-1980s. People hit hardest by structural

EXHIBIT 1   How People Become Unemployed

Reasons for Unemployment	1989 Expansion (percent)	1991 Contraction (percent)
Lost job—layoff or firing	46	54
Left job	16	12
Did not find job upon entering the labor force	10	9
Did not find job upon reentering the labor force	28	25
Total	100	100

This exhibit shows that only about one half of the unemployed became unemployed through a firing or layoff.
SOURCE: *Monthly Labor Review*

Cyclical and structural unemployment are matters of social and policy concern

unemployment are those who find it most difficult to relocate. Workers over fifty years old with a lifetime of work in the oil industry would find it difficult (and perhaps not economically worthwhile) to move to another industry in another region.

Labor Market Search

People become unemployed because they are fired or laid off, because they quit, or because they fail to find a job upon entering (or reentering) the labor force. Exhibit 1 shows how people become unemployed. With the exception of laid-off workers who choose to wait to be recalled, the unemployed are all searching for jobs.

When people become unemployed, they do not automatically step into their next job. If they did, there would be little unemployment. Instead, they begin a job search, which can be short or long. They search because they cannot possibly know about all possible jobs for which they are qualified. They find out about these jobs by telephoning, hiring professional placement counselors, going to factory gates, and so on. They must decide whether to take a job that is below their expectations or to search further in the hope of finding a better job.

People use common sense in making these decisions. If they pass up a job, they don't earn the income from that job. There are opportunity costs to continuing the search. People continue to search as long as they expect to gain more from searching than it costs.

When factors shorten average job searches, unemployment falls.

How people search for jobs has a big impact on unemployment. If something happens to make people shorten their job search (people accept jobs more readily), unemployment drops. If something happens to make people prolong their job search (people continue to search for jobs longer), unemployment rises.

Full Employment

Involuntary unemployment has both social and private costs. If an otherwise productive person remains involuntarily idle, society loses the output that that person could have produced. The unemployed lose the income they would have earned. Both individuals and society have reason to hold down the amount of unemployment. For both social and private reasons, the amount of unemployment should be kept near "full employment."

It is surprisingly difficult to define and measure full employment. Total elimination of unemployment is not required for full employment. There must be a certain amount of frictional unemployment. If unemployment rates are above those required for the "normal" changing of jobs in a dynamic economy, the unemployment rate is above full employment.

Full employment occurs at the **natural rate of unemployment** when the ever-shifting labor market is in *balance*. The labor market is in balance when the number of jobs being created roughly equals the number of qualified applicants available to fill those jobs. As new jobs are created or as people vacate established jobs, people with the appropriate skills and qualifications are entering the labor force or moving from other jobs to fill these vacancies. There may be imbalances in particular occupations or industries, but on average there can be a balance between the number of unfilled jobs and the number of qualified job seekers.

> The **natural rate of unemployment** is that unemployment rate at which there is an approximate balance between the number of unfilled jobs and the number of qualified job seekers.

No one knows for sure what the natural rate of unemployment is at any point in time. In the early 1960s, government officials felt that full employment was reached at an unemployment rate of around 4 percent. In the late 1970s, an unemployment rate of 5 to 5.5 percent was regarded as full employment. During the 1990s, the natural rate of unemployment was in excess of 6 percent.

Inflationary pressures remain the same in a balanced labor market. Inflation neither speeds up nor slows down. When an economy operates at its natural rate of unemployment, there is a general balance between jobs and job applicants. If the economy were below the natural rate, there would be more jobs than applicants, and wages and prices would rise. If the economy were above the natural rate, there would be more applicants than jobs, and wages and prices would fall. Only at the natural rate would inflationary pressures remain unchanged.

The natural rate of unemployment occurs when the labor market is in balance. Labor market balance is seen in inflationary or deflationary pressures.

Trends in Unemployment

Exhibit 2 shows long-term trends in unemployment since 1900. The unemployment rate has been subject to significant year-to-year fluctuations. It has varied from lows of near 1 percent to a high of 25 percent during the Great Depression of the 1930s. It is no wonder that the Great Depression had a great effect on macroeconomic theory and that many Americans who experienced the Great Depression firsthand harbor a deep fear of mass unemployment.

Since the 1960s, the unemployment rate has moved generally upward. The unemployment rate was in the range of 2.5 percent to 5.5 percent from 1945 to 1960. After 1960, unemployment rates generally rose. In the 1960s, the unemployment rate ranged from 3.4 percent to 6.5 percent. In the 1970s, the unemployment rate ranged from 4.8 percent to 8.3 percent. In the first half of the 1980s, the range was from 7 percent to 9.5 percent. In the second half of the 1980s to the early 1990s, the unemployment rate was between 5.5 and 7.5 percent.

The unemployment rate has generally moved up since the 1960s.

INFLATION

People worry about unemployment and inflation. Macroeconomics seeks to explain the causes of inflation and to offer ways to cure excessive inflation.

EXHIBIT 2   The Unemployment Rate, 1900–1992

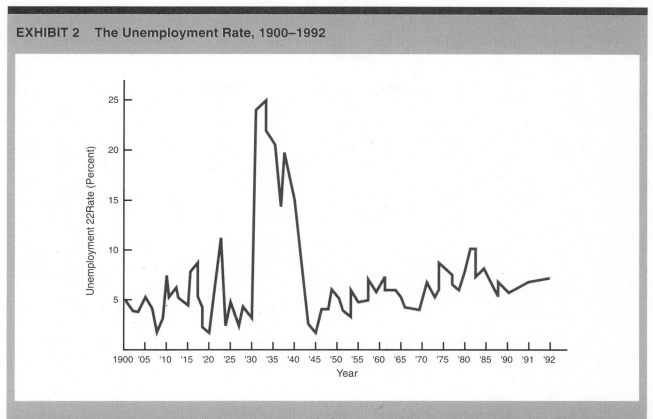

The unemployment rate has been rising in recent years, but it is far from reaching the level experienced during the Great Depression of the 1930s.

SOURCES: *Historical Statistics of the United States; Economic Report of the President*

Inflation occurs when prices rise generally throughout the economy. **Deflation** occurs when prices fall generally throughout the economy.

> **Inflation** is a general increase in prices as measured by a general index of price movements.

> **Deflation** is a general decline in prices.

Hyperinflation is a very rapid and accelerating inflation.

Inflation, defined as a general increase in prices, can be anything from a slow upward creep in prices to a runaway increase in prices, known as *hyperinflation*. Hyperinflation is a very rapid and often accelerating rate of inflation. Prices might double every month, or double daily or even hourly.

Most economies experience slow to moderate inflation. A number of countries, however, have experienced hyperinflation. Recently, Israel's annual inflation rate was 800 percent, and Bolivia's annual inflation rate was 25,000 percent in 1985. Germany had the best-known historical case of hyperinflation in the 1920s—it helped bring Hitler to power. The American South experienced hyperinflation during the Civil War. In Russia, prices were rising by more than 10 percent per month in the mid 1990s.

People who have witnessed the destructive power of hyperinflation know that it can cause the destruction of the established social order.

Measuring Inflation

If all prices rose at the same rate—say, 3 percent per year—the inflation rate would obviously be 3 percent per annum. But prices do not rise at the same rate; some prices rise more rapidly than others. Some prices even fall during inflations. The prices of pocket calculators, home computers, and silicon chips fell throughout the inflationary 1970s and early 1980s. On the other hand, between 1972 and 1981 crude oil prices rose five times faster than the average price increase before plummeting in the mid-1980s.

Because prices do not rise at the same rate, the different rates of price increase must be combined in a **price index** that shows the general increase in prices.

> A **price index** shows the cost of buying the same market basket of goods in different years as a percentage of the cost in some base year.

A **market basket** is the combination of goods and services consumed by a typical family. Price indexes measure the changing cost of purchasing the same market basket of goods in different years. If the typical market basket of goods costs $200 per week in 1990, $220 per week in 1991, and $230 per week in 1992, the price index in 1990 is 100 (the base year), 110 in 1991 ($220/$200 × 100), and 115 in 1992 ($230/$200 × 100). This price index shows that the typical market basket cost 10 percent more in 1991 than in 1990 and 15 percent more in 1992 than in 1991.

Government compiles the different indexes to measure the general change in prices. The most widely known price index is the Consumer Price Index, or CPI. The CPI measures changes in consumer prices paid by households. Currently, the CPI measures the changing cost of the typical market basket of goods and services purchased by households in the early 1980s.

Newspapers, radio, and television report monthly changes in the CPI that are closely followed by business, the public, and government officials. The wages of 9 million union workers and government employees are tied to the CPI: if the CPI goes up, wages are adjusted to reflect the higher cost of living. Many government pensions, including 38 million Social Security pensions and more than 3 million military pensions, are tied to the CPI. Since 1985, federal income tax schedules have been adjusted to reflect changes in the CPI. For these reasons, it is important that the CPI accurately gauges the rate of increase in consumer prices.

The CPI measures the prices only of consumer goods and services. In the early 1990s, 65 percent of the total output of the economy was for personal consumption. The remaining 35 percent went to business investment, government services, and exports and imports. A more general measure of inflation than the CPI is the *GDP deflator*. The GDP deflator measures the change in the prices of all final goods and services produced by the economy. The GDP deflator is a weighted average of prices of consumer goods, machinery and construction, government, and exports and imports.

The GDP deflator is the most general measure of inflation.

Trends in Inflation

Exhibit 3 shows the pattern of inflation since 1951. This chart shows why most people think of rising prices as one of the constants of life along with death and

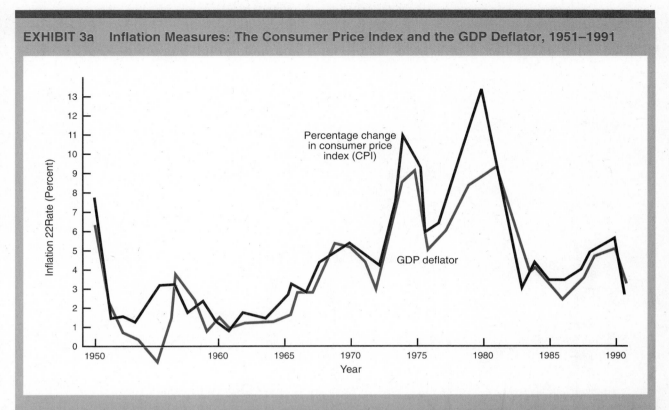

EXHIBIT 3a   Inflation Measures: The Consumer Price Index and the GDP Deflator, 1951–1991

The rate of inflation as measured by the CPI and GDP deflator accelerated sharply from the early 1960s to 1981. After 1981, the inflation rate slowed down. This figure shows why most Americans regard inflation as inevitable.

SOURCES: *Statistical Abstract of the United States; Economic Report of the President*

Historical data show that inflation is not inevitable, even though it may appear so to the current generation.

taxes: the CPI has decreased in only one of the last 36 years (1955). Moreover, the exhibit shows an upward drift in the inflation rate. The average annual inflation rate in the 1960s was 2.5 percent. In the first half of the 1970s it was 5.8 percent, and in the second half of the 1970s it was 7.6 percent. The period since the mid-1980s, however, has witnessed a retreat from the high inflation rates of the late 1970s and early 1980s.

Trends in inflation over the past two centuries are plotted in Exhibit 3b. The sustained increases in prices of the past half century years are a fairly new phenomenon, historically speaking. Up to 1930, prices were as likely to fall as to rise. Prior to the Second World War, deflations were just as common as inflations. The unusual feature of the years since World War II has been the notable absence of deflation.

Two Types of Inflation

A general rise in prices can occur because of demand-side inflation or supply-side inflation.

Demand-Side Inflation.   Inflation is "too many dollars chasing too few goods." **Demand-side inflation** is the "too many dollars" side of the inflation equation.

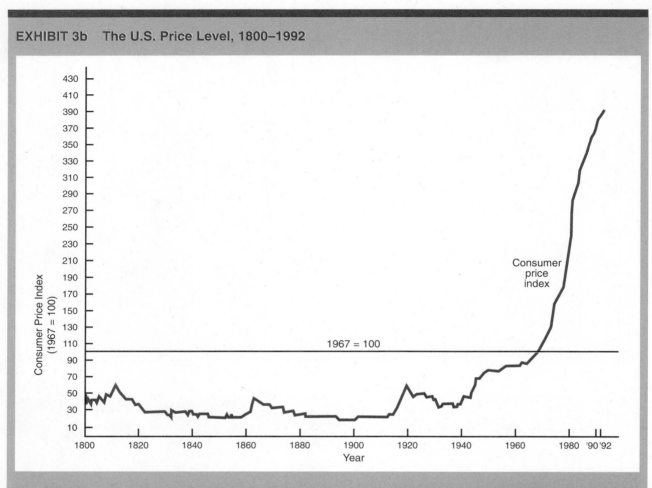

EXHIBIT 3b   The U.S. Price Level, 1800–1992

Consumer Price Index (1967 = 100)

1967 = 100

Consumer price index

Year

Prior to the 1930s, prices were as likely to rise as to fall. The price level has continuously risen since World War II, deviating from the pattern of the preceding 140 years.

SOURCES: *Historical Statistics of the United States; Economic Report of the President*

Demand-side inflation occurs when the demand for goods and services increases, placing upward pressure on prices.

The increase in demand pulls up prices. Demand-side inflation is caused by any event that motivates consumers, governments, or firms to desire to purchase more goods and services than they previously desired to purchase at prevailing prices.

Supply-Side Inflation.   **Supply-side inflation** is the "too few goods" side of the inflation equation.

Supply-side inflation occurs when the supply of goods and services offered by firms decreases, placing upward pressure on prices.

The willingness of firms to supply goods and services to markets at established prices depends on their costs of production. When costs of production rise, firms reduce their supply. With fewer goods and services on the market, prices are pushed up. An example of supply-side inflation is the increase in energy prices during the 1970s, when the formation of OPEC and the Iran-Iraq war raised production costs generally throughout the world economy.

Demand-side inflation is caused by an increased desire to purchase goods and services at prevailing prices. Supply-side inflation is caused by reductions in the supply of goods and services at prevailing prices. To understand inflation, therefore, we must understand why changes in demand and supply occur.

The two types of inflation are demand-side and supply-side inflation

Why People Fear Inflation

People fear inflation for a number of reasons—some justified, others not. Much confused thinking about the effects of inflation exists.

Inflation Lowers General Living Standards.   People fear that rising prices lower standards of living. Alarming increases in housing prices or food prices are cited as proof that standards of economic well-being are falling. While rising prices can indeed affect the living standards of specific individuals, general living standards are determined by the relationship between income and prices. What one person earns as income, the other person pays as a price (the plumber's fee is the plumber's income.) To assume that living standards automatically fall when prices rise is a logical fallacy that ignores the relationship between incomes and prices.

During inflations, prices of outputs and inputs, wages, rents, and interest rates tend to rise together. When the prices of the things we buy rise, so do the prices of the things we sell (such as labor). *Living standards are determined by the relationship between the income people have to spend and the prices they have to pay.* If earnings are rising faster than prices, living standards are rising; if earnings are rising slower than prices, living standards are falling. The relationship between changes in income and changes in prices determines the direction of change in economic well-being. Living standards can be rising when prices are rising and falling when prices are falling.

Living standard changes are determined by the relationship between price changes and income changes.

Inflation Redistributes Income.   People fear inflation because it redistributes income. Inflation redistributes income by increasing the incomes of some faster than prices are rising and the incomes of others slower than prices are rising. Inflation, however, does not automatically redistribute income from creditors to debtors or from the old to the young. Generally speaking, inflation redistributes income away from those who have underestimated the rate of inflation.

When people enter into multiyear money contracts (such as employment contracts or loan contracts), they try to anticipate inflation over the life of the contract. When Bradford lends Taylor money to be repaid at some future date, both must attempt to anticipate inflation. Errors can be costly. Suppose Bradford lends Taylor $10,000 for 5 years at an annual interest rate of 5 percent, but the actual inflation rate turns out to be 10 percent per year over the 5-year period. The $500 interest payment Bradford receives each year does not compensate for the loss in purchasing power suffered each year. Clearly, inflation has redistributed income from the lender (Bradford) to the borrower (Taylor). If the loan had been negotiated differently (say, at a 20-percent interest rate), income would have been redistributed from the borrower to the lender.

Similarly, wage contracts can redistribute income from employee to employer, or vice versa. When a union negotiates a 3-year wage contract with annual pay increases of 5 percent, and the annual inflation rate over this period turns out to be 10 percent, income has been redistributed from employee to employer. If the contract had called for a 20-percent annual pay increase, on the other hand, income would have been redistributed from the employer to the employee.

The income-redistribution effects of inflation depend on the ability to correctly anticipate inflation. The lender who anticipates inflation correctly will demand an interest rate that will compensate for inflation's eroding effect on interest and principal payments. Union negotiators will refuse to accept wage increases that do not compensate for inflation. (See Example 1.)

It is clearly in the interests of all who enter into contracts involving money payments over time to anticipate inflation correctly. Some people succeed; others fail. For the economy as a whole, inflation can be lower or higher than generally expected. When actual inflation is different from anticipated inflation, inflation redistributes income.

Inflation Creates Inefficiencies.   When inflation is rapid and erratic, it becomes very important to predict it accurately. If businesses believe that inflation will be 10 percent during the coming year, and inflation turns out to be 30 percent, they lose a lot of money.

Rapid and erratic inflation create two types of inefficiencies. First, businesses become more concerned with anticipating inflation than seeking out profitable business opportunities. Creative efforts are diverted from innovation and risk taking to anticipating inflation. Second, inflation leads to speculative practices that do not add to the economy's productive capacity. By trying to outwit everyone else, those who expect high inflation will speculate in real estate, foreign currencies, gold, and art objects. Such speculative investments are made *in place of* productive investments in plants, equipment, and inventories.

The negative effects of inflation on economic efficiency are most pronounced during hyperinflations. Workers become reluctant to accept their wages in money (preferring to be paid in products), and money is spent immediately. Businesses refuse to enter into fixed contracts, and most transactions involve barter exchanges of goods and services. In other words, hyperinflations result in the loss of the efficiency of money transactions.

Inflation Contributes to Business Cycles.   Inflation's role in provoking the ups and downs of business activity is one of the most important issues of macroeconomics. Does inflation cause more output to be produced *ceteris paribus?* Subsequent chapters will be devoted to this complex question. Some economists believe that inflation has a negligible effect on output and employment. Others say that inflation, especially when it is unanticipated, can significantly and positively affect output and employment.

If rising inflation can raise output and employment, then slowing inflation can lower output and employment. If the ups and downs of inflation contribute to the ups and downs of general business activity, one has another reason to be concerned about inflation.

STAGFLATION

Exhibit 2 showed that the unemployment rate tended to move upward from the 1960s to the early 1980s. Exhibit 3 showed that inflation also tended to rise from the 1960s to the beginning of the 1980s. Rising inflation and unemployment are not welcome in an economy that wishes to have both stable prices and low unemployment. Exhibit 4 combines this information to show the problem of **stagflation.**

Inflation redistributes income when actual inflation is different from anticipated inflation.

Economic efficiency can be harmed by rapid inflation, particularly by hyperinflation.

EXAMPLE 1

How Inflation Redistributes Income: Wages and Inflation

Inflation redistributes income when inflation is not anticipated. When inflation is anticipated, people enter into multiyear contracts that protect them from inflation. Employees typically enter into multiyear contracts with their employers either through individual bargaining or through collective bargaining through their labor unions. Employees try to avoid wage contracts that give them wage increases that do not keep up with inflation.

The accompanying chart shows the relationship between annual increases in money wages and annual inflation rates. It shows that wages do not keep up with inflation when inflation suddenly accelerates. Inflationary accelerations in 1974–1975 and 1979–1980 left workers with wage increases that failed to keep pace with inflation. On the other hand, workers benefited from sudden decelerations in the inflation rate. When inflation slowed down in 1976–1977 and in 1982–1983, wage increases outpaced inflation. These data show that people cannot anticipate *sudden* increases or decreases in inflation, and they therefore enter into multiyear contracts that do not properly protect them from inflation. Accordingly, income is redistributed. During sudden accelerations, it is redistributed from workers to their employers. During sudden decelerations, it is redistributed from employers to workers.

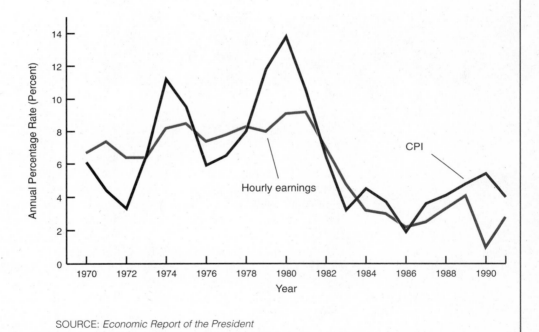

SOURCE: *Economic Report of the President*

Stagflation is the combination of high unemployment rates and high inflation over a period of time.

Starting in the mid-1960s, both inflation and unemployment began to rise together. In fact, between 1966 and 1975, the two rose in almost perfect tandem. After 1977, inflation and unemployment continued to move together, following

EXHIBIT 4   The Stagflation of the 1970s and 1980s

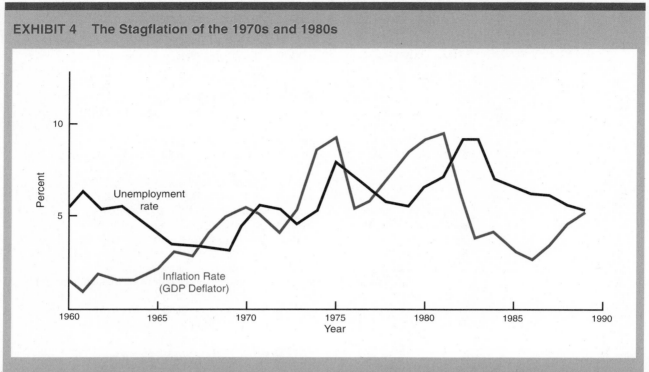

Inflation and unemployment both showed upward trends from the late 1960s to the early 1980s. The combination of high inflation and high unemployment is stagflation.

SOURCE: *Economic Report of the President*

clear upward trends until the early 1980s. In the mid-1980s, inflation declined more rapidly than unemployment.

The stagflation of the 1970s came as a surprise. Many macroeconomics had believed that high unemployment would drive down inflation and that low unemployment would raise inflation. During periods of high unemployment, job applicants would far exceed job vacancies, and wages and prices would decline. The combination of high inflation and high unemployment did not seem to make sense.

The stagflation of the 1970s (shown in Exhibit 4) forced macroeconomists to explain why high unemployment does not necessarily drive down inflation. In fact, stagflation spawned the new theories of macroeconomics that are discussed in Chapter 13 on inflation and unemployment. That same chapter explains how changing inflationary expectation can create the phenomenon of stagflation.

Stagflation creates a significant policy problem: Should we fight inflation or unemployment? (See Example 2.)

BUSINESS CYCLES

Trends in business activity are not smooth, neat, or predictable. Economies experience periods of reduced volume of total output and employment, which are followed by periods of rapid growth of output and employment. Unemployment rates rise and fall.

EXAMPLE 2

Stop-and-Go Policies: The Dance Between Inflation and Unemployment

High unemployment and rapid inflation are both "bads" that societies wish to avoid. In practice, however, it has proved difficult to achieve both high unemployment and low inflation. Unlike other governments such as Germany's which has a clear mandate to fight inflation first and foremost, the U.S. government has pursued "stop-and-go" policies to attack whatever economic problem—inflation or unemployment—that the public fears most at that particular time.

The accompanying table shows surveys by the Gallup Poll organization concerning problems that U.S. citizens fear most. These surveys show that when inflation is high, such as in the 1970s and early 1980s, people fear inflation more and don't particularly worry about unemployment. When unemployment is rising or high, such as in the early 1980s and early 1990s, people fear unemployment and have little concern about inflation. When inflation and unemployment are both high (such as in 1980), people worry more about inflation than unemployment.

U.S. government policy toward inflation and unemployment (a topic to be studied in later chapters) has changed with swings in public fears. When people are more worried about inflation, the government turns into a dedicated inflation fighter. When people are worried more about high unemployment, the government turns into a dedicated creator of jobs.

Critics point out that this jumping back and forth between "inflation fighter and jobs creator" has deprived the federal government of the opportunity to pursue a long-term policy aimed at jobs growth combined with price stability. The pursuit of "stop-and-go policies" has meant that the government is constantly chasing short-run goals rather than a consistent economic policy geared toward economic growth.

Public Opinion, Inflation, and Unemployment

The figure shows that people have consistently over the years rated current economic problems as the most important problem they face. During periods of high inflation, they consider inflation the most important problem. During periods of high unemployment, they consider unemployment the most important problem.

SOURCE: The Gallup Poll, *News Service,* Vol. 57, no. 18a, September 17, 1992.

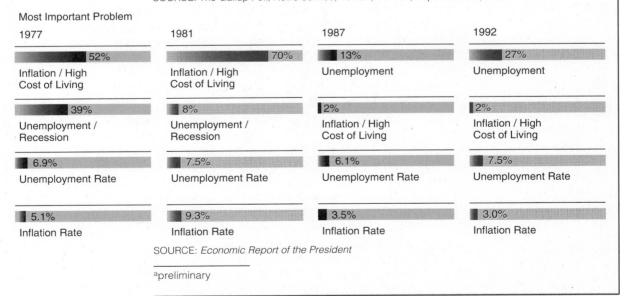

Most Important Problem

1977	1981	1987	1992
52% Inflation / High Cost of Living	70% Inflation / High Cost of Living	13% Unemployment	27% Unemployment
39% Unemployment / Recession	8% Unemployment / Recession	2% Inflation / High Cost of Living	2% Inflation / High Cost of Living
6.9% Unemployment Rate	7.5% Unemployment Rate	6.1% Unemployment Rate	7.5% Unemployment Rate
5.1% Inflation Rate	9.3% Inflation Rate	3.5% Inflation Rate	3.0% Inflation Rate

SOURCE: *Economic Report of the President*

_____

apreliminary

Over the very long run, economies increase their total output of goods and services. The labor force grows with population; capital accumulation increases the nation's capital stock; technological improvements raise productivity. The American economy of 1993 produced a volume of output more than 20 times that of 1893. There is an undeniable long-term trend toward increasing output. However, there are distinct movements in the level of business activity around the generally rising long-run trend. In some years, business activity expands rapidly; in other years it expands slowly or even contracts. These movements are called **business cycles.**

> A **business cycle** is the pattern of upward and downward movements in the general level of real business activity.

The Four Phases of the Business Cycle

Movements in the level of business activity occur in the four phases shown in Exhibit 5.

1. Downturn or recession (or depression if the decline is prolonged and severe). During the *recession* phase, the level of business activity is in general decline. The various indexes of business activity (building permits, total output, employment, business formation, new orders) indicate that the economy is producing a declining rate of output. The unemployment rate rises, and the number employed declines (or the rate of increase in employment slows down).
2. Trough. The *trough* (or lowest point) of the business cycle occurs when the various indicators of business activity stop falling. The economy has reached a low point from which recovery begins.
3. Recovery. During the *recovery* stage of business cycle, the various output indicators point to expanding output. The recovery phase is also called the expansion phase of the business cycle.
4. Peak. The final phase of the business cycle is reached at the *peak* when the various indicators of production and employment fail to yield further increases. When the next stage—recession—begins, the economy begins another business cycle.

The four phases of the business cycle are recession (downturn), trough, recovery (expansion), and peak.

The duration of a business cycle is the length of time it takes to move through one complete business cycle. The length of the business cycle can be measured either as the number of months between the peak of the cycle and the next peak or as the time it takes to move from trough to trough. No two business cycles are identical. The average duration of cycles of the U.S. economy is almost five years. The recession phase lasts, on the average, slightly less than one year. The expansion phase lasts, on the average, about four years.

There is a big difference between small cyclical swings where the economy stays near full employment and large swings from boom to depression. *Recessions* occur when the total output of the economy declines. Typically, declining output over a six-month period or more signifies recession. A recession can involve a fairly small reduction in output and increase in unemployment. During the recession of 1990–91, the total output of the economy fell less than 1 percent, while the unemployment rate rose from 6.1 percent to 7.6 percent. The recession of 1982 saw a 2 percent fall in total output and a rise in the unemployment rate from 7.5 percent to 9.5 percent. When the decline in output is severe and prolonged, the recession becomes a *depression*. During the Great Depression, the total output of the economy fell in 1933 to 70 percent of its 1929 level. The unemployment rate rose from 3.2 percent in 1929 to 24.9 percent in 1933.

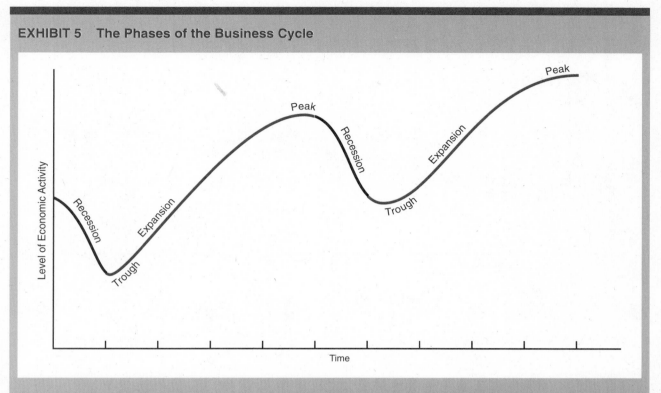

EXHIBIT 5   The Phases of the Business Cycle

Level of Economic Activity

Recession

Trough

Expansion

Peak

Recession

Trough

Expansion

Peak

Time

This figure illustrates the four phases of the business cycle. Since 1924, the average recession has lasted one year, and the average recovery has lasted four years. Each peak in the figure is higher than the previous one because of the long-term growth of the economy.

Business Cycles and the World Economy

The economic ups and downs of major industrial economies cause ripple effects throughout the world economy. National economies do not exist in isolation. They trade goods and services with one another. Their credit markets are interrelated, with multinational firms borrowing dollars in New York, London, Zurich, or Hong Kong. Rapid economic growth in one country causes that country to increase its purchases (imports) from other countries. High interest rates in one country can raise interest rates generally in world credit markets. The world's economies are interrelated through flows of goods and services and through flows of credit. Therefore, it is not surprising that business cycles tend to spread from country to country.

Exhibit 6 shows that the world's economies are interrelated. They tend to share common periods of rapid or slow growth. Industrial countries tend to experience common inflation and unemployment trends. Interest rates tend to rise and fall together. Business cycles do not move together in perfect harmony among countries. One country will experience recession before other countries, but over the long run, it is clear that there is a common general trend.

The next chapter will examine how to define and measure aggregate economic output (gross domestic product) and its various components.

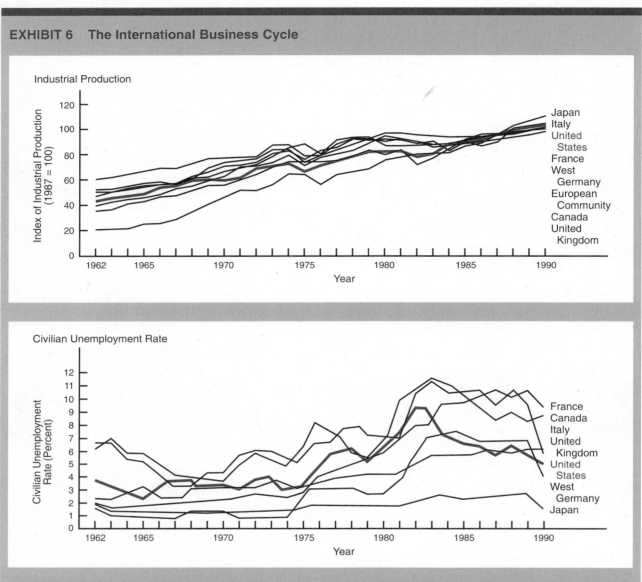

EXHIBIT 6   The International Business Cycle

Industrial Production

Index of Industrial Production (1987 = 100)

Japan
Italy
United
 States
France
West
 Germany
European
 Community
Canada
United
 Kingdom

Year

Civilian Unemployment Rate

Civilian Unemployment Rate (Percent)

France
Canada
Italy
United
 Kingdom
United
 States
West
 Germany
Japan

Year

SOURCE: *Economic Report of the President*

The most important point to learn from this chapter is: The objective of macroeconomics is to explain the causes and cures of inflation and unemployment.

1. Macroeconomics is the study of the economy in the whole. Macroeconomists study inflation, unemployment, and the business cycle.

How Should We Deal with Unemployment?

The Employment Act of 1946 requires the government to provide employment opportunities to U.S. citizens. The Great Depression of the 1930s created public support for the notion that it is government's responsibility to counteract unemployment. State and federal governments, along with private organizations such as unions, now provide financial assistance to unemployed workers. This financial assistance allows unemployed workers to survive spells of unemployment.

Few dispute the notion that the government should provide financial assistance to the unemployed. The public policy issue is the duration and magnitude of such assistance. Modern macroeconomics has shown that unemployed individuals weigh the costs and benefits of being unemployed. If the costs of being unemployed are low, they will stay unemployed longer. If unemployed workers receive unemployment benefits that make up a substantial fraction of their lost income and if these benefits can be drawn over a long period of time, there is less incentive to accept jobs.

Some empirical studies show that much of the rise in Europe's unemployment rate (from an average of 3 percent in the early 1970s to an average of near 10% in the early 1990s) is explained by the unconditional payment of unemployment benefits for an indefinite period. Studies of unemployment in the United States show that most unemployed workers find jobs in the week before their unemployment benefits expire.

Policy makers must strike the proper balance between cushioning the financial blow of unemployment and leaving appropriate incentives for searching for and accepting jobs. If unemployment benefits are too generous, the unemployment rate will remain stubbornly high.

SOURCES: Olivier Blanchard and Lawrence Summers, "Beyond the Natural Rate Hypothesis: Why Is Unemployment So High in Europe?" *American Economic Review* 78 (May 1988): 182–93. Richard Layard and Stephen Nickell, in *The Rise in Unemployment,* ed. Charles Bean et al. (London: Basil Blackwell, 1987).

2. A person is unemployed if he or she is not working, is currently available for work, and is actively seeking a job. There are three main types of unemployment: frictional unemployment (normal changing of jobs in a changing economy), cyclical unemployment (associated with general downturns in the economy), and structural unemployment (resulting from long-term economic declines concentrated in specific industries or regions). People who are unemployed search for jobs. Full employment is reached at the natural rate of unemployment.

3. Inflation is a general increase in prices measured by price indexes that determine the changing cost of buying a specific market basket of goods. Deflation is a general decrease in prices. The most important price indexes are the Consumer Price Index and the GDP deflator. The two types of inflation are demand-side inflation and supply-side inflation. Inflation can affect income distribution, efficiency, employment, and output. There is no simple relationship between inflation and general living standards.

4. Both the inflation rate and the unemployment rate took an upward trend from the mid-1960s to the early 1980s. Modern macroeconomics must explain the combination of high unemployment and high inflation, which is called *stagflation*.

5. A business cycle is the pattern of upward and downward movements in the level of business activity. The four phases of the business cycle are: recession, trough, recovery, and peak. The world economy appears to share common business cycles.

Policy Focus: **Public policy must strike a balance between cushioning the blow of unemployment and providing unemployment benefits that are too generous and prolong unemployment.**

Key Terms

labor force (p. 93)
unemployment rate (p. 93)
frictional unemployment (p. 94)
cyclical unemployment (p. 94)
structural unemployment (p. 94)
natural rate of unemployment (p. 96)
inflation (p. 97)

deflation (p. 97)
price index (p. 98)
demand-side inflation (p. 99)
supply-side inflation (p. 100)
stagflation (p. 102)
business cycle (p. 106)

Questions and Problems

1. Explain why there are both voluntary elements and involuntary elements to unemployment.

2. How would each of the following people be classified according to the official definition of unemployment?
    a. The high-school student casually looking for an after-school job.
    b. The person who quits his or her job to become a full-time homemaker.
    c. The laid-off autoworker waiting to be recalled to his or her previous job.
    d. The person who has quit a job to search for a better job.

3. Describe the relevant criteria by which government statisticians determine whether a person is "unemployed" or "not in the labor force."

4. Suppose economic conditions are generally good but that higher gasoline prices have caused a protracted slump in the automobile industry. How would you classify unemployment in the automobile industry?

5. In 1992, a typical market basket cost $500. In 1994, the same market basket cost $800. What is the price index for 1994, using 1992 as the base year?

6. By analogy to microeconomics, explain why "too many dollars chasing too few goods" can cause inflation.

7. Explain how inflation can redistribute wealth from lenders to borrowers. Why is it important whether the inflation is anticipated or unanticipated?

8. Explain why, in a society where prices are doubling every week, this hyperinflation would reduce economic efficiency.

9. Would an economy that is in a recession be operating at the natural rate of unemployment?

10. If normal frictional unemployment is 5 percent of the labor force, and the economy is currently operating at a 3 percent unemployment rate, speculate on what might happen to the inflation rate.

11. What inflation rate would you predict for 1994 if the annual inflation rates were either (a) 6 percent in 1991, 4 percent in 1992, and 5 percent in 1993, or (b) 10 percent in 1991, 0 percent in 1992, and 5 percent in 1993? With which set of numbers would you predict more confidently?

12. Jones lends $100 to Smith for one year. During this year the inflation rate is 5 percent. How much interest and principle would Jones have to receive to be able to buy the same physical quantities of goods and services when the loan is repaid as when the loan was made?

13. If recoveries last four times longer than recessions, what would you expect the long-term trend in real business activity to be?

14. Explain why the GDP deflator may be a better measure of inflation than the CPI.

Doing Economics

The Consumer Price Index (CPI) attempts to measure changes in the cost of living of a typical urban consumer. However, few individuals actually consume goods and services in the pattern described by the CPI's market basket. In the Government Documents section of your college library, locate a recent issue of the *CPI Detailed Report,* published monthly by the Bureau of Labor Statistics. Find the table describing the current prices of the components of the "CPI-U" series. (This index applies to typical urban consumers.) Note the column headed "Relative Importance." This column tells the percentages of the dollar expenditures of the "typical urban consumer" that are devoted to each category of goods and services. Now think about your own expenditures. Construct a simple market basket of about ten categories of items that constitute the bulk of your expenditures and attach approximate relative importance weights to each so that the weights sum to 100%. Compare the weights on these items to the weights of similar categories in the CPI. Now use the detailed price information in the *CPI Detailed Report* to construct your own personal CPI for a particular month. Was your CPI higher or lower than the official one for that month? Why?

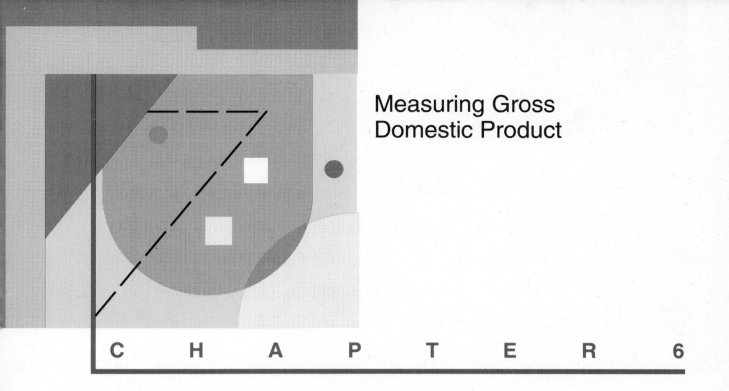

Measuring Gross Domestic Product

C H A P T E R 6

CHAPTER FOCUS   Macroeconomics, as the study of the economy in the large, requires methods for measuring the performance of the economy as a whole. Some of the measures of the economy in the large are straightforward. The number of persons employed, the number of homes built, and first-time unemployment claims all shed light on the state of the macroeconomy.

The most comprehensive measure of the economy in the large, however, is how much output the economy is producing. The total output of the economy, or gross domestic product (GDP), is the best single measure of whether the economy is expanding or contracting. The best single indicator of the business cycle is the rate of change of the total output of the economy.

This chapter explains how to measure the total output of the economy. It explains the accounting concepts used to determine what goods and services to count, how to eliminate the effects of inflation, and alternative ways of calculating total output.

After studying this chapter, you will be able to:

- Explain the concept of gross domestic product and how it is calculated.
- Differentiate between the different measures of output and income ranging from net national product to personal income.
- Understand why saving and investment are equal.
- Show why intermediate goods are not counted in GDP.
- Describe the activities that are excluded from GDP.
- Explain why GDP is an imperfect measure of material welfare.

NATIONAL-INCOME ACCOUNTING

Statisticians, government officials, and private economists puzzled for many years about how to measure the total output of the economy. After World War II agreement was reached on accounting methods for measuring an economy's total production. **National-income accounting** studies how to measure the total output of an economy.

> National-income accounting defines and measures the total output of an economy and its components.

The Circular Flow

The circular flow shows the fundamental national-income identity: the value of output equals the value of income.

The circular-flow diagram introduced in Chapter 2 illustrates the most important principle of national-income accounting: the *value of total output equals the value of total income*. If the economy produces a total output of $500 billion, then a total income of $500 billion will automatically be created in the process. Let's consider why.

In producing output, costs are incurred. Workers must be paid, capital costs must be paid, and land must be rented. The business owners receive any profits that remain after all costs are met. The act of producing goods and services, therefore, creates incomes for those supplying the factors of production. But what is to prevent the value of output from exceeding or falling short of the sum of factor payments? If $500 billion worth of output is produced and sold but only $450 billion is paid to (or earned by) the factors of production, the $50 billion remaining is profit for the owners of business firms—and profits are income, just like wages, rents, and interest. If $500 billion worth of output is produced and sold but $550 billion is paid to the factors of production, the $50 billion difference falls on business owners as losses, reducing their income.

A Simple Example

Consider a simple hypothetical economy consisting of five industries, whose annual sales are shown in Exhibit 1a. In this economy, steel is made from ore and coal (in addition to land, labor, and capital), autos are made from steel, and clothing is made from cotton. Goods used to produce other goods (such as the coal

Simon Kuznets (1901–1985)

Simon Kuznets is called the father of national-income accounting. The methodologies that Kuznets worked out for measuring the total output of the economy, supported by his own studies of U.S. GNP and of the U.S. business cycle, were adopted by the Department of Commerce and later by the United Nations. Virtually all countries (except the communist countries) use common accounting procedures to determine their GNPs, thanks in large part to Kuznets. In 1971 he was awarded the Nobel Prize in economics for his pioneering work in national-income accounting.

Born in Russia, Kuznets headed a statistical office in the Ukraine during the early years of Soviet rule. He later emigrated to the United States and received his Ph.D. from Columbia in 1926. Kuznets was a member of the research staff of the influential National Bureau of Economic Research. During World War II, he was associate director for Planning and Statistics of the U.S. War Production Board. He served as president of the American Economic Association and of the American Statistical Association. After teaching at the University of Pennsylvania and Johns Hopkins, Kuznets joined the Harvard faculty in 1960 and remained there until he retired.

Colleagues say that Kuznets was happiest spending many hours bent over a calculator. In a field long devoted to deductive reasoning, Kuznets insisted on facts and measurement. These facts and measurements are particularly important to macroeconomics, which is devoted to explaining aggregate output, employment, and the business cycle. Without accurate measure of output, modern macroeconomics would lack a factual foundation.

and ore used to produce steel) are **intermediate goods**. Goods consumed by final consumers are **final goods**.

> **Intermediate goods** are goods used to produce other goods such as wheat to make flour or flour to make bread.

> **Final goods** are goods that are destined for final use by consumers or firms, such as bread or investment goods.

In this example, the value of final goods is the sum of automobile sales and of clothing sales. There are no investment goods produced by this simple economy.

The circular-flow diagram describing this simple economy is given in Exhibit 1b. The upper circle shows the flows of goods and services from businesses to households. Only the final goods—cars and clothing—flow from businesses to households. The intermediate goods—ore and coal, steel, and cotton—flow from one firm to another but do not flow to households. As the cars and clothing flow to households, money payments for the clothing and automobiles flow from households to businesses.

In addition to buying intermediate goods, firms must also hire factors of production—land, labor, and capital—owned by households. The bottom half of the circular-flow diagram represents the flows of the factors of production from households to businesses and the factor payments made by businesses to households. The dollar flow of payments for goods and services in the upper half of the diagram exactly equals the dollar flow of factor payments in the bottom half.

EXHIBIT 1   A Simple Example of GDP

a. Annual Sales, Value Added, and GDP

	Value of Intermediate Goods (billions of dollars of annual sales)		Value of Final Goods (billions of dollars of annual sales)	Value Added of Each Industry (billions of dollars)
Ore, coal	20 ⟶		—	20
Steel		100	—	80
Autos			200	100
Cotton	50		—	50
Clothing			90	40
Total (GDP)			290	290

b. The Circular Flow

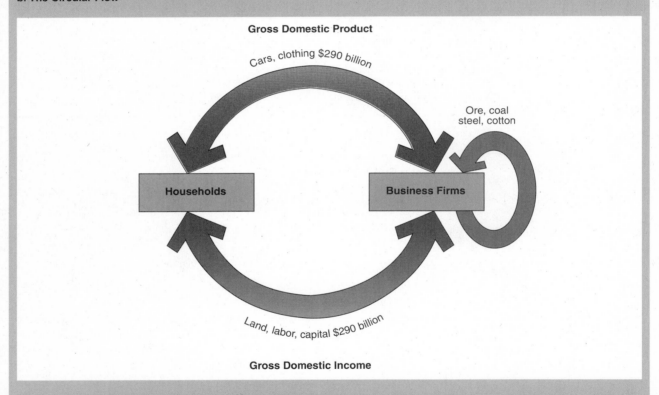

Gross Domestic Product

Cars, clothing $290 billion

Ore, coal steel, cotton

Households   **Business Firms**

Land, labor, capital $290 billion

Gross Domestic Income

The first column in Exhibit 1a shows the intermediate goods used to produce final goods. The arrows show the flow of intermediate goods through the production process. The second column shows the value of the final goods produced from intermediate goods and from the factors of production. GDP is the value of final goods, or $290 billion. The third column shows the value added of each industry—the value of sales minus purchases from other industries. Ore and coal and cotton are raw material industries that do not purchase materials from other industries. The value added of each industry equals its factor payments. The sum of value added ($290 billion) equals the value of final sales.

Exhibit 1b shows the circular flow of this economy. The upper part of the circle shows the flow of final products (automobiles and clothing) from businesses to consumers, whose personal consumption expenditures pay for the final products. The lower part of the circle shows the flow of factor services from households to businesses. Households receive payments for their factor services to equal the payments for final products in the top circle. Intermediate goods (ore and coal for making steel, cotton, for making clothing) remain within the business sector and are not counted in the GDP.

The circular-flow diagram provides a starting point for understanding the total output of an economy. The diagram includes only final goods in the flow of output from firms to households. Intermediate goods are not considered part of total output because they remain entirely within the business sector. Cotton is an intermediate good because it is used to produce another good—clothing. Automobiles are a final good because they are consumed by households and do not reenter the production process to produce other goods. The prices of final goods include the value of intermediate goods used in their production.

The table in Exhibit 1a is divided into three parts. Column 1 lists intermediate goods used within the business sector; column 2 shows the final goods that are produced. Intermediate goods are not important in their own right; they are simply a means to an end. Material well-being is determined by the final goods and services that the economy produces. Column 3 will be discussed later.

Only final goods flow to households. Intermediate goods remain within the business sector. Total output equals the value of final goods.

Gross Domestic Product: Definition

The most comprehensive measure of the total output of the economy is **gross domestic product (GDP)**.

Gross domestic product (GDP) is the market value of all final goods and services produced by the factors of production located in the country during a period of one year.

A *good* is a tangible object, such as a can of peaches or an automobile, that has economic value. A *service* is an intangible product, such as a movie or an airline trip, that has economic value. In our simple economy that produces only cars and clothing for final use, GDP equals the value of the automobiles and clothing produced by the economy in one year's time. The value of automobile production during one year is $200 billion, and the value of clothing manufacture during one year is $90 billion. GDP is, therefore, $290 billion.

GDP does not include the value of intermediate goods because some products would be counted two times or more. Including them in our example results in a total of $460 billion (= $20 + $100 + $50 + $200 + $90 billion). The value of ore and coal is already counted in the value of steel, and the value of steel is already counted in the value of autos. The value of cotton is already counted in the value of clothing. The measure of total output should not count products more than once.

GDP includes only final goods. If intermediate goods were included, they would be counted more than once.

GROSS DOMESTIC PRODUCT: THE SUM OF OUTPUT OR INCOME

Because the total output of the economy equals the total income of the economy, GDP can be calculated either by summing the value of all final goods and services produced in one year or by summing all factor incomes earned in one year. Both approaches yield the same outcome. (See Example 1.)

How the Commerce Department Ensures the Security and Neutrality of GDP Estimates

The Department of Commerce uses two teams of economists and statisticians to estimate GDP. Each team works independently, and then the two teams meet to reconcile their estimates. As this chapter shows, GDP can be estimated by calculating either the value of final output or the total of income. One Department of Commerce team uses Census Bureau surveys of firms to estimate the total output of consumption and investment goods. To these figures are added government purchases of goods and services and net exports. The second team uses census surveys of household income and business profits to which are added depreciation and indirect business taxes.

The national income accounting identity says that the two figures should conceptually add up to the same number. In earlier years, the two teams would meet 3 days before the GDP estimate was due to reconcile differences, but with growing concern over the security of the GDP figures, now they meet only 1 day before the deadline. Although it would appear that estimating GDP is a technical business that only requires adding up numbers, in reality a great deal of human judgment must be used, especially when the estimates of the two teams disagree.

Security and neutrality are preserved by having two independent teams that meet together to reconcile their results only one day before the figures are released.

SOURCE: Timothy Tregarthen, "Estimating GNP: A Leakproof Lockup?" *The Margin* (September/October, 1988), p. 12.

The Sum of Final Expenditures

In Exhibit 1, GDP is the sum of the sales of the two final products—clothing and automobiles—produced by the hypothetical economy. In this simplified example, only one type of final product is produced: goods for final consumption by households. In the real world, there are four types of final expenditures that are summed to calculate GDP:

1. Personal consumption expenditures, C.
2. Federal, state, and local government purchases of goods and services, G.
3. Investment expenditures, I.
4. Net exports, $X - M$.

Personal consumption expenditures are purchases of food, clothing, TVs, stereos, movie tickets, plane tickets, and auto repairs. These are all expenditures on final products that are used by households.

Federal, state, and local government purchases of goods and services are counted as final expenditures. Governments spend money to run the legal system, to provide for the national defense, and to operate the schools. Although some government expenditures resemble intermediate expenditures—such as government regulation of business or agricultural extension services—by convention, government expenditures for goods and services are counted as final goods and services. Because they are typically not sold to the final consumer, there is no market valuation for government services. Unlike other items that enter into GDP, government services are usually valued at the *cost of supplying* them. For example, the value of public education is taken to be the sum of public expenditures on education; the value of national defense is the sum of expenditures on national defense. Only government *purchases of goods and services* are counted in GDP. **Transfer payments** are not included.

> **Transfer payments** are payments to recipients who have not supplied current goods or services in exchange for these payments.

Transfer payments, as the term implies, are transfers of income from one person or organization to another. Transfer payments are made by both private and governmental organizations. A corporation may contribute to a worthy charity; government may transfer income from taxpayers to poor people through welfare programs. The largest transfer payments are handled by the Social Security Administration, which transfers incomes from those currently working to retired or disabled workers and their dependents. Government interest payments are considered transfer payments.

Investments are expenditures that add to (or replace) the economy's stock of *capital* (plants, equipment, industrial and residential structures, and inventories). Unlike intermediate goods, which are used up entirely in the process of making other goods (steel is used up to make autos, cotton is used up to make clothing), capital is only *partially* depleted in making other goods. A steel mill may have a useful life of 40 years. In producing steel in any one year, only a small portion (say, 1/40th) of the mill is consumed. The ore and coking coal, on the other hand, are entirely consumed in producing steel. A computer's working life may be seven years (before it becomes obsolete). The bank using the computer to manage its accounts uses up only a portion (say, 1/7th) of the computer in producing one year's banking services. The using up of capital is called **depreciation**. Depreciation is a business cost, just like labor costs or material costs.

> **Depreciation** is the value of the existing capital stock that has been consumed or used up in the process of producing output.

Investment is classified as either **inventory investment** or **fixed investment**. Both types increase the economy's productive capacity.

> **Inventory investment** is the increase (or decrease) in the value of the stocks of inventories that businesses have on hand.

> **Fixed investment** is investment in plant, structures, and equipment.

If business inventories are $200 billion at the beginning of the year and $250 billion at the year's end, inventory investment is $50 billion. Inventory investment is negative if year-end inventories that are smaller than at the beginning of the year.

All the final expenditures by households, businesses, and government added together do not equal the total output of the economy because some of the items purchased are produced by other countries (imported from abroad); these goods and services must be subtracted from total purchases. On the other hand, some of the domestic economy's output is exported to other countries; these goods and services must be added to total purchases. The total output of the economy is therefore the sum of final expenditures *plus* exports *minus* imports. The subtraction of imports from exports yields the *net exports* of goods and services $(X - M)$.

GDP is the sum of personal consumption expenditures, government purchases of goods and services, investment expenditures, and net exports:

$$GDP = C + G + I + X - M.$$

Exhibit 2 gives U.S. GDP by final expenditure categories.

GDP as the Sum of Incomes

As noted above, the total output of the economy can be calculated either as the value of final output or as the total income created in producing that output. As the circular-flow diagram shows, the value of final goods and services produced by an economy (GDP) exactly equals **gross domestic income (GDI)**.

Gross domestic income (GDI) is approximately the sum of all income earned by the factors of production.

GDI *approximately* equals GDP because GDI includes depreciation and sales and excise taxes that are not exactly payments to the factors of production.

With GDP = GDI, GDP can be calculated either by adding up the incomes earned by the factors of production located in the country or by summing the incomes paid out by producing enterprises. Both methods yield the same total. In the example of a hypothetical economy in Exhibit 1, the contribution to GDP produced by any one industry—by ore and coal, by steel, by automobiles, by cotton, or by clothing—does not equal each industry's sales because of double counting. The automobile industry's share would be overstated because the dollar value of its sales includes the dollar value of the steel that it uses to produce cars. Instead, each industry's contribution to GDP is its **net output**, or **value added**.

The **net output**, or **value added**, of an industry is the output of that industry minus its purchases from other industries.

Column 3 of the table in Exhibit 1a shows that the value added of the automobile industry is the sales of automobiles ($200 billion) minus purchases from the steel industry ($100 billion), or $100 billion. The value added of steel is the output of steel ($100 billion) minus its purchases from the ore and coal industries ($20 billion), or $80 billion. The value added of ore and coal equals its production ($20 billion) because in this example, ore and coal make no purchases from other industries. The value of industry output minus the purchases from other industries equals the payments to labor, capital, land, and entrepreneurship. Panel *a* shows that the sum of industry value added ($290 billion) is the same as the sum of the value of final products ($290 billion).

GDP can be calculated either as the value of final output minus the purchases from other industries or as the sum of incomes.

U.S. GDP for 1991 is calculated as the sum of incomes in and as the sum of industry value added in Exhibit 2b and c, respectively.

EXHIBIT 2 Three Ways to Calculate Gross Domestic Product (1991)

a. GDP by Final Expenditure

Expenditure Category		Amount (billions of dollars)	Percentage of Total
Personal consumption expenditures		3,887	69
Durable goods	445		
Nondurable goods	1,250		
Services	2,192		
Government purchases of goods and services		1,087	19
Federal government	445		
State and local government	642		
Gross private domestic investment		726	13
Nonresidential structures	175		
Equipment	376		
Residential structures	195		
Inventory investment	−20		
Net exports		−27	−1
GDP		5,673	100

b. Gross Domestic Product by Type of Income

Type of Income	Amount (billions of dollars)	Percentage
Compensation of employees	3,388	60
Proprietors' income	380	7
Rental income of persons	42	insig.
Corporate profits	324	7
Net interest	481	8
Depreciation, indirect business taxes, net payments to rest of world, and other adjustments	1,057	18
GDP = GDI	5,672	100

c. Gross Domestic Product by Net Output (value added)

Industry	Value Added (billions of dollars)	Percentage
Agriculture, forestry, fisheries	113	2.0
Mining	45	0.8
Construction	272	4.8
Manufacturing	1,032	18.2
Transportation and utilities	408	7.2
Wholesale and retail trade	822	14.5
Finance, insurance, real estate	856	15.1
Services	1,236	21.8
Government and government enterprises	877	15.3
Rest of the world	11	0.2
GDP	5,672	100.0

SOURCE: *Survey of Current Business*

REAL GDP

Because GDP is measured in dollar values, the GDP of an economy can rise either because the *quantities* of goods and services produced increase or because the *prices* of these goods and services rise. The concepts of nominal and real GDP serve to distinguish quantity changes from price changes.

GDP that is measured in current prices is **nominal GDP**, or **GDP in current dollars**.

> **Nominal GDP**, or **GDP in current dollars** is the value of final goods and services in that year's prevailing prices.

When nominal GDP rises, it is not immediately apparent whether the increase is a result of rising prices or increasing outputs of real goods and services. The distinction is significant because the material well-being of society is improved by increasing the output of goods and services but not when prices rise and the quantities of real goods and services remain constant. Thus, in order to compare GDP levels over a period of time, economists eliminate the effect of rising prices by measuring **real GDP**, or **GDP in constant dollars**.

> **Real GDP**, or **GDP in constant dollars**, measures the volume of real goods and services by removing the effects of rising prices on nominal GDP.

Between 1982 and 1991, nominal GDP rose from $3.2 trillion to $5.7 trillion, while real GDP rose from $3.2 trillion to $4.3 trillion (in the constant prices of 1982). Nominal GDP increased 78 percent; real GDP increased 34 percent. The difference was due to rising prices. Exhibit 3 shows U.S. real GDP and nominal GDP over the past two decades.

Real GDP shows movements in the level of real economic activity. The amount of employment (and unemployment) is related to real GDP. Recessions occur when real GDP declines; booms occur when real GDP expands rapidly. For these reasons, macroeconomists are more interested in real GDP than in nominal GDP.

FROM GDP TO DISPOSABLE INCOME

Gross domestic product is the broadest measure of the economy's total output. GDP includes items that do not represent new production, such as depreciation, and items that do not represent income for individuals or businesses, such as indirect taxes. Moreover, GDP does not show the amount of income flowing to households because it omits transfer payments and includes items that households do not receive, such as social security payroll taxes.

Exhibit 4 shows the step-by-step process for determining how much of gross domestic income households are actually free to spend and to save.

1. **Gross national product (GDP)**. Both GDP and GNP are defined in terms of goods and services produced, but different criteria are used to determine which goods and services to include in the calculations for each. GDP covers the goods and services produced by labor and property located in the United States. As long as the labor and property are located in the United States, the suppliers (that is, the

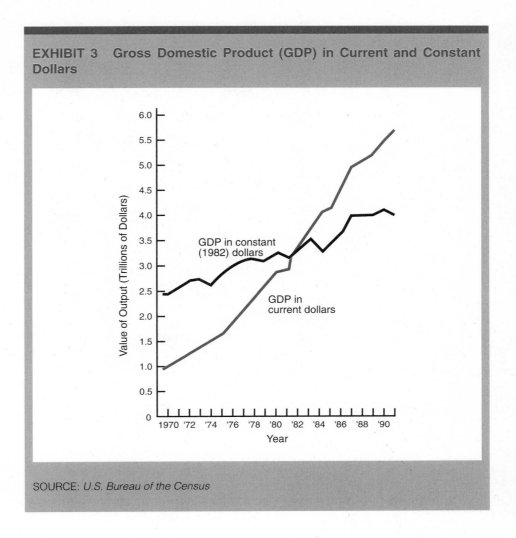

EXHIBIT 3 Gross Domestic Product (GDP) in Current and Constant Dollars

SOURCE: *U.S. Bureau of the Census*

workers and, for property, the owners) may be residents of either the United States or other countries. GNP covers the goods and services produced by labor and property supplied by U.S. residents. As long as the labor and property are supplied by U.S. residents, they may be located either in the United States or abroad.

To move from GDP to GNP one must add factor income receipts from foreigners, which represent the goods and services produced abroad using the labor and property supplied by U.S. residents, and subtract factor income payments to foreigners, which represent the goods and services produced in the United States using the labor and property supplied by foreigners. Factor incomes are measured as compensation of employees, corporate profits (dividends, earnings of unincorporated affiliates, and reinvested earnings of incorporated affiliates), and net interest. GDP measures the production taking place in the country, not the production produced by the factors of production owned by the country's citizens. Hence, GDP is regarded as a better measure of total production.

2. **Net national product (NNP)**. GNP includes depreciation, the value of the capital used up in producing output. If GNP is $2,500 billion and depreciation is $250 billion, then 10 percent of output simply replaces the capital that has been consumed. Net national product (NNP) measures the total value of *new* goods and services available to an economy in a given year.

EXHIBIT 4　From GDP to Personal Disposable Income, 1991

Item	Amount (billions of dollars)
Gross domestic product (GDP) = GDI	5,672
Factor income receipts from foreigners	135
Factor income payments to foreigners	−122
Gross national product (GDP) = GNI	5,685
Depreciation (capital consumption)	−623
1. Net national product (NNP)	5,062
Indirect business taxes*	−519
2. National income	4,543
Corporate taxes, undistributed corporate profit, Social Security contributions	−1,314
Transfer payments and government interest	+1,607
3. Personal income	4,836
Personal taxes	−618
4. Personal disposable income	4,218

*Minor items, such as business payments and government subsidies, are also subtracted here.

SOURCE: *Department of Commerce, Bureau of Economic Analysis*

Net national product (NNP) equals GNP minus depreciation.

3. **National income**. Included in NNP are a variety of sales and excise taxes—called *indirect business taxes*. Although they augment the revenues of government, sales and excise taxes do not generate income for individuals. When indirect business taxes are subtracted from NNP, national income—or the total payments to the factors of production in the economy—remains.

National income equals net national product minus indirect business taxes. National income equals the sum of all factor payments made to the factors of production in the economy.

4. **Personal income**. Not all national income is actually received by persons as income. Corporate profits that are retained by the corporation, corporate income taxes, and social insurance contributions are not received by persons. Personal income does include transfer payments and interest payments that individuals receive from government (which, remember, are not included in GNP).

Personal income equals national income *minus* retained corporate profits, corporate income taxes, and social insurance contributions *plus* transfer payments and government interest payments.

5. **Personal disposable income**. Individuals must pay federal, state, and local income taxes. In order to determine potential spending power, income taxes must be subtracted from personal income to yield personal disposable income.

> Personal disposable income equals personal income minus income tax payments.

6. **Personal saving**. Personal disposable income is the sum that persons actually have at their disposal. They can either spend it on personal consumption expenditures or they can save it.

> Personal saving equals personal disposable income minus personal consumption expenditures.

Personal saving is what remains of personal disposable income after personal consumption expenditures (Remember, income tax payments are already subtracted from personal income to get disposable income). Individuals save by refraining from consumption. When individuals save, they add to their assets by increasing funds in savings accounts, buying bonds, stocks, or precious metals. Accordingly, the amount of personal savings in the economy can be determined either by subtracting personal consumption from personal disposable income or by calculating the increase in the value of personal assets.

> Personal saving is achieved by refraining from consumption.

SAVING EQUALS INVESTMENT

Saving is necessary in order to carry out capital investment. Businesses invest in plant, equipment, and inventories by using their depreciation funds or retained earnings or by borrowing. At the economywide level, saving and investment will be equal. The equality of investment and saving does not mean that the amount savers want to save always equals the amount businesses want to invest. What it means is that forces in the economy cause the two to be equated.

Not all private saving in the economy is the personal saving of individuals. Businesses save by retaining profits and by setting aside funds to replace capital that is depreciating. The sum of personal saving and business saving is **private saving**.

> **Private saving** is the sum of the personal saving of individuals and of business savings (in the form of retained profits and depreciation).

Just as individuals save by not spending all their personal disposable income, so do economies save by not spending all their income. Personal saving is what is left over after consumption and income taxes. Private saving (S) equals the amount of income not spent on consumption (C) or used for taxes (T), or

$$S = \text{GDI} - C - T. \tag{1}$$

GDP equals the sum of final expenditures (we take the case where net exports are zero), or

$$\text{GDP} = C + I + G \tag{2}$$

Because GDP = GDI, the right-hand side of equation 2 can be substituted for GDI in equation 1.

$$S = C + I + G - C - T. \qquad (3)$$

From equation 3, one can see that investment equals the sum of private saving (S) and the government surplus (or deficit) ($T - G$).

$$I = S + (T - G). \qquad (4)$$

The government surplus (or deficit) (T – G) is *public saving*. Government is like a household (although government does not have to pay taxes). The government saves if its income (T) exceeds its expenditures (G). When this happens the government is running a surplus. The government dissaves if its income is less than its expenditures. When this happens, it is running a deficit. Deficits require government to increase its debt by borrowing.

Equation 4 shows that investment equals the sum of private and public saving (or dissaving). If investment in the economy is $200 billion, then the sum of public and private saving must also be $200 billion. If investment is $200 billion, and the government deficit is $50 billion, then private saving must equal $250 billion.

Investment can be financed through the private saving of persons and businesses and through government saving (or dissaving). A third source of investment finance—foreign saving (or dissaving)—is discussed in Example 2.

> When net exports are zero, investment equals the sum of private and public saving.

OMISSIONS FROM GDP

The definition of GDP leaves several gray areas. National income economists must consider what to do with nonmarketed goods and services, including household production, illegal activities, leisure, and economic "bads."

Nonmarketed Goods and Services

Many final goods and services are not acquired through regular market transactions. Vegetables can be grown in the backyard instead of bought at the grocery store. A leaky faucet can be repaired by the homeowner instead of by the plumber. These are examples of *nonmarketed goods and services* that have been consumed without using organized markets. In most cases, GDP includes only those transactions that take place through markets. Barter transactions and production within the household are not included.

The exclusion of nonmarketed goods and services has a substantial effect on the size of GDP. Life insurance companies advise families to carry life insurance on homemakers because it would cost the family tens of thousands of dollars per year to replace the homemaker. If services performed by homemakers were purchased—if dirty clothes were taken to the laundry or if babysitters were hired—these services would enter GDP. The inclusion of homemakers' services would raise GDP dramatically. There are currently more than 29 million homemakers in the United States. If each produces household services worth, say, $30,000 per year, then the total value of their services would equal $870 billion, or 150 percent of 1991 GDP. The less developed countries (LDCs) of Africa and Asia tend to have a larger

EXAMPLE 2

Foreign Saving as a Source of Investment Finance

The equality of saving and investment still holds in an economy with net exports, but **foreign saving** must be included in the calculations.

> **Foreign saving** equals imports minus exports.

Private saving (S) equals the amount of income not spent on consumption (C) or used for taxes (T), or

$$S = \text{GDI} - C - T. \tag{1}$$

GDP equals the sum of final expenditures, or

$$\text{GDP} = C + I + G + (X - M). \tag{2}$$

Because GDP = GDI, the right-hand side of equation (2) can be substituted for GDI in equation (1).

$$S = [C + I + G + (X - M)] - C - T. \tag{3}$$

Simplifying equation (3) and solving for I, investment equals the sum of private saving (S), public saving ($T - G$), and foreign saving ($M - X$):

$$I = S + (T - G) + (M - X). \tag{4}$$

In equation 4, ($T - G$) is *government saving* (or dissaving if a negative number). Imports minus exports ($M - X$) measures (approximately) the amount of foreign saving (if a positive number) or dissaving (if a negative number) in the domestic economy. When imports exceed exports, the country's earnings from the rest of the world (exports) are less than its expenditures (imports). The difference must be financed by a transfer of savings (mainly in the form of loans) from the rest of the world to the domestic economy.

Thus, domestic investment has three sources of financing: private saving, government saving (or dissaving), or foreign saving. As the accompanying table shows, 11 percent of U.S. domestic investment in 1990 was financed from foreign saving in the domestic economy. Federal government dissaving subtracted $140 billion from the saving pool, while foreign saving added $84 billion back in. Foreign saving allowed the U.S. economy to raise the amount of domestic investment by 11 percent. In effect, foreign saving allows an economy to consume more than it produces.

Categories in 1990 U.S. Saving and Investment Account	Billions of Dollars		Proportion of Investment Financed by Form of Saving	
Gross saving (including foreign saving)	795		100	
Personal saving	206		26	
Business saving (including capital-accumulation allowances)	644		81	
Government dissaving	−140		−17	
Federal dissaving		−165		−20
State and local saving		25		3
Net foreign saving from abroad	84		11	
Gross private domestic investment	705		—	

SOURCE: Department of Commerce, *Survey of Current Business* proportion of transactions outside of organized markets. Accordingly, GDP measures tend to understate the total output of LDC economies.

Illegal Activities

GDP does not include illegal goods and services—such as illegal gambling, murder for hire, prostitution, and illegal drugs—even though they *otherwise* meet all the requirements for inclusion in GDP: they are final products, and they are purchased in market transactions. Moonlighting activities—such as an electrician working for cash after hours—are not included because they are concealed.

No one knows the exact dollar volume of illegal market activities. The available estimates of the size of the American underground economy vary considerably.

The Internal Revenue Service estimates its volume at between 6 percent and 8 percent of GDP; private economists estimate a range up to 15 percent. Although the American underground economy is large in absolute size, it is much smaller in relative terms than in other countries, such as France and Italy, where it may reach 25 percent of GDP.

Should illegal activities be included in GDP? If GDP is to measure the level of economic activity, illegal economic activities would need to be included. Official GDP could show slackening production and employment when in reality activity has simply shifted from the legal to the underground economy. Government economic policies are based upon measured GDP and measured unemployment. If illegal activities are omitted, a false impression of economic activity, unemployment, and income may be obtained.

There are two basic arguments for not including illegal activities in GDP. First, it is impossible to obtain reliable statistics on the underground economy. Second, because most underground activities are illegal, legislators, at least, do not believe they raise the material well-being of society. In fact, according to prevailing legislation, such activities lower material well-being.

The Value of Leisure

The number of hours the average American works per year has declined dramatically over the past 50 years. In effect, our society has chosen to produce a smaller flow of goods and services in return for more leisure. Should GDP reflect this voluntary choice of leisure? After all, voluntary increases in leisure raise material well-being just as increases in goods and services do.

GDP would increase dramatically if the value of leisure were included. In 1900, workers in manufacturing worked, on average, a 60-hour week. By 1993, this figure had fallen to less than 40 hours per week. If American workers worked the same number of hours now as they did in 1900, personal income would be much larger than it actually is. The choice of leisure over higher money incomes indicates that people value leisure more than the extra earnings sacrificed.

Leisure is not included in GDP because GDP is narrowly defined to encompass only goods and services. It does not include intangibles such as the value individuals place on leisure.

Economic "Bads" and Measures of Economic Welfare

GDP measures only the final goods and services that an economy produces; it is not a measure of well-being. What if these goods and services are not economic goods but *economic "bads"*? Many "bads" are already excluded because they are illegal, but what about legal "bads" such as air, water, and noise pollution? What about the prison camps common in totalitarian countries or the cures sold by medical quacks?

EXAMPLE 3

GDP IN INTERNATIONAL PERSPECTIVE

How large is American GDP relative to that of other economies? To make this comparison, the GDPs of the United States and of other countries must be calculated in a common set of prices, such as U.S. dollars. There are two approaches to such a calculation. The first is to take the other country's GDP and convert it into dollars using the current exchange rate (the number of dollars it takes to buy the other country's currency). The second and preferred approach is to convert the other country's GDP into dollars using **purchasing power parity rates.** A purchasing power parity rate shows how much real goods and service one U.S. dollar can buy in the U.S. compared to what one unit of the foreign currency can buy in that country. To give a simple example, if $1 buys four loaves of bread and 1 German mark buys two loaves, then the purchasing power rate is $1 = 2 German marks. Purchasing power comparisons can be quite different from exchange rate calculations.

Country size is a prime determinant of relative GDP. U.S. GDP is many times that of Switzerland because the U.S. population is 250 million and Switzerland's population is less than 7 million. Another useful measure, therefore, is **GDP per capita**.

GDP per capita is a country's GDP divided by its population.

GDP per capita is a better comparative measure of a country's productivity, prosperity, and wealth. It shows how much output is available, on average, for each man, woman, and child in the country.

The accompanying table shows that the United States remained the world's "richest" country on the basis of purchasing power parity calculations of per capita GDP in 1990. However, using exchange rates, the United States fell below a number of countries. Most economists, however, believe that purchasing power parity better reflects relative output.

	Exchange Rate	Purchasing Power
U.S.	100	100
Belgium	90	80
Denmark	117	74
France	97	83
Germany	109	87
Italy	87	67
Japan	107	87
Netherlands	84	72
United Kingdom	79	67

SOURCE: *Handbook of Economic Statistics, 1991*, p. 56.

Economic "bads" such as pollution are particularly troublesome. Economists have long recognized that polluters, whether they be individuals or firms, do not bear the full costs of their polluting activities. Society must pay some of these costs.

Economic "bads" have caused some economists to argue for a different measure of total output, called the *measure of economic welfare*. The measure of economic welfare would subtract the value of economic "bads" from the value of economic goods. An accepted method of calculation, however, does not yet exist. How does one know whether something enters the measure of economic welfare as a plus or a minus and what its numerical value should be? (See Example 3 for international comparisons.)

The Importance of Independent Measures of Gross Domestic Product

The 1992 presidential campaign, which resulted in the unseating of the incumbent President George Bush by Democratic challenger Bill Clinton, illustrates the importance of having independent measures of GDP. The 1992 presidential campaign, most pundits agree, was decided primarily on the economic issues: how well the incumbent had handled the economy, and which candidate presented a better economic program for the future.

In order to answer these questions, the electorate needed unbiased measures of the state of the economy, the most comprehensive being the rate of growth of GDP. If GDP could have been shown as growing rapidly prior to the election, Bush's chances or reelection would have increased. If GDP growth was shown as sluggish, voters would conclude that Bush's economic program had failed.

In many other countries, most notably the formerly communist countries of Eastern Europe and Russia and in China, government statisticians produce statistical results to please the current leadership. If the leadership wants to show rapid growth, government statisticians show rapid growth.

In the United States, crucial steps have been taken to ensure that government statistical agencies, such as those of the Department of Commerce, are shielded from political pressure. (See Example 1.) The best evidence of the success of such measures is that the Department of Commerce estimated third quarter growth of GDP at 2.7 percent per annum several weeks prior to the election. Although this figure gave a slight boost to President Bush's campaign, it was not enough. Several weeks after the election, the Department of Commerce revised the estimate upward to a hefty 3.9 percent growth—a figure that might have given the incumbent enough of a boost to win the election.

This chapter explained how the economy's total output is measured and described its components. The next chapter will examine macroeconomic behavior.

Chapter Summary

The most important points to learn from this chapter are: GDP measures the total output of the economy. When the effects of inflation are removed from nominal GDP, the resulting real GDP measures changes in the real output of the economy. Because real GDP affects employment and unemployment, macroeconomics must explain the factors that cause real GDP to change.

1. National income accounting measures the total output of the economy. The value of total output equals the value of total income because the act of producing output automatically creates an equivalent amount of income. Gross domestic product (GDP) is the broadest measure of the total output of the economy. GDP is the dollar value of all final goods and services produced by an economy during a one-year period. Only final goods and services are included, in order to avoid the double counting of products.

2. GDP can be calculated by measuring the total value of final products or by measuring the total value of income. The total value of income can be calculated as the sum of factor payments or as the sum of the value added by all industries. Therefore, the three methods for computing GDP are
    a. GDP = Personal consumption expenditures + Government expenditures for goods and services + Investment + Net exports.
    b. GDP = Compensation of employees + Proprietors' income + Rental income + Corporate profits + Interest + Depreciation + Indirect business taxes.
    c. GDP = The sum of the value added of all industries. Value added equals the value of output minus purchases from other sectors. Value added also equals the sum of factor payments made by the sector.

3. Nominal GDP is the value of final goods and services in current market prices. Either increasing output or rising prices can cause nominal GDP to rise. Real GDP measures the volume of real output by removing the effects of changing prices.

4. Gross national product (GNP) measures the output produced by factors of production owned by a country's citizens, whether these factors are used at home or abroad. Net national product (NNP) equals GNP minus depreciation. National income equals NNP minus indirect business taxes. Personal income equals national income *minus* factor payments not received by individuals and social insurance contributions *plus* transfer payments. Personal disposable income equals personal income minus personal taxes.

5. Saving and investment are equal by definition. Investment is the addition to the economy's stock of capital. Saving is that portion of income that is not spent on consumption and taxes. Saving equals the sum of private saving and government saving (or dissaving).

6. Nonmarketed goods, illegal goods, and the value of leisure are not included in GDP. Some economists argue that the appropriate measure of total output is the measure of economic welfare, which equals GDP minus the cost of economic "bads."

7. The United States is the world's largest economy and has the world's highest per capita income.

Policy Focus: **If GDP statistics are produced without political influence, voters and policymakers can make informed decisions.**

Key Terms

national income accounting (p. 112)
intermediate goods (p. 113)
final goods (p. 113)
gross domestic product (GDP)(p. 115)
transfer payments (p. 117)
depreciation (p. 117)
inventory investment (p. 117)
fixed investment (p. 117)
gross domestic income (GDI) (p. 118)
net output (p. 118)
value added (p. 118)

nominal GDP (p. 120)
real GDP (p. 120)
gross national product (GNP) (p. 120)
net national product (NNP) (p. 121)
national income (p. 122)
personal income (p. 122)
personal disposable income (p. 122)
personal saving (p. 123)
private saving (p. 123)
foreign saving (p. 125)
GDP per capita (p. 127)

Questions and Problems

1. The economy produces final goods and services valued at $500 billion in one year's time but sells only $450 billion worth. Does this result mean that the value of final output does not equal the value of income?

2. Discuss the implications (in Exhibit 1) of $5 billion worth of coal being purchased directly by households to heat their homes. Assume nothing else in Exhibit 1 changes. How and why will this change affect GDP? Will it affect value added?

3. An industry spends $6 million on the factors of production that it uses (including entrepreneurship). It sells $10 million worth of output. How much value added has this industry created, and how much has this industry purchased from other industries?

4. Explain why investment is regarded as a final product even though it is used as a factor of production to produce other goods.

5. A large corporation gives a grant to a classical musician to allow her to train her skills in Europe. How will this payment enter into GDP? Into personal income? Will this payment differ from one made to an engineer employed by the corporation?

6. Which of the following investment categories can be negative: inventory investment, fixed investment, or net fixed investment (gross investment minus depreciation)? Explain your answer.

7. Explain why GDP measures may tend to overstate the GDP of rich countries relative to poor countries.

8. Personal disposable income is $100 billion, personal consumption expenditures are $80 billion, taxes are $40 billion, and government expenditures for goods and services are $50 billion. Net exports equal $0, and there is no business saving. How much total saving is there in the economy? How much is private saving?

9. In an economy, $300 billion worth of final goods and services are purchased. Explain under what conditions GDP will be more or less than $300 billion.

10. Calculate GDP, net national product, and national income from the following data: consumption equals $100 billion; investment plus government spending equals $50 billion; net exports equal $0; depreciation equals $10 billion; indirect business taxes equal $5 billion.

11. In year 1, nominal GDP was $200 billion. In year 2, nominal GDP was $300 billion. In year 1, the general price index was 100. In year 2, the general price index was 125.
   a. Express year 2 GDP in the prices of year 1.
   b. Calculate the growth of real GDP.

12. What happens to measured GDP when a person marries his or her housekeeper?

13. Explain why illegal goods are not counted in GDP.

14. In Nevada gambling is legal, whereas in most other states it is illegal. If one were to measure Nevada's final output, would it be necessary to include the net income produced by the gambling industry? What would happen to measured U.S. GDP if gambling were legalized in all states?

15. A corporation earns a profit of $10 million. It distributes $4 million of this profit to its shareholders. It also sets aside in its depreciation accounts a sum of $6 million to replace depreciating capital. How much money has this corporation saved?

16. In 1992, the federal government spent more than it took in as revenues. The revenues of state and local governments, however, exceeded their expenditures. Which government units were saving and which were dissaving? How would total government saving or dissaving be calculated?

Doing Economics

Obtain a copy of the annual budget for your college or university (or for another institution or firm). How are the items in the budget counted in the national income and product accounts? In particular, how are student expenditures on tuition, room and board, etc. counted under the expenditure breakdown of GDP? What components of the institution's expenses are intermediate goods? What is the value added of your institution? How much does your institution contribute to the major components of national income (wages and salaries, proprietors' income, etc.)?

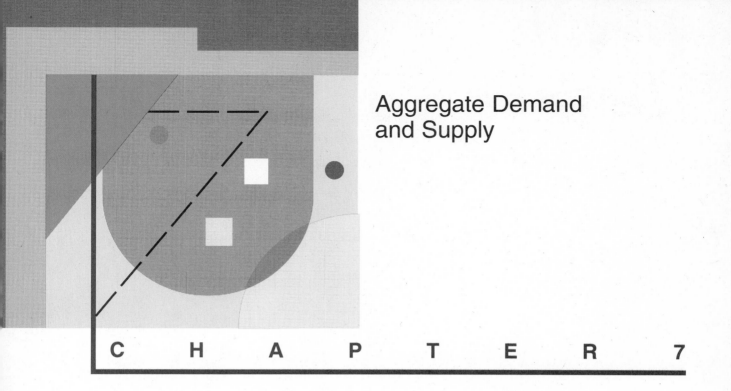

Aggregate Demand and Supply

C H A P T E R   7

CHAPTER FOCUS   Macroeconomics must explain inflation, unemployment, and the business cycle. Why does real GDP expand rapidly in some periods and fall in others? Why do we have high inflation and low unemployment in one period and high inflation and high unemployment in another?

Demand and supply are used in microeconomics to explain how much output is sold in a particular market and at what price. In macroeconomics, aggregate demand and aggregate supply are used to explain how much real output the economy produces and the economy's price level.

Aggregate supply and aggregate demand are powerful tools. They explain most of what we need to understand modern macroeconomics. The tools of aggregate demand and supply are, however, more difficult to master than demand and supply. To understand the workings of demand, one must understand the commonsense law of demand. To understand supply, one must understand why firms tend to supply more at higher prices.

There are no basic economic "laws" to explain aggregate demand and supply. For example, the law of demand does not explain why people wish to buy more real output at a higher price level. The law of demand depends on relative prices. If one good's price rises relative to others, people wish to buy less, *ceteris paribus.* If all prices rise, why should people wish to buy less of everything? If all prices and wages rise, why should business firms wish to supply more of everything?

This chapter introduces aggregate demand and supply. It explains the shapes of the aggregate demand and supply curves, the notion of macroeconomic equilibrium, and how shifts in aggregate demand and supply affect real GDP and the price level.

After studying this chapter, you will be able to:

- Understand why the aggregate demand curve slopes downward.
- Understand why the aggregate supply curve slopes upward.
- See how changes in aggregate supply and demand determine movements in output and prices.
- Explain how the economy automatically adjusts to the natural or full employment level of output.

AGGREGATE DEMAND

The GDP of an economy measures its output or, equivalently, the income of its productive factors. On the income side, GDP is simply the sum of all incomes. On the output side, $GDP = C + I + G + (X - M)$. This section focuses on the basic determinants of the **aggregate demand curve (AD)**. Essentially, the aggregate demand curve shows the level of output (real GDP) that people are willing to buy at different price levels. Exhibit 1 shows how the demands for the various components of GDP are added to derive the aggregate demand curve. For example, the curves labeled C and $C + I$ are, respectively, demand for consumer goods at different price levels, and the sum of consumption plus investment at different price levels. The AD line in Exhibit 1 shows that the aggregate demand curve is downward sloping: the lower the price level, the higher the aggregate quantity demanded.

> The **aggregate demand curve (AD)** shows the levels of real GDP that agents (households, businesses, government, and foreigners) are prepared to buy at different price levels.

Broadly speaking, the aggregate demand curve has a negative slope because as the price level falls, the purchasing power of the money supply increases. As a result, people feel richer, and people and firms can borrow money more easily, thus stimulating consumption and investment. A lower price level also facilitates exports to other countries.

These consequences point to three major factors that cause aggregate demand to decline as the price level rises: the real-balance effect, the interest-rate effect, and the foreign trade effect.

The Real-Balance Effect. Individuals accumulate money savings: cash, checking deposits, savings accounts, and certificates of deposits. The purchasing power of these assets rises and falls with the price level. For example, if you have $500 in the bank, a higher price level means that the real value of the $500 falls. If prices are generally falling, people realize that their money savings can buy more. Falling prices, *ceteris paribus,* motivate money-holding individuals to conclude that they are better off, and they tend to increase their purchases of goods and services. Rising prices reduce the purchasing power of money savings; people conclude they are worse off and reduce their purchases of goods and services. The effect of the change in the price level on real consumption spending is called the **real-balance effect**.

EXHIBIT 1   The Aggregate Demand Curve

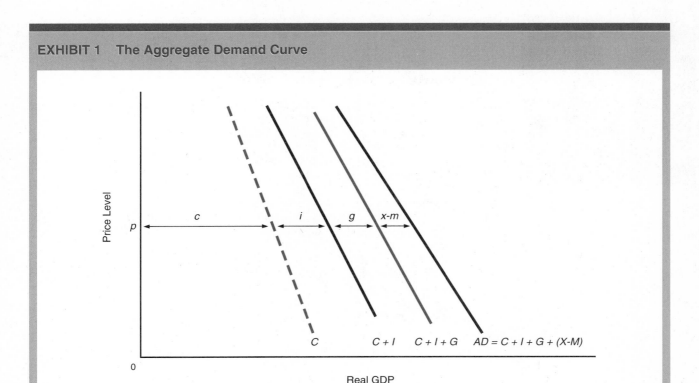

The aggregate demand curve AD = $C + I + G + (X - M)$ shows that people are willing to purchase larger aggregate quantities of goods at lower prices. At the particular price level p, people buy the quantities c, i, g, and $(x - m)$ of consumption, investment, government goods, and net exports (assumed positive for illustration purposes only), respectively. The *AD* curve shows a larger response to a price change than any of the components because it reflects the real-balance, interest-rate, and foreign trade effects of a lower price level.

> The **real-balance effect** occurs when price level changes alter the purchasing power of money savings. Price increases reduce purchasing power and reduce desired consumption at each income level; price declines raise purchasing power and raise desired consumption at each income level.

The real-balance effect changes consumer demand. As the price level rises, consumers desire to spend less on real consumption at each level of income. As the price level falls, real consumption increases.

The Interest-Rate Effect.   A higher price level, holding other factors constant, puts upward pressure on interest rates. With higher prices businesses and households must try to borrow more money to finance their investments and their purchases of cars and other durable goods. As people try to borrow more, interest rates are pushed up by the law of supply and demand. But as interest rates rise, investment demand will be reduced. Thus, in addition to the real-balance effect that reduces consumption spending there is an **interest-rate effect** that reduces investment spending.

> The **interest-rate effect** is that a rising price level raises interest rates and therefore, discourages investment spending.

GALLERY OF ECONOMISTS

John R. Hicks (1904–1989)

Sir John Hicks, one of the greatest economists of the twentieth century, was born in England and studied at Oxford University. He taught at the London School of Economics, Manchester University, and at Oxford until retiring in 1965. His most important theoretical contribution was *Value and Capital,* which broke new ground in both microeconomics and macroeconomics. Knighted in 1964, he received the Nobel Prize in Economics (jointly with American Kenneth J. Arrow) in 1972.

Hicks' writings are exquisite and rigorous. He had the ability to explain complicated mathematical economics in beautiful prose. Although one of the giants in economics, graduate students quickly learned that his door was always open.

Hicks wrote in many areas of economics: labor economics, microeconomics, monetary economics, and macroeconomics. He was an economists' economist. When Keynes' *General Theory* first appeared, economists did not fully understand its fundamental framework. In a short paper, Hicks definitively explained Keynesian economics to economists. Keynes wrote Hicks to say that he had ". . . next to nothing to offer by way of criticism." Hicks' approach to Keynesian economics became part of the equipment used by every macroeconomist.

The Foreign Trade Effect.   As the domestic price level rises relative to foreign price levels, holding constant the exchange rate (the value of the dollar in terms of foreign currencies), exporters will face stiffer competition and imports will appear cheaper. As a consequence, exports (X) will fall and imports (M) will rise. Thus, net exports ($X - M$) will fall. For example, if the U.S. price level rises, *ceteris paribus,* American farmers can export less of their wheat and American consumers will be encouraged to buy more Japanese cars and Swiss watches. As a consequence of this **foreign trade effect**, an increase in the domestic price level will cause net exports to fall. If the price level falls, the aggregate quantity demanded will increase because net exports will increase.

> The foreign trade effect occurs when a rise in the domestic price level (holding foreign prices and the exchange rate constant) lowers the aggregate quantity demanded by pushing down net exports ($X - M$).

The real-balance, interest-rate, and foreign trade effects cause the aggregate demand curve to have a negative slope.

The Slope of the Aggregate Demand Curve

The slope of the aggregate demand curve shows the aggregate responsiveness of the various components of demand to changes in the price level. In Exhibit 1, at the particular price level p, the economic agents purchase the specific quantities c, i, g, and ($x - m$) of domestic goods. The real-balance, interest-rate, and foreign trade effects explain why consumption, investment, and net exports rise as the price level falls. Consumption increases as the price level falls because of the real-balance effect on consumption and the interest-rate effect on the demand for consumer durables. Investment is the horizontal distance between the C curve and the $C + I$ curve; as the price level falls, the distance grows. Net exports, represented by the horizontal distance between the $C + I + G$ curve and the AD curve itself, also grow

EXHIBIT 2   Shifts in the Aggregate Demand Curve

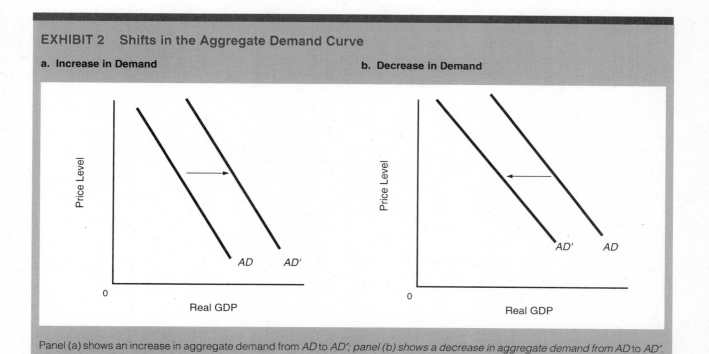

a. Increase in Demand

b. Decrease in Demand

Panel (a) shows an increase in aggregate demand from *AD* to *AD'*; panel (b) shows a decrease in aggregate demand from *AD* to *AD'*.

when p falls. The *AD* curve is flatter than the component curves because it reflects all of the reasons why the aggregate demand curve is downward sloping. It is clear that the aggregate demand curve will be flatter the larger the real-balance effect, the more sensitive investment is to interest, the easier it is to lower interest rates in response to credit availability, and the larger the price sensitivity of foreign trade (both exports and imports).

The Conditions of Aggregate Demand

Along the aggregate demand curve certain factors are held constant. Since government spending is a component of GDP, and private spending is influenced by the taxes that agents face, the spending and taxation policies of the government are taken as given. Private spending is also influenced by the amount of money in the economy. Since the money supply is determined in part by the government, we can say that government monetary policies are taken as given along a particular aggregate demand curve.

The aggregate demand curve also holds constant certain features of the private demand for domestic goods and services. The thriftiness and wealth of consumers must be held constant. People spend more if they become less thrifty or have greater wealth. The optimism of businesses toward the profitability of investment must also be held constant. If business firms expect greater profits from investment, they will spend more on plants and equipment. Finally, the ability of the economy to compete with the rest of the world, as represented by the costs of production and the availability of goods and services at home and abroad, must be held constant.

The aggregate demand curve will shift when any of these underlying conditions changes. For example, panel (a) of Exhibit 2 illustrates the effects of, say, an increase in the money supply or government spending on the aggregate demand curve: The entire curve shifts to the right. Panel (b) of Exhibit 2 illustrates the effects of, say, an increase in tax rates or a reduction in government spending on the aggregate demand curve: The entire curve shifts to the left.

AGGREGATE SUPPLY

The demand side of the macroeconomy rests on what output people will buy: Will people buy the output that is being produced at prevailing prices? By contrast, the supply side of the macroeconomy is based on the aggregate amounts of goods and services that are produced from the available resources with the available technology: Will businesses produce the quantity that people wish to buy at prevailing prices?

Wage Rigidities

How much businesses want to produce depends on their profits. In turn, profits depend on the margin between the prices they receive and the prices they pay. Their most important costs are the *wages* they must pay.

In the modern view of aggregate supply *in the short run,* wages are not perfectly flexible because some are fixed by implicit or explicit contracts. The wage of auto workers may be fixed by a two- or three-year contract. The wage of a laborer may fluctuate on a daily or weekly basis. The degree of short-run flexibility can vary from economy to economy and from time to time. *In the long run,* however, prices and wages are perfectly flexible in the upward or downward direction.

In the short run, workers and employees in many important industries, such as steel and automobiles, strike a bargain. Employers agree to pay workers a higher wage than they could earn elsewhere. In return for this higher wage, workers implicitly agree to wait to be recalled when laid off during bad times, and the employer agrees that laid-off workers will be the first to be recalled when business conditions improve. The employer will not necessarily reduce the wages of those who remain employed during business downturns. Rather wages tend to be held steady throughout the cycle. Improvements in business conditions—not lower wages—cause jobs to reappear.

The major reason for short-run wage inflexibility is that major union wage contracts typically cover a two- to three-year period. Such multiyear contracts set nominal wages *over the life of the contract.* If a three-year wage contract is negotiated during a period of optimism concerning future business conditions, it will call for wage increases over the life of the contract. If business conditions decline and there is less demand for labor, employers still must grant the agreed-upon wage increases in the second and third years of the contract. (See Example 1.)

Multiyear wage contracts reduce the flexibility of the economy to adjust nominal wages to changes in business conditions. They make wages less responsive to general labor-market conditions.

Aggregate Supply in the Short Run

Short-run aggregate supply *(SRAS)* is a schedule of the real GDP that business firms are prepared to supply at different price levels, holding other factors constant.

> **Short-run aggregate supply** *(SRAS)* is a schedule of the quantities of real output the economy is prepared to supply at different price levels, holding the anticipated price level and other factors constant.

Is Wage Flexibility Increasing?

This chapter argues that the speed with which wages and other costs adjust to changes in economic conditions is important. Many economists believe that wages are becoming more flexible and that changes in labor market conditions affect worker compensation more quickly than they did in the past. Economists cite several institutional changes as causes of this increase in the flexibility of wages. First, a decreasing proportion of the labor force is employed in contract-type labor markets. In highly unionized branches such as manufacturing, transportation, utilities, and construction, compensation is typically set by contract three years in advance, in anticipation of future labor market conditions. However, an increasing proportion of the labor force now works in nonunionized sectors, such as services, that are not subject to long-term employment contracts. Second, more and more union contracts include "reopener clauses" that allow the wage contract to be renegotiated in the case of significant changes in labor market conditions. Third, the share of fringe benefits as a percentage of total compensation has declined since 1980. Fringe benefits tend to be relatively fixed costs that cannot respond to changes in economic conditions. Fourth, almost 70 percent of union contracts include significant compensation payments (such as bonuses) that depend on the economic performance of the employer. These extra payments are not part of the base pay upon which future wage increases are calculated.

SOURCE: Erica L. Groshen, "What's Happening to Labor Compensation?" *Economic Commentary*, Federal Reserve Bank of Cleveland, May 15, 1988.

The most important condition that the short-run aggregate supply curve holds constant is the anticipated price level. This means that *business firms and workers signed a short-run contract that anticipated a particular price level to prevail.* The inflation that firms and workers expect determines the outcome of wage bargaining. If inflation is expected to be 10 percent over the next year, a worker may be satisfied with a 10-percent wage increase. If the same worker expected no inflation, he or she might agree to a zero percent wage increase. The higher are anticipated prices, the higher are the wages that business firms will agree to pay their workers.

In the short run, a great many wages are tied to the anticipated price level. *The actual price level that actually prevails need not be the same as the anticipated price level.* If prices rise faster than people expect, businesses will find themselves in a favorable position. Their selling prices will be rising faster than their contract wages and profits will increase. This will cause firms to want to expand output.

Suppose that people anticipate the price level to be 100. Wage rates for a significant fraction of the work force for the short run will be based on this expectation.

As long as there is some fixity in input costs (including labor costs), selling prices rise faster than costs during an unanticipated inflation, and production and employment are raised as business profitability improves. The short-run aggregate supply curve is positively sloped because unanticipated increases in the price level improve the relationship between selling prices and costs and cause firms to produce more output.

If the price level unexpectedly falls—say, from 100 to 95, as shown in Exhibit 3—business profitability will fall. Workers are on contracts calling for fixed or rising wages; firms have contracted to purchase materials at fixed prices. The selling prices of business firms are falling more rapidly than their costs, and firms

EXHIBIT 3   Short-Run Aggregate Supply

The short-run aggregate supply curve *SRAS* is based on an anticipated price level of 100. If inflation rises to a level higher than anticipated—say, to a price level of 105—output rises to y_1. Unanticipated inflation stimulates output. Unanticipated deflation discourages output.

respond by producing less. Firms become more willing to fire workers and to lay off workers not currently needed. An unanticipated decline in prices causes the economy to reduce real output.

SHORT-RUN EQUILIBRIUM

We now put aggregate demand and supply together in the same graph. **Short-run macroeconomic equilibrium** occurs where the *SRAS* and *AD* curves intersect. (See Exhibit 4).

> **Short-run macroeconomic equilibrium** occurs at that price level at which aggregate quantity demanded and short-run aggregate quantity supplied are equal.

Short-run macroeconomic equilibrium occurs when the *AD* and *SRAS* curves intersect.

If the economy were to settle at a price level at which the aggregate quantity demanded exceeded the aggregate quantity supplied, the price level would rise and output would increase. If the economy were to settle at a price level at which the aggregate quantity demanded fell short of the aggregate quantity supplied, the price level would drop and output would fall. Such adjustments would take place until the economy settled at a macroeconomic equilibrium where aggregate quantity demanded equaled aggregate quantity supplied.

CHANGES IN EQUILIBRIUM OUTPUT AND PRICES

The equilibrium price level and real GDP are determined by the intersection of the short-run aggregate supply curve and the aggregate demand curve. As in micro-

EXHIBIT 4   Short-Run Macroeconomic Equilibrium

Short-run macroeconomic equilibrium occurs where the
SRAS and *AD* curves intersect. If the price level is below *p*,
aggregate quantity demanded exceeds aggregate quantity
supplied; if the price level is above *p*, aggregate quantity
demanded falls short of aggregate quantity supplied.

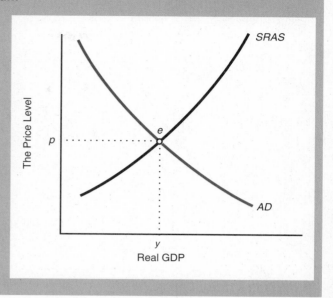

economic supply and demand analysis, changes in aggregate demand or aggregate
supply change equilibrium prices and quantities. Inflation (a rising price level)
results when aggregate demand increases or when aggregate supply decreases.
Falling real GDP occurs when aggregate demand falls or when aggregate supply
falls. In this section, we discuss those factors that cause shifts in the short-run
aggregate supply curve and in the aggregate demand curve.

Supply Shocks

Shifts in the short-run aggregate supply curve are caused by **supply shocks**.

> A **supply shock** occurs when costs of production rise due to changes
> external to the economy.

Examples of factors external to the economy that can cause general changes in
production costs are worldwide changes in harvests, oil shocks, or changes in
prices of imported goods. Supply shocks can be either in the direction of *raising*
costs of production or *lowering* costs of production. When the supply shock raises
costs, it is an *adverse* supply shock. When it lowers costs, it is a *favorable* supply
shock.

Panel (a) of Exhibit 5 shows the effect of an adverse supply shock on prices
and real output. The economy is initially operating at point *e* (the intersection of
SRAS and *AD*), where the level of output is *y* and price level is *p*. Suppose bad
harvests occur on a worldwide basis, and the prices of foods, fibers, and feed rise,
raising the production costs to firms. The short-run aggregate supply curve shifts
left from *SRAS* to *SRAS'*. The new equilibrium price level is *p'* and the new
equilibrium output is *y'*. The end result of an adverse supply shock is one-time
inflation and smaller real output. (See Example 2.)

EXHIBIT 5 Changes in the Short-Run Macroeconomic Equilibrium

a. Supply Shock

b. Demand Shock

The economy is initially operating at point *e* in panel (a). Aggregate supply is reduced (from *SRAS* to *SRAS'*) by disastrous harvests. As prices rise, the economy moves along *AD* (from *e* to *e'*) until a new equilibrium is established at *e'*. Supply shocks reduce real output and raise prices in the short run.

In panel (b), the economy is initially producing y at the price level *p*. Autonomous expenditures increase and aggregate demand shifts from *AD* to *AD'*. As prices begin to rise, the economy moves along its short-run aggregate supply curve until a new equilibrium is established at *e'*. An increase in aggregate demand raises prices and output.

Shifts in Aggregate Demand

Aggregate demand can change if at any price level consumption, investment, government spending, or net exports change. Panel (b) of Exhibit 5 illustrates the effects of an increase in aggregate demand on real output and prices. The economy is initially producing at point *e* where the short-run aggregate supply curve and aggregate demand curve intersect. An increase in investment spending shifts the aggregate demand curve from *AD* to *AD'*. At the initial price level, *p,* aggregate quantity demanded exceeds aggregate quantity supplied, so the price level begins to rise. As the price level rises, there is a movement up the short-run supply curve, *SRAS*, from *e* to *e'*. The new equilibrium is established at *e'*, where the economy is producing output *y'* at price level *p'*. The increase in aggregate demand has raised both output and prices.

> The effect of the increase in aggregate demand in the short run is to raise both real output and the price level.

INFLATIONARY AND DEFLATIONARY GAPS

Macroeconomic equilibrium occurs wherever the *SRAS* and *AD* curves intersect. In the short run, because these curves are independent, the equilibrium level of output may be larger or smaller than the real GNP required to have full employment of the labor force.

EXAMPLE 2

Supply Shocks: The Energy Crisis

The most dramatic case of a supply shock is the 1,475 percent rise in the price of imported oil between 1973 and 1980. When the Organization of Petroleum Exporting Countries (OPEC) discovered cartel pricing in 1973, the oil-importing countries of the world were hit with an enormous adverse supply shock. OPEC inflicted leftward shifts in the aggregate supply curves of every oil-importing country. The oil-induced reductions of supply pushed up the general price level. The accompanying table supplies data on the price of OPEC oil and the average inflation rate in seven major countries.

The upsurge of world inflation rates coincided with the increase in energy prices. Although OPEC was not the only cause of the inflation, the oil shock likely did contribute to the inflation of the 1970s.

Price shocks can also emanate from agriculture. Poor weather and bad harvests throughout the world can raise agricultural prices, and because agricultural goods are a major input for the world economy, this price rise can shift the aggregate supply curve. The year 1973 brought with it not only the beginning of the oil shock, but an increase in the price of wheat from $70 per ton to $140 per ton—due largely to a poor harvest in the United States in 1973 and a crop disaster in the Soviet Union the year before.

OPEC Crude-Oil Prices and Average Inflation Rates in the Big Seven Countries (U.S., Germany, Japan, France, Canada, Italy, and the U.K.), 1971–1983

Year	Oil Price (dollars per barrel)	Average Inflation Rate (percent)
1971–73	2.13	6.4
1974	10.77	14.5
1975	10.72	13.0
1976	11.51	10.0
1977	13.12	10.1
1978	12.93	7.6
1979	18.67	9.7
1980	30.87	9.1
1981	34.50	10.1
1982	33.63	8.4
1983	29.31	6.0
1984	28.17	5.4
1985	28.14	3.2
1986	15.35	2.5
1987	17.70	3.8
1988	19.00	3.3
1989	19.63	4.7
1990	20.47	5.0
1991	21.42	4.5

SOURCES: *Handbook of Economic Statistics*, James Griffin and Henry Steele, *Energy Economics and Policy* (New York: Academic, 1980), p. 18; *Economic Report of the President*, 1993.

The modern definition of full employment is the natural rate of unemployment. Chapter 5 defined the natural rate as the unemployment rate at which the prevailing rate of inflation can be sustained indefinitely. If the economy is at the natural rate of unemployment, and the inflation rate is zero, that inflation rate will continue (zero inflation) as long as the economy is at the natural rate of

EXHIBIT 6   Inflationary and Deflationary Gaps

a. Deflationary Gap

b. Inflationary Gap

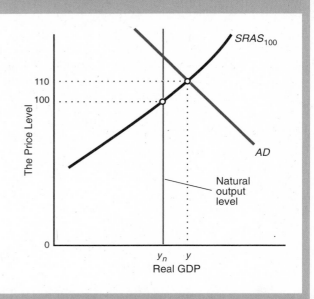

Panel (a) shows a deflationary gap. The anticipated price level is 100. The $SRAS_{100}$ curve intersects the AD curve where y is less than y_n, the natural output level. The equilibrium price level is 90.

Panel (b) shows an inflationary gap. The anticipated price level is 100. The $SRAS_{100}$ curve intersects the AD curve where y exceeds y_n. The equilibrium price level is 110.

unemployment. Associated with the natural rate of unemployment is a **natural level of output**.

> The **natural level of output** is the real GNP that the economy produces when its actual unemployment rate equals the natural rate of unemployment.

Exhibit 6 shows the possible relationships between the actual output of the economy (the result of the aggregate-demand/aggregate-supply equilibrium) and the natural level of output. The equilibrium output, y, in panel (a) of Exhibit 6, falls short of the natural level of output, y_n. In panel (b), the equilibrium level of output, y, exceeds y_n. Differences between actual output and y_n indicate a **deflationary gap** or an **inflationary gap**.

> A **deflationary gap** exists if the equilibrium level of output falls short of the natural level of output.

> An **inflationary gap** exists if the equilibrium level of output exceeds the natural level of output.

Subsequent chapters study how monetary or fiscal policy can be used to eliminate a deflationary or inflationary gap. See Example 3 for estimates of the gaps.

Inflationary and Deflationary Gaps

This chapter explains that a *deflationary gap* is present when the actual unemployment rate is above the natural rate. An *inflationary gap* is present when the actual unemployment rate is below the natural rate. The accompanying figure provides estimates of inflationary and deflationary gaps from 1930 to the present. Economists may disagree with these estimates of the natural rate, but most would agree with the general trends shown in the figure. The colored areas are periods of deflationary gaps. The black areas are periods of inflationary gaps. The figure shows the enormous deflationary gaps of the Great Depression, which persisted from 1930 to 1942. The World War II era was a period of inflationary gaps, as most able-bodied males were drawn into military service, creating exceptionally low unemployment. The 1950s and late 1960s were periods of inflationary gaps, whereas the early 1960s and the period from 1975 to 1984 were characterized by deflationary gaps.

SOURCE: Robert Gordon, "Inflation, Flexible Exchange Rates, and the Natural Rate of Unemployment," in *Workers, Jobs, and Inflation,* edited by Martin N. Bailey (Washington, D.C. Brookings, 1982); and Gordon, *Macroeconomics,* 5th ed. (New York: HarperCollins, 1990), Appendix A. The 1986–91 figures are estimated by the authors.

LONG-RUN EQUILIBRIUM: THE SELF-CORRECTING MECHANISM

Up to this point, we have discussed shifts in short-run aggregate supply or aggregate demand curves and their short-run effects on prices, real output, and unemployment. Shifts in short-run aggregate supply and aggregate demand can cause an inflationary or deflationary gap.

The *short run* is a period of time so short that wages and prices are not perfectly flexible and people cannot adjust their wage or price contracts to the change in the inflation rate. The short-run aggregate supply curve is upward sloping simply because people have not fully anticipated the change in prices. In our examples, economic agents initially expected the prevailing price level to continue into the future. Unanticipated inflation caught workers off guard with wage contracts that failed to protect them from the unanticipated inflation. Business firms had

EXHIBIT 7   The Self-Correcting Mechanism

a. A Self-Correcting Deflationary Gap

b. A Self-Correcting Inflationary Gap

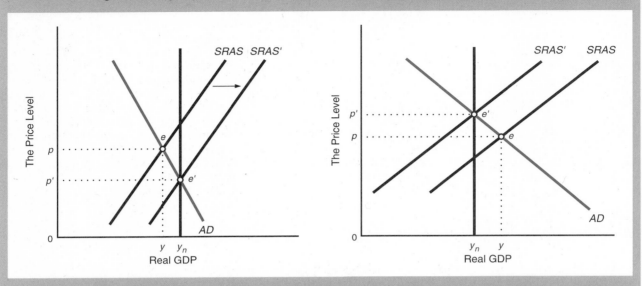

Panel (a) shows a deflationary gap where the economy's short-run aggregate-supply (SRAS) curve intersects the aggregate demand (AD) curve at e. At this point, y is less than y_n, and the unemployment rate exceeds the natural rate. Wages fall and prices fall. In the long run, the SRAS curve shifts to the right to reflect lower anticipated prices. Again, the long-run equilibrium occurs when the AD and SRAS curves intersect at the natural level of output, y_n. The fall in the price level from p to p' brings about this automatic adjustment.

Panel (b) shows an inflationary gap where the economy's short-run aggregate-supply (SRAS) curve intersects the aggregate demand (AD) curve at e, where y exceed y_n and unemployment is less than the natural rate. Wages rise and prices rise. In the long run, the SRAS curve shifts left to reflect higher anticipated prices. The long-run equilibrium occurs when the AD and SRAS' curves intersect at the natural level of output, y_n.

contracts for the purchase of inputs at prices that were rising less rapidly than selling prices.

The economy moves automatically to the natural level of output when people have time to adjust inflationary expectations because a *self-correcting mechanism* removes deflationary and inflationary gaps. This automatic adjustment takes place without any change in monetary or fiscal policy (studied in later chapters) to change aggregate demand. Most macroeconomists agree that the automatic process works; the disagreements are over how long the process takes.

The Automatic Removal of a Deflationary Gap

The adjustment to long-run equilibrium for a deflationary gap is illustrated in panel (a) of Exhibit 7. The economy is initially operating at point e, where the output level, y, is less than the natural level, y_n. In other words, the unemployment rate exceeds the natural rate of unemployment. Initially, the inflation rate is zero, and this is the inflation rate that people expect.

When there is a deflationary gap, prices will fall (or the rate of inflation will fall). In this case, there will be actual deflation of prices and wages. They might not be able to fall immediately because of contracts, but in the long run, old wage contracts expire. When they expire, firms will be able to pay workers lower wages because unemployment has increased and living costs have declined. Thus, wages

Can We Depend on the Self-Correcting Mechanism?

The self-correcting mechanism carries a soothing message: In the long run, economies will automatically return to the natural rate of unemployment (full employment). The theory of the self-correcting mechanism does not tell us how quickly this return will occur (whether it will take a few months or 5 years), but it does appear to rule out long-run economic disasters such as an ever-worsening unemployment rate. It recognizes that economies will be buffeted from all sides—by supply shocks, by fluctuations in investment spending, and by accelerating government spending—but that movements in wages and prices will eventually restore the economy to the natural rate of unemployment without any assistance.

Whether the self-correcting mechanism works and with what speed are crucial policy issues. If the self-correcting mechanism works reliably and quickly, there would be no need for government intervention. Full employment would be restored without government action. If the self-correcting mechanism is not reliable, a case for government action could be made. If the self-correcting mechanism works too slowly, society may not be able to tolerate long periods of excessive employment waiting for the self-correcting mechanism to work. As Keynes remarked, "In the long run, we are all dead."

The evidence suggests that the self-correcting mechanism worked reasonably well during the nineteenth century. Although reliable statistics on unemployment rates from the late nineteenth through the early twentieth centuries are hard to produce, the available evidence suggests that there was no long-term trend in unemployment rates from the 1880s to the Great Depression. Unemployment rates fluctuated from year to year, but they seemed to return to a fairly "normal" unemployment rate. In France, for example, the unemployment rate ranged from a low of 4.7 percent to a high of 10.2 percent from 1895 to 1913, yet it appeared to return after such fluctuations to a 6.5 percent unemployment rate. The German unemployment rate ranged from 0.2 percent to 7.2 percent between 1887 and 1922, yet always seemed to return to a rate of around 2 percent. From 1887 to 1920, the English unemployment rate ranged from 0.4 percent to 7.8 percent but seemed to return to a rate of around 3 percent. From 1890 to 1929, there was no discernible trend in the U.S. unemployment rate, which ranged from a low of 1.4 percent to a high of 18.4 percent and tended to return to an unemployment rate in the range of 4 to 5 percent.

The late nineteenth and early twentieth centuries witnessed many kinds of supply and demand shocks—wars, investment booms and busts, shifts of employment from agriculture to industry and services, stock market binges, major technological changes, new resource discoveries. It was also a period of laissez-faire macroeconomic policy. Governments did not consciously attempt to use monetary and fiscal policy to eliminate inflationary or deflationary gaps. The evidence from the nineteenth and early twentieth centuries is consistent with the theory of the long-run self-correcting mechanism.

One apparent reason for the potency of the self-correcting mechanism was the great degree of wage and price flexibility in the nineteenth and early twentieth centuries. Prices and wages were flexible, with extreme upward and downward movements taking place regularly. Part of this flexibility is explained by the greater importance of agriculture during this time period, but it is also explained by the lack of modern wage- and price-setting practices (unions, long-term price contracts, and so on) that limit wage and price flexibility.

The strongest reason for doubt about the self-correcting mechanism was its apparent inability to create recovery from the Great Depression of the 1930s. This matter will be discussed in the next chapter.

As long as the unemployment rate remains below the natural rate, falling wages and prices will in the long run move the economy to the natural rate of unemployment. This adjustment is self-correcting; it takes place without the need for changes in monetary or fiscal policy.

and costs will start to drift downward. When costs fall, business firms will begin to cut prices. *The short-run aggregate supply curve will eventually shift to the right from SRAS to SRAS′ as wages and costs fall.* Falling prices will move the economy down the aggregate-demand curve, *AD*, to a higher level of output. The economy moves from point *e* toward point *e′*. As long as the economy's output is less than y_n, prices will continue to fall and move the economy closer and closer to y_n. This process stops when the economy is finally producing y_n at price level *p′*. Falling prices have automatically restored the economy to full employment.

The Automatic Removal of an Inflationary Gap

Panel (b) of Exhibit 7 shows how the self-correcting mechanism can automatically eliminate an inflationary gap. The initial level of output is *y* and the price level is *p*. When there is an inflationary gap, the inflation rate will increase. As old wage contracts expire, workers bargain for higher wages because unemployment is low and wages have not kept up with living costs. Thus, wages and costs will drift upward. When costs rise, business firms will begin to raise prices. The short-run aggregate supply curve will begin to shift left. In long-run equilibrium, the *SRAS* curve shifts to *SRAS′* as wage rates rise. Increasing prices will move the economy up the negatively sloped aggregate demand curve, *AD*. The economy is in long-run equilibrium when the level of output is y_n.

There is a choice between the self-correcting mechanism and active government policy to eliminate inflationary or deflationary gaps.

There is an imbalance between the automatic removal of an inflationary gap and the automatic removal of a deflationary gap. The elimination of deflationary gaps requires falling wages and prices, while removing inflationary gaps requires rising wages and prices. Generally speaking, in the short run, wages and prices are far more flexible moving up than moving down. Workers and business firms do not like accepting lower wages and prices even if those cuts do not represent real wage or price cuts. On the other hand, workers and firms are eager to raise money wages and prices to prevent real wages or prices from falling or even to increase real wages or prices. A wage cut may cause a strike or extended negotiation. A wage increase will be praised. Thus, it may take longer to remove a deflationary gap by relying on the self-correcting mechanism.

Some economists prefer to rely on the self-correcting mechanism; others believe that the government should take an active role. The following chapters examine the mechanics of monetary and fiscal policies.

Chapter Summary

The most important point to learn from this chapter is: In the short run, aggregate demand affects the level of prices and the level of output; in the long run, aggregate supply determines output while aggregate demand determines only the level of prices.

1. The aggregate-demand curve is downward-sloping because as the price level rises, *ceteris paribus,* there is an increase in interest rates, the purchasing power of money balances falls, and exports fall. The increase in interest rates cuts investment, and the real-balance effect reduces consumption.

2. Money wages and prices are more flexible in the long run than in the short run. Contracts are affected by expected inflation. Multiyear contracts prevent wages and prices from adjusting quickly to changing economic conditions. In the long run, all

wages and prices are perfectly flexible upward or downward because in the long run all contracts can be renegotiated. The natural rate of unemployment can be sustained indefinitely without accelerating inflation or deflation. The natural level of real GDP is the real GDP that is produced when the economy is operating at the natural rate of unemployment.

3. The short-run aggregate supply (SRAS) curve is upward sloping because unanticipated increases in the price level relative to business costs encourage firms to produce more.

4. Short-run macroeconomic equilibrium occurs where the aggregate demand (AD) curve intersects the SRAS curve.

5. A deflationary gap prevails if the short-run equilibrium real GDP falls short of the natural level. An inflationary gap prevails if short-run equilibrium real GNP exceeds the natural level.

6. In the long run, there is a self-correcting mechanism that automatically removes inflationary or deflationary gaps.

Policy Focus: The reliability and speed of the self-correcting mechanism determine whether government intervention is required: If the self-correcting mechanism is potent, a laissez-faire macroeconomic policy is appropriate.

Key Terms

aggregate demand (p. 132)
real-balance effect (p. 132)
interest-rate effect (p. 133)
foreign trade effect (p. 134)
short-run aggregate supply (SRAS) (p. 136)

short-run macroeconomic equilibrium (p. 138)
supply shock (p. 139)
natural level of output (p. 142)
deflationary gap (p. 142)
inflationary gap (p. 142)

Questions and Problems

1. Give three reasons why the aggregate demand curve is downward sloping.

2. How does the shape of the aggregate supply curve alter the effect of a shift in the aggregate demand curve?

3. What is the difference between the interest-rate effect and the real-balance effect when the price level falls? How are they similar?

4. Why are wages and prices more inflexible in the short run than in the long run?

5. Assume that during a period when nominal wages are fixed the price level begins to fall. What effect will this drop in prices have on the employment decisions of firms?

6. Can actual unemployment be less than the natural rate of unemployment? How?

7. How is an increase in the expected price level reflected in short-run aggregate supply?

8. Explain why the SRAS curve is upward sloping.

9. What would happen to the slope of the SRAS curve if workers were covered by fewer long-term wage contracts?

10. How is the SRAS curve affected by each of the following events?
    a. An increase in the anticipated price level.
    b. An increase in the price level in the short run.
    c. An increase in labor productivity.

11. Assume that the anticipated price level is 110 and that the actual price level is 100. Under these conditions, what will be the relationship between aggregate demand and aggregate supply? Is there an inflationary or deflationary gap?

12. What does an inflationary gap imply about:
    a. the unemployment rate?
    b. the actual versus the anticipated price level?

13. Explain how the self-correcting mechanism drives unemployment to the natural level. Will the self-correcting mechanism work faster when wages and prices are inflexible? Why?

Doing Economics

Data on real gross domestic product (GDP) and its deflator are given in the tables at the end of the *Economic Report of the President* or elsewhere. Using graph paper or computer graphics software (usually available in spreadsheet programs), plot and label points representing 1971 through 1992 with output on the horizontal axis and the price level on the vertical axis. Think of each of these points as the intersection between an *AD* curve and an *SRAS* curve for that year. Based on this graph, try to determine for each year starting in 1972 whether the *AD* curve shifted up or down relative to the previous year or whether the *SRAS* curve shifted out (down) or back (up).

(You will only be able to determine one of the curves with certainty for each year.) Does aggregate demand seem to increase or decrease in most years? Why do you think this is true? Does aggregate supply seem to increase or decrease in most years? Explain. Consider the recession periods of 1974–75, 1982, and 1991. For each of these periods, use the graph to assess whether the recession was caused predominantly by a decrease (or unusually small increase) in aggregate demand or by a decrease (or unusually small increase) in aggregate supply. How do your conclusions compare with what you know about events of these years?

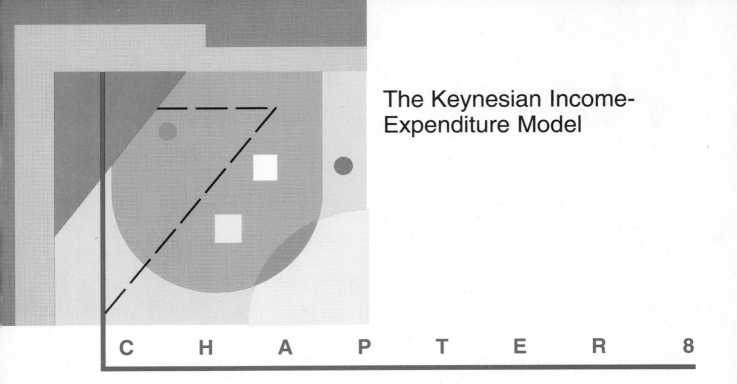

The Keynesian Income-Expenditure Model

C H A P T E R 8

CHAPTER FOCUS — The world-wide Great Depression of the 1930s caused a fundamental shift in the study of economics. Prior to that time so-called "classical" economists believed that employment was determined by the number of people wanting to work. The Great Depression led John Maynard Keynes to turn this on its head by arguing that employment was determined by the number of jobs available. According to "Keynesian" economics, aggregate demand and worker productivity determined the number of jobs available.

Keynes' ideas were widely accepted by the early 1960s, at which time most Western countries came to believe that it was government's responsibility to manage output and employment. However, by the 1980s, governments around the world found it difficult to keep unemployment at low levels. Indeed, unemployment drifted up throughout the 1970s, 1980s, and into 1990s. There has never been a revival of classical economics.

Classical economics may be regarded as the economics of full employment and growth; Keynesian economics is the economics of a Great Depression. This chapter explains that the basic difference between classical economics and Keynesian economics is in terms of how the labor market itself works.

LEARNING OBJECTIVES

After studying this chapter, you will be able to:

- Understand why the classical economists did not worry about unemployment or the business cycle.

- See how consumption spending responds to changes in income.

- Explain how the equilibrium level of real GNP is determined where there is substantial unemployment of resources.

- Discuss how the economy moves from one income-expenditure equilibrium level to another when there are changes in investment or government spending.

TWO VIEWS OF MACROECONOMICS

The last chapter explained how the current level of output is determined by the interaction of aggregate demand and aggregate supply. Two entirely different views of the macroeconomy can be explained by the same basic framework by a radical change in the shape of the aggregate supply curve. Exhibit 1, panel (a), shows that if the aggregate supply curve is perfectly vertical at the level of full employment, aggregate demand only influences the level of prices. This gives a simplified picture of what is called classical macroeconomics: output is supply determined. Exhibit 1, panel (b), shows that if the aggregate supply curve is perfectly horizontal up to the level of full employment, aggregate demand determines the level of output. This gives a simplified picture of what is called Keynesian macroeconomics: the level of output is determined on the demand side of the economy as long as aggregate demand falls short of the full employment level of output.

CLASSICAL MACROECONOMICS

Classical economics covers over a century of economic teaching. Classical theory owes its origin to the works of David Ricardo (1772–1823) and Jean Baptiste Say (1767–1832). It reached its most refined level of development in the works of A. C. Pigou (1877–1959).

The aggregate supply curve will be perfectly vertical if wages and prices are perfectly flexible in the upward or downward direction. As explained in the last chapter, the short-run aggregate supply curve is upward sloping because it reflects the fact that prices can rise faster or slower than wages, which may be fixed by contract or custom over the short run. Classical economists thought about labor markets the way we think about any highly competitive market: prices immediately register what is happening to demand and supply. Unemployed labor could not exist because an excess supply of labor would bid down wages until all workers who wanted a job would find one. Thus, the wages paid by business firms would be as flexible as the prices received by business firms. In general, rising and falling prices of goods would result in rising and falling wages so that there would be no general incentive for all businesses to expand or contract.

Say's Law

According to the classical economists, whatever GDP can be produced will be demanded (Say's law), and unemployment can only be the short-term conse-

EXHIBIT 1   The Role of Aggregate Supply

a. Classical Theory

b. Simple Keynesian

Panel (a) describes classical macroeconomics, where *AD* just determines the price level. Panel (b) describes simple Keynesian macroeconomics, where *AS* is horizontal at the current price level of full employment and *AD* just determines the level of GDP.

quence of money wages being temporarily too high. Determining GDP was no mystery because the economy was assumed to operate at the full-employment level. The classical theorists believed full employment to be the norm. National-income accounting demonstrates that it is always and everywhere true that *actual* aggregate income equals *actual* aggregate expenditures, but classical theorists went one step further. They argued that *aggregate supply creates its own demand*. This assertion is called **Say's law**.

> According to **Say's law**, *desired* aggregate expenditures can never depart from *actual* aggregate expenditures. Whatever output is produced will be demanded.

Say's law goes far beyond the vertical supply curve shown in Exhibit 1, panel (a). It means that the aggregate demand curve itself will not shift just because people decide they want to buy more goods and services. Suppose consumers decide, as a group, to save less and consume more. This decrease in saving will be matched by a decrease in investment that just offsets the increase in consumption. Accordingly, aggregate demand stays the same. How can this be?

Exhibit 2 shows how saving and investment are coordinated in the classical model. The rate of interest is measured on the vertical axis, and desired saving and investment are measured on the horizontal axis. The saving curve shows how saving responds to the interest rate. The higher the interest rate, the higher is desired saving. The higher the interest rate, the greater is the incentive to save more and spend less on personal consumption. The investment curve shows how desired investment responds to the interest rate. Generally speaking, the higher the

James Tobin (1918–   )

One of the leading Keynesian economists, this native of Champaign, Illinois was educated at Harvard and taught at Yale. A writer of grace, charm, and wit, Tobin was influential in applying Keynes' theory of income determination to macroeconomic problems in the early 1960s when Keynesian economics enjoyed great popularity. Even the greatest critic of Keynesian economics, Milton Friedman, said in the 1960s: "We are all Keynesians today."

When invited to join President Kennedy's Council of Economic Advisors, Tobin commented: "Mr. President, I'm an ivory-tower economist." Kennedy then quipped: "That's the best kind. I'll be an ivory-tower President." Tobin responded: "That's the best kind." The 1962 *Economic Report of the President* is the manifesto of Keynesian economics in its heyday. The press called it "the new economics," because the Council openly advocated the government's role in stabilizing the level of real output.

In the 1980s, Keynesian economics became less popular. In a lecture at Trinity University in San Antonio, Texas, Tobin said:

> The tides of political opinion and professional fashion have turned against me. . . . I do not despair over the present divisions of opinion in economics. Our subject has always thrived and advanced through controversy, . . . I haven't abandoned the field of battle myself. I hope I learn from the new, but I still think and say that Keynesian ideas about how the economy works and what policies can make it work better are relevant today—not just as Keynes wrote them, of course, but as they have been modified, developed, and refined over the last half-century.

Tobin's contributions to macroeconomics range from early estimates of the consumption/income relationship to the way in which assets and the stock market affect economic activity. For his pioneering work, he received the Nobel Prize in 1981.

---

interest rate, the less business managers and others want to invest in buildings, trucks, inventories, and equipment.

As Exhibit 2 shows, the interest rate will adjust to that rate at which *desired* saving equals *desired* investment. In the classical model, the interest rate coordinates saving and investment decisions. In Exhibit 2, the interest rate that equates desired saving and desired investment is 5 percent. At any interest rate above 5 percent, desired saving would exceed desired investment, and the interest rate would fall. At any interest rate below 5 percent, desired investment would exceed desired saving, and the interest rate would be driven up.

According to the classical model, in equating desired saving and desired investment, the interest rate automatically equates desired aggregate expenditures and aggregate income. If saving increases spontaneously, consumption falls by the amount of the saving increase. The increase in saving withdraws consumption expenditures from the spending stream. The increase in saving, however, pushes down the interest rate and the lower interest rate raises desired investment. The interest rate will fall until the increase in investment is enough to offset the decline in consumption.

Laissez-Faire Policy

The classical economists' views of aggregate supply and demand and the source of unemployment caused them to advocate **laissez-faire** economic policy for government.

EXHIBIT 2 The Interest Rate Equates Desired Saving and Investment in the Classical Model

The saving curve shows the amount of desired saving at different interest rates. The higher the interest rate, the greater is the amount of desired saving. The investment curve shows the amount of desired investment at different interest rates. In this example, the interest rate that equates desired saving and desired investment is 5 percent.

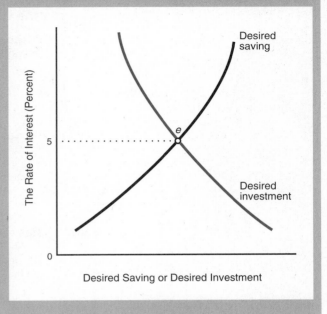

Laissez faire means a hands-off government policy toward the economy. Government intervention in macroeconomic affairs should be strictly limited.

Classical economists believed the economy was capable of healing itself by allowing flexible wages, prices, and interest rates to adjust to eliminate unemployment.

As long as aggregate supply creates its own aggregate demand, the government need not play a role in regulating the amount of aggregate demand. Aggregate demand would always equal the aggregate amount of production. As long as unemployment is caused by wages that are too high, the government need not intervene to create jobs. Sufficient jobs will be created simply by letting wages adjust to the equilibrium levels.

THE TRANSITION TO KEYNESIAN MACROECONOMICS

The Great Depression

The Great Depression of the 1930s shook economists' belief in the classical model. Between 1929 and 1933, real GNP in the United States declined by 30 percent. The 1929 output level was not regained until 1939. Unemployment rose from 3.2 percent of the labor force in 1929 to 24.9 percent in 1933 and was still 17.2 percent in 1939. Such a substantial downturn appeared to contradict the teachings of classical economics. There had been economic recessions and depressions before, but none this severe or sustained. (See Example 1.)

The Great Depression's impact on economic thinking and on public attitudes cannot be overestimated. A generation grew up during the Depression; for many

EXAMPLE 1

Images From the Great Depression

The Great Depression made a lasting impression on the generation that experienced it. People who lived through the Great Depression fear its return.

A "Southern Belle's" Account

It was my junior year, and I came home for Christmas. . . . I found the telephone disconnected. And this was when I realized that the world was falling apart. Imagine us without a telephone! When I finished school, I couldn't avoid facing the fact that we didn't have a cook any more, we didn't have a cleaning woman any more. I'd see dust under the beds, which is something I'd never seen before. I knew the curtains weren't as clean as they used to be. Things were beginning to look a little shabby.

An Oklahoma Resident's Account

There was thousands of people out of work in Oklahoma City. They set up a soup line, and the food was clean and it was delicious. Many, many people, colored and white, I didn't see any difference, 'cause there was just as many white people out of work than were colored. Lost everything they had accumulated from their young days. And these are facts. I remember several families had to leave in covered wagons. To Californy, I guess.

See, the oil boom come in '29. People come from every direction in there. A coupla years later, they was livin' in everything from pup tents, houses built out of cardboard boxes and old pieces of metal that they'd pick up—anything that they could find to put somethin' together to put a wall around 'em to protect 'em from the public.

I knew one family there in Oklahoma City, a man and a woman and seven children lived in a hole in the ground. You'd be surprised how nice it was, how nice they kept it. They had chairs and tables, and beds back in that hole. And they had the dirt all braced up there, just like a cave.

A Boston Financier's Account

A cigar stock at the time was selling for $115 a share. The market collapsed. I got a call from the company president. Could I loan him $200 million? I refused, because at the time I had to protect my own fences, including those of my closest friends. His $115 stock dropped to $2 and he jumped out of the window of his Wall Street office.

There was a man who headed a company that had $17 million in cash. He was one of the leaders of his industry and controlled three or four situations that are today household words. When his stock began to drop, he began to protect it. When he came out of the second drop, the man was completely wiped out. He owed three banks a million dollars each.

SOURCE: Studs Terkel, *Hard Times*, pp. 62, 85, 181–82, 468.

it remains a frightening experience. The political influence of the Great Depression was enormous. A *laissez-faire* economic philosophy that instructed the government to do nothing while one out of four was unemployed became a political liability. The question of the times became: "Why can't the government do something to help us?"

The Great Depression set the stage for the *Keynesian revolution*, which was sparked by the publication in 1936 of *The General Theory of Employment, Interest, and Money* by English economist John Maynard Keynes. In this landmark book, Keynes argued that economies can reach a fairly stable equilibrium—from which they will budge only slowly—at much less than full employment. Keynes' evidence was the Great Depression itself, which demonstrated that substantial sustained declines in economic activity were possible.

The Keynesian revolution opened up a new approach to macroeconomic policy: it argued that it is the responsibility of government to ensure that the economy operates at an acceptable rate of output and employment. Keynes believed that letting wage and price adjustments raise output and employment was too slow, unreliable, and unnecessary. Government economic action could be used to restore the economy to full employment more quickly and at much lower social costs.

Fixed Prices in the Keynesian Model

Keynes and his followers drew a picture of labor markets that is much different from the flexible labor market of the classical economists. According to the Keynesian school, the labor market can be inflexible because a variety of factors prevent money wages from falling when unemployment exists. These factors include the difficulty of *general* wage cuts, union contracts that fix wages for several years, minimum-wage laws, and unemployment insurance that gives unemployed workers a financial backstop. These factors make money wages sticky in the downward direction. "Sticky" money wages do not fall when the demand for labor falls. Instead, they remain stuck at a rate high enough to cause unemployment. If wages do not adjust smoothly and quickly, the economy is left with persistent unemployment.

This picture accurately represents England at the time Keynes was writing. From 1921 to 1936, the unemployment rate in Great Britain varied between 9.7 and 22.1 percent. In the period 1921 to 1929, the British unemployment rate averaged 12 percent; from 1930 to 1936, it averaged 17.8 percent. Throughout this entire period, prices declined very slowly, and money wages remained more or less at the same level. (See Example 2.)

In such severely depressed economies as 1930s America and Britain, it may be possible to coax more production out of existing resources without raising wages and prices. A large number of people are out of work and are willing and eager to work at going wage rates. People are waiting for some business firm to give them a job. In addition, there is much idle plant and equipment because factories are not running at capacity. The firm need not raise wages to get more workers; it simply puts the unemployed worker back on the job. Because unemployed workers are willing to work at the going money wage, it is possible to expand output without raising the price level. *At less than full employment, real GDP can increase without an increase in the price level.*

The Keynesian model analyzes economies that can expand or contract output without raising the price level.

THE INCOME/EXPENDITURE APPROACH

Keynes' *income/expenditure model* uses the relationship between income and expenditures to explain real output determination. Keynes sought to explain why economies can settle at less than full employment, contrary to the teachings of the classical economists. In the Keynesian model, an economy that is operating at less than full employment is in a position to increase its output without affecting prices.

The Classical and Keynesian Models and the Great Depression

The classical model predicted that high unemployment would be self-liquidating. For the Great Depression, which began in the late 1920s in Europe and spread to the United States in 1929, this prediction did not hold true. In Germany, France, the United States, and the Scandinavian countries, unemployment rates rose to 25 percent or even higher in the early 1930s. In Europe and the United States, unemployment rates stubbornly remained high for a decade. The accompanying diagrams show unemployment rates and wage and price indexes in Great Britain, the United States, and Germany during the Great Depression.

The figures for Great Britain clearly show why Keynes believed the classical model was not working: The British unemployment rate was higher than 10 percent from 1925 to 1937, rising to more than 20 percent in the early 1930s. During this same period, money wages in industry scarcely fell despite massive unemployment. Prices did decline somewhat, meaning that English real wages (money wages after adjustment for inflation) were actually rising during the Great Depression! It is no wonder that Keynes worried about the automatic self-correcting forces of falling wages and prices. The picture in the United States was slightly different. Money wages did fall substantially during the early 1930s, and prices fell more rapidly. The surprising feature of the U.S. experience was the fact that both wages and prices were rising in the mid-1930s, despite massive unemployment. The German case appears to conform most closely to the classical model. As the German unemployment rate rose to 30 percent of the labor force, the wage rate plummeted, falling more sharply than prices. Falling real wages accompanied high unemployment. Of the three cases, the German unemployment rate returned most quickly to pre-Depression levels. There are a number of reasons for this pattern (many cite Hitler's rearmament of the German military), but flexible wages and prices may have played a role.

SOURCES: *Historical Statistics of the United States,* Series D1–10; D802–810; B.R. Mitchell, *European Historical Statistics, 1750–1970,* Tables C–2, C–4.

This is shown in Exhibit 1, panel (b), where aggregate demand falls short of full employment.

Chapter 7 identified the major components of aggregate demand as personal consumption expenditures (C), private investment (I), government expenditures for goods and services (G), and net exports ($X - M$). To understand how economies settle at a particular level of output, one must consider how the desired levels of C, I, G, and $X - M$ are determined. Consumption is the major component of GDP; therefore, Keynes focused particularly on the determinants of consumption spending and its relationship to income.

Consumption, Income, and Saving

Keynes used two facts concerning consumption and income in the income/expenditure model. First, as income increases, people increase their consumption. If your income goes up by $1,000, you are likely to increase your consumption spending. What is true for individuals is true for the economy. As aggregate income increases, so does aggregate consumption. Second, for the economy as a whole (but perhaps not for a particular individual), consumption does not increase as much as income. If your income goes up by $1,000, your consumption will

EXHIBIT 3 The Consumption/Income and Saving/Income Schedules

a. Income, Consumption, and Saving

Output = Income, Y (1)	Consumption, C (2)	Saving, S (3)
100	125	−25
200	200	0
300	275	25
400	350	50
500	425	75
600	500	100
700	575	125
800	650	150

b. The Consumption/Income Curve

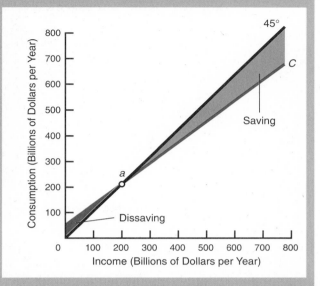

c. The Saving/Income Curve

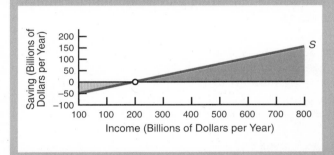

Columns 1 and 2 of panel (a) show the consumption/income schedule for our hypothetical economy. There are no taxes, so income and disposable income are the same. The marginal propensity to consume (MPC) in this example is 0.75 because for every $100 billion increase in income, consumption increases by $75 billion. The marginal propensity to save (MPS) is 0.25 because for every $100 billion increase in income, saving increases by $25 billion. Panel (b) graphs the consumption/income schedule of columns 1 and 2 as line, C. The 45-degree line shows when consumption equals income. The vertical distance between the C curve and the 45-degree line shows saving. Panel (c) graphs the saving/income schedule of columns 1 and 3 of panel (a) as the line S.

likely increase by less than the full $1,000. Part of the increase in income will find its way into an increase in saving. The same is true for the economy as a whole. An increase in income will cause consumption to increase by less than the increase in income.

These two facts are illustrated in Exhibit 3, which provides data on GDP (Y), consumption spending (C), and saving (S), for a hypothetical economy with no government spending, no taxes, and zero net exports. (Later on, we show what happens when there is government spending, taxes, and net exports.) *All variables are in real terms.* Because there are no taxes, every dollar earned is available as disposable income for either consumption or saving. In this special case, GDP equals disposable income.

Consumption varies with income. When income is $100 billion, then consumption is $125 billion, and saving is −$25 billion. At this level of income, households are borrowing or drawing down their financial assets (savings accounts, stocks, bonds). When income rises from $100 billion to $200 billion, consumption rises by $75 billion to $200 billion. At this income level, households are now just breaking even. A further increase in income from $200 billion to $300 billion raises consumption spending to $275 billion. Households are now more than breaking even; they have unspent income left over for saving. At $300 billion, saving is a positive $25 billion.

Exhibit 3 shows the **consumption/income schedule** and the **saving/income schedule**.

> The consumption/income schedule shows the amount of desired consumption at different levels of national income or output.

> The saving/income schedule shows the amount of desired saving at different levels of national income or output.

The consumption/income schedule is given in columns 1 and 2 of panel (a). The saving/income schedule is given in columns 1 and 3 of panel (a).

The Marginal Propensities

The income/expenditure model depends to a great extent on the relationship between increases in income and resulting increases in consumption. In the consumption/income schedule in columns 1 and 2, whenever income increases by $100 billion, consumption increases by $75 billion. Hence, every additional $1 of income increases desired consumption by $0.75.

Keynes called the fraction of additional income that is spend on consumption the **marginal propensity to consume** *(MPC)* because it refers to extra consumption induced by another dollar of disposable income.

> The **marginal propensity to consume** *(MPC)* is the change in desired consumption (*C*) per $1 change in income (*Y*):
>
> $$MPC = \frac{\Delta C}{\Delta Y}$$

The Greek delta symbol Δ placed before a variable is shorthand for "the change in" that variable. For example, if your income rises from $400 to $500, then for you $\Delta Y = \$100$.

Every time income increases, saving increases as well. The saving/income schedule in columns 1 and 3 shows that saving increases by $25 billion for every $100 billion increase in income. Every extra $1 of income increases desired saving by $0.25. Keynes called the fraction of the increase in income that is saved the **marginal propensity to save (*MPS*)**.

> The **marginal propensity to save** *(MPS)* is the change in desired saving (*S*) per $1 change in income (*Y*):
>
> $$MPS = \frac{\Delta S}{\Delta Y}$$

When there are no taxes in the economy (as in this hypothetical example), an additional dollar of income is either consumed or saved. Hence,

$$MPC + MPS = 1.$$

The graphs of the consumption/income and saving/income schedules are also shown in Exhibit 3. Consider first the consumption/income schedule in panel (b). The 45-degree line from the origin has the property that any point on it is the same distance from the two axes. For example, the vertical line drawn from an income of $600 billion on the horizontal axis to the 45-degree line will be the same length as a horizontal line drawn from a consumption-spending level of $600 billion on the vertical axis to the 45-degree line. Each point on the 45-degree line is an equal distance from both axes.

If the consumption/income curve were identical to the 45-degree line, all income would be spent on consumption at every level of income. The vertical distance between curve C and the 45-degree line is the difference between income and consumption, or a visual measure of saving. By comparing the 45-degree reference line with the consumption/income curve, the amount of saving at each level of income can be read directly from the diagram. For example, at an income level of $600 billion, saving equals $600 billion minus $500 billion, or $100 billion.

The intersection of the 45-degree reference line and the consumption/income curve (point a) is a very useful reference point. To the right of point a, saving is positive because consumption is below income. For example, when income is $400 billion, consumption is $350 billion, and saving is $50 billion. To the left of point a the economy is **dissaving** (saving is negative) because the economy's income is less than the amount of consumption spending. For example, when income is $100 billion, consumption is $125 billion and saving is −$25 billion.

> The economy is **dissaving**—total saving is negative—when consumption spending exceeds disposable income. The economy is either increasing its indebtedness or drawing down its accumulated savings.

At point a, the economy is neither saving nor dissaving. Saving equals zero. The intersection of the consumption/income curve and the 45-degree line occurs at an income level of $200 billion. At this income, the vertical distance to the 45-degree line is the same height as the vertical line to the consumption/income curve. At this point, income and consumption are the same; no income is left over for saving.

The corresponding relationship between saving and income is graphed in panel (c), which is directly below panel (a) in Exhibit 3. The saving/income curve shows the amount of saving at different levels of income. For income greater than $200 billion, saving is positive; for income less than $200 billion, saving is negative (there is dissaving). Like the consumption/income curve, the saving/income curve has a positive slope.

Other Factors That Affect Consumption

Income is not the only determinant of consumption. Other factors that affect consumption are expectations, stocks of assets, the price level, taxation, and attitudes toward thrift.

Expectations. Consumption expenditures respond to changes in consumer expectations about the future. People form expectations about how rapidly prices will rise, about the likelihood of becoming unemployed, or about whether a war will cause shortages of goods. Those who believe their jobs will remain secure may consume more than others earning the same income who believe they will lose their jobs. People who believe that inflation will accelerate may spend more than those who believe that inflation will slow down. If people suddenly become convinced that inflation will speed up, they may increase their consumption spending, to buy before the price is too high.

Wealth. Changes in the wealth of consumers can affect consumption. The wealth of individuals is the value of the assets they own (stocks, cash balances, real estate) minus their indebtedness. As the money value of assets rises, *ceteris paribus*, people feel that they are better off, and they increase their consumption expenditures. As the money value of assets falls, people feel that they are worse off, and they reduce their consumption expenditures.

Interest Rates. The rate of interest that consumers must pay on loans may also affect current consumption. If interest rates fall, consumers may borrow more on their credit cards to finance trips, restaurant meals, automobile repairs, and so forth. If interest rates rise, consumption spending may be discouraged. However, the effects of interest rates on consumption are small. For example, using estimates by Michael Boskin, an increase in interest rates from 6 percent to 10 percent would probably not decrease consumption by more than one percent.

The Price Level. The consumption of individuals can be affected by changes in the purchasing power of their money savings. An individual whose wealth consists of $25,000 in a savings account will realize that this wealth will buy less if prices rise by 10 percent. If prices fall by 10 percent, the same $25,000 will now buy more goods and services. As prices rise, the purchasing power of a given nominal value of money savings falls. As prices fall, the purchasing power rises. An increase in the price level, therefore, would be expected to reduce consumption, *ceteris paribus*. The real value of a given amount of money savings has fallen, and people feel that they are worse off. A reduction in the price level would be expected to increase consumption, *ceteris paribus,* because the real value of money savings has risen.

Taxation. As income taxes rise, disposable income falls, *ceteris paribus*. As taxes increase, one would expect less consumption spending for the same amount of income. As income taxes are cut, disposable income rises, *ceteris paribus*; thus, one would expect more consumption spending from the same level of income.

Attitudes Toward Thrift. How much people choose to save out of a given amount of disposable income can shift with changing public attitudes. If people suddenly become more thrifty, the amount of saving increases and consumption falls without there being any change in income.

Movements along the consumption/income curve must be distinguished from *shifts* in the consumption/income curve. A *movement along* the consumption/income curve occurs when income changes—with all other factors that affect consumption held constant. A *shift* in the consumption/income function occurs when a factor other than income changes.

In Exhibit 4 a change in income from y_1 to y_2 will cause a movement along the consumption/income curve from a to b. A change in a factor such as expectations, wealth, the price level, taxation, or thrift, shifts the entire curve from C to C'.

EQUILIBRIUM EXPENDITURES

The Keynesian income/expenditure model explains the determination of real output, Y. Remember that the Keynesian model deals with an economy in which more output can be produced without driving up the price level. The income/expenditure model explains real output. It does not explain the price level.

EXHIBIT 4 Shifts in the Consumption/Income Curve

The original consumption/income curve, *C*, is drawn, holding constant certain consumption-affecting factors other than income. Upward shifts in *C* are caused by increases in financial assets, reductions in the price level, reductions in taxes, or the development of a more negative attitude toward thrift.

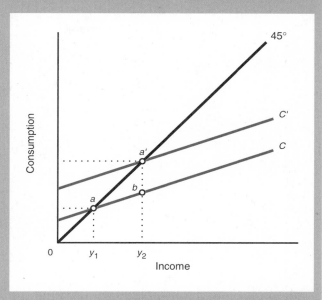

To explain real-output determination, one must explain total expenditures, not just consumption expenditures. Consumption (*C*) is only one component of total expenditures—although the most important since consumption is the ultimate goal of all economic activity. Total expenditures include investment (*I*), government spending (*G*), and net exports (*X* − *M*). To keep the explanation simple, we consider only one additional final expenditure: investment. Real-output determination can be effectively shown with only one additional expenditure component.

Desired Aggregate Expenditures

The consumption/income schedule relates the amount of consumption spending at each income level. It shows how much consumption would be *desired* at each income level. This desired amount of consumption will be *realized* only if the economy actually produces that amount of income. The amount of consumption spending therefore depends on the amount of income. Panel (a) of Exhibit 5 reproduces the consumption/income schedule from Exhibit 3 in columns 1 and 2. In panel (b), the consumption/income (*C*) curve is plotted from columns 1 and 2. For simplicity, we assume that business firms wish to invest $50 billion per year at all income levels as shown in column 4. This amount of desired investment must be added to the amount of desired consumption at each level of income to obtain desired **aggregate expenditures**. Column 5 shows the sum of desired consumption and investment. The aggregate-expenditure (*AE*) curve is plotted from columns 1 and 5, but is simply the *C* curve shifted up by the amount of investment.

The schedule of **aggregate expenditures** *(AE)* shows the desired amount of total spending (*C* + *I* + *G* + *X* − *M*) at each level of income.

EXHIBIT 5   The Keynesian Equilibrium of Real Output

a.

Output = Income, Y (1)	Consumption, C (2)	Saving, S (3)	Investment, I (4)	Desired Aggregate Expenditure, AE = C + I, (5)	Unintended investment (+), (6)	Change in GNP (7)
100	125	−25	50	175	−75	Increase
200	200	0	50	250	−50	Increase
300	275	25	50	325	−25	Increase
400	350	50	50	400	0	Equilibrium
500	425	75	50	475	25	Decrease
600	500	100	50	550	50	Decrease
700	575	125	50	625	75	Decrease
800	650	150	50	700	100	Decrease

b.   **c.**

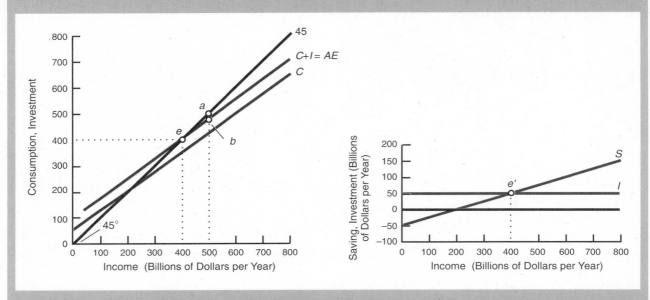

In panel (a), column 5 shows *AE* as the sum of columns 2 and 4. Panel (b) shows the *AE* curve as the sum of *C* + *I*. The intersection of the *AE* curve with the 45-degree line occurs at an income of $400 billion (point *e*). If the economy were to attempt to produce an income greater than $400 billion (to the right of *e*), aggregate output would exceed desired aggregate expenditures, and income would fall. If the economy were to attempt to produce an income less than $400 billion (to the left of *e*), desired aggregate expenditures would exceed aggregate production, and income would rise. Panel (c) shows how the economy reaches equilibrium by equating desired investment and desired saving.

Realization of Desired Aggregate Expenditures

The aggregate expenditure schedule shows the amount of desired spending at each level of income. *Desired* decisions are not necessarily *realized*. Which desired levels of aggregate spending are realized depends on the relationship between desired aggregate expenditures and aggregate output.

Panel (b) of Exhibit 5 shows how the equilibrium output is determined. The *AE* curve and the 45-degree reference line show the relationship between aggregate output (or income) and *desired* aggregate expenditures at each output level. Aggregate income (or output) can be measured along the horizontal axis or by the corresponding vertical distance to the 45-degree reference line at that level of income (or output). *Point e, which is the intersection of the aggregate expenditure curve with the 45-degree line, is the point where desired aggregate expenditures equal aggregate output.* To the right of point *e*, more output is being produced than the economy wishes to purchase; desired spending falls short of output at every income level. To the left of point *e*, less output is being produced than the economy wishes to purchase. The economy adjusts to such a disequilibrium by changing output until production and desired aggregate expenditures are equal (at $400 billion at *e*).

Let us consider what would happen if the economy attempted to produce an output of $500 billion. This decision is made by the hundreds of thousands of producers in the economy acting independently of one another. As Chapter 6 on national-income accounting demonstrated, the act of producing $500 billion worth of output creates an income of $500 billion. At an income of $500 billion, the economy would desire to spend $475 billion on consumption and investment, as shown in column 5 of Exhibit 5a or point *b* in Exhibit 5b. Desired aggregate expenditures would fall short of aggregate output by $25 billion, or the distance *ab* in panel (b).

The output rate of $500 billion worth of goods and services per year is, therefore, not an equilibrium output because the economy is producing output at a rate faster than purchasers in the economy are buying. Producers will realize that too much output is being produced because unsold goods will accumulate in inventories greater than producers want to hold; excessive inventories of unsold cars, TV sets, sewing machines, and the like will build up. The accumulation of unwanted or excessive inventories will signal to business firms that their current production rates are higher than the market is prepared to purchase. Producers will have to slow down the rate of output production. (Remember, we are assuming a Keynesian economy in which prices are constant. Firms do not sell excess output by lowering prices.)

If, on the other hand, business firms attempted to produce an output of $300 billion, desired aggregate expenditures would exceed output by $25 billion. Producers will realize that there is too little output because purchasers will be buying at too fast a rate. Inventories of goods will fall below normal levels. Normal inventories can be replenished only by speeding up the rate of production.

At an aggregate output of $500 billion, too much was produced, and firms reduced their output. At $300 billion, too little was produced, and firms increased their production. By adjusting the rate of output in response to total spending, the economy moves toward **Keynesian equilibrium**.

> **Keynesian equilibrium** occurs when the economy produces an output that equals desired aggregate expenditures.

Saving and Investment

Chapter 6 demonstrated that actual saving and investment are equal. There is no reason, however, why the desired saving *(S)* of individuals should equal desired investment *(I)* of business firms without a coordinating mechanism. The classical economists had supposed that the rate of interest would adjust to equate desired saving and desired investment (Say's law). To Keynes, on the other hand, the main mechanism that coordinated desired investment and desired saving was changes in the level of output.

Returning to Exhibit 5, the movement toward equilibrium output can be seen in the contrast of desired saving and investment decisions. The business community desires to invest $50 billion at all levels of income (or output). The amount of desired saving depends on the amount of income. At an output of $500 billion, desired saving equals $75 billion because consumption equals $425 billion. Desired saving exceeds desired investment by $25 billion at this output. There is too much saving; $25 billion of output is unsold and accumulates as unintended inventory investment. (*Inventory investment* is the addition to the inventories of goods and materials held by business firms.) When goods are unsold (because aggregate expenditures are insufficient), actual investment exceeds desired investment by the sum of unintended inventory investment. Note that this unintended accumulation of inventories raises actual investment to the level of $75 billion (the sum of desired and unintended investment) to equal desired (and actual) saving. **Unintended investment** is shown in column 6 of the table of Exhibit 5a. *It is clear that throughout the entire schedule, actual investment equals actual saving.*

> **Unintended investment** is the difference between desired saving and desired investment at each level of income. It can be positive or negative.

When unintended investment is taking place, output begins to fall. With prices fixed (as Keynes assumed), businesses have only one way to cut back on the amount of unsold goods piling up in unwanted inventories: they cut back on the rate of production. Because desired saving depends upon the amount of income, as output falls so does saving. As this adjustment continues, the disparity between desired investment and desired saving diminishes until income (or output) is $400 billion.

When desired saving is less than desired investment, there is too little saving. The withdrawal of saving from the spending stream is smaller than the injection back into the spending stream by investment. Businesses will see their inventories being drawn down to low levels, and there will be unintended *disinvestment* in inventories. Again with prices fixed, firms have only one way to build their inventories back up to normal levels: they increase the rate of production. As the amount of income increases, the amount of desired saving increases along with income. As desired saving increases, the gap between desired saving and desired investment disappears. The **Keynesian equilibrium** can be defined in a second way as the relationship between desired saving and desired investment.

> **Keynesian equilibrium** is attained at that output at which desired investment equals desired saving.

In panel (c) of Exhibit 5, the movement to equilibrium output is shown in terms of the relationship between desired saving and desired investment. Point e' is the intersection of the horizontal investment curve with the saving/income curve (at an output of $400 billion). Only at this income are desired saving and desired investment equal.

Two Definitions of Equilibrium Are One

In the simple Keynesian model, the economy will adjust its rate of output until:

1. aggregate output equals desired aggregate expenditures ($Y = AE$) or, equivalently,
2. desired investment equals desired saving ($I = S$).

These two conditions are really different ways of looking at the same thing. When desired investment equals desired saving, output equals desired aggregate expenditures. Saving is the withdrawal households make from the spending stream, and investment is the injection firms replace in the spending stream. Whenever desired saving exceeds desired investment, more is withdrawn from spending than is replaced (desired aggregate expenditure is less than output). When desired saving is less than desired investment, less is withdrawn by savers than is replaced by business investment, or desired aggregate expenditure exceeds output. Because saving must equal investment, paradoxically, an increase in the desire to save may not increase actual saving because of a drop in income.

MULTIPLIERS

Keynes' main interest was in explaining why the Great Depression took place and how to move the economy toward recovery. He was therefore interested in the causes of downward movements in equilibrium real GDP. Keynes noted that any change that shifts the aggregate expenditure (AE) curve will change equilibrium income. If the AE curve shifts upward, desired aggregate expenditures ($C + I$) will exceed the initial equilibrium output, y, and aggregate production will rise. If the AE curve shifts down, desired aggregate expenditures will be less than the initial equilibrium output, and aggregate production will decline.

Consider the case of an increase in desired investment spending. Exhibit 6 shows that an increase in investment spending from $50 billion per year to $100 billion per year shifts the AE_1 curve to AE_2. Graphically, a change in investment spending causes a vertical shift in the aggregate expenditure AE_1 curve by the amount of the change in I. The economy is now purchasing output at a rate faster than output is being produced; inventories are drawn down to subnormal levels; firms respond by increasing their production. Upward shifts in AE_1, therefore, shift equilibrium from e_1 to e_2 and increase output from y_1 ($400 billion) to y_2 ($600 billion) if there are unemployed resources. The increase in income is four times the increase in investment. How can this be?

The tendency for the increase in desired aggregate expenditures (in this case, an increase in investment) to cause magnified increases in output is called the **multiplier**. In the above example the economy has only two types of desired spending—consumption spending and investment spending. In a more complete analysis it is necessary to consider government spending, taxes, exports, and imports. But any shift in AE caused by an independent change in investment, government spending, or consumption will cause a multiplier effect.

> The **multiplier** ($\Delta Y / \Delta I$) is the ratio of the change in output to the shift in the AE curve (due to an independent change in investment, government spending, exports, or imports).

Why should an independent change in spending cause a much larger change in output? When investment expenditures are increased by $50 billion, the immediate effect is for incomes in the economy to increase by $50 billion. These

The $50 billion increase in investment shifts the aggregate expenditure curve up vertically by $50 billion, from AE_1 to AE_2. At the original equilibrium, output is $400 billion; desired aggregate expenditures now exceed aggregate production, and desired saving exceeds desired investment. The economy's producers will, therefore, increase their output. Equilibrium is restored at an output of $600 billion. The $50 billion increase in investment has caused a $200 billion increase in output.

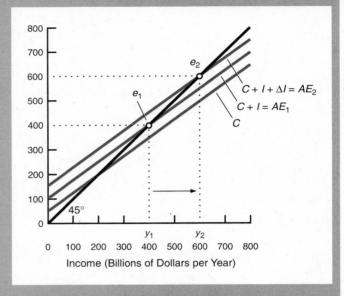

expenditures, after all, end up in the pockets and purses of the suppliers of the factors of production that produced the $50 billion worth of investment goods. If this immediate effect were the only effect, then the increase in investment would cause an equivalent increase in output. But the process does not stop here. *Those households whose incomes have gone up by a total of $50 billion will increase their consumption spending.* When income increases, consumption increases according to the economy's marginal propensity to consume, or by *MPC* times the increase in income. Aggregate incomes again increase by the amount of the injection of more consumption, and the recipients of this extra income again increase their consumption by *MPC* times the amount of the income increase. This process continues until the successive increases in spending dwindle to zero.

Exhibit 7 shows how an increase in investment leads to a magnified increase in output. A $50 billion increase in investment immediately creates $50 billion worth of additional income. With a marginal propensity to consume of 0.75, this increase in income causes an increase in consumption of $37.50 billion. In round 2, this $37.50 billion increase in consumption creates another $37.50 billion in income. Of this $37.50 billion, 75 percent ($28.125 billion) is spent on additional consumption, creating $28.125 billion of additional income. In round 3, this $28.125 billion worth of new income stimulates a consumption increase of another $21.09 billion (= $28.125 × 0.75), and so the multiplier process continues until the full effect of the multiplier is felt. In our example, the investment multiplier is 4 because the $50 billion increase in investment eventually causes a $200 billion increase in income.

At each stage, income is leaking out of the circular flow of expenditure in the form of saving. As Exhibit 7 shows, of the initial $50 billion increase in income, when $37.50 billion is consumed, $12.50 billion is saved. At the next stage, when $28.125 billion is consumed $7.04 billion of the newly generated $37.50 billion in

EXHIBIT 7 The Multiplier Principle Illustrated (Billions of Dollars)

Round	Amount of Increase in Income (ΔY)	Amount of Increase in Consumption (ΔC)	Leakages (increase in saving) (ΔS)
1	50.00	37.50	12.50
2	37.50	28.125	9.875
3	28.125	21.09	7.035
4	21.09	15.82	5.27
5	15.82	11.87	3.95
6	11.87	8.90	2.97
All others	35.62	26.71	8.91
Totals	200.00	150.00	50.00

income is saved, and so on. These leakages in the form of saving limit the ultimate increase in income in response to an increase in investment (or government spending). The increase in income stops when the total leakages equal the initial $50 billion increase because at that point what consumers are taking out of the spending stream in the form of saving is put back in in the form of investment. The same result would have been obtained if the original increase in spending had been in government spending or consumption spending.

One can see in Exhibit 7 that the *MPC* has a great deal to do with the value of the multiplier. If the *MPC* had been 0.9 rather than 0.75, the initial increase in consumption would have been larger in the first and in subsequent rounds. The smaller are the leakages (or the larger is the *MPC*), the greater is the amount of additional income created at each stage, and the larger is the multiplier. The larger are the leakages (or the smaller is the *MPC*), the smaller is the amount of income generated at each stage, and the smaller is the multiplier.

The formula for determining the multiplier ($\Delta Y/\Delta I$) is:

$$\Delta Y/\Delta I = \frac{1}{1 - MPC} = \frac{1}{MPS},$$

where there are no taxes ($MPC + MPS = 1$ in the absence of taxes).

The logic of the multiplier can be most directly seen in the $I = S$ condition for equilibrium. If investment increases by $1, in the new equilibrium, saving must also increase by $1 because $S = I$. If *MPC* equals 0.75, however, $MPS = 0.25$, and $4 of extra income is necessary to increase saving by the necessary $1. Thus, income must increase by $4 to generate the extra saving to match the $1 increase in investment. Algebraically, a simple derivation is to note that $\Delta S = \Delta I$. Because $\Delta S = MPS \times \Delta Y$, it follows that $\Delta I = MPS \times \Delta Y$, or $\Delta Y/\Delta I = 1/MPS$.

The higher is the *MPC*, the higher is the multiplier. An *MPC* of 0.75 yields a multiplier of 4; an *MPC* of 0.9 yields a multiplier of 10. The economy's response to autonomous expenditures, therefore, depends on the *MPC* (or *MPS*). The higher is the *MPC*, the higher are the induced expenditures from any given rise in income. In other words, the higher is the *MPC,* and the lower is the *MPS,* the more income must change in order to get the saving leakages to match the injection of new investment.

The higher the *MPC*, the higher is the multiplier. The lower the *MPC*, the lower is the multiplier.

Keynes, Multipliers, and Activism

Keynes attempted to provide the tools for controlling equilibrium aggregate expenditures. His multiplier analysis suggested that relatively small changes in investment spending, government outlays, or tax rates could bring about relatively large changes in real output. With a multiplier of 4, for example, a $10 billion increase in government spending would be sufficient to eliminate a deflationary gap of $40 billion. Excessive unemployment could be eliminated by means of manageable increases in government spending or by reductions in tax rates.

The Keynesian revolution, which swept the Western world in the 1960s, caused policymakers to believe that they could control the business cycle. In the heady days of the 1960s, some optimists even declared that the "business cycle is dead." Policymakers need simply open and close the government spending and taxation spouts when necessary to eliminate deflationary and inflationary gaps. In other words, governments could pursue *discretionary and activist* policies to control the business cycle. But since the 1960s, both unemployment and inflation are higher.

Subsequent chapters will show that the debate concerning the appropriateness of activist policy is far from over. Believers in Keynesian activist policy argue that, although we still are not able to control the macroeconomy well, it is better to use activism to control the business cycle. The alternative—doing nothing—is dangerous and could lead to depression.

Opponents of activist policy argue that we still lack the knowledge and tools to control the business cycle. They argue that we don't even know what the real-world multipliers will be.

The multipliers discussed in this chapter are valid only under a restricted set of circumstances. They apply to situations in which more real output can be produced without driving up prices, interest rates are stable, and the different types of final spending do not affect one another. Real-world multipliers must deal with the fact that rising real output drives up the price level, and a higher price level discourages consumption; that rising real output may drive up interest rates, and higher interest rates discourage investment; and that more final spending in one area may cause less final spending in another area. Increases in government spending on education, for example, may cause less personal spending on private education.

The magnifying effect of real-world multipliers is smaller than the simple multipliers discussed above. Increases in investment, for example, would be expected to drive up the price level and raise interest rates, thereby discouraging investment spending and consumption spending. Discouraging of investment and consumption spending reduces the multiplier effect. In some cases, it can cancel the effect on real output entirely.

Opponents of activism could ask: How can we conduct activist policy if we don't know what the multiplier will be? Moreover, opponents of Keynesian activism argue that we do not know enough about the current state of the economy to know what policy to apply and when. Even if government policymakers knew the appropriate policy, politics make it difficult to bring about the called-for changes in government spending or taxation.

The next chapter will study how government spending and taxes might be used to create full employment.

The most important point to learn from this chapter is: If the price level is fixed and many resources are unemployed, the equilibrium level of output is determined by desired aggregate expenditures. Moreover, any increase in equilibrium output is a multiple of the initial increase in spending.

1. Keynes studied economies operating with unemployed resources in which increases in aggregate expenditures could cause increases in real output and employment. Because of the emphasis on aggregate demand, Keynesian economics has been called *demand-side economics*. Keynes rejected the classical full-employment model. He rejected Say's law that supply creates its own demand and believed that money wages were not sufficiently flexible to eliminate involuntary unemployment. According to Keynes, desired saving and desired investment would be equated not through the interest rate but through changes in income. The Great Depression of the 1930s created the appropriate climate for the Keynesian notion that the government should ensure full employment.

2. Keynes assumed money wages were sticky in the downward direction. When there is substantial unemployment, additional workers are available at the going set of wage rates.

3. The Keynesian income/expenditure model explains how economies determine their real output. The consumption/income schedule shows the amount of desired consumption at each income level. The saving/income schedule shows the amount of desired saving at each income level. The marginal propensity to consume (*MPC*) is the fraction of an extra dollar of income that is consumed. The marginal propensity to save (*MPS*) is the fraction of an extra dollar of income that is saved. In a world without taxes, $MPC + MPS = 1$. Factors that shift the consumption/income (and saving/income) curves are expectations, the real value of assets, taxation, income distribution, age, and attitudes toward thrift.

4. The aggregate-expenditure (*AE*) curve shows the amount of desired aggregate expenditures, $C + I + G + X - M$, at each income level. The economy will produce that income at which (a) aggregate production equals desired aggregate expenditures or (b) desired investment equals desired saving. These two equilibrium conditions are two ways of looking at the same thing.

5. The multiplier is the change in equilibrium income divided by the increase in investment (or any type of autonomous spending). The multiplier equals $1/(1 - MPC) = 1/MPS$.

Policy Focus: **The Keynesian revolution called for activist policy to control the business cycle. A key tool in activist policy is the multiplier. Uncertainty about the real-world multiplier calls into question the use of activist policy.**

Key Terms

Say's law (p. 151)
laissez-faire (p. 152)
consumption/income schedule (p. 158)

saving/income schedule (p. 158)
marginal propensity to consume (*MPC*) (p. 158)
marginal propensity to save (*MPS*) (p. 158)

dissaving (p. 159)
aggregate expenditures (*AE*) (p. 161)
Keynesian equilibrium (p. 163)

unintended investment (p. 164)
multiplier (p. 165)

Questions and Problems

1. "Savers and investors are different people. There is no way desired saving will equal desired investment." Describe how classical economists and Keynesian economists might respond to this statement.

2. Explain why classical theorists believed that there would be no long-term involuntary unemployment.

3. What did Keynes assume about the labor market when the economy was in a depression?

4. What is Say's law?

5. How could the classical theorists believe that aggregate supply creates its own demand?

6. For the classical economists, what mechanism coordinates business investment with consumer saving?

7. What is the marginal propensity to consume? How is it related to the marginal propensity to save?

8. Using the consumption/income schedule in Table A,
   a. Calculate the saving/income schedule.
   b. Determine the marginal propensity to consume (*MPC*) and the marginal propensity to save (*MPS*).
   c. Determine at what level of income the break-even point of zero saving is reached.
   d. Determine the aggregate expenditure (*AE*) schedule if investment is a constant $50 billion.
   e. Find equilibrium output and demonstrate that, at this equilibrium, desired investment and desired saving are equal.
   f. Determine what happens to equilibrium output if investment falls to zero. What happens to the savings/investment equality?
   g. Answer part d if an increase in thrift occurs and people now desire to consume $50 billion less at each income level (they save $50 billion more at each income level); determine equilibrium income and compare income and saving both before and after the increase in thrift.

9. Define *unintended inventory investment*. How will businesses respond to unintended investment in the simple Keynesian model? If prices were flexible, would the response of businesses to unintended inventory investment perhaps be different?

10. In Keynesian economics, what mechanism coordinates business investment and consumer saving?

11. What would happen to the aggregate expenditure curve in each of the following cases?
   a. Investment demand increases.
   b. The amount of money people have increases.
   c. The price level increases.
   d. Consumers anticipate a sharp increase in prices in the next year.

12. *Optional question*: Suppose the consumption schedule is *C* = $100 billion + 0.75*Y*.
   a. Draw the consumption/income schedule for income levels of $200 billion, $400 billion, $600 billion, and $800 billion. What is the marginal propensity to consume?
   b. What is the equation for saving?
   c. If *I* = $50 billion, what is the equilibrium level of output?

TABLE B

Income (billions of dollars) *Y*	Consumption (billions of dollars) *C*
0	75
100	150
200	225
300	300
400	375
500	450
600	525

13. Assume that I = $25 billion, and the relationship between consumption and income *without taxes* is given in Table B. Neglect all other factors.
   a. What is *MPC*? What is *MPS*?
   b. What is the equilibrium output?

14. In the country of Friedmania, there is no government spending and no taxes. Evaluate the impact of an increase in investment from $30 billion to $50 billion, assuming that the price level is constant. The consumption schedule is given in Table C.
   a. What is *MPC*? What is *MPS*?

TABLE A

Income (billions of dollars) *Y*	Consumption (billions of dollars) *C*
0	50
100	100
200	150
300	200
400	250

b. What is the equilibrium income when investment spending is $30 billion? What is the equilibrium income when I = $50 billion?
c. What is the multiplier?
d. Assume that in Friedmania, investment spending is $30 billion. If investment falls to $20 billion, what is the impact on income and consumption?

15. Consider an economy with the same consumption/income curve as in Table B. Assume that I = $60 billion and that there is no government. Let exports (X) equal $30 billion, and assume that imports (M) are determined by the schedule shown in Table D. What is the equilibrium output?

TABLE C

Income (billions of dollars) Y	Consumption (billions of dollars) C
0	10
50	50
100	90
150	130
200	170
250	210
300	250

TABLE D

Income (billions of dollars) Y	Imports (billions of dollars) M
0	5
100	10
200	15
300	20
400	25
500	30
600	35

Doing Economics

One key element of the Keynesian macroeconomic model hinges on what people choose to do with additional income they may earn. To find out more about how some people would actually respond to an increase in their income, ask the following question of at least ten people: "If you received a tax-free windfall of $1,000, how much of it would you save and what would you buy with the remainder?" Try to get a varied sample of people rather than, for example, all students living in dorms. Based on your findings, what are the marginal propensities to consume and save, averaged across this group of individuals? How much variation exists among individuals in the *MPC* and *MPS*? What kinds of commodities appeared most often as potential purchases: durables, nondurables, or services? Based on this evidence, which of these categories would you predict to be the most and least sensitive to business-cycle fluctuations? *Optional:* Look at the time-series data on real (constant-dollar) personal consumption expenditures by category, which can be found in the tables at the end of the *Economic Report of the President* for any recent year. For the recessions years of 1974, 1982, and 1991, which categories of consumer spending responded most strongly to the fall in income and which continued to expand despite the decline? Does this evidence agree with your conclusions from above?

Macroeconomic Problems and Policies

P A R T   T H R E E

CHAPTER 9
Fiscal Policy and National Debt

CHAPTER 10
Money and Prices

CHAPTER 11
Commercial Banking and the
Federal Reserve

CHAPTER 12
Monetary Policy

CHAPTER 13
Inflation, Unemployment, Stagflation

CHAPTER 14
Stabilization Policy

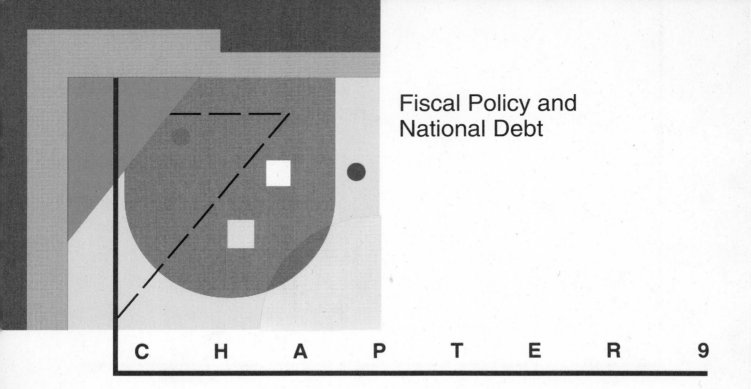

Fiscal Policy and National Debt

C H A P T E R 9

CHAPTER FOCUS   The presidential election of 1992 focused on fiscal responsibility. More was said about the alarming national debt than about any other campaign issue. Incumbent President Bush tried to paint his Democratic opponent, Bill Clinton, and the Democratic Congress as having a "tax and spend" philosophy, while claiming that he would ensure fiscal responsibility. The Democratic challenger gleefully pointed to the rise in the national debt that had occurred during the Reagan and Bush presidencies as proof that the Republicans could not be trusted to manage the public purse. Independent challenger Ross Perot based his campaign on the dangers of runaway spending and public debt. The American public was clearly alarmed and disturbed by a national debt that was approaching the $5 trillion mark.

The bitter congressional battle over President Clinton's taxation and spending proposals in the summer of 1983 showed that deficit reduction would be a key challenge of the Clinton presidency.

This chapter is about how the government collects and spends money and about the consequences of the government spending more than it earns.

After studying this chapter, you will be able to:

■ Define fiscal and monetary policy and distinguish between automatic stabilizers and discretionary fiscal policy.

■ Understand how discretionary fiscal policy can be used to eliminate deflationary and inflationary gaps.

■ Explain the differences between the Keynesian budget philosophy and the balanced budget philosophy.

■ Describe how the full-employment surplus can be used as a measure of discretionary fiscal policy.

■ Discuss why people fear public debt and discuss whether these fears are justified.

■ Explain the problems of fiscal policy—crowding out, lags, and uncontrollable expenditures.

POLICY GOALS

Chapter 7 showed that if the economy is in a deflationary gap (output below natural real GDP), an increase in aggregate demand would move the economy toward full-employment output. If the economy is in an inflationary gap (output above natural real GDP), a reduction in aggregate demand would move the economy back to the natural rate of output. If it were possible to manipulate aggregate demand perfectly and instantaneously, there would be no need to have inflationary or deflationary gaps. The business cycle could be avoided.

Two tools are available to manipulate aggregate demand—**fiscal policy** and **monetary policy**.

> **Fiscal policy** is the deliberate control of government spending and taxation to achieve macroeconomic goals.

> **Monetary policy** is the deliberate control of the money supply to achieve macroeconomic goals.

Monetary and fiscal policy are the two tools that can be used to control aggregate demand.

This chapter explains how fiscal policy can be used to affect aggregate demand and perhaps aggregate supply. Fiscal policy operates on aggregate demand by changing government spending and tax rates. Chapter 12 talks about monetary policy. Chapter 7 explained the factors that raise or lower aggregate demand. If there is an increase in desired investment spending or in government spending, aggregate demand increases. A reduction in taxes raises desired consumption expenditures and hence raises aggregate demand.

AUTOMATIC STABILIZERS VERSUS DISCRETIONARY POLICY

Governments can affect aggregate demand through government spending and the tax system. Fiscal policy manipulates government spending and taxes to achieve macroeconomic goals. Governments spend money and collect taxes on a continuous basis. Whether intended or not, their spending and taxing actions affect aggregate demand.

Many fiscal actions take place automatically and require no policy decisions—as in the case of an **entitlement program**, such as Social Security or unemployment-compensation payments.

> An **entitlement program** requires the federal government to pay benefits to anyone who meets the eligibility requirements of the program.

Payments for entitlement programs and tax collections depend on the general state of the economy.

To receive entitlement payments, recipients need only demonstrate that they qualify under established rules. Once the rules are set, the government does not determine the magnitude of such entitlement program payments. Instead, payments depend on general economic conditions. Once income tax rates and depreciation and personal exemption rules are set, government tax revenues depend on general economic conditions.

Other government revenues and expenditures are determined by deliberate, discretionary decisions. Rules concerning eligibility for entitlement programs can be changed; income tax rates can be raised or lowered; major new defense expenditure or public works programs can be started.

Government spending or taxation actions can be either **automatic stabilizers** or **discretionary fiscal policies**.

> **Automatic stabilizers** are government spending or taxation actions that take place without any deliberate government control and that automatically dampen the business cycle.

Automatic Stabilizers

The tax system and entitlement programs act as automatic stabilizers that moderate business cycles.

The Tax System.   The amount of income tax revenues government collects is determined by multiplying the average tax rate times the economy's taxable income. If an economy has an average tax rate of 20 percent, and if total taxable income is $100 billion, the government will collect $20 billion in income taxes. If total taxable income rises to $150 billion, the government will collect $30 billion. The amount of income tax collected rises and falls with income.

If the economy goes into a recession with falling income, tax collections fall, thereby cushioning the drop in consumption. In an inflationary boom, incomes rise, and tax collections rise to moderate the increase in consumption spending. People consume out of disposable income. The tax system cushions fluctuations in consumption by having tax collections fall during bad times and rise during good times.

Unemployment Compensation and Welfare Payments.   During cyclical downturns, more people are eligible for unemployment benefits. Moreover, families whose incomes decline because of fewer hours of work or unemployment become eligible for welfare assistance. Unemployment compensation and increased welfare payments prevent consumption expenditures from falling as much as they would have without these programs.

Unemployment compensation and welfare programs also moderate the business cycle on the upswing. Welfare recipients leave the welfare and unemployment compensation rolls as they find jobs, and increased deductions from payrolls (to state and local programs and union unemployment funds) reduce the amount of disposable income going to employed workers.

Automatic stabilizers cannot fully neutralize the business cycle. If the economy is operating at full employment and investment falls, the automatic stabilizers will neutralize only a part of the decline in output. Unemployment compensation and other welfare payments restore only a portion of lost disposable income. Falling tax collections restore only a portion of the decline in consumption spending.

Automatic stabilizers—the tax system, welfare payments, and unemployment compensation—soften the effects of the business cycle.

Discretionary Fiscal Policy

Automatic stabilizers can only moderate cyclical instability, not eliminate it. Discretionary macroeconomic policy can be used to attack directly the business cycle. The aim of discretionary policy is to eliminate inflationary and deflationary gaps. There are two types of discretionary macroeconomics policy—discretionary fiscal policy and discretionary monetary policy. This chapter is about discretionary fiscal policy.

Discretionary fiscal policy operates through **autonomous changes** in tax rates and government expenditures.

Autonomous changes can be contrasted with automatic stabilizers. Many changes in government spending and taxation are *not autonomous*. They are induced by changes in income. Tax collections decline because income is declining. Government welfare expenditures rise because incomes are declining. An autonomous change in government spending or taxation occurs not because of changes in income, but because of changes in policy. *Discretionary fiscal policy works through autonomous changes in taxes and in government spending.*

Eliminating a Deflationary Gap.   Exhibit 1a shows an economy in a deflationary gap, operating below the natural level of output. The long-run self-correcting mechanism would eventually restore the economy to full employment through falling prices, but discretionary fiscal policy offers an opportunity to restore the economy to full employment without waiting for deflation. Government tax authorities could lower tax rates. The government could deliberately spend additional money on dams or national defense. The government could liberalize unemployment compensation rules and eligibility requirements for welfare.

Exhibit 1a shows how an *expansionary fiscal policy* could be used to eliminate a deflationary gap.

> **Expansionary fiscal policy** consists of raising discretionary government spending and/or lowering tax rates.

If tax rates or discretionary spending are changed by the right amounts, the aggregate demand curve could be shifted to the right to intersect the short-run aggregate supply (*SRAS*) curve at *e′* at the natural level of output.

Eliminating an Inflationary Gap.   Exhibit 1b shows an economy in an inflationary gap. If left alone, inflation would return to the economy to the natural level of unemployment as aggregate supply falls. Alternatively, government taxing could raise tax rates and reduce discretionary government spending.

Exhibit 1b shows how *contractionary fiscal policy* can be used to close an inflationary gap.

> **Contractionary fiscal policy** consists of lowering discretionary government spending and/or raising tax rates.

If tax rates were raised or discretionary government spending reduced by the right amounts, the aggregate demand curve could be shifted to the left to intersect the *SRAS* curve at the natural level of output.

FISCAL POLICY AND DEFICITS

Government finances resemble household finances. Both governments and households take in income. Households receive income through factor payments and transfer payments; government takes in income by collecting taxes, receiving transfer payments from other government units, and selling services (such as municipal water or sewage connections, or tuition at state universities). Both governments and households spend their income. Households spend income on consumer goods and services; governments spend income on purchases of goods and services and on transfer payments. When a household spends more than its

EXHIBIT 1 Removing Deflationary and Inflationary Gaps

a. Expansionary Fiscal Policy for a Deflationary Gap

b. Contractionary Fiscal Policy for an Inflationary Gap

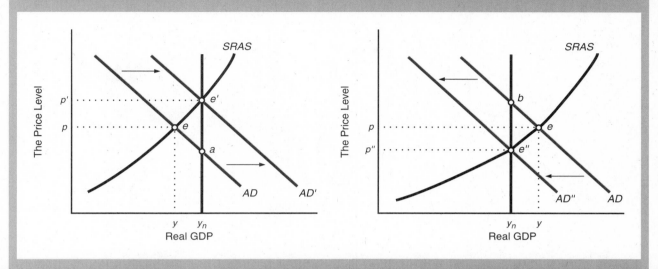

Panel (a) shows how expansionary fiscal policy could be used to eliminate a deflationary gap. By increasing autonomous government spending or by autonomously reducing taxes, the aggregate demand curve could be shifted to the right (from *AD* to *AD'*), restoring the economy to the natural rate of output, y_n. Panel (b) shows how contractionary fiscal policy could be used to eliminate an inflationary gap. By reducing autonomous government spending or by autonomously raising taxes, the aggregate demand curve could be shifted to the left (from *AD* to *AD''*) to restore the economy to the natural rate of output.

income, it is *dissaving*. Dissaving occurs when the household must borrow money (or draw down accumulated savings). Similarly, when government spends more than it takes in, it is dissaving. Government dissaving occurs when government must borrow money (or draw down accumulated savings).

Any difference between the total revenues and total outlays of a government unit is either a **government deficit** or a **government surplus**.

> A **government deficit** is an excess of total government spending over total revenues from taxes and fees.

> A **government surplus** is an excess of total government revenues from taxes and fees over total spending.

Deficits occur when government spends more than it takes in. Surpluses occur when government takes in more than it spends.

If total government revenues equal total government expenditures, the government unit has a *balanced budget*.

Facts and Trends

Exhibit 2 shows the pattern of government expenditures, revenues, surpluses, and deficits as a percentage of GDP since 1960. The figure reveals some basic facts about government finance.

First, the expenditures and revenues of total government (federal, state, and

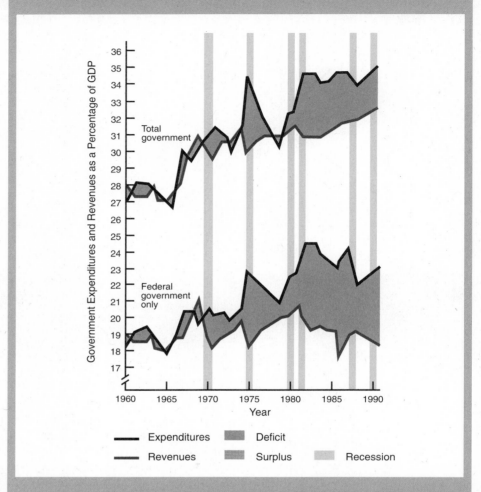

EXHIBIT 2   Government Expenditures, Revenues, and Deficits as a Percentage of GDP

This figure shows that, since 1960, deficits have tended to be associated with recessions. During recessions, government revenues fall while expenditures rise. The late 1960s (the Vietnam War years) were an exception to this rule.

SOURCE: *Economic Report of the President*

local) have generally risen as a percentage of GDP, with expenditures rising more rapidly than revenues.

Second, government deficits are far more common than government surpluses. There are only three years of small surpluses for total government and only one year of surplus for the federal government. Federal deficits have grown larger over time—from $13 billion in the 1950s to $75 billion in the 1970s to over $300 billion in the mid-1990s.

Third, government deficits widen during recessions. Deficits are wider during the periods marked by recessions, and they narrow during the recovery period. This tendency is shown by the black line in Exhibit 2.

Fourth, the color-shaded areas in the bottom part of the figure (representing federal deficits) are generally larger than the color-shaded areas in the top part (representing deficits of total government). The deficits of the federal government dominate, and state and local governments have even run small surpluses to partially offset federal deficits. The federal deficit typically exceeds the total government deficit (which is the sum of the federal deficit and the surplus of state and local government).

THE FULL-EMPLOYMENT DEFICIT

Taxes and government expenditures respond automatically to changes in output. Hence, the direction of fiscal policy cannot be gauged simply by looking at government spending, taxes, and the actual government surplus or deficit. During periods of declining real GDP, the government deficit tends to become larger. As income falls, tax revenues fall, but government obligations, in the form of unemployment compensation payments and welfare transfers, rise. During periods of prosperity, the deficit narrows as tax collections rise and entitlement spending falls.

The **cyclical deficit** and the **structural deficit** distinguish the effects of the business cycle from the effects of discretionary changes in fiscal policy.

> The **cyclical deficit** is that part of the deficit caused by movements in the business cycle.

> The **structural deficit** is that part of the deficit that would be present if there were no business cycle and the economy were operating at the natural level of real GDP.

It is possible to separate the effects of the business cycle from structural factors by comparing the actual deficit (or surplus), illustrated by the colored line, with the **full-employment deficit** (or **surplus**), illustrated by the black line in Exhibit 3.

> The **full-employment deficit** (or **surplus**) is what the government budget surplus or deficit would have been had the economy been operating at the natural level of output (full employment).

To understand how the full-employment deficit is calculated, assume that the natural rate of unemployment is 6 percent and the economy has 8 percent unemployment. Because the economy is 2 percentage points below full employment, the government must take extra payments for welfare and unemployment compensation, and it collects fewer tax dollars. The actual budget deficit (actual revenues minus actual expenditures) is $40 billion, but at full employment, revenues would have been $15 billion more and expenditures would have been $10 billion less. The full-employment deficit is therefore $15 billion (= $40 − $15 − $10)—much less than the actual deficit.

Because the effects of the cyclical deficit have been removed, the full-employment budget reveals the direction of discretionary fiscal policy. When the deficit is calculated as if the economy were steadily operating at the natural rate, any changes in that deficit must be caused by discretionary changes in government

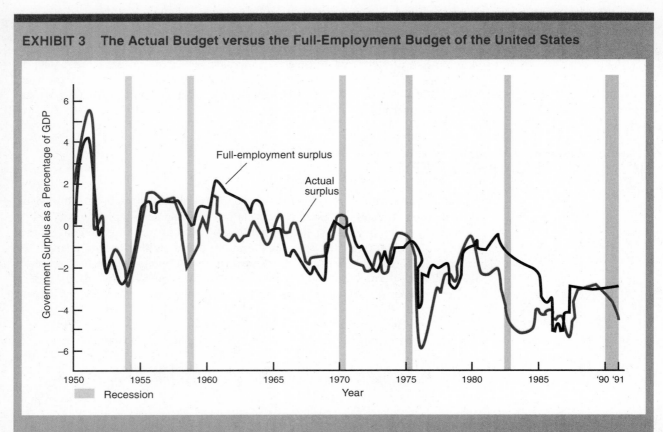

EXHIBIT 3   The Actual Budget versus the Full-Employment Budget of the United States

Full-employment surplus

Actual surplus

Recession

Year

The colored line shows the actual federal government surplus or deficit. The black line gives the full-employment surplus or deficit for the same years. The full-employment budget should reveal changes in discretionary fiscal policy over this period. The shaded bars are periods of recession.

SOURCE: Robert J. Gordon, *Macroeconomics*, 5th ed. (New York: HarperCollins, 1990), Appendix A. Updated by authors.

spending, eligibility requirements for entitlements, and tax rates. The movement from a full-employment surplus in the early 1960s to a full-employment deficit by the late 1960s signals a movement toward expansionary fiscal policies (associated with a tax cut in 1964 and accelerated military spending during the Vietnam War). The mid-1970s was a period of contractionary fiscal policies (as the full-employment deficit narrowed), but the fiscal policies of the 1980s and early 1990s were expansionary (as taxes were cut and military spending expanded).

The actual budget deficit (or surplus), shown by the colored line in Exhibit 3, tends to move with the full-employment deficit (or surplus), shown by the black line. For periods of low unemployment (as in most of the 1960s and the late 1980s), the two budget figures are close. During periods of high unemployment, the two lines diverge. For example, during the recession of 1958, the actual deficit was greater than 2 percent of GDP, while the full-employment budget was in balance. In the recession of 1982, the actual deficit was more than twice as large as the full-employment deficit. The differences between the two deficit measures show the cyclical deficit. The vertical distance between the two budget figures represents the cyclical component of the deficit.

THE EFFECTIVENESS OF FISCAL POLICY

The aim of discretionary fiscal policy is to eliminate inflationary or deflationary gaps more quickly than the self-correcting mechanism does. Critics of discretionary fiscal policy question its effectiveness.

Lags in Fiscal Policy

Because changes in taxation and government spending must be approved by Congress they often take several years from inception to enactment. Public works programs must be approved by Congress and are often handled on a case-by-case basis. Lacking line-item veto authority, the president must either accept or veto budgets forwarded by Congress, and logrolling often overrides considerations of stabilization.

Three lags impede fiscal policy. First, Congress and the president may be slow to recognize the need for a change in fiscal policy. Reliable statistics on real output become available only 6 months after the fact. No one is certain whether a downturn is temporary or the start of a serious recession. It is therefore difficult to recognize when a change in fiscal policy is required. This *recognition lag* makes fiscal policy difficult to initiate on a timely basis.

Second, fiscal policy is subject to a substantial *implementation lag*: by the time the program goes through Congress and is implemented, the policy may no longer be correct. By the time a tax cut has been passed, a tax increase may have been more appropriate.

Third, the *effectiveness lag* is the amount of time it takes between implementation of a fiscal policy and an actual change in economic conditions. Statistical evidence on the length of the effectiveness lag is mixed, but it appears to be long. Critics of activist fiscal policy ask whether a country can carry out effective activist fiscal policy when substantial lags are involved.

Permanent Income

Many modern economists, such as Nobel laureates Franco Modigliani and Milton Friedman, argue that people base their consumption decisions on life-cycle income, or **permanent income**, not on transitory changes in current income.

> **Permanent income** is an average of the income that an individual anticipates earning over the long run.

A transitory change in this year's income—resulting from a *temporary* tax increase—will have a minimal effect on current consumption. The impact of the tax on long-run income is so small that few people change their current consumption.

When people base their spending decisions on permanent income, the relationship between this year's income and this year's consumption is unstable. With its effects on private spending unknown, discretionary tax policy is therefore difficult to pursue.

Crowding Out

An increase in aggregate demand may crowd out private investment by pushing up interest rates. When this crowding out occurs, the growth of the nation's capital stock is retarded, and the long-run growth of the economy is reduced. Moreover, because the amount of crowding out is hard to anticipate, the exact effects of a fiscal stimulus are difficult to predict.

Increases in government spending can have other crowding-out effects, as well. For example, government expenditures on health care, education, police protection, roads, and parks could directly reduce some private expenditure. Thus, when government provides goods as substitutes for private goods, an increase in government expenditures could cause the **direct crowding out** of some private expenditures.

> **Direct crowding out** occurs when an increase in government spending substitutes for private spending by providing similar goods.

If direct crowding out is complete, aggregate expenditures do not increase when government spending increases. Complete crowding out means that the *increase* in government spending causes an equal *decrease* in private spending.

The debate over fiscal policy is about the ability of discretionary fiscal policy to smooth out the wrinkles in the business cycle. Given its slow-moving nature, fiscal policy cannot be used to counter every turn in the business cycle. Rather, it is better used to create a climate that is conducive to economic growth. Some economists argue that fiscal policy should operate through its effects on aggregate supply. (See Example 1.)

National Debt

When the federal budget is in deficit, the federal government *dissaves*. Like individuals who dissave, the federal government must borrow to finance the difference between expenditures and revenues. The federal government borrows by selling IOUs in the form of U.S. government bonds or bills to private individuals (both at home and abroad), to banks, to corporations, or even to the Federal Reserve banks. The cumulated outstanding debt of the federal government is the **national debt**.

> The **national debt** is (approximately) the sum of outstanding federal government IOUs upon which interest and principal payments must be made.

The *federal deficit* is the *annual addition* to the national debt. If the federal deficit in a particular year is $300 billion, the national debt will rise by that amount in that year.

Few economic issues generate as much emotion as the national debt. People complain, "We are going to bankrupt our children and grandchildren if we can't get the federal deficit under control." Others ask, "If we have to live within our means, why can't the government live within its means?"

Regardless of these widely expressed concerns and fears, the postwar period has seen only one year of federal government surpluses. Despite legislative efforts and numerous campaign promises, the federal deficit continues to rise.

Trends in the National Debt.   Exhibit 4a shows trends in the national debt. At the end of World War II, it was $204 billion. By 1960, the national debt had risen only to $291 billion. The national debt passed $1 trillion in 1981 and stood at almost $5 trillion in the mid-1990s. It is these numbers that have alarmed the public and politicians alike. Is the national debt out of control?

EXAMPLE 1

Supply-Side Economics

Supply-side economists argue that lower marginal tax rates for individuals and corporations increase aggregate supply. According to **supply-side economics**, lower marginal tax rates increase aggregate supply by increasing work effort and by encouraging risk taking and innovation. As people increase their work effort and as businesses modernize their plant and equipment, aggregate supply increases.

The accompanying contrasts the two potential effects of discretionary tax cuts. In panel *a*, the tax cuts cause an increase in aggregate demand only. In panel *b*, the tax cuts cause an increase in short-run aggregate supply only. In general, when tax rates fall, both aggregate demand and short-run aggregate supply increase. If the aggregate demand increase dominates, output increases and *prices increase*. If the aggregate supply increase dominates, output increases but *prices fall*. If authorities could cut taxes and count on substantial increases in short-run aggregate supply, the result would be the best of both worlds: more output and employment and lower prices.

Demand-Side versus Supply-Side Views of the Effects of a Tax Cut

a. The Demand-Side View of a Tax Cut   **b. The Supply-Side View of a Tax Cut**

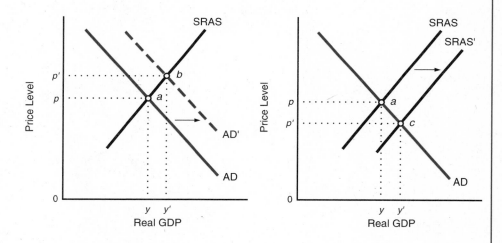

According to the demand-side view illustrated in panel (a), a tax cut will affect output and prices through an increase in aggregate demand (from *AD* to *AD'*). The increase in aggregate demand raises both output and prices. The supply-side view, in panel (b), is that the tax cut affects output and prices through an increase in short-run aggregate supply (from *SRAS* to *SRAS'*). The increase in short-run aggregate supply raises output and lowers prices.

Chapter 1 warned against using figures that are unadjusted for inflation or for growth in the general economy. Exhibit 4b shows the trend in national debt as a percentage of GDP. National debt fell as a percentage of GDP from the end of World War II to the mid-1970s. Since the early 1980s, the ratio of national debt to GDP has been rising.

The Burden of the Debt.   Probably the most widespread public concern is that high deficits will eventually result in a national debt that is "too large" to handle.

EXHIBIT 4 National Debt

a. The Size of the National Debt

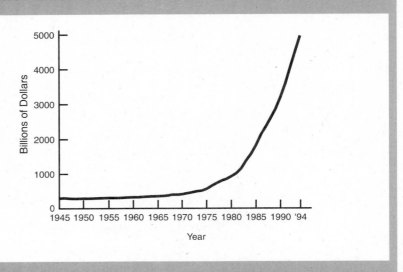

b. National Debt as a Percentage of GDP

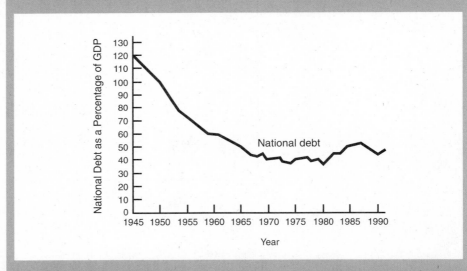

Despite growing concern about its absolute size, national debt as a percentage of GDP has been falling throughout the postwar period, although the percentage did rise between 1981 and the present.

SOURCE: *Economic Report of the President*

The burden of national debt can be measured in the same way that the burden of private debt is measured. The person who goes to a bank to borrow money will be asked about income and existing liabilities. The borrower with an income of $100,000 and no outstanding debts will be able to borrow much more than one with a $15,000 annual income and large debts. Debt must be judged relative to the ability of the debtor to pay the interest and principal on the debt.

What determines the U.S. government's ability to carry debt? Insofar as tax collections (the government's income) are closely tied to GDP, ultimately the federal government's income depends on the amount of GDP produced. Government tax receipts since 1960 have averaged around 20 percent of GDP. The 1992 GDP of almost $6 trillion gave the federal government an income of more than $1 trillion. A GDP of $10 trillion in the year 2000 would yield the government about $2 trillion. The amount of GDP produced now and in the future is a critical factor in determining the burden of the national debt.

As Exhibit 4b indicates, public debt as a percentage of GDP declined since the end of World War II. In 1945, public debt was 1.2 times GDP. By 1981, the ratio of debt to GDP had fallen to 34 percent. Between 1981 and 1993, the national debt rose from 34 percent to about 60 percent of GDP. By comparison, the average American family has personal debt equal to three-quarters of one year's income after taxes.

The burden of the public debt can also be measured by the proportion of current income required to pay interest and principal on the debt. In 1993, 17 percent of federal government expenditures was devoted to interest payments on the national debt. For the average American family, approximately 17.5 percent of personal disposable income was devoted to interest payments on mortgages and consumer debt in the same year. The burden of private debt appears to be about the same as national debt.

Will the United States ever go bankrupt by accumulating too much debt? As long as GDP grows as rapidly as debt, the burden of the debt will remain the same. If GDP outgrows debt, the burden of the debt falls.

> A growing economy is the best protection against an increasing burden of national debt.

Unlike private individuals or corporations, the federal government has a special guarantee of its ability to handle its debt. If the federal government runs a $50 billion deficit in a particular year, the U.S. Treasury can either sell $50 billion worth of bonds to the public or ask the Federal Reserve to buy the bonds, thereby pumping $50 billion worth of additional reserves into the economy. In other words, the federal government can finance its deficit by printing money.

The national debt affects different generations differently. Some are actual beneficiaries. If that generation receives more benefits from government than it pays in taxes, it is a beneficiary. (See Example 2.)

INTERNAL VERSUS EXTERNAL DEBT

Any country can have either **internal debt** or **external debt**.

> **Internal debt** is national debt owned by the citizens of that country.

> **External debt** is national debt owned by citizens of other countries.

If the debt is *internal*, the United States basically owes itself. When interest payments are made on the national debt, income is transferred from one U.S. citizen to another. The taxpayers' dollars are used to pay interest to the owners of

EXAMPLE 2

The Burden of the Debt on Different Generations

In an effort to determine the remaining net-payment burden placed on each generation by the present national debt, under current fiscal policies, the Congressional Budget Office has developed "generational accounts." These accounts, which include federal, state, and local government debt, also compute the average net-payment burden that will have to be imposed on members of all future generations if the government debt is eventually to be paid off.

The accompanying chart depicts these amounts for selected generations. Note that older generations are expected to be net recipients, since they pay low taxes but receive substantial Social Security and Medicare benefits. Younger generations will likely pay more than they receive because of their greater income, payroll, and sales taxes. Men aged 30 in 1989 could expect to pay out almost $200,000 more in taxes than they receive in benefits.

For both newborn and future generations, these numbers represent net-payment burdens to be paid over their entire lifetimes. A comparison of the results reveals a substantial generational imbalance.

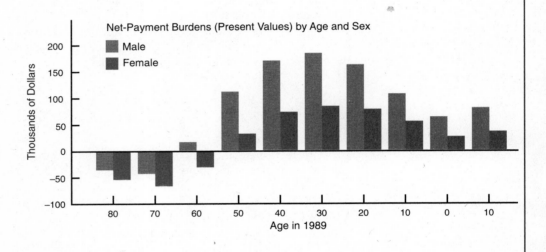

SOURCE: Federal Reserve Bank of Cleveland, *Economic Trends*, January 1992; Congressional Budget Office; *Budget of the United States Government*, fiscal year 1992.

government bonds. Insofar as recipients of interest payments are also taxpayers, the *net transfer* of income is small. Internal debt payments do not alter the amount of income in the country; they affect only the distribution of income between debt owners and nonowners.

An *external* debt works differently: Interest payments represent transfers of income from U.S. taxpayers to residents of other countries. The amount of income left in the country is affected by this type of transaction. In the 1950s, only 5 percent of national debt was owned by foreigners. By the early 1990s, the proportion exceeded 20 percent. Foreign ownership of the national debt has increased over the years for many reasons. The main reason

EXHIBIT 5   The Relationship Between Deficits and Inflation

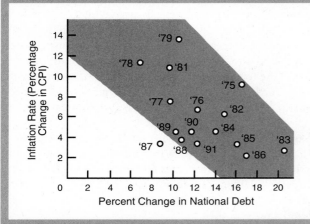

a. The Short-Run View (Annual Changes)

b. The Long-run View (Five-Year Changes)

The scatter diagram in panel (a) plots the inflation rate versus the yearly change in national debt. Although one would expect a positive relationship, the dots actually line up to suggest a negative relationship. The scatter diagram in panel (b) reveals a positive long-run relationship between five-year average inflation rates and five-year changes in the national debt.

is that the United States has come to be regarded as a safe haven by foreign investors.

External debt is not necessarily bad. Had the United States not borrowed abroad, U.S. interest rates might have been higher and private investment much lower. For other countries, such as those in Central and Latin America, external ownership of the debt is so large that interest payments abroad account for a large share of GDP.

Deficits, Inflation, and Interest Rates

In addition to worrying about the burden of debt, people fear that growing national debt causes inflation and raises interest rates.

Deficits and Inflation.   People fear that deficits cause inflation for two reasons. First, if the deficit is caused by increases in government spending, aggregate demand can increase and create an inflationary gap. Second, government deficits can increase the money supply, and increasing money supply can be inflationary. (This will be discussed in Chapter 10.)

Exhibit 5 shows the relationship between deficits and inflation. Panel (a) shows that, in the short run, the relationship between deficits and inflation is weak. During the recession phase the deficit grows, but product and labor markets are weak, and prices remain stable. During the recovery stage, the deficit falls, but product and labor markets are tight and inflation heats up. Increases in the deficit can have a number of causes: income and tax revenues can be falling, the government may be aggressively expanding government spending, taxes may have been cut. Each of these factors affects inflation differently.

Panel (b) shows that when cyclical effects are averaged out over the long run, there is a positive relationship between deficits and inflation. The effect of the business cycle on deficits obscures the long-run relationship between deficits and inflation.

Deficits and Interest Rates. People fear deficits because high deficits are supposed to cause high interest rates. When the government runs a deficit, it must borrow funds in credit markets just like any other borrower. A large deficit increases the demand for credit and should raise interest rates. As interest rates rise, private investment falls, and the federal deficit crowds out private investment.

Although the belief that deficits raise interest rates has gained wide acceptance, the empirical relationship between federal deficits and interest rates is surprisingly weak. Exhibit 6 plots interest rates and the federal deficit (as a percent of GDP) for the period 1960 to 1992. It fails to reveal the expected positive relationship between interest rates and the deficit. When interest rates rose in the late 1960s, the federal deficit was falling. Interest rates fell in the early 1970s as the deficit was rising. In the 1980s and 1990s, the deficit was generally rising while interest rates were falling. However, the high interest rates in the mid-1970s did correspond to rising federal deficits.

Four factors explain why the relationship between federal deficits and interest rates is weak. First, deficits are high during recessions when credit demand is low. Therefore, government borrowing does not push up interest rates because private credit demand is generally weak. Second, the deficits of total government (including state and local government) tend to be smaller than the federal deficit. In recent years, some of the federal deficit has been offset by budget surpluses at the state and local level. Third, the credit market is a world credit market. People with funds to loan can now place these funds in London, New York, Tokyo, Hong Kong, or Latin America on a moment's notice. If federal government deficits threaten to drive up interest rates in the United States, foreign saving flows into the U.S. to drive interest rates back down to world levels. Fourth, increases in government debt may motivate taxpayers to increase their saving. If taxpayers recognize that higher deficits now mean higher taxes in the future, they may increase private saving to handle the future tax burden. In this case, if the increase in private saving offsets the increase in public dissaving, the interest rate should be unaffected.

Problems of Deficit Reduction

Over the last decade, the impact of deficits on the economy has been hotly debated. Politicians, economists, and the general public favor deficit reductions. Although U.S. presidents have made strong deficit-reduction pledges in their campaigns, no president has been able to produce a balanced federal budget. Why is it so difficult to achieve a balanced budget in the last quarter century?

First, approximately 75 percent of all federal government spending is for relatively uncontrollable outlays—government expenditures whose level is determined by existing statutes, by contracts, or by other obligations. Federal government outlays for nondefense discretionary programs accounted for only 17 percent of the total in 1991. To cut the size of the federal deficit, federal revenues must be increased, federal outlays must be reduced, or a combination of the two must take place. In any particular year, budgetary authorities have little leeway for reduction. In addition to relatively uncontrollable outlays, tax revenues are also largely out of the control of budgetary authorities, insofar as they depend on the state of the economy.

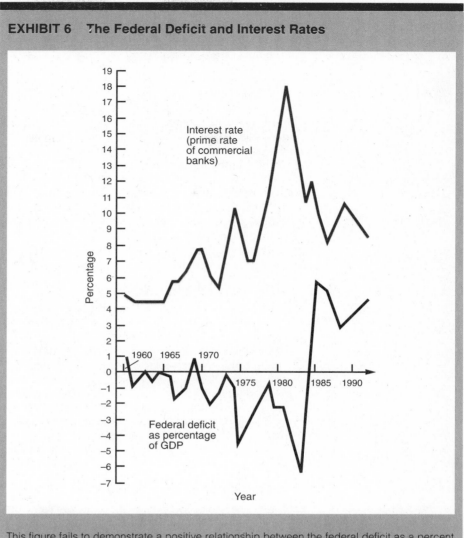

EXHIBIT 6   The Federal Deficit and Interest Rates

Interest rate
(prime rate
of commercial
banks)

Percentage

1960   1965   1970

1975   1980   1985   1990

Federal deficit
as percentage
of GDP

Year

This figure fails to demonstrate a positive relationship between the federal deficit as a percent of GDP and interest rates.

SOURCE: *Economic Report of the President*

There is no popular way to reduce the deficit. Spending cuts are vigorously opposed by those who benefit from the spending program; tax changes that raise government revenues are just as vigorously opposed by those who would pay higher taxes. Affected parties are able to lobby their elected officials, who then find it difficult to vote in favor of unpopular spending cuts or tax increases. Tax increase proposals are further complicated by the need to raise only those tax items that will not reduce work effort or capital formation. If work effort and capital formation drop, income drops and there is less income to tax. Although everyone favors deficit reduction, few are willing to pay the personal price of a lower deficit, particularly when it comes to giving up spending and tax programs that are of benefit to that individual. This fact, more than any other, explains why it is difficult to substantially reduce the deficit.

Should We Have a Balanced Budget?

Although the public has been taught to believe that deficits are bad and should be avoided, economists are divided on the policy question: Should we have a balanced budget?

In the early 1960s, economists and public officials almost unanimously embraced the Keynesian budgetary philosophy. Balanced budgets were no longer regarded as desirable *per se*; instead, budgets were supposed to meet macroeconomic goals. The decline in popularity of the balanced-budget philosophy signaled an important triumph for the Keynesian revolution.

The Keynesian budgetary approach did not advocate *sustained* deficits. Periods of excessive unemployment required budget deficits, but budget surpluses were required during inflationary upswings. Therefore, although no rule required that the budget should be balanced each year, budget surpluses and deficits should even out in the long run.

The expectation of a long-run balanced budget never materialized. Since 1960, the federal budget has had only 2 years of surpluses.

The Case for a Balanced Budget

Balanced budget advocates, including Nobel laureates James Buchanan and Milton Friedman, oppose a budgetary philosophy that calls for periodic deficits. They fear that politicians will not be able to limit government spending to socially necessary programs. Rational politicians know that spending programs that aid special-interest groups bring in votes. The average voter is generally poorly informed about government spending programs; special-interest legislation hurts each of a large number of voters in only a minor and poorly understood way; logrolling and vote trading are political facts of life. With the bias toward spending, balanced budget advocates fear that borrowing to pay for government programs will offer politicians the easy way out. If the budget must be balanced, the public would more likely want government spending limited to socially necessary programs. Balanced budget advocates cite the failure to follow Keynes' advice that surpluses should offset deficits as proof of their arguments.

Keynesian Budgetary Policy

The Keynesian proponents of discretionary fiscal policy maintain that government expenditures and taxes should be manipulated to keep the economy at full employment. If budget deficits are required to raise output to full employment, then these budget deficits are a necessary price to pay. The budget surplus or deficit should not stand in the way of important macroeconomic goals.

According to Keynesian budgetary philosophy, it would be unwise to keep the federal budget balanced. If a reduction in private investment reduces output below full employment, tax revenues fall. Therefore, to balance the budget, government expenditures must be reduced by the amount of the reduced tax collections. Reduced government spending reduces aggregate demand even more. To pursue a balanced budget during a cyclical downturn would only make the downturn worse. A balanced budget policy would also intensify inflationary cyclical upturns. A balanced budget requires that government expenditures rise with the increase in taxes; therefore, income will increase by the amount of the increase in government spending.

The policy debate over balanced budgets is reflected in the proposal to amend the U.S. Constitution with a balanced budget amendment. Currently a number of state constitutions have balanced budget provisions.

Advocates of balanced budgets argue that current political procedures are incapable of producing a balanced budget. Only a constitutional amendment can force a balanced budget. Opponents of the balanced budget amendment argue that it would do away with an important instrument of macroeconomic regulation.

The next chapter examines the role of money in the economy and effect of money on inflation.

The most important point to learn from this chapter is: Fiscal policy is hampered by lags and political obstacles. These factors have resulted in a steady stream of deficits that have not been countered by surpluses. Although people favor lowering the national debt, the political system has a bias toward deficits.

1. The objective of discretionary fiscal policy is to eliminate inflationary and deflationary gaps. Fiscal policy is the deliberate control of government spending and taxation to achieve macroeconomic goals. Monetary policy is the deliberate control of the money supply to achieve macroeconomic goals.

2. Government spending and tax collections depend on income. Tax collections fall as income falls; welfare payments and unemployment compensation rise as income falls. Such automatic stabilizers soften the business cycle, but they cannot eliminate it. Discretionary policies—autonomous changes in government spending and tax rates—are required to fully counteract cyclical disturbances.

3. Government budgets show the relationship between government revenues and outlays. A budget deficit occurs when the government unit is dissaving; a surplus occurs when the government unit is saving. Currently, the federal government is running deficits while state and local governments combined run a surplus.

4. Because of automatic stabilizers, economists use the full-employment budget as a yardstick to measure discretionary fiscal policy. The full-employment budget is the surplus or deficit that would have prevailed had the economy been producing full-employment output.

5. Critics question the effectiveness of fiscal policy because of lags, uncontrollable expenditures, and the crowding out of private investment. Deficit reduction is difficult because most federal spending is relatively uncontrollable in the short run.

6. The national debt is the sum of outstanding federal government IOUs. People fear the national debt because they believe it causes inflation, high interest rates, national bankruptcy or lower capital accumulation.

Policy Focus: **Economists and public officials debate the wisdom of requiring balanced budgets. Keynesian economists argue that deficits should be accepted if necessary to achieve full employment. The proponents of balanced budgets argue that budget deficits crowd out investment and that deficits should be based upon public finance considerations.**

Key Terms

fiscal policy (p. 175)
monetary policy (p. 175)
entitlement program (p. 176)
automatic stabilizers (p. 176)
discretionary fiscal policies (p. 176)
autonomous changes (p. 177)
expansionary fiscal policy (p. 178)
contractionary fiscal policy (p. 178)

government surplus (p. 179)
government deficit (p. 179)
cyclical deficit (p. 181)
structural deficit (p. 181)
full-employment deficit or surplus (p. 181)
national debt (p. 184)
crowding out (p. 184)

Questions and Problems

1. Private saving is $500 billion. Expenditures of the federal government are $700 billion, and its revenues are $650 billion. The combined expenditures of state and local government are $300 billion, and their combined revenues

are $350 billion. There is no foreign saving. What is the total amount of saving in the economy?

2. An economy is operating below the natural rate of output when autonomous government spending is increased by $50 billion. As a consequence of this action, private spending is reduced by $50 billion. What will be the impact of the increase in government spending on output and employment?

3. When an economy goes into a recession, tax collections fall. Would it be correct to call this fall in tax collections an *autonomous change*?

4. Which type of tax cut is more likely to affect aggregate output: a one-year tax surcharge or a permanent lowering of tax rates?

5. "If wages and prices are flexible in both inflationary and deflationary gaps, there is no need for activist macroeconomic policy." Evaluate this statement.

6. What is the difference between automatic stabilizers and discretionary fiscal policy? Are they not the same because they both work through government spending and taxes?

7. If actual government expenditures are $200 billion and actual government revenues are $100 billion, and if the economy is at less than full employment, would the full-employment budget show a larger or smaller deficit than the actual budget? Explain.

8. Why is crowding out important to the debate over discretionary policy?

9. "If the U.S. public debt keeps growing, the U.S. economy will become bankrupt." Evaluate this statement.

10. How is the federal budget deficit related to inflation and interest rates?

11. In 1992, the actual deficit was $100 billion, and the full-employment deficit was $80 billion. In 1993, the actual deficit was $200 billion, and the full-employment deficit was $80 billion. From these figures, speculate about what happened to the economy in this year.

12. If deficits are highest during recessions, explain why the link between large deficits and inflation may be weak.

Doing Economics

Consider yourself (or your family) as a representative member of the U.S. economy. You represent a very small share of the U.S. gross domestic product. To figure out what share, divide your family's gross income by the U.S. GDP, which can be obtained from the tables at the end of a recent edition of the *Economic Report of the President*. Multiply this share by the most recent number you can find for the U.S. national debt (also in the *Economic Report of*

the President) to get an estimate of your family's share of the debt. Does your family own any government bonds, either directly or indirectly through participation in mutual funds, retirement programs, or other intermediaries? Try to estimate your family's net government debt position, subtracting holdings of government securities from your share of the debt. Is this number positive or negative? Is it positive or negative for the average U.S. family? Explain.

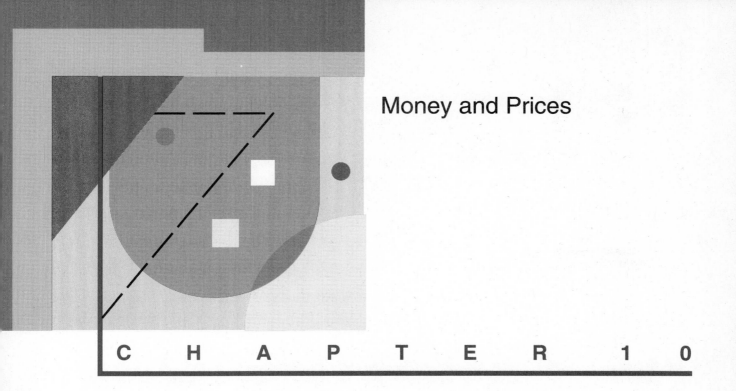

Money and Prices

C H A P T E R 1 0

CHAPTER FOCUS   Money is an integral part of our daily lives. We buy goods with cash, credit cards, or by writing checks. Department stores and gasoline stations are prepared to exchange valuable real goods for coins, currency, or signed checks, which have no inherent value in and of themselves. Money is as mysterious as it is common. Where does it come from? How is more of it created?

Most people understand that there is a linkage between money and prices. If there is a lot of money, prices should be high. If there is little money, prices should be low.

This chapter studies the nature of money and how money is created by the banking system.

After studying this chapter, you will be able to:

- Explain the purpose of money and the different roles it plays in the economy.
- Describe the different types of money that might be used.
- Understand how the money supply is defined.
- Show how the money supply is related to the price level.

THE FUNCTIONS OF MONEY

To economists, the term **money** means something that is generally accepted in exchange for goods and services. In itself, money does not give a country the power to produce anything. If this is so, why do we use money?

> **Money** is the medium of exchange used by an economy; it is something ordinarily used in transactions that transfer ownership of goods and services from one person to another.

Money facilitates trade and commerce in economies that are characterized by specialization and exchange. In such economies, money performs three basic functions. Money serves as:

1. a medium of exchange,
2. a unit of value, and
3. a store of value.

By performing these functions, money allows people to specialize according to their comparative advantage, and exchange goods and services with others. Money allows people to earn higher incomes and, hence, to consume more goods and services than would otherwise be possible. By performing its three functions, money increases the efficiency of the economy.

Money as a Medium of Exchange

Money's most important function is that of a medium of exchange. In a modern economic system, money enters almost all market transactions. The existence of a common object acceptable to all sellers eliminates the need for the *double coincidence of wants* that is necessary for barter transactions. In a barter economy, in which goods are traded directly for other goods, a seller of wheat who wants to buy some sugar must find a seller of sugar wanting to buy wheat. Because a double coincidence of wants is rare, in a pure barter economy the seller of wheat might first have to settle for potatoes, trade the potatoes for an ax, and then finally trade the ax for some sugar. The efficiency of the economy suffers as the efforts of the wheat grower (who wants sugar) are diverted from wheat cultivation into a long string of barter transactions.

Because barter is costly, customs and laws designate something to serve as the medium of exchange. Money allows the wheat farmer to sell wheat for money and to use the money to buy sugar. Converting wheat into sugar is easy—the wheat farmer can concentrate on wheat growing and the sugar grower can concentrate on sugar cultivation.

Irving Fisher (1867–1947)

Irving Fisher is probably the greatest American economist. Born in Saugerties, New York, in 1867, he attended Yale University, ranking first in his class and winning honors in every field of study. He received his Ph.D from Yale in 1891, and his doctoral dissertation broke new ground in economics.

After a brief sojourn in Europe, Fisher returned to Yale, where he taught from 1895 until his retirement in 1935. He was struck down by tuberculosis in 1898, but recovered to live a long and extremely productive life. His experience with tuberculosis made him resolve "to be a great man," and started him on a lifelong crusade for good health.

Fisher was an all-around genius. He invented a visible card index that was patented in 1913, and which made him wealthy. Today's Sperry Rand corporation absorbed Fisher's own firm in 1925. When Fisher lost his wealth in the October 1929 stock market crash, his reputation among noneconomists suffered; however, his contributions to economics were so broad and enduring that no other American economist has touched his academic reputation.

In economics, Fisher's hand can be found everywhere. His greatest work, perhaps, is *The Theory of Interest* (1930), in which he explained the real and monetary determinants of the rate of interest. He developed a model of people living through time that is used today by economic theorists. Fisher popularized the equation of exchange in his book, *The Purchasing Power of Money* (1911). Fisher believed that money caused both inflation and the business cycle. Today, Fisher's monetary views are preserved in the works of Milton Friedman, Robert Lucas, and many others.

Irving Fisher illustrates that even the greatest economist need not be able to predict the stock market. Economic expertise is not measured by one's ability to predict things that are inherently uncertain or random (stock prices, the exchange value of the dollar, tomorrow's interest rates), but by being able to understand the fundamental determinants of how the economy works.

Money's most important function is to serve as that which is generally acceptable as a means of payment (for buying things and paying debts).

Money is a social invention. The object that society uses as money or the medium of exchange could be almost anything. The list of things that have been used as money staggers the imagination. American Indians used *wampum* (a string of shells); early American colonists used tobacco, rice, corn, cattle, and whiskey. Gopher tails were used as money in North Dakota in the 1880s; cigarettes were used as money in prisoner-of-war camps. Farther from home more exotic things have been used: whale teeth in Fiji, sandalwood in Hawaii, fish hooks on the Gilbert Islands, reindeer in parts of Russia, red parrot feathers on the Santa Cruz Islands (as late as 1961), silk in China, slaves in Africa, rum in Australia. Our modern paper money is boring by comparison. (See Example 1.)

Money as a Unit of Value

The value of a good or service is that for which it can be exchanged in the market. In a barter economy, a cow might sell for two pigs, for an acre of land, for 50 bushels of corn, for a motorcycle, or for dozens of other things. It is, of course, inconvenient to keep track of the value of a cow or anything else in terms of every other thing for which it would trade. Barter is also inconvenient when the units cannot be divided, as in a case where a pig is worth half a cow. Choosing a common

EXAMPLE 1

The Stone Money of the Island of Yap

Anything acceptable as a medium of exchange by the population can serve as money. The island of Yap is a tiny U.S. trust territory in the South Pacific 500 miles from Guam. For money, the Yapese—10,000 strong—use stone wheels, from 1 foot to 12 feet in diameter, made from stones found only on distant islands. Most of the stones are 2 to 5 feet in diameter. Each stone has a hole in the middle so it can be carried on a tree trunk. A private citizen could produce money only by making what was often a treacherous sea journey. Thus, Yap money could be called a commodity money. Interestingly enough, the value of the stones is related to their size as well as to their scarcity and the difficulty of acquiring them.

Physical possession is not necessary for ownership. A particular large stone may be owned by many residents, each of whom has received some part of the stone in exchange for some product or service. Larger stones, thus, stay put, with legal ownership being transferred from person to person. How the Yapese keep their bookkeeping straight is not known. On at least one occasion, a family was considered wealthy because an ancestor was known to have discovered an extremely large and valuable stone that a storm sent to the bottom of the sea!

The Yapese have several media of exchange in addition to stone money: U.S. dollars, necklaces of stone beads, and large sea shells. The sea shells and stone beads are used as small change in traditional transactions, but U.S. dollars must be used to make deposits in banks or to buy goods in one of the few retail stores. Will the stone money last? Probably not. The informational requirements of stone money are too large (each stone has a history) for a complicated world. As retailing and banking displace traditional person-to-person exchange, stone money will doubtless become extinct.

As this example illustrates, money does not have to have intrinsic value, but money must be scarce. What works as money in one society need not work as money in another society. As societies become more complex and impersonal, money must become more standardized.

SOURCES: William Furness III, *The Island of Stone Money* (New York: J. B. Lippincott Company, 1910), pp. 92–100; "Fixed Assets, Or: Why a Loan in Yap Is Hard to Roll Over," *The Wall Street Journal*, March 29, 1984.

unit of value—money—saves much time and energy in keeping track of the relative prices or values of different things and solves the problem of converting units. When the money prices of a number of common objects are known, it is easy to appraise the *relative* price of any item just from its money price. If an apple costs $0.50, an orange costs $0.25, and a banana costs $0.10, we know immediately that an apple is twice as expensive as an orange and five times as expensive as a banana and that an orange is 2.5 times as expensive as a banana. Money prices can also be used to add together apples and oranges. By reducing different economic entities to their dollar values, homemakers can add apples and oranges, firms can subtract expenses from revenue to obtain profit, and accountants can subtract liabilities from assets.

Money serves as the common denominator in which the values of all goods and services are expressed.

Money as a Store of Value

People, on average, do not consume all their income, although some households do. When a family consumes less than its income, it saves, or (to say the same thing) it accumulates wealth. People can accumulate wealth in virtually any form that is not perishable—paintings, gold, silver, stocks, bonds, land, buildings, apartments—and money. A desirable characteristic of any *asset* (anything owned that has value) is that it should maintain or increase its value over time. During periods of rising prices, the value of money is eroded because the amount of goods and services one unit of money will purchase falls. Paper currency or coins that have a face value greater than the value of the substance of which they are made are particularly vulnerable to this erosion. Nevertheless, money, like other assets, serves as a store of value. If people accumulate wealth in the form of money, they can use this money at some future date to purchase goods and services. How good a store of value money is depends on the rate of inflation. The higher the rate of inflation, the less well money serves as a store of value.

Because money is a medium of exchange, it can also be used as a means of storing wealth.

THE SUPPLY OF MONEY

Money is anything that performs the three functions of money. Different objects and substances have served as money at different times and in different parts of the world. Money ranges from things that have no intrinsic value (such as a dollar bill) or little intrinsic value (such as a dime) to things that have considerable intrinsic value, such as gold coins.

Types of Money

Money comes in three basic varieties: *commodity money, fiat money,* and *bank money.*

Commodity Money.   Two important examples of **commodity money** have been gold and silver. Gold and silver have nonmonetary uses in jewelry and industry; they can be easily coined, weighed, and used for large and small transactions. In early history, governments started minting gold and silver coins to avoid costly weighings each time a transaction occurred. When gold or silver serve as commodity money, private citizens can produce money simply by taking mined gold to the government mint! In a commodity money system there can also be paper currency, but the paper can be exchanged for the commodity money at a fixed rate.

> **Commodity money** is money whose value as a commodity is as great as its value as money.

The most important example of a commodity money is the gold standard, where, say, one ounce of gold is minted as "$100" coins. If the amount of gold minted increases (because of new discoveries), there is more money in circulation, prices of goods and services are bid up, and one unit of money buys less. (The relationship between money and prices will be discussed later in this chapter.) In this case, gold's value as money has fallen. If the nonmonetary demand for the commodity increases (if the demand for gold fillings increases), there is less money in circulation, prices fall, and a unit of money buys more. In this case, gold's value as money has risen. In this way, the value of gold as a commodity and as money are kept equal. People cannot place a value on commodity money that is higher than its monetary value (dentists would never be willing to pay $110 for an ounce of gold when its monetary value is $100 per ounce) because gold would be shifted to commodity use whenever the commodity price threatened to exceed the commodity's value as money.

Commodity money suffers from an inherent problem, known as **Gresham's law** (named after the sixteenth-century banker and merchant, Sir Thomas Gresham). People try to hoard high-quality commodity money and spend low-quality money.

> **Gresham's law** states that *bad money drives out good.* When depreciated mutilated, or debased currency is circulated along with money of high value, the good money will disappear from circulation; only the bad money will remain in circulation.

When people shave or mutilate gold and silver coins, the bad currency will begin to circulate along with the good currency. The lesser-valued coins will be the ones spent while the more valuable coins will be hoarded. Tobacco money in colonial Virginia illustrates Gresham's law. Initially, tobacco of both good and poor quality circulated as money. As predicted by Gresham's law, people hoarded the good tobacco and used only the worst tobacco as money. Eventually, the tobacco used as money in colonial Virginia was only the scruffiest and foulest tobacco. This opportunism tends to raise the cost of using the commodity money as a medium of exchange because sellers of goods become suspicious of the money being used.

There is a direct cost to society for the use of commodity money: society must devote real resources to producing it. Gold and silver mines must be discovered and operated to produce gold or silver commodity money. This gold and silver must then be set aside to circulate as money and will not find its way into use as jewelry or dental fillings.

Fiat Money. If society could use something as money that costs little or nothing of society's resources (such as pieces of engraved paper), resources could be devoted to other activities. For this reason, societies began to use **fiat money**.

> **Fiat money** is money whose value or cost as a commodity is less than its value as money.

Governments usually have a monopoly over the issue of fiat money, for a simple reason: If everyone were allowed to produce fiat money, so much fiat money would be issued that its value as money would fall to its production cost. If anyone could go to private engravers and order paper currency that could be exchanged for goods and services, everyone would place large orders with engravers. A flood of paper money would saturate the economy and push up prices. This rush to print money would only cease when the purchasing power of one unit of money equaled the bill's commodity value, or the cost of producing the unit of paper money (which is very low). When the amount of fiat money in circulation is determined by government, however, fiat money exchanges for more than its cost of production. Because money is useful, people are willing to exchange goods and services for money in excess of the commodity value of money.

One criticism of a fiat-money system is that the absence of constraints on the government to issue more paper currency increases the chances of inflation.

The two basic forms of fiat money are coins and paper currency. U.S. coins are issued by the U.S. Treasury, and the value of the metal plus the cost of minting is less than the value of the coins used as money. Sometimes such coins are called *token money.* The most important example of fiat money in the United States is paper currency—called *Federal Reserve Notes* because they are issued by the Federal Reserve System rather than by the U.S. Treasury. (See Example 2.)

Fiat money has the advantage that it uses up little of society's resources. Critics of fiat money argue that it has one major flaw—there will be a constant temptation

Does Anything Back the Dollar?

The Federal Reserve System is a public agency charged with regulating the money supply and serving as the bankers' bank (the central bank). The Federal Reserve issues the paper currency of the United States, called *Federal Reserve Notes.* Nothing backs Federal Reserve Notes. If you examine one of these notes you will find that it states: "This note is legal tender for all debts public and private." You will also notice along the top of the note the words, "In God We Trust." Not too long ago, the legal declaration read: "This note is legal tender for debts public and private and is redeemable in lawful money at any Federal Reserve Bank." This statement, of course, was an empty promise because the Federal Reserve Notes themselves were the lawful money of the United States! In the 1950s, a Cleveland man tested this promise by requesting that a $20 bill be converted into lawful money. The Federal Reserve Bank sent him two $10 bills! The man persisted, sending in one of the $10 bills, and ended up with two $5 bills and a letter explaining that "lawful money" was not defined. Soon after this incident, the promise for redemption was dropped and the words "In God We Trust" were added!

This story vividly illustrates that nothing backs the U.S. dollar. At one time the dollar was based on gold. When the U.S. was on the gold standard, anybody could exchange dollars for gold. The U.S. dollar cut its link to gold in two stages. First, in the 1930s, President Franklin Roosevelt allowed only foreign central banks to convert dollars to gold. American citizens could not convert dollars to gold. Second, in the early 1970s, President Richard Nixon cut the final link to gold by not allowing foreign central banks to convert dollars into gold. Today, the U.S. still owns gold in Fort Knox, but the amount of gold is not related to the money supply.

for government to produce too much fiat money because it is so cheap and easy to produce. Governments, which have a monopoly over printing fiat money, may be tempted to produce more fiat money to pay their bills. As more fiat money floods the market, prices will be bid up throughout the economy, and the value of a unit of fiat money will fall.

Bank Money.   In a modern economy, most transactions are conducted using **bank money**.

> **Bank money** is a deposit in checking accounts.

About 90 percent of the dollar value of all transactions in the United States are carried out by writing a check. Payments can be made more safely by check. Checks are a better record of transactions, and money is more secure from theft if it is in a checking account than in someone's wallet. A checkable deposit at a local bank is money, simply because it is a generally acceptable medium of exchange in the nation's marketplaces. The details on how bank money is created are described in the next chapter.

Definitions of Money Supply

The definition of **money supply** incorporates all three types of money just described. A country's money supply is also known as its *stock of money*.

> The **money supply** of a country is the sum of all commodity money, fiat money, and bank money held by the nonbanking public as of a given date.

In the United States, there is no commodity money, so the U.S. money supply is the sum of fiat money and bank money. Note that the fiat money *held by banks* is not a part of the money supply. When someone cashes a check, the bank money the person holds in a checking account is converted to fiat money. Thus, the supply of fiat money in circulation has increased by the same amount as the supply of bank money has decreased. The fiat money the bank holds as cash is not counted in the money supply until it is held by someone outside the bank.

The money supply is a *stock variable* that can be defined as of a given moment in time—say, midnight on April 15. One's personal money supply on a given date would be the total amount of one's holdings of commodity money (which is zero in the United States), one's fiat money (paper money plus coins), and the balance in one's checking account on that date. The combined money supply of all individuals and nonbanking firms on that date is the total money supply of the country.

Currency and demand deposits are a medium of exchange, a store of value, and a unit of account. There is no question that they should be included in the money supply. But other types of assets can be converted to cash with varying degrees of ease. *Money market funds* and savings deposits on which checks may be written can be converted into cash quickly, but not on weekends or if one is out of town. Time deposits with a fixed maturity date can be converted to cash but with some penalty. Government and corporate bonds can also be converted into cash quickly but only when the banks are open or when the bond market is open. Also, when these bonds fall in value, they have to be sold at a loss. Even assets such as land or old paintings can be converted into cash, though a substantial penalty may be incurred if one cannot wait for the right buyer to come along. Where does one draw the line between *money* and *nonmoney*?

Because it is difficult to draw the fine dividing line between money and nonmoney, U.S. financial authorities use different definitions of the U.S. money supply for different purposes.

Exhibit 1 shows the two definitions of the U.S. money supply that are most frequently used by financial authorities, **M1** and **M2**. Basically, M1 is the money people have in cash and in checking deposits, while M2 includes savings deposits, money market mutual funds, and other items. The most important categories of checking deposits are ordinary *demand deposits*, which do not pay interest, and *NOW* (negotiable orders of withdrawal) accounts, which pay interest.

> **M1** is the sum of currency (paper money and coins), demand deposits at commercial banks, travelers' checks, and other checkable deposits such as NOW (negotiable order of withdrawal) accounts and ATS (automatic transfer services) accounts held by the nonbanking public.

> **M2** equals M1 *plus* savings and small time deposits plus money market mutual fund shares plus other highly liquid assets held by the nonbanking public.

In May 1993, M1 amounted to about $1,067 billion and M2 amounted to about $3,506 billion. In addition to including M1, M2 includes assets such as savings and other time deposits.

Why is the distinction between the different money supply definitions impor-

EXHIBIT 1　The U.S. Money Supply, M1 and M2, May 1993

Component	Amount (billions of dollars)
Currency and coin	304
plus	
Demand deposits[a]	359
plus	
Travelers' checks	8
plus	
Other checkable deposits[b]	396
equals	
M1	1067
plus	
Savings deposits at all depository institutions	1194
plus	
Small time deposits at all depository institutions[c]	838
plus	
Money-market mutual-fund shares	539
plus	
Other	935
equals	
M2	3506

[a]Demand deposits at all commercial banks other than those due to other banks, the U.S. government, and foreign official institutions.

[b]Other checkable deposits include NOW and ATS accounts, credit union share draft balances, and demand deposits at mutual savings banks. NOW (negotiated order of withdrawal) accounts pay interest and are otherwise like demand deposits. ATS (automatic transfer services) accounts transfer funds from savings accounts to checking accounts automatically when a check is written.

[c]A small time deposit is one issued in a denomination less than $100,000.

SOURCE: *The Federal Reserve Bulletin*

tant? Because the supply of money has an important effect on the economy, the supply of money is controlled by government monetary authorities. Whether monetary authorities control M1 or M2 will affect the extent to which individuals and firms substitute one form of money for another. Increasing M1 by, say, 10 percent may have very different effects than increasing M2 by 10 percent.

THE RELATIONSHIP BETWEEN MONEY AND PRICES

Economists have long been interested in the relationship between money and prices. This section discusses how changes in the money supply affect the price level. The next chapter examines how monetary authorities control the supply of money.

The Classical Quantity Theory of Money

The classical economists of the eighteenth century, such as David Hume and Adam Smith, proposed a theory to explain the relationship between money supply and price level. This theory was taken up by the great American economist Irving Fisher of Yale University (1867–1947) and by the great English economist Alfred Marshall (1842–1924) and has come to be called the *classical quantity theory of money*, or simply the *quantity theory*. The quantity theory preceded important modern macroeconomic theories. It is especially useful because it provides a powerful though simplified view of how the macroeconomy works. The key lesson to be learned is: the value of money is determined more by its *quantity* than by its *quality*.

Velocity of Circulation

The concept of **velocity of circulation** is essential to an understanding of the quantity theory.

> The **velocity of circulation** is the number of times the average dollar is spent on final goods and services in one year's time.

Because nominal GDP equals real GDP (denoted here by Q) multiplied by the price level, P, the velocity of circulation is:

$$V = \frac{PQ}{M},$$

where M represents money supply.

The higher the velocity of circulation, the faster people are turning over the available stock of money. Velocity can rise or fall with changing economic conditions. When inflation rates are rising for example, velocity tends to rise as people try to spend their money as fast as possible before its value declines even further. When the rate of inflation is falling, people are more inclined to hold their money longer.

The Equation of Exchange

By multiplying both sides of the velocity-of-circulation equation by M, the equation becomes

$$MV = PQ.$$

This equation is known as the *equation of exchange*.

In effect, the equation of exchange says that the amount of final purchases in the economy (GDP) must equal the amount of money in circulation times the average number of times each dollar changes hands. Were this not true, then the observed amount of final spending would not have been possible.

The equation of exchange can be used to explain the quantity theory. Irving Fisher and Alfred Marshall both believed that the equation of exchange summarized the relevant factors determining the link between the money supply and the price level.

Changes in Money Supply and Prices

The equation of exchange does not guarantee that money supply and the price level will rise at the same rate. If V rises while M is constant, total spending (PQ) must rise. Unless Q rises to take up the slack, P must rise. Thus, P could rise without there being any increase in M. There are two important assumptions the quantity theory makes. They are:

1. the velocity of circulation, V, is fixed and
2. real GDP, Q, is fixed in the short run.

These assumptions turn the equation of exchange into the *classical quantity theory of money*. The equation of exchange shows that if both Q and V are fixed, then P will be proportional to M.

The basic message of the classical quantity theory of money is that the price level is proportional to the money supply, and has nothing to do with the quality (that is, whether the money is fiat money or gold) of the monetary unit.

Why did the quantity theorists assume that velocity of circulation and real GDP were both fixed in the short run? They thought that velocity is fixed by the monetary habits and institutions of the community. A country with a large number of money substitutes may have a high velocity of circulation; a country with few money substitutes may have a low velocity. A country with frequent pay periods may have a high velocity; a country with few pay periods may have a low velocity. Whatever the case, because habits and institutions change very slowly, for all practical purposes, quantity theorists regarded velocity as constant.

The quantity theorists believed the size of real GDP is fixed in the short run by the size and productivity of the resources (land, labor, and capital) of the country. Land, labor, and capital grow slowly over time, but at any point in time they are essentially fixed in supply. The real output of the economy is fixed because resources will tend to be fully employed, particularly the most important resource—labor. In this view, changing resource prices ensure the full employment of resources. If workers are involuntarily unemployed, the wage rate will automatically adjust downwards until all those willing to work at the going wage will be employed. Over time as the labor force expands and technology improves, real output will rise. But in the short run, real output is fixed by the resource base and by technology.

The Money Sector and the Real Sector

The classical quantity theorists divided the economy into two sectors, a *real sector* and a *monetary sector*. In the real sector, resources are combined to produce full-employment output. The same amount of output will be supplied no matter what the price level. What counts is not the height of the general price level but the adjustment of relative resource prices to bring the economy to full employment. In the monetary sector, the price level is established by the amount of money in the economy. According to the quantity theorists, the two sectors do not overlap. Changes in money supply are not associated with changes in employment or real output, and vice versa.

The quantity theory, therefore, denies a link between the money supply and unemployment. According to the quantity theory, employment and output are determined in the real sector, and changes in money supply will affect only the price level, not real output or employment.

Aggregate Supply and Aggregate Demand in the Quantity Theory

Chapter 7 explained in detail the concepts of aggregate demand and aggregate supply. Aggregate supply-and-demand analysis can be used to illustrate the major propositions of the classical quantity theory. Aggregate demand (AD) is a schedule of the amount of real GDP demanded by the economy at different price levels. Aggregate supply (AS) is a schedule of the amounts of real GDP supplied at

EXHIBIT 2   The Classical Quantity Theory

The aggregate quantity demanded of goods and services at each price level, according to the classical quantity theory, is simply MV/P, where V is a constant and M is held constant. Because real GDP is fixed, the aggregate supply curve (AS) is vertical. If the money supply increases from M to M', AD shifts to the right, and the equilibrium price level increases proportionately from P to P'.

different price levels. Chapter 7 explained the negative slope of the AD curve and the positive slope of the aggregate supply curve in the short run.

What types of aggregate demand and aggregate supply curves are suggested by the quantity theory? To obtain the quantity theory aggregate demand curve, the quantity equation $MV = PQ$ can be rearranged as $Q = MV/P$. With this arrangement, the aggregate quantity demanded (Q) is a negative function of the price level (P). A higher P causes a smaller Q to be demanded, *ceteris paribus*. According to the quantity theorists, velocity is already constant, so the aggregate demand curve can shift only if the money supply changes.

With money supply and velocity fixed, the quantity equation says that the aggregate demand for real GDP will vary inversely with the price level. The higher is the price level, the lower will be the quantity of real goods and services demanded. When money supply increases, aggregate demand increases (AD shifts to the right). The demand equation, $Q = MV/P$, shows that when M increases, more will be demanded *at each price level*.

Exhibit 2 shows the aggregate demand and aggregate supply curves according to the classical quantity theory. The aggregate demand curve is negatively sloped, and the aggregate supply curve is a vertical line. AS is vertical because, according to the classical quantity theory, real GDP is fixed at full employment. Real GDP, therefore, cannot increase as the price level increases; all resources are already fully employed. With real GDP already determined, the intersection of AD and AS determines only the price level.

When the money supply increases, the aggregate demand curve shifts right proportionately, and the equilibrium price level, P, rises to P'. If M' is twice M, then P' will be twice P.

According to the quantity theory, *the value of money depends on its nominal quantity, not on the stuff from which it is made.* Money is valuable because of what it can buy. According to the quantity theory, it makes no difference whether the

How to Avoid Hyperinflation

Hyperinflations can ruin an economy just as depressions can ruin an economy. In fact, the father of the Russian revolution, V. I. Lenin, referred to hyperinflation as a "machine gun that could destroy capitalism." Fortunately, most countries have been able to avoid hyperinflation or have been able to limit the number of episodes of hyperinflation. Those who have experienced hyperinflation understand its destructive power. One reason given for the greater financial conservatism of the American South is that the South experienced hyperinflation during the Civil War while the North did not. Germany attributes its stubborn support of a strong German mark to its terrible experiences with hyperinflation during the early 1920s—a hyperinflation that contributed to Hitler's rise to power.

The trick to avoiding hyperinflation is well known: Hyperinflation is caused by excessive rates of growth of the money supply. Hyperinflation can be controlled by cutting back of the growth of money. If the solution to hyperinflation is so well known, how do countries fall into the hyperinflation trap?

Hyperinflation usually occurs when governments pay for their expenditures by printing money. They have obligations—interest payments, reparations, defense spending, industry subsidies— that are so large they cannot be covered by tax revenues. Accordingly, the government pays its bills by printing money. The Southern Confederacy paid its military expenditures by printing Confederate money at high rates. The Bolshevik government paid for the Russian civil war (1918–1921) by printing rubles. The German Weimar Republic paid its war reparations in the early 1920s by printing Reichmarks. The Yeltsin government in Russia has kept loss-making industries alive and has subsidized governmental salaries by printing rubles at rapid rates.

To stop hyperinflation, the government must stop printing money at such rapid rates. This may be easier said than done. Once a hyperinflation is underway, people have begun to anticipate hyperinflation, so they turn money over as fast as they can. With money changing hands at ever-accelerating rates, it becomes even harder to stop the hyperinflation.

It is for this reason that most hyperinflations have been halted by introducing a new currency—a process called monetary reform. In Bolshevik Russia, a new currency, the Chervontez, replaced the ruble in the early 1920s. In Weimar Germany, the Rentenmark replaced the Reichsmark. In the American South, the U.S. dollar replaced the Confederate dollar at the end of the Civil War. It is noteworthy that the Yeltsin government in Russia is considering replacing the ruble with a new currency.

money is made out of gold, platinum, or just plain old paper on which some engravings of famous people have been made. If the quantity of money is limited, the money will have value because it is the generally accepted medium of exchange.

This conclusion has policy implications. Why waste resources using a commodity money like gold or silver? Why not just print the money in a way that is difficult to counterfeit and limit its quantity? Skeptics doubt the ability of governments to resist the lure of printing too much money. For these critics, the cost of resources involved in commodity money is less than the inflationary costs of the excesses of government printing presses.

This chapter has explained what money is and how to measure the money supply and has introduced the simplest theory of macroeconomics: the quantity theory of money. The next chapter will explain how the money supply is actually determined in a modern economy and will describe the role of the banking system.

Chapter Summary

The most important points to learn from this chapter are: Money is anything people accept as money, and the value of money is determined more by its relative supply rather than by the material from which it is made.

1. Money is the medium of exchange ordinarily used in transactions. In addition, money serves as a unit of value and a store of value.

2. The money supply consists of commodity money, fiat money, and bank money. Commodity money's value as a commodity is as great as its value as money. Fiat money's value as a commodity is less than its value as money. Bank money consists of checking deposits.

3. The classical quantity theory of money suggests that changes in money supply and price level will be strictly proportional. This conclusion follows from the equation of exchange ($MV = PQ$) and from the assumptions that velocity and output are fixed.

Policy Focus: **Hyperinflations are caused by excessive growth of the money supply. Governments cause hyperinflations by printing money to pay their bills. Hyperinflations can therefore be avoided by having governments avoid the excessive printing of money.**

Key Terms

money (p. 196)
commodity money (p. 199)
Gresham's law (p. 200)
fiat money (p. 200)
bank money (p. 201)

money supply (p. 201)
M1 (p. 202)
M2 (p. 202)
velocity of circulation (p. 204)

Questions and Problems

1. "Anything is money that is legally declared by the government to be money." Evaluate this statement.

2. According to Adam Smith: "That wealth consists in money . . . is a popular notion which naturally arises from the double function of money, as the instrument of commerce and as the measure of value." What is Smith talking about?

3. Is the U.S. money supply fiat or commodity money?

4. Explain why the value of fiat money is determined by its relative abundance. What is the lowest limit to which the value of fiat money can fall?

5. Discuss the social costs of having a commodity money system. What are its benefits? How does Gresham's law enter into this issue?

6. If prices are rising 5 percent per year, what is happening to the value of money?

7. Assume that real GDP is increasing at a rate of 20 percent per year and that the supply of money is increasing

at a rate of 10 percent per year. What would you expect to happen to the value of money and to prices?

8. Why is the distinction between M1 and M2 important?

9. When answering the following questions, assume M = $100, Q = 400 units, and P = $2 per unit.
   a. What is the value of V?
   b. Determine the aggregate demand schedule when velocity is 8 times for a price level of $1, for a price level of $2, and for a price level of $3.
   c. If the money supply rose to $150, what would the aggregate demand schedule be for the three price levels listed in part b?
   d. Use this example to illustrate the basic proposition of the classical quantity theory.
   e. In this example, show that if V is unstable and unpredictable, the basic proposition of the classical quantity theory does not hold.

10. Assume that in Economy X rice is the sole form of money. A rice blight wipes out half this year's crop and also

spoils much of the rice in storage. Predict what effects these events will have on prices and output.

11.   Explain why houses are not considered money.

12.   Assume that in Economy Y cigarettes are used as money. What will happen to the price level if a health scare motivates people to reduce their commodity demand for cigarettes?

Doing Economics

Use the textbook definitions and calculate the approximate amount of M1 and M2 that you (or your family) presently hold. What factors went into the decision to hold this amount? (*Hint*: Think about what factors outside your control affect your holdings of money and what choices you make about your money balances.) Estimate your annual dollar expenditures and use this number to

13.   Economy A uses gold as money, and Economy B uses paper money without any commodity backing. Economy A's money supply is growing at a rate of 10 percent per year; Economy B's money supply is growing at a rate of 5 percent per year. As a quantity theorist, predict which economy will have the largest rate of inflation? Why?

14.   How might a fiat money system result in more inflation over the long run than, say, a commodity money system?

calculate your velocity of circulation for M1 and M2. Use the data at the end of the *Economic Report of the President*, or elsewhere, to calculate velocity for the entire U.S. economy. Is your velocity higher or lower than the national average? If your velocity is very different, can you think of some reasons for this difference?

Commercial Banking and the Federal Reserve

C H A P T E R 1 1

CHAPTER FOCUS   Most money is "bank money." We pay most of our bills by check, not by cash. To understand how the money supply increases, we must begin with the banking system.

Modern banking systems have a number of common characteristics. One of the most fascinating is that banks keep as reserves only a small fraction of deposits. The bank in which you have your checking account may have only a few cents in its vaults for every dollar of deposits. Another common feature of modern banking is that control over their loans and deposits is exercised by a central bank—a banker's bank. In the United States, this central bank is the Federal Reserve System. The Federal Reserve, or Fed, as it is called, can control the money supply and credit of the entire economy simply by purchasing or selling government bonds.

This chapter explains how commercial banks expand and contract credit in response to actions by the Fed.

After studying this chapter, you will be able to:

- Understand the balance sheet of a bank.
- Know why banks hold reserves.
- Describe the Federal Deposit Insurance Corporation.
- Explain the connection between banks and the Federal Reserve System.
- Show how open-market operations affect the money supply.
- Understand how banks create money by making loans.

FINANCIAL INTERMEDIATION

Most of us have had some experience with banks: a commercial bank cashes our checks, a savings-and-loan association handles our savings accounts, the credit union at our place of work gives us a loan for new furniture. What services do these banks perform for us? How do they earn profits?

A savings-and-loan association, an insurance company, a commercial bank, a mutual savings bank, a credit union, a retirement fund, and a mutual fund are all examples of **financial intermediaries**, or financial institutions that mediate between borrowers and lenders.

> **Financial intermediaries** borrow funds from one group of economic agents (people or firms with savings) and lend to other agents.

Financial intermediaries serve a useful purpose in our economy. The commercial bank, for example, accepts a deposit with the promise to pay the depositor a specified interest rate and then lends these funds to, say, a shopping center developer at a higher interest rate. You the depositor need not know the intricacies of shopping center development. The bank hires experts who specialize in many different lines of business. The financial intermediary profits from borrowing at wholesale and lending at retail.

COMMERCIAL BANKS

Prior to the mid-1970s, the differences between commercial banks and other financial intermediaries were more clear than they are now. Historically, a commercial bank could be defined as a financial institution that offered its customers checking accounts (as well as savings accounts) and made short-term loans to the general public and to businesses. Commercial banks were distinguished from *thrift institutions* by the checking account deposits that commercial banks offered.

Thrift institutions, such as savings-and-loan associations, mutual savings banks, and credit unions cater to noncommercial customers and traditionally could not offer checking account services; instead, thrift institutions could offer only different types of savings accounts (hence the name *thrift* institution). Thrift institutions now are able to offer checking accounts to both families and commer-

GALLERY OF ECONOMISTS

Knut Wicksell (1851–1926)

Johan Gustav Knut Wicksell was born in Sweden in 1851. He was Alfred Marshall and John Maynard Keynes rolled into one. Wicksell became a great economist even with a late start. He studied mathematics and physics while young, but he found that economics offered him an understanding of society that he could not obtain elsewhere. In 1887 he received a grant to study economics and, at the age of 53, finally became a full professor. Late in life he served as a consultant to the governor of the Bank of Sweden.

Wicksell's most important work was his *Interest and Prices* (1898). He argued that the inflationary process started when banks charged interest rates less than the "natural" rate of interest. Similarly, a deflationary process started when banks charged interest rates above the "natural" rate of interest. Wicksell's work leads directly to many Keynesian insights and gives us a deeper appreciation for the role of the banking system.

Wicksell's life makes fascinating reading. A man of great principle, he once chose to go to jail to test the freedom of speech guaranteed by the Swedish constitution, and he refused the oath to the Swedish monarch in his wedding ceremony.

During his lifetime Wicksell did not receive sufficient recognition for his creative contributions. His work was not translated into English until the 1930s. Wicksell's reputation has soared since then. Today, he is considered to be a giant in the history of economics.

cial firms. Recent legislation also enables the thrift institutions to make limited commercial loans.

How Commercial Banks Make Profits

A humorist once described bankers as "people who take care of your money by lending it to their friends." Humor and friends aside, this statement captures the essence of modern banking. Bankers ordinarily cannot earn substantial profits by lending only to their friends; to be profitable, a bank must lend funds only to businesses and households that offer the best return on their investment funds. Commercial banks make profits by borrowing from customers in the form of demand deposits and time deposits and then relending these funds in the form of automobile loans, real-estate loans, business loans, and student loans. As with other financial intermediaries, commercial banks earn profits by borrowing money at low interest rates and lending it at higher interest rates. But banks do not always make profits.

Balance Sheets

The concept of a **balance sheet** is essential to an understanding of how banks operate.

> A **balance sheet** summarizes the current financial position of a firm by comparing the firm's *assets* and *liabilities*.

The **assets** of a firm can be buildings, equipment, inventories of goods, money, or even IOUs. A balance sheet lists the claims to these assets.

> **Assets** are anything of any value that is owned.

The **liabilities** of a company include unpaid bills, tax obligations, and outstanding debt.

> **Liabilities** are anything owed to other economic agents.

The value (or net worth) of a company is measured as the excess of assets over liabilities. If a company owns assets worth $1 million and has liabilities of $900,000, the net worth of the company is $100,000.

Net worth = assets – liabilities

A bank's assets consist primarily of IOUs it holds of one kind or another—the loans it has made to persons and to firms, the government bonds it has purchased, the deposits it has with other banks. Its liabilities consist principally of the various deposits that its customers have made—demand deposits, savings deposits, and time deposits.

The combined balance sheet of America's commercial banks as of January 1993 is shown in Exhibit 1. As of that date transaction-account liabilities (demand deposits and NOW accounts) accounted for about 20 percent of liabilities, while savings and time deposits accounted for about 50 percent.

The asset side shows how commercial banks serve as financial intermediaries. Commercial bank deposits are loaned to individuals and businesses and are used to purchase securities. The asset statement shows that commercial banks are primarily in the business of making loans.

Bank **reserves** consist of two components: *vault cash*, which is simply currency and coin in the vaults of the bank, and the *bank's balances with the Federal Reserve System* (explained below). When you cash a check at your bank, you are paid out of its reserves.

> **Reserves** are the funds that the bank uses to satisfy the cash demands of its customers.

The combined balance sheet of Exhibit 1 shows that bank reserves are much less than the liabilities of the banking system. In January 1993, bank reserves equalled $57 billion, or 8 percent of the transaction-deposit liabilities to the nonbanking public. When savings deposits are included (because in practice banks also pay out these funds on demand), the ratio of reserves to deposits falls to 0 percent.

Why are depositors and the banks not alarmed by the imbalance between bank reserves and transaction-deposit or savings-deposit liabilities? As we will discuss later, deposits are insured. But such insurance is a modern invention. The system will work without insurance. On an ordinary business day, some customers deposit money in their checking accounts. Others withdraw money by writing checks on their accounts. If deposits come in at the same pace as withdrawals, bank reserves do not change. Reserves rise when deposits exceed withdrawals; they fall when withdrawals exceed deposits. The normal course of banking is for withdrawals and deposits to proceed at roughly the same rate.

EXHIBIT 1 Consolidated Balance Sheet of All Commercial Banks, January 1993

Assets (billions of dollars)		Liabilities (billions of dollars)	
Vault cash	32.6	Transaction deposits	717.6
Reserves at Fed	24.1	Savings deposits	737.7
Securities	792.2	Time deposits	997.6
Loans	2,247.4	Other borrowings	831.9
Other assets	459.5	Net worth	271.1
Total	3,555.8	Total	3,555.8

SOURCE: *Federal Reserve Bulletin*

THE FEDERAL RESERVE SYSTEM

The Federal Reserve Act of 1913 created the Federal Reserve System. Bankers use the Federal Reserve System as their banker. The *Federal Reserve System*—or *the Fed*—is the central bank of the United States. All modern countries have a central bank.

Functions of the Fed

The Fed, like other central banks throughout the world, performs two primary functions:

1. The Fed controls the nation's money supply.
2. The Fed is responsible for the orderly working of the nation's banking system. It supervises private banks; it serves as the bankers' bank; it clears checks; it fills the currency needs of private banks; it acts as a lender of last resort to banks needing to borrow reserves.

The control of the money supply is the Fed's most important function. The supply of money has an important effect on prices, output, employment, and interest rates. The Fed's control of the money supply, therefore, places it in a position to influence inflation, output, unemployment, and interest rates.

The Structure of the Federal Reserve System

The Federal Reserve Act divided the country into 12 districts, each with its own Federal Reserve bank. These banks are located in Boston, New York, Philadelphia, Cleveland, Richmond, Atlanta, Chicago, St. Louis, Minneapolis, Kansas City, Dallas, and San Francisco. Each Federal Reserve bank issues currency for its district, administers bank examinations, clears checks, and is the nominal lender of last resort to depository institutions in the district.

The Federal Reserve System is controlled and coordinated by a seven-member *Board of Governors* (formerly known as the Federal Reserve Board) located in Washington, D.C. This powerful group is appointed by the president of the United States. Each member of the Board serves a 14-year term. Terms are staggered so that the appointees of a single U.S. president cannot dominate the

Board. The president appoints the chair of the Board, who is the most powerful member and serves for four years.

Bank Regulation

It is useful to examine the key developments in bank regulation in the United States in order to understand the current system.

Restriction of Interest Payments on Deposits.   The Banking Acts of 1933 and 1935 imposed limits on the interest rates banks could pay on demand, savings, and time deposits. These acts prohibited interest payments on checking accounts and provided for the Fed to adjust the other rates periodically. The United States began to phase out these interest-rate ceilings in the early 1980s.

Deposit Insurance.   In the Great Depression, government-guaranteed deposit insurance was instituted for both commercial banks and savings-and-loans associations. The FDIC (Federal Deposit Insurance Corporation) insured bank deposits, and the FSLIC (Federal Savings and Loan Insurance Corporation) insured savings-and-loan deposits. In 1989, the two were merged under the FDIC. Deposits are insured up to $100,000. (See Example 1.)

Restrictions on Permissible Activities.   Until the early 1980s, savings-and-loan associations were restricted to making mortgage loans. Commercial banks were free to make consumer loans, commercial loans, and mortgage loans and to buy government securities. The Glass-Steagall Act of 1933 separated the activities of commercial banks from the securities industry. Commercial banks were prohibited from selling corporate securities. Investment banks (which could deal in corporate securities) were prohibited from engaging in commercial banking. Thus, the distinction between savings-and-loan associations, commercial banks, and investment banks is a legal one.

Capital Requirements.   All depository institutions must meet certain minimum capital requirements. There are two ways to finance the acquisition of assets: drawing the owner's equity or capital, and borrowing. Historically, there have been diverse capital requirements, depending on the size and location of the bank. Since 1983, the Fed and the Comptroller of the Currency have established the minimum capital requirement of 6 percent of a bank's assets. In other words, 6 percent of a bank's assets should be financed by the owners of the bank. This presumably makes the bank safer in case the bank enters a period of negative profits. Federal bank regulators have some discretion in enforcing the requirement for individual banks.

Inspection and Control of Riskiness.   The government has the power to examine depository institutions to determine the riskiness of their assets and liabilities.

Entry Restrictions.   To create a new bank, a new branch of an old bank, or a new savings-and-loan association, it is necessary to obtain permission from federal and state regulators.

Reserve Requirements

The 1980 Monetary Control Act expanded the power of the Fed to set required-reserve ratios for all depository institutions (not just national banks); all depository

EXAMPLE 1

The Problem of Bank Failures

In the early 1980s Congress removed many restrictions on the investment activities of commercial banks and thrifts. The combination of deregulation and deposit insurance proved lethal, and unintended consequences followed. Basically, the FDIC method of insuring deposits creates an incentive problem. Even though there is a $100,000 limit on insured deposits, any amount can be insured by spreading deposits over many banks and using intermediaries. There is no incentive for banks to provide, nor for consumers to demand, information on how well the bank is doing. Deposits are as safe in a poorly run bank as in the best-run bank. The incentive to monitor the performance of banks falls on the shoulders of regulators.

Deregulation meant that nobody was watching the banks. Thus, banks lent money to real-estate developers and corporations without examining the creditworthiness of their business plans. When these investments failed, so did banks and thrifts. Bank failure rates in the late 1980s and early 1990s increased tenfold over the bank failure rates in the 30 years from 1950 to 1980.

In response to this, Congress passed the Federal Deposit Insurance Corporate Improvement Act in 1991. Now there are strict requirements for loan collateral and documentation that make it difficult to categorize a loan as a high-quality one. Loans that do not meet these standards must have higher reserves backing them. But this caused problems in the recovery from the 1990–91 recession. The Fed found it difficult to get banks to increase their loans simply by providing more reserves.

institutions were given the right to borrow from the Fed; it phased out interest-rate ceilings on deposits by 1986; it authorized banks and thrift institutions to offer interest on checking accounts (NOW accounts).

Private profit-maximizing banks choose voluntarily to hold a portion of their assets in reserves. A prudent banker knows that sufficient reserves must be on hand to meet the cash demands of customers. In the United States the Fed imposes uniform **reserve requirements** on all commercial banks, savings-and-loan associations, mutual savings banks, and credit unions. U.S. banks are required by law to hold reserve levels that meet a standard **required-reserve ratio**.

> **Reserve requirements** are rules that state the amount of reserves a bank must keep on hand to back bank deposits.

> A **required-reserve ratio** is the amount of reserves required for each dollar of deposits.

A required-reserve ratio of 0.1 (10 percent) means that the bank must hold $0.10 in reserves for each dollar of deposits. Transaction accounts, such as checking accounts, have required-reserve ratios ranging from 3 to 10 percent, depending on the size of the bank. The reserve requirements on time and savings accounts range from 0 to 3 percent, depending on the size of the account and its maturity. The Fed has the power to raise or lower these required-reserve ratios and to impose supplemental requirements.

Borrowing from the Fed

Any depository institution holding reserves with the Fed is entitled to borrow funds from the Fed. Prior to the Monetary Control Act of 1980, only banks that were members of the Federal Reserve had such borrowing privileges.

Banks do not have unlimited access to Fed borrowing. They must have exhausted all reasonable alternative sources of funds before coming to the Fed. Banks can borrow from the Fed for temporary and immediate cash needs of the banks. They do not abuse their borrowing privileges because they may be audited.

The rate of interest the Fed charges banks is called the *discount rate*. The Fed sets the discount rate and can encourage or discourage bank borrowing by raising or lowering the discount rate. If the spread between the rate at which the banks themselves borrow (the discount rate) and the rates at which they lend is small, the bank's incentive to borrow from the Fed is reduced.

The Federal Open Market Committee

The control of the money supply is the responsibility of the Federal Open Market Committee (FOMC). The FOMC meets once a month and holds telephone conferences between meetings. The FOMC consists of the seven members of the Board of Governors and presidents of five of the regional Federal Reserve banks. The president of the New York Federal Reserve Bank is always one of these five; the presidents of the other regional Federal Reserve banks rotate in the four remaining slots.

The official function of the Federal Open Market Committee is to direct the buying and selling of government securities on the Federal Reserve's account. Because *government securities* are simply the IOUs of the federal government that are continuously traded on the open market, FOMC purchases or sales of government securities are called **open-market operations**.

> **Open-market operations** are purchases and sales of federal government securities by the Fed (as directed by the Federal Open Market Committee).

The Monetary Base

Congress has delegated its power to issue currency to the Fed. Because the Fed can print money, whenever the Fed buys something, it puts money into the economy; whenever the Fed sells something, it takes money out of the economy. Just as you and I do, the Fed buys things by writing checks. The Fed differs from you and me, however, in that it can cash its own checks by issuing newly printed currency. Imagine, for the moment, that you could print money; whenever you bought something with the money you printed, everyone else (taken together) would have more money; whenever you sold something, you would get some of your money back and everyone else (taken together) would have less money. Similarly, Fed purchases inject money into the economy; Fed sales withdraw money.

As this chapter will show later, the Fed normally buys and sells government securities. The Fed's purchases and sales directly affect the **monetary base**. When the Fed buys something, it issues a check. The check, in turn, can form the basis for a bank's reserves if the bank receiving the check simply deposits it in the Fed. Alternatively, the bank receiving the check can "cash it" at the Fed. The Fed can then issue currency equal to the value of the check. If you visit your nearest

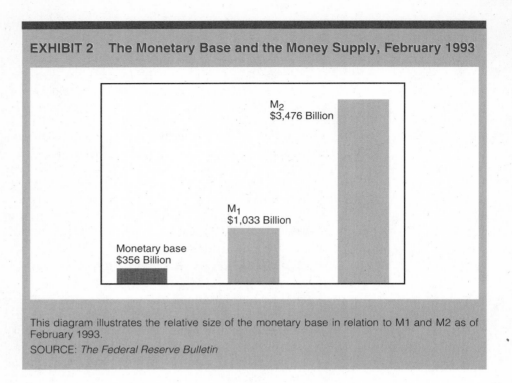

EXHIBIT 2   The Monetary Base and the Money Supply, February 1993

M2
$3,476 Billion

M1
$1,033 Billion

Monetary base
$356 Billion

This diagram illustrates the relative size of the monetary base in relation to M1 and M2 as of February 1993.
SOURCE: *The Federal Reserve Bulletin*

Federal Reserve bank, you will find that it has enormous stacks of unissued currency. Any bank can withdraw reserves. To meet these cash demands the Fed simply issues new currency. Thus, the monetary base consists of currency in circulation plus bank reserves.

> The **monetary base** is the sum of bank reserves and the currency in circulation.

We have shown that Fed purchases raise the monetary base and Fed sales lower the monetary base. The Fed can control the monetary base by varying the amounts of things it buys or sells (whether those things are goods and services or government bonds).

Exhibit 2 compares the monetary base with two concepts of the money supply (M1 and M2). In January 1993, for example, the money supply M1 was about $1,000 billion and the monetary base was about $350 billion. Where did the $650 billion difference between M1 and the monetary base come from? The difference is even larger between the monetary base and M2. One must consider how banks create money.

HOW BANKS CREATE MONEY

Banks can create bank demand deposits (money) by lending out the money that people and firms have deposited. Each bank is simply trying to make a profit from financial intermediation. By examining how banks create money, one can understand why the money supply exceeds the monetary base and how the Fed controls the money supply.

Money and Debt

Borrowers (business borrowers, home builders, car purchasers) come to the bank to borrow money. If the bank agrees to loan them money, an exchange takes place: the bank sets up a checking account equal to the sum of the loan, and the borrower gives an IOU to the bank spelling out the terms of repayment. In the process of this exchange, money has been created. Demand-deposit liabilities of the bank (remember, demand deposits are the main component of the money supply) have increased by the amount of the loan. Thus, banks create money through the purchase of debt with their own liabilities.

Consider what happens when someone makes a deposit of $100 in currency in Bank A. Suppose the depositor has been keeping the cash in an old shoe. Prior to the deposit, the bank was in equilibrium—it was neither making new loans or calling in old ones. The moment the $100 cash deposit is made, Bank A's balance sheet changes as shown on line (a) of Exhibit 3. Both vault cash and demand deposits have gone up by $100.

The cash deposit on line (a) does not create money because cash in the vault is not part of the money supply.

Nothing happens to the money supply as long as Bank A remains in this position. Currency in circulation has fallen by the amount that demand deposits have increased; the total money supply outside banks remains the same.

It is likely that Bank A will not be content to stay in this position. Banks have learned through experience that only a small fraction of deposits must be kept as reserves—the rest can be loaned out. The bank is not making any profit from the $100 cash in its vault. Because the bank is interested in making profits, the $100 deposit will allow Bank A to expand its loans. What fraction of the new deposit will Bank A keep? In the United States, banks must maintain the required-reserve ratio of reserves to demand deposits imposed by the Fed. If the Fed requires a reserve ratio of 10 percent, banks must keep $10 as reserves for each $100 of demand deposits.

The Fed's reserve requirements have typically been more conservative than the reserve ratio a profit-minded banker would consider safe and prudent. Hence, reserves above required reserves would likely be considered **excess reserves**. Excess reserves will usually be loaned out. Banks that have no excess reserves are said to be "loaned up."

> **Excess reserves** are reserves in excess of required reserves. Excess reserves equal total reserves minus required reserves.

Suppose that prior to the $100 cash deposit, the required reserves of Bank A equaled actual reserves (Bank A was loaned up). Assume the Fed's required-reserve ratio is 10 percent. Because the new $100 deposit would require a $10 increase in required reserves, the bank would have $90 in excess reserves after the deposit. The bank, therefore, makes $90 worth of new loans to eliminate the $90 of excess reserves. The moment the $90 loan is made, the borrower's demand-deposit account is credited with $90. Before the borrower spends this $90, Bank A's balance sheet changes as shown on line (b) of Exhibit 3.

Notice that on line (b) the money supply has increased by exactly $90. Bank A has created money! The bank exchanged the borrower's IOU for a demand deposit. The borrower's IOU *is not* money. The bank's IOU—the $90 demand deposit—*is* money. The bank has created money by monetizing debt. If demand deposits were not used as money or if the banks made no loans, banks could not create money.

Banks can create money when: (1) demand deposits are used as money, and (2) banks make loans out of excess reserves.

EXHIBIT 3   The Effects of a $100 Cash Deposit and a $90 Loan

	Change in Assets		Change in Liabilities
Bank A (a) After $100 cash deposit:	Cash in vault	+$100	Demand deposits +$100
(b) After $90 loan but before loan funds are spent:	Reserves Loans	+$100 +$ 90	Demand deposits +$190
(c) After $90 loan proceeds are deposited in Bank B:	Reserves Loans	+$ 10 +$ 90	Demand deposits +$100
Bank B			
(d) After the $90 deposit but before the new loans are made:	Reserves	+$ 90	Demand deposits +$ 90

The cash deposit in part (a) does not create money because cash in the vault is not part of the money supply. The $90 loan and corresponding $90 demand deposit on line (b) creates $90 worth of new money because demand deposits have increased and currency in circulation has remained the same. When the $90 loan is deposited in Bank B on lines (c) and (d), no new money is created until Bank B makes a loan.

Line (c) of Exhibit 3 takes this process a step farther. When the loan recipient spends the $90, Bank A loses $90 of its reserves. The department store, grocery store, or plumber who is paid the borrowed $90 will either cash the $90 check or deposit the $90 check in some other bank.

Whether the $90 ends up in cash that remains in circulation or in a checking account in another bank, the money supply has still increased by $90 as a result of the loan. If the check is cashed, the amount of cash in circulation goes up by $90 and Bank A's deposit liabilities go down by $90. If the check is deposited in another bank, the increase in the depositor's account equals the decrease in the check writer's account. Most transactions (in terms of dollar value) are in checks, and the $90 will likely end up as a checking account deposit in another bank.

Multiple-Deposit Creation

The expansion of the money supply does not end with the $90 increase in the money supply as long as transactions continue to be in the form of checks. In our example, we assume that when Bank A loses the $90 in reserves, some other bank—Bank B—gains the entire amount in new deposits. Our example assumes that there is no **cash leakage** from the banking system to the public.

> A **cash leakage** occurs when a recipient of a check converts it into cash rather than depositing it in a checking account. This cash remains in circulation outside of the banking system.

In this example, people are paid in checks, and they deposit these checks in their checking accounts.

Because Bank B receives $90 in new deposits, its balance sheet changes as shown on line (d) of Exhibit 3. The transfer of $90 from Bank A to Bank B has no

EXHIBIT 4   The Multiple Expansion of Bank Deposits

Bank	New Deposits	New Loans or Investments	Additional Reserves
Bank A	$ 100.00	$ 90.00	$ 10.00
Bank B	$ 90.00	$ 81.00	$ 9.00
Bank C	$ 81.00	$ 72.90	$ 8.10
Bank D	$ 72.90	$ 65.61	$ 7.29
Bank E	$ 65.61	$ 59.05	$ 6.56
Sum A–E	$ 409.51	$368.56	$ 40.95
Sum of remaining banks	$ 590.49	$531.44	$ 59.05
Total for whole banking system	$1,000.00	$900.00	$100.00

The banking system as a whole can create a multiple expansion of bank deposits; a single bank can create only as much money as it has excess reserves. If the reserve requirement is 0.10 (10 percent), a fresh deposit of $100 will lead to $1,000 in total deposits and $900 in new money, provided there are no cash leakages and no bank keeps excess reserves. The original deposit of $100 in Bank A leads to a $90 deposit in Bank B (because of Bank A's new loans), and so on. Thus, $10 is manufactured out of $1, or $9 is created by the multiple expansion of bank deposits.

immediate impact on the money supply. The amount of demand-deposit liabilities remains the same, and no additional money is created.

If Bank B were originally in equilibrium with no excess reserves, it would now have excess reserves of $81. Because deposits increased by $90, required reserves increased by $9 with a 10 percent reserve requirement. Like Bank A before it, Bank B will loan out its excess reserves of $81. When the recipient of Bank B's loan spends this $81 (with zero leakages of cash), Bank C will receive a new deposit of $81.

The moment Bank B made the loan of $81, the money supply increased by that amount. Bank C will keep 10 percent of the $81 deposit as reserves and lend out the rest—$72.90—which again increases the money supply. When the borrower of $72.90 spends the funds, Bank D receives a new deposit of that amount (again assuming zero leakages of cash).

The $100 increase in reserves has set into motion a pattern of multiple expansion of the money supply. If there are no leakages of cash out of the banking system, the original $100 cash deposit in Bank A leads to demand deposits of $90, $81, $72.90, and so on, with each succeeding figure being 90 percent of the previous deposit. If one sums $100 + $90 + $81 + $72.90 and so on down to the smallest amount, one obtains the total of $1,000.

Exhibit 4 shows what happens to each bank as a consequence of a $100 cash deposit in Bank A. The original $100 cash deposit has led to the creation of $900 in additional deposits, or a **multiple-deposit expansion**.

> A **multiple-deposit expansion** of the money supply occurs when an increase in reserves causes an expansion of the money supply that is greater than the reserve increase.

The banking system as a whole can create a multiple expansion of bank deposits; a single bank can create only as much money as it has excess reserves. If the reserve requirement is 0.10 (10 percent), a fresh deposit of $100 will lead to $1,000 in total deposits and $900 in new money, provided there are no cash leakages and no bank keeps excess reserves. The original deposit of $100 in Bank A leads to a $90 deposit in Bank B (because of Bank A's new loans), and so on. Thus, $10 is manufactured out of $1, or $9 is created by the multiple expansion of bank deposits.

Notice that one bank out of many cannot create a multiple expansion of bank deposits. Each single bank can lend out only a fraction of its new deposits. In the above example, each bank can create new money at a rate equal to only 90 percent of any fresh deposit; that is, each bank can loan out only its excess reserves. But when there is no leakage of cash out of the system, an original cash deposit of $100 will lead to a multiple expansion of deposits. As long as the extra cash reserves are in the banking system, they provide the required reserves against deposits. If the reserve requirement is 10 percent, a $100 reserve will support $1,000 worth of deposits. When each bank lends out its excess reserves, it loses those reserves to other banks; these reserves then become the basis for further expansion of the money supply by other banks. The $100 initial cash deposit continues to be passed through the banking system until $900 in new money is created for a total of $1,000 in deposits.

Thus, what is true of all banks taken together is not true of any single bank (believing otherwise is an example of the fallacy of composition).

> One bank can lend out only its excess reserves. However, the banking system as a whole can lend out a *multiple* of any excess reserves.

The Deposit Multiplier

Exhibit 4 showed how the banking system was able to turn a $100 increase in reserves into $900 of new money for a total increase in demand deposits of $1,000. The factor by which demand deposits expand is the **deposit multiplier**.

> The **deposit multiplier** is the ratio of the change in total deposits to the change in reserves.

A deposit multiplier of 10 indicates that for every $1 increase in reserves, demand deposits will increase by $10. We have already calculated the deposit multiplier when the required-reserve ratio is 10 percent (and when there are no cash leakages). With a 10 percent required-reserve ratio, banks will always lend out 90 percent of their excess reserves. Each dollar of new reserves adds $1 to deposits in Bank A, $0.90 to deposits in Bank B, $0.81 to deposits in Bank C, and so on. When all these deposits are added together, the result is a $10 increase in deposits for each $1 increase in reserves.

If the required-reserve ratio had been 20 percent in our example, the $1 increase in reserves would still add $1 to deposits in Bank A, but would now add $0.80 in Bank B, $0.64 in Bank C, and so on for a total increase of $5 in deposits. With a required-reserve ratio of 20 percent, the deposit multiplier is 5. These two examples suggest a formula for the deposit multiplier.

> The deposit multiplier is the reciprocal of the reserve ratio (RR) maintained by the banking system:
> Deposit multiplier = $\dfrac{1}{RR}$.

When the reserve ratio is 10 percent, $RR = 0.10$, and the deposit multiplier is 10. If the reserve ratio is 5 percent, $RR = 0.05$, and the deposit multiplier is 20. As the formula suggests, the deposit multiplier varies inversely with the reserve ratio.

The deposit multiplier works in reverse. If people draw cash out of the banking system, the money supply will fall by a multiplied amount. Money will disappear into thin air. (See Example 2.)

Money-Supply Expansion in the Real World

Our discussion of the multiple expansion of bank deposits assumed that no cash ever leaked out of the banking system and that banks keep excess reserves at zero. Both assumptions are not strictly true.

EXAMPLE 2

Stock Market Crashes and the Money Supply: Where Did All the Money Go?

The money supply can increase or decrease rapidly. From 1929 to 1933, money supply fell by 25 percent from $26.6 billion to $19.9 billion, yet the amount of currency held by the public actually increased. What happened to the missing $6.7 billion? Those who lived through the Great Depression will argue either that people had it under their mattresses or that Rockefeller had it all. Of course, the deposit multiplier tells us what happened. As people drew their cash out of the bank in response to the financial panic caused by the 1929 stock market crash, the amount of deposits fell by a multiplied amount. While the monetary base stayed about the same, the quantity of bank reserves fell. Hence, the money supply itself could fall. The money that existed was just an entry in a bank's books. The magic of the deposit multiplier simply caused the $6.7 billion to vanish into thin air.

From 1929 to 1933 the Fed did not attempt to pump reserves into the banking system. Today, if people began to withdraw cash, the Fed would step in with defensive open market purchases that would restore bank reserves and prevent the money supply from shrinking.

One of the crucial differences between the stock market crash of 1929 and the stock market crash of October 19, 1987, is in the role of the Fed and the FDIC. In 1929, there was no FDIC and the Fed was too inexperienced in the ways of central banking to know how to properly respond to a cash drain. In 1987, deposits were insured and the Fed would never repeat the 1929 mistake.

Cash Leakages. The public does not hold all of its money balances in demand deposits. When banks begin to create new demand deposits, it is likely that the public will also want to hold more currency. Thus, there will be leakages of cash into hand-to-hand circulation as the multiple creation of bank deposits takes place.

Cash leakages reduce the deposit multiplier. Returning to our numerical example, when $100 was initially deposited in Bank A and $90 was lent out, the next generation of banks—Bank B—might receive only $80 in new deposits rather than $90. Thus, Bank B could create only $72 in new deposits rather than $81. This erosion would occur all along the line in Exhibit 4 and would reduce the deposit multiplier accordingly.

If one knows the total cash leakage that will take place, one can apply the deposit multiplier $(1/RR)$ to the amount of the new reserves that are left with the banking system. Suppose that out of the $100 originally deposited with Bank A, $20 would eventually leak into hand-to-hand circulation. Because $80 of new reserves would remain in the banking system, then $800 of deposits must result from the $100 deposit. Thus, the 10-to-1 multiplier applies to the quantity of reserves permanently left with the banking system.

Excess Reserves. If RR in the deposit-multiplier formula is interpreted as the required-reserve ratio, the formula applies only when there are no excess reserves. However, RR in the formula can also be interpreted as the *desired-reserve ratio* of banks. The desired-reserve ratio will depend on the required-reserve ratio and on the profitability of making loans.

In recent years, most banks have kept very small excess reserves. Thus, the desired-reserve ratio has been only slightly larger than the required-reserve ratio. Before the Monetary Control Act of 1980, excess reserves remained at around 1 percent of total reserves. The 1980 act substantially lowered required reserves. The consequence is that excess reserves have increased slightly. In 1993, excess reserves were in the range of 1.5 percent to 2 percent of total reserves.

The Money Multiplier

The process of multiple expansion of reserves explains why the money supply can exceed the monetary base (currency in circulation plus bank reserves). We have shown that the banking system as a whole can, by lending out excess reserves, create deposits that are a multiple of banking-system reserves. The size of this multiple depends on required-reserve ratios, cash leakages, and banks' willingness to hold excess reserves.

The deposit multiplier measures by how much deposits increase for every $1 increase in bank reserves if there are no cash leakages. In reality, the deposit multiplier ($1/RR$) exaggerates the actual increase in the money supply from a $1 increase in reserves because there are substantial cash leakages. The *money multiplier* measures the increase in the money supply for every dollar increase in the monetary base. Because of cash leakages, the money multiplier is less than the deposit multiplier.

Exhibit 2 illustrated the relationship between the money supply and the monetary base: the money supply (currency in circulation plus checkable deposits) was about 3 times the monetary base in January 1993.

FEDERAL RESERVE POLICY

The Fed's most important function is to control the quantity of money. The quantity of money can affect prices, output, and employment; therefore, the Fed controls, to some degree, the pulse rate of the economy. By expanding the money supply, the Fed can speed up the pulse rate; by contracting the money supply (or by slowing down its rate of growth), the Fed can slow down the pulse rate.

The Fed controls money and credit by three major techniques:

1. controlling the monetary base through open-market operations,
2. controlling reserve requirements, and
3. setting the discount rate.

Open-Market Operations

As already mentioned, the Fed can inject or withdraw reserves from the economy by buying or selling. An injection of reserves normally leads to a multiple expansion of deposits; a withdrawal of reserves normally leads to a multiple contraction of bank deposits.

The Fed controls bank reserves by buying and selling federal government securities on the open market as directed by the Federal Open Market Committee. The Fed already owns a large sum of government securities.

The mechanics of Fed open-market transactions are the same whether the Fed is simply offsetting actions in the private economy to hold money supply steady or embarking on a course of monetary expansion or contraction.

Open-Market Sales. Suppose the Fed sells $10,000 worth of government securities to an individual (by means of some intermediary). The individual sends a personal check written on a commercial bank to the Fed (although the exact same effect is achieved if the individual pays cash). Part (a) of Exhibit 5 shows what

EXHIBIT 5   Two Open-Market Transactions

a. Effects of an Open-Market Sale of $10,000 in Government Securities

	Changes in Assets		Changes in Liabilities	
(1) Individual or household	Securities	+$10,000	No change	
	Demand deposits	−$10,000		
(2) Commercial bank	Reserves at Fed	−$10,000	Demand deposits	−$10,000
(3) The Fed	Government securities	−$10,000	Reserve balances of banks	−$10,000

b. Effects of an Open-Market Purchase of $10,000 in Government Securities

	Changes in Assets		Changes in Liabilities	
(1) Individual or household	Securities	−$10,000	No change	
	Demand deposits	+$10,000		
(2) Commercial bank	Reserves at Fed	+$10,000	Demand deposits	+$10,000
(3) The Fed	Government securities	+$10,000	Reserve balances of banks	+$10,000

Part (a) of this table shows the effect of an open-market sale by the Fed. Lines (2) and (3) of Part (a) show that commercial-bank reserves fall by the amount of the sale. Thus, Fed *sales* of government securities *lower* commercial-bank reserves. Part (b) shows the effect of an open-market purchase by the Fed. Lines (2) and (3) show that commercial-bank reserves rise by the amount of the Fed purchase. Thus, Fed *purchases* of government securities *raise* commercial-bank reserves.

happens to the balance sheet of the individual, the commercial bank, and the Fed. The individual's total assets stay the same. The individual's bonds increase by $10,000, and demand deposits decrease by $10,000. The commercial bank finds that its demand-deposit liabilities have fallen by $10,000, and its reserves with the Fed fall by $10,000. When the Fed receives the check drawn on the commercial bank, it reduces the bank's account by that amount. The Fed's stock of government securities falls by $10,000, and its reserve-balance liability to the commercial bank falls by $10,000.

As a consequence of the Fed sale, the money supply falls by $10,000 because demand deposits fall by that amount. In addition, the monetary base also falls by $10,000. By selling $10,000 in securities, the Fed extinguishes $10,000 in reserves. Writing a check to the Fed, unlike writing one to someone else, destroys money instead of transferring it.

The extinction of $10,000 in reserves (monetary base) will cause a multiple contraction of deposits. With a deposit multiplier of 10, the deposits could fall by $100,000.

Open-Market Purchases.   Now suppose the Fed purchases $10,000 worth of securities from a person (by means of some intermediary). That person receives a check from the Fed and deposits it in his or her bank. Part (b) of Exhibit 5 shows what happens to the balance sheets of the person, the commercial bank, and the Fed. The individual's total assets remain the same: demand deposits increase by $10,000, and government bonds decrease by $10,000. The commercial bank finds that its demand deposits have risen by $10,000, and its reserves with the Fed rise by $10,000. Finally, the Fed's government securities and reserve balances of commercial banks both rise by $10,000. The monetary base has risen by the amount of the purchase. This expansion of bank reserves will set into motion a multiple expansion of deposits.

Open-market purchases increase the monetary base; open-market sales lower the monetary base. Open-market operations are flexible because they can be transacted quickly and in almost any desired amount. Open-market operations are powerful because they have a magnified impact on the money supply.

As a comparison of parts (a) and (b) of Exhibit 5 shows, open-market purchases have the exact opposite effects as open-market sales.

Open-market sales destroy reserves, and open-market purchases create reserves. *The Fed uses these operations to control the size of the money supply by controlling the size of the monetary base.* Open-market operations are the most potent weapon of Fed policy because the Fed can quickly buy or sell small or large quantities of government securities.

Changes in Reserve Requirements

The Fed's power to change reserve requirements within broad limits is one of its tools for controlling the money supply. For example, increasing reserve requirements from 10 percent to 12.5 percent would force banks to contract demand deposits by 20 percent. Recall that the deposit multiplier is $1/RR$. When $RR = 0.10$, \$40,000 in reserves would support \$400,000 in demand deposits. If reserve requirements were raised to $RR = 0.125$, \$40,000 in reserves would support only \$320,000 in demand deposits; demand deposits would have to contract by \$80,000. Conversely, lowering reserve requirements can have a massive impact on increasing the money supply.

Increases in reserve requirements reduce the money supply; reductions in reserve requirements increase the money supply. Changes in reserve requirements, however, are a seldom-used instrument of monetary policy.

Traditionally, the Fed has been reluctant to use this tool of monetary policy. One argument against reserve-requirement changes is that they are too blunt. An open-market operation, for example, can be carried out to offset a seasonal currency drain without any fanfare of comment from the press. But a reduction in reserve requirements that is used to simply offset a seasonal currency drain might be interpreted by the financial press as a fundamental change in monetary policy.

Changes in the Discount Rate

The discount rate is the interest rate the Fed charges depository institutions that wish to borrow reserves to meet reserve requirements. Before 1980 only member banks had access to Fed borrowing. Now all depository institutions with balances at the Fed can borrow from the Fed.

The basic function of Fed borrowing is to perform the lender-of-last-resort function of the central bank. Unanticipated withdrawals from a bank can lead to a deficiency in reserves. The bank can make up this deficiency by borrowing from the Fed. The lower the discount rate relative to other interest rates that the bank can earn on its loans and investments, the less costly is it for the bank to keep a small margin of excess reserves. Thus, a lowering of the discount rate may encourage banks to follow a more lenient credit policy and may expand the money supply—but the effects are small.

Generally speaking, the Fed raises or lowers the discount rate in line with market interest rates on government securities. If market interest rates are rising on Treasury bills (government securities with a maturity of less than one year), banks will be tempted to invest all excess funds in such securities up to the loan limits imposed by reserve requirements. Raising the discount rate will reduce the temptation of banks to follow a more lenient loan-and-investment policy when interest rates are rising. Thus, raising the discount rate does not necessarily mean that the Fed is trying to lower the money supply; the Fed may only be trying to control money supply by restricting Fed borrowing.

This chapter explained the relationship between the Federal Reserve System and the money supply. The money supply is important because it affects total expenditures for goods and services. The next chapter will examine the use of monetary policy to control aggregate demand.

Should We Allow Private Money? Hayek's Proposal for Denationalizing Money

A most ingenious and radical solution to the inflation problem has been advanced by Nobel laureate Friedrich A. von Hayek. Were it not for Hayek's credentials, many would be inclined to write this solution off as a crazy scheme. Hayek proposes that each country of Europe and North America bind themselves to an agreement "not to place any obstacles in the way of the free dealing throughout their territories in one another's currencies or of a similar exercise of the banking business by any institution established in any of their territories." In short, Hayek proposes the denationalization of money and free competition among different types of money. Why should governments have a monopoly on the issue of money?

What Hayek supposes would eventually happen is that large banks would get into the profitable business of issuing currencies. The Bank of America might issue the BAM, the Bank of France the BAF, the First City Bank the FCB, and so on. These banks would then compete with one another for customers for their currency. Banks that succeeded in keeping the value of their currency stable would do well in this competitive struggle.

How would people manage with all these currencies? Within any one city there would be a number of currencies with different rates of exchange. Would money's value as a medium of exchange be hampered by the existence of different currencies? With computers, the checkout clerk at the grocery store need only pass each item over the eye of the computer, which will then announce each price and figure the total amount including change. Computers could easily handle 50 separate currencies simultaneously.

The idea of different currencies competing with one another is not as strange as it sounds. Long before the German hyperinflation had destroyed the value of the mark in the 1920s, foreign currencies had begun to circulate in Germany. Those familiar with American banking history will know of the history of wildcat banking during which American banks issued their own currencies. The system did not work well then, but that was before the age of the computer.

Denationalization of money means the end of monetary policy because the government no longer controls the money supply. Hayek would feel more comfortable if money were taken out of the hands of government where he believes it has been abused for centuries.

SOURCE: Friedrich A. von Hayek, *Denationalization of Money* (Great Britain: Institute of Economic Affairs, 1976).

Chapter Summary

The most important points to learn from this chapter are: Banks can create money out of thin air by making loans, and the Fed can increase the total amount of money created by purchasing government securities.

1. Banks are financial intermediaries. Financial intermediaries borrow money from ultimate lenders and lend this money to ultimate borrowers. Most lending in the United States is done by financial intermediaries.

2. Commercial banks are chartered by state banking authorities or by the U.S. Treasury. Commercial banks offer their customers checking account services and savings accounts. They earn money by loaning out funds they have borrowed or by investing these funds in government securities. Banks make profits by borrowing at a lower rate of interest than that at which they lend or invest. Bank balance sheets summarize the claims on the assets of a bank. Banks must maintain reserves to meet the cash needs of their depositors. Reserves are held in two forms: cash in the vault and reserve balances at the Fed. Reserves are always much less than the demand-deposit liabilities of the bank.

3. The Federal Reserve System is the central bank of the United States and was established in 1913. The Fed imposes reserve requirements on banks and thrift institutions. Depository institutions can borrow from the Fed to meet their temporary cash needs, and the interest rate at which they borrow is called the *discount rate*. By buying and selling things, the Fed injects money into the banking system and takes money out of the banking system. The monetary base equals reserve balances with the Fed, vault cash, and currency in circulation. The monetary base is smaller than the money supply.

4. The FDIC insures deposits and gives depositors the necessary sense of security. Banks are also subject to regulation.

5. Banks create money by monetizing debt. Banks can use reserves to make loans, and in the process of making loans, they create money. The deposit multiplier is the ratio of the change in deposits to the change in reserves. If there are no cash leakages and banks lend out all excess reserves, the deposit multiplier is the inverse of the required-reserve ratio.

6. The Fed has an arsenal of weapons to control the money supply: open-market operations, control of the discount rate, and control of the required-reserve ratio. By buying government securities, the Fed injects reserves into the system and expands the money supply. By selling government securities, the Fed withdraws reserves, and the money supply contracts. Changing reserve requirements can have a large impact on the money supply because it creates excess reserves (when the rate is lowered) and because it creates reserve deficiencies (when the rate is raised). This tool is seldom used. Changes in the discount rate have a modest effect on the money supply.

> *Policy Focus:* **Hayek has proposed the denationalization of money. He claims that private money would provide the best insurance against excessive inflation.**

Key Terms

financial intermediaries (p. 211)
balance sheet (p. 212)
assets (p. 213)
liabilities (p. 213)
reserves (p. 213)
reserve requirements (p. 216)
required-reserve ratio (p. 216)

open-market operations (p. 217)
monetary base (p. 217)
excess reserves (p. 219)
cash leakage (p. 220)
multiple-deposit expansion (p. 221)
deposit multiplier (p. 222)

Questions and Problems

1. "Banks get away with murder. They need not pay interest on your checking accounts, and then they turn around and lend your money to some poor borrower at 18 percent." Evaluate this statement.

2. Commercial banks hold about 10 percent of their transaction deposits in reserves. Explain how banks can get by with so few reserves.

3. Explain why even without required-reserve ratios bankers would maintain reserves.

4. Assume that the Fed sells all its old office furniture to XYZ corporation for $10 million. What effect will this sale have on the money supply? What will happen if the Fed sells XYZ corporation $10 million worth of its holdings of government securities?

5. Explain why banks can create money only if bank deposits are accepted as money and only if banks are willing to make loans.

6. Assume that the required-reserve ratio is 0.4 (40 percent) and that there are no cash leakages. The Fed buys a government security from Jones for $1,000. Explain, using *T*-accounts, what will happen to the money supply. Answer the same question assuming only that Jones (and only Jones) takes payment from the Fed as follows: $500 cash (which he puts under his mattress) and a $500 check.

7. Rework Exhibit 3 on the assumption that *RR* = 0.2. In this case, the deposit multiplier is 5, so that the $100 fresh deposit in Bank A will ultimately lead to $500 in total deposits, or $400 in new money.

8. Describe what happens to the monetary base with the following operations:
   a. The Fed sells $1,000,000 worth of used furniture.
   b. The Fed sells $1,000,000 worth of government securities.

   c. A customer cashes a check at the bank.
   d. A commercial bank invests $1,000,000 in government securities.

9. What would you predict would happen to commercial-bank borrowing from the Fed if the Fed were to raise the required-reserve ratio?

10. Assume that between year 1 and year 2, the amount of currency in circulation increased while the amount of vault cash and reserves at the Fed remained the same. Was the Fed purchasing or selling securities?

11. During the Christmas season, the public tends to withdraw large sums of cash from checking accounts. What effect do these withdrawals have on the nation's money supply?

12. If the Fed buys $1 billion worth of German marks, what would happen to the U.S. monetary base?

13. How does the money multiplier compare to the deposit multiplier?

Doing Economics

Locate the current (or a recent) issue of the *Federal Reserve Bulletin* in the Government Documents section of your library. In the statistical tables at the back, look up the current required reserve ratio against demand deposits. (There may be more than one rate, depending on the amount of deposits held at the bank.) Use that ratio to estimate the deposit multiplier if there are no cash leakages and no excess reserves. In a different table, find total bank reserves (including excess reserves) and calculate the ratio of total reserves to demand deposits. Are banks holding many excess reserves? Why? What would be the deposit multiplier based on banks' actual reserve ratio? Now calculate the actual money multiplier as the ratio of M1 to the monetary base for the current month. How does it compare to the deposit multipliers you calculated? Why?

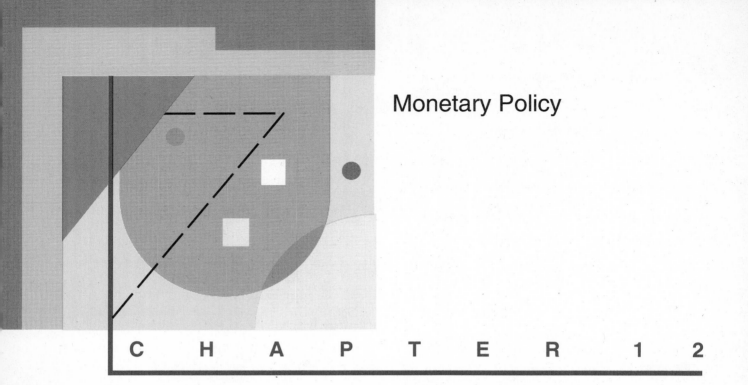

Monetary Policy

CHAPTER FOCUS   The Chairman of the Board of Governors of the Federal Reserve System, currently Alan Greenspan, has been called Washington's second most powerful person. Some even claim that the Fed Chairman's power over economic affairs exceeds that of the President and of Congress. Why is this so?

This chapter looks at how monetary policy can be applied to inflationary and deflationary gaps. It first describes the Federal Reserve System's tools for controlling the supply of money and then traces the Keynesian theory of the link between the money supply and aggregate demand. The chapter examines the targets and goals of monetary policy and evaluates the effectiveness of the Fed's monetary policy. Monetarism is introduced as a response to the limitations of monetary policy. The chapter closes with a discussion of the Fed's independence from the federal government.

LEARNING OBJECTIVES	After studying this chapter, you will be able to:

- Understand how the Fed uses open-market operations, discount rates, and reserve requirement changes to control the money supply.
- Trace the link between the money supply, interest rates, and output.
- Discuss the advantages of monetary policy over fiscal policy.
- Explain the difficulties the Fed faces in controlling the business cycle.
- See how monetarism differs from Keynesian monetary policies.

INSTRUMENTS OF MONETARY POLICY

Chapter 9 explained how fiscal policy could be used to deal with inflationary and deflationary gaps. This chapter explains the role of **monetary policy**.

> **Monetary policy** is the deliberate control of the money supply and, in some cases, credit conditions for the purpose of achieving macroeconomic goals, such as a certain rate of unemployment or inflation.

Whereas the Congress and the executive branch of government are responsible for fiscal policy, the Federal Reserve System (the Fed) is responsible for monetary policy. Monetary policy is conducted by changing the money supply. The previous chapter explained the Fed's three instruments of monetary policy—open-market operations, discount-rate changes, and changes in reserve requirements.

Open-Market Operations

The previous chapter defined the *monetary base* as the sum of currency in circulation and bank reserves. Increases in the monetary base increase the money supply. When the Fed buys government securities from the public in the open market, bank reserves or currency in circulation increase. Fed purchases of government securities increase the monetary base. When the Fed sells government securities in the open market, bank reserves or currency in circulation fall, and the money supply is reduced. Fed purchases and sales of government securities in open securities markets are called *open-market operations* (see previous chapter).

Because open-market operations give the Fed precise control over the monetary base, they are its most important instrument of monetary control. The Fed can either buy or sell large or small sums of government securities. When it buys government securities, the exact amount of its purchase is added to the monetary base. When the Fed sells, the exact amount of the sale is subtracted from the monetary base. These open-market operations are flexible. They can be carried out quickly and with little or no publicity. They can be used to offset unwanted increases or decreases in reserves or in the monetary base.

Open-market operations are the main instrument of monetary policy.

The Discount Rate

Commercial banks and thrift institutions can borrow from the Fed at the *discount rate*, as explained in Chapter 11. When banks are in financial trouble and cannot

Milton Friedman (1912–   )

Milton Friedman was born in New York City, the son of a poor immigrant. He studied at Rutgers University, the University of Chicago, and Columbia University. Friedman became a professor of economics at the University of Chicago in 1946. His major contributions to economics came after age 40. He solved an outstanding empirical puzzle about the relationship between consumption and income in his book, *A Theory of the Consumption Function* (1957). In 1959, he published *A Program for Monetary Stability*, which explained why he believed the government should not try to stabilize the economy. His major work, *A Monetary History of the United States*, was published in 1963 (with Anna Schwartz). In it, Friedman showed that misguided monetary and fiscal policies contributed to making the business cycle worse. It was Friedman who clarified the relationship between unemployment and inflation in his influential presidential address to the American Economic Association in 1967. Friedman was honored with the Nobel Prize in 1977.

Friedman is one of the most controversial figures in economics. He is most well-known perhaps as the founder of monetarism—the doctrine that the money supply or the monetary base should grow at a fixed rate. But Friedman is also one of the most eloquent defenders of the free market. His book, *Capitalism and Freedom* (1962), contains a complete statement of what Friedman regards as the proper role of government in a free society. His ideas address problems ranging from how to finance education to how to alleviate poverty. It is remarkable that whether one agrees with Friedman or not, his brilliant policy ideas are difficult to ignore.

The spread between bank lending rates and the Fed's discount rate affects bank borrowing from the Fed.

meet their reserve requirements, they can borrow from the Fed. The Fed is often said to be the "lender of last resort." Since the Fed has the power to print money, it can "lend" all it wants to banks. The monetary base increases when banks step up their borrowing from the Fed. The relationship between the discount rate and bank lending rates affects banks' willingness to borrow from the Fed. The discount rate is lower than bank lending rates. Banks have an incentive to borrow from the Fed when their lending rates well exceed the Fed's discount rate.

If banks can borrow from the Fed at, say, 6 percent and make loans to their best customers at, say, 9 percent, what prevents them from borrowing unlimited amounts? The Fed attempts to limit bank borrowing to seasonal borrowing needs or to help banks in financial trouble, and it can refuse to make loans. The Fed attempts to keep its discount rate in line with bank lending rates. When lending rates rise, the Fed typically raises its discount rate. Nevertheless, the higher are market interest rates relative to the discount rate, the greater is the incentive for banks to borrow from the Fed.

Because the Fed has a flexible instrument of money-supply control in its open-market operations, it does not use the discount rate in a major way to control the money supply. Some economists believe that the Fed uses the discount rate to indicate future monetary policy. They believe that increases in the discount rate indicate a tightening of monetary policy, and decreases indicate an easing of monetary policy. Discount-rate changes can have an *announcement effect* by letting people know what the Fed is doing.

Reserve-Requirement Policy

Changes in reserve requirements can be a potent instrument of monetary control. Chapter 11 showed that an increase in the required-reserve ratio reduces the deposit multiplier and hence cuts back on the money supply. Although changes in required-reserve ratios are available for wartime and other emergencies, the Fed does not use reserve-requirement changes as a tool of day-to-day monetary policy. Whatever can be achieved by changes in reserve requirements can be achieved with more precision and flexibility by open-market operations.

KEYNESIAN MONETARY POLICY

The income/expenditure model pioneered by Keynes viewed the role of money differently from the classical quantity theorists, whose views were summarized in Chapter 10. The classical economists believed that the supply of money affected the level of money expenditures directly. With velocity (V) constant and the economy operating automatically at full employment, the equation of exchange ($MV = PQ$) showed that money expenditures would rise at the same rate as the money supply (M). In the classical quantity theory, an increase in the money supply would *directly* lead to an increase in the price level (P) because output (Q) was fixed at full employment.

The classical quantity theorists felt that the quantity of money did not affect real GDP or employment. They believed that economies would tend to operate at the natural level of output whatever the existing money supply. Increases in money supply would translate into proportionate increases in the price level and would have no effect whatsoever on output and employment.

Keynes viewed the link between the money supply and desired aggregate expenditures in a different light. He rejected the two classical notions of fixed velocity and full employment. Keynes believed that both velocity and real GDP fluctuated unpredictably; therefore, the direct link between the money supply (M) and aggregate expenditures (PQ) was weak and unstable.

In the Keynesian model, monetary policy affects output *indirectly* through interest rates.

Instead, Keynes proposed an indirect link between the money supply and real GDP. This indirect relationship operated through the effect of money supply on interest rates. If changes in the money supply affected interest rates, then output and employment would be affected by the interest rate's effect on investment.

The link between money and output is discussed in the following sections. First, the relationship between the money supply and interest rates must be clarified.

Bond Prices and Interest Rates

The financial pages of the daily newspaper often contain accounts of interest rates and bond prices such as the following: "Bond prices drifted lower yesterday as interest rates moved up for the second day in a row." Such statements reflect the inverse relationship between bond prices and interest rates.

A *bond* is a promise to pay specified dollar amounts in the future. Because bonds promise fixed dollar payments in the future, the lower the price of bonds, the higher the interest rate yielded. Similarly, the higher the current price of bonds, the lower the interest rate. The simplest bond—the 3-month Treasury bill (called a *T-bill*)—illustrates this point. A $1,000 U.S. Treasury bill promises to pay the face amount—$1,000—of the bill in 3 months. The price of the T-bill will be some discount from $1,000. For example, if the price of the bill were $990, the buyer would earn $10 ÷ $990 = 1.0 percent interest over 3 months, or 4 percent per year (there are four 3-month periods in a year, so the annual rate of 4 percent is four times the 3-month rate of 1.0 percent). If the interest rate increased to 8 percent, the buyer would pay only about $980 for the 3-month T-bill ($20 ÷ $980 = 2 percent; 4×2 percent $= 8$ percent). *The interest rate on a T-bill rises if the price of the T-bill falls. The price of the T-bill falls when the interest rate on T-bills rises.*

The inverse relationship between the bond price and interest rate holds for any bond, but the calculations are harder if bonds pay interest periodically over a period of years.

When the financial section of the newspaper talks about a bond-market *rally* (bond prices rising), one knows that interest rates are falling. When the newspaper talks about the bond market being *bearish* (bond prices falling), interest rates are rising.

Fed open-market operations can affect interest rates. When the Fed purchases government bonds, the increase in demand for those bonds will drive up their prices and, thus, lower interest rates. When the Fed sells government bonds, the increase in the supply of those bonds will drive down their prices and, thus, raise interest rates.

Money and Interest Rates

The effect of changes in the money supply on interest rates depends on how responsive the quantity of money demanded is to the rate of interest. The Keynesian view of interest-rate determination is called the **liquidity-preference theory**.

> According to the **liquidity-preference theory**, the opportunity cost of holding money—a completely liquid asset—is the interest sacrificed, and the interest rate is determined by the supply of and demand for money.

Cash in one's pocket earns no interest. Money in a checking account earns little or no interest. Indeed, about two-thirds of all the M1 balances people hold pay no interest. The interest rate is the opportunity cost of holding money. The higher is the opportunity cost of holding money, the lower is the quantity of money demanded. Therefore, the money-demand curve (the demand curve for liquidity) will have a negative slope relative to the interest rate. At high interest rates, the opportunity cost of holding money is high, and the quantity of money demanded will be low. At low interest rates, the opportunity cost is low, so the quantity of money demanded will be greater.

The Demand for Money. Exhibit 1 shows a money-demand curve. The money-demand curve is also called a *liquidity-preference curve* because people demand liquidity when they demand money. The liquidity-preference curve is like any other demand curve in that the quantity demanded (money) is inversely related to the commodity's price (the interest rate). Like other demand curves, there are a number of demand factors that are held constant, which will be discussed later. The other factors, as we will see later, play a key role in interest-rate determination.

Interest-Rate Determination. The equilibrium rate of interest is that rate at which the quantity of money demanded equals the quantity of money supplied. In Exhibit 1, the initial money supply is represented by the vertical line, M. The equilibrium rate of interest is r.

At interest rates above the equilibrium rate (r), the quantity of money supplied will exceed the quantity demanded. When there is an excess supply of money, people find credit easier to obtain, and interest rates will fall. In other words, if there is an excess supply of money, people will buy bonds and drive interest rates *down* as bond prices *rise*. If the interest rate is less than the equilibrium rate (r), there will be an excess demand for money, and the interest rate will rise as people sell bonds.

Fed open-market purchases (which expand the money supply) tend to drive down interest rates. Fed open-market sales (which contract the money supply) tend to drive up interest rates.

The equilibrium interest rate is that rate at which the quantity of money demanded equals the quantity of money supplied.

EXHIBIT 1   The Demand and Supply of Money and the Interest Rate

The money-demand curve, or liquidity-preference curve, has a negative slope. The amount of money demanded by the economy is greater at low rates of interest because the interest rate is the opportunity cost of holding money. The supply of money is determined by monetary authorities. The interest rate (r) will be the equilibrium rate at which the quantity of money demanded (m) equals the quantity of money supplied. As monetary authorities increase the supply of money from m to m', the interest rate falls from r to r', ceteris paribus.

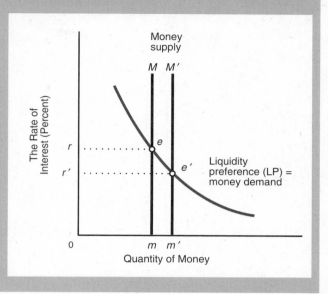

Fed Control of the Interest Rate.   According to the liquidity-preference theory, the Fed can control interest rates by means of its control of the supply of money. By increasing the money supply, the Fed can drive down the rate of interest. By reducing the supply of money, monetary authorities can raise the rate of interest.

In Exhibit 1, the interest rate falls from r to r' when the money supply increases from m to m', ceteris paribus. A greater supply of money induces lending institutions like banks and savings-and-loan associations to make more loans, which drives down the market rate of interest. As long as other factors that affect the demand for money change, an increase in the money supply lowers interest rates and a reduction in the money supply raises interest rates.

How Money Affects Aggregate Demand

Exhibit 2 shows the sequence of events that causes an increase in the money supply to affect the economy's level of output. In panel (a), when the Fed increases the money supply, the rate of interest falls (with a fixed money-demand curve) from r to r'. In panel (b), the fall in the rate of interest increases the quantity of investment demanded. This increased investment shifts up the aggregate expenditure (AE) curve in panel (c) and, hence, shifts the aggregate demand (AD) curve to the right in panel (d). The increase in aggregate demand causes a movement up the short-run aggregate supply curve, and real GDP increases.

Exhibit 2 shows that the effect of an increase in the money supply on aggregate demand depends on the interest rate's sensitivity to the increase in M and on the sensitivity of investment to lower interest rates. The more responsive investment is to the reduction in interest rates, and the more responsive interest rates are to a change in the money supply, the larger is the shift in the AD curve.

When the money supply increases, the increase in aggregate demand depends on the responsiveness of interest rates and investment to the money supply.

EXHIBIT 2 How the Money Supply Affects Real GDP

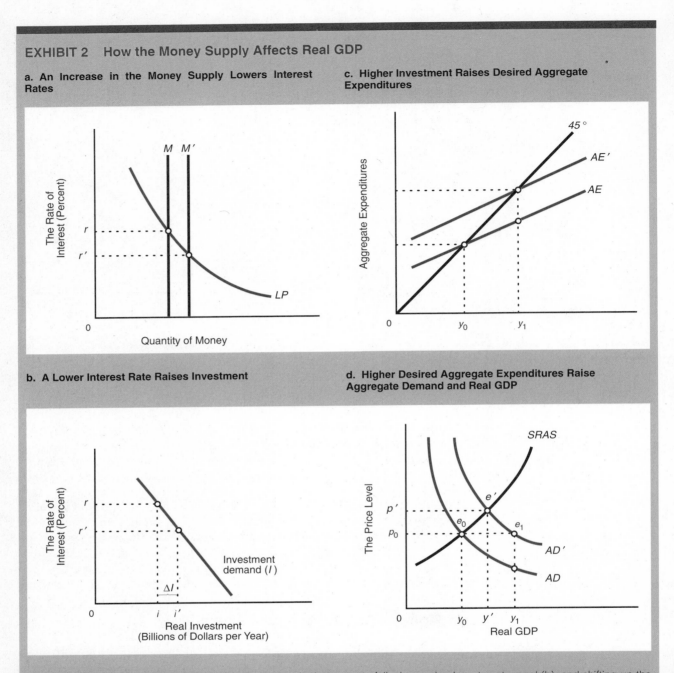

a. An Increase in the Money Supply Lowers Interest Rates

c. Higher Investment Raises Desired Aggregate Expenditures

b. A Lower Interest Rate Raises Investment

d. Higher Desired Aggregate Expenditures Raise Aggregate Demand and Real GDP

As panel (a) shows, when the money supply increases, the interest rate falls, increasing investment, panel (b), and shifting up the *AE* curve. The increase in aggregate expenditures, panel (c), results in a rightward shift in the *AD* curve, as shown in panel (d).

MONETARY POLICY AND DEFLATIONARY AND INFLATIONARY GAPS

Chapter 9 described how an expansionary fiscal policy could be used to eliminate a deflationary gap and how a contractionary fiscal policy could be used to eliminate an inflationary gap. Fiscal policy works through its effects on the aggregate

EXHIBIT 3   Monetary Policy and Inflationary and Deflationary Gaps

a. Using Monetary Policy to Close a Deflationary Gap

b. Using Monetary Policy to Close an Inflationary Gap

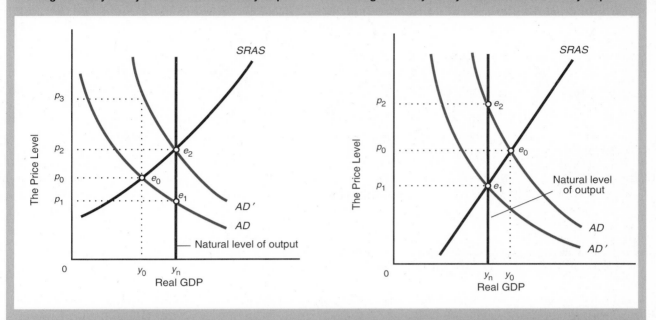

In panel (a), the economy is originally in short-run equilibrium at e_0, where the *AD* curve intersects the *SRAS* curve. A deflationary gap exists because y_0 is less than the natural level of output, y_n. The self-correcting mechanism would require deflation until the economy reaches e_1 on the *AD* curve. Increasing the money supply sufficiently, however, could shift the *AD* curve to *AD'*, thereby eliminating the deflationary gap.

In panel (b), the economy is originally in short-run equilibrium at e_0, where the *AD* curve intersects the *SRAS* curve. An inflationary gap exists because y_0 exceeds the natural level of output y_n. The self-correcting mechanism would require inflation until the economy reaches e_2 on the original *AD* curve. A sufficient decrease in the money supply, however, can shift the *AD* curve to *AD'*, thereby eliminating the inflationary gap.

demand curve. We have just seen how monetary policy—controlling the money supply—can be used to affect aggregate demand.

Exhibit 2 showed that an increase in the money supply can lead to an increase in aggregate demand. In the same way, a reduction in the money supply can lead to a reduction in aggregate demand. An *expansionary monetary policy* increases the money supply (or the growth rate of the money supply), and a *contractionary monetary policy* reduces the money supply (or reduces the rate of growth of the money supply).

Exhibit 3 shows how expansionary monetary policy can close a deflationary gap and how contractionary monetary policy can close an inflationary gap. Exhibit 3 compares a policy of discretionary monetary policy with a policy of waiting for the self-correcting forces of deflation or inflation to eliminate gaps between actual and natural output. Panel (a) shows that a deliberate monetary expansion to remove a deflationary gap restores the economy to the natural level of output at a higher price level than would have resulted from the self-correcting forces of deflation. Panel (b) shows that using deliberate monetary contraction to remove an inflationary gap restores the economy to the natural level at a lower price level than would have resulted from the self-correcting forces of inflation.

Keynes believed that waiting for deflation to remove a deflationary gap wasted far too many economic resources. Instead of letting the self-correcting mechanism return the economy to the natural level of output (which could be slow and painful), Keynes thought the money supply should be increased immediately. An appropriate increase in the money supply could remove the deflationary gap more quickly than waiting for the self-correcting mechanism to work. Modern Keynesians believe that the self-correcting mechanism will remove inflationary gaps more quickly than deflationary gaps. Prices and wages rise more readily than they fall. Hence, Keynesians tend to prefer action to nonaction more often with respect to expansionary monetary policy than with respect to contractionary monetary policy.

An important characteristic of Keynesian monetary policy is its potential *inflationary bias*. The money-supply increases are used to eliminate deflationary gaps and if the self-correcting mechanism is used to eliminate inflationary gaps, the money supply will increase in the long run. In this sense, Keynesian monetary policy is said to have an inflationary bias. This bias is not necessarily bad; it may be the optimal monetary policy if prices and wages are less flexible downward than they are upward.

> Because prices and wages are more flexible in an upward direction, the self-correcting mechanism works more quickly for inflationary gaps.

THE COMPLEXITIES OF MONETARY POLICY

The Fed's basic objective is to use monetary policy to counteract deflationary or inflationary gaps generated by the business cycle. If the business cycle were pushing the economy into a recession (a deflationary gap), the Fed would pursue an expansionary policy. If the business cycle were pushing the economy into an inflationary gap, the Fed would adopt a contractionary (or tight) monetary policy.

The Fed must make its policy decisions in a complex world. Although its basic job is dealing with the business cycle, the Fed has to deal with a wide variety of economic problems. Because fiscal policy is slow-moving and plagued by political difficulties, the Fed is often called upon to deal with a wide variety of short- and long-run problems. The Fed has to deal with the ups and downs of the *exchange rate* for the U.S. dollar (how much foreign currency it takes to buy a U.S. dollar); it has to worry about slumps in housing construction caused by high interest rates; and it has to worry about wild swings in stock markets.

Target Interest Rates or the Money Supply?

According to the Keynesian view of monetary policy, money affects the economy through interest rates. Fiscal policy is conducted (at least in theory) by selecting government spending levels and tax rates that will achieve macroeconomic objectives. To conduct monetary policy, the Fed can focus on either a desired **monetary aggregate target** (the money supply that it thinks will best achieve its macroeconomic objectives) or an **interest-rate target** (the interest rate that it thinks will achieve its macroeconomic objectives).

> An **interest-rate target** is a rate of interest that the Fed seeks to achieve through monetary policy.

> A **monetary-aggregate target** is a particular money supply or growth rate of the money supply that the Fed seeks to achieve through monetary policy.

Economists and monetary authorities have long debated whether the interest rate or the money supply is the proper target of monetary policy. Keynesian economists, who stress that monetary policy works through interest rates, have generally favored targeting interest rates. Monetarists, who believe that the money supply has a more direct effect on aggregate demand, have favored targeting the money supply.

The choice of monetary-aggregate targets or interest-rate targets is important. If a low monetary-aggregate target is selected, credit market funds may run short and interest rates may be driven to high levels. If a low interest-rate target is selected, a very rapid rate of monetary expansion may be required to keep the interest rate at its targeted level.

Interest-Rate Targeting

Until the end of the 1970s, the Fed set interest-rate targets. Once the interest-rate target was set, the money supply would be adjusted to maintain the targeted interest rate. Opponents of interest-rate targeting, however, argued that interest-rate targeting could destabilize the economy. As an example they cite what happens when monetary authorities (following an interest-rate policy) decide to hold to an interest-rate target during a period of rapid economic expansion. Economic expansion increases the demand for credit, and this increased demand starts to drive up interest rates. To hold interest rates down, therefore, the Fed must create even more money. The increase in money supply will further feed the boom. Likewise, when the economy is depressed, the demand for credit will contract and threaten to push down interest rates. For monetary authorities to hold the interest rate constant, they must reduce the supply of money, thereby depressing economic conditions even further.

Setting interest-rate targets would work if the Fed knew the interest rate compatible with achieving the natural level of output. The Fed could then change the money supply until that interest-rate target was achieved. Unfortunately, it is very difficult to know what interest rate will achieve the natural level of output.

Prior to October 1979, the Fed's monetary policy was directed toward interest-rate targets. This policy meant that the growth of the money supply was dictated by the interest-rate targets and the demand for money. If very rapid growth of the money supply were required to achieve a target rate of interest, so be it. During booms, more money was required to keep interest rates from rising.

Money-Supply Targeting: 1979–1982

In October 1979, the Fed decided to base monetary policy on monetary-aggregate targets and let interest rates settle at the level dictated by the targeted money supply. The Fed set a target range of growth rates for the money supply and used its instruments of monetary control to keep monetary growth within these target ranges. The policy was inspired by its then new chairman, Paul T. Volcker, who argued that control of the money supply was necessary to control inflation, which was running at an annual rate of 9 percent in 1979. While the Fed had set money-growth targets prior to 1979, the October 1979 decision meant that the Fed would stop manipulating interest rates and start taking the money-supply targets seriously. Indeed, the Fed reduced the growth rate of the money supply from 1979 to 1981, an action that caused a sharp reduction in the inflation rate.

Recent Fed Policy

The Fed's experiment with strict money-supply targeting did not last long. Initially, inflation increased from 9 percent in 1979 to 9.7 percent in 1981. But the reduced rate of growth in the money supply from 1979 to 1981 helped push the inflation rate, as well as real GDP, down by 1982. The inflation rate dropped to 6.4 percent in 1982, and unemployment rose to 9.5 percent. As the economy moved into a recession, the Fed suspended its 1982 target range of 2.5 to 5 percent monetary growth and allowed the money supply to rise by 8.5 percent during 1982. In 1983, the inflation rate dropped to 3.8 percent and unemployment remained high. The Fed again suspended its 1982 target range of 4 to 8 percent and increased the money supply by more than 10 percent. (See Example 1.)

As we learned in Chapter 10, one measure of the money supply is the sum of currency in circulation plus the checkable deposits and travelers checks the public holds in depository institutions, such as commercial banks and savings-and-loan associations. The above definition of money, known as M1, is quite narrow. A broader concept of money, M2, consists of M1 plus money-market deposit accounts, savings accounts, and small-denomination time deposits at all depository institutions. M2 is about $3^1/_2$ times as large as M1.

Since 1987 the Fed has stated a target range for M2 growth but not M1 growth. During 1993, the Fed targeted M2 growth to range between 2 and 6 percent. The Fed has turned away from M1 targeting because the velocity of M2 circulation is much more stable than the velocity of M1 circulation. For example, the velocity of M1 increased from 3.66 in 1960 to 6.6 in 1991; but the velocity of M2 has not strayed far from 1.7 over the past 30 years. In the mid-1980s, the Fed also found it difficult to meet its M1 target range, as phasing out interest-rate ceilings on some checking accounts led to explosive M1 growth. The Fed may return to M1 targeting in the future, however.

PROBLEMS OF MONETARY POLICY

We have seen that there are several problems with using fiscal policy to deal with deflationary and inflationary gaps. Fiscal policy is slow-moving; its multiplier effects are uncertain; there are strong political obstacles to using spending and tax policy to achieve macroeconomic goals. There are also problems with using monetary policy to deal with inflationary and deflationary gaps.

In contrasting monetary and fiscal policy, it should be noted that most economists now argue that *monetary policy is the more important macroeconomic policy tool.* Policymakers rely much more on monetary policy to deal with macroeconomic problems than on fiscal policy. While fiscal policy is paralyzed by contradictory political forces, monetary policy is conducted by the Fed, largely out of the public eye. The Fed can move quickly and flexibly to deal with macroeconomic problems, largely independent of political constraints.

Because of its flexibility, monetary policy is now the major instrument of macro policy.

Problems of Controlling the Money Supply

The old saying, "You can take a horse to water but you can't make him drink," can be applied to monetary policy. Basically, all the Fed can do to expand the money supply is make additional monetary reserves available to the banking system. It cannot force banks to lend out these reserves. Nor can it force businesses to increase their investment borrowing when interest rates drop. Using monetary policy to induce the economy to increase investment can be ineffective. Monetary

EXAMPLE 1

The Policy Directive of the FOMC

The Federal Open Market Committee (FOMC) is the major operating arm of the Fed. The FOMC directs the buying and selling of government securities. The FOMC meets once a month and issues a policy directive to the Manager of Domestic Operations. The content of this directive is secret for several months.

The directive consists of three parts. First, it states the goals of the FOMC. For example, it might state that the Committee seeks monetary conditions that foster price stability, promote economic growth, and improve the value of the U.S. dollar on foreign exchange markets. Second, the manager will be given operating ranges for the monetary aggregates. It may state, for instance, that the annual growth of M2 should be in the range of 3 to 7 percent. Finally, it will instruct the manager to keep close tabs on the federal funds rate. The federal funds rate is the rate of interest on overnight loans between banks with excess reserves and banks with a shortage of reserves. The FOMC might desire to keep the federal funds rate in the range of, say, 4 to 6 percent. If the federal funds rate rises to 6 percent, the Fed will supply additional reserves through open-market purchases; if the federal funds rate falls to 4 percent, the Fed will absorb reserves through open-market sales.

If the above objectives are not met, the chairman of the Fed may call for a consultation of all the members of the FOMC before the next meeting.

policy is more effective when it contracts the money supply by withdrawing reserves and forcing a contraction of the money supply.

The link between the money supply and desired aggregate expenditures in the Keynesian model is very fragile. The link can be broken at any point in the chain. If increases in money supply fail to lower interest rates, or if changes in interest rates fail to elicit changes in investment, changes in money supply will exert no pressure on desired aggregate expenditures. Moreover, even if the chain is not broken, the effects may be very slight or take time to occur. Interest rates may respond only slightly to changes in money supply; investment demand may be insensitive to changes in interest rates.

For these reasons, Keynes believed that monetary policy would be less effective than fiscal policy in combating severe unemployment.

> Keynesians originally believed that monetary policy would be ineffective in dealing with severe unemployment.

Knowing the Money Multiplier

The Fed does not directly control the money supply; it controls the monetary base (the sum of checking account money and currency in circulation). The **money multiplier** shows how much the money supply will increase for every dollar increase in the monetary base.

> The **money multiplier** is the ratio of the money supply to the monetary base.

When the Fed purchases $100 million of government securities in the open market, it adds exactly $100 million to the monetary base. How much this adds to the money supply depends on banks' willingness to hold reserves and on how much currency the public wants to hold. If banks use the extra monetary base to build up reserves or if the public increases its currency holding relative to checking account money, the impact of the increase in the monetary base will be reduced.

EXAMPLE 2

Money and Unintended Consequences

The monetary base is the amount of currency in circulation plus the reserves of the banking system. Some of this currency is in circulation outside the United States. The U.S. dollar is often used as the preferred means of payment in countries with unstable currencies, such as Russia's rouble or Israel's shekel. It is also used by Colombian drug dealers, smugglers, and other people engaged in illegal economic transactions.

This creates a potential problem for Fed policy. The Fed does not know who is demanding the currency component of base money. If the demand for base money increases from Russia or Colombian drug dealers, the Fed may unwittingly supply the currency to fuel their activities. Supplying Russia with currency may be beneficial, but providing Colombian drug dealers with their means of payment may be detrimental. The law of unintended consequences is difficult to circumvent.

Changes in the money multiplier make it difficult for the Fed to control the money supply in the short run.

When the Fed buys or sells government securities, it cannot be sure what the ultimate effect on the money supply will be because the money multiplier can change when bank reserve policy changes and when the currency-holding habits of the public change. (See Example 2.) Though the Fed's ability to control the money supply is imperfect, experts find that it is more imperfect in the short run thàn in the long run. The Fed can control the money supply in the long run.

The Problem of Lags

If the monetary authorities can recognize and deal with inflationary or deflationary gaps on a timely basis, discretionary monetary policy can stabilize the economy. Discretionary monetary policy is made more difficult, however, by a **recognition lag** and an **effectiveness lag**.

> A **recognition lag** is the time it takes the Fed to decide to change the supply of money in response to a change in economic conditions.

> An **effectiveness lag** is the time it takes the change in the money supply to affect the economy.

Modern economists, even with modern data-gathering facilities, can never be sure of *current* economic conditions. GDP is not known until several months after the fact. Inflation and trade data come in more quickly but are a month old. To know whether an expansionary or contractionary policy is required, one must be able to compare actual unemployment to the natural rate of unemployment. Economists are not even certain about what the natural unemployment rate is or whether deviations from it are temporary aberrations or a part of a serious trend. Nobody knows for sure what is happening right now. The recognition lag may be about 4 months; the Fed may need 4 months or so to identify an inflationary or deflationary gap and to initiate the appropriate technical procedures to expand or contract the money supply.

Estimates of the effectiveness lag vary widely. Some economists believe it is short and predictable—from 5 to 10 months; other economists believe it is long and variable—from 6 months to 2 years.

If lags are short, the argument in favor of discretionary monetary policy is stronger. With short lags the monetary authorities stand a better chance of adopting the correct countercyclical policy. If a deflationary gap develops (threatening a recession), a 5-month total lag means that an expansionary monetary policy will be felt 5 months after recognizing the problem. A 2-year lag means that the effects of the policy will be felt 2 years after recognizing the problem. By that time, the economy may be in a boom that requires a contraction in the money supply.

Keynesian economists tend to believe that lags are short and that activist policy can be used to iron out many fluctuations in real GDP. However, even if lags are short but variable, monetary policy should not try to iron out every small inflationary or deflationary gap. If a deflationary gap is relatively small, the self-correcting mechanism may do the job better. Most Keynesians now believe that policymakers should not try to *fine-tune* the economy but should aim only at correcting significant inflationary or deflationary gaps.

THE INDEPENDENCE OF THE FED

The Fed's power to set money-supply and interest-rate targets is independent of Congress and the executive branch of the government. The Fed does not require financing from Congress; it is self-supporting. Moreover, members of the Board of Governors have 14-year, nonrenewable terms. The Fed can make decisions that the Secretary of the Treasury, the president of the United States, and congressional leaders all oppose. The authors of the 1913 Federal Reserve Act believed the Fed should be independent of political pressures. Opponents of an independent Fed disagree.

There are three arguments for independence. First, if the Fed were under the direct control of politicians, the Fed would be more inclined to follow inflationary policies because, it is argued, politicians like to spend money but do not like to tax. With a dependent Fed, government deficits could be easily financed by money expansion and inflation would be encouraged. Many countries with high rates of inflation have a central bank that is not independent. It is easier for nonelected, relatively anonymous central bankers to adopt anti-inflationary policies than it would be for elected officials to do so.

Second, proponents of independence argue that the Fed can carry out long-term plans better than politicians who can see no farther than the next election. Proponents fear a so-called "political business cycle" brought about by politicians who might try to engineer Fed policy to help get themselves reelected.

Without political independence, the Fed would be more short-sighted and would be more likely to pursue inflationary policies.

Third, proponents of Fed independence argue that the Fed will never go too strongly against the wishes of the electorate because the independence of the Fed is somewhat constrained by political reality. If the Fed gets out of hand, Congress can pass legislation reducing the Fed's independence.

Critics of Fed independence cite two arguments. First, independence means that those who control the most important policy tool available to the government are not accountable to the electorate. If the public does not like Alan Greenspan (the Fed chairperson appointed by President Reagan in June 1987) or the other members of the Board of Governors, there is nothing that can be done. Fed officials cannot be thrown out of office as could an unpopular and, perhaps, incompetent politician. Many believe that in a democracy, policy should be sensitive to the wishes of the public.

Second, critics of Fed independence point out that monetary and fiscal policy

Monetarism

Nobel laureate Milton Friedman is the patron saint of a monetary policy rule known as *monetarism*. Instead of the monetary authorities trying to erase inflationary and deflationary gaps, monetarists argue that the Fed should simply fix the rate of growth of some monetary aggregate, such as M2, at some constant level year after year. The rate of growth usually suggested is 3 percent per year.

The logic of monetarism begins with the observation that monetary policy affects the economy with a lag that varies between about 10 months and 28 months. Thus, the lag is long and of uncertain duration. As a consequence, any attempt to remove a deflationary gap may be too late. Recessions tend to last about one year, on the average, so that by the time the effects of monetary policy are felt, the expansion may no longer be needed. It is possible, according to Friedman, that a discretionary monetary policy designed to stabilize GDP would actually destabilize GDP growth! In other words, Friedman believes that the business cycle is in part just the "dance of the dollar," caused by the Fed's discretionary policy.

A major criticism of monetarism is that the Fed should not focus on M2 or M1 but rather on the monetary base. The idea is that the money multiplier depends on the state of the economy. When the economy is booming, the money multiplier is large; when the economy is in recession, the money multiplier is small. Thus, keeping the reins on M2 will require the Fed to have a stop-and-go policy on the monetary base. Sometimes the Fed might have to increase the monetary base by double-digit percentage rates in a recession, then turn around and reduce the monetary base in prosperous times.

Holding the rate of growth in the monetary base constant would result in sharp expansions and contractions in the money supply as the economy speeded up or slowed down. When the economy speeds up, more money is needed; when the economy slows down, less money is needed. Proponents of this view tend to believe that the business cycle is driven by real factors rather than monetary factors.

Keynesians, of course, criticize monetarism, but for entirely different reasons. They believe that the rate of monetary growth should be speeded up when the economy slips into a recession.

should be coordinated. Under the current system, monetary and fiscal policy can work at cross-purposes. For example, take the case of the large government deficit. The U.S. Treasury may want the Fed to expand the money supply rapidly to stimulate economic growth and, thus, reduce the deficit through increased tax revenues. On the other hand, if the Fed maintains a low rate of money supply growth, the government deficit is likely to be higher because GDP and tax revenues will be lower.

The next chapter examines stagflation and the tradeoff between inflation and unemployment.

Chapter Summary

The most important point to learn from this chapter is: Monetary policy is the most flexible tool of macroeconomic policy. There is

disagreement, however, over the appropriate targets and whether discretionary policy should be used.

1. The Fed can change the money supply through its open-market operations, reserve-requirement changes, and discount-rate changes. Open-market operations are the principal tool of Federal Reserve monetary policy.

2. Keynesian monetary policy is based on the indirect link between money supply and real GDP. Because bond prices and interest rates move inversely, increases in the money supply lower interest rates, *ceteris paribus*. The quantity of investment demanded rises when interest rates fall. In principle, inflationary and deflationary gaps can be removed by changes in the money supply.

3. The Fed's use of interest-rate targets rather than monetary-growth targets can destabilize the economy. Prior to October 1979, the Fed's interest-rate targets had priority over money-growth targets. Since October 1979, the Fed's policy has been more flexible.

4. Keynesians believe that monetary policy should be used to remove major deflationary and inflationary gaps.

5. Defenders of Fed independence stress that being independent reduces the inflationary bias of government policy and allows the Fed to have a longer time horizon. An independent Fed can follow politically tough policies. Critics of Fed independence worry about the Fed being unresponsive to the electorate and working at cross-purposes with fiscal policy.

Policy Focus: **Monetarism argues that the Fed should fix the rate of monetary growth of M1 or M2 because to do otherwise destabilizes the economy. A recent criticism comes from those who believe the business cycle is caused by real factors beyond the Fed's control. They believe the Fed should concentrate on holding the rate of growth of the monetary base constant. Keynesians disagree with both policy prescriptions.**

Key Terms

monetary policy (p. 231)
liquidity preference theory (p. 234)
interest-rate target (p. 238)
monetary-aggregate target (p. 238)

money multiplier (p. 241)
recognition lag (p. 242)
effectiveness lag (p. 242)

Questions and Problems

1. Describe briefly how the Fed uses its three major instruments of monetary control.

2. What is the most important instrument of monetary policy and why?

3. Define the money multiplier. How does it affect the Fed's control over M1?

4. Explain the relationship between interest rates and bond prices.

5. If the newspaper reports, "The bond market is in the doldrums; it has been depressed all week," what is happening to interest rates?

6. Compare the impact on interest rates of a change in the money supply when:

   a. the quantity of money demanded is highly responsive to interest rates.
   b. the quantity of money demanded is relatively insensitive to interest rates.

7. How does a change in the money supply increase real GDP?

8. What problems could arise to reduce the impact of a change in the money supply on real GDP?

9. How does the sensitivity of investment to interest rates affect the impact of a change in the money supply on the shift in the aggregate-demand curve?

10. How would the sensitivity of interest rates to the money supply affect the impact of a change in the money supply on the shift in the aggregate-demand curve?

11. What decision did the Fed make in October 1979? Did this decision result in a lasting change?

12. Why might interest-rate targeting destabilize the economy?

13. Describe recent Fed policy.

14. How do lags in the effectiveness of monetary policy affect the design of good monetary policy?

15. How can Fed independence reduce inflation?

16. How can Fed independence result in poor monetary policies?

Doing Economics

The influence of monetary policy on spending is often supposed to occur through changes in interest rates. Capital investment and consumer durables are usually assumed to be most sensitive to interest rates. Interview one or more individuals who are involved in selling automobiles, residential real estate, construction services, or industrial capital goods. Ask them what national or regional economic conditions or variables have the strongest impact on the demand for their products. If they do not list interest rates, ask whether rises in interest rates reduce their demand significantly. Try to get as much information as you can about how these people think interest rates affect their markets.

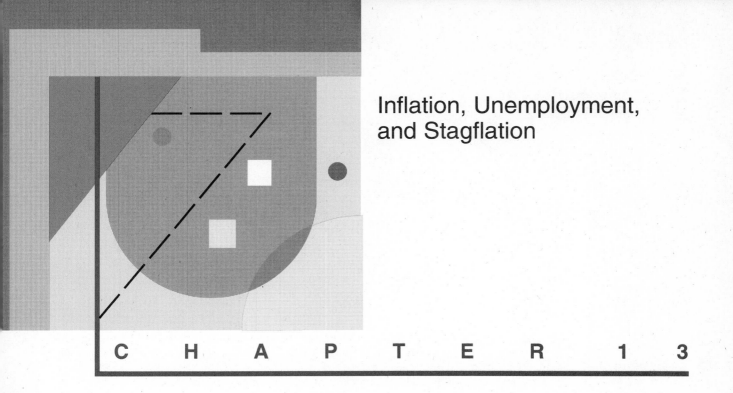

Inflation, Unemployment, and Stagflation

C H A P T E R   1   3

CHAPTER FOCUS   The combination of high unemployment and high inflation (stagflation) in the
1970s and early 1980s shattered belief in an inevitable tradeoff between
inflation and unemployment and prompted a search for new understanding of
the relationship between inflation and unemployment. Frustrated
commentators of the 1970s proclaimed that the "laws of economics" were no
longer working. How could inflation and unemployment rise together?

The stagflation of the 1970s was not limited to the United States. Virtually
all industrialized countries experienced both rising inflation and rising
unemployment during this period.

Stagflation presents a serious policy dilemma. Contractionary monetary
and fiscal policies are the traditional remedy for inflation, whereas high
unemployment calls for expansionary policies. If an economy has both
unemployment and inflation, what should policymakers do? If they fight high
unemployment, they will worsen inflation. If they fight inflation, they will
worsen unemployment.

After studying this chapter, you will be able to:

■ Discuss the difference between demand-side and supply-side inflation.

■ Describe the wage-price spiral.

■ Understand why the natural rate of unemployment changes.

■ Explain how the relationship between inflation rates and unemployment depends on anticipated inflation.

■ Consider the policies that can be used to fight inflation and unemployment.

INFLATION

To deal with inflation, one must understand its sources. Aggregate supply-and-demand analysis points to two general types of inflation; *demand-side* and *supply-side* inflation.

Demand-Side and Supply-Side Inflation

Exhibit 1 illustrates both types of inflation using aggregate supply-and-demand analysis.

Panel (a) of Exhibit 1 illustrates **demand-side inflation**. The economy is initially operating at point e, where output is y and the price level is p. The short-run aggregate supply curve, *SRAS,* is positively sloped—which means that a higher price level will cause the economy to produce more output. If aggregate demand increases—through an increase in the money supply, a lowering of taxes, or an increase in government spending—the aggregate demand curve, *AD,* shifts to the right. At the new equilibrium, e', more output (y') is produced (and unemployment falls). The increase in demand has caused the equilibrium price level to rise (to p').

Demand-side inflation raises both prices and output.

> **Demand-side inflation** occurs when aggregate demand increases and pulls prices up.

Panel (b) illustrates **supply-side inflation**. The economy is initially operating at point e again, producing output y at price level p. A reduction in aggregate supply—because of poor harvests, increases in world energy prices or some other reason—shifts the aggregate supply curve to the left from *SRAS* to *SRAS'*. The drop in aggregate supply shifts the equilibrium to e''. The reduction in aggregate supply has raised both the price level and unemployment.

Supply-side inflation raises prices but reduces output.

> **Supply-side inflation** occurs when aggregate supply declines and pushes prices up.

Demand-side and supply-side inflation are often confused when inflation is moderate. Suppose an increase in aggregate demand. As each sector of the economy seeks to meet the increase in demand, its prices and wages rise. Business managers do not see the increase in aggregate demand; they see only that their

EXHIBIT 1   Demand-Side Versus Supply-Side Inflation

a. Demand-Side Inflation   **b. Supply-Side Inflation**

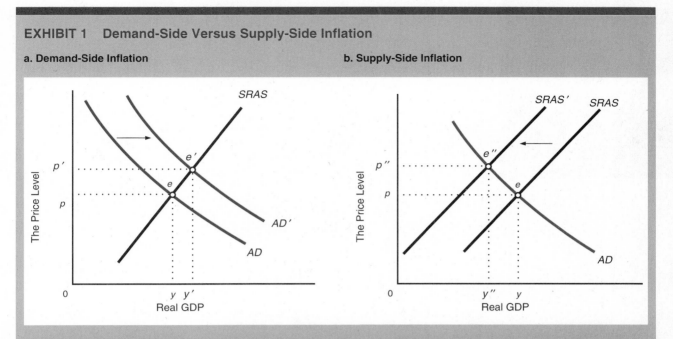

Panel (a) illustrates demand-side inflation. The economy is initially in equilibrium at point *e*. Aggregate demand increases from *AD* to *AD'* and raises the price level from *p* to *p'* as the economy moves up along the short-run aggregate supply curve, *SRAS*, to point *e'*. In the short run, output increases from *y* to *y'*. Panel (b) illustrates supply-side inflation. The economy is initially in equilibrium at point *e*. A reduction in short-run aggregate supply from *SRAS* to *SRAS'* causes a movement back along the aggregate demand curve from point *e* to point *e''*. Prices rise from *p* to *p''*; output declines from *y* to *y''*; unemployment increases.

wage costs, material costs, and interest charges are rising, and they raise prices in response to higher costs. Demand-side inflation looks like supply-side inflation on an individual level.

During hyperinflations, there is less chance people will think that demand-side inflation is really supply-side inflation. People are generally aware that the government is creating money at excessive rates (the lowest-denomination bill may be in the millions!). They know that prices are soaring because of demand increases, not because of supply reductions.

Monetary Growth and Sustained Inflation

Inflation can be caused either by increases in aggregate demand or by reductions in aggregate supply. Reductions in aggregate supply are unlikely to explain *protracted* or *sustained* inflation because aggregate supply reductions (weather, oil shocks, etc.) are usually of a one-shot nature. Good weather follows bad weather. Drops in world oil prices follow increases in world oil prices. The sources of protracted inflation are to be found on the demand side.

Exhibit 2 shows the positive long-run empirical association between the growth of the money supply and inflation. Although both money and prices have risen together, money has grown faster than prices. The money supply (M1) rose about 70 times while the price level rose by more than 13 times over the 1915–1991 period.

The classical quantity theory (discussed in Chapter 11) predicts that money will grow faster than prices. Recall that the equation of exchange is $MV = PQ$.

A. W. Phillips (1914–1975)

A. W. Phillips was born in Te Rehunga, New Zealand, into a farming family. Leaving school at 16, he worked in an Australian mining camp and studied electronics in the evening. He later emigrated to England, served in the Second World War, and was taken prisoner while in the Far East. After the war he enrolled in the London School of Economics to study sociology. Fascinated by economics, especially by the concept of the circular flow, he pictured the economy as a hydraulic machine. Together with another student, Phillips built a mechanical Keynesian model of the economy using flows of colored water. He published a paper on his mechanical water model and was offered a teaching job at the London School of Economics in 1952. Phillips left England to teach at Australian National University in 1967. After suffering a stroke, he returned to New Zealand, where he taught until his death.

Phillips became famous for a single paper: "The Relation Between Unemployment and the Rate of Change of Money Wage Rates in the United Kingdom, 1861–1957." Published in 1958, the paper gave birth to the "Phillips curve." Called the most influential macroeconomic paper of the century by Nobel laureate James Tobin, Phillips' paper showed that there had been a stable trade-off between inflation and unemployment in the United Kingdom for almost a century. Subsequent research on U.S. data appeared to show a stable trade-off for the United States as well. Phillips' work once again seemed to make economics a dismal science: inflation was the cost of low unemployment; high unemployment was the cost of low inflation.

Because of Phillips' work and that of others, economists and policymakers in the 1960s began to regard a trade-off between inflation and unemployment as a "law" of economics, much like the law of demand or the law of scarcity. When both inflation and unemployment began to rise together in the 1970s, it was thought that the laws of economics (the Phillips curve) were no longer working.

Suppose velocity is constant (or nearly so). The money supply grows more rapidly than the price level because some of the increase in money is required to accommodate the larger quantity of real GDP. Between 1915 and 1991, real GDP increased 12 times. More money was required just to keep prices constant. In the long run, money tends to grow more rapidly than prices because rising real output holds down price increases.

> Protracted (sustained) inflation is most likely caused by persistent increases in aggregate demand resulting from excess monetary growth.

The data in Exhibit 2 explain why many economists believe that protracted inflation (such as we have experienced since the early 1930s) is a *monetary phenomenon*.

Exhibit 2 reveals that sustained inflation has been with us only since the 1930s. Prices in the nineteenth century were not notably different from prices in the eighteenth century. Prices in 1940 were approximately the same as prices in 1920, and the money supply in 1940 was also about the same as the money supply in 1920. The U.S. economy has had a clear inflationary pattern only since the 1930s. (See Example 1.)

Cases of Supply-Side Inflation

Supply-side inflation tends to be a one-shot affair. Such inflation can take time for the supply shock to work its way through the economy and it can reinforce demand-side inflation. The most dramatic supply-side inflation in recent years is the 1,475 percent rise in the price of imported oil between 1973 and 1980. The oil-induced reductions of aggregate supply pushed up the general price level.

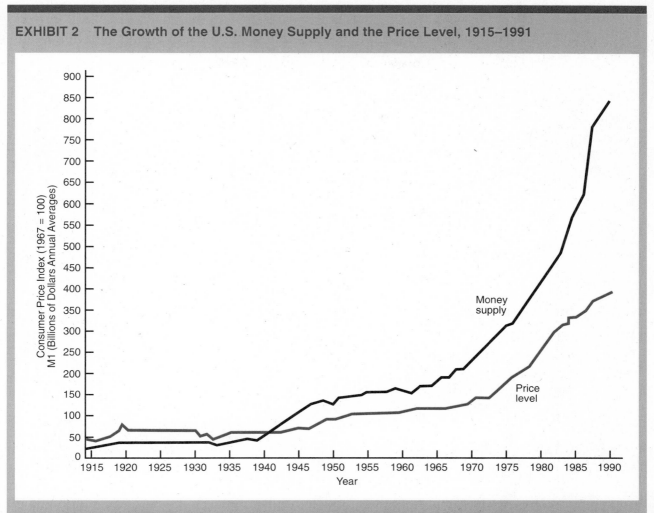

Changes in the money supply and changes in the price level have tended to move together, although without exact agreement. M1 has grown faster than the price level because the increase in real GDP over time absorbs some of the increase in M1.

SOURCES: *Historical Statistics of the United States*, 1970, 210–11, 992; *Economic Report of the President*

The upsurge of world inflation coincided with the increase in energy prices. World inflation rates accelerated in the mid- and late 1970s with the increase in oil prices. They abated as oil prices stabilized or dropped. The year 1973 brought with it not only the beginning of the oil shock, but an increase in the price of wheat from $70 per ton to $140 per ton, largely as a result of a poor harvest in the United States in 1973 and a crop disaster in the Soviet Union the year before.

The oil shocks of the 1970s and droughts are examples of supply-side inflation.

Inflation and Interest Rates

Inflation and interest rates are intimately connected. Rising inflation typically leads to rising interest rates. Higher interest rates crowd out investment spending and hurt industries like automobile and home construction. Higher interest rates tend to depress stock markets.

EXAMPLE 1

Inflation, Death, and Taxes

People today believe that inflation is one of life's inevitabilities. They believe the only question is how rapidly prices will increase each year. Inflation is not inevitable in the sense that the sun will rise everyday. In fact, modern industrial economies—like Germany—have even experienced years of deflation (generally falling prices) in recent years. Inflation is not inevitable; in fact, inflation has not always been with us. The accompanying diagram shows that prior to the 1930s deflation was just as likely as inflation. The prices of the early 1940s were not much different from the prices in the year 1800!

The U.S. Price Level, 1800–1992

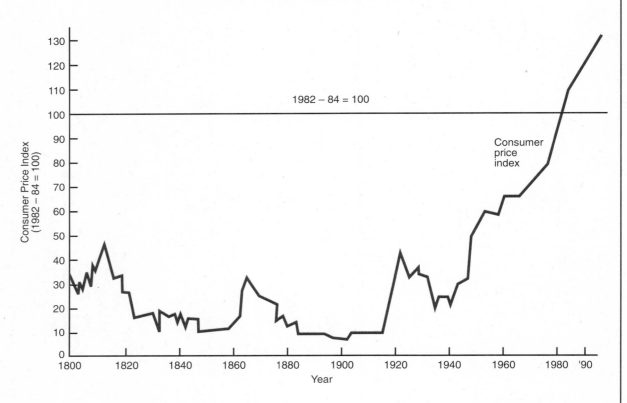

The price level has continuously risen since World War II, deviating from the pattern of the preceding 140 years.

SOURCES: *Historical Statistics of the United States; Economic Report of the President*

It is important to distinguish between **nominal interest rates** and **real interest rates.**

The **nominal interest rate** is the cost of borrowing expressed as an annual percentage rate unadjusted for the effects of inflation.

The real interest rate is the nominal interest rate adjusted for inflation. It is the rate of return in terms of the goods and services money will buy.

> The **real interest rate** is the nominal interest rate minus the expected rate of inflation.

Interest rates on home mortgages, bank loans, and government bonds are nominal interest rates, unadjusted for the impact of inflation. The real interest rate is calculated by deducting the expected rate of inflation from the nominal interest rate. For example, if the expected inflation rate is 5 percent and the interest rate is 9 percent, the real interest rate is 4 percent ($= 9 - 5$) because lenders are expecting to be paid back in 5 percent cheaper dollars.

When people begin to anticipate more inflation, the nominal interest rate rises. When more inflation is anticipated, lenders will be less willing to lend at prevailing interest rates because they know they will be paid back with cheaper dollars. Borrowers will be more anxious to borrow at prevailing interest rates because they can pay back their loans with cheaper dollars. Thus, rising inflationary expectations drive up nominal interest rates.

High interest rates accompany high inflation.

How Inflationary Expectations Are Formed

Nominal interest rates are the sum of expected inflation and the real rate of interest. Chapter 5 noted that people have a strong interest in anticipating what the inflation rate will be. Whether they make good or bad decisions on wage contracts, stock market purchases, or their home mortgage depends on how well they anticipate inflation.

There is no way to know for sure how people form inflationary expectations. Different people might form them in different ways. Economists offer two competing hypotheses of the way expectations are formed.

One view is that people form **adaptive expectations** concerning future inflation exclusively on the basis of what has happened in the past.

> **Adaptive expectations** are expectations of the future that people form from past experience and only gradually modify as experience unfolds.

For example, if the annual inflation rate has been 5 percent year in and year out for the past 10 years, people would probably expect the inflation rate to remain at 5 percent. If the inflation rate jumps to 15 percent, adaptive expectations predict that people would not immediately adjust their expected inflation up to 15 percent. In the first year, they might raise their expected rate of inflation to 10. As inflation continues at 15 percent, people would continue to adjust upward each period until they finally reach a 15 percent expected inflation rate. Until they reach 15 percent, actual inflation exceeds expected inflation.

Adaptive expectations says that it takes time for people to adjust to a new rate of inflation thus creating a difference between actual and anticipated inflation.

With adaptive expectations, when the rate of inflation rises, the anticipated rate of inflation will rise by less than the actual rise. If the rate of inflation falls, the anticipated rate of inflation will fall by less than the actual decline. Only gradually will people raise or lower their anticipated rate of inflation to bring it in line with the actual rate of inflation.

The other view is that people use **rational expectations** to form inflationary expectations.

Rational expectations assume that people change their expectations more quickly and use all available information in forming their expectations. A major difference between adaptive and rational expectations is the speed of adjustment of expectations. People can change the anticipated rate of inflation simply on the basis of a policy pronouncement from monetary or fiscal authorities. For example, if they believe monetary reform will halt hyperinflation, inflationary expectations can drop overnight.

Rational expectations allow a more rapid adjustment of inflationary expectations than adaptive expectations.

The Wage/Price Spiral

When inflation has continued for some time, workers and firms will no longer be caught off guard by inflation; their actions will anticipate inflation. Contracts between workers and employers will reflect the anticipated rate of inflation. Workers who anticipate a 10 percent annual inflation rate over the life of a wage contract will negotiate contracts that will protect them from this amount of inflation. When inflation is anticipated, higher wages will be demanded, and firms can pass wage increases along in the form of higher prices. Sellers entering into sales contracts will also factor the anticipated rate of inflation into their sales contracts.

In such a situation, the economy can get caught in a **wage/price spiral** of accelerating inflation.

In a wage/price spiral, workers anticipate inflation and demand higher wages. Higher wages raise production costs and shift the aggregate supply curve in Exhibit 3 to the left. *The reduction in aggregate supply reduces output and raises unemployment.* To prevent unemployment from increasing, the monetary authorities increase aggregate demand and drive prices even higher. Workers now anticipate a higher price level; they demand higher wages; aggregate supply falls again; the whole process repeats itself.

Is the wage/price spiral supply-side or demand-side inflation? If workers did not demand higher wages (thereby reducing aggregate supply), it would not be necessary to increase the money supply to hold down unemployment. Or if the money supply had never increased and the economy were not on an inflationary path, workers would not demand wage increases. The debate over who has caused the wage/price spiral is much like the argument over which came first, the chicken or the egg.

Supply shocks tend to have a one-shot effect on the economy if there is no increase in aggregate demand. If the economy suffers an adverse supply shock and monetary authorities decide to prevent the drop in unemployment, aggregate demand increases. The increase in aggregate demand pushes up prices even more. The increase in prices raises inflationary expectations, and there is a further reduction in aggregate supply.

Without increases in aggregate demand, an adverse supply shock would not lead to a wage/price spiral.

EXHIBIT 3   The Wage/Price Spiral

The economy is initially operating at e_1—producing y_1 at price level p_1. When short-run aggregate supply falls from SRAS to SRAS', the price level rises to p_2, and output falls to y_2 (the unemployment rises). The government increases aggregate demand from AD to AD' to prevent a rise in unemployment. The price level rises to p_3, and output (and unemployment) returns to its original level at e_3. If workers now anticipate higher inflation, there will be another reduction of aggregate supply, and a wage/price spiral begins.

UNEMPLOYMENT

Chapter 5 presented the basic facts of unemployment. It showed that persons are unemployed if they are without work, seeking a job, and currently available for work. The unemployed are all, by definition, looking for work.

Matching People to Jobs

The unemployment rate depends on how millions of individuals make decisions about whether they should go to school, stay home to raise children, retire at age 60, or remain in the labor force. Once people decide to be in the labor force, they must decide whether to remain at their current job (if employed) or to seek another job. People without jobs must decide what kinds of jobs they want and how to go about finding them. The labor market must match an incredible variety of jobs—from brain surgeon to store clerk—to an equally staggering variety of workers.

The unemployed seek jobs that are consistent with skills, qualifications, and work experience. The unemployed construction worker does not seek work as a certified public accountant. Because people have different educational and work-experience backgrounds, they restrict their search to jobs that they regard as suitable. The unemployed automotive design engineer will likely not take a job managing a fast-food restaurant. If people's job expectations are not met, they typically choose to remain unemployed or even drop out of the labor force. Matching available jobs with worker qualifications underscores the difficult distinction between voluntary and involuntary unemployment. The matching problem also explains why unemployment exists even in an economy with a large number of unfilled positions.

The labor market must match people with jobs for which they are qualified through job searches.

EXHIBIT 4   Unemployment Rates

The unemployment rate has shown a general tendency to rise since the 1950s.

SOURCE: *Economic Report of the President*

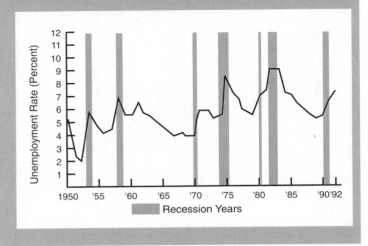

The Long-Run Rise in Unemployment

The unemployment rate has been generally rising, as Exhibit 4 shows. Unemployment rates during recovery periods have become successively higher, as have unemployment rates during successive recessions. The fact that unemployment rates have been rising from cyclical peak to cyclical peak (or from trough to trough) indicates that the *natural rate of unemployment* has been rising. In the 1960s, the natural rate was in the 3–3.5 percent range. In the 1980s, the natural rate was in the 5–5.5 percent range. In the 1990s, the natural rate is believed to be around 6 percent. A number of factors explain the rise in the natural rate of unemployment.

The Changing Composition of the Labor Force.   Exhibit 5 shows unemployment rates of different segments of the labor force. Young people and women, especially women who maintain families, have higher unemployment rates than experienced workers and married men. Over the past 40 years, the numbers of women and young workers in the labor force have been rising. This change in the composition of the labor force has pushed up the natural rate of unemployment.

Multiple Earners.   Currently more than half of the women over the age of 16 have jobs. In 1960, only one in four had jobs. The trend toward two-earner families has affected the unemployment rate. Before 1960, the loss of a job by the household head meant the almost total loss of family income. In the early 1990s, the loss of a job by one family member is cushioned by the earnings of the second. Only about one-quarter of the families with an unemployed member has no employed person in the household. Multiple-earner households allow people more time to find a suitable job and hence raise the unemployment rate.

Unemployment Insurance.   Currently the average unemployed worker can count on state and federal programs to cover roughly one-half of his or her after-tax wage income. This figure does not include employer-provided benefits or

EXHIBIT 5   Why the Natural Rate has Risen: Unemployment Rates of Different Segments of the Labor Force

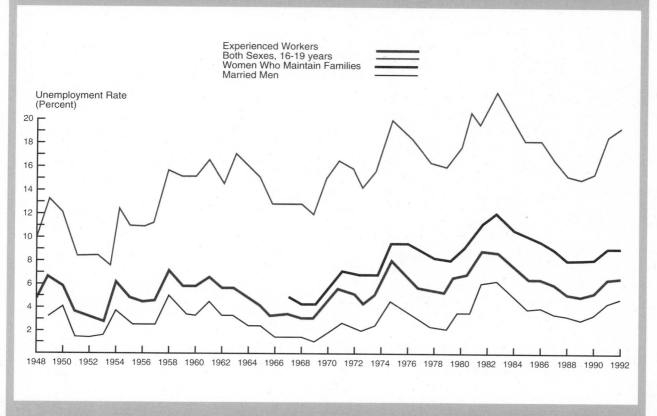

Experienced Workers
Both Sexes, 16-19 years
Women Who Maintain Families
Married Men

Unemployment Rate
(Percent)

Teenagers and women, especially women who maintain families, have experienced high and generally rising unemployment rates. Their share of the labor force has risen. This factor explains some of the rise in the natural rate of unemployment.

The natural rate of unemployment has risen because of the changing labor force, multiple-earners, and improved unemployment benefits.

union unemployment funds. Unemployment benefits and the percentage of the work force covered by unemployment benefits have risen sharply over the past quarter century.

Other factors that have raised the unemployment rate over the years are more difficult to quantify. These factors include minimum wage laws, the effects of the tax system, and how labor markets are organized.

STAGFLATION

Just as the Great Depression of the 1930s motivated Keynes to question the economic theories of the classical economists, the stagflation of the 1970s and early 1980s motivated economists to revise their views of the relationship between inflation and unemployment.

The 1970s and the early 1980s showed that high unemployment and high inflation could occur simultaneously. A new term entered the economist's vocabulary: **stagflation**.

> **Stagflation** is the combination of high unemployment and high inflation.

The stagflation of the 1970s was particularly troubling because it represented the worst of all possible worlds. Journalists and politicians began to speak of a "misery index"—the sum of inflation and unemployment.

The Phillips Curve

Data on the relationship between U.S. inflation and unemployment from 1961 to 1992 (Exhibit 6) show why stagflation surprised economists and politicians in the early 1970s. Prior to the 1970s, high unemployment was usually accompanied by low inflation, and vice versa.

The inflation/unemployment rate combinations for the 1960s are connected with a colored line in Exhibit 6. The 1960s dots show that unemployment fell from 5–7 percent in the early 1960s to 3–4 percent in the late 1960s while inflation rose from 1–2 percent in the early 1960s to 4–5 percent in the late 1960s.

The combination of high unemployment with low inflation (or high inflation with low unemployment) in the 1960s appears logical. At low rates of unemployment, labor markets become "overheated" and push up wage inflation. Conversely, at high rates of unemployment, labor markets are "loose," and wages tend to fall.

The colored line connecting the 1960s dots traces out a negatively sloped curve called the **Phillips curve** (see Gallery of Economists).

> The **Phillips curve** graphs the relationship between the unemployment rate and the inflation rate. Its negative slope for the 1960s suggested a difficult policy choice between inflation and unemployment.

The Phillips curve of the 1960s suggested a tradeoff between inflation and unemployment.

The policy implication of the Phillips curve of the 1960s was that inflation could be eliminated only if society was prepared to tolerate an unemployment rate well above full employment. Inflation was the price of low unemployment!

The Breakdown of the Phillips Curve

Panel (a) of Exhibit 6 shows that the combinations of inflation and unemployment for the 1970s and the 1980s fail to show a neat trade-off between higher inflation and lower unemployment. The colored line connects the years 1969 to 1992. Instead of the neat negative relationship of the colored 1960s line, the colored line of the 1970s and 1980s dissolves into a *swirling pattern*. For the 1970s as a whole, both unemployment and inflation rose together. Commentators of the 1970s proclaimed that the "laws of economics" no longer worked. We will return to panel (b) after a discussion of the new Phillips curve.

The New Phillips Curve

Modern macroeconomics must explain why there is a trade-off between inflation and unemployment in one period and stagflation in another period. Milton Friedman and Edmund S. Phelps provided an explanation: a *tradeoff* will exist *when inflationary expectations are constant*, and *stagflation* will be present when

EXHIBIT 6   Inflation and Unemployment in the United States Since 1960

a. Inflation/Unemployment Combinations

b. Shifts in Short-Run Phillips Curves

Panel (a) plots the inflation/unemployment combinations since 1960. The 1960s are connected with a colored line that shows a negatively sloped Phillips curve. The colored line connecting the 1970s and 1980s reveals a swirling pattern, rather than the expected tradeoff between inflation and unemployment. In panel (b), freehand curves are drawn through the dots for the 1960s, early 1970s, late 1970s, and early 1980s. These curves show shifts in the short-run Phillips curves as inflationary expectations change.

inflationary expectations are rising. With stable inflationary expectations, the inflation-unemployment dots will look like the 1960s. With rising inflationary expectations, there will be a rising pattern of both inflation and unemployment.

Exhibit 7 shows how the relationship between inflation and unemployment depends on whether inflationary expectations are constant or rising. We start with a period in which inflationary expectations are constant. The lower curve labeled PC_0 shows the relationship between inflation and unemployment for a constant anticipated inflation rate of zero percent.

Consider what would happen to unemployment if the inflation rate unexpectedly rises, while people continue to expect zero inflation. The actual inflation rate is higher than the anticipated rate. Many business costs are tied to the expected inflation rate. Wage bargains were struck expecting no inflation. As inflation pushes up the prices of the product the business firm sells, business profits rise. Firms raise their production and unemployment falls. *Higher than expected inflation reduces unemployment.*

The Phillips curve that results when inflationary expectations are constant is called the **short-run Phillips curve**.

The short-run Phillips curve yields a tradeoff between inflation and unemployment because inflationary expectations are constant.

The **short-run Phillips curve** shows the relationship between inflation and unemployment when inflationary expectations are constant. It gives a negative relationship between inflation and unemployment.

EXHIBIT 7   The New Phillips Curve

The economy is initially operating at the natural rate (assumed to be 5 percent) at point c on the Phillips curve PC_0. The actual and anticipated inflation rates are 0 percent. An increase in aggregate demand raises the inflation rate, and the unanticipated inflation moves the economy to point a, where the unemployment rate is 4 percent. If the economy had been instead at point c' with an anticipated inflation rate of 5 percent, the Phillips curve would be PC_5. On PC_5, a 7 percent inflation rate is required to move the economy to point a', where the unemployment rate is again 4 percent.

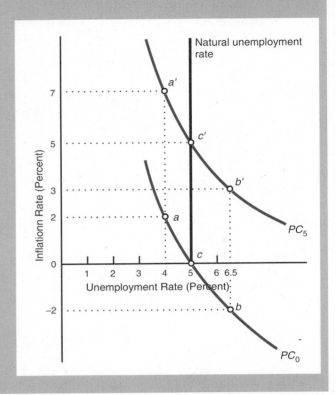

In Exhibit 7, PC_5 is the short-run Phillips curve for a higher anticipated inflation rate of 5 percent. It is drawn *above* the short-run Phillips curve for an anticipated inflation of zero percent, PC_0. If people expect an inflation rate of 5 percent, and the actual inflation rate is greater than 5 percent, output expands and unemployment falls.

Upward Shifts of Short-Run Phillips Curves

An increase in the anticipated inflation rate causes short-run Phillips curves to shift up. As they shift up, both unemployment and inflation rise—the phenomenon of stagflation. Let us consider why this happens.

Recall from Chapter 5 that the natural rate of unemployment occurs where the number of qualified job seekers and the number of vacant jobs are in balance. At the natural rate, people are properly anticipating inflation; they are not caught off guard. As long as inflation is properly anticipated, workers and firms are aware that real wages or the relationship between costs to selling prices are not changing. Business firms know that 20 percent increases in both wages and selling prices do not change the real profitability of employment.

As long as actual and anticipated inflation are the same, there will be no change in output, employment, and unemployment. It makes no difference whether the actual inflation rate is minus 10 percent, zero percent, or plus 10 percent. Anticipated inflation will have no effect on output and unemployment.

Exhibit 7 shows that short-run Phillips curves shift up every time anticipated

> Workers and firms do not change employment or output decisions if there are no changes in real wages or in the ratio of business costs to selling prices. If inflation is correctly anticipated, there will be no change in output or employment.

inflation increases. There is an entire family of short-run Phillips curves—one for each anticipated rate of inflation. We have already shown that inflation greater than the anticipated rate moves the economy up the short-run Phillips curve. Inflation less than anticipated moves the economy down the short-run Phillips curve. When actual inflation is different from anticipated inflation, a tradeoff exists between inflation and unemployment. In the long run, however, the economy comes to anticipate a higher rate of inflation, and the short-run Phillips curve shifts up as anticipated inflation increases.

In Exhibit 7, we began with the economy at the natural rate of unemployment and with people expecting zero inflation. The economy is at point c on PC_0. When the actual inflation rate is 2 percent, the actual inflation rate is 2 percentage points above the anticipated inflation rate. The unemployment rate falls from 5 percent to 4 percent (the movement from c to a). Unexpected inflation pushes the actual unemployment rate below the natural rate.

As inflation continues at 5 percent, people eventually come to anticipate a 5 percent inflation rate. In the long run, new wage and delivery contracts will be agreed to based on the higher (correctly anticipated) inflation rate of 5 percent. Firms that had been encouraged to provide more employment by the unexpected inflation now find that their wages and production costs are rising at the same rate as their selling prices. They accordingly reduce their output and unemployment rises. In terms of the diagram, the short-run Phillips curve shifts up from PC_0 to PC_5 when the economy raises its inflationary expectations from zero percent to 5 percent.

Understanding the Swirls

We are now able to make more sense out of the confusing swirls of panel (a) in Exhibit 6. Four freehand curves are superimposed over the dots in panel (b): one through the dots of the 1960s, one through the dots of the early 1970s and the mid-1980s, one through the dots of the late 1970s, and one through the dots of the early 1980s. The result is four short-run Phillips curves. Each short-run Phillips curve has a negative slope, and each successive one is higher than the previous one. These freehand representations show how the short-run Phillips curves have been shifting upward as inflationary expectations rose from the 1960s to the 1980s. As one would expect, the dots for 1984–91 fall below the 1980–83 short-run Phillips curve. As inflationary expectations fell, there was a drop in the short-run Phillips curve.

Note the tendency for the short-run Phillips curves to shift both up *and* to the right. The rightward shift reflects the above-mentioned increase in the natural rate of unemployment from the 1960s to the 1980s.

POLICY CHOICES

Countries can face a high inflation rate, a high unemployment rate, or both (stagflation). How does a country fight inflation without raising unemployment? How does a country lower unemployment without increasing inflation?

Lowering Inflationary Expectations

The new Phillips-curve analysis suggests that there may be substantial unemployment costs to reducing inflation if expectations are slow to adjust. Anti-inflationary monetary policy will raise the unemployment rate if inflationary expectations do not drop at the same rate as the inflation rate. If actual inflation is below anticipated inflation, unemployment will rise.

How do policymakers lower the anticipated inflation rate without first lowering the inflation rate and causing more unemployment?

There are two proposed solutions. One method requires government-imposed wage and price controls. Such controls will, it is hoped, somehow encourage the public to lower its expectations of inflation. The United States attempted wage and price controls in the early 1970s, but that policy failed because it did not bring down inflationary expectations. Brazil attempted a similar policy in the mid-1980s, but the policy failed because Brazil (like the United States) continued expansionary monetary and fiscal policies. (See Example 2.)

A second method for reducing inflationary expectations is for the government to persuade the public that it will follow a policy of slow monetary growth. The public, upon being convinced of the government's anti-inflation program, then lowers its anticipated inflation rate. The most famous example was the German hyperinflation of the 1920s. The German government announced a monetary reform (changing the monetary unit and balancing the government budget). The government convinced the public that it was serious and the monetary reform ended the hyperinflation without sending the economy into a deep recession.

To limit the unemployment costs of reducing inflation, inflationary expectations must fall rapidly.

The Unemployment Costs of Lowering Inflation

Unless the public can somehow be convinced to lower their inflationary expectations immediately, an anti-inflationary program will raise unemployment. It will also raise interest rates. Any program that raises both unemployment and interest rates will likely face political opposition.

Exhibit 8 illustrates this problem. The economy is initially operating at the natural rate of unemployment (5 percent) with an inflation rate of 10 percent. Actual and anticipated inflation are equal. How can the economy move from a high rate of inflation to a zero rate of inflation without raising unemployment (how can it move from c' to c)?

According to the new-Phillips-curve analysis, getting from c' to c is very difficult because inflationary *expectations* must be beaten down to zero percent! If expectations are adaptive, there will be a number of years in which the actual rate of inflation is less than the anticipated rate. But unemployment will rise when actual inflation is below anticipated inflation.

During the period when actual inflation is less than anticipated inflation, the path of the economy might look something like the curve $c'bc$. The economy starts at c' with inflation at 10 percent, unemployment at 5 percent, and the anticipated inflation rate at 10 percent. When contractionary policies are applied, the economy moves to point b. At the intermediate point b, the unemployment rate has risen to 8 percent and the inflation rate has dropped to 4 percent, but the anticipated inflation rate is 8 percent. Unemployment above the natural rate has been caused by an anticipated rate of inflation higher than actual inflation. The hardships of unemployment at point b are considerable. As the inflation rate continues to drop towards zero percent, inflationary expectations will continue to drop. Once the economy reaches point c, the natural rate of unemployment is restored, and the actual and anticipated rates of inflation are both zero percent.

Gradualism

To move from c' to c in Exhibit 8 requires an extreme contractionary monetary policy. Even if this contraction is accomplished all at once—say, monetary growth

EXAMPLE 2

The Nixon Wage/Price Controls

It has been suggested that one way to defeat rising inflationary expectations is for the government to impose wage and price controls. When the government controls wages and prices, people will know that inflation is "under control" and will begin to expect lower prices. The experience with wage and price controls from August 1971 to April 1974 demonstrates why wage and price controls do not work.

On August 15, 1971, President Richard Nixon announced a 90-day freeze on almost all wages and prices. Controls were introduced because stagflation was beginning to rear its ugly head. The 5.1 percent inflation rate from 1969 to 1971 appeared alarming and the unemployment rate had roughly doubled between 1969 and 1971. It was hoped that controls would reduce inflationary expectations, leaving the government free to fight unemployment.

The controls program ran through four phases and was dismantled in late 1973 and early 1974. Phase I was the 90-day freeze from which only taxes, mortgage interest rates, and raw agricultural commodities were exempted. Phase II began in November 1971. A Pay Board was established that set a standard for wage increases of 5.5 percent per year with certain exceptions. Phase III began in January 1973. The Pay and Price Boards were abolished; the 5.5 percent wage-increase standard was retained, but standards for passing on cost increases were loosened. Inflation accelerated alarmingly during Phase III, and a second freeze was announced in June of 1973. The second freeze froze prices but not wages! Phase IV went into effect in August 1973; the standards and regulations of this phase were very much like those of Phases II and III. On April 30, 1974, the president's authority to control wages and prices lapsed, and the experiment with wage/price controls ended.

What happened to inflation and unemployment during this period? During Phase I prices were basically unchanged. During Phase II the inflation rate averaged 3.6 percent. There was an alarming resurgence of inflation during Phase III—inflation rose to 9.1 percent. At the end of the controls program (1974), the inflation rate was 9.4 percent. In the two years after controls were lifted (1975 and 1976), inflation averaged 5.9 percent. During the controls program unemployment remained between 5 percent and 6 percent. After the controls were lifted, the unemployment rate rose to 8.5 percent.

The controls program failed to meet its objective to bring down inflation and unemployment at the same time. Economists who have studied the controls program conclude that the controls likely held down the inflation rate somewhat when they were in effect, but they raised the inflation rate when the controls were removed. The controls did not hold down inflationary expectations because the public was aware that wages and prices would play a game of catch-up after the controls were lifted.

SOURCE: Alan Blinder, *Economic Policy and the Great Stagflation* (New York: Academic Press, 1979), chaps. 3 and 6.

---

is cut from 13 percent to a permanent 3 percent—the economy may require 3 to 5 years to complete its adjustment. During these years, the economy would have to endure considerable unemployment. A gradualist policy might reduce unemployment costs. Instead of reducing the growth of money supply from 13 percent to 3 percent all at once, monetary authorities might do it gradually over a period of, say, 5 years. Moreover, in order to persuade the public to lower its expectations about inflation, the monetary authorities would announce in advance the scheduled reductions in the rate of monetary growth. If expectations are rational, when people believe the government policy announcements they will immediately lower the anticipated rate of inflation. If the people do not believe the government's

EXHIBIT 8 The Unemployment Costs of Reducing Inflation

The economy is initially operating at point c′—at the natural rate of 5 percent unemployment with an anticipated inflation rate of 10 percent (which equals the actual inflation rate.) Monetary authorities reduce the growth of the money supply, and the rate of inflation begins to slow down. The economy begins to move along the curve c′bc. Point b is a representative intermediate point: at b, the inflation rate is 4 percent, but the anticipated inflation rate is 8 percent; unemployment is 10 percent. Until the expected rate of inflation falls to 0 percent, the economy will continue to experience unemployment above the natural rate.

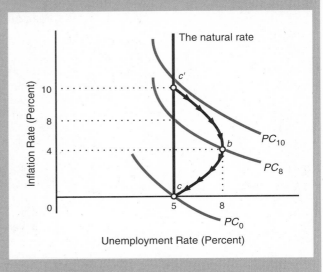

Gradualism may reduce the unemployment costs of reducing inflation.

monetary-growth plans (they may have long ago lost faith in such pronouncements), the anticipated inflation rate will drop only when people see the actual inflation rate dropping.

Human-Resource Policies

The stagflation policy problem has been made more difficult by the long-run rise in the unemployment rate. The changing composition of the labor force, multiple-earner families, unemployment benefits, and a variety of other factors explain this increase. Governments can use **human-resource policy** to limit the rise in the natural rate of unemployment.

> **Human-resource policy** is the use of government training programs and unemployment services to lower the natural rate of unemployment.

Human-resource policy aims at reversing long-run trends that have raised the natural rate of unemployment over time. Human-resource policies—such as government-sponsored vocational training programs, jobs corps, and government employment commissions—aim at improving the efficiency of labor markets and providing job skills to those with limited training and experience. If human-resource programs are successful, the rightward shift of the short-run Phillips curve would be halted, and policymakers would be less likely to try to hold the actual unemployment rate below the natural rate.

The last two chapters discussed inflation and unemployment and have suggested possible policies to deal with inflation without driving up unemployment. If the problem of inflation were solved, the economy would still be subject to ups and downs in unemployment because of the business cycle. The next chapter explores how the business cycle can be stabilized.

The Case for Zero Inflation

Since the early 1980s, the United States has experienced inflation rates between 3 percent and 5 percent. It is clear that double-digit inflation, such as that experienced in the mid- and late 1970s, is destructive and should be avoided. Is moderate inflation, however, a sufficient worry to warrant adopting policies to achieve zero inflation?

Proponents of zero inflation make the following arguments:

1. Even moderate inflation causes people to engage in economically unproductive activities, such as investing in land or precious metals, instead of making more productive investments in plant and equipment. These unproductive activities reduce economic efficiency and growth.

2. Through the tax system, moderate inflation reduces long-term gains on invested capital. An investment that has earned 20 percent over a four-year period, earns virtually nothing after adjustment for moderate inflation, especially after investment earnings have been taxed.

3. Moderate inflation causes price system distortions. When prices are generally rising, information on relative prices becomes obscured. People do not know what the cheapest input combinations are or what the best buys are. When the price level is stable, however, people can be well informed about relative prices and make "good" economic decisions.

4. There is no long-run tradeoff between unemployment and inflation.

Advocates of zero inflation also point to the empirical finding that inflation tends to be negatively related to economic growth. The economies of countries with high inflation grow more slowly than those with low inflation. Proponents cite this finding as evidence that countries should aim for a zero rate of inflation.

Chapter Summary

The most important point to learn from this chapter is: Stagflation (the combination of high unemployment and high inflation) occurs when inflationary expectations are rising. Stagflation is therefore cured by lowering inflationary expectations. If inflationary expectations cannot be lowered quickly, unemployment will remain high while inflation is falling.

1. There are two types of inflation: demand-side, in which the aggregate demand curve shifts to the right; and supply-side, in which the short-run aggregate supply curve shifts rightward.

2. Higher anticipated inflation rates raise normal interest rates. The adaptive expectations hypothesis states that people base their anticipated inflation rate on past experience; the rational expectations hypothesis states that people use both past information and projected policy effects to anticipate inflation.

3. Unemployment arises because it is difficult to match people to jobs. The natural rate of unemployment has risen because of the changing composition of the labor force,

the increase in the number of multiple-earner families, and increased unemployment insurance.

4. Stagflation is the combination of high unemployment and high inflation. Modern macroeconomic theory says that the Phillips curve will shift up with the anticipated rate of inflation.

5. The short-run Phillips curve shows a negative relationship between inflation and unemployment when inflationary expectations are constant.

6. It may be possible to lower the anticipated rate of inflation by using price and wage controls or a preannounced policy of monetary restraint, but such policies are difficult to implement. Inflation can be reduced by permanently lowering the rate of growth of the money supply, but until inflationary expectations fall, the unemployment rate will rise. The unemployment costs of fighting inflation can extend over a period of years. Gradualism is one solution to the problem of fighting inflation without creating too much unemployment in the process. Human-resource policies could be applied to reduce the natural rate of unemployment.

> *Policy Focus:* **Zero inflation will cause more productive investments, increase gains on invested capital, and limit price-system distortions. If there is no long-run tradeoff between inflation and unemployment, the case for zero inflation is even stronger.**

Key Terms

demand-side inflation (p. 248)
supply-side inflation (p. 248)
nominal interest rate (p. 252)
real interest rate (p. 252)
adaptive expectations (p. 253)
rational expectations (p. 253)

wage/price spiral (p. 254)
stagflation (p. 258)
Phillips curve (p. 258)
short-run Phillips curve (p. 259)
human-resource policy (p. 264)

Questions and Problems

1. The owner of the apartment you are renting complains: "Wages, utilities, and other costs are rising too rapidly. I have no choice but to raise your rent." Is this increase in price a case of supply-side inflation?

2. Economists classify inflation as either supply-side inflation or demand-side inflation. Using aggregate supply-and-demand analysis, explain the differences between these two types of inflation. Is it possible to distinguish between the two types of inflation from observed information on output, employment, and prices?

3. How does the rational expectations hypothesis differ from the adaptive expectations hypothesis? If the Fed reduces monetary growth during a period of rapid inflation, would adaptive expectations or rational expectations be expected to cause a more rapid drop in inflation?

4. Using aggregate supply-and-demand analysis, explain why supply-side inflation combines the worst of two worlds: more inflation and higher unemployment.

5. The wage/price spiral is blamed on friction between unions and management and on expansionary economic policy. Explain why it is difficult to accurately assign the blame for the wage/price spiral.

6. Imagine an economy with only one person (Robinson Crusoe). Would there be any unemployment? Why or why not?

7. Give three reasons why the natural rate of unemployment has been increasing.

8. Explain why the short-run Phillips curve shows a negative relationship between inflation and unemployment. Explain why the Phillips curve would shift up.

9. What happens to the unemployment rate in the following situations?
   a. Initially, the anticipated rate of inflation is 5 percent, and the actual rate of inflation is also 5 percent.
   b. In the next period, there is an unexpected decline in the inflation rate to 2 percent.
   c. In the following period, inflationary expectations

drop to 2 percent, and the actual inflation rate is also 2 percent.

10. You observe two economies: one has a 20 percent nominal interest rate, the other has a 5 percent nominal interest rate. Which economy would you expect to have the higher inflation rate? Why?

11. Why might lowering the inflation rate be more difficult politically than raising the inflation rate?

Doing Economics

The theory of the Phillips curve asserts that, for fixed inflationary expectations, a higher rate of inflation occurs when the unemployment rate is low, and lower inflation is associated with a high unemployment rate. This theory is almost always tested by looking at the behavior of national inflation and unemployment rates over time. However, under certain assumptions, the theory might also apply across geographic regions. What assumptions are necessary to extend the Phillips curve theory to imply that cities with higher inflation rates will have lower unemployment rates than those in which prices are rising less quickly? The Bureau of Labor Statistics publishes both a consumer price index and unemployment rates for major cities in the United States. Choose a sample of at least ten large cities across the United States and collect data for a recent year on their local rates of inflation and unemployment. You can find these data in appropriate issues of *Monthly Labor Review,* which can be found in the Government Documents section of most large libraries. Using graph paper or the graphics software in a computer spreadsheet program, plot your observations for cities with the inflation rate on the vertical axis and the unemployment rate on the horizontal axis. In your sample, do you find a negative relationship between inflation and unemployment? If not, can you explain this result in terms of the assumptions you identified above?

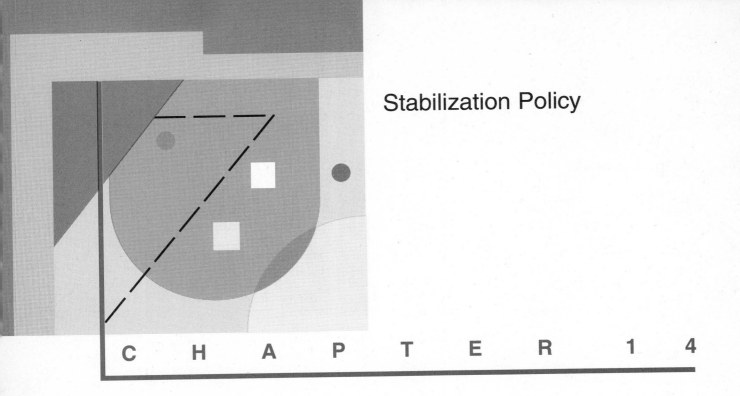

Stabilization Policy

C H A P T E R   1 4

CHAPTER FOCUS   The most controversial question in macroeconomics today is how to stabilize business cycles. Economists agree generally about many things, but there are two issues on which they disagree: how to control inflation and how to control unemployment. The average person also worries about these issues and looks to policymakers and economists for answers.

Keynesian economics created the expectation that the government should stabilize the business cycle through activist monetary and fiscal policy. In the 1960s, there was even talk of activist policy being so efficient as to eliminate entirely the business cycle. Belief in the government's ability to manage the business cycle has been shaken over the past decade. A number of economists now question whether we would be better off without activist policy.

After studying this chapter, you will be able to:

- Explain what activism and nonactivism mean.
- Present the activist case for discretionary policy and offer supporting evidence.
- Present the nonactivist case for rules and offer supporting evidence.
- Understand the role of the self-correcting mechanism in the activist-nonactivist debate.
- Discuss whether U.S. policymakers have used activism or nonactivism and explain why.

THE POLICY OPTIONS

Activism

Activist policy deliberately manipulates fiscal and monetary policies to iron out fluctuations in the business cycle.

> An **activist policy** selects monetary and fiscal policy according to perceived economic conditions, which in turn change as economic conditions change.

Activist policy does not include the use of built-in fiscal stabilizers (like progressive taxes or unemployment compensation) that change automatically with the business cycle. Activist policy includes deliberate changes in monetary or fiscal policy undertaken to soften the business cycle. Few economists argue for frequent policy changes in response to every change in the business cycle. Policy should be adjusted only in response to major movements in real GDP and inflation.

Activists argue that the economic costs of inaction are too high.

Nonactivism

The major spokesperson for nonactivism, Milton Friedman, argues for stable monetary and fiscal rules that do not change with economic circumstances. Nonactivists believe that attempts to deliberately manage monetary and fiscal policy are ineffective and even harmful; they argue that **nonactivist policy** will yield macroeconomic results that are superior to those of activism.

> A **nonactivist policy** is independent of prevailing economic conditions and is held steady when economic conditions change.

Friedman's proposal for nonactivism has two parts:

1. There should be a fixed monetary rule that requires constant (or nearly constant) growth of the money supply year after year at a rate equal to the long-run average growth rate of real GDP.
2. The federal budget should be balanced over the business cycle. Surpluses

Robert Lucas (1937–   )

Robert Lucas was born in Yakima, Washington. His B.A. degree in history and Ph.D. in economics were both from the University of Chicago, and, in 1978, it was to that university that he returned to teach. Lucas edited the influential *Journal of Political Economy* and created a new school of macroeconomics. The New Classical Economics argued that activism is likely to be ineffective. Lucas' theories are summarized in his *Studies in Business-Cycle Theory*, published in 1981.

Lucas applied the rational expectations theory of J. F. Muth to the macroeconomy and used it to explain why Keynesian monetary and fiscal policies were largely ineffective during the early 1970s. In a 1961 article, Muth had presented the idea of rational expectations to show how the prices of stocks or commodities traded on speculative markets reflect all available information. When, for example, an orange freeze threatens to reduce the supply of oranges, or if there is going to be a large increase in IBM's profits, speculators have this information, and prices will rise immediately to reflect these developments.

According to modern macroeconomics, monetary and fiscal policies affect output and employment by creating unanticipated inflation or deflation. Yet Lucas argued that people do their best to avoid being surprised by price changes caused by monetary and fiscal policies. They use all the information available about impending policy actions and their effects on the economy. If people's rational expectations concerning the effects of policy actions are correct, price changes will be anticipated, and activist policy will have no effect on output and employment.

Writing with Thomas Sargent, Lucas commented on policy during the 1970s: ". . . the inflationary bias on average of monetary and fiscal policy during this period should . . . have produced the lowest average unemployment rates for any decade since the 1940s. In fact, as we know, they produced the highest unemployment since the 1930s. This was . . . failure on a grand scale."

Nonactivists favor fixed monetary growth and a balanced budget over the business cycle.

during the recovery phase should cancel out deficits during the recession stage. Government spending should be dictated by the need for public spending and not by the needs of discretionary fiscal policy.

Nonactivists argue that stable monetary and fiscal rules provide the proper setting for long-run economic stability. Stable rules would rule out major surprises and policy mistakes. Recessions and inflations would be cured by wage and price adjustments (the self-correcting mechanism), and the economy would experience stable growth without excessive inflation or unemployment.

Self-Correction Versus Demand Management

The choice between activism and nonactivism can be illustrated using the now-familiar tools of aggregate demand and aggregate supply. Exhibit 1 shows an economy (at point *a*) that is in a deflationary gap—producing below the natural level of output. The short-run aggregate supply curve is upward sloping, meaning that an increase in aggregate demand would bring higher prices. The goal is to return the economy to the natural level of output, y_n. Panel (a) shows the ideal activist approach. In response to the prevailing deflationary gap ($y < y_n$), expansionary monetary and fiscal policies are applied. Aggregate demand increases from AD to AD'. The economy moves up the short-run aggregate supply curve from *a* to *e′*, and the economy returns to producing the natural level of output y_n. The increase in aggregate demand has raised the price level (from p to p').

EXHIBIT 1   The Policy Options

a. Activist Policy

b. Nonactivist Policy

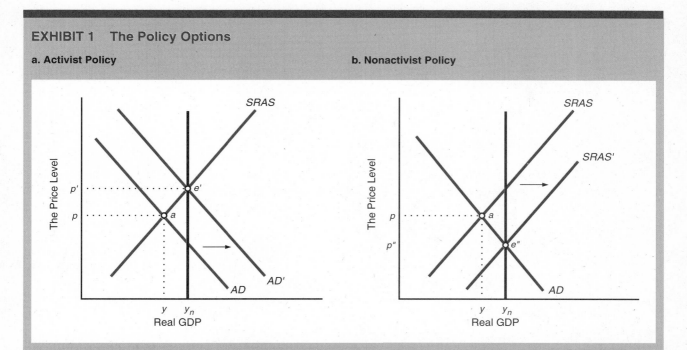

Panel (a) shows how activist policy can be used to eliminate a deflationary gap. The economy is initially operating at point a in a deflationary gap. Expansionary monetary or fiscal policy increases aggregate demand (shifting AD to AD'), causing the economy to produce a greater output y_n and the price level to rise from p to p'.

Panel (b) shows the nonactivist approach to restoring equilibrium through the self-correcting mechanism. The economy is initially operating at point a in a deflationary gap. As a consequence of operating below the natural level of output, the price level falls, and firms supply more output. The short-run aggregate supply curve shifts to the right, from $SRAS$ to $SRAS'$. The price level continues to fall until the natural level of output is restored, so the aggregate supply shifts until the economy reaches point e'', where it is producing y_n at the new price level p''.

Panel (b) shows how nonactivism (working through the self-correcting mechanism) raises output and employment to the natural level. Because the economy is producing less than y_n, the price level falls. As prices and wages fall, short-run aggregate supply increases from $SRAS$ to $SRAS'$. The economy is restored to producing y_n, and the price level has fallen from p to p''.

Activism eliminates a deflationary gap by raising aggregate demand. Nonactivism works through deflation's effect on aggregate supply.

As these diagrams show, both activism and nonactivism (if followed properly) yield the same output result: the economy produces the natural level of output. In the activist case, there has been an increase in the price level (from p to p'). In the nonactivist (self-correcting) case, the price level has fallen (from p to p''). The following discussion focuses on the pros and cons of the activist and nonactivist approaches when applied to real policy choices.

POLICY INSTRUMENTS AND ACTIVISM

The two major activist **policy instruments** are monetary policy and fiscal policy. Monetary policy deliberately controls the money supply (and sometimes credit conditions) for the purpose of achieving macroeconomic goals. Fiscal policy deliberately controls government spending and taxation for the purpose of achieving macroeconomic goals.

> The **policy instruments** are the money supply, tax rates, and discretionary government spending.

The presence of more than one policy instrument means that policymakers may be able to select the appropriate blend of monetary growth, credit restrictions, government-spending level, and tax rates to achieve their macroeconomic goals.

Monetary Policy

Monetary policy is conducted by the Fed. As noted in the chapter on monetary policy, the Fed was designed to be insulated from current political pressures, but its independence is not complete. Although the Fed must consider major political factors, it is generally agreed that the Fed is more independent of political pressures than the president, the Treasury, or the Congress. The Fed can act quickly and quietly to change the money supply. The Fed can buy or sell government securities daily or once a year, largely hidden from public view. On a more visible level, the Fed can raise or lower the discount rate, change reserve requirements, and even impose credit controls. The Fed's control of the money supply is not perfect (especially in the short run), but the Fed does possess the flexibility to change monetary policy on short notice.

The Fed has sufficient flexibility and independence to conduct monetary policy.

Fiscal Policy

The two instruments of fiscal policy are discretionary government spending and tax policy. The president submits spending budgets to Congress, but only Congress can authorize actual spending. The president must either sign or veto the spending bills approved by Congress. The president does not have the authority to cut out parts of approved spending packages; instead, the president must accept or reject the entire bill. On occasion, the president can decide not to spend the money authorized by Congress (called *impounding*), but the constitutional legality of this practice is questionable, and Congress can force the spending of appropriated funds. Although Congress has sought to develop procedures for gearing the total amount of federal spending to specific macroeconomic goals, this approach has never worked out well. Given the current appropriation system, it is very difficult to conduct macroeconomic policy by manipulating federal-government spending.

Congress has the final word on tax policy. Tax proposals can be made by the Treasury or can originate within Congress. The tax system is very complex and is influenced by special-interest groups. Congress has succeeded in passing a number of tax bills specifically designed to achieve macroeconomic goals. Taxes were lowered in 1964, 1975, and 1981 for the purpose of stimulating economic activity. The tax reform passed in 1986 was designed to change tax rates and deductions rather than to manipulate aggregate demand. (See Example 1.)

Congress has not used control of federal spending to achieve macroeconomic goals. Tax changes have been used to achieve macroeconomic goals.

Because of Fed independence and the flexibility of open-market operations, the money supply is the most flexible policy instrument. Monetary policy is the most frequently used instrument of activist policy because of its greater flexibility and independence. Because of the inflexibility and uncontrollability of federal spending, the major instrument of fiscal policy has been tax policy.

Matching Policies to Macroeconomic Goals

There is no single goal of macroeconomic policy. Everyone agrees that it would be desirable to have full employment, stable prices, and steady real-GDP growth.

Economic Policymaking

This text continually refers to economic policymakers. Who exactly are the economic policymakers? On the executive side, the principal policymakers are the Fed, the Treasury, the Office of Management and Budget, the Council of Economic Advisors, and the White House staff. The Treasury is responsible for debt management, the balance of payments, and for estimating government revenues. The Office of Management and Budget prepares the annual budget and coordinates government expenditures. The Council of Economic Advisors estimates GDP growth and advises the president on economic affairs. On the congressional side, several committees in the House and Senate, a joint committee, and congressional leaders are responsible for economic policy. The House Ways and Means Committee is responsible for revenue bills and social security. The House Appropriations Committee is responsible for government expenditures. The House Banking, Finance, and Urban Affairs Committee is responsible for price control legislation, and the House Education and Labor Committee is responsible for human-resource policy. In the Senate, the Finance Committee and the Appropriations Committee are the two most important economic policymaking bodies.

The Fed conducts monetary policy on an ongoing basis through open-market operations, and periodic changes in reserve requirements and discount rates. Initiatives for tax reform are prepared by the Department of the Treasury for action by various House and Senate subcommittees. The Federal budgeting process begins with the formulation and submission of the president's budget to Congress according to the following schedule:

The Federal Budget Process

A minimum lead time of 20 months is required between the planning and execution of the federal budget. This lag makes it difficult to conduct discretionary fiscal policy. Final data trickle in throughout the following year; e.g., final GDP data are in 9 months after the year ends.

Everyone agrees that it would be desirable to avoid the ups and downs of the business cycle (especially the downs). Businesses and families prefer low interest rates. In the international arena, most people would like to avoid extreme fluctuations in the international value of the dollar and would like to achieve stable and growing world trade.

The full-employment target was established as a national economic goal by the Employment Act of 1946. Although politicians understand that people generally do not like high inflation rates (and the accompanying high interest rates), price stability has not been a legislative goal that legally binds policymakers. In making decisions on macroeconomic policy, politicians must be conscious not only of the economic health of the nation but also of their election prospects.

Rather than pursuing one single goal, macroeconomic policy aims to achieve a combination of goals: full employment combined with reasonable price stability and steady economic growth; equilibrium in our trade dealings with other countries; avoiding recessions and inflationary booms.

Policymakers pursue a combination of economic goals.

THE CASE FOR ACTIVISM

The main conflict between the activists and nonactivists is whether or not deliberate monetary and fiscal policy should be used to stabilize the economy. Modern Keynesians support an activist policy.

The Costs of Lost Output

Modern Keynesian economists do not deny the self-correcting mechanism. They acknowledge that the private economy automatically moves to the natural rate of unemployment in the long run without activist monetary or fiscal policy. Even Keynes believed that in the long run the economy would tend toward full employment.

In spite of the self-correcting mechanism, modern Keynesian economists assert that sharp fluctuations in real GDP and employment will naturally occur if monetary and fiscal policy are held constant. The economy is subject to all kinds of shocks. Investment is naturally unstable because of changing expectations; supply shocks can disrupt the economy; unpredictable shifts in consumer demand take place. Changes in spending cause magnified changes in real GDP and unemployment through the multiplier. If the economy is beset by adverse supply shocks, both unemployment and prices can be pushed up.

Modern Keynesians support activism because it is too costly to wait for the self-correcting mechanism.

The modern Keynesian rationale for activist stabilization policy is that *waiting for the economy to cure itself by wage and price adjustments (the self-correcting mechanism) is too costly.* As Keynes remarked, "In the long run, we are all dead."

When the economy experiences an adverse shock, it operates below full employment. In addition to the private anguish of unemployment, society must bear a social cost—the cost of lost output. If the economy had been able to remain at full employment, a larger real GDP would have been produced. The **GDP gap** measures this loss of output.

The objective of activist policy is to limit the private and social costs of unemployed resources by speeding the adjustment toward full employment.

> The **GDP gap** is the difference between current GDP and *potential GDP* (the output the economy would conceivably have produced at full employment).

The GDP gap is the price society must pay while waiting for the self-correcting mechanism to work. In the Keynesian view, the economy can be restored to the natural rate quicker by using activist monetary and fiscal policies.

Modern Keynesians believe that the self-correcting mechanism is sluggish. They point to the Great Depression when real wages actually rose in the U.S. after 1932 even though there was massive unemployment. They point to the experience of England during the Great Depression when money wages refused to fall despite massive unemployment.

Modern Keynesians point to a number of wage and price inflexibilities in today's economies. Wages set in multiyear contracts are not free to respond to changing economic conditions. Moreover, laid-off union workers often wait to be recalled to former jobs rather than searching for a new job. By not searching for new jobs, they do not depress wages generally throughout the economy. Prices are also subject to rigidities. Oil and natural gas prices have been set by long-term delivery contracts. Prices of many industrial raw materials are fixed in long-term contacts with suppliers.

Important wages and prices are not free to respond to market conditions. In modern economies, key wages and many prices are set in long-term contracts, not in **auction markets**.

> In an **auction market** the market price is renegotiated on a regular basis.

For example, the prices of stocks are determined in auction markets (the various stock exchanges) in which prices are renegotiated virtually every minute. The wage rate of day laborers who gather at hiring halls is determined every morning. Most basic commodities (wheat, cotton, coffee, sugar, corn, soybeans, cattle, oats, gold, silver) are bought and sold in auction markets.

Activists believe that wage and price rigidities slow down the self-correcting mechanism.

Whenever wages and other input prices are set in long-term contracts, they are not free to change when economic conditions change. When wages and prices are not free to fall, the self-correcting mechanism will restore the economy to full employment slowly.

Activism Versus Nonactivism

Proponents of activism admit that discretionary activist policy is difficult to devise. They readily admit that mistakes have been made in the past and that mistakes will be made in the future. Activists have never promised perfect activist policy. Rather, they mainly argue that imperfect activist policy is superior to a do-nothing policy. The best criterion for judging activism is whether it has produced results better than those that have been produced by nonactivism.

Especially from the 1960s on, a variety of activist policies were used to combat the business cycle. Discretionary monetary and fiscal policies attempted to soften unemployment and inflation. Yet the last 30 years have seen considerable unemployment, recessions, inflation, and even stagflation.

Keynesians cite two pieces of evidence in support of activism. First, the historical data show that, while the business cycle has not been eliminated, it has become less severe since activist policies came into use. Exhibit 2 plots the annual rates of growth of real GNP and unemployment rates from 1890 to 1992. It is clear that since the 1950s, fluctuations have been significantly smaller than in preceding periods. Second, advocates of activism point to the successful use of tax cuts in 1964 and 1981 to create the prolonged expansions of the 1960s and 1980s.

Activists point to the smaller business cycles of recent years and to the success of tax cuts to support activism.

Activists argue that there is no way to know how the economy will behave if policymakers commit themselves to fixed rules. With a cyclically balanced budget rule, what would happen if a severe recession drove down government revenues? How would one know when to suspend a balanced-budget rule? With fixed-monetary-growth rules, how should the Fed respond to unforeseen types of new monies that the banking system is so good at creating? Would we be able to suspend the fixed-monetary-growth rule in a national emergency? In effect,

EXHIBIT 2 GDP Growth and Unemployment in the United States

a. The Annual Rate of Growth of Real GDP

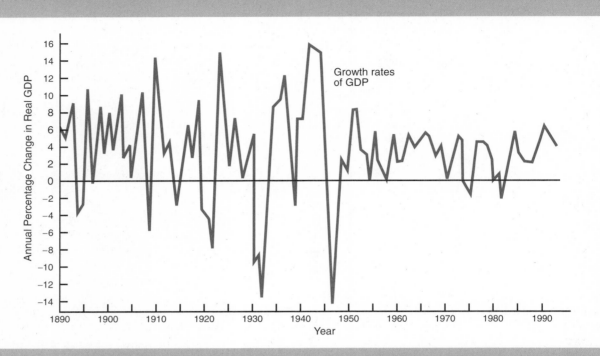

b. The Unemployment Rate

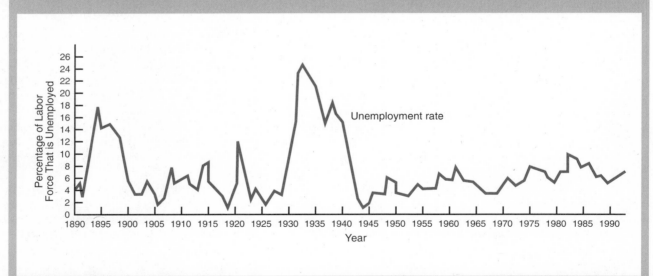

Both the GDP growth rate in panel (a) and the unemployment data in panel (b) show less cyclical volatility after 1948. Panel (c) shows the monetary growth was more stable after 1948.

Chapter 14   Stabilization Policy

EXHIBIT 2   GDP Growth and Unemployment in the United States *(Continued)*

c. The Annual Growth Rate of the Money Supply in the United States

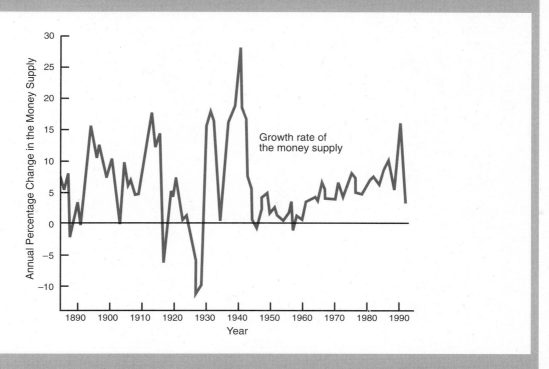

SOURCES: *Historical Statistics of the United States; Economic Report of the President; Survey of Current Business; Federal Reserve Bulletin.* The percentage growth rate in money supply is based on M1 for the years from 1915 to 1981 and includes time deposits (formerly M2) for the years from 1890 to 1915.

activists argue that nonactivism represents uncharted waters for a complex, modern economy. The unknown risks of nonactivism may be great.

THE CASE FOR NONACTIVISM

Nonactivists fall into two related groups: **monetarists** and **rational expectations economists**. Monetarists want fixed monetary growth; rational expectations economists hold that monetary or fiscal policy has unpredictable effects on the economy and is incapable of controlling the business cycle.

> **Monetarists** advocate a policy of constant monetary growth, such as 3 percent growth in the money supply per year.

> **Rational expectations economists** maintain that anticipated monetary and fiscal policies cannot stabilize the economy.

Monetarists and rational-expectationists believe that it is better to do nothing in the face of demand and supply shocks and to let the self-correcting mechanism work without interference.

The monetarists, led by Milton Friedman, maintain that activist policies either fail to improve the business cycle or actually make the cycle worse. The rational expectations school, led by Robert Lucas (see Gallery of Economists), maintains that activist policies affect only inflation, not unemployment. Activist policies can make inflation better or worse but have no lasting effect on reducing real GDP fluctuations.

The Difficulty of Devising Activist Policy

Monetarists argue that countercyclical policy historically has failed to soften the business cycle. *Instead, activist policies have actually made the business cycle worse.* Monetarists give three reasons why activist policy has served to worsen the business cycle.

1. *There are long and variable lags in the effect of money on the economy.* If monetary authorities decide to combat a rising unemployment rate by increasing the growth of the money supply, the effect on real output and unemployment will not be immediate. Milton Friedman's own research shows that there is a lag of 6 months to 2 years before changes in money supply affect GDP. Thus, monetary authorities can never be sure when the change in money supply will begin to affect real output and employment. If the lag is short, the chances are less that the monetary policy will be inappropriate, but if the lag is long (say, 2 years), the policy may be the wrong one when the effects take place.

2. *It is difficult for policymakers to know if the economy is entering a recession.* Because of the lagged effects of activist policy, it is very important to be able to anticipate changes in the business cycle. If policymakers knew 6 months in advance, for example, that a recession was coming, it would be much easier to devise countercyclical policy. But recessions vary in length and in predictability. Through computer models of the economy and various early-warning measures, policymakers attempt to anticipate recessions, but there are no accurate guides to the future course of the economy. When activist monetary and fiscal policies are carried out at the wrong time, they destabilize the economy. Monetarists believe policymakers do not possess sufficient information to diagnose and cure the disease before it spontaneously corrects itself. By acting without adequate information, authorities may actually use the wrong medicine and make the patient even worse.

3. *Activist policies can aim for the wrong target.* The appropriate target of activist policy is the natural rate of unemployment. If the economy is operating with an unemployment rate above the natural rate, expansionary policies can lower unemployment without accelerating inflation. But policymakers may not know what the natural rate is at any point in time. The natural rate varies with changes in the composition of the labor force, raw material prices and labor-force behavior. Because the natural rate itself fluctuates, it is difficult to achieve it with deliberate policy actions.

The Counterproductive Effects of Activism

Exhibit 2 shows that the swings of the business cycle have narrowed in the postwar period—after activist policies came to be used. The trauma of the Great Depression has not been repeated. The fact that further great depressions have been

EXAMPLE 2

The Policy Blunders of the 1930s

Nonactivists point to the policy blunders of the 1930s as a reason for relying on fixed rules rather than discretion. The policy blunders of the 1930s were as follows.

1. From 1929 to 1933, the nominal supply of money (MI) fell 25 percent. The price level also fell nearly 25 percent. Therefore, there was no change in the real money supply, even though an increase in the real money supply was needed to get the economy moving again. If monetary policy had been stable in the early 1930s, falling prices would have increased the real money supply; the economy would not have fallen into the Great Depression.

2. As Nobel Prize winners James Tobin and Milton Friedman have pointed out, various government actions taken by Roosevelt's New Deal program raised wages and prices after 1933 amid massive unemployment, even though the self-correcting mechanism required falling wages and prices. The New Deal increased the power of labor unions, gave more monopoly power to business firms, and encouraged them to raise prices. In short, from 1933 to 1936, a supply-side inflation in the middle of a deep depression retarded the move toward full employment.

3. In 1937, in an incredible act of self-destruction, the Federal Reserve System doubled reserve requirements. The banking system did have large excess reserves at the time, but excess reserves were being held by banks because of the prevailing economic situation. Accordingly, the increase in the reserve requirement brought the needed money growth to a halt and sent the economy into another recession within the Great Depression.

4. Large tax increases were passed in 1932 and 1937 during periods of massive unemployment.

The nonactivists blame these four policy blunders for the Great Depression. They believe that if policymakers had pursued a policy of steady monetary growth and nonintervention in wage and price determination, the Great Depression would have been avoided.

SOURCES: James Tobin, "Inflation and Unemployment," *American Economic Review* 62 (March 1972): p. 14; Milton Friedman, *Dollars and Deficits* (Englewood Cliffs, NJ: Prentice Hall, 1968).

avoided is an important argument for activism, but the monetarists do not share this view. They believe that activist policy blunders caused the Great Depression in the first place. The Great Depression would not have occurred had a hands-off policy been followed by monetary and fiscal authorities. (See Example 2.)

While Keynesians maintain that activist countercyclical policy is responsible for reducing business fluctuations after the Second World War, monetarists argue that greater cyclical stability is a consequence *not* of countercyclical policies but of a more stable money-supply growth.

The monetarists evidence is presented in Exhibit 2c, which shows the annual growth rate of the money supply since 1890. The reduced range of GDP fluctuations coincides with the sharply reduced range of money-supply growth. The greater relative stability over the past 40 years may not be the result of activist policy but of the increased stability of the growth of the money supply.

If the business cycle is caused by fluctuations in the growth of money supply, cyclical instability can be reduced by eliminating the unstable monetary growth. This conclusion is the rationale for Friedman's 3 percent rule that monetary authorities should expand the money supply at a constant rate year in and year out and that monetary authorities should be denied the use of activist monetary policy.

Monetarists argue that monetary authorities should be ordered to expand the money supply at a constant rate to reduce cyclical instability and inflation.

Rational Expectations Theory and Activist Policy

The rational expectations theory argues that activist policies—*if predictable*—will have no impact on the business cycle.

Suppose monetary and fiscal authorities adopt activist expansionary policies to reduce unemployment. As aggregate demand increases, the price level rises. As earlier chapters have demonstrated, if inflation is unexpected, it raises output and reduces unemployment. If wages are inflexible selling prices are pushed up more rapidly than costs, and firms expand their hiring and reduce layoffs. The unanticipated inflation has reduced unemployment and expanded real output.

Rational expectations theory goes one step further and maintains that unanticipated inflation can raise output and reduce unemployment *even if wages and prices are fully flexible*. People and firms can process only a limited amount of information on prices and wages, so they specialize in the wages and prices most important to them. People typically know by how much their wages are changing, but they have trouble keeping up with the prices of the hundreds or thousands of things they buy. Businesses sell a few things but must buy many things to produce their products. Hence, businesses can keep up with the prices of the things they sell better than the prices of the things they buy. Because price information is unevenly distributed, unanticipated inflation can fool people and firms into taking actions they would not otherwise have taken.

Unanticipated inflation can fool wage earners into thinking that their real wages have risen (wage earners know that the nominal wage has gone up but are uncertain about what has happened to prices). The perceived rise in real wages motivates people to accept job offers more readily and remain out of work for shorter periods of time. Unanticipated inflation can fool firms into thinking that their selling prices are rising faster than their costs. Accordingly, the firm expands its employment and output.

If people correctly anticipate the inflationary effects of activist policies, policies will not affect output or unemployment. Suppose that people and firms have come to recognize that expansionary monetary policy increases inflation. Whenever the Fed speeds up monetary growth, people expect a higher rate of inflation. When the higher inflation actually materializes, it is fully anticipated. People recognize that rising wages and rising selling prices are a part of the general rise in prices. Unless people can be fooled into thinking their real wages have changed, or unless firms can be fooled into thinking their prices are rising faster than costs, there will be no change in output, employment, or unemployment. The expansionary policies will cause nominal GDP to rise with inflation, but real GDP will remain unchanged.

Rational expectations theorists maintain that activist policies work only if people do not understand their effects. Initially, monetary expansions or tax cuts might cause changes in output and employment because people do not immediately understand how they work. After several uses, however, people should start to catch on and anticipate the effects of these policies. Once the effects are anticipated, activist policies have no impact on output or employment. Rational expectations theory adds another degree of complexity to activist policy. Policymakers must not only be able to select the correct policy with the proper timing, they must also know whether people and firms will be able to anticipate the effects of these policies.

> Rational expectations theory argues that unanticipated inflation causes people and firms to mistake nominal wage and price changes for real wage and price changes. Accordingly, activist policies can affect employment and real output if they cause *unanticipated* changes in inflation.

> Rational expectations theory says that activist policy works only when people are caught offguard by the policy.

A REDUCTION IN DIFFERENCES?

The disagreement between activist Keynesians and nonactivist monetarists and rational expectationists appears profound. One side believes in activist policy; the other side believes that countercyclical policies either do not matter or make matters worse.

Signs of agreement between activists and nonactivists are beginning to emerge. First, the two positions have come much closer in the last 30 years. The Keynesians began with the notion that the money supply scarcely mattered at all; now Keynesians and monetarists hold a more balanced view that both monetary and fiscal policy matter. Because of its greater flexibility of monetary policy, even Keynesians regard monetary policy as the major tool of activist policy. Modern Keynesians have also largely abandoned the notion of *fine-tuning*—the constant fiddling with the dials of discretionary policy. Activist policy should be used to respond only to major cyclical disturbances.

Activists acknowledge that policymakers have committed costly errors in the past. It is unlikely that policy blunders as large as those committed in the 1930s will ever be repeated. Presumably, the ability to forecast the business cycle improves over time; we learn from experience. Yet economists are far from reaching the point where monetarists would be confident that policymakers know enough to devise error-free activist policy.

Monetarists and rational expectations economists have shown that, with crowding out, lags, and unpredictable inflationary expectations, the effects of any monetary or fiscal policy will be extremely difficult to predict.

The activists have pointed out the potential weaknesses of fixed rules. If a balanced-budget rule is followed, what kind of provisions must be made to trigger its suspension? Would a war or severe recession be sufficient cause to suspend the balanced-budget rule? Activists have pointed out the difficulties faced by the Fed in setting monetary-growth targets during a period of rapid changes in financial institutions. The creation of money substitutes makes it difficult for monetary authorities to know whether interest-bearing deposits are used for savings or transactions.

The activists and nonactivists do share an important common ground. They wish to achieve the same targets: full employment, moderate inflation, and real economic growth. Both dislike unnecessary unemployment; both recognize the private and social costs of recessions. Both activists and nonactivists believe that the self-correcting mechanism works in the long run. The disagreement is basically over the amount of time it takes for the self-correcting mechanism to work. Activists argue that it is important to use discretionary policy to speed up the return to full employment. According to them, the self-correcting mechanism works slowly, and activist policy (however imperfect) can return the economy to equilibrium more quickly than relying on automatic forces. Nonactivists maintain that the self-correcting mechanism works with sufficient speed. Even if it were slow-moving, the nonactivists would argue that the chances of activist policy blunders are too great to warrant interfering with automatic forces.

Activists have pointed out possible problems with fixed monetary and budgeting rules.

ACTIVISM AS THE CHOICE OF U.S. POLICYMAKERS

U.S. policymakers have chosen the activist-policy approach. Monetary-growth rates have fluctuated considerably over the years, although the fluctuations have decreased in recent years. Activist monetary policy (either directed toward interest-rate targets or monetary-growth targets) has aimed at moderating the business cycle. The Fed has never followed a fixed-monetary-growth rule—even after October 1979 when the Fed placed a higher priority on monetary-growth targets. There is an important distinction between following monetary-growth targets (which can be changed as economic conditions change) and a fixed-

Should the Monetary Authority Be Independent?

The principal policy issue of this chapter is whether activist policies should be pursued by government economic authorities. A second policy issue is: Should activist policy, if we choose to pursue an activist policy, be carried out by policymakers who are independent of the electorate? Should the electorate, through its elected officials, decide on activist policy?

Earlier chapters pointed out that contractionary policies are automatically unpopular. Spending programs must be cut, taxes raised, or credit made more tight. Expansionary programs are automatically popular. This raises the question: If contractionary policies are unpopular, must we have a politically independent body to carry them out?

Insofar as budget and tax policy are decided upon by the legislative and executive branches, fiscal policy will not be independent of politics. Monetary policy is conducted by the central bank, and the central bank can be either independent or dependent. In the United States, Switzerland, and Germany, for example, the central bank is independent of politics. In Russia, the central bank is under the control of the elected legislature. In the United States, Germany, and Switzerland, the central bank typically acts to limit inflation. In Russia, the central bank follows the orders of the legislature to expand the money supply at a rapid rate.

Empirical studies show that countries that have an independent monetary authority have lower rates of inflation. The less independent the central bank, the higher is the rate of inflation. Empirical studies also show no correlation between economic growth, unemployment, and the independence of the monetary authority. Loose monetary policy does not generate more growth or less unemployment.

The independence of the Federal Reserve System of the United States has been subject to numerous challenges by Congress. Members of Congress have argued that the Federal Reserve should follow the will of the Congress. World experience shows that when the monetary authority loses its dependence, the result is higher inflation without creating more jobs or more economic growth.

SOURCE: J. Bradford DeLong and Lawrence Summers, "Macroeconomic Policy and Long-Run Growth," *Federal Reserve Bank of Kansas City Economic Review*, Fourth Quarter, 1992, pp. 5–25.

U.S. policymakers have chosen activism over rules.

monetary-growth rule. Activist monetary policy is perfectly consistent with monetary-growth targets.

U.S. policymakers have made relatively frequent use of activist tax policy since the 1964 tax cut. In the postwar era, there have been four tax revisions that have been passed largely for activist-policy reasons. These tax revisions have had different degrees of success, but it is clear that U.S. policymakers regard tax revision as a major instrument of activist fiscal policy. U.S. policymakers have not followed the balanced-budget rule advocated by the nonactivists. In fact, the inability of policymakers to balance the budget over the cycle despite the best intentions of several presidents makes one skeptical about our ability to implement any balanced-budget rule. President Clinton's 1993 tax increases and spending cuts fall far short of balancing the budget.

The debate between activism and nonactivism continues. As new middle ground is discovered, new differences of opinion will emerge. The next chapter looks at the determinants of long-run economic growth and development.

Chapter Summary

The most important point to learn from this chapter is: The major unresolved policy issue in macroeconomics is whether or not we should use activist policy to deal with the business cycle. Modern Keynesians say that activist policies make matters better. Monetarists and rational-expectations economists argue that activism either makes matters worse or has no effect; they therefore favor fixed rules.

1. The two policy options are activism and nonactivism. Activist policies aim to stabilize the business cycle using discretionary monetary and fiscal policy. Nonactivist policy uses two fixed rules: (a) let the money supply grow at a constant rate and (b) have a cyclically balanced budget.

2. The policy instruments of macroeconomic policy are monetary policy and fiscal policy. Monetary policy is the most flexible policy instrument, and it has been used as the main instrument of activist policy.

3. The chief argument for activism is that the self-correcting mechanism is too slow. The main evidence in favor of activism is the reduction in GDP fluctuations since the Second World War, the successful tax cuts of the 1960s and 1980s, and the unknown dangers of fixed rules.

4. The case for nonactivism rests on the following points: the economy is not as unstable as the activists believe; instability has been caused by policy blunders; the reduced GDP fluctuations since the Second World War are the result of smaller fluctuations in monetary growth. Activist policy tends to be destabilizing because lags make it difficult to devise discretionary policy and because the effects of fiscal policy are uncertain. Rational expectations theory maintains that activist policy will not stabilize the economy if policy is anticipated.

5. Modern Keynesians now take into account many of the monetarist points. Monetarists increasingly recognize the difficulty of using the money supply as a policy target when financial innovations create new types of money.

6. U.S. policymakers have used activist policy to try to moderate the business cycle and have not followed a cyclically balanced budget rule or a fixed-monetary-growth rule.

Policy Focus: **An independent monetary authority allows a country to pursue necessary but unpopular macroeconomic policies.**

Key Terms

activist policy (p. 269)
nonactivist policy (p. 269)
policy instruments (p. 271)
GDP gap (p. 274)

auction market (p. 275)
monetarists (p. 277)
rational expectations economists (p. 277)

Questions and Problems

1. Modern Keynesians argue that activist policy has made things better. What examples do they cite to support this position?

2. Explain the role of fiscal policy in the conduct of activist policy.

3. If there is agreement among activists and nonactivists that the self-correcting mechanism automatically moves the economy toward full employment, how can anyone advocate activist policy?

4. Advocates of nonactivism must demonstrate that

activist policies tend to worsen the business cycle. What evidence is there that activism actually makes matters worse?

5. How could we have had the Great Depression of the 1930s if there is a self-correcting mechanism at work in the economy?

6. The rational expectations argument is that expectations can defeat activist policy. Assume Congress decides to pass a tax cut to stimulate the economy. How could rational expectations defeat the purpose of the tax cut?

7. Explain the difference between monetary targets and monetarism. Is it correct to call the Fed's decision in October 1979 to follow monetary-growth targets a victory for monetarism?

8. What is the activist defense of activist policy given the fact that lack of data, lags, and changing expectations make it difficult to devise activist policies?

9. Both activists and nonactivists use the greater stability of the economy after the Second World War to support their positions. Explain how both sides can use the same data to support entirely different positions.

10. Some studies suggest that wages have responded more sensitively to unemployment in the 1980s than in the 1960s. For which period would the case for non-activism be stronger if this conclusion is indeed the case?

11. Suppose that, to combat inflation, Congress passed a tax increase. Would the expected effect be greater if the bill called for a permanent increase in tax rates or a one-year increase in tax rates?

12. Explain why both activists and nonactivists appear to agree that monetary policy is the most important policy instrument.

Doing Economics

The Federal Open Market Committee (FOMC) is the body within the Federal Reserve System that makes major monetary policy decisions. The FOMC meets about every six weeks in Washington, D.C. Minutes of these meetings are released about a month later and published in the *Federal Reserve Bulletin*, which is probably available in your library's Government Documents department. Choose several dates, at least one of which is during a recessionary period (1974–75, 1979, 1982, 1991) and read the minutes of an FOMC meeting. Based on your reading, was the Fed following an activist policy? Did the degree of activism you detected vary between meetings? Did there seem to be a difference between meetings held in prosperous economic times and meetings held during recessions? Between meetings when inflation was high and meetings when inflation was moderate?

The Global Economy

P A R T   F O U R

CHAPTER 15
Productivity, Growth, and Development

CHAPTER 16
International Trade and Protection

CHAPTER 17
The International Monetary System

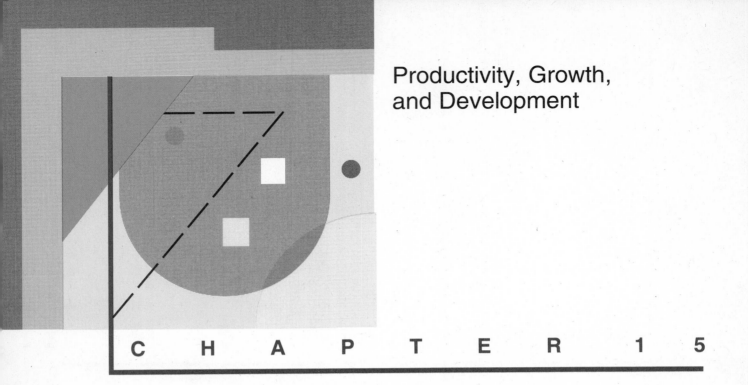

Productivity, Growth, and Development

C H A P T E R   1 5

CHAPTER FOCUS

Sometime in the early eighteenth century, the United Kingdom began to experience the world's first case of sustained economic growth and industrialization. The world had previously seen transitory periods of economic growth in the rises and falls of the great civilizations of Egypt, Greece, and the Roman Empire. Yet each of these experiments failed to produce the sustained economic growth necessary to improve living standards. By contrast, the United Kingdom's industrial revolution raised living standards to unprecedented levels.

From the United Kingdom, the industrial revolution spread to the European continent and to North America and Australia, but then it stopped. It failed to move to Latin America, Asia, and Africa. Since the initial industrial revolutions in the eighteenth and nineteenth centuries, only a few countries have successfully made the transition from poverty to affluence. The most prominent example is Japan, and the most recent contenders are Taiwan, Singapore, South Korea, and Hong Kong. This chapter examines the mystery of economic development. What are the sources of economic growth? Why is sustained economic growth and prosperity confined to such a small percentage of the world's population? What can countries do to raise their growth?

Thomas R. Malthus (1766–1834)

Thomas R. Malthus was born in Surrey, England, the son of a country gentleman. Malthus was educated in private schools and by his father, a friend of the noted philosophers David Hume and Jean-Jacques Rousseau. In his youth, Malthus was exposed to the main intellectual currents of the late eighteenth century. At the age of nineteen, Malthus received a theological degree from Cambridge University. Although an ordained clergyman, his main interest was in social problems rather than in the ministry. Malthus married, had three children, and taught history at Haileybury College. With David Ricardo and James Mill he founded the Political Economy Club in London in 1821.

While a student at Cambridge, Malthus distinguished himself as a scholar, and his father was so impressed with his son's view of the law of nature that he encouraged him to publish his work, *Essay on the Principle of Population,* which appeared anonymously in 1798.

In this essay, Malthus presented his famous theory. It held that there was an inexorable tendency for population growth to outstrip the means to support that population. Malthus wrote that "population, when unchecked, increases in a geometric ratio," while "subsistence only increases in an arithmetic ratio."

The publication of Malthus' essay set off considerable controversy. Although the Prime Minister and England's most famous theologian were favorably impressed with his arguments, indignant critics accused him of favoring wars and famine and letting the poor starve. In the second and expanded edition of his *Essay on the Principle of Population,* Malthus responded to these criticisms and recommended "moral restraint" to prevent overpopulation. It was only in the second edition that Malthus acknowledged his authorship.

Malthus' views have had a far-reaching impact on economics and biology. Both Charles Darwin and Alfred Russell Wallace (the codiscoverer of the theory of evolution) acknowledged their intellectual debt to Malthus.

ECONOMIC GROWTH

Economic growth is defined in terms of changes in real GDP in two ways.

> Economic growth is an increase in real GDP from one period to the next.

> Economic growth is an increase from one period to the next in *real GDP per capita,* which is real GDP divided by the country's population.

When economists study economic growth, they are interested in the growth of real output (or output per capita) over an extended period of time. Long-term economic growth is the long-term trend in real output, ignoring the short-run deviations around this trend caused by the business cycle. In effect, economic growth is the expansion of the natural level of real GDP.

The two measures of economic growth provide different information about economic performance. The growth of real GDP measures the rate at which total output is expanding. As such, it measures the degree to which an economy is growing in both scale and importance. For instance, Japan's phenomenal growth

EXAMPLE 1

Are Economic Growth Rates Increasing?

A lesson of this chapter is that an economy can experience growth in per-capita output because of capital accumulation and technological progress. Measured by the growth rate of real per-capita GDP, the advanced capitalist countries appear to have experienced increasing growth rates over the past several centuries. Angus Maddison has collected the best available data on GDP and populations for 14 advanced capitalist countries going back to 1820. The accompanying table shows that from 1820 to 1870 the annual growth rate of the 14 countries averaged only 0.9 percent, but from 1870 to 1989 the average annual growth rate was 1.6 percent.

Paul Romer has explained the increase in growth rate by the basic nature of technological change. Inventions are carried out to make a profit, but every new product or invention lowers the cost of additional inventions or products. For example, the invention of the cathode ray tube lowered the cost of inventing television; the invention of the gasoline engine lowered the cost of developing the automobile. Each new invention may contribute to a new idea consisting of all previous ideas. Technical progress can thus accelerate, causing the rate of growth of the economy to increase.

The Romer vision may, however, be overly optimistic. Critics might point out that since 1973 growth rates have headed downward. Romer would reply that his theory deals with long-run growth rather than short-run cyclical developments.

Growth Rates of Real Per Capita GDP (annual average)

	1820–1870	1870–1989
Australia	1.9	1.2
Austria	0.6	1.8
Belgium	1.4	1.5
Denmark	0.9	1.8
Finland	0.8	2.3
France	0.8	1.8
Germany	0.7	2.0
Italy	0.4	2.0
Japan	0.1	2.7
Netherlands	0.9	1.5
Norway	0.7	2.2
Sweden	0.7	2.1
United Kingdom	1.2	1.4
United States	1.5	1.9
Average	0.9	1.6

Sources: Paul Romer, "Increasing Returns and Long-Run Growth," *Journal of Political Economy,* 95 (October 1986): 1002–1037; Angus Maddison, *Dynamic Forces in Capitalist Development* (New York: Oxford University Press, 1991).

after World War II allowed it to join the select group of advanced industrialized nations. (See Example 1.) If the current rapid growth of countries such as Taiwan and South Korea continues, they too will soon be advanced industrialized countries. The growth of real GDP per capita measures the growth of average living standards. People who live in countries with high per capita GDP are better off materially (on average).

The two rates of economic growth can be quite different. Some countries with rapid GDP growth also have rapid population growth; such countries can have a smaller increase in living standards than a country in which GDP growth is more

> Economic growth can be measured by the growth of real GDP or real GDP per capita.

modest but in which there is little or no population growth. The difference between the two measures of economic growth is evident from comparisons of small, rich countries with large, poor countries. The total output of the People's Republic of China in 1985 was $354 billion; Switzerland's output was $92 billion. On a per capita basis, the output of China was $346 and that of Switzerland was $14,154. Although the total output of Switzerland was less than that of China, Swiss living standards were 40 times those of China.

THE HAVES AND THE HAVE NOTS

The modern world is divided into "have" and "have not" nations, according to the **level of economic development**.

> The **level of economic development** is measured by per capita GDP, industrial structure, population dynamics, and the health and education of the population.

Although there is no single indicator of the level of economic development, per capita GDP comes as close as possible to being the most comprehensive. However, a country can have a high GDP per capita and yet lack the other characteristics of economic development, such as a highly educated population or an industrial structure geared to industry and services.

The industrialized countries of North America, Europe, Australia, and Japan have attained a high level of economic development. The **less developed countries (LDCs)** have not.

> A **less developed country (LDC)** is a country with a per capita income far below that of a typical advanced country.

Exhibit 1 shows that approximately three out of every four persons lives in an LDC. Only 15 percent of the world's population lives in the highly developed capitalist countries of the United States, Canada, Australia, Japan, and Western Europe, and 10 percent of the world's population lives in the former communist countries of the U.S.S.R. and eastern Europe. The LDCs' share of world population has been rising since 1900 and is projected to rise throughout the twenty-first century.

A comparison of the distribution of world population with the distribution of world income dramatizes how unequally income is distributed among the different countries of the globe. The developed countries, which account for only 25 percent of the world's population, account for 83 percent of the world's GDP. The LDCs account for 75 percent of world population but only 17 percent of world GDP. World output is concentrated in the United States, western Europe, and Japan. The unequal distribution of income among countries also leads to an unequal consumption of natural resources between the rich and poor countries. The industrialized capitalist countries, for example, consume 71 percent of the world's oil production. Only 9 percent of the world's oil production is available for the LDCs.

The LDCs' share of world production has been falling as its share of world population has been rising. In 1800, the LDCs accounted for 44 percent of world production. By 1900, the LDCs' share of world production had fallen to 19

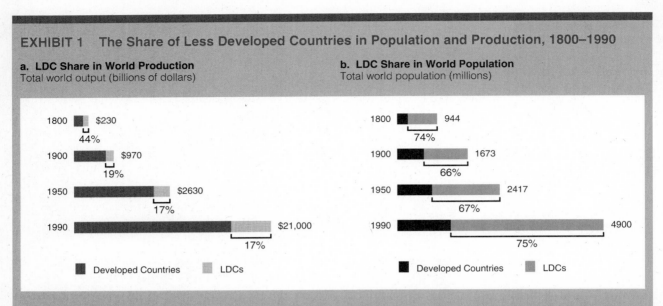

EXHIBIT 1 The Share of Less Developed Countries in Population and Production, 1800–1990

a. LDC Share in World Production
Total world output (billions of dollars)

1800	$230 44%
1900	$970 19%
1950	$2630 17%
1990	$21,000 17%

■ Developed Countries   ▨ LDCs

b. LDC Share in World Population
Total world population (millions)

1800	944 74%
1900	1673 66%
1950	2417 67%
1990	4900 75%

■ Developed Countries   ▨ LDCs

This exhibit shows that the less developed countries' share of the world's population far exceeds their share of income. It also shows the decline in their share of world output since 1800.
SOURCES: Adapted from World Bank, *World Development Report 1984*, 6, and from *Handbook of Economic Statistics*, 1990

percent. The declining LDCs' share of world production has been the result of rapid growth in the developed countries combined with slow or stagnant growth in the LDCs after 1800.

Life in a low-income LDC is very different from life in the United States. Only one of five people in a low-income LDC lives in an urban area (as opposed to 78 percent in the industrial market economies). One out of every seven children dies before the age of four (as compared with one out of every 200 in the industrial market economies). In a community of 6,000 people, there is one physician (as opposed to eleven in the industrial market economies). Life expectancy is 58 years in a typical low-income LDC and 75 years in a typical industrial market economy. In an LDC, only one out of every two adults can read or write, and only one out of four school-age children attends secondary school. There is a better than 50:50 chance that a girl will never attend school. Only two out of every 100 persons own their own radio, and a private automobile is a virtually unheard-of luxury. LDC residents come from large families and plan on having a large number of children, many of whom will not survive their infancy.

ECONOMIC GROWTH OF THE HAVES

The industrial revolution discussed in this chapter opener resulted in the acceleration of the growth of real GDP and of population. The growth of output exceeded the growth of population, and per capita GDP began to grow at a sustained or increasing rate.

The principal feature of modern economic growth has been its sustained nature. There is no simple explanation for why the industrialized world began to sustain economic growth in the eighteenth century, for the first time in human history. The industrial revolution was accompanied by a technological revolution. Productivity-increasing inventions produced by eighteenth- and nineteenth-century science, including the steam engine, the mechanized cotton spindle, and the blast furnace, help explain modern economic growth. Modern economic growth was also accompanied by the expansion of trade and the growth of free-market institutions.

Modern economic growth brought about substantial changes in life-styles. The share of economic activity devoted to industry and services rose; the share of agriculture declined. These changes in the structure of the economy were accompanied by rising urbanization; the typical worker was no longer a farmer but an industrial laborer. Rising per capita income made it possible for real wages to rise, and items that had previously been available only to the rich—quality textiles, long-distance transportation, phonographs, automobiles—became available for mass consumption. With rising living standards, birth rates began to fall. After the initial acceleration of population growth, the rate of population growth began to decline in industrialized countries. In the late twentieth century, a number of affluent countries even worry about declining population.

Extensive and Intensive Growth

Since the beginning of modern economic growth, industrialized economies have experienced sustained growth of GDP and of GDP per capita. Although there have been cyclical episodes of zero or negative growth—such as the Great Depression of the 1930s—the industrialized economies have grown consistently over the long run. (See Exhibit 2.)

Economies expand their real GDP because of both **extensive growth** and **intensive growth**.

> **Extensive growth** occurs when the total amount of land, labor, and capital inputs expands.

> **Intensive growth** occurs when available inputs are used more effectively.

The more effective use of inputs shows up as increases in output per unit of input—that is, as increases in **factor productivity**.

> An increase in **factor productivity** occurs when more output is produced per unit of factor input.

To expand labor inputs, people must sacrifice leisure or household production to produce more market output. To expand capital inputs, people must sacrifice current consumption for future consumption. Compared to these costs of extensive growth, the costs of intensive growth are smaller. Such sacrifices are not necessary when output is increased through intensive growth.

Extensive growth occurs when factor inputs expand. Intensive growth occurs when factor productivity increases and there is more output per unit of input.

The Role of Productivity

Does economic growth result from the growth of inputs or from the growth of productivity? Exhibit 3 supplies long-term data for American economic growth. The first column gives the growth rates of real GDP for different periods from

Country	1929–1950 Growth Rate (percent)		1950–1960 Growth Rate (percent)		1960–1990 Growth Rate (percent)	
	GDP	GDP per Capita	GDP	GDP per Capita	GDP	GDP per Capita
United States	2.9	1.8	3.2	1.4	3.3	2.1
Canada	3.2	1.8	4.6	1.9	4.4	3.0
France	0.0	−0.1	4.6	3.6	3.7	3.2
West Germany	1.9	0.7	8.0	6.4	3.1	2.9
Italy	1.0	0.3	5.5	4.8	4.0	3.4
Japan	0.6	NA	8.0	6.9	6.4	5.4
United Kingdom	1.6	1.2	2.8	2.4	2.5	2.3
U.S.S.R.	5.4*	3.5*	6.0	4.2	3.4	2.0

*1928–1940

SOURCES: *Statistical Abstract of the United States; Handbook of Economic Statistics*

1800 to 1988. The next two columns give the corresponding growth rates of labor inputs (measured in hours) and of capital inputs. The fourth column gives the growth rates of labor and capital combined. From data on real GDP growth and factor input growth, one can calculate productivity.

Three measures of productivity are shown in Exhibit 3, **labor productivity, capital productivity**, and **total factor productivity**.

Labor productivity measures output per unit (usually per hour) of labor input.

Capital productivity measures output per unit of capital input.

Total factor productivity measures output per unit of combined labor and capital input.

The three measures of productivity are usually expressed as rates of growth. The growth rate of labor productivity measures the growth rate of output per unit of labor input. The growth rate of total factor productivity measures the growth rate of output per unit of combined inputs. *The growth rate of productivity is approximately the growth rate of real output minus the growth rate of the factor input.*

By comparing the growth of real GDP, factor inputs, and factor productivity, one can determine how much economic growth is attributable to the expansion of inputs (extensive growth) and how much is due to the expansion of productivity (intensive growth). Because inputs grew at an annual rate of 1.5 percent between 1948 and 1988 in the United States, 47 percent (1.5/3.2) of the 3.2 percent annual output growth is explained by the growth of inputs. The remaining 53 percent is accounted for by productivity growth. The data for the periods 1855 to 1948 (the period of U.S. industrialization) show that productivity growth explains the major portion of U.S. economic growth. (See Example 2 for an international perspective.)

Productivity growth accounts for more than half of U.S. growth.

EXHIBIT 3 Growth Rates of U.S. GDP, Factor Inputs, and Productivity, 1800–1988

Period	Real GDP (1)	Labor Inputs (hours) (2)	Capital Inputs (3)	Annual Growth Rate (percent)					
				Combined Inputs (4)	Labor Productivity (5) = (1) – (2)	Capital Productivity (6) = (1) – (3)	Total Factor Productivity (7) = (1) – (4)	Proportion of Growth Explained by Inputs (percent) (8) = (4) ÷ (1)	Unexplained Residual (percent) (9) = (5) ÷ (1)
1800–1855	4.2	3.7	4.3	3.9	0.5	–0.1	0.3	93	7
1855–1898	4.0	2.8	4.6	3.6	1.1	–0.6	0.3	90	10
1899–1919	3.9	1.8	3.1	2.2	2.0	0.7	1.7	46	54
1919–1948	3.0	0.6	1.2	0.8	2.4	1.6	2.2	20	80
1948–1988	3.2	0.9	3.7	1.5	2.3	–0.2	1.7	47	53

SOURCES: John W. Kendrick, "Survey of the Factors Contributing to the Decline in U.S. Productivity Growth," Federal Reserve Bank of Boston, *The Decline in Productivity Growth*, Conference Series No. 22, June 1980, 2: U.S. Department of Labor, Bureau of Labor Statistics, *Trends in Multifactor Productivity, 1948–81*, September 1983, 24; Edward Denison, *Trends in American Economic Growth, 1929–1982* (Washington, DC: Brookings, 1985); *World Development Report 1991*, pp. 43–44.

EXAMPLE 2

Productivity as a Source of Growth: World Experience

This chapter explains that economic growth can be either extensive (resulting from the growth of capital and labor inputs) or intensive (resulting from technology advances, better business methods, and so on). The example of the industrialized West shows that productivity growth, rather than the growth of inputs, has been the most important source of economic growth.

The accompanying table, prepared by the World Bank, shows that the poor regions of the world, Africa, Latin America, and East Asia, have a different long-term growth experience from the industrialized countries. Africa and Latin America had no growth of factor productivity between 1960 and 1987. In South Asia, there was only slight growth of factor productivity. Hence, virtually all growth in these regions was extensive in nature. In the industrialized countries, on the other hand, more than half of the growth was accounted for by factor productivity growth.

SOURCE: *World Development Report 1991: The Challenge of Development* (New York: Oxford University Press, 1991), 43–45.

The Growth of GDP, Inputs, and Total Factor Productivity, 1960–1987

Region, Group, or Economy	GDP	Capital	Labor	Total Factor Productivity	Percentage of Growth Explained by Factor Productivity
Developing economies					
Africa	3.3	6.3	2.2	0.0	0
East Asia	6.8	10.2	2.6	1.9	28
Latin America	3.6	6.3	2.6	0.0	0
South Asia	4.4	7.7	2.1	0.6	14
Sixty-eight economies	4.2	7.2	2.3	0.6	14
Industrial economies					
France	3.9	4.8	−0.2	1.7	78
Germany[a]	3.1	4.2	−0.6	1.4	87
United Kingdom	2.4	3.1	−0.2	1.2	78
United States	3.0	3.4	1.8	0.5	50

Note: Estimates for developing countries are based on a sample of sixty-eight economies. Estimates for industrial economies are based on data from 1960 to 1985.

[a] The Federal Republic of Germany before reunification with the former German Democratic Republic.

SOURCE: *World Development Report 1991*, 43–44.

Labor Productivity

Exhibit 3 also shows the annual rate of growth of labor productivity from 1958 to 1990. Labor productivity growth—as measured by the rate of growth of real GDP per hour of labor—fluctuates significantly from year to year. These fluctuations make it difficult to see long-run trends in labor productivity. The period from the late 1950s through the mid-1960s was one of high labor productivity growth. From the late 1960s to 1991, labor productivity growth was erratic, generally falling with recessions and rising with recoveries.

Exhibit 3 illustrates why fears of a long-term productivity decline were widespread in the 1970s and early 1980s. From high and steady productivity

EXHIBIT 4   Long-Term Trends in U.S. Labor Productivity Growth

Period	Average Annual Growth Rate in Output per Hour (percent)
1900–1916	1.5
1916–1929	2.3
1929–1948	1.6
1948–1965	3.3
1965–1973	2.3
1973–1990	1.4

SOURCE: Michael Darby, "The U.S. Productivity Slowdown: A Case of Statistical Myopia," *American Economic Review* (June 1984): 302. Darby's figures are updated from *Economic Report of the President.*

growth in the 1960s, the economy experienced negative productivity growth in the mid- and late 1970s. The economic recovery after 1982 generated positive and reasonably rapid labor productivity growth, underscoring the fact that labor productivity is heavily dependent on the state of the business cycle. We do not know whether the 1990s will be a time of steady and high or slow and erratic labor productivity growth.

Exhibit 4 shows that fears of a long-term decline in labor productivity may not be justified. Productivity growth since 1973 has been close to the long-run average for earlier periods. In fact, the early postwar period was one of exceptionally high labor productivity growth.

WHY THE LDCs ARE POOR

Sustained productivity growth explains why the developed countries are affluent. What explains why the LDCs are poor? The "stationary state" of the classical economists provides a first explanation of LDC poverty.

The Classical Growth Model

Economists first became interested in economic growth in the late eighteenth and early nineteenth centuries. The classical economists, particularly David Ricardo and Thomas Malthus, sought to explain why predominantly agricultural economies reach an upper limit to economic growth, which they called a *stationary state.* From the perspective of the classical economists writing at the very beginning of the industrial revolution, the stationary state of zero growth seemed to be the normal state of affairs; there was very little growth of output or of population prior to 1750, the approximate starting point of modern economic growth in Great Britain.

Diminishing Returns.   The classical economists were interested in explaining the growth of a traditional agrarian economy. In such an economy, modern science and technology had yet to be applied to agriculture, and capital equipment (such as hoes or plows) was a relatively minor input. Output was produced primarily by combining land and labor, and agricultural land was essentially fixed in supply.

The *law of diminishing returns* applies to situations in which more and more units of a variable factor (labor) are being added to a fixed factor of production (land). According to the law of diminishing returns, at low levels of population and labor force, increases in labor initially yield fairly substantial increases in output, but as more and more labor is combined with a fixed amount of land, additional inputs of labor bring in smaller and smaller additions to output. The average product of labor, after first rising, falls as diminishing returns set in.

Panel (a) of Exhibit 5 shows the aggregate output of an economy in which more and more units of a variable input (labor) are combined with a fixed input. Initially, output rises at an increasing rate, but the increase in output tapers off as more units of labor are added. Panel (b) shows how the average product of labor first rises but then declines.

The law of diminishing returns suggests that an agricultural economy with a fixed amount of land, primitive technology, and rudimentary capital resources should avoid excessively large inputs of labor insofar as these labor injections drive down the average product of labor. Labor productivity determines real wages; therefore, an economy whose population and labor force are too large should expect to experience falling real wages and falling living standards.

Malthusian Population Laws.   Because of the writings of Thomas R. Malthus, whose *Essay on the Principle of Population* was published in 1798, classical economics came to be called the "dismal science." Malthus believed that there would be a long-term disproportion between the rate of growth of population and the rate of growth of food production. Population, Malthus argued, tends to increase at *geometric* rates (in which the *ratio* between each number and its predecessor is constant) because the "passion between the sexes" and factors such as disease and war remain constant throughout human history. On the other hand, food production tends to increase at *arithmetic* rates (in which the *difference* between each number and its predecessor is constant), following the law of diminishing returns. Because a geometric series, such as 1, 2, 4, 8, 16, . . . , grows at a faster rate and will inevitably overtake an arithmetic series, such as 10, 11, 12, 13, . . . , Malthus believed that humanity would usually find itself on the verge of starvation, living at subsistence wages.

The crux of the Malthusian population problem is that wages can never rise above the subsistence level for long periods of time because when they do, reproduction tends to increase. Thus, once wages rise above the subsistence level, the population and labor force will expand geometrically, and the increase in the supply of labor will drive wages back down to the subsistence level. If wages fall below the subsistence level, famine and higher mortality rates will reduce the population and allow wages to rise back to the subsistence level.

The Stationary State.   The classical economists came to the pessimistic conclusion that there are distinct limits to growth. In the long run, economies would end up in a stationary state characterized by (1) a zero growth rate of output, population, and per capita output, and (2) subsistence wages.

In panel (c) of Exhibit 5, the downward-sloping labor demand curve shows the economy's demand for labor at different wage rates, and the upward-sloping labor supply curve shows the amounts of labor supplied at different wage rates. The subsistence wage (w_s) is drawn as a horizontal line.

In the short run, the supply of labor is determined by the size of the population and by the proportion of the adult population that works—both of which change slowly over time. In the short run, wages can rise above the subsistence level; they

Diminishing returns explains low real wages in economies with fixed land and capital and primitive technology.

EXHIBIT 5   The Classical Growth Model

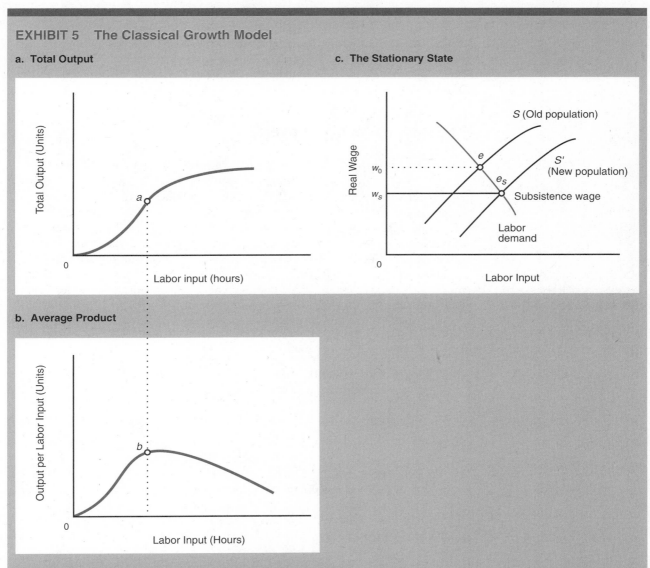

a. Total Output

c. The Stationary State

b. Average Product

In this economy, the amount of agricultural land is fixed. As the variable factor, labor, is combined with the fixed factor, output initially rises at an increasing rate. Panel (a) shows that as more and more units of the variable factor are added beyond point a, the rate of increase in output slows. Panel (b) shows that the average product of labor first increases and then decreases. Panel (c) shows that in the short run, the market wage rate will be w_0—the equilibrium wage rate. The horizontal line shows the subsistence wage rate, w_s. If the market wage is above the subsistence level, as it is in this case, population will expand, and the labor supply curve will shift to the right (supply will increase). As long as the market wage remains above the subsistence level, population will continue to expand, thereby driving wages down even further. Population growth will cease when the market wage is driven down to the subsistence level. At this point, the economy is in a stationary state. The growth of output ceases, and wages are stuck at the subsistence level.

Malthus predicted starvation and subsistence wages because of the disproportion between population and food production.

are determined by the forces of supply and demand. If the wage rate rises above the subsistence level, the birth rate will rise and death rates will fall as a result of better nutrition and health. The increase in population will increase the labor supply (the curve will shift to the right), thereby driving down the equilibrium wage rate. Population growth will not cease until population growth shifts the labor supply curve to S'. At this point, wages stabilize at the subsistence level.

If a severe famine or war reduces the number of workers, wages will temporarily rise above the subsistence level, the population will begin to reproduce, and wages will be driven back to the subsistence level. During the Black Death plague of the Middle Ages, which destroyed one-third of Europe's population, real wages rose substantially but declined thereafter as population growth accelerated.

The Sources of LDC Poverty

The classical growth model has relevance to today's LDCs. LDCs are typically economies that rely primarily on agricultural output for their income, where arable land is limited in supply, where population is growing at a rapid rate, and where technological improvements are limited. Thus, LDCs contain the basic ingredients of the stationary state. Population pressure forces such an economy to operate with diminishing returns as technological progress fails to offset declining labor productivity. Wages are kept near the subsistence level, and population growth is regulated by rising and falling mortality. Good harvests cause lower mortality but more population pressure. Poor harvests cause higher mortality and less population pressure.

LDCs have many of the ingredients of the classical stationary state.

The classical model suggests what could be done to release the LDCs from the stationary state:

1. If the rate of population growth were to decline, the pressures of diminishing returns would be abated.
2. If capital formation could be accelerated, labor productivity could be raised.
3. If technological progress could be achieved, diminishing returns could be avoided.

Population Pressures.   The rate of growth of per-capita GDP equals the rate of growth of GDP minus the rate of growth of population. Per-capita growth can, therefore, be accelerated either by increasing the growth of GDP or by decreasing the growth of population. This simple arithmetic explains why many analysts of LDCs tend to regard rapid population growth as an enemy of economic development.

Why is population growth more rapid in the LDCs than in the developed countries? Demographers have long studied a "law" of population growth called the **demographic transition**.

The **demographic transition** is the process by which countries change from rapid population growth to slow population growth as they modernize.

In a country's premodern era, there is little or no population growth because the birth rate and death rate are roughly equal, and there are no net additions to the population. However, as modernization begins, there is an acceleration of population growth. Modernization brings with it better health care and nutrition, and the death rate declines, especially infant mortality rates. In addition, rising incomes may cause birth rates to rise in the early phases of modernization. The first phases of modernization are, therefore, characterized by an accelerated rate of population growth.

As modernization proceeds, further reductions in the death rate become harder to achieve. Mortality attributable to infectious diseases has already become rare, and medical science is left with harder-to-combat chronic diseases, such as heart disease and cancer. Modernization eventually causes the birth rate to decline. As married couples become more educated, they more effectively regulate family size through birth control practices, and the number of children decreases. In modern societies, a large number of children no longer assure old-age security. Reduced infant mortality makes it unnecessary to have many children to ensure that some will survive to adulthood. Employment opportunities for women improve, and the opportunity costs of having children increase. All of these facts combine to reduce the birth rate.

These forces cause a demographic transition from high rates of population growth to low rates. The Malthusian specter of overpopulation is removed, and some advanced societies must even start to worry about underpopulation—about negative population growth.

The LDCs have failed to participate in the demographic transition for a number of reasons.

1. Unlike the industrialized countries, declines in death rates in the LDCs were not coordinated with rising modernization and prosperity. Instead, public-health improvements (such as typhoid and cholera immunizations) were introduced by the colonial powers prior to significant economic development. Improved health care and sanitization in the LDCs caused significant declines in mortality *prior* to modernization.

2. In many LDCs—which remain rural societies without government old-age-security programs—children are still the only guarantee that one will be looked after in one's old age. Parents with many children stand a better chance of health and income security in their old age.

3. In many LDCs, there are century-old traditions that favor large families. The proof of manhood may be the number of children fathered. Immortality is considered assured by having many children, grandchildren, and great-grandchildren.

4. As long as the country remains underdeveloped and employment opportunities are primarily in agriculture, the opportunity costs to women of having additional children are low. In many LDCs, having a baby means the loss of only a few days or weeks. At an early age, children work in the fields and help their parents.

Many LDCs have not experienced the demographic transition from high to low rates of population growth.

For these reasons, the LDCs are caught in a vicious circle: rapid population growth inhibits increases in per-capita income; without substantial increases in per-capita income (and the modernization that accompanies rising incomes) it is difficult to bring about substantial reductions in birth rates.

Capital-Formation Problems. The LDCs encounter another vicious circle in the area of capital formation. The major portion of a nation's saving is carried out by the affluent; the poor save little or nothing. Therefore, if a whole country is poor—with most of its population living near a subsistence level of income—its saving rate should be low. Moreover, the wealthy in the LDCs tend to invest their savings in nonproductive areas, such as land speculation, precious metals, and foreign bank accounts. The wealthy are simply reacting to the realities of LDC life: the political uncertainties and the apparently poor development prospects of their own countries.

Modern economic growth began in the developed countries after centuries of preparation. Canals, schools, roads, and cathedrals had been built in the centuries that preceded the industrial revolution. By the time of the industrial revolution, the developed countries had accumulated an impressive stock of this *social overhead capital*. The LDCs have not had the luxury of centuries of steady accumulation of social overhead capital which, in effect, is required before real economic development can take place.

Technological Backwardness.   On the surface, it would appear that the industrialized countries have already developed modern technology that should simply be borrowed by the LDCs. The technology of the industrialized countries represents a response to the factors that are present in these countries. Relative to the LDCs, capital is abundant in the developed countries; the quantity of labor is scarce, but the quality of each worker (in training, health, and education) is quite high. Because of these factor endowments, the industrialized countries have developed over the years technologies that emphasize labor saving and require inputs of highly skilled labor and capital.

The modern production techniques of the developed countries are, therefore, not well suited for the LDCs. The LDCs require technologies that take advantage of their abundant supplies of unskilled labor and do not place heavy burdens on their more limited resources—skilled labor and capital. Although a wealth of sophisticated technology is on hand in the industrialized countries, the LDCs remain in the ironic position of having to develop their own technologies. Although there is evidence that Japan was successful in adapting modern technology to its particular needs, most LDCs have been less successful.

Signs of Progress?

Is material life in LDCs getting better? Have there been significant improvements? Exhibit 6 gives data on average rates of growth of population and per capita GDP and on changes in two social indicators from 1960 to 1986. On the whole, there is little evidence that the LDCs are catching up with per-capita incomes in the developed countries. The low-income LDCs have fallen further behind since 1950 (although they grew rapidly in the 1980s), while the middle-income LDCs have just about held their own. LDCs have clearly experienced more rapid population growth than the developed countries. Both the low- and middle-income LDCs have experienced GDP growth as rapid as or more rapid than that of the developed countries, but more rapid population growth has meant equivalent or slower per-capita GDP growth.

In terms of life expectancy and literacy, the LDCs have indeed been catching up with the developed countries. The developed countries are approaching natural upper limits (one cannot raise the literacy rate above 100 percent, and human beings are mortal), and the LDCs have succeeded in improving the health and education of their populations. Moreover, a number of countries have made significant progress in achieving agricultural self-sufficiency.

Trade Policies

The examples of Great Britain in the nineteenth century and Hong Kong, Taiwan, and Singapore today show how extensive international trade can bring many benefits to a country. Trade harnesses the power of specialization to raise national income beyond what is possible in isolation. Some LDCs have tried to grow by denying the benefits of specialization and have attempted to copy the industrialized countries. They want their own automobile and steel industries even though it is cheaper to purchase cars and steel indirectly by producing goods for which the economy's resource base is suited (textiles, natural resources). Countries such as Argentina and India have attempted to follow the inward-looking policy of **import substitution**.

	1950–1960	1960–1970	1970–1980	1980–1989
Rate of population growth				
Developed countries	1.2	1.0	0.7	0.7
Middle-income LDCs	2.4	2.5	2.4	2.1
Low-income LDCs	2.0	2.4	1.9	2.1
Rate of per capita GDP growth				
Developed countries	2.5	4.0	2.3	2.3
Middle-income LDCs	2.8	3.7	3.0	0.5
Low-income LDCs	1.8	2.1	1.0	4.1

	1960	1970	1980	1986
Life expectancy (years)				
Developed countries	68.9	71.8	74.9	75.0
Middle-income LDCs	50.6	54.9	59.9	60.0
Low-income LDCs	40.8	45.3	58.4	59.0
Adult literacy (per 100)				
Developed countries	96.9	98.3	98.9	99.0
Middle-income LDCs	44.0	56.2	65.2	67.0
Low-income LDCs	22.6	31.0	51.0	53.0

SOURCES: World Bank, *World Tables*; World Bank, *World Development Report 1991*, published for the World Bank by Oxford University Press

Import substitution occurs when a country substitutes domestic production for imports by subsidizing domestic production through tariffs, quotas, and other devices.

Cases of successful import substitution are rare, primarily because the products manufactured with the assistance of tariffs and other forms of protection are not competitive.

An alternative course followed by countries such as Hong Kong, South Korea, Taiwan, Brazil, and Singapore has been the outward-looking policy of **export promotion**—encouraging exports through various types of incentive schemes.

Export promotion occurs when a country encourages exports by subsidizing the production of goods for export.

In general, those LDCs that have followed export promotion policies have done better as a group than those that followed import substitution policies. The major success stories in the developing world are those countries that have become fully integrated into the world economy, competing successfully with more affluent countries in the area of manufacturing.

External Assistance

Can the LDCs realistically expect to develop on their own, or must they have outside assistance? The issue of assistance from the industrialized countries is an explosive one in developing countries. Direct foreign assistance is one means by which the industrialized countries assist the LDCs. The LDC bloc in the United

Policy for Growth

We know enough about the determinants of economic growth to develop policies that will increase economic growth. Economists have determined what factors enhance economic growth and what factors detract from economic growth.

Growth-enhancing factors include increased schooling and investments in human capital, increased saving, investments in equipment, and private expenditures on research and development. It is therefore clear what public policies will lead to greater economic growth. Policies that increase education and training will increase growth. Tax incentives that encourage saving, investment, and research and development increase growth. Countries that desire to raise their growth must install a tax system that encourages saving, investment, and research and development, and must gear public expenditures to promote health and education.

Growth-reducing factors include trade barriers, political instability (such as revolutions and assassinations), government consumption, and socialism. International experience has shown that countries that have erected trade barriers to protect their home industries have grown more slowly than those countries that have not protected their home markets but have relied more on export promotion—encouraging exports through various types of incentive programs. Empirical studies show that countries with high rates of government consumption (government spending for bureaucracy and public expenditures) grow slower. Big government is a hindrance to economic growth. Empirical studies also show that the choice of economic system—capitalism and socialism—affects economic growth. Those countries that have chosen the socialist path of economic development have grown more slowly than those that have chosen a capitalist path.

Growth-neutral factors include public expenditures on research and development and population growth. Although there has been considerable policy debate on the issue of government support of research and development, empirical analysis shows that the rate of return to publicly supported research and development is well below that of private research and development at costs that are probably below benefits. Although there has been considerable focus on the need for the LDCs, in particular, to restrain their population growth, there is no empirical relationship between population growth and the growth of per-capita income.

SOURCES: David Gould, "What Determines Economic Growth?" *Economic Review of the Federal Reserve Bank of Dallas*, Spring 1993; Allen C. Kelley, "Economic Consequences of Population Change in the Third World," *Journal of Economic Literature* 31, 4 (December 1988): 1685–1728.

Nations expresses the view that the current level of foreign assistance is grossly inadequate. The LDCs call for a doubling of foreign assistance, requiring the industrialized countries to donate approximately 1 percent of their GDP to the LDCs. Few industrialized nations, including the United States, contribute anything close to the 1 percent figure.

Most LDCs trade raw materials, and they feel that their dependence on raw-material exports places them at a disadvantage in the world economy. Their earnings from raw materials—coffee, rubber, flax, sugar, ores—fluctuate more than the prices of manufactured goods. The LDCs believe that there is a long-run tendency for the prices of raw materials to fall relative to manufactured goods. To deal with these problems, the LDCs have called for a new international economic order. The cornerstone of the new order would be a commodity stabilization program that guarantees the LDCs stable earnings from raw-material production.

In addition to more foreign aid and commodity stabilization, the LDCs have called for improved access to the markets and technology of the industrialized countries and for reforms of the international monetary system.

Chapter Summary

The most important point to learn from this chapter is: Affluence is still limited to an exclusive group of countries. Most people still live in less-developed countries at low levels of material well-being.

1. Economic growth is an increase in real GDP or an increase in real GDP per capita.

2. The industrialized countries have grown at a sustained rate since the mid-eighteenth century. Modern economic growth is characterized by sustained growth of per-capita GDP and by structural changes in the economy.

3. Economies grow because the total amount of factor inputs increases and because output per unit of input (or productivity) increases. The major factor causing economic growth is the growth of productivity.

4. Classical economists Thomas Malthus and David Ricardo predicted that economies would reach a stationary state of zero growth and subsistence living standards. The stationary state would be caused by the law of diminishing returns and by the tendency of the population to expand whenever wages rose above subsistence level.

5. The classical stationary-state model provides a first explanation of LDC poverty. The combination of rapid population growth and limited technological progress has caused diminishing returns to be a serious problem in LDCs. Possible solutions to the diminishing-returns problem are reduced population growth, increased capital formation, and more rapid technological progress. The demographic transition is the process by which countries change from rapid to slow population growth during the course of modernization. The LDCs have yet to experience the demographic transition. The LDCs suffer from inadequate capital formation. Although it may appear that the LDCs could borrow the advanced technology of the developed countries, this technology is generally not well suited to the factor endowments of the LDCs.

6. The LDCs must choose between import-substitution and export-promotion policies of economic development. The LDCs have asked the industrialized countries for more foreign aid, commodity-stabilization programs, and improved access to markets. The LDCs must decide whether planned or market-allocation systems offer them a better chance for economic development.

Policy Focus: **Public policy can contribute to economic growth by adopting policies that encourage saving, human capital, and improvements in health and education.**

Key Terms

economic growth (p. 287)
level of economic development (p. 289)
less developed country (LDC) (p. 289)
extensive growth (p. 291)
intensive growth (p. 291)

factor productivity (p. 291)
labor productivity (p. 293)
capital productivity (p. 293)
total factor productivity (p. 293)
demographic transition(p. 298)

Questions and Problems

1. Explain why the two measures of economic growth can yield different results.

2. The amount of land in the world is fixed. The law of diminishing returns indicates that, with a fixed input, the marginal productivity of variable inputs will ultimately decline. Will we not ultimately reach the classical stationary state?

3. Malthus maintained that whenever wages rise above the subsistence level, the population will grow. Has this prediction proven to be true in the industrialized countries? Explain.

4. Why is intensive growth less costly than extensive growth?

5. In the economy of Malthusia, over a 10-year period, real output grew at 5 percent per year, combined inputs at 2 percent per year, and population at 1 percent per year. What is the annual growth rate of per-capita GDP? What is the annual growth rate of factor productivity? What proportion of the 5 percent growth rate is explained by productivity growth (the residual)?

6. From 1973 to 1981 capital grew twice as fast as labor hours (approximately). If capital grows at three times the rate of labor hours, what would you expect to happen to labor productivity?

7. Describe the characteristics of the classical stationary state.

8. In the economy of Gregoria, the number of hours worked grew by 2 percent per year, and the capital stock grew by 5 percent per year. What effect would these trends have on labor productivity?

9. Explain why GDP or GDP per capita can be an imperfect measure of the level of economic development in a country.

10. "The stationary state of Ricardo and Malthus is not an accurate description of the situation in industrialized countries. On the other hand, it does appear to describe accurately conditions in the LDCs." Evaluate this position.

11. Describe the *demographic transition*. Why has the demographic transition not occurred in many of the LDCs?

12. Contrast the different trade policies that an LDC might pursue in trying to promote its economic development.

13. Evaluate the following statement: "The LDCs should not have any problem with technology. All they have to do is adopt the technologies that have been developed in the industrialized world."

14. Using the data presented in this chapter, indicate in which area—economic growth or social indicators—the LDCs have made the most progress relative to the industrialized world.

Doing Economics

One of the principal inputs to the production process of your college or university is its faculty. Thus, a crude measure of faculty productivity could be obtained by dividing the number of students at the school (or, better yet, the number of full-time-equivalent students) by the number of faculty. Look through the current catalog and old catalogs for your school from ten, twenty, and thirty years ago. Try to find information on the number of full-time-equivalent faculty and students in each year. (If you cannot find the information easily in the catalog, ask someone in the administration. All schools have this information.) By this measure, what has happened to faculty productivity in recent decades? Does this make sense? What other important factors have not been taken into account? Are these factors important in industries other than higher education? How might one attempt to account for them?

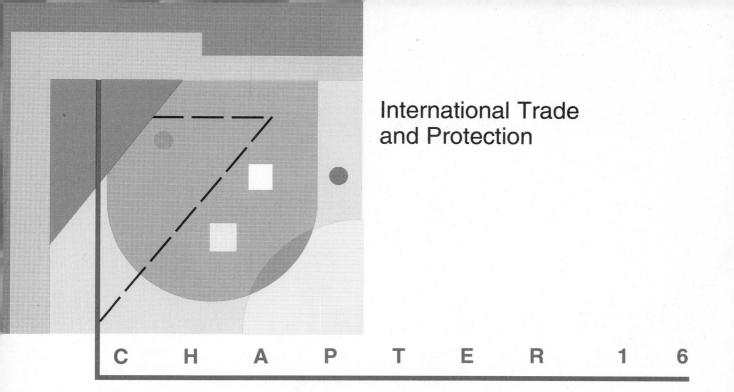

International Trade and Protection

CHAPTER FOCUS It pays for both individuals and countries to specialize in the goods and services they best produce. This chapter examines the reasons for and consequences of international trade, and the effects of tariffs and quotas on trade. We shall see that the gain from international trade consists more in its imports than its exports. Through international trade, as John Stuart Mill (1806–1873) said, "a country obtains things which it either could not have produced at all, or which it must have produced at a greater expense of capital and labor than the cost of the things which it exports to pay for them."

After studying this chapter, you will be able to:

■ Understand how the law of comparative advantage guarantees that every country can gain from exporting and importing.

■ Explain how countries can even export goods in which they have absolute cost disadvantages.

■ Discuss the similarities and differences between tariffs, import quotas, and voluntary export restraints.

■ Determine the relative costs and benefits of protecting a particular industry from international competition.

THE REASONS FOR INTERNATIONAL TRADE

International trade allows a country to specialize in the goods and services that it can produce at a relatively low cost and export those goods in return for imports whose domestic production is relatively costly. As a consequence, international trade enables a country—and the world—to consume and produce more than would be possible without trade. We shall later show that a country can benefit from trade even when it is more efficient (uses fewer resources) in the production of *all* goods than any other country. Adam Smith noted:

> *What is prudence in the conduct of every private family can scarce be folly in that of a great kingdom. If a foreign country can supply us with a commodity cheaper than we ourselves can make it, better buy it with some part of the produce of our industry employed in a way in which we have some advantage.*

Aside from the tangible benefit of increasing the world's output of goods and services, trade has intangible benefits as well. Trade offers diversity to our lives and work. The advantages of particular climates and lands are shared: the United States imports oil from the hot desert of Saudi Arabia to drive cars in cool comfort; Americans can enjoy coffee, bananas, and spices without living in the tropics; and we can have the economy and durability of Japanese cars without driving in hectic Tokyo. Thus, international (and interregional) trade enables us to enjoy a more diverse menu of goods and services than would be possible without trade. World trade also encourages the diffusion of knowledge and culture because trade serves as a point of contact between people of different lands.

THE UNITED STATES IN WORLD TRADE

The Volume of U.S. Trade

The world's largest exporting countries are Germany and the United States. Exhibit 1 shows the merchandise exports of West Germany, the United States, Japan, France, the United Kingdom, Italy, Canada, and the Netherlands. These countries account for about half of world trade. Because of its size and diversity, the United States is less dependent on trade than any of the other seven countries, as the lower U.S. ratio of exports to GDP demonstrates.

David Ricardo (1772–1823)

Born in London in 1772, David Ricardo made a fortune by the time he was 25, retired, became one of the world's greatest economists, and then entered politics. Starting as a stockbroker he soon became a multimillionaire even by today's standards. Wealth gave him the leisure to study economics, mathematics, chemistry, mineralogy, and geology. At the age of 27 he borrowed a copy of Adam Smith's *Wealth of Nations*, and the rest is history. Today we have the Ricardian theory of trade, the Ricardian theory of value, the Ricardian theory of distribution, and the Ricardian equivalence theorem. Perhaps no other economist is honored by so many theorems. This is all the more remarkable because he was an active economist for only fourteen years.

Ricardo had the rare ability to switch from the abstract to the concrete. He could speculate in corn, or foreign exchange, or wheat, and make a handsome profit; he would then turn his enormous analytical skills to the mechanisms determining the price of corn or the price of foreign exchange. In his practical life, he concentrated on day-to-day movements in prices. In his scholarly investigations, he thought in terms of the long run—years or even decades.

Ricardo's most important work was his classic *Principles of Political Economy and Taxation*, published in 1817. Among its many insights, Ricardo's law of comparative advantage stands out as perhaps the most enduring. Because foreign wages need not be the same as domestic wages, Ricardo pointed out, "the labour of 100 Englishmen cannot be given for that of 80 Englishmen, but the produce of the labour of 100 Englishmen may be given for the produce of the labour of 80 Portuguese, 60 Russians, or 120 East Indians."

U.S. Exports and Imports

Exhibit 2 shows the principal commodity exports and imports of the United States in 1992. About 8 percent of American exports consist of agricultural goods, such as wheat, soybeans, corn, cotton, and tobacco. Chemicals, business machines and computers, and aircraft make up about 16 percent of total merchandise exports. Consumer products and automobiles dominate American imports. The American propensity to drive foreign cars, wear clothes made in Taiwan or shoes made in Italy or Brazil, and watch Japanese TV sets shows up in the heavy imports of consumer goods and automotive vehicles. These aggregate statistics hide the fact that the United States is almost entirely dependent on foreign suppliers for bananas, cocoa, coffee, diamonds, manganese, cobalt, nickel, natural rubber, tea, tin, natural silk, and spices.

Exhibit 3 shows how the U.S. involvement in foreign trade has increased from 1960 to 1992. In 1960, the United States exported about 4 percent of GDP, and imports were only 3 percent of GDP. In 1992, imports had grown to about 11.2 percent of GDP, and exports had risen to about 10.7 percent of GDP. The much-discussed U.S. merchandise trade deficit shows up clearly for recent years. Notice that up until the 1970s the U.S. had a merchandise trade surplus.

THE LAW OF COMPARATIVE ADVANTAGE

In Chapter 2 we saw how the **law of comparative advantage** could be used to explain the benefits people enjoy from specialization. Individuals are made better

EXHIBIT 1 Size of Exports in Eight Major Countries, 1990

Country	Exports as Percent of GNP	Total Exports (billions of dollars)
West Germany	30	398
United States	7	393
Japan	10	287
France	20	210
United Kingdom	20	185
Italy	20	181
The Netherlands	50	131
Canada	21	127

SOURCE: *Statistical Abstract of the United States*, 1992, p. 848.

EXHIBIT 2 Principal Commodities of U.S. Merchandise Trade, 1992

Commodities	Quantity (billions of dollars)	Percentage of Total*
Exports		
Industrial machinery	137	31
Agricultural	36	8
Chemicals, bus. machines, and comp.	31	7
Civilian aircraft	38	9
Other exports	197	45
Total	439	100
Imports		
Consumer goods (nonauto)	123	23
Automotive vehicles	91	17
Petroleum	56	10
Metals	30	6
Coffee, cocoa, sugar	3	1
Other imports	233	44
Total	536	100

*Totals may not sum to 100 due to rounding.
SOURCE: U.S. Department of Commerce, *Survey of Current Business*, March 1993, Table 2.

off by specializing and engaging in trade with other people. The law of comparative advantage can also help explain the gains from international specialization. Interpersonal trade and international trade are very similar because many of the individual traits of persons and nations cannot be transferred to other persons and nations. David Ricardo (see Gallery of Economists) proved in 1817 that international specialization pays if each country devotes its resources to those activities in which it has a comparative advantage.

EXHIBIT 3   U.S. Merchandise Exports and Imports

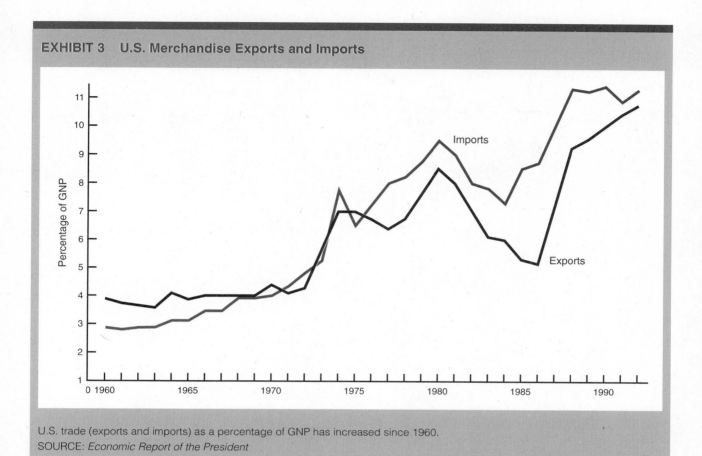

U.S. trade (exports and imports) as a percentage of GNP has increased since 1960.
SOURCE: *Economic Report of the President*

The **law of comparative advantage** states that people or countries specialize in those activities in which they have the greatest advantage or the least disadvantage compared to other people or countries.

Profound truths are sometimes difficult to discover; the real world is so complex it can hide its basic nature. Ricardo's genius was to provide a simplified model of trade without the irrelevant details that cloud our vision. He considered a hypothetical world with only two countries and only two goods. The two "countries" could be America and Europe; the two goods could be food and clothing. For the sake of simplicity, let us assume also that:

1. labor is the only productive factor, and there is only one type of labor;
2. labor cannot move between the two countries (this assumption reflects the relative international immobility of productive factors compared to goods;
3. the output from a unit of labor is constant (in other words, productivity is constant no matter how many units of output are produced);
4. laborers are indifferent between working in the food or clothing industries, provided only that wages are the same; and
5. there is no unemployment (each worker can produce food or clothing on his or her own without being attached to a firm that has capital).

Exhibit 4 shows the hypothetical output of food or clothing from one unit of labor in each of the two hypothetical countries. America can produce 6 units of

Trade patterns depend on comparative, and not on absolute, advantages. In our hypothetical example, America is 6 times more efficient than Europe in food production and twice as efficient in clothing production. America has an absolute advantage in both food and clothing but has only a comparative advantage in food production. Europe has an absolute disadvantage in the production of both goods but has a comparative advantage in clothing production. Europe will export clothing to America in return for food, and both will gain by this pattern of trade.

Country	Units of Food Output from 1 Unit of Labor	Units of Clothing Output from 1 Unit of Labor
America	6	2
Europe	1	1

food with 1 unit of labor and can produce 2 units of clothing with 1 unit of labor. Europe can produce either a unit of food or a unit of clothing with 1 unit of labor. America is 6 times more efficient than Europe in food production (it produces 6 times as much with the same labor); America is only twice as efficient in clothing production (it produces twice as much with the same labor).

We have deliberately constructed a case where America has an **absolute advantage** over Europe in all lines of production.

> A country has an **absolute advantage** in the production of a good if it uses fewer resources to produce a unit of the good than any other country.

Even under these circumstances, however, both countries stand to benefit from specialization and trade according to comparative advantage, as demonstrated below.

The Case of Self-Sufficiency

Assume that each country in our hypothetical world is initially self-sufficient and must consume only what it produces at home.

America. A self-sufficient America must produce both food and clothing. American workers can produce 6 units of food or 2 units of clothing from a unit of labor (see Exhibit 4). Thus, in the marketplace, 6 units of food will have the same value as 2 units of clothing. In other words, 3 units of food (F) will have the same value as 1 unit of clothing (C), because these quantities use the same amount of labor. In opportunity-cost terms, to acquire 1 unit of clothing, a worker must sacrifice 3 units of food.

America's opportunity cost of 1 unit of clothing is 3 units of food:

$$3F = 1C.$$

Under conditions of self-sufficiency, the American price of a unit of clothing will be 3 times the price of a unit of food.

These same facts are shown in panel (a) of Exhibit 5. Panel (a) shows America's production-possibilities frontier. Labor is the only factor of production, and a total of 15 units of labor are assumed to be available to the American economy. America's production-possibilities frontier is a straight line because

EXHIBIT 5 Hypothetical American and European Production-Possibilities Frontiers

a. America

b. Europe

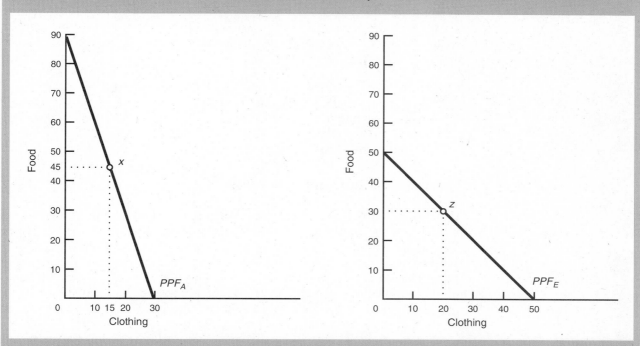

Panel (a) shows a hypothetical production-possibilities frontier for America. Based on the labor-productivity rates in Exhibit 4, if 15 units of labor are available and labor is the only factor of production, America could produce either 30 units of clothing, 90 units of food, or some mixture of the two—such as that combination represented by point *x*, where 45 units of food and 15 units of clothing are produced. Panel (b) shows a hypothetical *PPF* for Europe, where 50 units of labor are available. Europe could produce 50 units of clothing, 50 units of food, or a combination, such as that represented by point *z*, where 30 units of food and 20 units of clothing are produced.

opportunity costs are constant in our example. If everyone worked in clothing production, 30 (= 15 × 2) units of clothing could be produced. If everyone worked in food production, 90 (= 15 × 6) units of food could be produced. The economy would likely produce a mix of food and clothing to meet domestic consumption. Such a combination could be point *x* where 45 units of food and 15 units of clothing are produced and consumed in America. Without trade, America consumes 45*F* and 15*C*, the combination of which reflects America's preferences.

Europe.   In a self-sufficient Europe, workers can produce 1 unit of food or 1 unit of clothing with a unit of labor. A unit of clothing and a unit of food have the same labor costs and, hence, the same price. In other words, Europeans must give up 1 unit of food to get 1 unit of clothing.

Europe's opportunity cost of a unit of clothing is a unit of food:

$$1F = 1C.$$

Panel (b) of Exhibit 5 shows Europe's production-possibilities frontier. In our example, Europe is more populous than the United States; it has 50 units of labor available. Europe has a straight-line production-possibilities frontier as well and can produce either 50 units of food, 50 units of clothing, or some combination of the two. A likely situation would be for Europe to produce and consume at a point such as z, where 30 units of food and 20 units of clothing are produced. Without trade, Europe consumes $30F$ and $20C$, the combination that reflects Europe's preferences.

Without trade, each country must consume on its production-possibilities frontier. To produce (and consume) more requires either a larger labor force or an increase in the efficiency of labor.

The World.   If both Europe and America were self-sufficient, the total amount of food and clothing produced would be the amount produced by America ($45F$ and $15C$ plus the amount produced by Europe ($30F$ and $20C$). Thus, the total amount of food produced would be 75 units ($45F + 30F$), and the total amount of clothing produced would be 35 units ($15C + 20C$).

The Case of International Trade

If trade opened between Europe and America (as described in Exhibit 4), an American trader would find that 1 unit of clothing sells for 1 unit of food in Europe but sells for 3 units of food in America. If the trader applies 1 unit of labor in American food production and ships the resulting 6 units of food to Europe, he or she can obtain 6 units of clothing instead of only 2 by producing it at home! It makes no difference that clothing production is half as efficient in Europe. What matters is that in Europe food and clothing use the same amount of labor, and so food and clothing sell for the same price in Europe.

Americans would soon discover that clothing could be brought more cheaply in Europe than at home. Soon the law of supply and demand would do its work. Americans would stop producing clothing to concentrate on food production and would begin to demand European clothing. This increased demand would drive up the price of European clothing. Europe would presumably shift from food production to clothing production; eventually the pressure of American demand would lead Europe to specialize completely in clothing production.

The end result would be that Americans would get clothing more cheaply (at less than $3F$ for $1C$) than before trade; Europeans would receive a higher price for their clothing (at more than $1F$ for $1C$).

In making trade decisions, each country needs to know how much clothing is worth in terms of food, or the **terms of trade**.

> The **terms of trade** is the rate at which two products can be exchanged for each other between countries.

The terms of trade between Europe and America will settle some place between America's and Europe's opportunity costs. If America's opportunity cost of 1 unit of cloth is 3 units of food, and Europe's opportunity cost of 1 unit of cloth is 1 unit of food, the terms of trade will settle between $1C = 3F$ and $1C = 1F$. Europe is willing to sell 1 unit of cloth for at least 1 unit of food; America is willing to pay no more than 3 units of food for 1 unit of cloth.

The cheap imports of clothing from Europe will drive down the price of clothing in America. When Europe exports clothing to America, the European price of clothing will rise.

Although the final equilibrium terms of trade cannot be determined without knowing each country's preferences, one can determine that the final terms of trade will be somewhere between $3F$ and $1F$ for $1C$. If the world terms of trade at which both Europe and America can trade are set by the market at $2F = 1C$, Americans would no longer get only 2 units of clothing for 1 unit of labor but could produce 6 units of food and trade that food for 3 units of clothing (because $2F = 1C$) in Europe. Europeans would no longer have to work so hard to get a unit of food. They could produce 1 unit of clothing and trade that clothing for 2 units of food instead of getting only 1 unit of food for the hour of work.

When the terms of trade in the world are $2F = 1C$, Americans will devote all their labor to food production, and Europeans will devote all their labor to clothing production. Each country completely specializes because we made the simplifying assumption of constant rather than increasing costs of production. With increasing opportunity costs, America would likely produce some cloth and Europe some food because as each country specialized their costs of production would become more similar.

THE GAINS FROM TRADE

When American workers are specialized in food production and European workers are specialized in clothing production, the gains to each may be measured by their sacrifices before and after trade. Americans before trade sacrificed 3 units of food for 1 unit of clothing. After trade, Americans need sacrifice only 2 units of food for a unit of clothing (with terms of trade $2F = 1C$). Europeans before trade sacrificed 1 unit of clothing for 1 unit of food. After trade, Europeans need sacrifice only half a unit of clothing (because clothing sells for twice as much as food after trade).

The gains from trade are shown more dramatically in Exhibit 6. Before trade, America is at point x in panel (a), and Europe is at point z in panel (b). When trade opens up at the terms of trade $2F = 1C$, America moves its production to point p_A (specialization in food production), as the arrows show. Thus, America increases its food production from 45 units to 90 units. America can now trade each unit of food for half a unit of clothing. America trades 40 units of food for 20 units of clothing. Now America consumes at point c_A, with consumption at 50 units of food and 20 units of clothing. Trade enables America to consume above its production-possibilities frontier. In this example, trade shifts consumption from x to c_A. The dotted line shows the consumption possibilities available to Americans when $2F = 1C$ in the world market.

Europe's story is told in panel (b) of Exhibit 6. Europe shifts production from z, where $30F$ and $20C$ are produced, to point p_E, where 50 units of clothing are produced. The terms of trade are $2F = 1C$; when Europe trades 20 units of clothing for 40 units of food, Europe's consumption shifts from z to c_e—which is above the original production-possibilities frontier. Europe is also better off. The dotted line in Exhibit 6 shows the consumption possibilities available to Europeans when $2F = 1C$ in the world market.

In this simple world, the benefits of trade are dramatic. Everybody is made better off; nobody is hurt by trade. In effect, trade has the same effect on consumption as an increase in national resources or an improvement in efficiency of resource use. As a consequence of trade, countries are able to consume beyond their original production-possibilities frontiers. (See Example 1.)

In the real world, imports of goods from abroad displace the domestic production of competing goods, and in the process some people may find that their income falls. Because the Ricardian model assumes only one factor of production, the model simply cannot account for changes in the distribution of income. The

The law of comparative advantage guarantees that the most productive countries can gain from imports and that the least productive countries will be able to export something.

EXHIBIT 6 The Effects of Trade

a. America

b. Europe

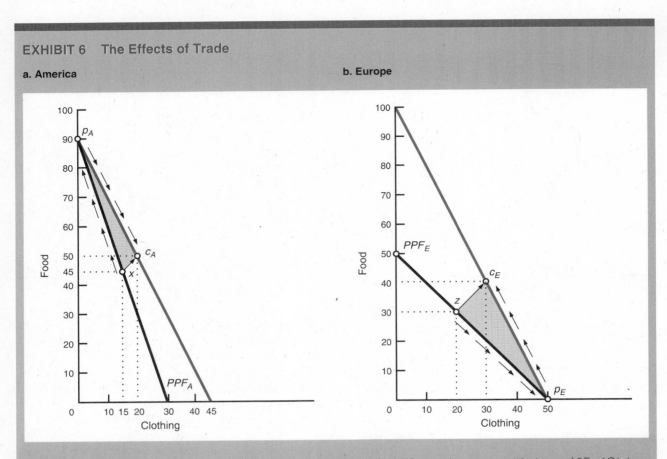

As shown in panel (a), before trade America produces and consumes at point x. When trade opens up at the terms of $2F = 1C$ (where F = units of food and C = units of clothing), America produces at p_A, specializing in food production, and trades 40 units of food for 20 units of clothing. America, therefore, consumes at point c_A, where it consumes 50 units of food and 20 units of clothing. Trade shifts American consumption from x to c_A. As shown in panel (b), before trade Europe produces and consumes at point z. When trade opens up, Europe shifts production to p_E, specializing in clothing production, and trades 20 units of clothing for 40 units of food. Europe, therefore, shifts consumption from z to point c_E, where 30 units of clothing and 40 units of food are consumed. The arrows pointing up in panel (a) and down in panel (b) show the effects of trade on domestic production, and the arrows pointing down in panel (a) and up in panel (b) show the effects of trade on domestic consumption. Both countries consume somewhere on the red line above their original production-possibilities frontiers.

model does demonstrate that in a world with many factors and shifts in distribution of income, trade increases average real income. Although trade makes the *average* person better off, some people are made even better off than the average while others are made worse off.

PROTECTIONISM

The American dairy industry contends that imported cheese and ice cream hurt its business. Americans love dairy products, but the U.S. government loves the dairy industry even more. Thus, cheese and ice cream imports are severely limited. This happens in other industries. Why?

When each country specializes and trades according to comparative advantage, each country can consume more than would be possible if it had to produce

EXAMPLE 1

U.S. Comparative Advantage

According to Ricardian theory, every country has a comparative advantage in something. But what determines comparative advantage in the real world? A country tends to export those goods that intensively use the productive factors the country has in abundance. For instance, if labor is plentiful relative to land or capital, a country's wages will be lower than wages in countries with abundant land or capital. Even if technical know-how were the same across countries, labor-cheap countries would have a comparative advantage in the production of labor-intensive goods. While the Ricardian theory assumes only one factor and takes cost differences as given, in the real world comparative advantage is the consequence of differences in the relative abundance of different factors.

The United States abounds in highly skilled technical labor and has a comparative advantage in manufactured goods that require intensive investment in research and development (R&D) such as the laser optical computer shown in the photograph. Industries with relatively high R&D expenditures contribute most to American export sales. Chemicals, nonelectrical or electrical machinery, aircraft, and professional and scientific instruments are the major R&D-intensive industries. These industries generate a surplus of exports over imports. The manufacturing industries that are not in this category—like textiles or paper products or food manufacturers—generate a trade deficit (a surplus of imports over exports).

The products of R&D industries tend to be new products, which are nonstandardized and not well suited to simple, repetitive mass-production techniques. The production processes for these products—such as hand-held calculators—become more standardized each year. The longer a product remains on the market, the easier it is for it to become standardized and the less need there is for highly trained workers. When new goods become old goods, other countries can gain a comparative advantage over the United States. The United States then moves on to the next new product generated with its giant research establishment and abundant supply of engineers, scientists, and skilled labor in order to fulfill its comparative advantage. The U.S. comparative advantage in manufacturing is in new products and processes.

at home everything that it consumed. As shown earlier, with **free trade** a country can consume above its production-possibilities frontier.

> **Free trade** is international trade unimpeded by artificial barriers such as tariffs (import taxes) or import quotas.

Is it to a country's advantage to adopt complete free trade or is it to a country's advantage to interpose some trade barriers between it and the rest of the world?

TRADE BARRIERS

Tariffs

An import **tariff** raises the price paid by domestic consumers as well as the price received by domestic producers of similar or identical products.

A tariff on clothing from Taiwan will raise the prices paid by American consumers of clothing imports and the prices charged by American clothing producers.

Suppose a country levies a $1 tariff on imported shoes that cost $10 in the foreign market. If domestic and foreign shoes are the same, both imported and domestically produced shoes will sell for $11 in the home market. Because consumers will pay more for shoes than otherwise, the tariff discourages shoe consumption. Because the domestic producer of shoes will be able to charge more for shoes, the tariff encourages domestic production. The $1 tariff discourages shoe imports and foreign shoe production.

The same result (of discouraging shoe consumption and encouraging domestic production) could also be accomplished by taxing domestic consumption of shoes by $1 and giving every domestic firm a $1 subsidy per pair of shoes produced.

Import Quotas

An **import quota** sets the number of units of a particular product that can be imported into the country during a specified period of time. U.S. import quotas on imported steel, for example, might specify the number of tons of steel of a specified grade that can be imported into the United States in a particular year.

Generally speaking, importers of products that fall under quota restrictions must obtain an import license to import the good. By limiting the number of licenses issued to the number specified by the quota, the quantity of imports cannot exceed the maximum quota limit.

Import licenses can be distributed in a variety of ways. One option is for import licenses to be auctioned off by the government in a free and fair market. If import licenses are scarce (more importers want licenses than are available), they will sell for a price that reflects their scarcity. In such a case, an import license is similar to a tariff: it restricts imports and raises revenue for the government.

Import licenses may also be handed out on a first-come-first-served basis, on the basis of favoritism, or according to the amount of past imports by the importer. When import quotas are not auctioned off, the potential revenue that the government could collect goes to the lucky few importers who get the scarce import licenses. For this reason, some importers, especially those who are likely to obtain import licenses, prefer import quotas to tariffs. Instead of the government collecting the revenue, the importers can cash in on the scarcity value of the import licenses. The license permits them to buy a product cheaply in the world market and then to sell it at a handsome profit in the home market. For example, in late 1993, world sugar prices were about $0.10 a pound. The U.S. sugar quota keeps domestic sugar prices at about $0.20 a pound. The importers collect the difference! American consumers pay higher prices, and the government gains no revenues.

Voluntary Export Restraints

A **voluntary export restraint** is a popular trade barrier in use by the United States.

A **voluntary export restraint** is an agreement between two governments in which the exporting country voluntarily limits the export of a certain product to the importing country.

The U.S. government has negotiated a number of voluntary export restraints with foreign governments that limit the foreign country's volume of commodity exports to the U.S. market. Unlike tariffs or import quotas, voluntary export restraints do not generate any revenue for the importing country or its government. Instead, foreign exporters or the foreign government collect the scarcity value of the right to export to the huge American market.

Voluntary export restrictions are particularly widespread in textiles. An agreement among 29 countries restricts trade in textiles. The importing country induces the exporting country to impose export quotas under the threat of imposing tariff or import quotas. Under these quota agreements, not all those who wish to export textiles to the United States can do so. First, they must acquire scarce export licenses. The privilege to export textiles to the United States is a property right that can be bought and sold in several Asian countries. The voluntary export quotas imposed by Japan on automobile exports to the United States is another example. When the U.S. threatened to impose an import quota, the Japanese government ordered its auto companies to voluntarily limit exports to the United States to about 1.8 million units a year from 1981 to 1985. In 1985, the "voluntary" export limit was raised to 2.3 million units per year. A Brookings Institution study concluded that before the export limit was raised the Japanese-American curb boosted average car prices by about $2,500.

Like import tariffs, import quotas and voluntary export restraints limit the quantity of foreign goods available in the domestic market. Such nontariff barriers raise the price paid by domestic consumers and the price that can be charged by domestic producers on their import-competing products. Domestic producers benefit from quotas by being able to charge higher prices. The importer who receives a license to buy cheap imports gains, or, if licenses are auctioned, the government gains some revenues. The loser from quotas is the consumer, who pays higher prices.

Other Nontariff Barriers

The importance of nontariff barriers in world trade has grown in the last decade. It has been estimated that nearly 50 percent of world trade is conducted under some sort of nontariff barrier. Import and voluntary export quotas are not the only nontariff barriers. Three other major impediments to trade are *government procurement practices, technical standards*, and *domestic-content rules*. Governments tend to give preferential treatment to domestic producers when they purchase goods and services. Further, the free flow of products can be impeded by technical standards that imported products must meet. For example, imported cars must pass American pollution-control and safety standards; imported foods and drugs must meet U.S. food and drug standards. American autoworker unions have proposed domestic-content rules, which would require domestic automakers to use American-made parts for a certain fraction of a car's cost. Recent talks among the major trading nations indicate a desire to limit such nontariff barriers, but no agreements have been forthcoming on limiting import quotas or voluntary export restraints.

Tariffs and nontariff barriers raises costs to consumers and protect the domestic producers of import-competing products. The following discussion of the economics of protection applies to tariffs, but tariff and nontariff barriers have similar effects.

THE CASE AGAINST PROTECTION

Economists' enthusiasm for free trade has remained steadfast for more than two hundred years because it is easy to demonstrate that the benefits of protection are outweighed by the costs.

Measuring Benefits and Costs

According to the law of comparative advantage, specialization benefits the country as a whole, while tariffs or quotas eliminate or reduce those gains from specialization. The argument for free trade presented thus far has rested on the rather simple Ricardian model which, for simplicity, ruled out the existence of different types of land, labor, and capital. In the real world, when trade opens, some people are hurt. The import of Japanese cars keeps domestic car prices lower than otherwise, which keeps car buyers happy but certainly hurts domestic auto producers. The export of American wheat keeps domestic prices of bread higher than otherwise but makes wheat farmers happy. The law of comparative advantage, however, guarantees that the *net* advantages are on the side of trade rather than protection.

Exhibit 7 shows why consumers benefit from lower prices. If the price of a video game is $36, the demand curve in Exhibit 7 shows that 6,000 games are demanded. If the price of the game were to fall to $24, about 9,000 games would be demanded. The gain to consumers of the lower price is the area $G + H$. The people who would have bought 6,000 units at $36 have to pay only $24 and, therefore, save $12 per unit. Their gain is $12 × 6,000, or $72,000 (area G). When the price is $24, new customers come into the market who buy 3,000 additional video games. The average new customer would have been willing to pay $30 (the average of $36 and $24). Since new customers are paying only $24 per game, their gain is $6 × 3,000, or $18,000 (area H). Thus, if the price falls from $36 to $24 per game, consumers gain $G + H$. Conversely, if the price rises from $24 to $36, consumers lose $G + H$.

The demand curve in Exhibit 7 showed how consumers benefit from lower

EXHIBIT 7   Consumer Benefits from Lower Prices

When the price falls from $36 to $24 per video game, consumers benefit by the area $G + H$. Those who would buy 6,000 units at $36 each (point *a*) benefit by area G because they save $12 per unit. Those new customers who buy the 3,000 additional units when the price is $24 (point *b*) benefit by area H.

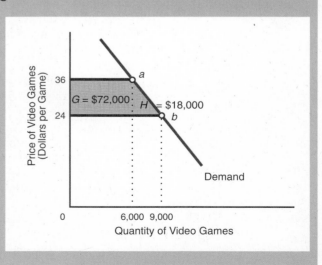

prices. Similarly, the supply curve in Exhibit 8 can show how producers benefit from higher prices. If the price of a ton of coal is $140, Exhibit 8 shows that at that price 9 million tons of coal will be supplied. If the price of coal were $200, 12 million tons would be supplied. The gain to producers from raising the price from $140 to $200 is the area $J + K$. Coal producers who would have suppled 9 million tons at a price of $140 receive $200 per ton (a $60 gain on each of the 9 million tons). Their gain is $60 × 9 million, or $540 million (area J). When the price rises to $200 per ton, 3 million additional tons are produced. The average producer of this new coal would have been willing to receive $170 (the average of $200 and $140) for a ton of coal. Because the new suppliers are in fact receiving $200, their gain is $30 × 3 million, or $90 million (area K). Thus, if the price of a ton of coal rises from $140 to $200, producers gain $J + K$. Conversely, if the price falls from $200 to $140, producers lose $J + K$.

Why Tariffs Impose Net Costs

Exhibit 9 shows the supply and demand conditions in a country whose imports of a particular good are so small relative to the world supply that the world price (p_w) is taken as given. The amount imported by this country will not affect the world price.

With a zero tariff, consumers can purchase all they want at the prevailing world price, p_w. According to Exhibit 9, the quantity represented by the distance between q_1 and q_4 would be imported because this quantity is the difference between the quantity demanded at p_w and the quantity supplied by domestic producers.

When a tariff (t) is imposed, the price rises to $p_w + t$; the new domestic price equals the world price plus the tariff rate. The country now imports only that quantity represented by the distance between q_2 and q_3.

The tariff benefits domestic producers of the competitive product by the area N. The government (or public) benefits by area T, which equals the revenue from the tariff (the tariff rate times the quantity of imports). The loss to consumers from the increase in price is the sum of areas $N + R + T + V$. If the gains (area $N + T$)

EXHIBIT 8   Producer Benefits from Higher Prices

When the price rises from $140 to $200, producers benefit by the area $J + K$. Those who would sell 9 million tons at $140 per ton (point c) benefit by area J. Those new suppliers who sell 3 million additional tons when the price is $200 per ton (point d) benefit by area K.

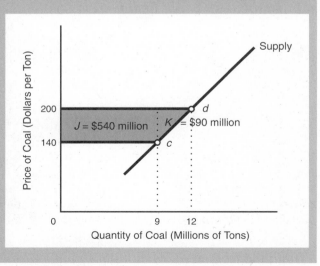

EXHIBIT 9   The Effects of a Tariff

Before the tariff, the price of the product is p_w. The tariff raises the price to $p_w + t$, that is, the world price plus the amount of the duty. Consumers lose area $N + R + T + V$. Producers gain area N. The government gains the tariff revenue of area T, which equals the tariff per unit times the quantity of imports. The net loss is area $R + V$. The tariff lowers imports from $(q_4 - q_1)$ to $(q_3 - q_2)$.

are subtracted from the losses (area $N + R + T + V$), the tariff imposes a net loss to the country of area $R + V$.

The bottom line is that protection imposes costs on society that are greater than the benefits received by the individual industries being protected. Trade barriers raise prices and lead to economic inefficiency (shifting resources from efficient to less efficient industries). One way to look at the costs of protection is to examine the cost of maintaining a job through protection. A trade barrier increases the number of jobs available in the protected industry (but not necessarily in the economy). Example 2 estimates the annual costs to consumers per job protected by different trade barriers. In general, the cost per job is more than twice as much as the average earnings in that job. In other words, if trade barriers save a $20,000-a-year job, that job costs the rest of the community more than $40,000.

Such losses may be an underestimate, according to economists Gordon Tullock and Anne Krueger. Tullock and Krueger argue that because producers have an incentive to expend resources to get the tariff passed, the import-competing industry may form a committee, lobby Congress, or advertise the plight of its industry. When the color-TV industry was hurt by imports, the industry formed COMPACT (the Committee to Preserve American Color Television). Such expenditures reduce gains to protected producers and, thus, further increase the costs of protection.

The Explanation for Tariffs

Since exports of things must pay for the imports of things, restricting imports will ultimately restrict exports.

The exports of goods, services, and securities must equal the imports of goods, services, and securities. If the United States, or any country, restricts imports, it necessarily restricts exports. In other words, subsidizing import-competing industries by means of tariff or nontariff barriers penalizes a whole host of unseen export industries. Imports can be more visible than exports.

If tariffs impose a cost on the community, why do they exist? Why would a representative democracy, which is supposed to represent consumer interests, establish trade barriers?

EXAMPLE 2

Measuring the Costs of Protection

The accompanying table shows the annual cost to consumers for each job protected in a few selected industries. Trade barriers protect jobs in particular industries at the cost of higher prices for consumers. What is the ratio of annual costs to benefits? The table shows that the ratio of cost to benefits ranges from 10 for citizens band transceivers to 3.6 for autos. In other words, the trade barrier for citizens band transceivers costs consumers $85,539 for each $8,500 job saved! The trade barrier for autos costs consumers $85,400 for each $23,566 job saved. Thus, the hidden costs of protection far exceed the visible benefits.

Product and Restriction	Number of Jobs Protected	Average Earnings	Cost per Job	Ratio of Cost to Earnings
Citizens band transceivers (tariffs, 1978–81)	587	$ 8,500	$85,539	10.1
Apparel (tariffs, 1977–81)	116,188	6,669	45,549	6.8
Footwear* (tariffs and quotas, 1977)	21,000	8,340	77,714	9.3
Carbon steel* (tariffs and quotas, 1977)	20,000	24,329	85,272	3.5
Autos* (proposed local content law, 1986–91)	58,000	23,566	85,400	3.6

*In 1980 dollars.

SOURCE: Keith E. Maskus, "Rising Protectionism and U.S. International Trade Policy," Federal Reserve Bank of Kansas City, *Economic Review* (July/August 1984), pp. 3–17.

Tariffs are explained by the fact that the costs they impose are highly diffused among millions of people, while the (smaller) benefits are concentrated among specific sectors of the economy associated with the protected industry. The costs imposed on the community are large in total but so small per person that it is not worth the trouble to any one person to join a committee to fight tariffs on each and every imported good, while the benefits to protected sectors are well worth the costs of lobbying. For example, assume people devote about 0.5 percent of all consumption to sugar (in all its various forms). A trade barrier that raises the price of sugar by 50 percent helps domestic sugar producers enormously, but it raises the cost of living to consumers by only 0.25 percent (50 percent of 0.5 percent). To the consumer, this cost is just too small to worry about. The costs of fighting against each request for protection are prohibitive.

The benefits of protection are relatively small but concentrated on the few, while the costs are relatively large but diffused among the many.

U.S. TRADE POLICIES

The tariff history of the United States is shown in Exhibit 10, which shows that tariffs have fluctuated up and down with the ebb and flow of protectionism in the U.S. Congress. In modern times, tariffs hit their peak with the infamous Smoot-Hawley Tariff of 1930. Economists were so appalled by the prospect of this tariff bill that in a rare show of agreement, 1,028 of them signed a petition asking

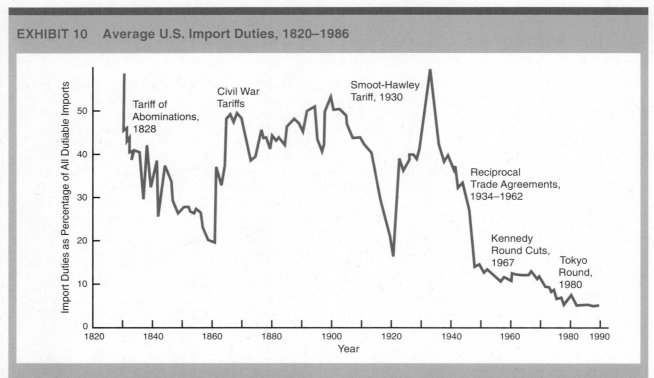

EXHIBIT 10   Average U.S. Import Duties, 1820–1986

Import Duties as Percentage of All Dutiable Imports

Tariff of Abominations, 1828

Civil War Tariffs

Smoot-Hawley Tariff, 1930

Reciprocal Trade Agreements, 1934–1962

Kennedy Round Cuts, 1967

Tokyo Round, 1980

Year

As attitudes toward free trade and protectionism have fluctuated in the United States, average tariff rates have also fluctuated but have shown a distinct downward trend.

SOURCES: *Historical Statistics of the United States; Statistical Abstract of the United States*

President Hoover to veto the bill. Because politics tends to override economics in tariff legislation, the bill was signed.

The Trade-Agreements Program and GATT

The Smoot-Hawley tariff, like most of the preceding 18 tariff acts stretching back to 1779, was the result of political *logrolling* in the U.S. Congress. Logrolling occurs when some politicians trade their own votes on issues of minor concern to their constituents in return for other politicians' votes on issues of greater concern to their constituents. Tariffs, historically, are the best example of the sacrifice of general interests for special interests.

Having established the highest tariff rates in U.S. history, the Smoot-Hawley Act triggered angry reactions overseas, as predicted by economists. As one nation after another erected trade barriers, the volume of world trade declined more than it would have due to the Great Depression. The export markets of the United States shrank at the time of a very deep domestic depression.

In order to secure a larger market for U.S. exports, Congress amended the Tariff Act of 1930 with the Reciprocal Trade Agreements Act of 1934. The President was authorized to negotiate reciprocal agreements that promised to lower U.S. trade barriers or tariffs in return for similar concessions abroad. The fact that Congress did not have to approve the tariff cuts marked a significant change in the power of special interests to influence U.S. tariff policy.

The trade-agreements program has been broadened under successive exten-

Free Trade

The law of comparative advantage has a clear policy implication: A country can gain from free trade even if its trading partners have import restrictions. Why? Trade pays because goods can be purchased more cheaply abroad than they can be produced at home as measured by opportunity costs.

There is perhaps no clearer example of the benefits of international trade than a comparison of less-developed countries that have encouraged trade and those that do not.

In 1960, India, South Korea, and Thailand were at about the same stage of development—extreme poverty. South Korea and Thailand embarked on a course that encouraged expanded international trade, whereas India looked inward and emphasized the protection of domestic industries from cheaper foreign imports. The consequences could not be more dramatic. By 1990, South Korea's per capita income was over seven times that of India, and Thailand's per capita income was over four times that of India.

Experiences like these can be multiplied many times. Free-trade success stories like Hong Kong, Singapore, and Taiwan have ushered in the Pacific century. Many countries—even India—are now jumping on the free-trade bandwagon. Mexico once banned many imports and levied tariffs above 100 percent on some goods. Beginning in 1986 Mexico unilaterally opened its markets to foreign goods. Mexico sought a free-trade agreement with the United States. In 1992, Canada, Mexico, and the Bush administration signed a free-trade agreement (which must be approved under the Clinton administration).

Many studies have shown that the per-capita incomes of free-trade countries grow at about 1 percent more per year than the per-capita incomes of protectionist countries over several decades. Moreover, the gains come quickly. One study of 30 episodes of trade liberalization found that within just one year, the growth rate of GDP increased by an average of about 1 percent.

Trade pays not only because of the gains from increased specialization, but also because it forces innovation and speeds the diffusion of technology. For example, the competition from Japanese cars almost certainly improved the quality of the cars produced by Ford and Chrysler.

In the face of all of this evidence, there are still a few calls for managed trade over free trade. Presumably, managed trade would mean that trade policy might be used to pry open foreign markets or to promote selected domestic industries. The evidence is not clear on this issue. When we argue that "free" trade is better than "protection," we are simply saying that countries that have "freer" trade do much better than those countries that have more protection. That is all we know. We do not know whether a little bit more or little bit less free trade is beneficial. The difficulty with such attempts to manage trade is that it bolsters the case of special-interest groups trying to protect their own industries.

sions and modifications. The Trade Expansion Act of 1962 gave the president the power to reduce tariffs by up to 50 percent and to remove duties of less than 5 percent. Under the authority of this act, the United States engaged in multilateral negotiations, known as the Kennedy Round, which resulted in an average reduction of 35 percent on industrial tariff rates. The Trade Reform Act of 1974 allowed the president to reduce tariffs by up to 60 percent and to eliminate duties of less than 5 percent. This act resulted in the Tokyo Round (1980) of multilateral reductions, in which the United States agreed to cut tariffs on industrial goods by 31 percent, the European Community agreed to cut tariffs by 27 percent, and

Japan agreed to cut tariffs by 28 percent. The Trade and Tariff Act of 1984 authorized the president to enter into a new round of multilateral reductions in trade barriers (called the Uruguay Round).

Clearly, the trade-agreements program has been an enormous success. In 1932, the average tariff rate was about 59 percent; today the average tariff rate is about 5 percent. The trade-agreement obligations of the United States and other countries are carried out under the General Agreement on Tariffs and Trade (GATT), established in 1948. All of the major countries belong to GATT, and members are responsible for about 85 percent of world trade. GATT is an agreement that spells out rules on the conduct of trade and procedures to settle trade disputes. GATT is also the forum in which international tariff negotiations take place.

Chapter Summary

The most important point to learn from this chapter is: Every country gains by exporting those goods in which their advantages are the greatest, or their disadvantages are the smallest, and by importing those goods in which their advantages are the smallest, or their disadvantages are the greatest.

1. The United States and Germany are the world's largest exporting countries, but trade as a percentage of GDP is smaller in the United States.

2. In a simple two-country, two-good world, even if one country has an absolute advantage in both goods, both countries can still gain by specialization and trade. If the two countries were denied the opportunity to trade, they would have to use domestic production to meet domestic consumption. With trade, specialization allows them to consume beyond their domestic production-possibilities frontiers by producing at home and then trading the product in which the country has comparative advantage. Countries will specialize in those products whose domestic opportunity costs are low relative to their opportunity costs in the other countries. Through trade, countries are able to exchange goods at more favorable terms than those dictated by domestic opportunity costs.

3. The major trade barriers are tariffs, import quotas, voluntary export restraints, and other nontariff barriers. A *tariff* is a tax levied on imports. It raises both the price paid by the domestic consumer and the price received by the domestic producer of the import-competing product. *Import quotas* limit the amount of imports of specified products. They raise the prices paid by domestic consumers and the prices received by domestic producers of import-competing products. Quotas are normally regulated by import licenses. If import licenses are sold to importers, the government receives their scarcity value. If they are not sold, private importers benefit from their scarcity value. *Voluntary export restraints* direct governments to restrict their exports to another country.

4. The basic argument against protection is that the costs of protection outweigh the benefits of protection. The loss to consumers from a tariff is greater than the gain to the protected producers.

5. The politics of tariffs explains why tariffs are passed. Although the costs of tariffs are large in total, these costs are small per person. Special-interest groups, therefore, lobby and spend funds to obtain tariff protection.

6. U.S. trade policies have changed over the years. The Smoot-Hawley tariff of 1930 caused a further restriction of trade during the Great Depression by setting very high

tariff rates. Since then, legislation has been passed that allows the U.S. president to negotiate tariff reductions.

Policy Focus: **Free trade pays such obvious dividends that more and more countries are liberalizing their trade. The evidence for managed trade is not compelling.**

Key Terms

law of comparative advantage (p. 307)
absolute advantage (p. 310)
terms of trade (p. 312)
free trade (p. 315)

tariff (p. 315)
import quota (p. 316)
voluntary export restraint (p. 316)

Questions and Problems

1. Name the three largest exporting countries in the world.

2. Suppose that 1 unit of labor in Asia can be used to produce 10 units of food or 5 units of clothing. Also suppose that 1 unit of labor in South America can be used to produce 4 units of food or 1 unit of clothing.
    a. Which country has an absolute advantage in food? In clothing?
    b. What is the relative cost of producing food in Asia? In South America?
    c. Which country will export food? Clothing?
    d. Draw the production-possibilities frontier for each country if Asia has 10 units of labor and South America has 20 units of labor.
    e. What is the range for the final terms of trade between the two countries?
    f. If the final terms of trade are 3 units of food for 1 unit of clothing, compute the wage in Asia and the wage in South America, assuming that a unit of food costs $40 and a unit of clothing costs $120.

3. What happens to the answers to parts (a), (b), and (c) of question 2 when the South American productivity figures are changed so that 1 unit of labor is used to produce either 40 units of food or 10 units of clothing?

4. What are the differences and similarities between an import duty and an import quota?

5. What is the difference between an import quota and a voluntary export restraint.

6. Economists agree that tariffs hurt the countries that impose them. Yet nearly all countries impose tariffs. Is something wrong with the economists' argument?

7. Assume a country can export all the wheat it wants at the world price of $5 per bushel. Using an analysis parallel to the discussion of Exhibit 9 in the text, show the impact of imposing a $1-per-bushel export tariff on every bushel exported. Does the benefit to consumers and government exceed the cost to producers of wheat? (*Hint:* An export tariff means that if a foreigner purchases wheat, he or she must pay the domestic price plus the $1 export duty.)

8. A country imports shoes. The world price of shoes is $20 a pair. Show that a tariff of $5 per pair will impose larger costs on shoe consumers than the sum of the benefits to domestic shoe producers and the total tariff revenue from shoe imports.

Doing Economics

Consider the economy of your home state. What are its major exports? How does its comparative advantage in these products come about? (*Hint:* Think about the conditions or factors of production that are abundant. Is labor cheap or expensive? Are there raw materials present that are important? Is climate or proximity to ports important?) Are there any industries that seem to defy the law of comparative advantage? Why do you think they are present?

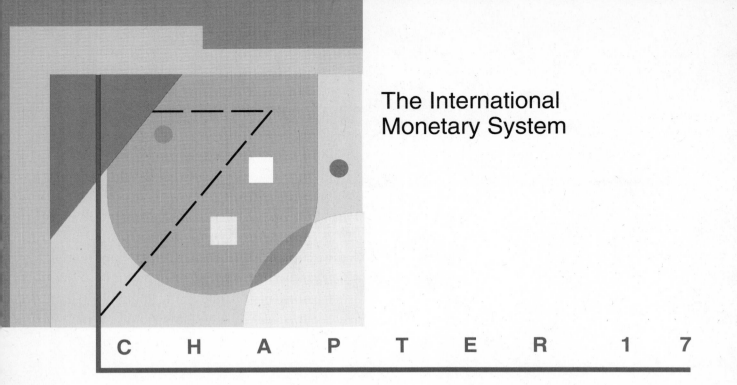

The International Monetary System

C H A P T E R   1   7

CHAPTER FOCUS   This chapter will examine the monetary mechanism behind the international
exchange of goods and services. It discusses the U.S. balance of payments,
international capital movements, and the coordination of monetary and fiscal
policies among countries. The daily news is filled with stories about trade
deficits and falling (or rising) exchange rates. This chapter will provide you
with a framework for understanding the meaning of such events.

After studying this chapter, you will be able to:

- Understand the main factors that cause exchange rates to fluctuate.
- Discuss how a fixed exchange rate system works.
- See how trade deficits or surpluses are related to the balance of payments.
- Explain how the current international monetary system developed.
- Know how international monetary coordination works.

INTERNATIONAL MONETARY MECHANISMS

The Foreign-Exchange Market

Money is the medium of exchange for domestic transactions because it is accepted by all sellers in exchange for their goods and services.

When an international transaction takes place, buyers and sellers reside in different countries. Sellers generally want the national currency of their own countries. Thus, Americans want U.S. dollars, the English want pounds sterling, the Japanese want yen, Germans want marks, and the French want francs. An American farmer sells wheat to a British miller or a British firm sells a bicycle to an American cyclist. To make the purchase, the buyer needs the currency of the seller's place of residence. The currency of another country that is needed for international transactions is called **foreign exchange**.

> **Foreign exchange** is the national currency of another country that is needed to carry out international transactions. Normally, foreign exchange consists of bank deposits denominated in the foreign currency but may sometimes consist of foreign paper money when foreign travel is involved.

Buyers of international goods and services obtain their currency requirements from the foreign-exchange market. Exchange between different currencies takes place around the world between large banks and brokers. For example, an American importer of a British bicycle priced in pounds sterling pays in sterling that is deposited in a British bank. The money is transferred by a check or draft or cable that is purchased with dollars from the importer's American bank that holds a sterling deposit in a British bank. These sterling deposits come from British importers of American goods who want dollars and supply pounds sterling.

The price of one currency in terms of another is the *foreign-exchange rate*. These exchange rates change from day to day and from hour to hour. In July 1993, the British pound cost about $1.50, the German mark about $.58, the French franc about $.17; and $1 was worth about 105 Japanese yen.

Foreign-exchange rates are needed to convert foreign prices into American prices. When the exchange rate is expressed in terms of dollars per unit of foreign currency, the rate can be multiplied by the foreign price to obtain the American price. For example, if a British bicycle costs 90 pounds ($\pounds$), the American importer pays $162 when the pound is worth $1.80 (because $162 = 1.80×90). When the exchange rate is expressed in terms of foreign currency per dollar, the foreign price can be divided by the rate to obtain the American price. For example, a Japanese

Harry G. Johnson (1923–1977)

Canadian-born Harry Johnson was truly an international economist on the grand scale. He wrote over 500 professional articles and over 40 books and pamphlets, was a Distinguished Professor at the University of Chicago, and held a Chair at the London School of Economics. He was constantly on the go, attending conferences, editing journals, giving public lectures, and receiving honors from most of the countries where he lived and worked. While ordinary mortals slept, Johnson wrote. While attending lectures or conferences, he would make beautiful wood carvings, but he could summarize the lecture or conference better than the note-takers in attendance.

Although involved in nearly every branch of economics, Johnson's main contributions dealt with international monetary economics. Johnson believed strongly in flexible exchange rates. Extremely small countries like Panama might use fixed exchange rates, but he thought that most countries such as his native Canada or his adopted United States should let the exchange rate seek its own market-equilibrium level. He developed the monetary approach to the balance of payments by arguing that under fixed exchange rates surpluses and deficits reflected misguided monetary policies. As he said: "[A] balance-of-payments deficit implies *either* dishoarding by residents, *or* credit creation by the monetary authorities." Throughout his career, he was suspicious of government intervention. For example, he criticized schemes to solve international monetary problems by giving resources to poor countries: "My reason for refusing to endorse such schemes is not that I am opposed to the less developed countries receiving more development assistance, but I think no useful purpose is served by misapplying economic analysis for political ends."

car costing 780,000 yen costs \$6,000 when 130 yen equal \$1 (780,000 ÷ 130 = 6,000).

Floating Exchange Rates

How the exchange rate is determined depends on whether the rate is a **fixed exchange rate** or a **floating exchange rate**.

> A fixed exchange rate is an exchange rate that is set by government decree or intervention within a small range of variation.

> A floating exchange rate is an exchange rate that is freely determined by the interaction of supply and demand.

The real world is a blend of these two polar cases. The floating system is easier to understand and roughly corresponds to the present regimen adopted by the United States, Great Britain, Canada, Japan, and other nations. Many small countries maintain fixed exchange rates against the dollar, the English pound, the French franc, or some basket of currencies. The major European countries have attempted to form a European Monetary System and maintain fixed exchange rates relative to each other but not relative to the United States. Some countries have adopted a dual exchange-rate system involving multiple exchange-rate quotations (depending on what is exchanged).

Americans demand foreign exchange to buy imported commodities, to use foreign transportation services and insurance, to travel abroad, to make payments to U.S. troops stationed abroad, to remit dividends, interest, and profits to the foreign owners of American stocks, bonds, and business firms, to grant foreign aid, and to make short-term and long-term investments in foreign assets.

America's supply of foreign exchange is generated by foreigners' demand for American dollars to buy American exports, to travel in America, to pay American owners of stocks, bonds, and businesses, and to invest in American assets.

To simplify the explanation of the foreign-exchange market, imagine that the world consists of two countries: America and England. The American demand for foreign exchange is, thus, a demand for British pounds sterling. Also assume that exports and imports of goods and services are the only things traded internationally.

Exhibit 1 shows the demand curve for foreign exchange by Americans. The vertical axis measures the dollar price of pounds; the horizontal axis measures the flow of pounds into the foreign-exchange market during the relevant period of time. The demand curve is downward-sloping because the higher is the price of pounds in dollars, *ceteris paribus*, the higher is the cost of British goods to American importers. For example, if a British bicycle costs 90 pounds and the pound price rises from $1.80 to $2.00, the bike's price rises from $162 to $180 for the American importer. This price increase will induce Americans to buy fewer bikes or switch to an American-made brand. Thus, the higher is the price of pounds, the lower is the quantity of foreign exchange demanded by Americans.

The American supply curve of foreign exchange depends on British importers of American goods. When the English buy American wheat, they supply pounds to the foreign-exchange market (because pounds must be exchanged to buy U.S. goods). The supply curve tends to be upward-sloping because when the dollar price of pounds rises—or when the dollar falls in value—American goods appear cheaper to foreigners. As a result, they will buy more American goods, thereby increasing the quantity of pounds supplied to Americans in the foreign-exchange market. For example, if a bushel of U.S. wheat costs $2.40, a fall in the value of the

EXHIBIT 1   The Foreign-Exchange Market

The dollar price of a British pound is measured on the vertical axis, the flow of pounds on the foreign-exchange market per unit of time is measured on the horizontal axis. The equilibrium exchange rate is $1.80 = £1. If the exchange rate was $2.00 = £1, the excess supply of pounds on the market would drive down the price. At a price of $1.60 per pound, there would be an excess demand for pounds on the market, bidding the price up.

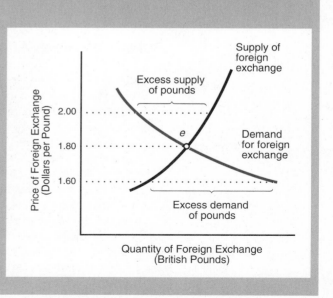

dollar from £1 = $1.60 to £1 = $2.00 will lower the cost of a bushel of wheat to foreigners from £1.50 to £1.20. The English will then shift their demand for wheat from British to American wheat and increase wheat consumption, stimulating American exports.

When the price of pounds is $2.00, Exhibit 1 shows that there is an excess supply of pounds on the foreign-exchange market. At the $2.00 exchange rate, desired U.S. exports exceed U.S. imports. With a floating exchange rate, there cannot be a permanent excess supply. An excess supply of pounds bids the price of pounds down, as in any competitive market. Similarly, at a price per pound of $1.60, there would be an excess demand for pounds, and the price of pounds would be bid up. The market-clearing price of $1.80 per pound in Exhibit 1 not only equates the supply and demand for foreign exchange but also maintains an equilibrium between U.S. exports and imports. Equilibrium between imports and exports is achieved because they are the mirror image of the demand and supply for foreign exchange.

The above analysis assumes that there are no other factors besides exports or imports requiring use of the foreign-exchange market. For example, international tourism, dividend and interest payments to foreigners, and foreign investments require the use of foreign exchange. Suppose in addition to exporting and importing, some foreigners wish to invest in American securities. The demand (D) and supply (S) curves in Exhibit 2 reflect America's exports and imports of goods. New investments in America shift the supply curve of foreign exchange outward to S'. The dollar price of pounds falls, or the dollar rises in value. This appreciation in the dollar, or depreciation in the pound, makes American goods more expensive, and brings about the required excess of imports over exports needed to accommodate the inflow of foreign capital to America.

A currency is said to *depreciate* if it falls in value on the foreign-exchange market (if it buys less foreign exchange) and to *appreciate* if it rises in value on the foreign-exchange market (if it buys more foreign exchange).

In our example, the appreciation of the dollar is the same thing as the depreciation of the pound because the dollar/pound exchange rate reflects the relative values of the two currencies: when one goes up the other must go down. In the actual world, of course, the dollar can rise in terms of the pound while falling in terms of the franc or the mark. To determine whether the dollar is rising or falling *in general* it is necessary to compute an index of the value of the dollar in terms of a bundle of currencies.

Market Forces Affecting the Exchange Rate

Why do exchange rates change? The above theory suggests how the underlying demand and supply curves for foreign exchange shift. The most important factors influencing exchange rates are:

1. *Changes in relative price levels.* If country A's prices are rising faster than country B's prices, A's currency will depreciate. The reason: the demand for B's exports will increase and the demand for A's exports will decrease.

Inflation rates in different countries play an important role in determining floating exchange rates. Countries that have enormous inflation rates can still trade with the rest of the world because the exchange rate reflects the relative purchasing power of the two currencies in their respective countries.

2. *Relative productivity changes.* If country A's productivity is increasing relative to country B's, in general A will become more competitive on world markets. Thus, the demand for A's exports will increase and A's currency will appreciate.

3. *Changes in relative interest rates.* If A's interest rates increase relative to country

EXHIBIT 2   The Effect of an Increase in Foreign Investment in America

If foreigners decided to invest more in America, the supply curve for foreign exchange would shift from S to S'. The equilibrium price of pounds would fall to $1.40 and would allow a surplus of imports over exports.

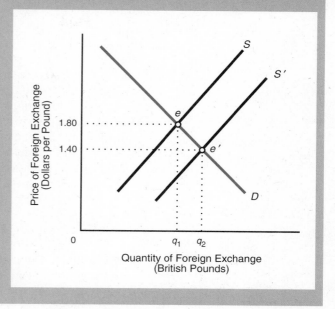

B's, international investors will increase their demand for A's currency and cause A's currency to appreciate.

4. *Changes in product preferences.* If country B develops a taste for country A's wines, the demand for country A's currency will increase and cause A's currency to appreciate.

5. *Changes in the "news."* If country A elects a new president that follows policies favored by the international business community, A's exchange rate is likely to rise.

Fixed Exchange Rates and the Gold Standard

The gold standard is the prototype of the fixed-exchange-rate system. The classical gold standard was in its heyday before World War I, from about the 1870s to 1914. The United Kingdom was on the gold standard as far back as the 1820s and used both gold and silver during the eighteenth century—the century in which David Hume and Adam Smith lived.

When Spain conquered the New World, it brought back enormous quantities of gold. As the quantity theory predicts, a major consequence of the inflow of gold into Spain was inflation of wages and production costs. This inflation made it more difficult for Spain to compete with other European countries in world markets. Thus, Spain developed an excess of imports over exports and shipped gold to pay for the difference. Eventually, this gold caused inflation elsewhere, and Spain's exports and imports were brought into approximate balance.

The gold standard can be explained using our hypothetical two-country world. If America defined the dollar as equal to 1/20 of an ounce of gold and England defined the pound as equal to $\frac{1}{4}$ of an ounce of gold, an English pound would contain 5 times as much gold as a U.S. dollar. England would convert gold into pounds (and vice versa) at the established rate of £1 = $\frac{1}{4}$ of an ounce of gold; America would convert gold into dollars at the rate of $1 = 1/20 of an ounce of gold. Under these circumstances, the exchange rate would be $5 = £1. No rational person would pay more than $5 for an English pound, because $5 would buy ¼ of an ounce of gold from the U.S. Treasury and that amount of gold would buy one pound note from the British Treasury. The next key ingredient of the gold standard is that England and America let their money supplies depend on how much gold was in their national treasuries.

If America had a surplus of exports over imports in our hypothetical world, gold would be shipped from England to America to pay for the surplus of exports over imports. This gold shipment would raise the money supply in America and reduce the money supply in England. As a result, inflation of costs and prices would occur in America, and a deflation of costs and prices would occur in England. Thus, America's exports would become less competitive, and England's exports would become more competitive. As America's exports decreased and England's exports increased, America's surplus of exports over imports would disappear—as long as the rules of the gold-standard game were followed.

The equilibrating mechanism of the international gold standard is the *relationship between the domestic money supplies and the state of the balance of payments.* If the country with a payments deficit allows its money supply to fall, while the country with a payments surplus allows its money supply to rise, automatic adjustment mechanisms will tend to restore equilibrium.

In the country gaining gold, the expansion of the money supply will (1) lower exports because of higher prices and costs, (2) raise imports because prices and costs are now cheaper abroad, and (3) raise imports because real GDP may be increased because of the expansion in the money supply. In the deficit country, which is losing gold, the contraction of the money supply will (1) raise exports because prices and costs are lower, (2) lower imports because prices and costs are now higher abroad, and (3) lower imports because real GDP may be lower because of the contraction of the money supply.

A fixed exchange rate imposes significant costs on an economy because gold surpluses and deficits may produce unwanted inflationary or deflationary pressures. During the Great Depression, with its enormous unemployment, countries could no longer afford to allow a deficit to produce further deflation and unemployment. Hence, country after country left the gold standard during the 1930s.

Gold is not necessary to establish a fixed-exchange-rate system that works like the gold standard. Fixed exchange rates can be established by official decree reinforced by central-bank intervention in the foreign-exchange market. For example, in Exhibit 3, America is assumed to maintain its currency at a $2 exchange rate against the English pound, but the equilibrium exchange rate is $1.75. Thus, at the official rate there is an excess supply of foreign exchange, because the pound is overvalued (or the dollar is undervalued). To maintain the $2 price of pounds, America's central bank must purchase the excess supply of pounds coming onto the foreign-exchange market. While America is experiencing this balance-of-payments surplus, the American central bank is adding to its inventory of pounds. This inventory of pounds can later be used as international reserves to defend the value of the dollar when a deficit appears—when the supply and demand curves intersect above the $2 official price.

The surplus of exports over imports in the above example will not persist if America and England follow the rules of the gold-standard game. If America lets its money supply rise and England allows its money supply to fall, mechanisms will be set in motion that will shift the demand curve to the right and the supply curve to the left. When America suffers inflation relative to England, America exports less (decreasing supply) and imports more (increasing demand).

EXHIBIT 3   American Balance of Payments

If the exchange rate were $1.75 = £1, America's balance of payments would be in equilibrium. If the dollar price of pounds is fixed at $2.00 = £1, however, the dollar will be undervalued (the pound will be overvalued), and America's balance of payments will be in surplus by the excess supply of pounds on the foreign-exchange market. These pounds will have to be purchased by the central banks of either America or England.

THE BALANCE OF PAYMENTS AND INTERNATIONAL CAPITAL MOVEMENTS

The Balance of Payments

A country's **balance of payments** summarizes information about the country's exports, imports, earnings by domestic residents on assets located abroad, earnings on domestic assets owned by foreign residents, international capital movements between countries, and official transactions by central banks and governments.

> A country's **balance of payments** is a summary record of its economic transactions with foreign residents over a year or any other period.

The balance of payments is a two-sided summary of international transactions. Each transaction is recorded by standard double-entry bookkeeping. In other words, every transaction has two sides, each of which is entered on one of the two sides of the balance-of-payments account. For example, when America exports wheat, the foreign importer might simply give an IOU in exchange for the wheat. The wheat sale is recorded on the minus (debit) side and the IOU is recorded on the plus (credit) side. Because each amount recorded on the minus side is recorded on the plus side, the balance-of-payments record will always be *in balance*.

Although the balance of payments always balances if all transactions are considered, specific *accounts* of the balance of payments need not balance. U.S. merchandise exports need not equal U.S. merchandise imports, for example. Thus, a specific account of the balance of payments may have a surplus or deficit, but all the surpluses in the balance of payments as a whole will cancel out the deficits. Because the balance of payments as a whole must balance, a deficit on one account implies a surplus on some other account.

These observations should serve as a warning that a deficit in a particular account should not be treated as unfavorable, nor should a surplus be treated as favorable to a country. Mercantilists—those seventeenth and eighteenth century writers whom Adam Smith and David Hume criticized—treated a surplus of exports over imports as a good thing and even called it a "favorable trade balance." That such a surplus benefits a country more than an "unfavorable" trade balance is a fallacy. A trade deficit may be a good thing. If a country is importing more than it is exporting, more goods are being brought in than are being sent out. Mercantilists committed the fallacy of treating exports as business sales and imports as business expenses. The **mercantilist fallacy** still lingers on in many press reports and in the minds of many people.

> The **mercantilist fallacy** is that exporting is better than importing.

The mercantilistic fallacy that exports are good and imports bad still persists in the popular mind. However, the economic reckoning of costs and benefits suggests that the exact opposite holds in general.

International-trade economists view exports as the cost of imports. When the U.S. imports Japanese cars, Americans have more cars to drive. When the U.S. exports wheat, Americans have less bread to eat. From the standpoint of the economy, exports are like a business firm's costs and imports are like a business firm's sales. Costs are something that a business firm sends out, just like exports; sales are something a business firm brings in, just like imports. To the modern-day international economists, the mercantilists turned the truth upside-down.

Exhibit 4 shows the U.S. balance of payments for the year 1992. While the U.S. imported more goods and services than it exported, it exported more securities than it imported. When a country exports securities, it is importing financial capital from another country; when it imports securities, it is exporting capital to other countries. To fully understand the balance of payments, a brief study of international capital movements is necessary.

International Capital Movements

International capital movements considerably complicate a country's balance of payments. Without such capital movements, exports of goods and services would more closely approximate imports of goods and services, and there would be fewer measures of deficit or surplus in the balance of payments.

Capital movements enable capital-importing nations to raise their physical capital stocks—dams, buildings, roads—above what such stocks would be in the absence of international capital flows. When a country exports capital, it is furnishing residents of another country with funds for financing investments in plants and equipment. Thus, capital exports divert one country's saving into investments in another country. Saving still equals investments in the world as a whole, but when international trade is involved, this equality need not hold for any individual country.

Recall from Chapter 6 that GDP = consumption (C) + government spending (G) + investment (I) + exports (X) − imports (M). Because GDP equals income, GDP = consumption (C) + saving (S) + taxes (T). If government spending and taxes are assumed to be zero (for simplicity),

$$C + S = C + I + X - M,$$

or

EXHIBIT 4   The U.S. Balance of Payments, 1992

Item		Amount (billions of dollars)
1. Exports of goods and services		+727
a. Exports of merchandise	+439	
b. Other	+288	
2. Imports of goods and services		−758
a. Imports of merchandise	−489	
b. Other	−269	
3. Net unilateral transfers abroad		−31
a. U.S. government grants and pensions	−17	
b. Private remittances	−14	
4. Balance on current account		−62
5. Net capital movements		+75
a. U.S. capital outflow	−45	
b. Foreign-capital inflow	+120	
6. Allocations of new SDRs to U.S. by IMF		0
7. Statistical discrepancy		−13
8. Total		0

SOURCE: *Survey of Current Business*, March 1992 (Categories may not add to totals because of rounding errors.)

$$S = I + X - M,$$

or

$$S - I = X - M.$$

This equation shows that the excess of saving over investment in a country is reflected in the excess of exports over imports. The excess of saving over investment is the net export of capital to other countries. Thus, the export of capital is transferred into physical goods through the current-account surplus. Similarly, an excess of investment over saving will match the excess of imports over exports. This excess investment corresponds to the import of capital, which describes the U.S. position in the 1980s and 1990s.

Capital movements take place for two reasons: investors wish to take advantage of earning a higher interest rate on their capital, or investors wish to gain some measure of security. Capital seeks higher returns and lower risks.

The capital account of any country's balance of payments contains both capital inflows and outflows because investors are seeking to diversify their investments and securities portfolios. A fundamental principle of sound investment strategy is not to put all of one's eggs in one basket. By holding a portfolio of international securities—for example, investments in German companies, Japanese companies, and American companies—an investor can reduce the risk of achieving a given expected rate of return.

The movement of net capital is governed by the desire for higher interest rates. For example, in a simple world with no risks, investors would place their capital in the country that paid the highest interest rate (the highest rate of return on investments). This process of capital exportation would raise interest rates in low-interest-rate regions and lower interest rates in high-interest-rate regions. This allocation of capital gives rise to greater production everywhere in the world and, thus, a more efficient utilization of the world's scarce stock of capital.

The U.S. Trade Deficit

The balance of payments must always sum to zero. This means that the exports of goods, services, and securities plus gifts from foreigners must equal the imports of goods, services, and securities plus gifts to foreigners. A study of Exhibit 4 also reveals an item called the "statistical discrepancy," which results from errors and omissions in the reporting process.

In 1992, as well as most other years since 1971, the U.S. recorded a trade deficit. That is, the exports of merchandise fell short of the imports of merchandise. The only way this can take place is for the United States to be a net borrower; that is, this country must be a net capital importer. To say that a U.S. trade deficit is undesirable is equivalent to asserting that borrowing capital from other countries reduces the real income of the American people.

However, importing capital takes place for a reason. It happens because the U.S. is not saving enough to match the investments that are being made. Other countries, such as Japan and Germany, are saving more than their domestic economies are absorbing in investment. Presumably, every country is made better off by this exchange. Americans are paying less for their capital; and Germans and the Japanese are earning more on their capital. To put the point another way, if Americans can borrow capital at 6 percent and invest it at 7 percent, America is the winner. If the Germans and the Japanese can invest at 6 percent instead of 5 percent, they are winners. To worry that the U.S. is living on borrowed money is to concentrate on the cost side of the borrowing equation and to ignore the benefit side.

The question is somewhat complicated by the fact that the U.S. government is also running a deficit. Government spending exceeds tax revenues. The trade deficit, then, reflects two forces: the excess of investment over saving and the excess of government spending over tax revenues. Thus, the trade deficit cannot be evaluated independently of the federal budget deficit. This issue was analyzed in Chapter 9. (See Example 1.)

THE EVOLUTION OF THE INTERNATIONAL MONETARY SYSTEM

In 1870, the world was not on an international gold standard; by 1900, the world had moved to an international gold standard. The gold standard was dead in 1945 and was replaced by a system of fixed but adjustable exchange rates. By 1973, that system was dead, and today the world is on a system of floating exchange rates with active exchange-rate-stabilization policies by the major central banks. To understand the current system, it is useful to take a backward look at this evolution.

The Breakdown of the Gold Standard

An international gold standard requires (1) that each country set a price for its currency in terms of gold, (2) that each country allow anyone to convert gold into its currency and vice versa at the set price, and (3) that the domestic money supply be tied to the domestic stock of monetary gold so that deficits reduce the money supply and surpluses increase the money supply. Under a gold standard, balance-of-payments deficits are defined as the reduction in the supply of monetary gold used for financing an excess of debits over credits by ordinary market participants; a surplus means the supply of monetary gold rises.

If these rules are followed, each country gives up its own monetary autonomy because the money supply takes a course dictated by the state of the balance of

Competitiveness

The long-lasting U.S. trade deficit from 1971 to the present has given rise to much discussion over the declining competitiveness of the U.S. economy. But the theory of comparative advantage tells us that every economy is competitive in the goods in which it has a comparative advantage; and every country has such goods. Countries become less competitive in particular goods and services as comparative advantages move from one country to another, but countries do not become less competitive in all goods.

Trade deficits basically occur because a country begins to borrow heavily, or in the long run the country has lent so much to other countries that when the income from those foreign investments is spent the country enjoys a trade deficit, that is, it spends more than the income being produced within the country. Both of these scenarios occurred in the United States.

There is nothing bad about trade deficits. This is a case where the language we use to describe a situation is taken as the economic diagnosis. We speak of government deficits, trade deficits, health deficits, and so forth as if to mean that the situation is bad and ought to be reversed. But a trade deficit is really a surplus: it is a surplus in the value of goods coming into the country versus the value of goods leaving the country.

Trade deficits do not cause unemployment, they do not lower economic growth, and they do not mean that the country is losing relative to the rest of the world. Trade deficits are a natural occurrence resulting from the flow of international capital around the world.

payments. Indeed, the gold standard may be considered a rather cumbersome way of setting up a world currency. A more straightforward method would be to set up a world currency directly with a single central bank or monetary authority.

The pre-1914 gold standard, centered in the United Kingdom, appeared to work well from 1870 to 1914. The balance-of-payments adjustment mechanism worked smoothly to eliminate surpluses and deficits. After World War I, the gold standard broke down. While a "new" gold standard was established in the 1920s, the turbulent 1930s saw it end. With widespread unemployment, deficit countries would never accept the discipline of further unanticipated deflation and more unemployment. Indeed, countries tried to do precisely the opposite; that is, they tried to export their unemployment to other countries. The opposite of the gold standard is to engage in so-called *competitive devaluations*. If Country A can unexpectedly devalue its currency, its exports will become more competitive, and it will find importing more expensive. With widespread unemployment, an unanticipated competitive devaluation (without retaliation from other countries) might increase employment at home at the expense of employment abroad.

The Bretton Woods System

The International Monetary Fund (IMF) was established in 1947 after a 1944 conference in Bretton Woods, New Hampshire. The monetary arrangements set up are now called either the "old IMF" system or the "Bretton Woods" system.

Each member of the IMF was assigned a quota that was determined by its trade and national income. A country contributed 25 percent of its quota in gold or U.S. dollars and 75 percent in its own currency. Thus, the IMF consisted of a pool of gold, dollars, and all other major currencies that could be used to lend assistance to any member country having balance-of-payments difficulties.

The Bretton Woods system was based on the theory that balance-of-payments *deficits* and *surpluses*—reductions or increases in international reserves—were usually temporary in a fixed-exchange-rate system. Thus, the discipline of the Hume reserve-flow mechanism—deflation for deficit countries and inflation for surplus countries—could in many cases be avoided. Thus, each country pledged to maintain a par value for its currency in gold or in dollars that were worth 1/35 of an ounce of gold and to maintain the exchange rate of its currency within 1 percent of this par value. Should a deficit develop, the country could rely on its international reserves to help it weather the storm until a surplus balance of payments developed. In the meantime, the country would not experience the adjustment of a domestic deflation.

If the deficit did not reverse itself, the country was considered to be facing a "fundamental disequilibrium" and was then allowed to adjust its exchange rate. A country in fundamental deficit could devalue its currency; a country in fundamental surplus could revalue its currency.

The Fall of Bretton Woods

The United States was the center of the Bretton Woods system. Under the old IMF system, countries tied their currencies to the U.S. dollar. The United States, in turn, tied the dollar to gold. Until 1971, the United States allowed foreign monetary authorities to convert dollars into gold at the rate of $35 an ounce. The dollar became a critical source of international reserves. Countries obtained dollars by accepting dollar payments in exchange for their goods and services. With other countries needing international reserves, the United States benefited from being able to buy the goods and services of the rest of the world with its own dollars, and it was in a very enviable position. Thus, by various measures, the U.S. had a payments deficit.

It was expected that when the U.S. payments deficit came to an end, the Bretton Woods system would begin to work smoothly. In the 1950s and 1960s the United States had a deficit in its official accounts virtually every year. But the turning of the country's deficit into a surplus or at least equilibrium never happened.

The fact that the U.S. dollar was the international money of the world also made it very difficult for the United States to adjust the value of its own currency. If the United States devalued the dollar, every country holding dollars as reserves would find itself losing a substantial fraction of its wealth. Thus, the most important member of the IMF could not use its safety valve when its deficit was permanent.

Speculation.   In addition to the U.S. official deficit, another problem was that the currency-adjustment system itself suffered from incompatibility with relatively free international capital movements. If a country had a fundamental deficit and needed to devalue its currency, speculators would know this fact better than anyone else. The chances of the country revaluing or raising the value of its currency would be virtually zero. The speculators would be in a no-lose situation if they sold weak currencies and bought strong currencies. For example, the British pound was often weak and the German deutsche mark (DM) was often strong. Accordingly, speculators found it advantageous to sell pounds and buy deutsche marks. This action made the deficit worse in the United Kingdom and increased the surplus in Germany.

EXAMPLE 2

The European Monetary System

The European community has attempted to design a uniform currency system. As a first step, it set up the European Monetary System, in which the exchange rates of each country are allowed to fluctuate only 2.25 percent above and below some specified par value.

The basic mechanism of the European Monetary System was virtually the same as the Bretton Woods system established for the world economy after World War II. The Bretton Woods system broke down in the 1970s because fixed exchange rates without common inflation rates results in speculation against weaker currencies. The United States has a common currency area that works because no single state has its own separate monetary policy.

Those who ignore history are destined to repeat it. The European Monetary System allowed each country to have its own central bank. Accordingly, the weak currencies were subject to enormous speculative pressures. Germany and France were the strong currencies, Britain and Italy were the weak currencies. In September 1992, Britain and Italy withdrew from the European Monetary System. Late in 1992 even the French franc came under speculative attack. The reason is that it is almost a no-lose proposition for speculators: If a currency is weak under a fixed exchange rate system, the authorities are unlikely to increase its fixed value and highly likely to devalue the currency. As a consequence, the European Monetary System is no longer working.

In 1971, speculators began to bet against the U.S. dollar by selling dollars and buying stronger currencies. President Nixon, in August 1971, changed the fundamental character of the IMF system when he severed the dollar's link with gold. No longer could countries convert dollars into gold at $35 an ounce; the dollar was essentially set free to fluctuate. After a few attempts to fix the system, by March 1973 all major world currencies were on a managed floating system, and the Bretton Woods system was shattered. (See Example 2.)

The Current International Monetary System

At a conference in Kingston, Jamaica, in early 1976, the original IMF charter was amended to legalize the widespread managed floating that replaced the Bretton Woods par-value system.

According to the new agreements—called the Jamaican agreements—each country could adopt whatever exchange-rate system it preferred (fixed or floating). Countries were asked to "avoid manipulating exchange rates . . . in order to prevent effective balance-of-payments adjustment or to gain an unfair competitive advantage over other members." The IMF was directed to "oversee the compliance of each member with its obligations" in order to "exercise firm surveillance of the exchange-rate policies of its members." Monetary authorities of a country could buy and sell foreign exchange in order to "prevent or moderate sharp and disruptive fluctuations from day to day and from week to week," but it was clearly considered unacceptable to suppress or to reverse a long-run exchange-rate movement.

The currencies of all the major countries are floating against the dollar. A number of small countries are tied to the dollar, and some others are tied to the French franc and the pound sterling. Thus, the entire system is one of individual

Managed Exchange Rates

Economists are currently divided over whether governments should try to manage exchange rates. The argument for managing exchange rates rests on three points. First, the government can determine the fundamental equilibrium exchange rate. Second, floating exchange rates have been too volatile. Third, under floating exchange rates, currencies can become significantly overvalued or undervalued.

The first and third points are related. If the information exists for determining whether an exchange rate is in "fundamental equilibrium," it is possible also to determine whether a currency is overvalued or undervalued (misaligned). A currency is overvalued if the exchange rate is higher than can be explained by changes in relative inflation rates or improvements in the country's productivity relative to other countries.

Critics of floating rates also argue that excessive exchange-rate volatility reduces the volume of international trade by making international transactions more uncertain.

Supporters of the current system argue that the very concept of currency misalignment supposes that economists have the correct model of exchange-rate determination. Economists' exchange-rate models have not worked very well (such models focus on fundamentals), but is the exchange rate misaligned or are the models simply wrong? According to the law of aerodynamics, a bumblebee cannot fly. According to some economic models of exchange rates, the U.S. dollar is too high because of the trade deficit. Until better models of exchange rates are developed, economists should be slow in pronouncing whether an exchange rate is "over-valued" or "undervalued" (loaded terms).

Supporters of floating exchange rates point out that volatile exchange rates may or may not have reduced the volume of international trade. The evidence is mixed. Moreover, it is clear that exchange rates have shown excessive volatility. For example, in the United States, Canada, Germany, Great Britain, and Japan, both interest rates and their domestic stock markets have been more volatile than their exchange rates.

floating, joint floating, and intervention in the foreign-exchange markets to keep the exchange rate from appreciating or depreciating too sharply.

When exchange rates are flexible, one country's monetary policy does not have to be dictated by the monetary policies of other countries. If everybody else wants to inflate, a country can maintain stable prices simply by following a long-run monetary policy of tight money (low monetary growth) and allowing its exchange rate to appreciate relative to the countries that choose to follow inflationary policies. Likewise, flexible exchange rates enable a country that chooses to do so to follow highly inflationary policies by just simply allowing its rate of exchange to depreciate.

Under a fixed-exchange-rate regime, a deficit can be solved by internal deflation or unemployment. If this solution is not in the best interests of the country, a flexible exchange rate allows a country to depreciate its currency rather than undergo the discipline of Hume's reserve-flow mechanism. It is much easier to lower the value of a country's currency than to lower every internal commodity price and wage rate!

The most dramatic achievement of the current system occurred when the OPEC countries quadrupled the price of oil in 1973–74, and the resulting shock to the world economy was absorbed by floating exchange rates. The enormous deficits that developed in the oil-importing countries and the necessity of the oil-exporting countries to invest their oil revenues meant that the foreign-exchange markets had a lot of oil revenues to recycle. The previous Bretton Woods system could not have accomplished this recycling. Indeed, the Bretton Woods system could not take much smaller pressures. While exchange rates fluctuated dramatically after the oil shock, the system worked. It did not break down or cause crises like those that the world witnessed in the late 1960s and early 1970s.

Chapter Summary

The most important point to learn from this chapter is: When there are international capital movements, trade deficits and surpluses are normal and necessary for economic efficiency.

1. Foreign exchange is the national currency of another country that is needed to carry out international transactions. America's demand for foreign exchange increases when U.S. residents demand more foreign goods and services. America's supply of foreign exchange increases when residents of foreign countries demand more U.S. goods and services. The demand curve for foreign exchange is downward-sloping because the higher is the dollar price of foreign currency, the higher is the cost of foreign goods to American importers. The supply curve of foreign exchange tends to be upward-sloping because as the dollar price of foreign currency rises, American goods appear cheaper to foreigners. Under a floating-exchange-rate system, the exchange rate is allowed to float to the point where the demand for foreign exchange equals the supply. Under a fixed-exchange-rate system, equilibrium in the demand for and supply of foreign exchange is brought about by Hume's gold-flow mechanism.

2. A country's balance of payments provides a summary record of its economic transactions with foreign residents over a period of one year. It is a two-sided (credit/debit) summary that must always be in accounting balance. International capital movements raise the physical capital stocks in the capital-importing countries and lower them in the capital-exporting countries.

3. Today the world operates on a system of floating exchange rates with active exchange-rate stabilization by the major central banks. The Bretton Woods system set up after World War II broke down because a currency-adjustment system is fundamentally in conflict with free international capital movements. Speculation destroyed the old Bretton Woods system. The new international monetary system involves a mixture of floating and fixed exchange rates. Since 1973 the U.S. dollar has floated with respect to all the major currencies of the world.

Policy Focus: **There are great difficulties involved in exchange-rate management because no economic model currently predicts exchange rates.**

Key Terms

foreign exchange (p. 327)
fixed exchange rate (p. 328)
floating exchange rate (p. 328)

balance of payments (p. 333)
mercantilist fallacy (p. 334)

Questions and Problems

1. In April 1988, the West German mark was worth $0.60 (in U.S. dollars) and $1 was worth about 125 Japanese yen. How much would a Mercedes-Benz cost in U.S. dollars if the German price were 30,000 deutsche marks (DM)? How much would a Toyota cost in U.S. dollars if the Japanese price were 1,200,000 yen?

2. Table A shows part of an actual newspaper report on the foreign-exchange market. Did the British pound rise or fall from Monday to Tuesday? Did the Japanese yen rise or fall from Monday to Tuesday? What happened to the U.S. dollar in terms of the pound? What happened to the U.S. dollar in terms of the yen?

TABLE A

	Foreign Currency in Dollars		Dollar in Foreign Currency	
	Tues.	Mon.	Tues.	Mon.
British pound	1.6005	1.5880	0.6248	0.6297
Japanese yen	0.006592	0.006605	151.7	151.4

3. If there were a floating exchange rate between Japan and the United States, which of the following events would cause the Japanese yen to appreciate? Which would cause the yen to depreciate? Explain your answers.
   a. The government of Japan orders its automobile companies to limit exports to the United States.
   b. The United States places a quota on Japanese automobiles.
   c. The United States increases its money supply relative to Japan's money supply.
   d. Interest rates in the United States rise relative to Japanese interest rates.
   e. More Japanese people decide to visit America.
   f. Japanese productivity growth rises relative to U.S. productivity growth.

4. Indicate whether each of the following transactions represents a debt (a supply of U.S. dollars) or a credit (a demand for U.S. dollars) in the U.S. balance of payments:
   a. An American commercial airline buys the European-made Airbus (an airplane competing with Boeing 747).
   b. A European airline buys an American Boeing 747.
   c. An American makes a trip around the world.
   d. A French company pays dividends to an American owning its stock.
   e. An American buys stock in a French company.
   f. An American company borrows from a European investor.
   g. A Canadian oil company exports oil to Japan on an American tanker.
   h. An American banker makes a loan to a European manufacturer.

5. Explain the mechanism under which U.S. restrictions on its imports will lead to fewer U.S. exports under a floating-exchange-rate system.

6. What would happen if Mexico and the United States had a fixed exchange rate, but for 20 years Mexico had more inflation than the United States experienced?

7. Why can exchange-rate volatility probably be reduced more by international policy coordination than by market intervention?

8. Assume in Germany a Mercedes-Benz costs 60,000 marks. In 1984, a German mark costs $0.35. In early 1988, a German mark costs $0.61. What would happen to the dollar price of a Mercedes-Benz?

9. "A gold standard will work well; a perfectly flexible exchange rate will work well; however, trying to combine fixed and floating exchange rates is asking for trouble." Evaluate this statement.

Doing Economics

This chapter identifies several factors that might cause exchange rates between currencies to change. Among these, differing inflation rates and changes in relative interest rates are among the most prominent. Information on exchange rates, price levels, and interest rates for many countries are published in *International Financial Statistics* by the International Monetary Fund. Many libraries subscribe to this monthly publication. Choose a pair of countries and two dates several years apart. Look up the value of each one's exchange rate against the dollar, its consumer price index (or the closest comparable price index you can find), and an interest rate such as the prime rate that seems comparable across the countries. Based on the difference between inflation and interest rates in the two countries, how well can you explain the difference in the behavior of their exchange rates based on the theory outlined in this chapter? Do you know of other factors that changed in one or both of the countries that would explain any deviations? Explain.

Microeconomics and the Product Markets

P A R T   F I V E

CHAPTER 18
Elasticity of Demand and Supply

CHAPTER 19
Demand and Utility

APPENDIX 19
Indifference Curves and Demand

CHAPTER 20
Business Environment: Firms, Information, and Contracts

APPENDIX 20
Corporate Finance and Financial Markets

CHAPTER 21
Costs and Productivity

CHAPTER 22
Perfect Competition

CHAPTER 23
Monopoly

CHAPTER 24
Oligopoly and Monopolistic Competition

CHAPTER 25
Regulation, Deregulation, and Antitrust

CHAPTER 26
The Economics of Agriculture

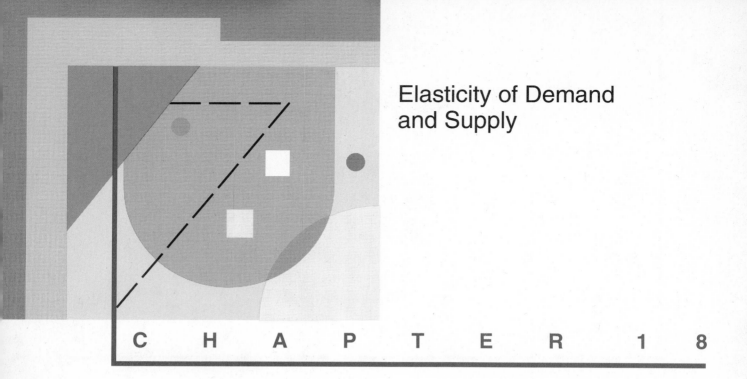

Elasticity of Demand and Supply

CHAPTER FOCUS   When prices rise, buyers look for substitutes. Higher prices encourage businesses to produce more of that product and less of others. In some cases, changes in prices evoke dramatic changes in consumer purchases and in businesses' willingness to sell products.

Elasticities describe responses to price changes. The sensitivity with which consumers and producers respond to prices depends on the product. Consumers are more sensitive to price changes when good substitute products are available. If no good substitutes are available, consumers won't cut back as much when the price rises.

Consumer price sensitivity affects pricing behavior in the marketplace. If firms know that an increase in price will cause a significant loss of markets, they will be hesitant to raise prices. If they know that people will continue to buy at higher prices, there will be less pressure on them to hold the line on prices.

Elasticity and policy are intertwined. The elasticity of consumer purchases has been used by the courts as a test of the degree of monopoly. The elasticity of consumer and producer responses to price changes has been used to determine the burden of proposed taxes. The degree to which markets are related can be judged by how much a price change in one market affects another market.

After studying this chapter, you will be able to:

- Measure the price elasticity of demand.

- Understand the relationship between price elasticity, price, and total revenue or expenditure.

- Predict how the price elasticity of supply changes between the immediate run, the short run, and the long run.

- Discuss how the burden of an excise tax is divided between consumers and producers.

- Understand how the income elasticity of demand is used to determine the dividing line between necessities and luxuries.

THE PRICE ELASTICITY OF DEMAND

The demand curve introduced in Chapter 3 shows how quantity demanded changes in response to changes in price, *ceteris paribus*. Economists use the **price elasticity of demand** to measure the *degree of responsiveness* of quantity demanded to a change in price. How does one measure how large or small the market response is to price changes? Absolute changes in price or quantity demanded are poor measures of responsiveness. If a $1 increase in the price of coal lowers quantity demanded by one ton, is this a large or small response? If the initial price is $2 per ton, a $1 change in price represents a 50 percent increase in price. If the initial price is $1,000, a $1 change in price represents a miniscule change in price. If the initial quantity were 1 million tons, the one ton change is very small, but if the original quantity were two tons, then the one ton change is large. To get a sense of whether a particular change in price is large or small, one must determine how large the change is relative to some initial position. In short, it is necessary to use *percentage* changes in quantity or price.

> The **price elasticity of demand** (E_d) is the percentage change in the quantity demanded divided by the percentage change in price.

The price elasticity of demand shows the percentage fall in quantity demanded per 1 percent rise in price. It also shows the percentage rise in quantity demanded per 1 percent fall in the price. For example, say the price of apples rises by about 10 percent (say, from $.50 a pound to $.55). If the quantity of apples demanded falls by 20 percent (say, from 1,000 bushels to about 800 bushels), the price elasticity would be 2 = 20 percent ÷ 10 percent. This means that every 1 percent increase in the price of apples will lower quantity demanded by 2 percent. Equivalently, a price elasticity of 2 means that a 1 percent reduction in the price will increase quantity demanded by 2 percent.

Calculating Price Elasticity of Demand

To compute the price elasticity of demand, one must calculate the percentage changes in quantity and in price. Imagine the price of pizza rises from $8 to $12. The percentage increase in the price appears to be 50 percent ($4 ÷ $8). But consider reducing the price of pizza from $12 to $8. Now the percentage fall in the price appears to be 33 percent ($4 ÷ $12). The price elasticity of demand between $8 and $12 should be the same for a movement from one price to another whether the price change is an increase or decrease. There should not be one elasticity for price decreases and another one for price increases. If percentage changes are calculated by dividing the change in price by the *average* price and the change in quantity by the *average* quantity, they will be the same for increases or decreases. In the above example, the percentage change in the price of pizza from $8 to $12 is 40 percent because the $4 price change is divided by $10—the average of $8 and $12. Because average prices and quantities represent the midpoints between the two prices and two quantities, this is called the **midpoints formula** for calculating price elasticity of demand.[1]

The **midpoints formula** for determining the elasticity of demand E_d for a given segment of the demand curve is:

$$E_d = \frac{\text{Percent Change in Quantity Demanded}}{\text{Percent Change in Price}}$$

$$= \frac{\dfrac{\text{Change in Quantity Demanded}}{\text{Average of Two Quantities}}}{\dfrac{\text{Change in Price}}{\text{Average of Two Prices}}}$$

---

[1] In symbols, if p_1 and p_2 are the two prices and q_1 and q_2 are the two quantities, the midpoints formula can be simplified as follows:

$$E_d = \frac{q_2 - q_1}{(q_1 + q_2)/2} \div \frac{p_2 - p_1}{(p_1 + p_2)/2} = \frac{q_2 - q_1}{p_1 - p_2} \times \frac{p_1 + p_2}{q_1 + q_2}.$$

EXHIBIT 1   Total Revenue and Elasticity

a. Elastic Demand

b. Unitary Elastic Demand

c. Inelastic Demand

d. Demand Schedule

Price (dollars per unit), P (1)	Quantity (units), Q (2)	Total Revenue, TR = P × Q (3) = (1) × (2)	Direction of Change in Revenue (4)	Percentage Change in Quantity Demanded, $\frac{\Delta Q}{(q_1 + q_2)/2}$ (5)	Percentage Change in Price, $\frac{\Delta P}{(p_1 + p_2)/2}$ (6)	Coefficient of Price Elasticity, E_d (7) = (5) ÷ (6)	Conclusion (8)
(a) 9	15	135	Increase	$\frac{10}{20}$ = 50%	$\frac{2}{8}$ = 25%	$\frac{50}{25}$ = 2	Elastic
(b) 7	25	175	No change	$\frac{10}{30}$ = 33.3%	$\frac{2}{6}$ = 33.3%	$\frac{33.3}{33.3}$ = 1	Unitary Elastic
(c) 5	35	175	Decrease	$\frac{10}{40}$ = 25%	$\frac{2}{4}$ = 50%	$\frac{25}{50}$ = 0.5	Inelastic
3	45	135					

The demand curve, *D*, is the same in panels (a), (b), and (c). Between the prices of $9 and $7, the elasticity of demand (E_d) is 2; demand is elastic. Panel (a) shows that a reduction in price raises revenue. The color shaded rectangle shows the revenue lost due to the lower price, and the black shaded rectangle shows the revenue gained due to the greater number of units sold. Because the black rectangle is greater in area than the colored rectangle, more revenues is gained than lost.

Between prices $7 and $5, E_d equals 1; panel (b) shows that the reduction in price has no impact on revenue. Finally, between the prices of $5 and $3, E_d is 1/2; demand is inelastic. Panel (c) shows that the reduction in price lowers revenue because more revenue is lost (color shading) than gained (black shading). Thus, the elasticity of demand varies along a linear demand curve with constant slope. Elasticity and slope are different.

The midpoints formula can be illustrated using the numbers in the demand schedule in Exhibit 1. Consider a change in price from $9 to $7. The change in price is $2, and the average price is ($7 + $9)/2 = $8. The percentage change in price is 25 percent ($2/$8 = 25 percent). When price falls from $9 to $7, quantity demanded rises from 15 to 25 units. The change in quantity is 10 units, and the average quantity is 20 units. The percentage change in quantity demanded is 50 percent (10/20 = 50 percent). Dividing the percent change in quantity demanded (50 percent) by the percent change in price (25 percent) yields a price elasticity of demand E_d of 2, as given in column 7 of Exhibit 1. The calculated elasticity is 2 whether the price rises from $7 to $9 or falls from $9 to $7.

Elastic and Inelastic Demand

Price elasticities of demand fall into three broad categories called elastic, inelastic, and unitary elastic:

1. When $E_d > 1$, demand is *elastic* (Q is strongly responsive to changes in P).
2. When $E_d < 1$, demand is *inelastic* (Q responds weakly to changes in P).
3. When $E_d = 1$, demand is *unitary elastic* (a borderline case).

Think of the dollar sales or revenue of the sellers of some product. The response of **total revenue** to price changes depends on elasticity.

> The **total revenue** of sellers *TR* is equal to the price of the commodity times the quantity sold:
>
> $$TR = P \times Q.$$

Along a demand curve, since price and quantity demanded always move in opposite directions, a change in price tugs total revenue in two directions. When the price falls, total revenue is tugged down because each unit sells at a lower price. However, the resulting increase in the quantity sold pulls revenue up. The net result depends on which effect dominates. What actually happens to total revenue when the price changes depends on the price elasticity of demand.

If the price elasticity of demand is greater than 1 (demand is elastic), the percentage rise in quantity demanded is greater than the percentage fall in price. Revenue *increases* because the increase in quantity demanded more than offsets the *decrease* in price. This is illustrated in Exhibit 1. When the price changes from $9 to $7, a 25 percent change by the midpoints formula, quantity demanded changes by a larger percentage amount from 15 units to 25 units—a 50 percent change. As a consequence, total spending by consumers—which is the revenue received by sellers—rises from $135 (= $9 × 15) to $175 (= $7 × 25). In panel (a), the area shaded in color shows the loss in revenue from selling the first 15 units at $7 rather than $9; and the gray shaded area indicates the revenue gained from selling more units. Revenue rises because the gray shaded area exceeds the color shaded area when demand is elastic. Conversely, an increase in the price of the good from $7 to $9 will lower total revenue. Price and revenue move in opposite directions.

When $E_d > 1$, *TR* will move in the opposite direction of price because changing the price will change the quantity demanded by a greater percentage in the opposite direction.

If the price elasticity is less than 1 (demand is inelastic), the percentage rise in quantity demanded is less than the percentage fall in price. Revenue *falls* because the *decline* in price is not offset by the relatively small rise in quantity. Demand is inelastic between the prices of $5 and $3 in Exhibit 1. When price falls by 50 percent from $5 to $3, the percentage increase in quantity demanded is 25 percent from 35 to 45. The relatively small percentage increase in quantity demanded is not enough to prevent revenue from falling. Revenue falls from $175 (= $5 × 35) to $135 (= $3 × 45). In panel (c), the color shaded area corresponding to the revenue loss exceeds the gray shaded area representing the revenue gain. Conversely, if the price rises from $3 to $5, total revenue rises. Price and revenue move in the same direction when demand is inelastic.

When $E_d < 1$, *TR* will move in the same direction as price because changing the price of the good will change quantity demanded by a smaller percentage in the opposite direction.

If the price elasticity of demand = 1 (unitary elastic), the percentage rise in quantity demanded equals the percentage fall in price. Revenue is unchanged because the decline in price is just offset by the rise in quantity. In Exhibit 1, demand is unit elastic between the prices of $7 and $5. When the price falls from

EXAMPLE 1

Vanity Plates and College Tuition: When Do Higher Prices Yield More Revenue?

The recession of the early 1990s forced states to seek out additional sources of state revenue. Insofar as raising the fees for various government services did not require voter approval, most states reexamined existing fees (tuition, licenses, and charges) to uncover additional sources of revenue.

All of the 50 states have public colleges and universities that charge tuition and fees, usually at highly subsidized rates. Most of the states offer vanity plates that permit users to have their own initials or a favorite slogan on their license plate.

Elasticity of demand explains why the states used increases in tuition and fees rather than increases in the price of vanity plates. Standard license plates are close substitutes for vanity plates. If the price of vanity plates rises, people cut back considerably on their purchases of vanity plates—so much so that the revenue from sales actually drops. The elasticity of demand for vanity plates is greater than unity. Students enrolled in state universities, however, will not drop out of school if tuition is raised. They may cut back somewhat on the number of courses, but enrollment tends to remain steady and revenues from tuition increase. The elasticity of demand for state college courses is less than unity. An increase in the price will raise revenue.

$7 to $5, 33 percent by the midpoints formula $(2 \div 6)$, the quantity demanded increases from 25 to 35—again 33 percent $(10 \div 30)$. The percentage changes are the same. Revenue stays constant at $175. In panel (b), the color shaded area is the same as the gray shaded area so that the loss in revenue due to lowering the price is just matched by the gain in revenue from selling more units. Alternatively, if price increases, the quantity demanded of the good will fall by exactly the same percentage so total revenue will still remain constant. Changes in the price of the good have no impact on total revenue when demand is unitary elastic (See Example 1.)

When $E_d = 1$, *TR* will not change because price and quantity move by exactly offsetting amounts.

As the above example shows, one can determine whether demand for a particular product is elastic, inelastic, or unitary elastic by observing what happens to total revenue when price changes. This is called the **total-revenue test**.

> The **total-revenue test** is:
> 1. If price and total revenue move in different directions, $E_d > 1$ (demand is elastic).
> 2. If price and total revenue move in the same direction, $E_d < 1$ (demand is inelastic).
> 3. If total revenue does not change when price changes, $E_d = 1$ (demand is unitary elastic).

Elasticity and Slope

The elasticity and the slope of the demand curve are not the same. In Exhibit 1, the slope of the demand curve is constant between every pair of prices (the demand curve is a straight line). Yet, the price elasticity of demand falls as the price is reduced. For movements between $7 and $9, the price elasticity of demand was 2. For movements between $3 and $5, the price elasticity of demand was a lower $1/2$. Why is the price elasticity of demand higher at high prices than at low prices?

When the demand curve is a straight line, the quantity demanded increases by the same absolute amount for every $1 reduction in the price. But when price is high, and quantity is low, the percentage increase in price is small while the percentage increase in demand is large. Thus, elasticity will be high when the price is high. When the price is low, a $1 reduction in price means a higher percentage reduction in price for a smaller percentage increase in quantity demanded. Thus, elasticity will be low when the price is low. Along a straight-line demand curve, the price elasticity of demand falls as the price falls.

Perfectly Elastic or Perfectly Inelastic Demand Curves

The highest degree of elasticity possible—the greatest responsiveness of quantity demanded to price—is a perfectly horizontal demand curve. In Exhibit 2, any amount on demand curve D can be sold at the indicated price ($5). Such a horizontal demand curve demonstrates **perfectly elastic demand**. In other words, the market is willing to take any quantity of the good the sellers are prepared to supply at the going price.

Perfectly elastic demand curves are common in the real world. In perfectly competitive markets—defined in Chapter 3 as markets in which no single producer is large enough to influence the market price—each seller can sell all he or she wants at the market price. Single sellers do not have to lower their prices to sell more. Each corn or wheat farmer can sell all he wants at the prevailing market price and can't sell anything at a higher price.

> A horizontal demand curve illustrates **perfectly elastic demand**, in which case quantity demanded is most responsive to price.

The lowest degree of inelasticity possible—the least responsiveness of quantity demanded to price—occurs when the demand curve is perfectly vertical. In Exhibit 2, the vertical demand curve D' demonstrates **perfectly inelastic demand**. With demand curve D', 75 units of the good will be sold regardless of the price. The elasticity of demand is zero because if the price were to rise above $5, the percentage change in the quantity demanded would be zero.

A perfectly inelastic demand curve suggests that no matter how high the price rises, consumers will not cut back on the quantity demanded. The closest example would be insulin for the diabetic, but even in this case if the price rose higher and higher, eventually diabetics might reduce their dosages and accept some health loss rather than pay the higher price.

Demand curves can be perfectly inelastic *within a range of prices*. If insulin prices were to rise by 10 percent, the quantity demanded of insulin would probably not change. If the price of salt were to rise from $0.20 to $0.21 per pound, the quantity demanded would probably stay the same.

> A vertical demand curve illustrates **perfectly inelastic demand**, in which case quantity demanded is least responsive to price.

Determinants of Price Elasticity of Demand

The price elasticity of demand measures the degree to which consumers respond to changes in prices. The four determinants of the price elasticity of demand for a good are:

EXHIBIT 2   Perfectly Elastic and Perfectly Inelastic Demand Curves

The demand curve *D* is perfectly elastic; it is perfectly horizontal, or parallel to the quantity axis. The demand curve *D′* is perfectly inelastic; it is perfectly vertical, or parallel to the price axis. The elasticity-of-demand coefficient of *D* is infinitely large along the entire demand schedule. The elasticity-of-demand coefficient of *D′* is zero along the entire demand curve.

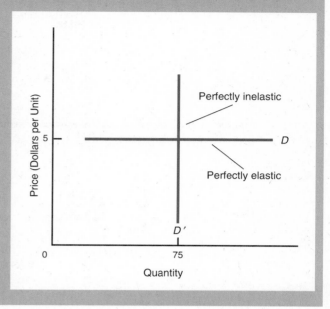

1. the availability of substitutes,
2. the relative importance of the good in the budget,
3. the amount of time available to adjust to the price change, and
4. whether the good is a necessity or luxury.

The Relative Importance of the Good in the Budget.   The more important a good is in the consumer's total spending, the more elastic should be the demand. When the price of salt changes, or toothpicks, or many other inexpensive items, a change in the price brings about a small change in quantity demanded. Why? A higher price of, say, salt does not cause the consumer to search out many new substitutes in order to save money. On the other hand, if the price of gasoline rises, an important item in the consumer's budget, it pays people to use less gasoline by driving smaller cars, riding bicycles, or taking the bus.

Time to Adjust to Price Changes.   Demand is more elastic the longer consumers have to adjust to price changes. Consider the response of consumers to higher electricity prices. Immediately after electric utility rates are increased, consumers can do little more than lower their heating thermostats in the winter and raise their air-conditioning thermostats in the summer. As time passes, additional substitutes for electricity become available. Extra insulation and more energy-efficient heating and air-conditioning equipment can be installed. If natural-gas prices have not risen as much, consumers can convert to natural-gas appliances when replacing the old system.

Many expenditures are conditioned by habit formation. Consumers are accustomed to buying certain products, and habits are hard to break. A family used to setting the thermostat at 72 degrees and to eating fresh vegetables will find it difficult to change when heating costs and vegetable prices rise.

Necessities Versus Luxuries.   As this chapter will discuss later in more detail, economists distinguish necessities from luxuries by defining *necessities* as products whose demand increases less rapidly than income.

Luxuries tend to have a higher price elasticity of demand than necessities. Chapter 3 noted that a reduction in price increases real income. Higher real incomes stimulate the demand for luxuries more than the demand for necessities, if everything else (the availability of substitutes, the importance of the good in the budget, the time allowed for adjustment) is equal.

THE INCOME ELASTICITY OF DEMAND

In Chapter 3 we saw that consumer demand depends not only on the product's own price, but also on consumer preferences, the prices of substitutes and complements, and consumer income. The elasticity concept is also applied to the other factors affecting demand.

A rise or fall in consumer income will affect the demands for different products. As consumer income rises, the demand for most products increases. The responsiveness of demand to consumer income is measured by the **income elasticity of demand** (E_i).

> The income elasticity of demand (E_i) is the percentage change in the demand for a product divided by the percentage change in income *holding all prices fixed*.[2]

The income elasticity of demand is positive for most goods because the higher their incomes, the more consumers spend. If the income elasticity equals unity, a 1 percent increase in income will lead to a 1 percent increase in the demand for the good. Hence, consumers would continue to spend the same fraction of their income on the good as before income increased. If the income elasticity exceeds 1, people will spend a larger fraction of their incomes on the good as income rises. If the income elasticity is less than 1, people will spend a smaller fraction of their incomes on that good as income rises. The definitions of **necessities** and **luxuries** given earlier in this chapter can be refined using the income-elasticity-of-demand concept.

> **Necessities** are those products that have an income elasticity of demand less than 1.

> **Luxuries** are those products that have an income elasticity of demand greater than 1.

Using these definitions, goods such as food items would be necessities, while recreational vehicles would be luxuries. Notice, though, that the economist allows

---

[2]The midpoints formula for the income elasticity of demand is:

$$E_i = \frac{q_2 - q_1}{(q_1 + q_2)} \div \frac{i_2 - i_1}{(i_1 + i_2)},$$

where i denotes consumer income.

the terms *luxury* and *necessity* to be defined by the market choices people make rather than by individual perceptions about what is more "necessary" than something else.

THE CROSS-PRICE ELASTICITY OF DEMAND

A useful elasticity concept is the **cross-price elasticity of demand** that relates the responsiveness of the demand for one good to the price of some other good. The cross-price elasticity between coal and oil tells us the percentage increase in the demand for coal that results from a specified increase in the price of oil. For example, a cross-price elasticity of 0.5 tells us that a 10 percent increase in the price of oil increases the demand for coal by 5 percent. On the other hand, a cross-price elasticity of −0.25 between bacon and eggs tells us that a 10 percent increase in the price of eggs *reduces* the demand for bacon by 2.5 percent. Thus, the cross-price elasticity provides us with information about the extent to which the demand for one good falls or rises in response to a given percentage increase in the price of some other good.

> The **cross-price elasticity of demand** is the percentage change in the demand for the one good by the percentage change in the price of the other good.

THE PRICE ELASTICITY OF SUPPLY

The price elasticity of demand measures the responsiveness of *consumers* to price change. The **price elasticity of supply (E_s)** measures the responsiveness of *producers* to price changes. The elasticity of supply is calculated in the same way as the elasticity of demand, only now the Qs refer to quantities *supplied,* not quantities demanded. Indeed, the terms elastic, inelastic, and unit elastic have the same meanings on the supply side as on the demand side.

> The **price elasticity of supply (E_s)** is defined as the percentage change in the quantity supplied divided by the percentage change in price.

The price elasticity of supply is measured in the same way as the price elasticity of demand. The formula is the same as the midpoints formula above. The only difference is that the quantities refer to quantities supplied rather than quantities demanded.

Perfectly Elastic and Perfectly Inelastic Supply Curves

The highest degree of elasticity possible for a supply curve is a perfectly horizontal supply curve. In Exhibit 3, supply curve *S* illustrates the case of **perfectly elastic supply**. At the price of $10, producers of the good are willing to supply any amount of the good to the market at that price.

Most of the supply curves that the average consumer deals with are perfectly elastic. The grocery store is willing to sell any person all the milk, canned goods, and dairy products that person wants to buy at the prices set. Under normal

EXHIBIT 3   Perfectly Elastic and Perfectly Inelastic Supply Curves

The supply curve *S* is perfectly elastic because at a price of $10 any quantity of output can be offered on the market by sellers. The supply curve *S'* is perfectly inelastic because no matter how much the price rises, the quantity supplied remains the same.

circumstances, however, all buyers together (the market) must offer higher prices to induce producers to increase the quantity supplied.

The lowest degree of elasticity occurs when the supply curve is perfectly vertical, as shown by supply curve *S'*. Such a supply curve demonstrates **perfectly inelastic supply**. The price elasticity of supply in this case equals zero. An increase in price has no effect on quantity supplied; therefore, the percentage change in quantity supplied is zero.

> A horizontal supply curve demonstrates **perfectly elastic supply;** quantity supplied is most responsive to price.

> A vertical supply curve demonstrates **perfectly inelastic supply;** quantity supplied is least responsive to price.

Elasticity of Supply in Three Time Periods

Just as the elasticity of demand depends on the amount of time the consumer has to respond to price changes, the elasticity of supply also depends on time. In general, the longer the period of time the producer has to adjust to changes in prices, the greater is the elasticity of supply.

Economists distinguish between three time periods during which producers adjust their supply to the new prices: the **immediate run**, the **short run**, and the **long run**.

> The **immediate run** is a period of time so short that the quantity supplied cannot be changed at all. In the immediate run—sometimes called the *momentary period* or *market period*—supply curves are perfectly inelastic.

Consider the case of a day's fish catch by fishermen selling to the Gulf Coast fresh fish market. In the immediate run, the fish catch is already in. If the price were to double unexpectedly at sundown, fishermen cannot return to their boats to bring in more fish. The immediate run supply curve is a vertical line (perfectly inelastic) as shown in Exhibit 4, panel (a).

In the short run, the fishermen have an opportunity to either increase or decrease their daily catch in response to price changes. If prices rise, they can work longer hours and hire additional helpers. The extra hours and extra help allow them to bring more fish to market in response to higher prices. Because of this flexibility, the short-run supply curve is not vertical but is upward-sloped. (See panel (b) of Exhibit 4.)

> The **short run** is a period of time long enough for existing firms to produce more goods but not long enough for existing firms to expand their capacity or for new firms to enter the market. Thus, output can be varied but only within the limits of existing plant capacity.

In the long run, the fishermen have even more opportunities to adjust their daily catch to changing prices. They have time to acquire new boats and equipment and to invest in new fish-finding technology. New fishermen can enter

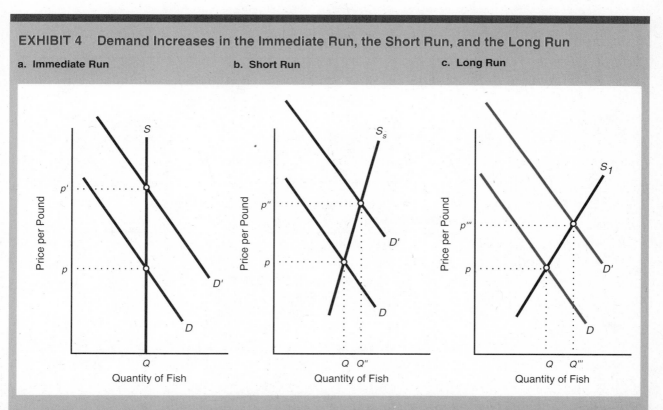

EXHIBIT 4   Demand Increases in the Immediate Run, the Short Run, and the Long Run

a. Immediate Run   b. Short Run   c. Long Run

In the immediate run, panel (a), the supply is fixed, and the supply curve is vertical. The increase in demand (from D to D') raises only the price (from p to p'), not the quantity. In the short run, producers can respond in a limited fashion to higher prices; hence the supply curve in panel (b) has a steep positive slope. As the market moves from the immediate run to the short run, the price drops from p' to p'' and the quantity increases from Q to Q''. In the long run, producers have the greatest flexibility to respond to higher prices. The long-run supply curve in panel (c) is even less steeply sloped. As the market moves from the short run to the long run, the price drops further (from p'' to p''') and the equilibrium quantity rises further from Q'' to Q'''.

EXAMPLE 2

Elasticities: Theory and Practice

Price Elasticities of Demand

	Short Run	Long Run
Tobacco products	0.46	1.89
Jewelry	0.41	0.67
Toilet articles	0.20	3.04
Owner-occupied housing	0.04	1.22
China and glassware	1.55	2.55
Electricity	0.13	1.89
Water	0.20	0.14
Medical care and hospitalization	0.31	0.92
Tires	0.86	1.19
Auto repairs	0.40	0.38
Durable recreation equipment	0.88	2.39
Motion pictures	0.88	3.69
Foreign travel	0.14	1.77
Gasoline	0.15	0.78

Source: Hendrick S. Houthakker and Lester D. Taylor, *Consumer Demand in the United States: Analyses and Projections* (Cambridge, Mass.: Harvard University Press, 1970), pp. 166–67; James L. Sweeney, "The Demand for Gasoline: A Vintage Capital Model," Department of Engineering Economics, Stanford University.

Price Elasticities of Supply

Wheat[a]	—	.93
Corn[a]	—	.18
U.S. oil[b]	—	.76
Natural gas[c]	—	.20
Urban housing[d]	—	5.30

Sources: [a]M. Nerlove, "Estimates of the Elasticities of Supply of Selected Agricultural Commodities," *Journal of Farm Economics* (May 1956); [b]E. W. Ericson, S. W. Millsaps, and R. M. Spann, "Oil Supply and Tax Incentives," *Brookings Papers on Economic Activity* (1974); [c]J. D. Khazzoom, "The FPC Staff's Econometric Model of Natural Gas Supply in the United States," *The Bell Journal of Economics* (Spring 1971); [d]B. A. Smith, "The Supply of Urban Housing," *Journal of Political Economy* (1976).

Income Elasticities

Motion-picture tickets[a]	3.4
Foreign travel[a]	3.1
Toys[a]	2.0
Automobiles and parts[b]	1.7
Clothing and shoes[b]	1.1
Furniture[b]	.9
Beef[c]	.5
Pork[c]	.3
Lard[c]	−.1

Sources: [a]H. S. Houthakker and L. D. Taylor, *Consumer Demand in the United States* (Cambridge, MA: Harvard University Press, 1970). [b]L. Philips, *Applied Consumption Analysis* (Amsterdam: North-Holland, 1974). [c]G. E. Brandow, "Interrelations among Demands for Farm Products and Implications for Control of Market Supply," Pennsylvania State University Agricultural Experiment Station Bulletin 680, 1961.

Calculated price elasticities of demand generally support theory. Long-run elasticities are larger than short-run elasticities. Elasticities appear to rise with the availability of substitutes. Medical care has fewer good substitutes than most of the other products listed, and it has lower short-run and long-run elasticities than products such as motion pictures, recreation equipment, gasoline, and foreign travel. In the short run, electricity has no good substitutes, and the short-run elasticity is low.

Income elasticities show that some items are highly elastic (movies, travel, and toys), while other goods (pork and lard) are inelastic.

the business. Accordingly, fish suppliers can respond more flexibly to changing prices. In the long run, the supply curve is more elastic than in the short run. (See panel (c) of Exhibit 4.)

> The **long run** is a period of time long enough for new firms to enter the market, for old firms to disappear, and for existing plants to be expanded. In the long run, firms have more flexibility in adjusting to price changes.

The elasticity of supply is larger in the long run than in either the short run or the immediate run. When the demand for a product increases, the immediate-run price will be higher than the short-run price, and the short-run price will be higher than the long-run price.

The effect on equilibrium prices and quantities of an increase in the demand for fish depends on the amount of adjustment time. Exhibit 4 shows that in the immediate run, an increase in demand raises price considerably, but does not affect quantity. In the short run, the increase in demand raises both price and quantity. Because fishermen are able to increase their catches by working longer hours and hiring more help, the increase in quantity supplied will hold down the price increase somewhat. In the long run, fishermen have even more flexibility in responding to higher prices, and there is an even larger increase in quantity supplied. This increase holds down prices even more.

The three time periods cannot be closely associated with calendar time. The amount of calendar time required to move from the short run to the long run varies with the type of industry. The electric-power industry may require a decade to expand existing power-generating facilities and to bring new plants on line. On the other hand, the fast-food industry can construct and open a new outlet in a few months.

Elasticity allows us to understand the extent to which changing prices and income affect supply and demand. The next chapter will look behind the demand curve to explain the law of demand. (See Example 2.)

Chapter Summary

The most important point to learn from this chapter is: The price elasticity of demand measures the degree to which Q responds to P for any good or service and indicates how total revenue changes along the demand curve.

1. The *price elasticity of demand* (E_d) is the percentage change in quantity demanded divided by the percentage change in price. Whether E_d exceeds, equals, or falls short of 1 determines how total revenue changes along the demand curve. E_d is typically calculated using the midpoints formula; the change in quantity is divided by the average quantity, and the change in price is divided by the average price.

Taxing Gasoline—Who Pays?

In the 1992 presidential election, third-party candidate Ross Perot proposed a $.50 per gallon tax on gasoline. The United States consumes about 110 billion gallons of gasoline per year at an average price of about $1.10 per gallon. How much would the price rise with a $.50 per gallon tax? Will consumers bear the entire burden and pay $1.60? How much revenue will be collected? In the newspapers it was often argued that $55 billion would be collected ($.50 × 110 billion). To illustrate the importance of the concepts of price elasticity of demand and supply, let us try to answer these questions.

   To make the calculations simple we will suppose that the current price of gasoline is $1 and that 100 billion gallons are consumed per year. In the accompanying graph, this is shown as point *e* where the pretax demand and supply curves intersect.

The Burden of Tax

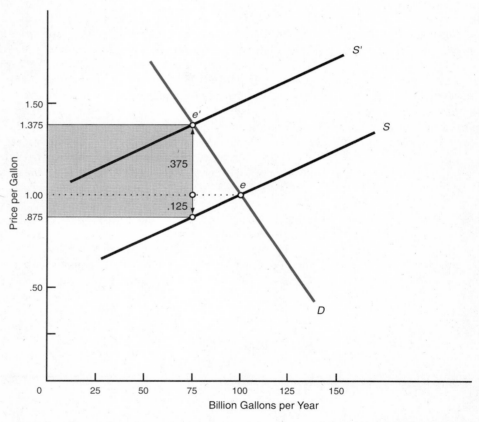

Curves *D* and *S* are the demand and supply curves for gasoline before the tax; the equilibrium price is $1. A tax of $.50 per gallon on sellers shifts the supply curve upward by exactly $.50 as sellers recoup their tax payments to the state. The new equilibrium price to buyers is found where the new supply curve, *S'*, intersects the old demand curve, *D*, at point *e'*; thus, the new price is $1.37¹/₂ to buyers. Sellers must send $.50 (per gallon sold) to the tax collector; hence, sellers keep only $.87¹/₂ after paying tax. Notice that three-fourths of the burden of the $.50 tax ($0.37¹/₂) falls on buyers and one fourth of the burden ($0.12¹/₂) falls on sellers. This incidence reflects the fact that the elasticity of supply is approximately 4 times greater (E_s = 2.4) than the elasticity of demand (E_d = 0.6).

The tax of $.50 per gallon changes the supply curve. In order for sellers to earn $1 a gallon (after paying the tax), they must now charge $1.50; to earn $.87$\frac{1}{2}$ they must charge 1.37\frac{1}{2}$. The tax will shift the supply curve up by exactly $.50—the amount of the tax. The tax does not change the demand curve. At each price (including taxes), consumers should continue to demand the same quantities as before. The new equilibrium must be less than $1.50 (the original price plus the tax) because at $1.50, the quantity demanded falls while the quantity supplied remains the same. Thus, at $1.50, there would be a surplus of gasoline on the market.

The new equilibrium point is *e'* at the price of 1.37\frac{1}{2}$ and a quantity of 75 billion gallons per year. Sellers receive $.87$\frac{1}{2}$, with the tax collector picking up the $.50 difference. The government collects $37.5 billion in tax revenue ($.50 × 75 billion). This is much closer to what would happen to tax revenues than the estimates made in the newspapers.

The equilibrium price paid by consumers rises by $.37$\frac{1}{2}$ and the net price (price minus the tax) received by sellers falls by $.12$\frac{1}{2}$. Thus, consumers pay three-fourths of the tax and sellers pay one-fourth of the tax. Why is it that the consumer has the greater part of the burden than the seller in this particular example? The answer is found in the elasticities of demand and supply.

The demand curve in the accompanying exhibit is less elastic than the supply curve, as shown by the fact that curve *S* is flatter than curve *D*. Consumers, therefore, respond less to the price than do sellers. Since consumers are less sensitive to changes in the price of gasoline, they will pay more of the tax because they reveal less inclination to avoid the tax. We have assumed that the elasticity of demand along *D* between $1 and 1.37\frac{1}{2}$ is approximately 0.6, and that the elasticity of supply along *S* is approximately 2.4.

In other cases, such as a tax on perfume, the elasticity of demand may exceed the elasticity of supply. In these cases, sellers will pay the greater burden of the tax because they are less sensitive to price changes than consumers. The consumer bears the greater burden of taxes when demand elasticities are less than supply elasticities, as is typical in the long run.

2. The cross-price elasticity is the percentage change in the demand for one good divided by the percentage change in the price of some other good. The income elasticity of demand is the percentage change in the demand divided by the percentage change in income. If this number is greater than 1, the good is a luxury; if it is less than 1, the good is a necessity.

3. The price elasticity of supply is the percentage change in quantity supplied divided by the percentage change in price. The price elasticity of supply depends on the time period of adjustment. Elasticity of supply is greater in the long run than in the short run and greater in the short run than in the immediate run.

4. The elasticites of demand and supply determine whether producers or consumers will bear the greater burden of a tax on a particular good. The group (producers or consumers) that bears the greater burden has the lowest price elasticity of demand or supply.

Policy Focus: **This chapter shows that it is elasticities that determine the incidence of a tax.**

Key Terms

price elasticity of demand (p. 345)
midpoints formula (p. 346)
total revenue (p. 348)

total-revenue test (p. 349)
perfectly elastic demand (p. 350)
perfectly inelastic demand (p. 350)

income elasticity of demand (p. 352)
necessities (p. 352)
luxuries (p. 352)
cross-price elasticity of demand (p. 353)
price elasticity of supply (p. 353)

perfectly elastic supply (p. 353)
perfectly inelastic supply (p. 354)
immediate run (p. 354)
short run (p. 354)
long run (p. 354)

Questions and Problems

1. Using the demand schedule in Table A, calculate the price elasticities of demand for each successive pair of rows.

TABLE A

Price (dollars)	Quantity (units)
5	1
4	2
3	3
2	4
1	5

2. Suppose the long-run price elasticity of demand for tobacco is 2. A new tax increases the price of tobacco to consumers from $10 to $11 per carton. If Mr. Iron-lungs smokes 500 packages of cigarettes per year, what percentage decrease in quantity demanded would you predict? Approximately how many packages would be smoked at a price of $11 per carton (assuming 10 packages to a carton)?

3. Suppose the price of gasoline falls from $1.20 per gallon to $0.60 per gallon. Why would a driver's short-run adjustment to this price change be different from the long-run adjustment?

4. Assume that the basic monthly charge for a private telephone is $10.50 per month. If the rate were to rise to $11.00, would you expect a substantial reduction in the quantity demanded? Explain your answer. If, on the other hand, the basic monthly charge were $250.00 per month and the rate were to rise by the same percent as in the first case, what is your prediction about the change in quantity demanded?

5. When a professional football team raises its ticket prices by 10 percent, its sales revenues decline. From this information, what can you say about the price elasticity of demand for its tickets?

6. The University of Cowtown faces an inelastic demand for its dormitory rooms. What would you recommend that the university do in its annual budge meeting: raise the price, lower the price, or maintain the same price of dormitory rooms?

7. The income elasticity of demand for all services taken together is greater than one. As the economy grows, what would you expect to happen to the share of service industries in total output?

8. Used-car sales typically rise during economic recessions, while new-car sales decline during recessions. Explain why.

9. Assume that oranges have the following characteristics. The elasticity of demand is 0.2 and the elasticity of supply is 2. If government imposes a tax of $1 per crate of oranges, who would pay more of the tax (bear the larger burden of the tax): the consumer or the producer? Why? Draw a diagram illustrating your argument.

10. Evaluate the following statement: "The elasticity of demand for oranges is 0.2; therefore, California orange growers could raise their income by restricting their output."

11. Suppose the supply curve for the product X shifts to the right (supply increases). What happens to the total expenditure of consumers under each of the following conditions?
   a. The demand for X is price elastic.
   b. The demand for X is price inelastic.
   c. The demand for X is perfectly elastic.
   d. The demand for X is perfectly inelastic.

12. Suppose the supply curve for the product X shifts to the left (supply decreases). What happens to the total expenditure of consumers under each of the following conditions?
   a. The demand for X is price elastic.
   b. The demand for X is price inelastic.
   c. The demand for X is perfectly elastic.
   d. The demand for X is perfectly inelastic.

13. Suppose the demand for product X increases. What happens to the total revenue of sellers under each of the following conditions?
   a. The supply of X is elastic.
   b. The supply of X is inelastic.

14. Using the determinants of the price elasticity of demand, indicate for each of the following pairs of goods which one has the highest elasticity.
   a. Wheat and grains.
   b. Soft drinks and beverages.
   c. Cars and clothing.
   d. Toothpicks and beef.

15. Double the quantities demanded at each price in Table A above (for example, when the price is $5, assume 2 units are demanded; when the price is $4, assume 4 units

are demanded; and so on). What happens to the slope of the demand curve? What happens to the elasticity of demand between each successive pair of prices?

16. Who bears the burden of a tax on a good in each of the following circumstances?
   a. The supply curve is upward-sloping; demand is perfectly inelastic.
   b. The supply curve is upward-sloping; demand is perfectly elastic.
   c. The demand curve is downward-sloping; supply is perfectly inelastic.
   d. The demand curve is downward-sloping; supply is perfectly elastic.

17. The price elasticity of supply of perfume is 1. The price elasticity of demand for perfume is 2. How is the burden of the tax divided between producers and consumers?

Doing Economics

Has your campus cafeteria or bookstore changed the price of an item by a significant amount lately? If so, ask whether they would share information about the change in weekly or monthly sales that resulted from the price change. Based on the information that you receive from them, calculate the price elasticity of demand for the product. Does your estimate conform to your expectation based on the determinants of elasticity discussed in this chapter? Using this method for measuring elasticity assumes that the change in price moved quantity demanded along a fixed demand curve. This means that tastes, incomes, and the prices of related goods must be constant. Are these reasonable assumptions in this case? Explain.

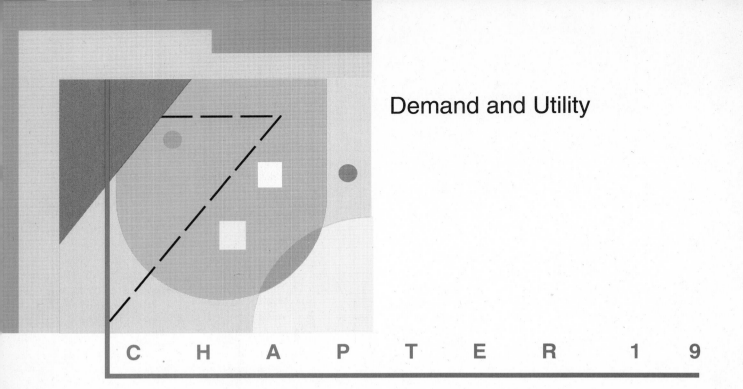

Demand and Utility

CHAPTER FOCUS Why is there a law of demand? The answer that economists give is that people buy more when the price of something is low because that makes them better off. For example, in 1990s America, television entertainment is very cheap: more channels are available, and high-quality color TV sets sell for a fraction of what low-quality black-and-white TV sets cost two decades earlier. Are consumers better off? *TV Guide* took a survey of its readers and found that about half would refuse to give up television for less than a million dollars! In other words, the value placed on watching television is astronomical compared to the actual price.

When people have only a limited amount to spend, they must spread their expenditures over the available goods and services to get as much satisfaction as possible. In doing so, they must weigh the costs of the good compared to the extra satisfaction that it yields. Consumption is increased until the price of the good just equals what one more unit of the good is worth at the margin. As the TV example indicates, people may therefore get a lot of satisfaction from something that has a very low price. This chapter focuses on how the law of demand is the result of the rational calculation of costs and benefits to consumers.

<table>
<tr><td rowspan="2" style="vertical-align:top">LEARNING OBJECTIVES</td></tr>
</table>

LEARNING OBJECTIVES

After studying this chapter, you will be able to:

- Understand how consumer preferences differ from demand.
- Know the law of diminishing marginal utility.
- Explain the principles under which the consumer's choices are in equilibrium.
- See how the law of demand is related to the law of diminishing marginal utility.
- Define the difference between income and substitution effects.
- Understand how to go from individual demand to market demand.

RATIONAL CONSUMER BEHAVIOR

The most important assumption of economics—the assumption upon which most economic ideas are based—is that individuals act to further their own self-interest. As buyers of goods and services, individuals spend their money to gain maximum satisfaction from their limited income. As owners of businesses, individuals operate their businesses to gain a maximum profit. As owners of factors of production, individuals use those factors to gain a maximum return. Economists assume that people act "rationally" in their own self-interest. Rational behavior does not mean that people are indifferent to family, friends, and society. People are entirely rational in helping others if they gain satisfaction from such benevolence.

Rational consumers spend their limited income buying goods and services. Consumers behave rationally when using their limited income to gain maximum satisfaction from the goods and services they consume.

CONSUMER PREFERENCES

Demand denotes the goods and services that households are prepared to buy given relative prices and consumers' income levels. If relative prices change or consumer income changes, the amounts people are prepared to buy change.

The amounts of goods and services that households are prepared to purchase depend not only on relative prices and income, but also on preferences or tastes. People have personal evaluations or **preferences** over the alternatives they face among the vast array of goods and services available.

> **Preferences** are a person's evaluations of goods and services independent of budget and price considerations.

People exhibit a wide variety of preferences. To satisfy the preference for entertainment, one person watches television, another goes to a movie, another learns how to pilot an airplane, yet another buys a book. Consumers' preferences determine how they would rank different combinations of goods and services in all conceivable situations. Smith prefers three apples and two oranges to one apple and five oranges, independently of apple and orange prices. Johnson prefers one apple and five oranges to three apples and two oranges, independently of apple and orange prices. Smith and Johnson have different preferences.

Nineteenth-century economists introduced a simple way of representing preferences. They assumed people's preferences for goods or services are based on how goods or services add to their **utility**.

> **Utility** is the satisfaction that a person enjoys from consuming goods and services.

Marginal Utility

It is not possible to attach a meter to someone to measure satisfaction from consuming goods and services. (The appendix to this chapter explains why it is not even necessary to measure utility in specific units.) Suppose, however, that one could measure utility in terms of imaginary *utils*, or units of utility. From consuming 50 gallons of water per week, for example, a consumer enjoys 3,000 utils of satisfaction. From consuming 51 gallons, a consumer enjoys 3,010 utils.

The **marginal utility (*MU*)** of water is the extra utility enjoyed by increasing water consumption by one gallon. If 50 gallons yield 3,000 utils and 51 gallons yield 3,010 utils, the marginal utility of the 51st gallon of water is 10 utils.

> The **marginal utility (MU)** of any good or service is the increase in utility that a consumer experiences when consumption of that good or service increases by one unit, holding the consumption of all other goods and services constant. In general,
>
> $$MU = \frac{\Delta TU}{\Delta Q},$$
>
> where *TU* is total utility and *Q* is the quantity of the good.

The Law of Diminishing Marginal Utility

The **law of diminishing marginal utility** states that, as a general rule, as more of a good or service is consumed, its marginal utility declines. Thus, the first gallon of water per week has an enormous marginal utility because a consumer who has no water would have to use the first gallon to sustain life. The 20th gallon of water has a relatively small marginal utility because a person who already has 19 gallons would be able to use the 20th gallon for less important purposes. The marginal utility of water should decline rapidly as more water is consumed. Because the first gallon of water is essential to sustaining life, its marginal utility is astronomical. As more water becomes available, water can be applied to less urgent uses: to washing oneself, to washing clothes, to feeding pets, and eventually even to watering the lawn. By the time sufficient water is available for watering the lawn, the marginal utility of the last gallon is much smaller than the marginal utility of the first gallon. (See Example 1.)

> The law of diminishing marginal utility states that as more of a good or service is consumed during any given time period, its marginal utility declines, holding the consumption of everything else constant.

The **total utility** from all 20 gallons of water would be the sum of the marginal utilities of all units. Marginal utility is more important to explaining consumer demand than is total utility.

> Total utility is the amount of satisfaction (utility) obtained from consuming a particular quantity of a good or service. It is the sum of the marginal utilities of each successive unit of consumption.

MARGINAL UTILITY AND THE LAW OF DEMAND

The law of diminishing marginal utility explains the law of demand. Consumers will allocate their income among all the various goods in such a way that their total utility is maximized. When the price of any good falls, the consumer is motivated to buy more of the good.

Consider an individual consumer, Adam Smith. Adam Smith lives in a part of rural Scotland where only two goods can be bought—ale (A) and bread (B).

Adam Smith's preferences for both ale and bread are summarized in Exhibit 1. They do not change as time passes and as other things change. Columns 2 and 6 show the total utility of ale (TU_A) and bread (TU_B), respectively; columns 3 and 7 show the marginal utility of ale (MU_A) and bread (MU_B), respectively. These utility schedules apply to Adam Smith's consumption over a week's time period. In Smith's case, the utility of ale does not depend on how much bread he consumes, or vice versa.

Adam Smith's marginal utility schedule for ale is shown in Exhibit 2 and is graphed from the data in Exhibit 1. The first pint of ale (per week) yields a marginal utility of 40 utils; the second yields 30 utils; the third yields 20 utils; the fourth pint of ale yields a marginal utility of 10 utils. The total utility from consuming different quantities of ale is the sum of the bars up to the quantity of ale consumed. The total utility from consuming three pints of ale, for example, is 90 (= 40 + 30 + 20).

EXAMPLE 1

Why Diamonds Cost More Than Water

Adam Smith, in the *The Wealth of Nations* (1776), noted that "nothing is more useful than water; but it will purchase scarce anything; scarce anything can be had in exchange for it. A diamond, on the contrary, has scarce any value in use; but a very great quantity of other goods may frequently be had in exchange for it." The question at the root of this paradox is why prices often fail to reflect the usefulness of goods. Goods such as water and salt, without which human beings would perish, have low relative prices, whereas goods that have little practical value, such as diamonds, gold, and high fashion, have high relative prices.

Why is it that diamonds, whose total utility is much less than that of water, have a higher relative price than water? The law of diminishing marginal utility provides the answer to this paradox. On the one hand, the consumption of water takes place at a low marginal utility because the supply of water is large; on the other hand, the supply of diamonds is usually so limited that consumption takes place at a relatively high marginal utility. Although water's total utility is high, its marginal utility is low. Therefore, no one will sacrifice very much for an additional gallon.

The terms of the diamond/water paradox hold under normal supply conditions, but what happens when these conditions are disrupted? In the confusion at the end of World War II, food supplies were interrupted, and people gladly exchanged diamonds and precious metals for bread and potatoes in parts of Europe. The availability of food products was so limited that food products yielded a higher marginal utility (by preventing malnutrition) than did diamonds and precious metals. Similarly, when the American West was being settled in the nineteenth century, range wars were fought (and people were killed) over the control of water holes, and in arid parts of the world (Africa, the Middle East), armed conflicts still break out over water.

We know only Adam Smith's preferences for ale and bread. We cannot go from preferences to demand without knowing how much Smith has to spend on bread and ale per week and the prices of bread and ale. As noted in Chapter 3, demand depends not only on consumer preferences, but also on consumer income and prices. The combination of preferences, income, and prices explains the relationship between quantity demanded and price.

Adam Smith has $8 to spend on ale and bread per week. The price of ale (P_A) is $2 per pint, and the price of bread (P_B) is $0.50 per loaf. Smith could spend the entire $8 on ale, buying 4 pints of ale, or he could spend all $8 on bread, buying 16 loaves of bread. The most likely case, however, is that Smith will spend part of the money on ale and part on bread. For instance, he could purchase 3 pints of ale costing a total of $6 and 4 loaves of bread costing a total of $2 for a total weekly expenditure of $8. Smith is confronted with a choice: he can afford a number of combinations of ale and bread. Which combination will he actually select?

> To achieve maximum utility, consumers allocate their budget on goods in such a way that it is impossible to improve their total satisfaction by spending a bit more on one good or a bit less on the other.

As a rational consumer, Adam Smith will spend his limited income in such a manner as to obtain maximum satisfaction. Exhibit 1 shows that Adam Smith gets utility from consuming more of both ale and bread. How will he decide what affordable combination gives him the most satisfaction?

We will now demonstrate that Adam Smith maximizes his satisfaction when his budget is spent so that *the last dollar spent on each product (ale and bread) yields the same marginal utility.* This rule makes a lot of sense: If marginal utility per dollar of the last dollar spent is not the same for two products, the consumer can get more utility by switching the last dollar to the good with the greater marginal utility per dollar and still remain within budget.

Quantity of Ale (pints), Q_A (1)	Total Utility of Ale (utils), TU_A (2)	Marginal Utility of Ale (utils), MU_A (3)	Marginal Utility of Ale per Dollar (utils), MU_A/P_A (4)	Quantity of Bread (loaves), Q_B (5)	Total Utility of Bread (utils), TU_B (6)	Marginal Utility of Bread (utils), MU_B (7)	Marginal Utility of Bread per Dollar (utils), MU_B/P_B (8)
1	40	40	20	1	15	15	30
2	70	30	15	2	23	8	16
3	90	20	10	3	30	7	14
4	100	10	5	4	35	5	10
5	105	5	2.5	5	38	3	6
6	107	2	1	6	40	2	4

The table lists the quantities of ale and bread consumed per week by the consumer along with the utility the consumer attaches to each quantity. The marginal-utility-per-dollar figures are calculated by dividing marginal utility by price. The price of ale equals $2 per pint and the price of bread equals $0.50 per loaf.

EXHIBIT 2   Declining Marginal Utility

This figure graphs the data in columns 1 and 3 of Exhibit 1. The width of each bar represents one pint of ale. The vertical height or area of each bar represents marginal utility for that extra unit of ale. Total utility up to some quantity of ale is the sum of the areas of the bars to the left of that quantity of ale. For example, the total utility of 2 pints equals 70 (= 40 + 30); the total utility of 5 pints equals 105 (= 40 + 30 + 20 + 10 + 5).

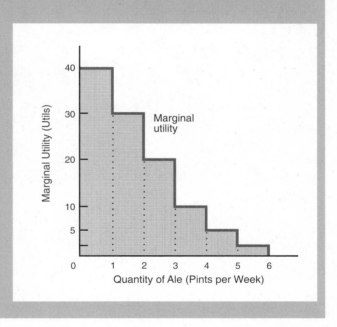

Maximum satisfaction requires that marginal utility per extra dollar spent on *A* be the same as the marginal utility per extra dollar spent on *B*.

Consumers select the affordable combination of goods that gives them maximum satisfaction by comparing marginal utility per dollar. In columns 4 and 8 of Exhibit 1, **marginal utilities per dollar** of ale and bread are calculated by dividing marginal utility by the price.

The **marginal utility per dollar** is the ratio *MU/P* and indicates the increase in utility from another dollar spent on the good.

EXHIBIT 3 The Steps to Consumer Equilibrium

	Available Choices	Decision	Income Remaining
1st Purchase ↓	1st pint of ale: $MU_A/P_A = 20$ 1st loaf of bread: $MU_B/P_B = 30$	Buy 1st loaf of bread for $0.50	$8.00 − $0.50 = $7.50
2nd Purchase ↓	1st pint of ale: $MU_A/P_A = 20$ 2nd loaf of bread: $MU_B/P_B = 16$	Buy 1st pint of ale for $2.00	$7.50 − $2.00 = $5.50
3rd Purchase ↓	2nd pint of ale: $MU_A/P_A = 15$ 2nd loaf of bread: $MU_B/P_B = 16$	Buy 2nd loaf of bread for $0.50	$5.50 − $0.50 = $5.00
4th Purchase ↓	2nd pint of ale: $MU_A/P_A = 15$ 3rd loaf of bread: $MU_B/P_B = 14$	Buy 2nd pint of ale for $2.00	$5.00 − $2.00 = $3.00
5th Purchase ↓	3rd pint of ale: $MU_A/P_A = 10$ 3rd loaf of bread: $MU_B/P_B = 14$	Buy 3rd loaf of bread for $0.50	$3.00 − $0.50 = $2.50
6th Purchase and 7th Purchase	3rd pint of ale: $MU_A/P_A = 10$ 4th loaf of bread: $MU_B/P_B = 10$	Buy 3rd pint of ale for $2.00 and 4th loaf of bread for $0.50	$2.50 − $2.00 = $0.50 $0.50 − $0.50 = $0 ⎫ Equilibrium ⎬ ⎭

This table shows the step-by-step process by which a consumer makes purchasing decisions that will maximize satisfaction. In choosing at each step between a unit of ale and a unit of bread, the consumer determines which commodity has the highest marginal utility per dollar and buys that commodity. The data are taken from Exhibit 1. The consumer has $8 to spend. The consumer ends up buying 3 pints of ale and 4 loaves of bread, which is the equilibrium combination because marginal utility per dollar is equal for the two goods and all income is spent.

Note that the concept of marginal utility per dollar is a rate measure like miles per hour. Just as one can drive 50 miles per hour without driving for a full hour, marginal utility per dollar does not require the spending of a full dollar.

Exhibit 3 shows a step-by-step process by which Adam Smith could allocate his income between bread and ale. The first loaf of bread costs $0.50 and yields a marginal utility of 15; the marginal utility *per dollar* is 30 (= 15/$0.50) for the first loaf. The first pint of ale costs $2 and yields a marginal utility of 40, but the marginal utility *per dollar* is only 20 (= 40/$2) for the first pint. Because the first loaf of bread has a higher marginal utility per dollar, Smith would first buy one loaf of bread at a cost of $0.50, leaving $7.50 to spend. Smith now finds that the marginal utility per dollar is higher for the first pint of ale (20) than for the second loaf of bread (16), so he purchases a first pint of ale for $2, leaving $5.50 to spend. Marginal utility per dollar is higher for the second loaf of bread (16) than for the second pint of ale (15), so Smith's third purchase is the second loaf of bread. Smith continues to select the product with the higher marginal utility per dollar until his

$8 budget is exhausted. Smith is in **consumer equilibrium** when he buys 3 pints of ale and 4 loaves of bread—where he has spent his entire income of $8 (3 pints at $2 each and 4 loaves at $0.50 each) and where the marginal utility per dollar is 10 utils for both ale and bread.

> Consumer equilibrium occurs when the consumer has spent all of the budget and marginal utilities per dollar are equal on each good purchased ($MU_A/P_A = MU_B/P_B$).

The consumer is not inclined to change purchases from an equilibrium position where marginal utilities per dollar are equal unless some other factor changes. How other factors—such as income or changes in preferences—affect consumer equilibrium will be discussed below.

The Law of Demand

The law of demand follows from the analysis of consumer behavior. When the price of ale is $2, Adam Smith purchases (demands) 3 pints of ale, given that his income is $8 and the price of bread is $0.50. The price/quantity combination of $2/3 pints of ale is one point (*r* in Exhibit 4) on Smith's demand curve.

Other points on the demand curve can be calculated by repeating the whole process at a different price of ale, keeping income at $8 per week and the bread price at $0.50 per loaf.

If the price of ale falls from $2 to $1 per pint, the marginal utility per dollar for ale is now higher than the marginal utility per dollar for bread at the old equilibrium of 3 pints of ale and 4 loaves of bread. Ale purchases will be increased because it now yields more satisfaction for each additional dollar spent. Expenditures will be reallocated between the two goods until the $8 is spent and marginal utilities per dollar are again equal—this time at 5 pints of ale and 6 loaves of bread purchased. Thus, when the price of ale is $1, the quantity demanded of ale is 5 pints. This price/quantity combination of $1/5 pints is a second point (*t*) on the demand curve

EXHIBIT 4   From Marginal Utility to the Demand Curve

This curve shows Adam Smith's demand curve for ale calculated from Exhibit 1. If the price of bread is $0.50 per loaf and weekly income is $8, consumer equilibrium can be calculated at the price of ale equal to $2 per pint. The equilibrium quantity of 3 pints of ale is the quantity of ale demanded when the price of ale equals $2 (point *r*). The equilibrium quantity can also be calculated for a price of ale equal to $1 per pint. The resulting equilibrium quantity of ale (5 pints) is the quantity of ale demanded when the price of ale equals $1 (point *t*).

EXAMPLE 2

Marginal Utility, "All You Can Eat for $10," and the Daily Newspaper

Many restaurants offer buffets where customers can eat all they want for a specified price. Such offers are possible because the marginal utility of food diminishes rapidly. Depending on the individual's appetite, extra helpings yield smaller and smaller marginal utilities. In fact, they rather quickly yield negative marginal utility—the consumer's utility was higher before the extra helping. Although more food costs the consumer nothing, people will limit the amount of food they consume.

Rapidly diminishing marginal utility explains why the daily newspaper is dispensed from coin-operated boxes that permit people to take as many copies as they want. Newspaper companies know that the marginal utility of a second newspaper is zero for most people and they don't worry about people taking more than one. Owner's of coin-operated dispensers of other products (soft drinks, candies, etc.) know that they cannot give the customer the opportunity to take more than one.

in Exhibit 4. The law of demand holds because, holding all other facts constant, a decrease in the price causes an increase in the quantity demanded. (See Example 2.)

Every point on a given consumer's demand curve satisfies the conditions that MU/P is the same for all goods the consumer is buying and that all income is spent—that is, the consumer is maximizing utility at that price/quantity combination.

Income and Substitution Effects

When the price of a good falls, two things happen. First, consumers can buy the goods and services they used to buy *plus* what can be bought with their new savings. A decrease in price is like an increase in income in the sense that it enables consumers to purchase more goods of any type, including more of the good whose price has fallen. The part of the increase in quantity demanded caused by such an increase in income is called the **income effect**. Second, the cheaper good now yields a higher marginal utility per dollar. Consumers bent on maximizing satisfaction will substitute this now cheaper good for other products. This part of the increase in the quantity demanded of the cheaper good is called the **substitution effect**.

> When the price of a good falls people buy more of it because of the **income effect**—a price reduction is like an increase in income that in itself normally leads to larger demands for all goods and services, including the one whose price has fallen.

> When the price of a good falls, people buy more because consumers tend to substitute the good whose price has fallen for other relatively more expensive goods. This is called the **substitution affect**.

In Exhibit 4, before the drop in the price of ale from $2 to $1, the consumer purchased 3 pints of ale and 4 loaves of bread for a total of $8 worth of ale and bread. At the lower price of $1 per pint of ale, the consumer can purchase the same 3 pints of ale and 4 loaves of bread for $5. The consumer now has $3 left over that can be spent on either ale or bread. This $3 is like an increase in income. The effect of this increase in real income on purchases of ale is the income effect.

In addition to having the extra $3, the relative price of ale has dropped (the ratio of ale price to bread price has fallen from 4 to 2). Because of the lower relative price of ale, the consumer is now getting more marginal utility *per dollar* out of ale than bread, and therefore switches to buying more ale. This switch from bread to ale is the substitution effect.

The size of the income effect from a price change depends on how much of the good is being consumed. If the price of a Rolls-Royce goes up or down, there is no income effect for the vast majority of people. But if the price of gasoline rises, every driver would be affected—and those who used the most gasoline would be affected the most. Thus, the income effects for changes in the prices of food, clothing, and housing can be quite substantial. The income effects of changes in the prices of goods that are relatively unimportant in the consumer's budget are small or trivial.

The size of the substitution effect depends on the ease with which other goods can be substituted for a good. There are more substitutes for a movie than for a pair of eye-glasses, and the substitution effect would be correspondingly larger.

The theory of rational consumer behavior predicts that the law of demand holds true. The theory of rational consumer behavior explains why people consume a variety of goods and services.

MARKET DEMAND

We have used the law of diminishing marginal utility to demonstrate that a rational consumer will purchase less of a product, *ceteris paribus*, if its price rises. In other words, the demand curves of individual consumers have negative slopes.

But prices are established in markets, and the individual consumer is usually only a small part of the market. The **market-demand curve** for a particular good combines the demand curves of all participants in that market.

> The **market-demand curve** shows the total quantities demanded by all consumers in the market at each price. It is the summation of all individual demand curves in that market.

Exhibit 5 shows the demand curves for ale for two consumers, Jones and White, who constitute all the buyers in the market for ale. (In reality, there would be many buyers of ale, but two buyers allow us to make the point as simply as possible.) At a price of $3 per pint, Jones demands 0 pints and White demands 1 pint. The market quantity demanded at the $3 price can be obtained by adding the two quantities demanded together (0 + 1 = 1 pint). At a price of $2 per pint, Jones demands 2 pints and White demands 3 pints. The market quantity demanded at the $2 price is 2 + 3 = 5 pints.

The market-demand curve is downward-sloping for the same reasons that the individual demand curves are downward-sloping. In addition, as price decreases more consumers might be enticed to buy a product. For example, when the price of ale is above $3 Jones is not in the market; at a price of $0.50, even more buyers may enter the market.

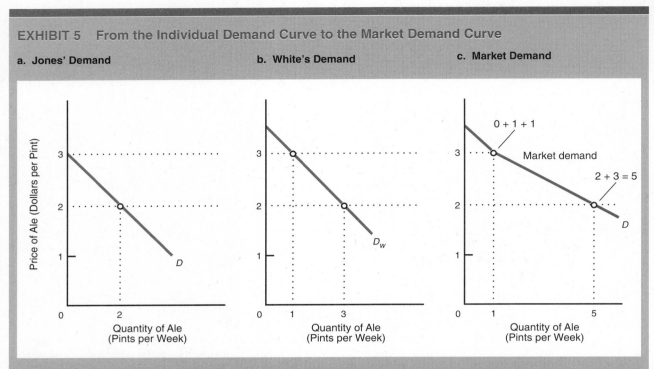

EXHIBIT 5 From the Individual Demand Curve to the Market Demand Curve

a. Jones' Demand

b. White's Demand

c. Market Demand

The market-demand curve is the horizontal summation of all individual demand curves; it is calculated by summing all individual quantities demanded at each price. Here, the market has only two consumers, but the principle applies to markets with any number of consumers.

This chapter examined the relationship between consumer behavior and the demand curve for goods and services. The next chapter shifts to the supply side of the market and examines how businesses are organized and the markets in which they operate.

Chapter Summary

The most important point to learn from this chapter is: When the consumer is in equilibrium the ratio of marginal utility to price is the same for each good purchased. The law of demand follows from this equilibrium condition.

1. Preferences are people's evaluations of goods and services independent of budget and price considerations. *Demand* denotes the goods and services that consumers are prepared to buy given income and relative prices.

2. The satisfaction that is obtained from consuming goods and services is called utility. Marginal utility is the increase in total utility obtained when consumption of a good is increased by one unit. The law of diminishing marginal utility states that the marginal utility declines as more of a good or service is consumed.

3. The law of diminishing marginal utility explains the law of demand. When the price of a commodity drops, two effects will be set in motion: The income effect occurs when

Should We Allow Price Gouging?

Natural disasters raise prices. After massive hurricanes such as Hurricane Andrew, which destroyed much of the Florida coast in the summer of 1992, the prices of building-repair materials tend to shoot up. With the many destroyed homes, gaping roofs, and open store windows, the marginal utility of building materials such as plywood increases, and the market demand increases.

Many states have ordinances that protect consumers from "price gouging" in the wake of natural disasters. These ordinances require that shop owners and speculators not benefit from the hardship of others. Even though people are prepared to pay a higher price of plywood after hurricanes, merchants cannot raise prices. If they do, they can be fined or even jailed!

Are anti-price-gouging laws really in society's best interest? Let us take a simplified example. The accompanying diagram shows a price of $5 per unit of plywood before the hurricane. Assume each "customer" buys 1 unit of plywood. At this price, two customers buy plywood. The hurricane increases demand. Without price controls, the price would rise to $11 with three customers buying at this price. If the law requires that the original $5 price be held, six people now wish to buy plywood, but only two customers can be satisfied.

The demand curve shows what people would have been willing to spend at different prices. After the hurricane, one customer would have been willing to pay $15, another $13, another $11. The first three customers would have been willing to pay $11 or more; the next three customers would have been willing to pay from $5 to $9.

This chapter teaches that the price people are willing to pay reflects that good's marginal utility to that person. The person willing to pay $15 places a higher value on plywood (perhaps to replace a missing roof) than the person willing to pay $5 (to

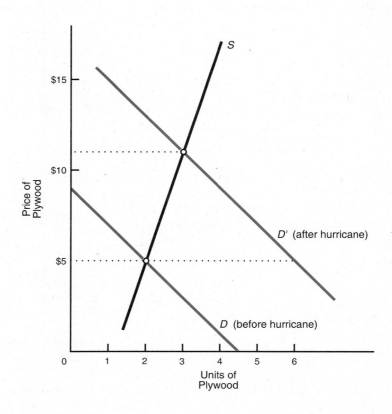

replace part of the front porch). If the price is held at $5, plywood will be distributed to two lucky customers according to the luck of the draw. If the person willing to pay only $5 is standing in line before the person willing to pay $15, plywood goes to a buyer who places a low value on the good. Let's assume that the luck of the draw results in customers 5 and 6 getting the plywood. For them, the plywood has a combined value of $12 ($5 + $7). For the excluded customers 1 and 2, the plywood would have a combined value of $28 ($15 + $13).

Goods allocated by price will always go to those buyers who place the highest value on the good. If goods are allocated by standing in line or by the luck of the draw, buyers who place a high value on the good may lose out to those who place a much lower value on the good. There is a loss to society if the person who desperately needs plywood to replace a roof cannot buy plywood, while the person who needs plywood for a minor front-porch repair can buy plywood.

the price decrease raises the real income of the consumer and when this increase in income is used to purchase additional goods and services. The substitution effect occurs because the fall in the relative price of the good motivates the consumer to substitute the good for other goods.

4. The marked-demand schedule summarizes the demand schedules of all individuals participating in the market. The market-demand curve will have a negative slope because individual demand curves have negative slopes.

Policy Focus: **Anti-price-gouging laws may not be in society's interest because they may result in goods going to buyers who place a relatively low value on them.**

Key Terms

preferences (p. 363)
utility (p. 364)
marginal utility (*MU*) (p. 364)
law of diminishing marginal utility (p. 365)
total utility (p. 365)

marginal utility per dollar (p. 367)
consumer equilibrium (p. 369)
income effect (p. 370)
substitution effect (p. 370)
market-demand curve (p. 371)

Questions and Problems

1. People spend a much larger fraction of their income on transportation in the 1980s than they did in the 1880s, when the horse and buggy was popular. Does this mean that consumer preferences for transportation services are basically unstable?

2. One of the most basic changes in consumer buying patterns in the late 1970s and early 1980s was the switch from "gas guzzlers" to fuel-efficient cars. Does this switch indicate that consumer preferences changed between the late 1970s and early 1980s?

3. For which good do you think marginal utility will decline more rapidly: hot dogs or best-seller paperbacks?

4. Use the marginal-utility information in Exhibit 1 to calculate the quantity demanded of ale at a price of $4 per pint. What do you do when marginal utility per dollar cannot be exactly equated on the last units sold?

5. Again using Exhibit 1, calculate the quantity demanded of ale at the price of $2 but at a weekly income of $11. Compare this result with the answer at $8. Which is larger? Why?

6. There are 1,000 identical consumers in the market with the same income and the same preferences. When the price of *X* is $50 per unit, the typical consumer is prepared to purchase 20 units of *X*. When the price is $40 per unit, the typical consumer is prepared to purchase 25 units of *X*. Construct the market-demand curve for *X* (assume the demand curve is a straight line).

7. A consumer spends total weekly income on goods *A*

and *B*. The last penny spent on *A* yields a marginal utility of 10; the last penny spent on *B* yields a marginal utility of 20. Is it possible for the consumer to be in equilibrium? If so, what are the exact conditions?

8. Ms. White consumes only goods *X* and *Y*. Column 1 of the table below shows the marginal utility she derives from various units of *X*; column 2 shows the marginal utility she derives from various units of *Y*. Her income is $20, the price of *X* is $2 per unit, and the price of *Y* is $4 per unit. Use Table A to answer the following questions:
   a. How much of *X* and *Y* will Ms. White demand?
   b. Check your answer by using the consumer-equilibrium conditions. (Is all income spent? Does $MU_x/P_x = MU_y/P_y$?)

TABLE A

Units of X	MU_x	Units of Y	Mu_x
1	20	1	2,000
2	16	2	200
3	12	3	20
4	10	4	10
5	6	5	4

9. Can the equilibrium conditions be applied to more than two goods? How?

10. The price of ale is $10, the price of bread is $5, and the marginal utility of bread is 50 utils when the consumer is in equilibrium. Can you deduce how much is spent on ale? Can you deduce the marginal utility of ale?

11. The price of oranges is $0.25 each, and the price of grapefruit is $0.50 each. Assuming that all income is spent in each case, determine whether or not the consumer is in equilibrium in each of the following circumstances. If consumer equilibrium does not occur, determine the good of which the consumer will purchase more and explain why.
   a. The marginal utility of oranges, MU_O, equals 10, and the marginal utility of grapefruit, MU_G, equals 15;
   b. $MU_O = 50$ and $MU_G = 100$;
   c. MU_O is twice that of MU_G;
   d. MU_G is twice that of MU_O.

12. Ms. Jones buys 100 cokes per year at $0.50 per coke and 20 pizzas at $5 each. Does doubling the price of cokes to $1 per coke have a larger or smaller income effect than raising the price of pizzas to $6? Explain your answer.

Doing Economics

One difficulty in applying supply-and-demand analysis is dealing with goods or services that are similar but not quite identical. For example, an apartment close to the center of a city (or close to campus) offers similar services to one far away, but is more desirable to some consumers because it reduces the amount of time spent commuting. Consumers choose between close-apartment/short-commute and distant-apartment/long-commute alternatives. From the analysis in this chapter, you know that a consumer (in equilibrium) balances the *MU/P* of each consumption alternative. Assuming that consumers are in equilibrium, you may be able to infer something from the differential in price about how much people dislike long commutes. From newspaper ads or personal inquiry, collect information on rents asked for otherwise comparable apartments in several areas at varying distances from the center of your city (or from your campus, if most of the apartments you consider are rented to students). Estimate the length of the commute from each area. What can you infer about the marginal disutility of commuting a particular length of time? What potential problems exist in this analysis?

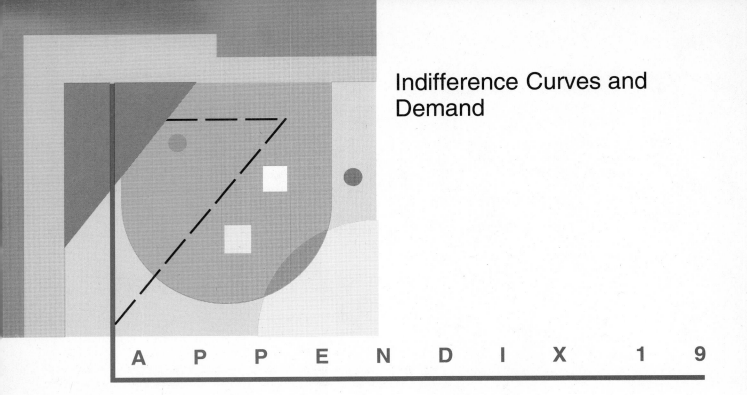

Indifference Curves and Demand

APPENDIX FOCUS   The preceding chapter on demand and utility showed how the law of diminishing marginal utility can be used to explain the law of demand. In equilibrium, consumers will equate marginal utilities per dollar on the last unit of items consumed. If the price of good *A* rises, the marginal utility per dollar of *A* will be *less* than that of other goods. The law of diminishing marginal utility states that the marginal utility of *A* will increase if less of *A* is consumed. Therefore, consumer equilibrium is reattained by consuming less of *A*. Because of diminishing marginal utility, there will be a negative relationship between price and quantity demanded.

The law of diminishing marginal utility does explain the law of demand, but it requires that people be able to measure the *utility* they obtain by consuming various quantities of goods and services.

Because of skepticism about the measurement of utility, economists were forced to find an alternative approach to understanding consumer behavior. The search culminated in *indifference-curve theory*.

CONSUMER PREFERENCES

Indifference-curve theory does not require that consumers be able to measure utility in any specific units of measurement but does assume that consumers are able to rank their preferences for combinations of goods. The consumer should be able to choose between 4 pints of ale and 5 loaves of bread on the one hand and 8 pints of ale and 1 loaf of bread on the other. If the consumer does not prefer one combination to the other, the consumer is said to be *indifferent*.

Exhibit 1 diagrams the preferences of a particular consumer. The horizontal axis measures the quantity of ale consumed by the individual per week. The vertical axis measures the quantity of bread consumed by the individual per week. At point *a*, 6 loaves of bread and 1 pint of ale are consumed. At *a*, the consumer is willing to give up 3 loaves of bread for 1 more pint of ale. This trade-off would move the consumer to point *b* where 3 loaves of bread and 2 pints of ale are consumed. At point *b*, the consumer is no longer willing to give up 3 loaves of bread to acquire 1 more pint of ale. The consumer is now willing to give up only 1 loaf of bread to acquire 1 more pint of ale. This trade-off would put the consumer at point *c*, consuming 2 loaves of bread and 3 pints of ale per week. Finally, to acquire 1 more pint of ale, the consumer is willing now to give up only half a loaf of bread, moving the consumer to point *d*. The consumer is indifferent between points *a, b, c,* and *d* and feels equally well off at any of these points.

A curve can be drawn, through points *a, b, c,* and *d*, which represents all the possible consumption patterns that keep the consumer at the same level of satisfaction. This curve is called an **indifference curve** because every point on the curve yields the same satisfaction even though the consumption pattern is different at each point. The indifference curve shows that a person can be flexible, and is willing to substitute one good for another.

> An **indifference curve** shows all the alternative consumption patterns that yield the same total satisfaction to a particular consumer and among which the consumer is indifferent.

An indifference curve is downward-sloping because as long as both goods yield satisfaction, more is better than less. The only way for the consumer's satisfaction to stay the same when more of one good is consumed is to consume less of the other good.

The Law of the Diminishing Marginal Rate of Substitution

The shape of an indifference curve provides useful information about preferences. Indifference-curve analysis substitutes the concept of the **marginal rate of substitution (MRS)** for the concept of marginal utility.

> The **marginal rate of substitution (MRS)** is how much of one good a person is just willing to give up to acquire one unit of another.

Thus, the marginal rate of substitution is just a fancy name for an acceptable trade-off between two goods or for the person's *valuation* of an additional unit of one good in terms of the other. For example, consider how many hot dogs you would be willing to sacrifice for an additional pizza. If you would give up 3 hot dogs

EXHIBIT 1   An Indifference Curve

When given the choice among the commodity bundles along an indifference curve, the consumer is indifferent. Consumption pattern *a* yields the same satisfaction to the consumer as *b*, *c*, or *d*. The absolute value of the slope of an indifference curve is the marginal rate of substitution and shows—in this case—how much bread the consumer is just willing to sacrifice for one more pint of ale.

for 1 pizza, your marginal rate of substitution of hot dogs for pizza is 3. That quantity of hot dogs is your personal valuation of pizza in terms of hot dogs.

In Exhibit 1 the marginal rate of substitution of bread for ale from point *c* to point *d* is 0.5 (one-half of a loaf of bread for 1 pint of ale). Geometrically, the absolute slope of the tangent at any point on the indifference curve measures the marginal rate of substitution of good *B* for good *A*. The flatter is the slope of the indifference curve, the lower is the relative valuation the consumer places on *A* (compared to *B*).

An indifference curve is always convex when viewed from below (bulges toward the origin). The convex curvature of the indifference curve is explained by the **law of diminishing marginal rate of substitution**: as more ale is consumed relative to bread, the consumer is willing to give up less and less bread to acquire additional units of ale because bread is getting more valuable and ale is getting less valuable. When one moves from point *a* down to point *d* and beyond, the indifference curve gets flatter and flatter because the relative valuation placed on ale is decreasing compared to bread.

> The **law of diminishing marginal rate of substitution** is that as more of one good (*A*) is consumed along a given indifference curve, the amount of the other good (*B*) that the consumer is willing to sacrifice for one more unit of good *A* declines.

Indifference curves can be drawn to represent any level of satisfaction. Exhibit 2 shows the same consumer at three different levels of satisfaction. Higher indifference curves for any one consumer represent higher levels of satisfaction. Each consumer has an entire map of indifference curves, one for every level of satisfaction. Exhibit 2 shows only three indifference curves. Whether a person is poor or well off is determined by the person's income and the relative prices of goods.

EXHIBIT 2   The Map of Indifference Curves

There is an infinite number of indifference curves for each consumer; three indifference curves for a particular consumer are shown here. The higher the indifference curve, the greater is the well-being of the consumer. The indifference map shows that commodity bundle *e* is preferred to bundle *d* because the former is on a higher indifference curve. Indifference curve U_3 represents a higher level of satisfaction than U_2 and U_2 represents a higher level than U_1. The level of satisfaction along each indifference curve is constant.

Indifference curves are subjective and unique to each person. Nevertheless, they have in common the following five properties:

1. Indifference curves that show preferences between two goods from which consumers derive benefits are downward-sloping.
2. They are bowed toward the *origin* (the point where the axes meet), which reflects the law of diminishing marginal rate of substitution.
3. Consumers are better off when they move to a higher indifference curve.
4. Indifference curves cannot intersect each other, because an intersection would indicate that the consumer is simultaneously worse off and better off. (Even though indifference curves do not intersect, they need not be parallel.)
5. The set of indifference curves does not move as a result of market circumstances (changes in income or prices).

A consumer's equilibrium position on an indifference curve is determined by the consumer's budget. What the consumer can buy depends on income and prices. The consumer can buy more when income rises for given prices; the consumer can buy more when prices fall for a given income.

The Budget Line

Suppose the price of ale is $2 per pint and the price of bread is $0.50 per loaf. Assume the consumer has $8 to spend per week on ale and bread. If the entire $8 is spent on ale, the consumer can buy 4 pints of ale. This combination corresponds to point *m* in Exhibit 3. If the entire $8 is spent on bread, 16 loaves of bread can be purchased. This combination corresponds to point *n*. The **budget line** connecting points *m* and *n* represents all the other combinations of ale and bread the consumer is able to buy by spending the entire $8 income on the two goods.

EXHIBIT 3   The Budget Line

With a budget of $8, the consumer can buy 16 loaves of bread at a price of $0.50 per loaf or 4 pints of ale at a price of $2 per pint. Spending $4 on each good would buy 8 loaves of bread and 2 pints of ale (point *p*). The budget line shows the choices open to the consumer. The consumer can afford to buy any combination of goods on the budget line. Points above the budget line, such as *k*, cannot be purchased with the consumer's income. The slope of the budget line is the ratio of the price of ale to the price of bread; in this case, the slope is 4.

The **budget line** is all the combinations of goods the consumer is able to buy given a certain income and set prices. The budget line shows the consumption possibilities available to the consumer.

The budget line in Exhibit 3 has a negative slope with an absolute value of 16/4 = 4. This negative slope is the price of ale in terms of bread: $P_A/P_B = \$2/\$0.50 = 4$. The slope indicates that if the consumer wants to buy one more pint of ale, the consumer must give up 4 loaves of bread. In other words, 4 loaves of bread represent the opportunity cost of consuming one more pint of ale.

Algebraically, point *m* in Exhibit 3 is income divided by the price of ale because point *m* shows the maximum possible consumption of ale. Point *n* is income divided by the price of bread. The absolute value of the slope of the line *nm* is then determined as follows:

$$\text{Slope} = \frac{\text{Income}}{P_B} \div \frac{\text{Income}}{P_A} = \frac{P_A}{P_B}.$$

Indifference curves show how the consumer ranks *different* market baskets; the budget line shows what the consumer *is able* to buy. Combining the information represented by the indifference curve and the budget line shows what combination of goods the consumer *will* buy.

CONSUMER EQUILIBRIUM

The consumer achieves equilibrium by choosing a consumption pattern that maximizes the consumer's satisfaction on the budget line. Exhibit 4 shows

EXHIBIT 4   Consumer Equilibrium

The consumer's optimal consumption pattern is at point *e*. A point like *d* is attainable (on the budget line) but is not as good as *e* because it places the consumer on a lower indifference curve (U_0). Point *f* is better than *e* (the consumer is on a higher indifference curve, U_2) but is not attainable with the given set of income and prices. At *e*, the indifference curve U_1 is tangent to the budget line. Thus, the slope of the indifference curve equals the slope of the budget line. This tangency is equivalent to the marginal-utility rule for maximizing utility ($MU_A/P_A = MU_B/P_B$) discussed in the chapter.

The consumer is in equilibrium when the budget line is just tangent to the highest attainable indifference curve. Two conditions are then satisfied: (1) The consumer is on the budget line. (2) The consumer's marginal rate of substitution of bread for ale equals the price ratio of ale to bread (P_A/P_B).

The marginal rate of substitution of bread for ale (*MRS*) equals the ratio of the ale's marginal utility (MU_A) to the bread's marginal utility (MU_B):

$$MRS = \frac{MU_A}{MU_B}.$$

the optimal consumption pattern. The consumer is *able* to locate anywhere on the budget line, but *the rational consumer will select that consumption combination that falls on the highest attainable indifference curve*. This combination is point *e*: by consuming 4 loaves of bread and 3 pints of ale the consumer can reach indifference curve U_1. Any other point on the budget line will fall on a *lower* indifference curve. At the optimal consumption pattern, represented by point *e*, the budget line is tangent to (touches the curve only at one point and has the same slope as) the indifference curve.

Equivalently, consumer equilibrium occurs at that point on the highest attainable indifference curve where the marginal rate of substitution equals the price ratio. At point *e*, the consumer's marginal rate of substitution is 4 because the consumer is willing to trade off 4 units of bread for one unit of ale. The price ratio, as we have shown, is also 4.

There is a link between indifference-curve analysis and marginal-utility theory. The marginal rate of substitution of bread for ale can also be indicated by the marginal utilities of ale and bread. For example, if the marginal utility of ale (MU_A) is 20 and the marginal utility of bread (MU_B) is 5, it takes 4 extra loaves of bread to compensate the consumer for the loss of only 1 pint of ale. But if $MU_A = 10$ and $MU_B = 5$, the marginal rate of substitution of bread for ale is only 2.

The condition for equilibrium can now be translated into the equal-marginal-utility-per-dollar rule for consumer equilibrium described in this chapter. At point *e*, the slope of the indifference curve is MU_A/MU_B. The slope of the budget line is P_A/P_B. The indifference-curve equilibrium rule is equivalent to $MU_A/MU_B = P_A/P_B$. A little algebraic manipulation shows that this equation is equivalent to the marginal-utility-per-dollar rule for equilibrium: $MU_A/P_A = MU_B/P_B$.

EXHIBIT 5   The Effect of an Income Change

When the price of ale is $2 per pint and the price of bread is
$0.50 per loaf, a fall in income from $8 to $4 causes a parallel
shift in the budget line from nm to hj. The equilibrium changes
from e_1 to e_0, which is on a lower indifference curve.

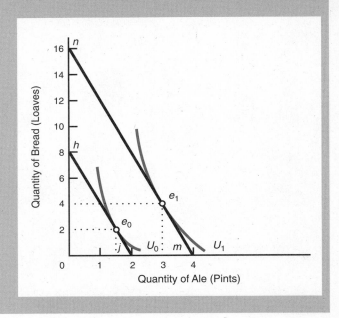

THE EFFECT OF AN INCOME CHANGE

The consumer's equilibrium position will be affected if income changes, if the
price of ale changes, or if the price of bread changes. Exhibit 5 shows how a
reduction in the consumer's income from $8 to $4 leads to a reduction in the
demand for both ale and bread. We assume the price of ale stays at $2 per pint and
the price of bread remains at $0.50 per loaf. The budget line shifts down from *nm*
to *hj*, because now the consumer can purchase a maximum of only 2 pints of ale or
8 loaves of bread. Instead of 4 loaves of bread and 3 pints of ale being consumed,
now only 2 loaves of bread and 1.5 pints of ale are consumed at the new
equilibrium (point e_0).

Notice that when income changes, holding prices constant, the budget line
shifts in a parallel fashion. This shift occurs because the slope of the budget line is
P_A/P_B, which has been assumed constant. The budget line shifts down when
income falls and up when income rises. Clearly, utility falls as income falls and rises
as income rises.

THE EFFECT OF A PRICE CHANGE

Now consider the effects of a change in one of the prices, holding income and the
other price constant. Exhibit 6 shows how a fall in the price of ale from $2 to $1 per
pint leads to an increase in the quantity of ale demanded. The initial equilibrium
situation is represented by the combination e_1, where the price of ale is $2 and the
price of bread is $0.50. Reducing the price of ale to $1 will allow the consumer the
option of purchasing as many as 8 pints of ale, because the income remains $8.
The budget line will now swing outward from *nm* to *nr*.

EXHIBIT 6 The Effect of a Price Change on Consumer Equilibrium: The Law of Demand

Assuming that income is $8 and the price of bread is $0.50, when the price of ale falls from $2 to $1 per pint, the budget line swings outward from nm to nr because the consumer is able to buy as many as 8 pints of ale. The consumer seeks out a new equilibrium combination, e_2, where the indifference curve U_2 is tangent to the new budget line nr. A fall in the price of ale from $2 to $1 thus increases the quantity of ale demanded from 3 pints at point e_1 to 5 pints at point e_2.

When the price of one good falls, an increase in real income occurs, as shown by an outward swing of the budget line.

The new equilibrium position occurs at e_2. At this point, the consumer buys 5 pints of ale and 6 loaves of bread. Before the price change, the consumer bought 3 pints of ale and 4 loaves of bread. The law of demand is confirmed: lowering the price of ale increases the quantity of ale demanded.

The consumer is clearly made better off (moves to a higher indifference curve) by the fall in the price of ale. Clearly, the consumer gets a bonus from low prices; the lower is the price of a good bought by a consumer, holding income and other prices constant, the greater is the consumer's welfare.

Why are demand curves downward-sloping? The chapter pointed out that there are two reasons for the law of demand: the substitution effect and the income effect. When the price of a good falls, people will tend to substitute the good for other goods because its relative price has fallen. Thus, the substitution effect tends to increase the quantity of a good demanded when the price falls. In addition, when the price of a good falls, people have more money to spend on all goods. If you are accustomed to buying one $10,000 car per year, a price reduction to $8,000 is like a $2,000 increase in income! If a good is normal, increases in income increase demand for the good. Thus, the income effect of a price reduction will also increase the quantity demanded of the good. Indifference-curve analysis can be used to illustrate the income effect and the substitution effect.

Exhibit 7 shows a consumer with the initial budget line vw and the initial equilibrium at point e. The consumer is purchasing q units of ale. When the price of ale falls, the budget line shifts to vz. The quantity of ale demanded is now q'' at the new equilibrium point, e''. The consumer is better off after the drop in the ale price because curve U'' is higher than curve U.

The change in equilibrium from e to e'' can be broken down into a two-step process to isolate the roles of the *income effect* and the *substitution effect* on the change in the equilibrium position.

When the price of ale falls, the ratio of the price of ale to the price of bread changes. *If the consumer were interested only in maintaining the current level of welfare*

EXHIBIT 7   Substitution and Income Effects

When income is $8 per week, bread costs $0.50 per loaf, and ale costs $2 per pint, the initial equilibrium is point *e*. When the price of ale falls from $2 to $1 per pint, the budget line swings outward from *vw* to *vz*. The new equilibrium is point *e″*. The substitution effect is obtained by drawing the budget line *st* parallel to *vz* but tangent to the original indifference curve, *U*. Thus, the substitution effect is the distance *qq′* and the income effect is the distance *q′q″*. In the case of a normal good, the income effect reinforces the substitution effect.

achieved on curve U, the consumer would increase the quantity demanded of ale until he or she reached the point on curve *U* where line *st* is tangent to *U* (*st* is a budget line with a slope that reflects the *new* ratio of ale price to bread price that results when the price of ale falls). The point on curve *U* where *st* is tangent to *U* is point *e′*. At *e′*, the consumer buys more ale and less bread without changing the level of satisfaction. This change in the quantity demanded of ale from *q* to *q′* is the **substitution effect** of the change in the price of ale.

> The **substitution effect** is the change in quantity of *X* demanded that occurs when the price of *X* changes and the consumer is compensated to keep utility constant.

At point *e′*, however, the consumer is not spending all the income available to him or her. Because of the drop in the price of ale, the consumer has more income available to spend on *both* bread and ale. The consumer's new budget line resulting from the lower ale price is *vz*, which has the same ale-price-to-bread-price ratio as *st* but which makes possible for the consumer a position on a higher indifference curve. The consumer who wished to maximize satisfaction would not stay at *e′* but would shift to *e″*, a point on the highest indifference curve attainable given budget line *vz*. The consumer making this shift would increase the quantity demanded of ale still further from *q′* at *e′* to *q″* at *e″*. This new equilibrium, unlike *e′*, *does* satisfy all the conditions of consumer equilibrium. The increase in quantity demanded from *q′* to *q″* as a result of the additional income made available is the **income effect** of the change in the ale price.

> The **income effect** is the change in the quantity of *X* demanded that is attributable to the welfare change that accompanies the price change.

The importance of the distinction between the substitution and income effects is that we can see that for normal goods the demand curve must be downward-sloping. In Exhibit 7, the price of ale falls and the substitution effect increases quantity demanded from q to q' along the convex indifference curve U. The move from e' to e'' is like any income increase. If ale is a *normal* good, for which demand increases with income, more ale will be consumed. In effect, a reduced price of ale gives the consumer more income to spend on both ale and bread. Thus, for a normal good, the income effect also indicates more ale will be consumed. It follows from the above analysis that if a good is normal, the demand curve for the good must be downward-sloping.

Appendix Summary

1. Indifference-curve analysis requires only that consumers be able to state whether they prefer one combination of goods to another combination or whether they are indifferent. An indifference curve plots those combinations of goods that yield the same level of satisfaction to the consumer. In indifference-curve analysis, the law of the diminishing marginal rate of substitution replaces the law of diminishing marginal utility. It states that the greater is the quantity of good X that the individual consumes relative to good Y, the smaller will be the quantity of good Y that the consumer is willing to sacrifice to obtain one more unit of good X. The budget line shows the choices of goods open to the consumer.

2. Maximizing satisfaction requires that the consumer seek out the highest indifference curve while remaining on the budget line. This point occurs at the tangency of the indifference curve and the budget line.

3. A change in income causes a parallel shift in the budget line. The budget line shifts down if income decreases and up if income increases. The new equilibrium is simply the new tangency of the new budget line with an indifference curve.

4. A reduction in the price of one commodity swings the budget line outward. The new equilibrium takes place at the point of tangency between a higher indifference curve and the new budget line. The consumer is made better off by the price reduction because the consumer is able to locate on a higher indifference curve. The effects of a price change on quantity demanded can be broken down into a substitution effect, which maintains the existing utility level, and an income effect, which results from the change in the consumer's level of utility.

Key Terms

indifference curve (p. 123)
marginal rate of substitution (*MRS*) (p. 123)
law of diminishing marginal rate of substitution (p. 124)

budget line (p. 125)
substitution effect (p. 130)
income effect (p. 130)

Questions and Problems

1. Assume that the consumer's income is $100, the price of ale is $5 per pint, and the price of bread is $4 per loaf
   a. Draw the consumer's budget line.
   b. How does the budget line shift if the price of bread rises to $10, holding the price of ale at $5.
   c. How does the budget line shift if the price of ale rises to $10 holding the price of bread at $10?
   d. How does the budget line shift if income doubles at $200, holding the prices of ale and bread at $5 and $10, respectively?

2. Why are indifference curves downward-sloping? Why are they bowed toward the origin?

3. Why must the equilibrium position be a point of tangency between the budget line and an indifference curve?

4. Illustrate a situation in which income increases and the demand for one of the goods falls.

5. Deduce the law of demand for a normal good using the distinction between substitution and income effects when the price of the good rises.

6. Assume that the marginal rate of substitution of good *X* for good *Y* is *MRS* = 6, that the price of good *X* is $1 per unit, and that the price of good *Y* is $3 per unit.
   a. Illustrate the consumer's current position on the budget line relative to an indifference curve.
   b. Explain why the consumer would buy more of good *Y*.

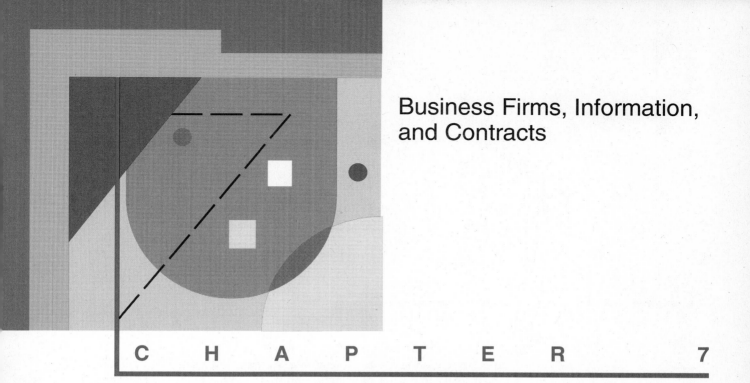

Business Firms, Information, and Contracts

CHAPTER 7

CHAPTER FOCUS   In olden times, businesses were run simply. One or several individuals would own the business, take the risks, and make the decisions. Most modern businesses cannot be run in such a direct way. Millions or even billions of dollars of capital are required—much more than one or two owners could manage. The failure of a such a large venture would destroy the personal wealth of the owners if they were held personally liable. Modern businesses employ thousands of persons spread among various divisions both at home and abroad.

The complexity of modern business fostered new forms of business organization. The corporation now accounts for most production. Modern corporations are run by professional managers whose goals and interests may differ from those of the owners (the shareholders). Relations among businesses are coordinated by contracts that may prove to be unfavorable if not constructed properly.

The modern corporation raises a fundamental question: How to run a company in which there is a separation of ownership from management. There is general agreement that companies should serve the interests of the owners. When professional managers run the show, contracts are complex, and information is scarce, devising an organization that actually serves the interests of the owners is not easy.

After studying this chapter, you will be able to:

- Define the goals of business firms.
- Understand the advantages and disadvantages of corporations, partnerships, and individual proprietorships.
- Know how information costs affect the contracts between parties to a business contract.
- Understand how opportunistic behavior affects business contracts.
- Understand the role of intermediaries as information specialists.

BUSINESS FIRMS AND THEIR GOALS

Business firms can take on a variety of legal forms, and they operate in different competitive conditions when selling their outputs and buying their inputs. Business firms have an owner or owners, who stand to receive the firm's profits. They are run by managers, who can be either the firm's owners or a hired management staff. The firm's managers direct the factors of production controlled by the firm to carry out tasks. The fourth factor of production (after labor, land, and capital), the **entrepreneur**, motivates the firm to discover profit-making opportunities.

> An **entrepreneur** organizes business firms to take advantage of profit opportunities. The entrepreneur evaluates risks, introduces innovations, and foresees new markets. The entrepreneur benefits from the firm's success and suffers the consequences of the firm's failure.

The business firm has external and internal dealings. On the outside, it deals with other firms in markets. It buys materials and services from other businesses and it sells its products to other businesses. Its transactions with other firms are coordinated by markets. General Motors buys its steel and plastics from other manufacturing firms, and it sells its automobiles to GM dealers. Resources are also allocated *within* the business firm by managerial coordination. Business firms own some factors of production (like plant and equipment). They also have contractual relationships with factors of production. The firm has labor contracts with its employees. It has contractual leases with the owners of buildings and land. The firm's manager has the authority to direct such factors of production to carry out specified tasks. The managers of GM can assign tasks to GM workers. The management of GM can use the plant and equipment owned by GM as it sees fit. Such managerial coordination of factors of production takes place without the use of markets.

Production is carried out by business firms whose goal is profit maximization.

The chapter on demand and utility emphasized that consumers want to spend their limited income to obtain maximum utility. Business firms have a primary goal: **profit maximization**.

> **Profit maximization** is the search by firms for the product quality, output, and price that give the firm the highest possible profits.

The search for profits is a dominating force in business life. The owners of the business firm are compensated with the profits that the firm earns. The value of the firm ultimately depends on its profits. The firm that earns no profits will have no value in the long run. Firms that do not maximize profits may be forced out of business by competitors who offer higher quality products produced at lower cost. They can be taken over by someone else who knows how to earn a higher profit.

FORMS OF BUSINESS ORGANIZATION

Businesses are organized as sole proprietorships or as corporations. Each form has its advantages and disadvantages.

Business enterprises are organized as *sole proprietorships, partnerships,* and *corporations.* Which form a business enterprise takes determines who makes business decisions, how capital is raised, who bears the risk of business failures, and how profits are taxed. (See Exhibit 1 for a profile of American business.)

Sole Proprietorships

The **sole proprietorship** is the least complex form of business enterprise.

> The sole proprietorship is owned by one individual who makes all the business decisions, receives the profits that the business earns, and bears the financial responsibility for losses.

The individual who has accumulated or borrowed funds can set up a sole proprietorship. No legal work is required, although the individual proprietor will often seek legal and accounting advice. Once in business, the proprietor is responsible for all business decisions—how many employees to hire, what products to produce, how to market these products. Other than being required to

EXHIBIT 1   A Profile of American Business

a. Proprietorships, Partnerships, and Corporations, 1991

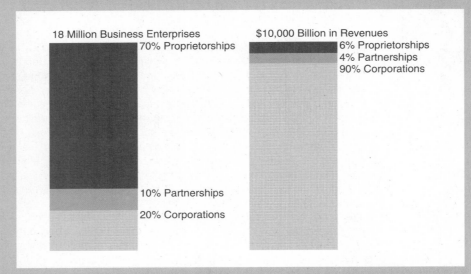

18 Million Business Enterprises
70% Proprietorships
10% Partnerships
20% Corporations

$10,000 Billion in Revenues
6% Proprietorships
4% Partnerships
90% Corporations

SOURCE: *Statistical Abstract of the United States.* Updated by authors.

b. Proprietorships, Partnerships, and Corporations, by Industry, 1991

Industry	Number of Firms (thousands)			Business Revenues (billions of dollars)		
	Nonfarm Proprietorships	Partnerships	Corporations	Nonfarm Proprietorships	Partnerships	Corporations
Mining	168	65	45	19	29	315
Construction	1,467	77	339	80	30	446
Manufacturing	304	27	312	17	24	3,873
Transportation, public utilities	551	21	138	37	11	995
Wholesale and retail trade	3,032	238	1,010	322	114	3,239
Wholesale						
Retail						
Finance, insurance, real estate	1,172	843	556	40	88	1,559
Services	5,211	324	986	177	108	582

SOURCE: *Statistical Abstract of the United States.* Updated by authors.

observe the law and honor legal contracts, the owner is free to make wise or foolish decisions.

For the sole proprietorships, decision-making authority is clear-cut: it resides with the owner. The individual proprietor receives profits that the business earns, and this income will be taxed only once. (As we shall show, this is not true of the corporation, whose income is often taxed twice.)

The main disadvantage of the sole proprietorship is that the owner has *unlimited liability* (responsibility) for the debts of the company. The owner enjoys

EXHIBIT 1   A Profile of American Business *(Continued)*

c. Business Failures in the United States, 1970–1991

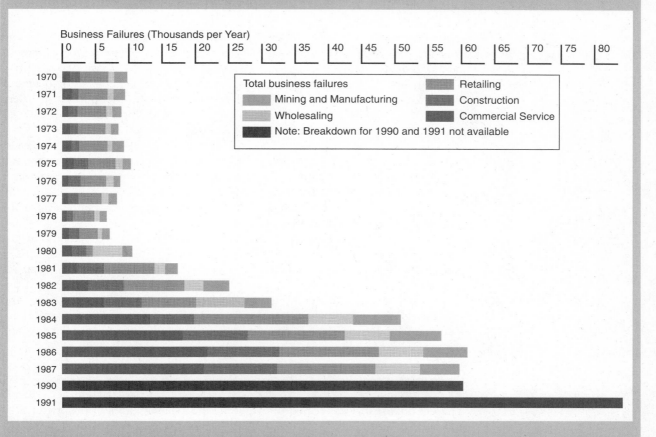

SOURCE: *Survey of Current Business;* Dun and Bradstreet Corp., Monthly Failure Report.

Panel (a) shows that although the proprietorship dominates in terms of numbers, the corporation produces 90 percent of output. Panel (b) shows that partnerships and proprietorships are important in services and construction. Panel (c) shows the rising rate of business failures in the United States.

the profit of the business if it is successful, but if the business suffers a loss, the owner is personally liable. If the company borrows money, purchases materials, and runs up other bills that it cannot cover, the owner must personally cover the losses. Sole proprietorships have a *limited ability to raise financial capital.* The owner can raise financial capital by reinvesting profits or borrowing. Lending money to a sole proprietorship can be risky, because so much depends upon the owner. As a consequence, sole proprietorships cannot raise as much financial capital as other business forms.

Partnerships

A **partnership** is much like an individual proprietorship but with more than one owner.

> A **partnership** is owned by two or more people (called partners) who make all the business decisions, share the profits of the business, and bear the financial responsibility for any losses.

Like the individual proprietorship, partnerships are easy to establish. Most partnerships are based on an agreement that spells out the ownership shares and duties of each partner. The partners may contribute different amounts of financial capital to the partnership; there may be an agreement on the division of responsibility for running the business; partners may own different shares of the business. One partner may make all the business decisions, while the other partner (a "silent partner") may only provide financial capital. A partnership can be a corner gas station or a nationally known law firm or brokerage house.

Partnerships are also easy to set up. The company profits go to the partners and are taxed only once. Partnerships offer a greater opportunity to specialize and divide managerial responsibility: the better salesperson will be in charge of the sales department, the talented mechanical engineer will be in charge of production. Partnerships can raise more financial capital than a sole proprietorship because the partners can pool their borrowing power.

The main disadvantage of partnerships is the unlimited liability of the partners. A business debt incurred by one is the responsibility of all partners. Each partner stands to lose money if the company is a commercial failure. "Two heads are better than one" *if* the two heads agree. But if partners disagree, decision-making can become quite complicated. There is no longer one single person who is in charge. Partnerships can be immobilized when partners disagree on fundamental policy. Partnerships become more complicated as the number of partners grows.

Corporations

The **corporation** was created to overcome the disadvantages of proprietorships and partnerships.

> A **corporation** is a business enterprise that is owned by its stockholders. The corporation has the legal status to act as a single person. The stockholders elect a board of directors that appoints the management of the corporation. Management is charged with the actual operation of the corporation.

A *corporate charter* is required to set up a corporation. The laws of each state are different, but, typically, for a fee, corporations can be established (incorporated) and can become legal "persons" subject to the laws of that state. Officers of the corporation can act in the name of the corporation without being personally liable for its debts. If corporate officers commit criminal acts, however, they can be prosecuted as individuals.

The corporation is owned by individuals (stockholders) who have purchased shares of *stock* in the corporation. A stockholder's share of ownership of the corporation equals the number of shares owned by that individual divided by the total number of shares outstanding. Owners of shares of stock have the right to vote on corporate matters (like electing the board of directors). The management of the corporation is required by law to issue periodic reports to its shareholders describing the corporation's financial and business activities. The profits of the corporation can either be reinvested or distributed to shareholders as dividends.

Corporations often have thousands or millions of shares outstanding, and these shares are typically owned by a large number of stockholders. Billionaire H. Ross Perot's 11 million shares of General Motors stock made him GM's largest shareholder (with 2 percent of GM stock) before he sold his shares in early 1987. There are usually too many shareholders to involve them in decision-making. For this reason, there is usually a *separation of ownership and management*. The board of directors appoints a management team that makes decisions for the corporation. The board of directors can fire the management team if it sees fit.

The main advantage of the corporation is *limited liability*. The owners of the corporation (the stockholders) are not personally liable for the debts of the corporation. The corporation's creditors can lay claim to the assets of the corporation (its bank accounts, equipment, supplies, and real-estate holdings), but they cannot file claims against the stockholders. The worst thing that can happen to stockholders is that the value of their stock will decline (in extreme circumstances, it can become worthless).

Corporations have more options than other business forms to raise financial capital. Proprietorships and partnerships can only raise financial capital outside the firm by borrowing from lending institutions. Corporations, on the other hand, can sell bonds and sell new shares of stock. Limited liability makes it easier to sell new shares (called issuing stock) because buyers of the new stock are not personally liable for the debts of the corporation. Lenders (such as buyers of corporate bonds) are more willing to make long-term loans to corporations because corporations can remain in business for a long time. (How corporations raise capital is described in more detail in the appendix to this chapter.) Many major U.S. corporations are more than a century old. Few corporations have the same owners and officers that they had when the corporation was founded.

The corporation offers limited liability to its owners. Corporations have more options in raising financial capital.

Separating ownership and management allows the corporation to recruit a professional management team and to bring in new management. The owners of businesses (individuals with money to invest) do not always make the best managers.

The profits (earnings) of the corporation can either be distributed to shareholders as dividends or reinvested (plowed back) into the corporation. The profits of the corporation are subject to a federal income tax. In many states, corporations must also pay a state income tax. If the corporation chooses to plow back all profits into the company, corporate profits will be taxed only once, but if it distributes some of its profits to shareholders in the form of dividends, shareholders must pay income taxes on these dividends. Corporate profits can, therefore, be taxed twice, first by the corporate income tax and second by the personal income tax on dividends.

Corporations can have thousands or even millions of different owners (stockholders). It is difficult to get the owners to agree (or even assemble), even when important issues are at stake. Power struggles among shareholder factions can paralyze decision making. It is difficult to mobilize widely dispersed stockholders to get rid of incompetent management. Shareholders want the best return from their shares of stock; however, the professional management team may be more interested in preserving their jobs or in maximizing their personal income or perquisites than in profit maximization. (See Example 1.)

Limited liability and an ability to raise large sums of capital have made the corporation the dominant form of business organization. Corporations can be huge, employing hundreds of thousands of people both at home and in foreign branches. The largest U.S. corporations are profiled in Exhibit 2.

The three different forms of business organizations have their advantages and disadvantages. The fact that the major portion of the U.S. economy's output is produced by corporations attests to the advantages of the corporation (See Exhibit 3 for a summary of advantages and disadvantages of the different business forms.)

EXAMPLE 1

Unlimited Liability and Lloyds of London

Lloyds of London, the centuries-old insurance syndicate headquartered in London, England, made its reputation for its willingness to insure virtually anything. Lloyds insured actresses's legs, renowned jewels, and hazardous shipments. Lloyds is one of the last great businesses that operates on the basis of unlimited liability. Various insurance packages are underwritten by "Names"—individual investors who must make good on claims, even if they must draw on all their personal assets to do so.

The years 1991 and 1992 were disastrous for the insurance industry. The Gulf War, numerous national disasters and airline crashes, and product liability claims caused billions of dollars of losses for Lloyds of London insurance syndicates. Lloyds of London Names therefore had to sell virtually all their personal assets to cover these losses. One Name—a former heavyweight boxing champion—had to sell his championship belts. Other Names had to sell their noble titles and their estates.

As a consequence of these losses, Lloyds of London is no longer willing to insure many high risk activities. Policies that were previously sold by Lloyds of London are no longer available. Hence, Lloyds of London has decided to restructure its way of doing business so that its investors may underwrite insurance with limited liability. The world's last major example of unlimited liability is in the process of disappearing.

PRINCIPALS AND AGENTS

Most economic dealings are governed by contracts. In some cases, these contracts are not written but parties to the contract implicitly understand its terms. Examples of contracts are employment contracts negotiated by unions, contracts for the delivery of natural gas at specified prices, or leasing contracts for office buildings.

Sole proprietorships, partnerships, and corporations enter into business contracts in which they act either as a **principal** or as an **agent**.

> A **principal** engages an agent to act subject to the principal's control and instruction.

> An **agent** is a party that acts for, on behalf of, or as a representative of a principal.

Firm A is a principal when it signs a contract with an employee (the agent) that calls for the employee to perform specific services at a specified wage for Firm A. The Boeing Corporation acts as a principal when it contracts with Rolls Royce (the agent) to supply jet engines for its aircraft. Chrysler Corporation acted as a principal when it hired Lee Iacocca (the agent) to serve as its chief executive officer.

Contracts and Information Costs

Business firms use contracts to specify the relationship between the principal and the agent. A typical contract requires the agent to perform services for the principal (to deliver goods, to build a house, to perform a certain type of work). Some

EXHIBIT 2   The Fifty Largest U.S. Industrial Corporations, Ranked by Sales

Rank 1987	Rank 1986	Company	Sales (millions of dollars)
1	1	GENERAL MOTORS Detroit	101,781.9
2	2	EXXON New York	76,416.0*
3	3	FORD MOTOR Dearborn, Mich.	71,643.4
4	4	INTERNATIONAL BUSINESS MACHINES Armonk, N.Y.	54,217.0
5	5	MOBIL New York	51,223.0*
6	6	GENERAL ELECTRIC Fairfield, Conn.	39,315.0*
7	8	TEXACO White Plains, N.Y.	34,372.0*
8	7	AMERICAN TEL. & TEL. New York	33,598.0
9	9	E.I. DU PONT DE NEMOURS Wilmington, Del.	30,468.0
10	11	CHRYSLER Highland Park, Mich.[1]	26,257.7
11	10	CHEVRON San Francisco	26,015.0*
12	12	PHILIP MORRIS New York	22,279.0*
13	15	SHELL OIL Houston[2]	20,852.0*
14	13	AMOCO Chicago	20,174.0*
15	17	UNITED TECHNOLOGIES Hartford	17,170.2
16	19	OCCIDENTAL PETROLEUM Los Angeles	17,096.0
17	18	PROCTER & GAMBLE Cincinnati[3]	17,000.0
18	20	ATLANTIC RICHFIELD Los Angeles	16,281.4
19	14	RJR NABISCO Atlanta	15,868.0
20	16	BOEING Seattle	15,355.0
21	21	TENNECO Houston	15,075.0
22	35	BP AMERICA Cleveland[4]	14,611.0*
23	22	USX Pittsburgh	13,898.0*
24	27	DOW CHEMICAL Midland, Mich.	13,377.0
25	26	EASTMAN KODAK Rochester, N.Y.	13,305.0
26	23	MCDONNELL DOUGLAS St. Louis	13,146.1
27	24	ROCKWELL INTERNATIONAL Pittsburgh[5]	12,123.4
28	25	ALLIED-SIGNAL Morristown, N.J.	11,597.0
29	34	PEPSICO Purchase, N.Y.	11,500.2
30	30	LOCKHEED Calabasas, Calif.	11,370.0
31	37	KRAFT Glenview, Ill.	11,010.5*
32	31	PHILLIPS PETROLEUM Bartlesville, Okla.	10,721.0
33	28	WESTINGHOUSE ELECTRIC Pittsburgh	10,679.0
34	32	XEROX Stamford, Conn.[6]	10,320.0
35	29	GOODYEAR TIRE & RUBBER Akron, Ohio	10,123.2
36	46	UNISYS Blue Bell, Pa.	9,712.9
37	39	MINNESOTA MINING & MANUFACTURING St. Paul	9,429.0
38	44	DIGITAL EQUIPMENT Maynard, Mass.[3]	9,389.4
39	36	GENERAL DYNAMICS St. Louis	9,344.0
40	40	SARA LEE Chicago[3]	9,154.6
41	59	CONAGRA Omaha[7,8]	9,001.6
42	•	BEATRICE Chicago[2]	8,926.0[10]
43	33	SUN Radnor, Pa.	8,691.0
44	50	GEORGIA-PACIFIC Atlanta	8,603.0
45	41	ITT New York[6]	8,551.0
46	45	UNOCAL Los Angeles	8,466.0*
47	43	ANHEUSER-BUSCH St. Louis	8,258.4*
48	47	CATERPILLAR Peoria, Ill.	8,180.0
49	51	HEWLETT-PACKARD Palo Alto, Calif.[11]	8,090.0
50	53	JOHNSON & JOHNSON New Brunswick, N.J.	8,012.0

Listed are the 50 largest U.S. industrial corporations ranked by business sales. The annual sales of certain large U.S. industrial corporations—like General Motors and Exxon—exceed the annual output of many industrial economies. The annual sales of General Motors, for example, equal the annual production of Belgium. The annual sales of the six largest U.S. industrial corporations exceed the annual production of the United Kingdom—a fact that underscores the importance of big business in the U.S. economy.

SOURCE: *Fortune*, April 28, 1988; Updated from *Fortune*, April 1993.

EXHIBIT 3   Advantages and Disadvantages of Different Forms of Business Organization

Type of Firm	Advantages	Disadvantages
Individual Proprietorships	1. Business is simple to set up. 2. Decision making is clear-cut; the owner makes the decisions. 3. Earnings are taxed only once as personal income.	1. The owner has unlimited liability; the owner's personal wealth is at risk. 2. The company has a limited ability to raise financial capital. 3. Business dies with owner.
Partnership	1. Business is relatively easy to set up. 2. More management skills are available; two heads are better than one. 3. Earnings are taxed only once as the personal income of the partners.	1. There is unlimited liability for the partners. 2. Decision-making can be complicated. 3. The company has a limited ability to raise capital. 4. Partnerships can be unstable.
Corporation	1. There is limited liability for owners. 2. Company is able to raise large sums of capital through issuing bonds and stock. 3. Company has an unlimited life span. 4. Company is able to recruit professional management and to change bad management.	1. Corporate income is taxed twice; once as corporate profits, then as personal income (dividends). 2. There are greater possibilities for management disagreements. 3. There is the possibility of conflicting goals between the owners of the corporation (the *principals*) and management (the *agents*).

contracts set the rules for principal/agent relationships within the firm. An employment contract, for example, spells out the duties and responsibilities of the employee (the agent). Other contracts set rules for principal/agent relationships among firms. A delivery contract, for example, calls upon the supplier of a good (the agent) to provide the principal with specified goods at specified prices.

Business firms operate with imperfect information. They are unable to specify contracts with agents containing every last detail, and they are unable to monitor perfectly the agent's performance. Business firms operate with imperfect information *because information is costly.*

> **Information is costly because resources are required to gather and process information.**

Opportunistic Behavior

Just as firms must economize on the use of land, labor, and capital inputs used to produce output, so must they economize on the resources devoted to gathering and processing information. As a consequence of imperfect information, firms enter into contracts that permit agents to engage in **opportunistic behavior**.

> **Opportunistic behavior** occurs when the agent is able to formally fulfill a contract while engaging in behavior that is not in the interests of the principal.

Costly information requires that principals write contracts with agents that specify only the agent's general obligations. Employment contracts, for example, specify that the employee work a specified number of hours. The contract does

EXAMPLE 2

Carl Icahn, Texaco, and the Principal/Agent Problem

As we have seen in this chapter, corporate management's goals may differ from shareholders' goals. At times, management may act in its own interest rather than in the interest of the shareholders. This conflict is called the principal/agent problem.

Two giant oil concerns—Texaco and Pennzoil—became involved in a massive legal battle over Texaco's acquisition of Getty Oil. Texas courts ruled that Texaco had illegally acquired Getty Oil at the expense of Pennzoil and ordered Texaco to pay $10 billion in damages to Pennzoil. The possibility that Texaco would have to pay such a huge settlement pushed down Texaco's share prices, but the uncertainty about whether Pennzoil would ever collect failed to raise Pennzoil's share price. Here was a situation in which shareholders of both Texaco and Pennzoil would benefit from a settlement.

The noted corporate raider, Carl Icahn, owned significant shares of both Pennzoil and Texaco at the time. (Icahn was Texaco's largest single shareholder). As a major shareholder, Icahn stood to gain from a settlement, and he pressured Texaco's officers to settle with Pennzoil for $3 billion in cash. In an interview, Icahn told of a conversation with Texaco's president, Jim Kinnear, concerning the need to settle the suit and get on with Texaco's business.

> Icahn asked Kinnear, "What happens if you can't make a deal?" And he said, "Well I can just go fishing." And I said, "What happens if there's no company when you get back?" And he said, "Well I'll still have my fishing pole." That's sort of amazing, because Kinnear might have his fishing pole, but what would all the shareholders have? The other shareholders wouldn't even have a fish.

SOURCE: "Icahn: 'We're Fed Up': The Raider Talks About His Stake in Texaco," *Newsweek*, January 4, 1988, p. 36.

---

not specify the quality of work that must be performed. Contracts for the delivery of spare parts cannot specify to the last detail the exact qualities and specifications of the spare parts. Even if such employment or delivery contracts specified the obligations of the agent to the last detail, the principal would find it too costly to monitor every last detail of contract fulfillment. (See Example 2.)

Costly information gives agents the opportunity to fulfill the general terms of the contract, while engaging in opportunistic behavior. Workers can work the specified number of hours but work carelessly and do low-quality work. Spare-parts suppliers can substitute cheaper materials.

By devoting more resources to monitoring and by devising incentive systems, business firms can limit opportunistic behavior. To prevent sales personnel from slacking off, business firms can offer employees bonuses that depend on increased sales. Corporations can offer executives incentives to act in the best interests of the shareholders. Business firms can deny repeat business to suppliers who have behaved opportunistically. The real world supplies many examples of incentive schemes that successfully limit opportunistic behavior.

> Because information is costly, agents can engage in opportunistic behavior.

In some cases, it is not possible to set up monitoring systems or to devise incentive schemes that effectively control opportunistic behavior. Military contracting appears to be one example. Assembly-line production appears to be another example. It is especially hard to control opportunistic behavior when agents are able to alter their behavior after entering into a contract. (See Example 3.)

EXAMPLE 3

Moral Hazard and Contracts

Business firms find it particularly difficult to devise contracts when agents have an opportunity to change their behavior after the contract is signed. This difficulty is called the *moral-hazard problem*.

The basic consequence of the moral-hazard problem is that firms can offer only those contracts that will not be flagrantly abused by their agents. The kinds of contracts offered must be limited to those that will minimize the moral-hazard problem. In some instances, the moral-hazard problem is so severe that certain contracts cannot be written at all, at least not by private profit-maximizing companies.

A moral-hazard problem would be present if a manufacturing firm agrees to buy highly specialized machine tools to produce specialized component parts for a diesel engine manufacturer. It would be difficult to devise a contract that would protect the component-parts manufacturer against abuse by the diesel manufacturer, who would be the firm's only potential customer. The diesel manufacturer could give every assurance that it would deal fairly with the component-parts manufacturer, but there is no guarantee that the diesel manufacturer would not alter its behavior after the contract was signed. A moral-hazard problem would also be present if a pump manufacturer were to enter into contracts with industrial users to replace without charge any pump that fails within a five-year period. The industrial user might fail to service the pump properly or even sabotage the pump to obtain a new one free of charge.

Contracting parties who stand to suffer will adopt measures to prevent opportunistic behavior. The pump manufacturer's guarantee may put the burden of proof on the pump user to demonstrate that the pump broke under normal usage and with proper maintenance. Or the manufacturer may insist on a stiff installation fee for replacement pumps. The component-part manufacturer would insist upon a long-term contract that guaranteed a certain level of purchases by the diesel manufacturer at specified prices before acquiring the specialized tools.

INTERMEDIARIES AND THE INFORMATION BUSINESS

Any business transaction or contract requires two parties. In business contracts, there must be a principal and an agent. In business transactions there must be a buyer and a seller. In order for transactions to take place and for contracts to be signed, the parties must be aware of each other's existence. They must have information concerning the fact that the other party is a potential participant in a business deal. The fact that information is costly applies not only to the monitoring of agents by principals but also to the information required to consummate business deals.

The Role of Intermediaries

Most business firms specialize in producing goods or services. Business firms must find buyers for their goods, and they must find factors of production and materials. Business firms require information in order to survive.

While most firms produce and sell goods and services, some produce "information" that enables other firms to conduct their transactions. Such firms

How Can Boards Reclaim the Company for Its Owners?

The 1980s and early 1990s were characterized as the "era of greed." Prominent Wall Street bankers and brokers were sent to jail. The terms "greenmail" and "poison pills" were originated to describe the selfish behavior of corporation presidents who placed their own interests above the company. (See Example 2.) The chief executive officer of the corporation was often the chairman of the board of directors, a situation akin to students grading their own papers. A much-publicized trip to U.S. executives to Japan in 1992 succeeded in focusing attention on their astronomical salaries despite poor operating performance.

Public policy can be used to prevent corporate abuse of the interests of shareholders, and in the early 1990s, changes were made in the governance of corporations. The basic approach has been to create legal conditions that encourage and even force the board of directors to act in the interests of the shareholders. Insofar as many boards of directors are dominated by professional management, public policy has aimed at making the outside directors of the board more active and responsive.

In 1989, in the wake of the savings-and-loan scandals, federal regulators were given the power to require boards of directors to pick up more of the costs of federal bailouts. In June 1992, the Securities and Exchange Commission enacted reforms that gave shareholders greater power to force change in poorly performing companies. Specifically, corporations had to provide shareholders with details of executive pay and how it related to the company's stock performance.

The most highly publicized consequence of these reforms was the forced resignation of General Motors' chairman and chief executive officer in October 1992. General Motors, over the years, had acquired a reputation of management waste, complacency, and lack of innovation. GM's share of the automobile market had fallen, and management had made a number of disastrous errors in the design and implementation of new models. Said one specialist: "GM's been the type of . . . nonperforming company whose board should have stepped in long before this."

GM had 11 outside directors drawn either from high-level positions in other industries or from academe. These outside directors hired their own counsel, appointed an outside director to head its executive committee, and finally forced the resignation of GM's chief executive officer. As a consequence of this action, declared one specialist, "CEOs are starting to learn that it's not their company, it's not their board, and directors are starting to say their accountability is to the shareholders."

SOURCE: "The High Energy Board Room," *New York Times*, October 28, 1992, C1.

Firms run by intermediaries specialize in information concerning exchange opportunities.

are run by **intermediaries**, or "middlemen," who specialize in information concerning exchange opportunities between buyers and sellers.

> **Intermediaries** specialize in information either to bring together two parties to a transaction or to buy in order to sell again.

Real-estate brokers, grocery stories, department stores, used-car dealers, auctioneers, stockbrokers, and travel agents are all intermediaries. All these professions "mediate" or stand between ultimate buyers and sellers in return for a fee.

Why are firms willing to pay for information from information specialists? Suppose that a company is willing to sell its multimillion-dollar corporate jet for no less than $20 million and that somewhere a potential buyer is willing to pay at most $25 million for such an airplane. Someone with information about this exchange opportunity could act as an intermediary and bring the two together. It would be possible for the seller to get $20 million, for the buyer to pay $25 million, and for the intermediary to charge as much as $5 million for the service of bringing the two together. The intermediary could collect the difference either in the form of a fee or buy the jet for $20 million and then resell it for $25 million. In both cases, the intermediary is receiving a fee for information.

The Value of Intermediaries

Transactions arranged by intermediaries take place all the time. Home buyers and sellers are brought together by realtors who charge a fee. Stock-market brokers bring together buyers and sellers of a particular stock. Auction houses bring together sellers of rare works of art and potential buyers and charge a fee for this service.

Do intermediaries "earn" their fees? Parties to transactions can in most situations avoid paying the intermediary fee. Homemakers could drive to farmers' markets and to wholesale distributors of meats and dairy products. The seller of the corporate jet could try to find a buyer without using an intermediary. The intermediary, by specializing in bringing together buyers and sellers, is able to provide the service at a lower cost than if the individuals involved performed the service themselves. As long as people voluntarily pay for the services of intermediaries, the intermediary is supplying information at a lower cost than could the user of information services.

We have seen that business organization is the first step in the supply side of product markets. The next chapter examines the role of production costs in determining product supply. The appendix to this chapter discusses financial markets for corporate stocks and bonds and how corporations raise financial capital by selling bonds and issuing stock.

Chapter Summary

The most important points to learn from this chapter are: Corporations are the dominant form of business organization because of limited liability. The owners of corporations are not personally liable for the corporation's debts. Limited liability allows the corporation to raise more financial capital and to deal better with uncertainty.

1. Business firms allocate the land, labor, and capital resources they control by managerial coordination. Business firms work both through market allocation in their dealings with other firms and consumers and through managerial allocation.

2. The goal of business firms is the maximization of profits.

3. The three forms of business organization are the *sole proprietorship* (a business owned by one individual), the *partnership* (a business owned by two or more partners who share in making business decisions), and the *corporation* (a business enterprise owned by stockholders).

4. Business enterprises operate in a world of imperfect information. They enter into contractual relationships with the factors of production and with other business firms.

A principal/agent problem exists when agents are able to act opportunistically contrary to the interests of the principal. Principals must devise monitoring and incentives schemes to limit opportunistic behavior.

5. Information is costly. Some firms therefore specialize in information. Whenever individuals and firms voluntarily purchase information from intermediaries, the intermediary is supplying the information at lower cost than they themselves would have incurred.

Policy Focus: **The separation of ownership and management in the corporation requires policy measures to ensure that corporations are run in the interests of their owners, the shareholders.**

Key Terms

entrepreneur (p. 134)
profit maximization (p. 134)
sole proprietorship (p. 135)
partnership (p. 137)
corporation (p. 138)

principal (p. 140)
agent (p. 140)
opportunistic behavior (p. 142)
intermediaries (p. 145)

Questions and Problems

1. What are some of the reasons business firms maximize profits?

2. What are some disadvantages of the sole proprietorship?

3. Sole proprietorships are, on average, smaller than partnerships and partnerships are smaller, on average, than corporations. Use the legal features of business organizations to explain why.

4. In the real world, limited partnerships exist in which the liability of each partner for the debts of the company is limited. Explain why such partnerships may be more attractive than the traditional form of partnership.

5. Explain why corporations can issue bonds that mature in the next century while partnerships and proprietorships can borrow for only short periods of time.

6. Indicate which of the following is an advantage of the corporate form of business:

a. conflicts of interest between stockholders and management.
b. continuity of management.
c. double taxation of corporation income.
d. limited liability.

7. Explain what is meant by limited liability.

8. What prevents principals and agents from always being in complete agreement?

9. For the following transactions, explain which party is the principal and which is the agent and why:
a. Smith hires a remodeling company to add a room to her house.
b. A university buys a computer from IBM.
c. An engineer signs a contract with Aramco to work for a year in Saudi Arabia.

10. What is the information in which intermediaries specialize?

Doing Economics

The association between a college or university and its students has a rich pattern of principal-agent relationships and information problems. Potential students have imperfect information about the quality of the education that they can obtain from alternative schools. How did you go about gathering quality information on colleges you considered? What measurable pieces of information did you use to signal quality? Do intermediaries play an important role in this market? How do you monitor quality as you progress through your studies? Is there a moral-hazard problem?

Another information problem in schools relates to grading. Faculty must ensure that each student has achieved a sufficient level of understanding to be certified as passing the course. Explain why this problem is one of moral hazard. How do faculty resolve this problem? Why is the problem different in, say, a math class versus a literature class? How do the means used by instructors reflect these differences?

Yet another problem relates to how the school monitors the behavior of its faculty. How does the school get information on faculty performance? (Ask one of your instructors if you do not know.) How is this information used to provide incentives for good performance? How does the tenure system affect these incentives?

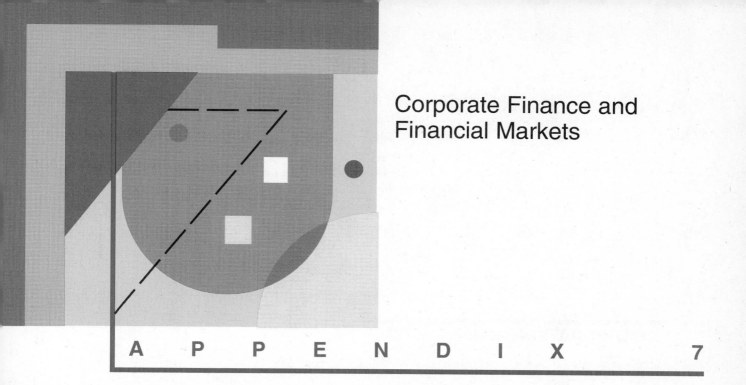

Corporate Finance and
Financial Markets

A P P E N D I X 7

APPENDIX FOCUS The corporation has a number of advantages over proprietorships and partnerships. One advantage is its greater ability to raise capital in financial markets. This appendix explains how corporations raise funds by selling bonds and by issuing stock. Interest rates and bond prices are determined in bond markets. The appendix discusses bond prices and the inverse relationship between interest rates and bond prices. Stock prices are determined in stock markets. The appendix shows that stock prices depend on the present and future earnings of the company. It discusses the efficient stock market hypothesis and explains how stock markets influence the allocation of resources.

After studying this appendix, you will be able to:

- Calculate the present value of an asset.

- Explain how the prices of bonds are established and the relationship between interest rates and bond prices.

- Understand why the stock price reflects the present value of future earnings and why the price/earnings ratio is a barometer of future earnings.

- Know the meaning of a stock price index.

- Comprehend the rational stock market hypothesis.

- Discuss how stock markets serve as guides to resource allocation.

HOW CORPORATIONS RAISE CAPITAL

Limited liability and continuity give corporations an edge in raising financial capital. Corporations have options for raising capital that are not available to sole proprietorships or to partnerships. Corporations, like proprietorships and partnerships, can borrow money from banks and from other lending institutions, and they can plow profits back into the business. In addition to these traditional forms of raising capital, corporations can:

1. sell bonds, or
2. issue (sell) new shares of stock.

Corporations raise capital by selling bonds and issuing new shares of stock.

Corporations sell **bonds** through intermediaries to individuals and businesses that have accumulated savings.

> Corporate **bonds** are IOUs that obligate the corporation to pay a fixed sum of money (the principal) at maturity and a fixed sum of money annually (the *interest* or *coupon*) until the maturity date.

Like other things, bonds have a price. The price of a bond is the sum people pay to acquire the bond. Bond prices and interest rates are intimately linked because the interest payments are paid over a period of time. To understand the linkage between bond prices and interest rates, one must first understand present value.

Present Value

Bonds are obligations to make payments at specific dates over a specified period of time. The payments of interest and principal are spread out over time. Some money will be received in the near future; other money may be received in the distant future. When dealing with money payments that are spread out over time, one must keep in mind a fundamental principle: A dollar today is worth more than a dollar tomorrow because it can earn interest.

A dollar today is worth more than a dollar tomorrow because it can earn interest.

Consider the following example in which 10 percent is the prevailing annual rate of interest paid throughout the economy. When $100 is deposited in a savings account, $10 interest will be earned at the end of one year. At 10 percent interest,

$100 today will be equal to $110 a year from now. If the interest rate had been 20 percent, $100 today would be equal to $120 a year from now.

Look at the process in reverse. If a bank were to offer to pay $110 one year from now, what would people be willing to pay today for this offer? At 10 percent interest, the most people would be willing to pay now in order to receive $110 in one year is $100. Thus, the **present value (*PV*)** of a future payment of $110 is $100 at 10 percent interest.

> The **present value (*PV*)** of money to be received in the future is the most anyone would pay today in order to receive the money in the future; alternatively, the present value of a future sum of money is the amount that must be invested today to generate that future sum of money.

The price of an IOU such as a bond that promises to make specified payments at specified future dates is the present value of those payments. We just showed that no one would pay more than the present value, and no one could buy for less than the present value. At 10 percent interest, $110 a year from now is worth $100. If I offer $105, no one would sell.

Formulas explain how to calculate present values. The longer the time period over which payments are made, the more complicated the formula. The present value (*PV*) of each dollar to be paid in one year at the interest rate i (i stands for the rate of interest in decimals) is:

$$PV = \frac{\$1}{1 + i}.$$

If the interest rate is 10 percent, then $i = 0.10$ and $1 + i = 1.10$. The *PV* of each dollar equals $0.9091. If $10,000 is the sum to be paid in one year, the *PV* equals $9,091 ($10,000 times 0.9091). The price of an IOU of $10,000 to be paid in one year's time is $9,091 at a 10 percent interest rate.

The present-value formula becomes more complicated when the time span is greater than one year. At an annual interest rate of 10 percent, how much would someone be willing to pay now for an IOU that paid $121 two years from now? The answer follows the same reasoning as before. Consider how much money would have to be deposited today at a 10 percent interest rate to have $121 in two years? If the sum *PV* were deposited at interest rate i, it would be worth $PV \times (1 + i)$ one year from now. That sum would then earn a second year's interest and by the end of the second year would be worth $PV \times (1 + i) \times (1 + i)$, or $PV (1 + i)^2$. Setting the sum, $PV(1 + i)^2$, equal to $121 and dividing by $[(1 + i)^2]$ yields:

$$PV = \frac{\$121}{(1 + i)^2}.$$

At a rate of interest of 10 percent, the present value of $121 to be received two years from now is $100 (= $121/1.1^2$). At 10 percent interest, the price of a $121 IOU to be paid in two years would be $100.

This result can be generalized. The present value of a sum to be received in three years is that sum divided by $(1 + i)^3$; the present value of a sum to be received in four years is that sum divided by $(1 + i)^4$; and so on. The present value (*PV*) of a dollar to be received in n years is

$$PV = \frac{1}{(1 + i)^n}.$$

The present value (*PV*) of a dollar to be received in n years is

$$PV = \frac{1}{(1 + i)^n}.$$

The further out in the future
the money is to be paid, the
lower is its present value.

The present value of a dollar
to be received in the future
falls as the interest rate rises
and rises as the interest rate
falls.

At a 10 percent interest rate, $100 received one year from now has a present value of $90.91; $100 to be received five years from now has a present value of only $62.27. The further out in the future the money is to be received, the lower is its present value.

Present-value formulas show that the present value of money to be received in the future falls as the interest rate rises. In the above example, the present value of $121 to be received two years from now is $100 at an interest rate of 10 percent ($121 ÷ 1.1^2 = $100). At an interest rate of 20 percent, the *PV* of $121 to be received two years from now falls to $84 ($121 ÷ 1.2^2 = $84). There is an inverse relation between present value and interest rates.

This principle is illustrated by an IOU that pays interest forever. Suppose someone has a bond that pays $100 per year *in perpetuity* (forever). What is this IOU worth (its market price) today? If the interest rate were 10 percent, a $1,000 deposit would earn $100 per year in interest. This $1,000 is the present value of the $100 perpetual interest stream. If the interest rate doubled to 20 percent, a $500 deposit would earn $100 a year in perpetuity. Hence, $500 would be the present value of the $100 perpetual income stream at a 20 percent rate of interest.

The formula for the present value (*PV*) of an asset that yields a perpetual income stream is:

$$PV = \frac{R}{i}$$

where R = the annual income and i = the rate of interest expressed in decimal form. At an interest rate of 10 percent, the present value of $100 a year in perpetuity is $100 ÷ 0.10, or $1,000. (This formula is important in understanding stock prices, as explained later in this appendix.)

Bond Prices

Corporations acquire funds to finance business expansion by selling bonds. Once the bond is sold, the buyer can resell it, but such sales of second-hand bonds do not add directly to the corporation's financial capital. The interest and principal payments on corporate bonds represent a legal obligation for the corporation, just like any other debt it has. The purchaser of the bond has loaned the corporation money, and in return the corporation has promised the lender fixed interest payments until maturity and payment of the principal at the date of maturity. Interest and principal payments on corporate bonds have a claim on company earnings prior to dividends. The company has no choice but to make interest payments unless it is declared **bankrupt**.

Interest payments on bonds
represent a legal obligation of
the corporation.

A corporation can be declared **bankrupt** if it cannot pay its bills or its interest obligations.

Because purchasers of corporate bonds have prior claims on company earnings, bonds offer a relatively secure return. As long as the corporation does not become bankrupt, the bondholder will receive the promised annual interest payment (as well as the principal payment at the date of maturity).

Nevertheless, corporate bonds are not a riskless investment because bond prices fluctuate in the second-hand market. If the bond owner wishes to sell the bond before the date of maturity, the price received for the bond may well be less than the price paid for the bond.

Chapter 7   Corporate Finance and Financial Markets

Bond prices, like the price of any IOU, are the present discounted value (PV) of the fixed interest payments and principal. But as demonstrated above, there is an inverse relationship between interest rates and present values. As interest rates rise, investors pay *less* for the bond's stream of interest payments. As interest rates fall, investors will pay *more* for the bond's stream of interest payments.

As interest rates fall, bond prices rise and vice versa.

Stock Issues

Corporations can sell additional shares of **stock** as a second means of raising financial capital.

> A share of **stock** represents the ownership of 1/n percent of the corporation, where n is the number of shares outstanding. Owners of shares can vote on corporate matters and receive dividends proportional to their share holdings.

Suppose ZYX corporation has 100,000 shares of stock that are already owned by stockholders. These outstanding shares of stock can be bought and sold in markets for second-hand stock, called stock exchanges. Each share of stock currently sells for $10 on the second-hand market for stocks.

The corporation decides that it needs to raise $500,000 to build a new plant and arranges with an intermediary to sell 50,000 new shares of stock to potential buyers. The company will prepare a statement called a *prospectus* that describes the financial condition of the company and the proposed uses to which the raised funds will be put.

The amount of money potential buyers will be willing to pay for the 50,000 new shares depends upon their assessment of the impact of the proposed investment on ZYX corporation earnings. If investors expect the new plant to raise company earnings substantially, they will offer a higher price than if they expect the investment to have a small effect.

Experts believe that corporations will issue new stock only if they can avoid a decline in the price of the stock in the second-hand market. Let us suppose this is the case with ZYX corporation. The 50,000 new shares sell for a $10-per-share price, and ZYX corporation raises $500,000 through the stock issue.

The corporation now has 150,000 shares owned by stockholders rather than the previous 100,000. The owners of the new 50,000 shares are entitled to vote on corporate matters and to receive dividends. Unlike corporate bonds that legally obligate the corporation to pay fixed interest payments, the corporation is not obligated to pay dividends. The corporation pays dividends only if sufficient profits are left over after meeting interest and other obligations. When corporations experience hard times, dividends are frequently cut or even omitted.

Stock Markets

Stock prices (the prices of shares of stock of corporations) are determined by supply and demand in second-hand markets, called **stock exchanges**.

> A **stock exchange** is a market in which shares of stock of corporations are bought and sold and prices of shares of stock are determined.

There are many organized stock exchanges in the United States and in other countries, located in New York City, London, Denver, Frankfurt, Tokyo, Zurich, and Paris. In each stock exchange the shares of particular corporations are traded. The shares of French companies are traded in Paris, the shares of Japanese companies are traded in Tokyo, and so on. The world's largest stock exchanges are located on New York City's Wall Street: the New York Stock Exchange (NYSE) and the American Stock Exchange (ASE). The New York Stock Exchange lists about 50 billion shares of stock, and most days millions of shares worth hundreds of billions of dollars change hands. The shares of the largest American and multinational corporations are traded on the New York Stock Exchange, which provides a good example of how stock exchanges works.

Stock prices are determined by supply and demand in stock exchanges.

Stock Prices.   Like any organized market, the NYSE brings together all buyers and sellers of a particular commodity. In this case, it brings together all buyers and sellers of shares of corporations like General Motors, Kodak, or IBM. The number of shares of IBM stock outstanding is fixed (unless IBM decides to issue new shares of stock), and the owners of these shares will be prepared to sell their shares at different prices. The supply curve of IBM shares on September 3, 1993, is shown as curve *S* in Exhibit 1. The higher is the price, the greater is the number of IBM shares current owners will be prepared to sell; the supply curve is positively sloped. On the demand side of the market are potential buyers of IBM stock. Their demand curve for IBM shares on September 3, 1993, is shown as curve *D*. The lower is the share price, the greater is the number of IBM shares people will be prepared to buy, and the demand curve is negatively sloped. The equilibrium price of IBM shares (on September 3, 1993) is that price ($46.75) at which the number of shares demanded equals the number of shares supplied. The equilibrium number of shares traded (8.2 million) is referred to as the *volume* of IBM transactions.

Stock prices, like other market prices, are determined by supply and demand. When the supply or demand curves shift, stock prices change. For example, on

EXHIBIT 1   Determination of IBM Stock Prices

This figure diagrams the supply (*S*) and demand (*D*) curves for shares of IBM stock on September 3, 1993. The supply curve is positively sloped because owners of IBM stock will offer more shares for sale at high prices than at low prices. The demand curve is negatively sloped because buyers of IBM shares will be prepared to buy more at low prices than at high prices. The equilibrium price is that price at which the quantity demanded equals the quantity supplied. Share prices fluctuate daily because of shifts in supply and demand. This equilibrium price reflects the consensus present value of the future earnings per share of IBM.

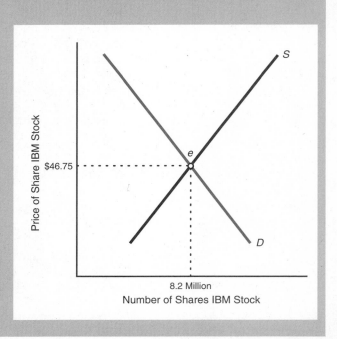

September 3, 1993, the price of IBM shares reached a low of 44\frac{1}{2}$ and a high of 46\frac{3}{8}$. The change in the price of IBM shares would be caused either by an increase in demand, a reduction in supply, or a combination of the two.

Exhibit 1 explains in a mechanical way how stock prices are determined, but it does not explain what lies behind the supply and demand curves: the different assessments of the future profits of the corporation. The owner of a share of stock benefits from the profits that the corporation earns now and in the future. The share owner of a corporation receives dividends that the corporation pays out of profits (if any) and benefits from reinvested profits that increase future profits. Share prices, therefore, depend on the present and future earnings of the corporation. Present earnings may be known, but future earnings are uncertain. They depend on factors such as the general state of the economy, the quality of management, and shifts in consumer demand. Because the future is unknown, different people will have different views of what the future holds. Some will see a bright future of rising profits and dividends. Others will foresee a bleak future of declining economic fortunes.

Stock prices depend on the present and future earnings of the corporation.

Stock Prices as Present Values.   The price of a share of stock is determined by the present and future profits of the corporation. The price depends upon the anticipated future profits per share of outstanding stock, or **earnings per share**.

> Earnings per share (*EPS*) is the annual profit of the corporation divided by the number of shares outstanding.

No one knows for sure what future profits will be. Suppose Jones, an optimist, expects earnings per share of ZYX Corporation to be $10 from now to eternity (in perpetuity). Smith, a pessimist, on the other hand, expects earnings per share of ZYX Corporation to be $5 from now to eternity. As the earlier discussion of present value showed, money to be earned in the future is worth less than money now. The anticipated future profits of ZYX Corporation need to be converted by both Jones and Smith into a present value. Applying the perpetuity formula (at a 10 percent interest rate), the present value of the anticipated profit stream of one share of stock is $100 ($10/0.10) for Jones and $50 ($5/0.10) for Smith. Jones would be a willing seller of ZYX stock at a price greater than $100 and a willing buyer at a price less than $100. Smith would be a willing seller at a price above $50 and a willing buyer at a price below $50. At a $75 price, Smith would sell and Jones would buy.

The price of a share of stock is the perceived present value of the future earnings per share of the stock.

The demand and supply curves of stock show that potential buyers and sellers assess differently the future earnings of corporations. The share price settles at that price at which the quantity of shares demanded equals the quantity supplied. This equilibrium price is the consensus of participants in the market concerning the present value of the future earnings of the corporation.

Price/Earnings Ratios.   Stock prices fluctuate because the future is unknown. No one knows for sure what the future earnings of any company might be. There will be disagreement among those who currently own the stock and those who are considering buying the stock. No one can predict for sure the future behavior of the economy. No one can predict for sure whether a particular company's fortunes will improve, deteriorate, or remain the same. When a company announces the development of a new product, the investment community may be convinced that this development will raise future earnings. This event will change investors' assessments of the present value of the company, and the stock price will rise.

The **price/earnings (*PE*) ratio** signals whether investors believe that the

A high *PE* ratio indicates that investors believe that current profits understate the future profits of the corporation.

profits of the company, or earnings per share, will rise or fall from their current profit levels.

> The **price/earnings** (*PE*) ratio is the stock price divided by the earnings per share.

If the average company has a *PE* ratio of 6, companies with a *PE* ratio greater than 6 are expected to have profits rising at above-average rates. Companies with a *PE* ratio less than 6 are expected to have profits rising at below-average rates.

Stock Indexes.   The share prices of corporations reflect the present discounted value of future profits. At times, share prices tend to rise generally in stock exchanges. At other times, they tend to fall generally. **Stock-price indexes** measure the ups and downs of average stock prices.

> A **stock-price index** (such as the Dow Jones Industrial Average, the Standard & Poor Index, or the New York Stock Exchange Index) measures the general movements of stock prices.

The different stock-price indexes measure movements in general stock prices differently. The Dow Jones Industrials Index measures the movement of 30 industrial stocks (such as Exxon, AT&T, and Du Pont). The New York Stock Exchange Index measures the average price of all stocks exchanged on the New York Stock Exchange. Although the different stock-price indexes do not yield identical results, they typically agree that stock prices are generally rising or falling but disagree on the magnitude of the rise or fall.

If buyers and sellers of stocks generally expect corporate profits to rise more rapidly, average stock prices should rise. The present value of future corporate earnings would rise, and buyers would be willing to pay more for stocks. Rising optimism about future corporate profits should cause stock-price indexes to register increases. When interest rates rise, the present values of future corporate earnings fall (because of the inverse relationship between present value and interest rates). The falling present values of corporate earnings should generally depress stock prices.

Anticipated corporate profits and interest rates are only two factors that explain general movements in stock prices. There are literally millions of participants in modern stock markets. Rumors of war, deaths of political leaders, drought, pronouncements of Wall Street gurus, and even trivial events can cause fluctuations in stock prices. It is often said that anyone who really understands the stock market is so rich that they do not have to bother dispensing advice to others on how to get rich.

The Efficient Stock Market Hypothesis

The efficient stock market hypothesis says that stock prices change because information about the company changes.

There are two opposing views of why stock prices change. One view is that the stock market is *irrational*. Potential buyers and sellers of stock are subject to changes in moods and whims. They turn overnight from being optimists to being pessimists for no apparent reason. They try to guess what other potential buyers and sellers are thinking. The opposing view—the **efficient stock market hypothesis**—is that the stock market reacts rationally to changes in information.

The **efficient stock market hypothesis** states that stock prices are determined by the information currently available on the present and future earnings of corporations. Changes in stock prices are due to changes in the information available on present and future earnings of corporations.

As noted above, the price of IBM shares on September 3, 1993, varied from a low of $44^1/8$ to a high of $46^3/8$. The efficient stock market hypothesis says that these price fluctuations would have been due to changes in the information available concerning IBM's current and expected profits. Proponents of the irrationality of stock market theory would argue that such changes occurred for no rational reason.

The efficient stock market hypothesis appeared to suffer a setback on "Black Monday," October 19, 1987, when in one day stock prices plummeted by almost one quarter. Analysts were hard pressed to explain how stock prices could fall in value so much in one day, when there was no apparent change in information concerning expected corporate profits.

Stock Prices and Resource Allocation

Corporations can issue new stock to raise financial capital. Once the stock is issued, it is traded on the various stock exchanges, and the buying and selling of stock do not have a *direct* effect on the corporation's financial capital. The gains from rising stock prices accrue to the individual holders of the issued stock.

The price of stocks does have an important effect on the allocation of capital resources. Consider what would happen if ZYX corporation's research-and-development team develops a promising anticancer drug and obtains Food and Drug Administration approval to market this drug. The investor community will realize (probably well before government approval is even granted) that ZYX corporation's earnings will rise substantially, so the price of the stock will rise rapidly. In our earlier example, the price of ZYX stock was $10, and the company was able to raise $500,000 by selling 50,000 new shares of stock. If, on the other hand, the prospect of the new drug raises the price of the stock to $50 (the new plant would be built to manufacture the new drug), the issue of 50,000 new shares would raise $2,500,000 instead of $500,000.

Rising stock prices make it easier for corporations to raise financial capital.

As stock prices rise, corporations find it easier to raise financial capital for expansion. Corporations with falling stock prices cannot raise large sums of money for expansion. In this sense, the second-hand markets for corporate stocks serve as barometers that signal the direction of the allocation of financial capital. Stockholders can express their dissatisfaction by "voting with their feet." By selling their shares, they drive down the price of the stock. If dissatisfaction is widespread, the stock price can fall considerably, preventing the firm from raising much capital by selling new shares.

Appendix Summary

1. A dollar today is worth more than a dollar tomorrow. The present-value formula allows one to compute what a stream of dollars to be received in the future is worth today.

2. The price of a bond reflects the present value of the interest payments and principal. If interest rates rise, this present value falls. Hence the relationship between bond prices and interest rates is inverse.

3. Corporations raise capital by issuing new shares of stock. Once issued, stock is bought and sold in stock exchanges. The price of a share of stock is the present value of the future earnings per share of stock. The price/earnings ratio signals whether stock markets believe that profits will be rising or falling.

4. Stock indexes measure general movements in the prices of shares.

5. The efficient stock market hypothesis maintains that stock prices depend upon the information that is currently available concerning the present and future profits of the corporation. Changes in stock prices are due to changes in this information.

6. Rising share prices allow a corporation to raise more financial capital by issuing new shares of stock. Hence rising stock prices tend to affect the allocation of resources.

Key Terms

bonds (p. 150)
present value (p. 151)
bankrupt (p. 152)
stock (p. 153)
stock exchange (p. 153)

earnings per share (p. 155)
price/earnings ratio (p. 155)
stock-price index (p. 156)
efficient stock market hypothesis (p. 156)

Questions and Problems

1. Without any change in information concerning a corporation's earnings prospects, the price of the corporation's stock falls by 25 percent. Would this fall support the efficient stock market hypothesis? Explain your answer.

2. Using the present-value formula, explain why a rise in the interest rate would tend to drive down stock prices.

3. The earnings per share of ABC corporation was 10, then dropped to 5. What does this change tell us about people's evaluation of the future earnings of ABC corporation?

4. What is $150,000 to be paid two years from today's date worth now? Do you have enough information to answer the question?

5. Answer the previous question at an interest rate of 10 percent and an interest rate of 5 percent. Compare the answers and explain what fundamental present-value principle is illustrated.

6. What is $100,000 put in a 5 percent saving account going to be worth in three years?

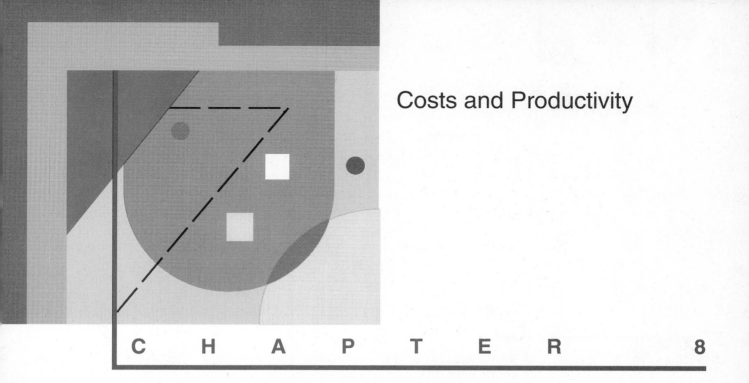

Costs and Productivity

C H A P T E R   8

CHAPTER FOCUS   This chapter shows that the costs that affect economic decision-making are opportunity costs. If a firm takes a particular action, like producing more output or purchasing new equipment, the costs of that action are what must be given up or sacrificed.

Instinct suggests incorrectly that the costs that really matter to businesses are their dollar costs. If an automobile dealer buys 20 cars for $12,000 and another 20 at $16,000 after the price has risen, the opportunity cost to the dealer of selling a car is $16,000, not $12,000 or $14,000. If the dealer sells one of the $12,000 cars, it will cost $16,000 to replace.

This principle of costs applies generally. If a shopping center, which cost $200,000 to build, is destroyed by a hurricane, the cost of this disaster is not $200,000 but how much it would cost to replace the shopping center (which could be more or less than the original cost).

Opportunity costs measure the resources that have to be sacrificed in order to take an action. Resources must be paid their opportunity costs. If they are offered a return less than their opportunity costs, they will go into an alternate activity.

After studying this chapter, you will be able to:

- See why opportunity costs include explicit and implicit costs.
- Explain the difference between economic profits and accounting profits.
- Understand the average/marginal rule.
- Define marginal physical product and use it to explain the law of diminishing returns.
- Distinguish between fixed and variable costs.
- Discuss the relationships between average variable, average total, and marginal costs.
- Explain the difference between the short-run and the long-run cost curves (and the shape of the long-run curve).

OPPORTUNITY COSTS

Business decisions are based upon opportunity costs. The notion of opportunity cost was introduced in Chapter 1: the opportunity cost of any action is the next best alternative that has to be sacrificed. In this chapter, we look more closely at opportunity costs in the context of the business firm.

Explicit and Implicit Costs

Economists look at costs in a way that differs from the common perception of costs as something that must be paid out of one's pocket. Consider the following case. Suppose your rich aunt gives you a brand new sports car, which has a market value of $15,000. She tells you: "This car is yours to keep or to sell. If you sell it, the $15,000 is yours. If you keep it, I'll pay for all gas, oil, maintenance, repairs, and insurance." This car is a generous gift. But is the car truly free? In fact, the car is not free. There is a cost to *using* the car.

The opportunity cost of using the car under these conditions may actually be higher than the annual cost of a small car. Consider selling the car today as opposed to keeping the car for one year. If the car were sold today for $15,000 and the money invested at 6 percent interest, the money would grow to $15,900 ($900 is the interest on $15,000 at 6 per cent per year). On the other hand, if the car were sold in one year, its resale value would decline due to depreciation. Suppose the resale value falls to $11,000. Selling the car today brings $15,900 in one year; selling in one year brings $11,000 in one year. Hence, the decision to sell the car today means that in one year you will have $4,900 more money than if the car is sold in one year. Using the car for one year will cost you exactly $4,900. The "free" car is far from free if the car is used! The lesson is that *costs are not necessarily what has been paid but what has been given up by taking one action rather than another.* **Opportunity cost** is the measure of what has been given up.

Economists use opportunity costs that include both explicit and implicit costs.

> The **opportunity cost** of an action is the value of the next best forgone alternative.

As the car example shows, an opportunity cost may be an **implicit cost** or an **explicit cost**.

Johann Heinrich von Thunen (1783–1850)

J. H. von Thunen was born in Germany in 1783. With the help of a small inheritance he bought a run-down 1,200-acre estate named Tellow that became a model farm and attracted visitors from all over Europe. The farm was his economic model. Thunen kept incredibly accurate records on the relationship between inputs and outputs. Years ahead of his time, he even offered his employees a profit-sharing plan. His major study, *The Isolated State with Respect to Agricultural and Political Economy,* was published in 1826 after more than twenty years of work and established him as an international authority on agriculture. Thunen was so excited about his discoveries in economics that he had one of his laws engraved on this tombstone.

Thunen put marginal productivity and costs on a secure foundation. His meticulous records revealed the law of diminishing marginal productivity. He conceived the experiment of recording the consequences of changing the input of capital, holding labor constant, or changing the input of labor, holding capital constant. Not only did he discover the law of diminishing marginal product, he stated the rules that would minimize a firm's costs of production and discovered many of the principles that govern the economics of how the city and farm interact.

An **explicit cost** (also called an *accounting cost*) is incurred when an actual payment is made.

An **implicit cost** is incurred when an alternative is sacrificed but no actual payment appears to be made.

Business firms must pay the factors of production their opportunity costs to attract resources. If firms make offers below opportunity costs, resources will seek out alternate employment.

Consider a business firm that produces stereos. Resources are required to produce stereos. Skilled workers must be hired, component parts must be purchased, and precision machinery must be available. The business firm could not acquire these resources without paying their owners. Skilled workers have alternative employment opportunities. The component parts are used by other manufacturers. How much would the business firm have to offer? The firm must offer each factor of production its opportunity cost. If skilled workers could earn $25 per hour in their next best employment alternative, the stereo manufacturer must offer at least $25 per hour. If the owners of the precision machines could rent them for $5,000 per month in their next best alternative, the stereo firm must offer at least that. (See Example 1.)

Opportunity Costs as the Sum of Explicit and Implicit Costs

Some of the business firm's factor payments are explicit (as money changes hands), and some may be implicit. The manager of the firm must consider the opportunity costs (the value of those resources if used in their next best alternative) of the resources owned by the firm. The hired resources (labor, land, equipment) have explicit costs that must be paid to acquire them.

For example, pharmacist Smith owns and operates Smith's Drugstore. Smith has put $60,000 of her own money into the business. As a pharmacist, Smith could earn $2,000 per month from a chain drugstore. Smith's capital investment in the drugstore may earn $500 per month invested elsewhere. This $2,500 (= $2,000 + $500) is an *implicit* cost of doing business. (Although this $2,500 is a true opportunity cost, no money changes hands.) The explicit (accounting) costs are Smith's rent payments on the building, inventory costs, business taxes, and wage payments to clerks and other pharmacists. These explicit monthly payments add up to $37,000 per month. Smith's total opportunity cost (per month) is the sum of explicit costs ($37,000) and implicit costs ($2,500), or $39,500.

Economic Profits

Economists measure profits using opportunity costs. Conventional accounting measures of profits often leave out implicit costs. Thus, **economic profits** are not always the same as profits reported by the usual accounting standards. Accounting profits can give a misleading picture of the firm's well-being, because they can sometimes ignore important implicit costs. Economic profits—which consider both explicit and implicit costs—signal whether or not resources are being directed to their best use.

Economic profits consider both explicit and implicit costs.

> **Economic profits** are the excess of revenues over total opportunity costs.

If Smith's Drugstore has monthly sales of $40,000, it has accounting profits of $3,000 per month because accounting costs = $37,000. Smith's economic profit, however, is only $500 because accounting costs ignore the implicit costs that must be paid to Smith for using Smith's entrepreneurial talents and funds. She is earning $500 more than the sum of money necessary to persuade the entrepreneur/owner to commit her talent and financial resources to the business. If accounting profit were below $2,500, the entrepreneur would not enter the business because Smith would be better off working for a chain pharmacy and drawing interest on her savings.

What would happen if revenues exactly equaled total opportunity cost (which would occur at an accounting profit of $2,500)? In this case, Smith would just be enticed to enter the business because she is earning the opportunity costs on the personal resources she devotes to the business. When revenues and total opportunity costs are equal, economic profit is zero.

Average/Marginal Rules

In economics, the relationship between *average* values or quantities and *marginal* values or quantities comes up again and again. This chapter examines the relationship between average costs and marginal costs. Later chapters will discuss the relationship between average revenues and marginal revenues. There is a common arithmetical background to all average/marginal relationships that can be illustrated with a familiar example.

Suppose that you are taking a course in chemistry and that there are eight (equally weighted) examinations. Your performance for the course is determined by your average score on all exams. Exhibit 1 shows how the average score is computed and graphs both marginal and average scores. On test number 1, you score 80 points; your average is 80. On test number 2, you score only 50; your *total* score is now 130 (= 80 + 50), and your average falls to 65 (= 130/2). Your average is the total accumulated points scored divided by the number of exams taken.

The marginal score is the increase in the total accumulated points obtained by taking one more exam. The marginal score is simply your score on the last examination taken. On the first exam your average and marginal scores are the same: 80. The second exam score is 50, which is below the previous average of 80.

Whenever the marginal value exceeds the previous average value, the new average value will rise. Whenever the marginal value is below the previous average value, the new average value will fall.

What will happen to the new average? *Whenever the marginal value is below the previous average value, the new average will fall.* In this case, the average falls from 80 to 65 because it is *pulled down* by the low marginal test score. The third exam score is 100, well above the 65 average to that point. What will happen to the new average? *When the marginal score is above the previous average test score, the new average will rise.* The average will be *pulled up* by the high marginal score.

A second rule is illustrated by the final marginal test score. The average test score of the first seven exams is 70. The eighth exam score is 70. Because the marginal score, thus, *equals* the previous average score, the new average will remain the same because the marginal value will pull the average neither up nor down.

If the marginal value equals the previous average value, the new average will not be changed.

Baseball fans are also familiar with these average/marginal rules. If a batter enters a game with a batting average of 0.250 (25 hits every 100 times at bat) and goes two for four on that day, the average will rise because the marginal score (0.500) is higher than the previous average score (0.250). If the player had gone one for four on that day, the average score would not have changed because the marginal score equals the previous average. If the player had zero hits, the average would have fallen because the marginal score was below the previous average.

COST CURVES IN THE SHORT RUN

A business firm expands the volume of its output by hiring or using additional resources. Every good or service is produced by a combination of resources (land, labor, capital, raw materials, entrepreneurial or managerial talent). The package of resources used depends on the prices and productivity of resources and on the time available to the firm for altering output. Prices and productivity are important because profit-minded businesses will use resources depending on their prices and productivity. Time is important because time is required to change the level of resource use. Some resources can be adjusted immediately. Other resources require considerable time to change.

EXHIBIT 1   Average and Marginal Relationships

a. Test Scores

Test	Test Score = Marginal Score	Average Test Score	Explanation
0		0	
1	80	80	Average and marginal values are the same.
2	50	65	When the marginal score is below the previous average, the new average falls.
3	100	76.67	When the marginal score is above the previous average, the new average rises.
4	70	75	When the marginal score is below the previous average, the new average falls.
5	60	72	When the marginal score is below the previous average, the new average falls.
6	50	68.22	When the marginal score is below the previous average, the new average falls.
7	80	70	When the marginal score is above the previous average, the new average rises.
8	70	70	When the marginal score equals the previous average, the new average is unchanged.

b. Graph of Test Scores

Panel (b) graphs the data from panel (a). Whenever the marginal score is less than the previous average score, the average score declines. Whenever the marginal score is greater than the previous average score, the average score rises. If the marginal score equals the previous average score, the average score will not change.

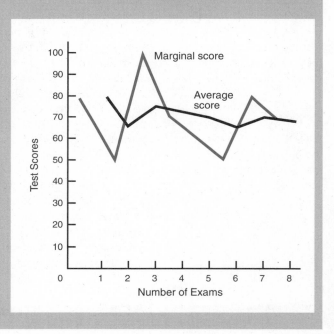

Short Run and Long Run

Suppose economic conditions are such that a business firm wishes to expand its volume of output. To expand output, it must expand resources. Some resources can be expanded quickly. The firm could ask its employees to work overtime. It may be able to recruit new employees on a moment's notice. Additional raw materials may be only a telephone call away. The firm's other inputs cannot be

In the short run, some factors of production are fixed. In the long run, all factors are variable.

expanded quickly. The installation of a new piece of capital equipment or the construction of a new plant may require significant time. The firm may have to wait for a lease to expire before moving into larger quarters. The business firm must wait for some resources to be expanded. In the meantime, the firm has to expand output by increasing those inputs that can be readily increased.

Economists distinguish between the **short run** and the **long run** when considering the time necessary to change input levels.

> The **short run** is a period of time so short that the existing plant and equipment cannot be varied; such inputs are fixed in supply. Additional output can be produced only by expanding the variable inputs of labor and raw materials.

> The **long run** is a period of time long enough to vary all inputs.

The long run is not a specified amount of calendar time. The long run may be as short as a few months for a fast-food restaurant, a couple of years for a new automobile plant, or a decade or more for an electrical power plant. Generally speaking, engineering complexity determines whether the long run is a matter of weeks or years in actual calendar time.

Fixed and Variable Costs

In the short run, there are both fixed and variable costs. In the short run, some factors (such as plant and equipment) are fixed in supply; even if the firm wanted to increase or reduce them, it would not be possible in the short run. The costs of these fixed factors are **fixed costs (FC)**. The firm pays these costs even if it produces no output. In the short run, greater output is obtained by using more of the *variable inputs* (such as labor and raw materials); the costs of these variable factors are **variable costs (VC)**. The sum of variable and fixed costs is **total costs (TC)**.

> Fixed costs (*FC*) are those costs that do not vary with output.

> Variable costs (*VC*) are those costs that do vary with output.

> Total costs (*TC*) are fixed costs plus variable costs:
>
> $$TC = VC + FC.$$

In the short run some costs are fixed. As the time horizon expands, more and more inputs can be varied. *In the long run, all costs are variable.* In other words, in the long run fixed costs are zero.

In the long run, all costs are variable. Thus, in the long run, fixed costs are *zero*. In the short run, some costs are fixed, and total costs consist of fixed plus variable costs.

We have seen that the costs of an action are measured in terms of the next best alternative sacrificed. In the short run there is no way to change fixed costs; they remain the same no matter what the firm decides. If the firm is considering expanding its output, this action has no effect on resources that are fixed. In the short run, fixed resources have no alternate use. The decision to increase output in the short run means an increase in variable inputs and, therefore, in variable costs. Variable inputs do have alternative uses, and they must be paid their opportunity costs.

The Law of Diminishing Returns

Production costs depend on input prices and technology. Production costs rise as input prices rise, *ceteris paribus,* and they fall as productivity improves, *ceteris paribus*. In this section, we are interested in what happens to the costs of production as firms expand the level of output in the short run.

The prices of the land, labor, and capital used in the enterprise are determined by conditions outside the firm (in the markets for those resources). Except in unusual circumstances, input prices would not be affected by the decision of a firm to expand its output. The firm's technology is determined by the ability of the management team to absorb the engineering and technical knowledge relevant to the firm's business. For all practical purposes, the firm's technology is fixed in the short run. The firm's technology dictates the relationship between increases in inputs and increases in outputs in the short run. In fact, the relationship between increases in input and increases in output follows a distinctive pattern in the short run, called the **law of diminishing returns**.

> The **law of diminishing returns** states that as ever larger amounts of a variable input are combined with fixed inputs, eventually the extra product attributable to each additional amount of the variable input must decline.

The extra product that is attributed to an additional unit of an input, holding other inputs fixed, is called the **marginal physical product (*MPP*)** of the input. It is calculated by taking the ratio of the change in output to the change in the variable input. The law of diminishing returns asserts that as more of a variable input is used, diminishing or declining marginal physical product must eventually be encountered by any firm. Alternatively, the law means that additional units of output become harder to produce when the point of diminishing returns is reached.

> The **marginal physical product (*MPP*)** of a factor of production is the change in output divided by the change in the quantity of the input, holding all other inputs constant.

To understand the law of diminishing returns, think about the average daily output of a shrimp boat along the Texas Gulf Coast. The fixed inputs would be the boat, along with its engine and nets (and other fishing equipment), as well as the ocean. The variable inputs would be the number of workers (shrimpers) used. Exhibit 2 shows the daily output (in terms of bushels) as a function of the number of shrimpers. Panel (b) shows the total output curve, panel (c) shows the marginal product curve, and panel (a) shows the underlying data.

If the boat is operated by only one shrimper, his or her time must be divided between piloting the boat, setting the nets, pulling in the nets full of shrimp, and unloading the nets. A lone shrimper catches 2 bushels per day. A second shrimper brings the total output to 12 bushels per day. An additional shrimper will allow the two persons to specialize somewhat and to save time switching from job to job. A third shrimper proves even more valuable, raising daily output to 32 bushels. The fourth shrimper raises output to 62 bushels, the fifth to 82, the sixth to 92 and so on.

Panel (c) and column 3 of panel (a) show the marginal physical product (*MPP*) of each additional shrimper. By definition, the *MPP* is the change in output per unit change in the input. Raising the input of shrimpers from 0 to 1 raises

EXHIBIT 2 The Law of Diminishing Returns, Shrimp Fishing

a. Total Product and Marginal Physical Product Schedules

Number of Shrimpers	Daily Output	Marginal Physical Product
0	0	
		2
1	2	
		6
		10
2	12	
		15
		20
3	32	
		25
		30
4	62	
		25
		20
5	82	
		15
		10
6	92	
		7.5
		5
7	97	
		4
		3
8	100	
		2.5
		2
9	102	
		1.5
		1
10	103	

This exhibit shows the relationship between the variable inputs and output. Panel (b) shows the total daily output; panel (c) shows the marginal physical product. Both graphs are based on the data in panel (a). When the total daily output is increasing rapidly, the marginal physical product curve (*MPP*) is increasing. When the total daily output is increasing but at a slower and slower rate, the *MPP* curve is declining.

b. Total Product

c. Marginal Physical Product

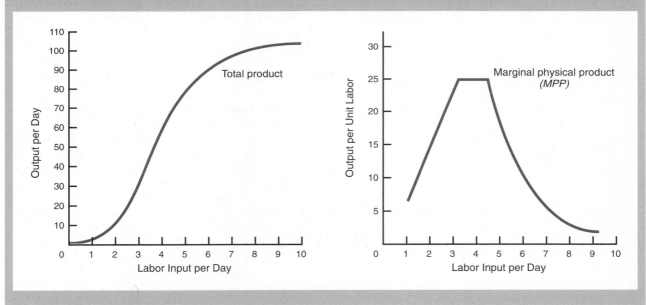

output by 2 bushels. Adding the 6th shrimper raises output from 82 to 92 bushels for an *MPP* of 10 bushels. Adding the 10th shrimper raises output from 102 to 103 bushels for an *MPP* of 1 bushel.

Marginal physical product can be calculated for one-unit increases in the input (as done above) or for increases of more than one unit. Consider the calculation of *MPP* when the number of shrimpers is increased by two. Raising the input of shrimpers from 0 to 2 increases output from 0 to 12 bushels. *MPP* is the change in output (12 bushels) divided by the change in inputs (two units)—or 6 bushels. The *MPP* of moving from 8 to 10 shrimpers is 1.5 units (3 bushels/2 shrimpers).

In panel (a) the *MPP* of increasing the number of shrimpers by one unit is given *in between* the relevant rows. When the *MPP* is calculated by increasing the labor input by 2 units, the results are given in boldface. For example, when the input increases from 4 to 6, output increases by 30 units from 62 to 92; thus, the *MPP* for the input level 5 (in between 4 and 6) is 15 (= 30/2) in boldface.

As the graph in panel (c) shows, diminishing returns set in after the fourth shrimper. Prior to the fourth shrimper, each additional shrimper had a higher *MPP*. Starting with the fourth shrimper, each additional shrimper has a lower *MPP* than the previous shrimper. What is the explanation? As more shrimpers are added to the fixed inputs of a boat and fishing equipment, the benefits from each shrimper being able to specialize in a particular activity are soon exhausted. By the time the fifth shrimper is added, the variable inputs may start to get in each other's way. The tenth shrimper adds only 1 bushel of shrimp to the daily output.

The law of diminishing returns—illustrated with the shrimp-boat example—applies to the production of any good or service. When some inputs are fixed, adding more variable inputs means that each variable input has less of the fixed input with which to work. When the fixed input becomes "crowded" with variable inputs, the law of diminishing returns sets in.

The law of diminishing returns explains why *MPP* eventually declines in the short run.

Marginal and Average Costs

The behavior of costs depends on the law of diminishing returns. Indeed, productivity and costs are inversely related. The higher the productivity, the lower are the costs; the lower the productivity, the higher are the costs.

Marginal Costs.   Recall that total cost equals variable costs plus fixed costs. Notice that as output increases, both total cost and variable cost increase by the same amount. Suppose, for example, that when the output of shrimp increases by 2 bushels, total (and variable) costs rise by $10. The change in costs divided by the change in output is called the **marginal cost (*MC*)** of production. In this example, *MC* = $5 = ($10 ÷ 2). In other words, *MC* is the increase in cost per unit increase in output. If the increase in output is only one unit, the *MC* is simply the increase in costs associated with increasing output by one unit. Marginal cost can be determined for any increase in output—one unit, two units, or any number.

> Marginal cost (*MC*) is the change in total cost (or equivalently in variable cost) divided by the increase in output or, alternatively, the increase in costs per unit increase in output.
>
> $$MC = \frac{\Delta TC}{\Delta Q} = \frac{\Delta VC}{\Delta Q}.$$

Business decisions are based on marginal costs (See Example 2.)

Average Costs.   While marginal costs look at the change in costs per unit change in output, average costs spread total, variable, or fixed costs over the entire quantity of output.

To determine whether the firm should operate in the short run or temporarily close down, the firm must consult its **average variable cost (*AVC*)**. By definition, *AVC* is obtained by dividing variable costs by output. Fixed cost per

EXAMPLE 2

Why Economic Decisions Are Based on Marginal Costs

Economic decisions are based on the marginal (opportunity) cost. Suppose you are in a supermarket and the manager announces that in the next five minutes you can buy two bottles of your favorite soft drink for the price of one. You hurry over and buy two bottles for $1 (the normal price of one bottle). When you arrive back at your home, your neighbor, who has unexpected company, asks to buy from you one bottle. What price would you charge? You have purchased two bottles for $1, for an average price of $0.50. There are three options: (1) Assume the bottle you are selling your neighbor is the "free" bottle and charge nothing. (2) Charge the average price of $0.50. (3) Charge $1. As a profit-maximizer, you should choose option 3. Why? It would cost you $1 to buy another. The two-for-one offer has expired, and you must now pay the regular price. The marginal cost of the action (parting with the bottle of soft drink) is $1. If you part with the bottle for the average cost ($0.50), your wealth would be reduced by $0.50 when you replace the bottle at a $1 price. The moral of this story is that profit-maximizing people and businesses make economic decisions on the basis of opportunity costs, not dollar costs.

SOURCE: Thomas Wyrick, "Marginal-Cost Policy Making and the Guy Next Door," *Wall Street Journal*, April 12, 1984.

unit produced is called **average fixed cost (AFC)** and is calculated by dividing fixed costs by output. To determine whether the firm is making economic profit on each unit produced, the firm must calculate its **average total cost (ATC)**; it is calculated by dividing total cost by output. Alternatively, ATC is just the sum of AFC and AVC.

Average variable cost (AVC) is variable cost divided by output:

$$AVC = VC \div Q.$$

Average fixed cost (AFC) is fixed cost divided by output:

$$AFC = FC \div Q.$$

Average total cost (ATC) is total cost divided by output, or the sum of average variable cost and average fixed cost:

$$ATC = TC \div Q = AVC + AFC.$$

The Cost Curves

Exhibits 3 and 4 assemble cost and output information for a hypothetical firm that produces a single product. The costs shown include all opportunity costs (explicit and implicit). The firm is operating in the short run because fixed costs are present. The enterprise has fixed costs of $48 per day. It consists primarily of the interest on the firm's capital, lease payments, and depreciation. As more output is produced, variable costs must rise because more inputs, such as labor and raw materials, must be hired or purchased. Exhibit 4a graphs total costs, variable costs,

EXHIBIT 3　The Short-Run Costs of a Hypothetical Enterprise

Cost Schedules in the Short Run for a Hypothetical Enterprise

Quantity of Output (units), Q (1)	Variable Cost (dollars), VC (2)	Fixed Cost (dollars), FC (3)	Total Cost (dollars), TC (4) = (2) + (3)	Marginal Cost (dollars), MC (5)	Average Variable Cost (dollars), AVC (6) = (2) ÷ (1)	Average Fixed Cost (dollars), AFC (7) = (3) ÷ (1)	Average Total Cost (dollars), ATC (8) = (4) ÷ (1) = (6) + (7)
0	0	48	48			∞	∞
				20			
1	20	48	68	15	20	48	68
				10			
2	30	48	78	8	15	24	39
				6			
3	36	48	84	5	12	16	28
				4			
4	40	48	88	6	10	12	22
				8			
5	48	48	96	10	9.6	9.6	19.2
				12			
6	60	48	108	16	10	8	18
				20			
7	80	48	128	26	11.4	6.9	18.3
				32			
8	112	48	160	38	14	6	20
				44			
9	156	24	180				

This exhibit shows the family of cost schedules for a hypothetical business enterprise operating in the short run with total fixed cost of $48. The table shows the basic data. *Variable cost* (column 2) rises with the level of output. *Total cost* (column 4) is the sum of total fixed cost and total variable cost. *Marginal cost* is shown in column 5; and *average variable, average fixed,* and *average total cost* are shown in the remaining columns.

The family of short-run cost curves consists of *MC, AVC, ATC,* and *AFC.*

and fixed costs; panel (b) graphs average variable costs, average total costs, and marginal costs. Exhibit 3 gives the basic underlying data for the firm.

In Exhibit 3, variable and total costs are shown in columns 2 and 4. Exhibit 4a shows the same data graphically. The marginal-cost figures in column 5 are shown *in between* the various output levels, because they are in this case the extra cost of going from one output level to another. The boldface figures are the marginal costs of increasing output by 2 units and are shown in between the respective output levels. For example, the *MC* of going from 0 units of output to 2 units of output is $15. This $15 *MC* figure between the output levels of 0 units and 2 units is displayed at the output level of 1. Similarly, the marginal cost in going from output level 5 to output level 7 is $16, because the increase in variable cost is $32 (from $48 to $80) and the increase in output is, again, 2. Thus, the *MC* figure for $Q = 6$ is $16 (= $32/2).

In the example, *MC* at first falls and then rises. Marginal costs first fall because as the first few units of output are produced, the variable inputs experience higher and higher marginal physical products as they specialize in different aspects of production. But eventually the law of diminishing returns sets in. At this point, it takes a larger increase in the variable inputs to produce a given increase in output. The law of diminishing returns dictates that marginal costs must eventually rise as output increases. As diminishing returns set in, marginal costs rise.

In Exhibit 3, column 6 divides variable costs by output to arrive at *AVC.*

EXHIBIT 4   The Short-Run Costs of a Hypothetical Enterprise

a. Total, Variable, and Fixed Costs

b. The Cost Curve

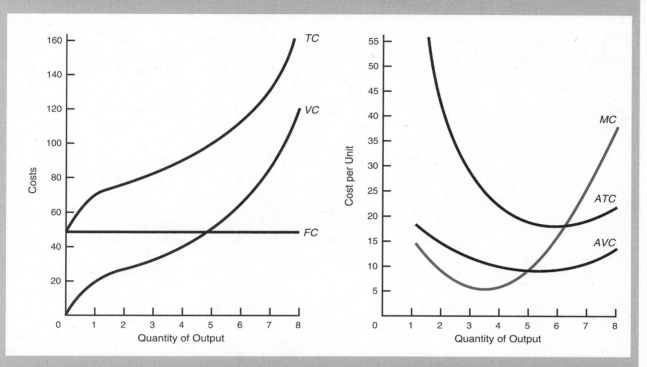

In Exhibit 4, the marginal and averages figures (except for average fixed costs) are graphed. Average total cost is the sum of average variable cost and average fixed cost. Note that *ATC* approaches *AVC* as output grows and that *MC* intersects both curves at their minimum points.

Column 7 divides fixed costs by output to arrive at *AFC*. Notice that *AFC* declines throughout because the same fixed cost is being spread out over more and more units of output. Finally, column 8 divides total cost—column 4—by output to obtain *ATC*.

Exhibit 4b shows the graphical relationship between marginal cost and average variable cost or between marginal cost and average total cost. Recall the average/marginal relationship, explained earlier. When *MC* is below *AVC* (or *ATC*), the margin is pulling down the average. Thus, in increasing output from 3 units to 4 units, *AVC* falls from $12 to $10, and *ATC* falls from $28 to $22. (Also see the data in Exhibit 3, columns 6 and 8.) The marginal cost of $4 is below *AVC* and *ATC* and pulls them both down. When output is 5 units, *MC* is slightly above *AVC,* and so just begins to pull *AVC* upward. When output is larger than 5 units, *MC* exceeds *AVC* and is pulling average variable costs up. When output is smaller than 5 units, *MC* falls short of *AVC* and is pushing average variable costs down.

Cost curves show what happens to costs of production as the level of output changes. Exhibit 4b illustrates an important principle: the *MC* curve intersects the *AVC* and *ATC* curves at their minimum points because of the average/marginal rule. At the minimum point, the average value is neither rising nor falling; therefore, the marginal and average values must be equal.

Notice that minimum *ATC* occurs after the minimum *AVC*. This must occur because when AVC reaches its minimum point, by definition, MC is equal to AVC but is still below ATC. Thus, when AVC is minimized, the ATC curve must still be falling by the average-marginal rule. When the ATC curve reaches its minimum point, the plant is being operated at its most efficient level. We shall see in the next chapter that competition forces the firm to produce at such a level.

MC equals ATC and AVC at their respective minimum values.

Because $ATC = AVC + AFC$, the distance between the AVC and ATC curves represents AFC. As a given fixed cost is spread over a larger and larger output, AFC gets smaller and smaller. Thus, the AVC and ATC curves get closer together as output rises.

LONG-RUN COSTS

The basic characteristic of the long run is that enterprises do not have any fixed costs; all costs are variable. In the long run, the business enterprise is free to choose any combination of inputs to produce output. Once long-run decisions are executed (the company completes a new plant, the commercial-farming enterprise signs a 10-year lease for additional acreage), the enterprise again has fixed factors of production and fixed costs. In the long run, enterprises are free to select the cost-minimizing level of capital, labor, and land inputs. Long-run cost-minimizing decisions are based on the prices the firm must pay for land, labor, and capital.

Shifts in Cost Curves

Take the case of Acme Steel Company, which produces steel tubes. Acme Steel can determine the average total cost curves it would face with different-size plants. With a small plant and highly unspecialized machinery, Acme Steel would face the average total cost curve ATC_1 in Exhibit 5. Notice that with this cost curve, ATC reaches its lowest point at output level q_1. With a slightly larger plant and somewhat more specialized equipment, Acme Steel's average total cost would be lower for sufficiently larger levels of output, such as at q_2. The average total cost curve associated with the larger plant and more specialized equipment is ATC_2. The remaining ATC curves show the average costs for even larger plants. The curve ATC_3 yields the most efficient plant size for producing the output level q_3.

The Long-Run Cost Curve

Exhibit 5 demonstrates that there is a different ATC curve for each level of fixed input. For every plant size, there is a different average total cost curve. If there is an infinite number of fixed input levels from which to choose, there would be an infinite number of associated ATC curves. Recall that in the long run all costs are variable; therefore, there is no distinction between long-run variable costs and long-run total costs—there is only **long-run average cost ($LRAC$)**.

> Long-run average cost ($LRAC$) consists of the minimum average cost for each level of output when all factor inputs are variable (and when factor prices and the state of technology are fixed).

In the long run, the enterprise is free to select the most effective combination of factor inputs because none of the inputs is fixed. The long-run cost curve "envelopes" the short-run cost curves, forming a long-run curve that touches each

EXHIBIT 5   Shifts in Cost Curves with Changing Plant Size

In this exhibit, economies of scale are achieved with larger plant sizes up to the plant size ATC_3. When diseconomies of scale are encountered, larger plant sizes entail larger unit costs, as with ATC_4 and ATC_5.

short-run curve ($SRATC$) at only one point, as shown in Exhibit 6. In the short run, the fact that some factors of production are fixed causes the average-total-cost curve to be U-shaped. The law of diminishing returns need not apply to the long run because, in the long run, all inputs are variable.

Economies and Diseconomies of Scale

The long-run average-cost curve will also be U-shaped, as shown in Exhibit 6. Why would long-run average costs ($LRAC$) first decline as output expands and then later increase as output expands even further? The reason is that firms experience first economies of scale, then constant returns to scale, and finally diseconomies of scale as output expands.

Economies of Scale.   The declining portion of the $LRAC$ curve is due to economies of scale that arise out of the indivisibility of the inputs of labor and physical capital goods or equipment. In a large firm, the division of labor will be much more specialized than in a small firm. Workers are able to specialize in various activities, increase their productivity or dexterity through experience, and save time in moving from one task to another. People are simply indivisible: it is difficult for one person to be one part mechanic, two parts supervisor, and three parts electrician and still remain as efficient as one who specializes in just one of these tasks. The classic example of worker specialization is the assembly line of an automobile plant. The same principles apply to machines. A small firm might have to use general-purpose machine tools whereas a large firm might be able to build special equipment or machines that will substantially lower costs when large quantities are produced. Small-scale versions of certain specialized machines simply cannot be made available.

Economies of scale can occur because of the greater productivity of specializa-

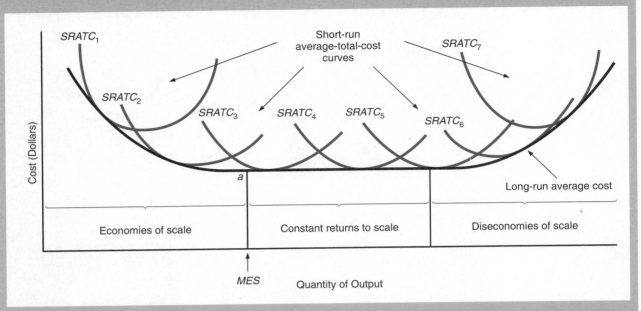

For each level of fixed input, there is a corresponding short-run average-total-cost curve. The long-run average-cost curve is the envelope of the short-run average-total-cost curves. The long-run average-cost curve is *U*-shaped. The declining portion shows economies of scale. The rising portion shows diseconomies of scale. The horizontal portion shows constant returns to scale.

tion in any of a variety of areas, including technological equipment, marketing, research and development, and management. The optimal rate of utilization for some types of machinery may occur at high rates of output. Some workers may not be able to perfect specialized skills until a high rate of output allows them to concentrate on specific tasks. As the output of an enterprise increases with all inputs variable, average costs will decline because of the **economies of scale** associated with increased specialization of labor, management, plant, and equipment. (See Example 3.)

Long-run costs decline because of economies of scale.

> Economies of scale are present when an increase in output causes average costs to fall.

Constant Returns to Scale.   Economies of scale will become exhausted at some point when expanding output no longer increases productivity. The evidence suggests that for a large range of outputs there will be **constant returns to scale**, where the average costs or production remain constant.

> Constant returns of scale are present when an increase in output does not change average costs of production.

Diseconomies of Scale.   As the enterprise continues to expand its output, eventually all the economies of large-scale production will be exploited, and

EXAMPLE 3

The Do-It-Yourself Car: Economies of Scale

Classic Motor Carriages, a company located in Florida, sells to do-it-yourself hobbyists a kit of automobile parts that can be assembled in one's own garage. Not included is the automobile drive train (which contains the engine and transmission), which the hobbyist can obtain already assembled. Even with the advantage of starting with an assembled drive train, Classic Motor Carriages estimates that it would take a person 200 hours to assemble the car. To get some idea of the advantages of specialization and large-scale production, consider General Motors' assembly plant in Tarrytown, New York. The plant employs 2,000 workers per 8-hour shift and turns out approximately one car per minute (about 500 cars per day). Dividing 500 cars by the 2,000 workers yields one car for every four workers—or, equivalently, one-fourth of a car per worker per day. Under conditions of specialization, large capital use, and mass production, the average worker produces one complete car every four days. The difference between four days (or 32 hours) per worker and 200 hours per worker illustrates in dramatic fashion the concept of economies of large-scale production.

SOURCES: Roger W. Shmenner, *Production/Operations Management: Concepts and Situations* (Chicago: SRA, Inc., 1981), chap. 5, and the authors.

long-run average costs will begin to rise. The rise in long-run average costs as the capital stock of the enterprise expands is the result of **diseconomies of scale**.

> **Diseconomies of scale** are present when an increase in output causes average costs to increase.

Diseconomies of scale can be caused by a series of factors. As the firm continues to expand, management skills must be spread over a larger and larger firm. Managers must assume additional responsibility, and managerial talents may eventually be spread so thin that the efficiency of management declines. The problem of maintaining communications within a large firm grows, and red tape and cumbersome bureaucracy become commonplace. Large firms may find it difficult to correct their mistakes. Employees of large firms may lose their identity and feel that their contributions to the firm are not recognized. As the output of an enterprise continues to increase, average cost will eventually rise because of the diseconomies of scale associated with the growing problems of managerial coordination.

Because of economies and diseconomies of scale, the long-run average cost curve is U-shaped.

This chapter examined how production costs behave in the short run and in the long run. The next chapter will study how perfectly competitive firms use these costs to determine their output level.

Chapter Summary

The most important point to learn from this chapter is:
Marginal costs increase because of the law of diminishing returns.

Two Prices for Natural Gas?

In the United States, the price of natural gas has been regulated since 1938. The latest act, the Natural Gas Policy Act of 1978, deregulated must of the natural-gas industry, allowing the prices of "new" gas to be set by the marketplace. "Old" gas remains a significant exception to market pricing. Natural gas previously committed to pipelines remains subject to price regulations that have kept the price of "old" gas significantly below the price of "new" gas.

Legislators argue that because "old" gas was discovered at a time when costs were low, it would be inappropriate for the producers of "old" gas to receive as much as "new" gas producers, who produce at a higher cost. Allowing the price of natural gas from all sources to be set by supply and demand would give windfall profits to producers of "old" gas.

This chapter teaches that opportunity cost appropriately measures the costs of an activity. With the price of "old" gas held below market rates, the natural-gas price paid by users is an average of the cost of producing "old" and "new" gas. Assume, for example, that "old" gas costs $1 per million btu and "new" gas costs $3 per million btu, and that half the gas is "old" gas and half is "new" gas. The price the consumer pays is therefore approximately $2. The opportunity cost of "old" gas is, however, $3. Once this gas is used, the producer must incur a cost of $3 to replace that gas.

In effect, the consumer is buying natural gas (at $2) at less than its opportunity cost ($3). The consumer will therefore be encouraged to use natural gas in uses that are worth only $2 to that consumer, below the opportunity cost of $3.

Economists have noted another defect of controlling the price of "old" gas. Modern technology (water flooding, fracturing, chemical treatment) allows producers of "old" gas to increase their production. It may be cheaper to increase the production of gas from old fields than to discover and develop new fields. Yet with the price of "old" gas controlled, producers of "old" gas have no incentive to use these new methods. They are better off developing new fields at higher costs than improving old fields.

This analysis suggests a full deregulation of natural gas to allow the prices of both old and new gas to be determined by supply and demand.

SOURCE: Ronald Braeutigam and R. Glenn Hubbard, "Natural Gas: The Regulatory Transition," in Leonard Weiss and Michael Klass (eds), *Regulatory Reform: What Actually Happened* (Boston: Little, Brown & Co., 1986), pp. 137–168.

1. The opportunity cost of an action is the value of the next best forgone alternative. Economic profit is defined as total revenue minus opportunity costs. When economic profits are zero, the firm is still earning an accounting profit. The average of a series of values falls when the marginal value is below the previous average value; the average stays constant when the marginal value equals the previous average; the average rises when the marginal value exceeds the previous average.

2. In the short run, the time period is so short that existing plant and equipment cannot be varied; in the long run, all inputs are variable. Variable costs are those costs that vary with output; fixed costs do not vary with output. In the long run, all costs are variable.

3. Marginal physical product is the increase in output divided by the change in the quantity of an input, holding all other inputs constant. The law of diminishing returns states that as one input is increased (holding other inputs constant), the marginal physical product of the variable input will eventually decline.

4. Marginal cost is the increase in cost divided by the increase in output. Average variable cost (AVC) is variable cost divided by output; average total cost (ATC) is total (fixed plus variable) cost divided by output. The average-variable-cost and average-total-cost curves tend to be U-shaped, with the MC intersecting AVC and ATC at their minimum values.

5. In the long run, there are different-sized plants. Associated with each size of plant is a particular short-run average-total-cost curve. The envelope of all such short-run average-total-cost curves is the *long-run average-cost curve.* The long-run average-cost curve gives the minimum unit cost of producing any given volume of output. Along the long-run average-cost curve, the firm is choosing the least-cost combination of inputs. Economies of scale prevail when increasing output lowers average costs of production. Constant returns to scale prevail when increasing output does not change average costs of production—in which case, the long-run average-cost curve in constant or horizontal. Diseconomies of scale prevail when increasing output lowers the average unit costs of production.

Policy Focus: **Charging prices below opportunity costs for "old" gas creates a gap between what people pay for natural gas and its opportunity cost.**

Key Terms

opportunity cost (p. 414)
explicit cost (p. 415)
implicit cost (p. 415)
economic profits (p. 416)
short run (p. 419)
long run (p. 419)
fixed costs (FC) (p. 419)
variable costs (VC) (p. 419)
total costs (TC) (p. 419)
law of diminishing returns (p. 420)

marginal physical product (MPP) (p. 420)
marginal cost (MC) (p. 422)
average variable cost (AVC) (p. 422)
average fixed cost (AFC) (p. 423)
average total cost (ATC) (p. 423)
long-run average cost (LRAC) (p. 426)
economies of scale (p. 428)
constant returns to scale (p. 428)
diseconomies of scale (p. 429)

Questions and Problems

1. In Lower Slobovia, the army is recruited by a draft and each recruit is paid $50 a month. In Upper Slobovia, the army is voluntary and each recruit must be paid $500 a month. Is the cost of the military cheaper in Lower Slobovia?

2. Why do economists measure profit differently than accountants?

3. A firm's accounting costs are $15,000 per month. In addition, the firm's implicit opportunity costs are $5,000. What are the firm's total opportunity costs? If revenue were $22,000, how much economic profit would the firm earn?

4. Your uncle gives you a "free" car and pays for the insurance, gas, oil, and repairs. You are told you may sell the car any time. Assume the car is now worth $20,000 and will have an estimated value of $12,000 after one year. If the interest rate is 10 percent, how much does it cost you to use the car for one year?

5. Contrast the average-total-cost (ATC) curve of a firm that has very large fixed costs relative to variable costs with the ATC curve of a firm that has very small fixed costs relative to variable costs.

6. Explain why fixed costs should not affect business decisions in the short run.

7. Answer the following questions using the production-function information in Table A.
   a. What is the MPP between 3 and 5 units of output?
   b. Derive the MPP schedule. Does it obey the law of diminishing returns?

TABLE A

Labor (units)	Output (units)
0	0
1	5
2	15
3	20
4	23
5	24

8. At the current output level, the average total cost (*ATC*) is $25, and marginal cost (*MC*) is $15. If output were increased by one unit, what would happen to the new average total cost? To the new average variable cost? If *ATC* were to stay at $25 and *MC* were to increase to $25, what would happen to the next *ATC*?

9. Suppose *FC* = $25, *VC* = Q^2, and *MC* = $2Q$. Draw the *AFC, AVC, MC,* and *ATC* curves. At what output level does the minimum *ATC* occur?

10. What is the role of the law of diminishing returns in explaining the shape of the marginal cost curve?

11. If *MC* rises, what conclusion can be drawn about whether *ATC* or *AVC* is rising or falling?

12. What is the opportunity cost of a worker to a firm that mistakenly pays the worker $40 an hour instead of the worker's wage of $25 an hour?

13. A firm increases its output by 50 units and finds that its costs, in the short run, increase by $200. What is its marginal cost of production over this range?

14. Suppose 30 units of labor produce 100 widgets and 40 units of labor produce 200 widgets. If each unit of labor is paid $10, what is the marginal cost of producing widgets between those two output levels?

15. Using Table B, plot all the short-run total-cost and average-cost curves discussed in this chapter. Do the cost curves have the expected shapes? Explain your answer.

TABLE B

Output (units)	Fixed Costs (dollars)	Variable Costs (dollars)
1	10	5
2	10	8
3	10	12
4	10	20
5	10	40

Doing Economics

If there is an empty seat next to you in economics class, it appears that the marginal cost (from the point of view of the college) of adding a student is zero. Is this true? Explain. It is profitable to fill the seat if the increased revenue the college receives exceeds its marginal cost. What implications does this have for the pricing and supply behavior of your college?

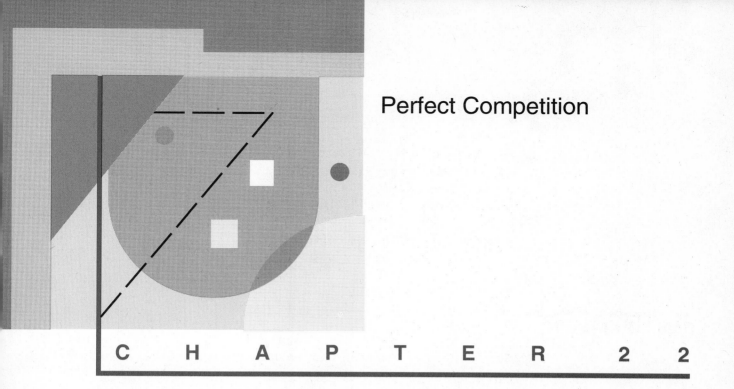

Perfect Competition

CHAPTER 2 2

CHAPTER FOCUS   Most people have seen competition and the lack of competition. If they work for a manufacturing or service company, they know that rival firms are competing with them for customers. They know the importance of holding their market share. In their jobs, people understand that other people are willing to take their place or that another company may want to hire them away. Accordingly, they encounter competition in the job market, just as their employer encounters competition in the market for products. If they work for the electric light company or for the only cable television company in town, they see that they have to hustle less to sell their product and have to worry less about the actions of rival firms.

Adam Smith in his *Wealth of Nations* emphasized the benefits of competition. It is competition that makes the self-centered baker or shoemaker produce the products desired by consumers. It is competition that causes firms to seek out new ways of doing things and to develop new products.

This chapter describes how businesses operate in the most competitive of all markets—the perfectly competitive market.

After studying this chapter, you will be able to:

■ See why perfectly competitive firms are price takers, and why price equals marginal revenue.

■ Understand the profit maximization conditions for the firm under perfect competition.

■ Discuss how the supply curve of the market is related to the marginal cost curves of each firm.

■ Determine the shape of the long-run supply curve for both constant-cost and increasing-cost industries.

■ Explain why perfect competition is efficient.

THE FOUR MARKET MODELS

An industry is a collection of firms producing a similar product (such as steel, aluminum, milk, wheat, or automobiles). Each industry is characterized by how much competition is present. Economists distinguish among four basic market models: *perfect competition, monopolistic competition, oligopoly,* and *monopoly.*

These markets will be discussed in detail later on. Briefly, *perfect competition* exists in an industry where individual firms have no control over the market price, and new firms are perfectly free to enter the industry. Perfect competition is most likely in an industry where there are many small producers of a homogeneous product, such as farming. *Monopolistic competition* prevails when there are many small producers of a differentiated product and new firms can enter freely. Local supermarkets and service stations are examples of monopolistic competitors. When firms are large relative to the market (such as General Motors or Ford), and there are impediments to the entry of new firms, the industry is *oligopolistic.* Automobile companies, steel companies, soap manufacturers, and cereal producers are examples of oligopolies. Finally, a *pure monopoly* exists when an industry's product is supplied by only one firm. Examples of pure monopolies are the local telephone service or cable-TV service.

The remainder of this chapter deals with firms that operate in perfectly competitive markets. The three other markets are discussed in the following chapters.

CHARACTERISTICS OF PERFECT COMPETITION

Almost every seller exercises some influence over price, but the more competition the seller faces the less control the individual seller can exercise over the prices charged. In the limiting case, the seller has absolutely no control over price. When the price is given to the individual seller by the market, the seller is said to be a **price taker**. In a perfectly competitive industry, each individual seller faces so much competition from other sellers that the market price is taken as a given. The price is something to which the perfectly competitive firm reacts. It cannot influence the market price through its actions.

A **price taker** is a seller that does not have the ability to control the price of the good it sells.

The characteristics of perfectly competitive markets account for the inability of a single firm to influence the market price. In perfect competition, all firms in the industry sell a homogeneous or identical product. No firm exercises an advantage over other firms in terms of quality, location, or other product features. If Firm A charges a higher price than Firm B for the identical product, no rational buyer will buy from A. In a perfectly competitive market, buyers have perfect information about the prices charged by different sellers. Every buyer would know if Firm B's price is lower than Firm A's price. Moreover, there are so many firms that no single firm can affect market supply by increasing or decreasing its output.

> In an industry characterized by **perfect competition:**
> 1. There is a large number of buyers and sellers in the market.
> 2. Each buyer and seller has perfect information about prices and product quality.
> 3. The product being sold is homogeneous; it is not possible (or even worthwhile) to distinguish the product of one firm from that of other firms.
> 4. There are no barriers to entry into or exit from the market; there is freedom of entry and exit.
> 5. All firms are price takers: No single seller is large enough to exert any control over the product price, so each seller accepts the market price as given.

The Conditions for Perfect Competition

Most industries are not perfectly competitive, but the model of perfect competition is much more useful than the strict conditions would indicate. In real-world markets, there are many industries that closely *approximate* the conditions of perfect competition. In such markets, the number of producers may not be large

Competition and World Trade

Economics teaches that a market consists of all potential buyers and sellers of a good or service. Both domestic and foreign firms serve as sellers in markets, and the presence of foreign sellers increases the amount of competition in a market. Competition in a market is determined by the number of foreign and domestic competitors.

The last thirty years have seen a dramatic expansion in world trade. From 1970 to 1988, world trade increased more than 6 percent per year, which is about twice the growth of economic activity in general. The high growth of international trade was made possible by the dismantling of barriers to international competition any by the development of modern telecommunications. Business enterprises no longer operate in isolated national markets. They must compete not only with domestic rivals, but also with rival producers located thousands of miles away. Around the globe, more and more businesses find that their chief competitors in markets are located in other countries.

The growth of international trade and competition means that it is no longer valid to measure competition according to the number of domestic producers in a market. Although there are only three major U.S. automobile manufacturers, they face stiff competition from rivals located in Germany, Italy, France, Japan, Brazil, and South Korea. Restaurants in Paris, Frankfurt, and Tokyo must compete for customers with McDonalds and Burger King. Buyers of precision machinery receive competitive bids from manufacturers in Switzerland, Hong Kong, Canada, and New Zealand.

The growth of international competition has made the theory of competition more relevant. International trade has increased the amount of competition in world markets.

---

enough to make each firm a perfect price taker, but the amount of control over price may be negligible. Information on prices and product quality may not be perfect, but consumers may have a significant amount of information at their disposal. The product may not be perfectly homogeneous, but the distinctions among products may be inconsequential. The number of firms actually in the industry may not be exceptionally large, but a large number of firms may be waiting in the wings to enter on short notice if economic profits are earned. (See Example 1.)

This chapter shows that perfect competition yields important insights into the functioning of markets. It describes the competitive forces that attract resources from one industry to another. It describes how businesses that have little control over price select the level of output that is best for them. It shows that firms operating in competitive markets produce output at minimum average cost in the long run. The model of perfect competition also shows why profits to be driven down to normal returns in competitive markets.

The Firm and the Industry

The difference between the perfectly competitive firm and the market (or the industry as a whole) is illustrated in Exhibit 1. Panel (b) shows the market demand curve, D, for the product. When the market price is $7, the quantity demanded in the market is 10,000 units. The individual firm, shown in panel (a), can sell all it wants (from a practical standpoint) at the going market price of $7. Whether the firms sells 3 units or 10 units, the price is still the $7 market price.

EXHIBIT 1 Market Demand Versus Firm Demand

a. The Firm   **b. The Market**

The market demand curve, *D*, in panel (b) shows the total market demand for a homogeneous product being produced by many relatively small firms. The demand curve, D_1, in panel (a) shows how the demand is perceived by the individual firm. Because the individual firm is so small relative to the market, it cannot significantly influence the market price. The firm is, thus, a price taker and can sell all it wants at the going price.

The demand curve facing the perfectly competitive firm is *horizontal* or *perfectly elastic* at the going market price.

The perfectly competitive firm can sell all it wants at the prevailing market price. This means that the demand curve *that the individual firm faces is perfectly elastic.*

The individual firm in a perfectly competitive market produces very small amounts relative to the market as a whole. An individual firm cannot change the market price by altering the quantity of the good it offers in the marketplace. Because the individual firm faces a perfectly elastic demand schedule, the firm is a price taker. If the firm tried to sell at a price higher than the market price, it would sell nothing.

THE SHORT-RUN SUPPLY CURVE

Perfectly competitive firms have no control over price; they are price takers. They do not have to decide what price to charge. The market does that. Therefore, the major decision they must make is how much output to produce. In the short run, a perfectly competitive firm makes its output decisions by varying the quantity of its variable inputs (such as labor, raw material, or energy) that are used with its fixed plant and equipment.

Selecting Output to Maximize Profit

Business firms use marginal analysis to decide *how much* to produce. The firm determines whether it is producing the "right" amount of output by considering what would happen if it either increased or reduced the level of output. If producing another unit of output raises the *profit of the firm (or reduces its losses),* more output should be produced. If reducing output by one unit raised profit, output should be reduced. Adjustments in the level of output will continue to be made as long as each change adds more profit or reduces losses.

Marginal costs play a key role in the firm's search for the right level of output. The preceding chapter showed that marginal cost (*MC*) is the increase in costs that results from increasing output by one unit. Marginal costs tell the firm what is happening to costs as it considers marginal changes in output. In considering marginal changes in output, the firm must compare marginal costs with changes in revenues.

The **profit-maximization rule** is that output should be produced up to the point where the extra cost of an additional unit of output (marginal cost) is just equal to the extra revenue derived from the additional unit of output, or the **marginal revenue (*MR*)**.

> Marginal revenue (*MR*) is the increase in total revenue (*TR*) that results from each one-unit increase in the amount of output:
>
> $$MR = \frac{\Delta TR}{\Delta Q}.$$

> The **profit-maximization rule** is that a firm will maximize profits by producing that level of output at which marginal revenue (*MR*) equals marginal cost (*MC*).

As long as an extra unit of output adds more to revenues than to costs, the profits of the firm are increasing (or its losses are being reduced). If the marginal cost of an additional unit of output exceeds its marginal revenue, the profits of the firm would be reduced (or its losses increased) if output is expanded. The profit-maximizing rule is a general rule that applies to all firms—be they perfectly competitive, oligopolistic, or monopolistic. Each firm will produce that level of output at which marginal revenue and marginal cost are equal.

The relationship between marginal revenue and price is different for perfectly competitive firms than for other types of firms (the importance of this distinction will be clear after studying the next chapter). For example, a monopolist can determine the price. By setting a high price, the monopolist loses sales; by setting a low price, the monopolist gains sales. Briefly, for a monopolist, marginal revenue will generally be less than the price because increasing the number of units sold lowers the price. But the competitive firm can sell all it wants at the going market price. To a competitive firm, the price (*P*) measures the extra revenue of an additional unit of output, or the marginal revenue (*MR*), because the extra unit sold is sold without depressing the market price. The increase in revenue brought about by increasing output by one unit, therefore, equals *P*.

Consider the hypothetical competitive firm described in Exhibit 2. The costs are the same as the firm studied in Exhibit 3 of the previous chapter. Both the table and the graph can be used to show how much the firm decides to produce. Panel (b) shows the basic data. The firm's average variable costs (*AVC*) for different levels of output are shown in column 2. The firm's average total costs (*ATC*) are shown in column 3. Total costs are shown in column 4, and the firm's marginal costs (*MC*) are shown in column 5. Panel (a) shows the same information in

EXHIBIT 2   The Profit-Maximizing Firm

a. Short-Run Profits

The market price is $26. The firm maximizes profits at an output level of 7 units (where $P = MC$). At $P = 26, price exceeds ATC by the distance bc. Total profit is the rectangle $abcd$ in panel (a) and is $54, as shown by column 8 of panel (b).

b. Cost and Revenue Schedule

Output (1)	Average Variable Cost (2)	Average Total Cost (3)	TC (4)	Marginal Cost (5)	P = Marginal Revenue (6)	Revenue (7)	Profit (8)
0	—	∞	$48		$26	$0	−$48
				$20			
1	$20	$68	68	15	26	$26	−32
				10			
2	15	39	78	8	26	52	−26
				6			
3	12	28	84	5	26	78	−6
				4			
4	10	22	88	6	26	104	16
				8			
5	9.6	19.2	96	10	26	130	34
				12			
6	10	18	108	16	26	156	48
				20			
7	11.4	18.3	128	26	26	182	54
				32			
8	14	20	160	38	26	208	48
				44			
9	17.3	22.7	204				

graphical form. The graphs of the various cost curves show again that the difference between the *ATC* and *AVC* curves measures average fixed cost (*AFC*) and that the *MC* curve intersects both the *AVC* and *ATC* curves at their minimum points.

The minimum points on the *AVC* and *ATC* curves are important to keep in mind. In Exhibit 2b, column 2 shows that the minimum average variable cost is $9.60—which occurs when output equals 5 units. Column 3 shows that the minimum average total cost is $18 and occurs when output equals 6 units.

Whether the firm can make a profit or not depends upon the price.

Three Cases

In the short run, the firm's objective would be either to maximize profits or, if necessary, to minimize losses. Once the market price is set, the firm can find itself in one of three positions:

1. the price may be high enough that the firm can make economic profits;
2. the price may be low enough that the firm stays in business but produces at a loss; or
3. the price may be so low that the firm's best option is to temporarily shut down and hope for the price to rise.

As the above three outcomes illustrate, prices affect output decisions. At very low prices, the firm may have to shut down. At higher prices, it produces a positive amount of output. The firm's supply curve shows how much it is prepared to sell at each price. We shall demonstrate that the quantity supplied at each price is simply the firm's profit-maximizing output (or its loss-minimizing output).

The Profitable Firm. Let us start with the price of $26. Because the firm is perfectly competitive, $P = MR = \$26$. Columns 4, 7, and 8 in Exhibit 2b show the total cost, total revenue, and the profit (positive or negative) of the firm. If the firm produces 5 units, where the average total cost (*ATC*) is $19.20, it can make a profit of $34. However, the firm can do better. When output is 5 units, *MC* equals $10. Since $MR = \$26$, the firm can increase its profits by producing more units. The increase in revenue exceeds the increase in costs. If output is increased to 6 units, profit increases to $48. Profit increases from $34 to $48 because the increase in revenue ($26) exceeds the increase in costs ($12) by $14. As long as $MR > MC$, the firm can do better by producing more output. Profit will be maximized when $MR = MC$. This occurs when output equals 7 units and profit is $54.

The graph in Exhibit 2a tells the same story. The line labeled $P = MR$ shows the marginal revenue (which is the same as price) of the firm. At any point along this line, the firm's total revenue equals the price times the quantity at that point. When $P = \$26$, profit is maximized where the $P = MR$ line intersects the *MC* curve—which occurs at an output level of 7 units. The vertical difference between the $P = MR$ line and the *ATC* curve at that point—the distance *bc*—shows profit per unit of output. Total profit is determined by multiplying this difference by the output of 7 units. Total profit is measured by the rectangle *abcd*.

The Loss-Minimizing Firm. Let us turn to the second case where the market price is not high enough for the firm to make a profit. Since the minimum *ATC* is $18, any lower market price must bring about losses. Consider a price of $16. The firm cannot make a profit. Instead, it must worry about minimizing its losses. Exhibit 3a and 3b uses the same cost figures, but columns 6, 7, and 8 of the table now reflect the lower $16 price. If the firm produced an output of zero, column 4

EXHIBIT 3 The Loss-Minimizing Firm

a. Short-Run Losses

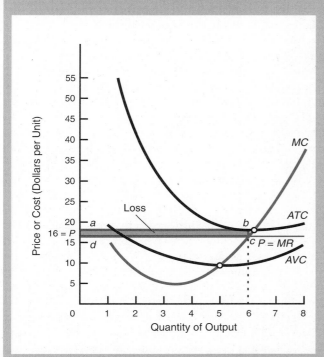

In this case, minimum *ATC* is $18, but *P* = $16. The firm loses money. But the firm minimizes its losses by adjusting output to 6 units, where *P* = *MC*. By shutting down, the firm would lose its fixed costs of $48. By producing where *P* = *MC*, the firm's losses are only $16 because the firm can cover not only its variable costs but also some portion of its fixed costs.

b. Cost and Revenue Schedules

Output (1)	Average Variable Cost (2)	Average Total Cost (3)	TC (4)	Marginal Cost (5)	P = Marginal Revenue (6)	Revenue (7)	Profit (8)
0	—	∞	$48		$16	0	−$48
				$20			
1	$20	$68	68	15	16	$16	−52
				10			
2	15	39	78	8	16	32	−46
				6			
3	12	28	84	5	16	48	−36
				4			
4	10	22	88	6	16	64	−24
				8			
5	9.6	19.2	96	10	16	80	−16
				12			
6	10	18	108	16	16	96	−12
				20			
7	11.4	18.3	128	26	16	112	−16
				32			
8	14	20	160	38	16	128	−32
				44			
9	17.3	22.7	204				

shows that total costs would still be $48—the firm's fixed costs do not go away if it shuts down. The firm's revenue would be zero, as shown in column 7, and its loss (its negative profit) would be −$48.

If the firm shuts down, it loses its entire fixed costs of $48. Can the firm do better? If the firm's revenue exceeds its variable costs, something will be left over to cover some portion of its fixed cost. If the firm can pay even a small portion of its fixed costs by staying in business, it is better off. The minimum AVC ($9.60) occurs when output is 5 units. By producing 5 units, the firm's price exceeds AVC by $6.40. The difference between the price and AVC generates revenues that can be used to cover some of the fixed costs. If the firm produced 5 units of output, its loss is −$16, as shown in column 8. At an output of 5 units, the firm is still not minimizing its losses. The price of $16 still exceeds the marginal costs of $10. An additional unit of output would add $16 to revenue and only $10 to costs. According to the profit-maximizing rule, the firm should produce more. The firm's losses are minimized when the output is 6 units, where $P = MC$. In panel (a), this occurs at point c, where the $P = MR$ line intersects the MC curve. The firm's losses *per unit of output* are measured by the distance bc, or $P − ATC = \$16 − \$18 = −\$2$. When it produces 6 units, the firm loses $2 per unit. The firm's total losses of −$12 (the 6 units times the $2 loss per unit) are shown by the rectangle $abcd$.

The Shutdown Case. In both cases so far, the price of the product exceeded the minimum AVC of $9.60. If the price falls short of the minimum AVC, what should the firm do? The firm should temporarily shut down. After all, if the price falls short of average variable cost, the firm's revenues must fall short of variable costs. In this case, it loses not only its fixed cost, but also that portion of its variable cost that is not covered by dollar sales. Thus, the firm's **shutdown rule** holds that output should be zero when the price is less than minimum average variable cost.

> The **shutdown rule** is: If the firm's price at all levels of output is less than average variable costs, it minimizes its losses by shutting down.

Exhibit 4 shows the competitive firm when the price is only $8. Column 8 in panel (b)'s table shows that its losses are minimized when output is zero. When the firm produces nothing, its losses are limited to its fixed cost of $48. Any additional output, since the price does not cover AVC, must increase the firm's losses. By producing the first unit, for example, the firm's AVC is $20. Since the price is only $8, the firm loses −$12 on the first unit. Thus, its losses increase from −$48 to −$60 as output rises from 0 to 1 unit. The $P = MR$ line is less than AVC for any output. The firm's losses are minimized when output equals zero. In column 8, its losses are −$48 for output equal to 0. For any positive level of output, the firm loses more money than by shutting down. In panel (a)'s graph, the price line $P = MR$ lies everywhere below the AVC curve.

The three cases explain the competitive firm's supply curve. The supply curve shows the output levels that competitive firms are prepared to supply at each price. In each case, the profit-maximizing level of output increased as the price increases.

The Industry Supply Curve

The behavior of the profit-maximizing firm explains the short-run behavior of the perfectly competitive industry of which it is a part. Recall that the short run is a period so short that old firms cannot build new plants and equipment; new firms cannot enter; old firms cannot leave. There are a fixed number of competitive

---

Perfectly competitive firms choose that level of output where $P = MC$—or, in graphical terms, where the P (=MR) line intersects the MC curve—provided price is greater than the minimum level of AVC. This holds whether the firm is maximizing its profit or minimizing its losses.

The competitive firm's supply curve (how much it is willing to sell at different prices) is that portion of the firm's MC curve above the AVC curve. It shows the profit-maximizing level of output for the firm at different price levels. Because the marginal cost curve is positively sloped, the competitive firm's supply curve is also positively sloped.

EXHIBIT 4   The Shutdown Case

a. Zero Output

The firm minimizes its losses by shutting down if the price is less than AVC. In this case, P = $8 and the minimum AVC is $9.60.

b. Cost and Revenue Schedules

Output (1)	Average Variable Cost (2)	Average Total Cost (3)	TC (4)	Marginal Cost (5)	P = Marginal Revenue (6)	Revenue (7)	Profit (8)
0	—	∞	$48		$8	0	−$48
				$20			
1	$20	$68	68	15	8	$8	−60
				10			
2	15	39	78	8	8	16	−62
				6			
3	12	28	84	5	8	24	−60
				4			
4	10	22	88	6	8	32	−56
				8			
5	9.6	19.2	96	10	8	40	−56
				12			
6	10	18	108	16	8	48	−60
				20			
7	11.4	18.3	128	26	8	56	−72
				32			
8	14	20	160	38	8	64	−96
				44			
9	17.3	22.7	204				

firms of given sizes. Each firm's supply curve is its MC curve above its AVC curve.

In the short run, the **market** or **industry supply curve** is the sum of the profit-maximizing or loss-minimizing outputs of every firm at each price. Exhibit 5 shows how the market supply curve is derived in the simple case of four identical firms, but the principles are the same for any number of firms. To simplify, we have considered an even simpler marginal cost curve than in the previous example.

> In the short run, the **market supply curve** is the horizontal summation of the supply curves of each firm, which in turn are their MC curves above minimum AVC.

The marginal cost curve (above AVC) for a single firm is shown as $S_1 = MC$. The firm wishes to sell 0 units at a price of \$15, 2 units at a price of \$20, 3 units at a price of \$25, 4 units at \$35, and 5 units at \$50. The curve S_4 shows the market supply curve for all four firms. Graphically, the market supply curve is the *horizontal* summation of each firm's supply curve. With four identical firms, no industry output is supplied at a price of \$15. At a price of \$20, 8 units are supplied (the four firms times 2 units each). At a price of \$50, the industry is prepared to supply 20 (four firms times 5 units each). The supply curves S_2 and S_3 show what the market supply curves would be with only two and three firms in the industry. Additional firms simply shift the market supply curve to the right.

EXHIBIT 5 The Market Supply Curve

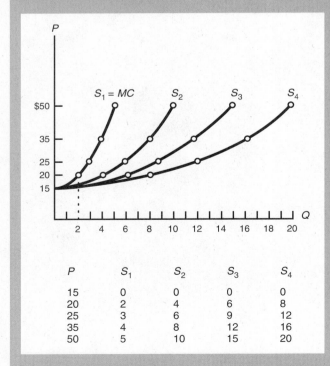

The market supply curve is the horizontal summation of each firm's supply curve. In the present simplified case, there are four identical firms. Each firm has the MC curve S_1. As additional firms are added, the supply curve shifts rightward to S_2 (for two firms), S_3 (for three firms), and finally to the market supply curve S_4 for all four firms.

P	S_1	S_2	S_3	S_4
15	0	0	0	0
20	2	4	6	8
25	3	6	9	12
35	4	8	12	16
50	5	10	15	20

Short-Run Equilibrium

The market or industry equilibrium is determined when the market price equilibriates the market supply with the market demand for the good. Exhibit 6 shows how the short-run equilibrium price is determined, using the hypothetical firm of Exhibits 2 through 4. Panel (a) shows the individual firm, and panel (b) an industry consisting of 1,000 such firms. The supply curve *S* in panel (b) is the horizontal summation of each firm's *MC* curve above *AVC*. For example, at the price $26 each firm sells 7 units and the industry sells 7,000 units. The market demand curve, *D*, intersects the market supply curve at the price of $26. At $26, the quantity demanded equals the quantity supplied (7,000). The $26 price becomes the firm's horizontal demand curve. In response to this price, the firm produces 7 units of the output, where the *MC* curve intersects its demand curve. The profit-maximizing behavior of the individual firm is consistent with the profit-maximizing behavior of all the firms in the market.

Panel (a) shows a representative firm that is *making an economic profit: ATC* at the profit-maximizing output level of 7 units is $18.30; therefore, the firm is making a per-unit profit of $7.70 (= $26 − $18.30) on each of the 7 units for a total of $54 economic profit. The representative firm could just as easily have made losses, because in the short run the firm will not shut down as long as it can pay part of its fixed costs.

EXHIBIT 6   Short-Run Equilibrium: The Firm and the Market

a. The Firm   b. The Market

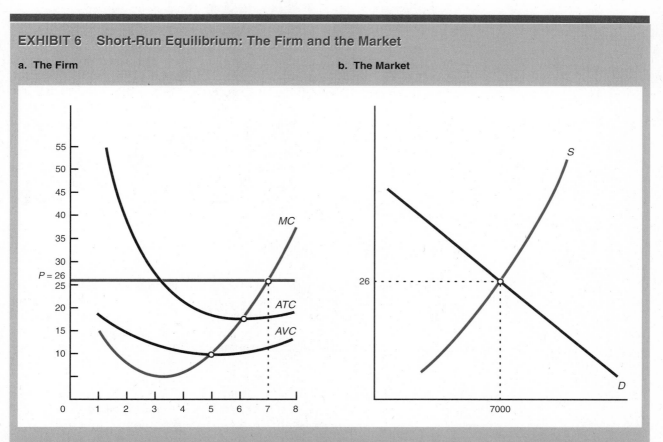

Panel (a) shows the representative firm; panel (b) shows the market, in which there are 1,000 firms. Firm demand is when market demand and supply are in equilibrium at the point of a $26 price and an equilibrium market output of 7,000 units. The individual firm produces 7 units of output and makes a profit of $54 ($7.70 × 7 units) from the per-unit profit of approximately $7.70.

LONG-RUN SUPPLY

The effect of economic profits on perfectly competitive industries is felt primarily in the long run when new firms can enter the industry and established firms can exit. As competitive firms respond to economic profits or losses, the industry short-run supply schedule shifts, and prices change.

Economic Profit Attracts Resources

Profit equals revenue minus costs. As noted in the preceding chapter, *economic profits* equal revenues minus opportunity costs, not just revenue minus accounting costs. *Opportunity costs* are the best alternatives sacrificed by the business firm when it engages in some particular production plan. *Included in these alternatives is the return that could be earned by the owner/entrepreneur if the owner's money capital, labor, and managerial time had been used elsewhere.* Economic losses are incurred when the return to the resources used in the business firm is less than the normal return those resources could earn in the next best alternative. When economic profits are zero, the business firm is earning a **normal profit**.

> A **normal profit** requires zero economic profit or accounting profit equal to a normal competitive return on the resources used in the firm.

The persistence of economic profits ($P > ATC$) or economic losses ($P < ATC$) is not a stable or equilibrium situation in the long run for a competitive industry. If economic profits continue, there will be an incentive in the long run for new firms to enter the industry. New firms will cause the price of the good to fall and economic profits to disappear. On the other hand, if there are economic losses, some firms will choose to exit from the industry. When long-term leases expire or an unprofitable plant can be sold, the firm no longer has these fixed costs and is free to leave the industry. The disappearance of firms will raise the price of the good and eliminate the losses. Thus, economic profits and losses tend to the normal level. Only when a normal profit is being earned will the industry be at rest—in long-run equilibrium. Long-run equilibrium occurs when firms no longer wish to either enter or leave the industry.

Entry and Exit

Perfectly competitive industries move toward normal profit by the entry and exit of firms. For the economy as a whole, entry and exit are opposite sides of the same coin. If it is profitable to enter one industry, resources must be exiting another industry. In other words, if revenue exceeds opportunity costs in some industries, revenue falls short of opportunity costs in other industries.

Entry. Consider the perfectly competitive industry consisting of 100 firms shown in panel (b) of Exhibit 7. Panel (a) shows the ATC and MC curves of a typical firm in this industry; ATC is the short-run average-total-cost curve in an efficient scale of plant. Panel (b) shows the market supply curve derived by summing the supply curves of 100 such firms. When the market demand curve is D, the equilibrium price is $10. At this price, the representative firm is making zero profits (a normal profit). The demand curve facing the representative firm is D_1; each of the 100 firms produces 7 units of the product, making for a market output

EXHIBIT 7   The Effect of Entry on Economic Profits

a. The Firm   b. The Industry

The initial long-run equilibrium is e_1, at the intersection of D and S in panel (b). When demand shifts to D', the short-run equilibrium price rises to \$12 (point a), creating economic profits for the individual firm facing the new demand curve D_2 in panel (a). In the long run, new firms enter until the supply curve shifts to S'. The long-run equilibrium is established at point e_2, where price again equals \$10. Each firm returns to producing 7 units of output, but the number of firms rises from 100 (700 ÷ 7) to 140 (980 ÷ 7).

of 700 units. The industry is in long-run equilibrium. With a normal profit, there is no inducement either to enter or exit.

Suppose that consumers increase their demand for the product, and the market demand curves shifts from D to D'. The short-run equilibrium price rises to \$12, and the short-run equilibrium output of the industry rises to 800 units. At this higher price, the firm's short-run equilibrium is now at 8 units of output, where price and marginal cost are equal. The typical firm now makes economic profits. In the short run, which may be a few months or many years, the individual firm will enjoy above-normal returns. This is not a long-run equilibrium because economic problems act as an inducement for new firms to enter the industry.

In the long run, above-normal profits will attract more firms. *As these new firms enter the market, the supply curve shifts to the right,* because the market supply is the sum of individual supply curves. The entry of new firms will continue as long as economic profits are positive. But as the supply curve shifts to the right (to S'), the market price falls, putting a squeeze on profits. Eventually, in the new long-run equilibrium, economic profits must again be zero. The new long-run (and short-run) equilibrium is e_2, which is at the old equilibrium price of \$10. In the new long-run equilibrium, the individual firm again produces 7 units, but there are now 140 such firms producing 7 units each (or 980 total units for the market as a whole).

Exit.   The reverse of entry is exit. Like entry, the exit of firms leads to a long-run equilibrium with the representative firm earning a normal profit. In part (b) of Exhibit 8, the initial demand and supply curves are D and S in panel (b). The

Long-Run Supply

EXHIBIT 8   The Effect of Exit on Economic Losses

a. The Firm   **b. The Industry**

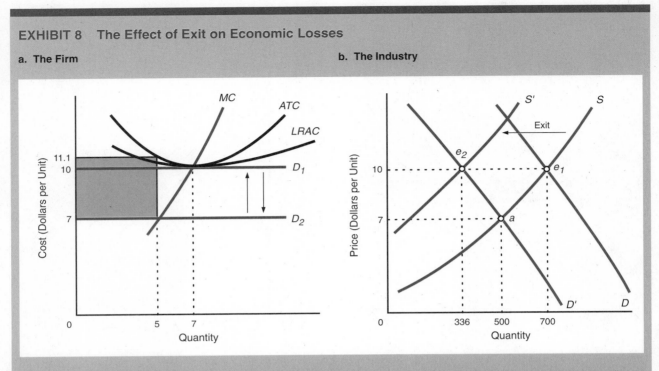

The initial long-run equilibrium is e_1, the intersection of D and S in panel (b). Demand drops to D', causing the short-run equilibrium price to fall to \$7 (point a). The representative firm in panel (a) makes losses as D_1 shifts downward to D_2. The exit of firms in the long run shifts the supply curve to S', which lifts the price back to \$10 and eliminates losses. Each firm returns to producing 7 units of output, but the number of firms falls from 100 (700 ÷ 7) to 48 (336 ÷ 7).

equilibrium is at e_1, which is both a short-run and a long-run equilibrium. There are 100 firms. Point e_1 is a short-run equilibrium point because, in Exhibit 8b, the market quantity supplied equals the market quantity demanded and because, in Exhibit 8a, $P = MC$ for the representative firm. The market is in long-run equilibrium because when price is \$10 (the firm demand curve is D_1), the representative firm makes a normal profit.

Suppose now that consumers reduce their demand for the product, and the market demand curve shifts from D to D' in Exhibit 8b. When the demand curve shifts from D to D', the short-run equilibrium shifts from e_1 to a. The short-run price falls to \$7, and the short-run quantity falls to 500 units, with the representative firm producing 5 units. Because \$7 is less than ATC, the representative firm has economic losses. In the long run, firms will begin to exit (the weaker ones first). The exit of firms shifts the industry supply curve to the left until economic losses are eliminated (at S'), and price is driven back up to the original \$10. The new equilibrium is at e_2, where total output is 336 units, and there are now only 48 firms, which again produce an average of 7 units each.

Characteristics of Long-Run Equilibrium

Exhibits 7 and 8 show a perfectly competitive market in long-run equilibrium. The industry is brought to a long-run equilibrium by entry in response to economic profits and exit due to losses. Consider the characteristics of this long-run equilibrium.

Perfectly competitive firms will operate at maximum efficiency (produce at minimum *LRAC*) in the long run. Long-run equilibrium occurs for the competitive industry when economic profits are zero and long-run average costs are minimized.

In the long run, the firm operates at an efficient scale of operation. The *ATC* curve for the optimal plant will have a minimum average cost equal to the minimum average cost on the long-run average-cost curve. The long-run equilibrium for the representative firm occurs at q_0, where $P = ATC = LRAC$.

When $P = MC$ and $P = ATC = LRAC$ at the long-run equilibrium output, and when MC intersects ATC at its *minimum point,* the perfectly competitive firm is producing at the lowest average cost in the long run.

Both forces together bring about *efficient* production, or production in which the good is being produced at the minimum cost to society. The firm in a competitive industry cannot be inefficient in the long run; the firm cannot select an inappropriate plant size. The plant size in Exhibit 7 must be the best possible size for producing 7 units, or the firm would not be around in the long run.

The Long-Run Industry Supply Curve

In Exhibits 7 and 8, increases or decreases in demand serve to raise or lower price in the short run. But in the long run, prices remain the same! In the case of Exhibit 7, the increase in demand is answered by an increase in supply that drives the price back down to the original level. Similarly, in Exhibit 8, the decrease in demand is answered by a decrease in supply that drives the price back up to the original level. The **long-run industry supply curve** determines what happens to price when demand changes.

> The **long-run industry supply curve** shows the quantities that the industry is prepared to supply at different prices *after* the entry or exit of firms is completed.

Constant-Cost Industries. The long-run industry supply curve corresponding to Exhibits 7 and 8 is perfectly elastic (horizontal) at the price of $10, which equals the minimum unit cost of production (minimum *LRAC*). The case of a perfectly elastic industry supply curve is illustrated in Exhibit 9, where S_L is the long-run industry supply curve. Shifts in demand, such as the shift from D to D', simply change the equilibrium quantity in the long run; there is no change in prices or costs. When shifts in demand do not change prices or cost in the long run, the industry is a **constant-cost industry**.

If the individual firms' cost curves remain the same when the industry expands (or contracts), the industry will be a constant-cost industry. Firms in constant-cost industries purchase labor, raw materials, lands, and the like at the same prices whether the industry is expanding or contracting. The constant-cost industry's demand for resources is a relatively small part of the total demand, and the industry's factor inputs usually are not highly specialized. (See Example 2)

> A **constant-cost industry** is relatively small and, hence, can expand or contract without significantly affecting the terms at which factors of production used in the industry are purchased. The long-run industry supply curve for a constant-cost industry is horizontal.

Increasing-Cost Industries. As the number of firms in an **increasing-cost industry** expands, the prices of the factors of production used by that industry are bid up. Industries whose factor purchases make up a large percentage of the market and industries that use factors of production specialized to that industry are

EXHIBIT 9   Long-Run Supply Curves

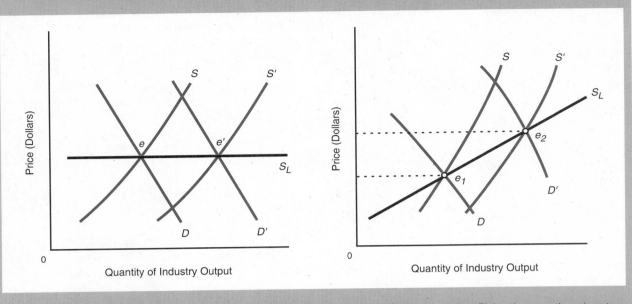

a. Constant-Cost Industry

b. Increasing-Cost Industry

Costs are constant for a constant-cost industry. In Panel (a), when demand increases, as from D to D', in a long run the price stays the same and only quantity increases as supply increases by a corresponding amount from S to S'. Price must stay the same to keep economic profits at zero. Thus, the long-run supply curve, S_L, is perfectly elastic. For an increasing-cost industry, costs increase when demand expands. In Panel (b), initially D and S are the demand and supply curves. When demand shifts to D', the long-run equilibrium price increases from p_1 to p_2. The entry of new firms and the rise in costs cause the short supply curve to shift only to S'. The long-run supply curve, S_L, is upwardly sloping but is still more elastic than the short-run supply curves, such as S or S'.

usually increasing-cost industries. Thus, when the industry is expanding, the individual firms must pay higher prices for their resources—so their costs of production will rise.

> As an **increasing-cost industry** expands, the factor prices of resources used in the industry are bid up. As the industry contracts, the prices of these factors fall. Hence, the long-run industry supply curve for an increasing-cost industry is upwardly sloping.

The long-run adjustment in an increasing-cost industry is illustrated in Exhibit 9. The equilibrium is initially at e_1, with the demand curve at D. The demand curve shifts to D', raising the price in the short run to the level indicated at point a. The typical firm now earns economic profits. New firms enter, the industry expands, and the price of the good itself falls, squeezing profits toward zero, as in a constant-cost industry. But factor prices are also bid up as the industry expands, and this increase in factor costs and the increase in the number of firms cause the supply curve to shift from S to S'. In the final equilibrium, indicated at e_2, profits have been squeezed to zero by the entry of new firms *and* rising costs. The long-run supply curve is shown as S_L.

Two of the most important characteristics of perfectly competitive industries are: (1) that perfectly competitive firms will operate at minimum average cost in

EXAMPLE 2

Competition, Freedom of Entry, and One-Hour Photo Processing

As recently as 10 years ago, people had to wait overnight for film to be developed. In the early 1980s, French and Japanese manufacturers revolutionized the photo-processing industry by developing low-cost minilabs that could fit into a corner space in a pharmacy or any other small retail establishment. When introduced, these minilabs required an investment of $33,000. As technology was perfected, the price of the minilabs dropped substantially.

The one-hour photo-processing business is characterized by minimal barriers to entry. Anyone who wants to enter the business can do so by buying the necessary equipment. The first entrepreneurs to offer one-hour processing made considerable, but transitory, profits. Later investors, attracted by these profits, entered the business and competed for customers without restriction.

Economic theory states that entry into competitive businesses will cease when all participants earn normal profits. The one-hour photo-processing industry reached this level of saturation in the early 1990s, when one-hour processing was available in virtually every pharmacy, in addition to specialized outlets.

the long run and (2) that perfectly competitive firms will produce that quantity of output at which price equals marginal cost in both the short run and the long run. These characteristics will be important to keep in mind when evaluating the other types of markets—monopoly, oligopoly, and monopolistic competition—that will be studied in the chapters that follow.

The next chapter will examine the behavior of firms that are able to exercise some control over price. Monopolists exercise considerable control over their prices; monopolistically competitive firms have only limited control over their prices.

Chapter Summary

The most important point to learn from this chapter is: In a perfectly competitive market, price equals marginal cost and, in the long run, competition forces firms to produce at the minimum point on their long-run average-cost curves.

1. A perfectly competitive market exists when there is a large number of sellers and buyers, when buyers and sellers have perfect information, when the product is homogeneous, and when there is freedom of entry and exit. These conditions ensure that each seller will be a price taker.

2. In the short run, the number of firms in the industry is fixed, and the firm has fixed costs. In the long run, the number of firms can change through entry and exit, and fixed costs become variable costs. If the market price covers average variable cost, the competitive firm will produce that quantity of output at which price and marginal cost are equal. The firm's supply curve is its marginal cost curve above average variable cost. The industry supply schedule is the horizontal summation of all the

Does the U.S. Need an Industrial Policy?

Critics of U.S economic policy argue that the United States has lost its competitive edge because it does not have an industrial policy. "Industrial policy" can mean a number of things, but in this context it means that the U.S. government should be actively involved in assisting companies or entire branches of the economy in their development. This assistance could be in the form of guaranteed loans, research-and-training grants, or tariff protection. Basically, the government would identify potential "winners" in the international marketplace and then give these winners the assistance they need to establish themselves in the world marketplace.

There are good reasons to oppose active industrial policy. Experience has shown that competitive markets do a good job in weeding out winners from losers. If a business has a good business plan, it will be able to convince private capital markets to fund it. It does not need government funding or subsidized funding if the idea is good. Private entrepreneurs are better at identifying and seeking out profit opportunities than are government bureaucrats sitting in Washington. A government agency in charge of picking winners would be more likely to pick losers than winners.

The most important business ideas and innovations have come from private entrepreneurs. The personal computer market, for example, was pioneered by lone individuals working out of their garages or basements. Larger computer companies passed up the opportunity to develop the personal computer and had to force their own bureaucracies to get involved in personal computers. Major innovations in automobile marketing and manufacturing were the results of Henry Ford's ideas at the turn of the century. The common feature of these innovations was that they were the result of the entrepreneurial drive of a small number of individuals working under competitive conditions. It is unlikely that this drive could be unleashed by an entrenched government bureaucracy, which would naturally favor the larger established firms, lacking in necessary entrepreneurial drive.

Advocates of U.S. industrial policy point to Japan, where the powerful Ministry for Industry and Trade (MITI) has purportedly provided the assistance and guidance that promoted the emergence of Japanese electronics and automotive manufacturers as world leaders.

Japan's industrial policy has not only been a small part of the economy, but the agency in charge, MITI, has been consistently wrong. For example, MITI first wanted only one automobile company. Market forces led them to continually revise their targets until MITI eventually recognized the need for seven automobile companies. The Japanese consumer products that have been so important on world markets (TVs, stereos, automobiles, and VCRs) are not the industries fostered by industrial policy in Japan in the last two decades. They targeted steel and semiconductors, but both industries have generated lower rates of return than other nontargeted industries. No one knows whether these industries created enough positive spillover effects on the rest of the Japanese economy to justify the subsidies.

supply schedules of individual firms in the industry. The price at which the quantity supplied equals the quantity demanded is the market price.

3. In the long run, firms enter competitive industries where economic profits are being made. They exit from industries where a below-normal profit is being earned. Economic profits must be zero for the competitive industry to be in equilibrium. In the long run, goods are produced at minimum average cost with price equal to marginal cost for the average competitive firm.

4. Constant-cost industries have horizontal long-run supply curves, increasing-cost industries have upwardly sloping long-run supply curves.

Key Terms

price taker (p. 434)
perfect competition (p. 435)
marginal revenue (*MR*) (p. 438)
profit-maximization rule (p. 438)
shutdown rule (p. 442)

market or industry supply curve (p. 444)
normal profit (p. 446)
long-run industry supply curve (p. 449)
constant-cost industry (p. 449)
increasing-cost industry (p. 449)

Questions and Problems

1.   A firm can sell all it wants at the price of $49.73. What is the firm's marginal revenue?

2.   A firm is contemplating whether to produce its 10th unit of output and finds its marginal costs for the 10th unit are $50 and its marginal revenue for the 10th unit equals $30. What advice would you give this firm?

3.   A firm has fixed costs of $100,000. It receives a price of $25 for each unit of output. Average variable costs are lowest (equal to $20) at 1,000 units of output. What advice would you give this firm? Would this advice be the same in the short run as in the long run?

4.   How is the firm's supply curve related to its marginal cost curve?

5.   The representative firm in the widget industry, which is perfectly competitive, is making a large economic profit. What predictions can you make about what will happen in this industry in the long run?

6.   What is the difference between a constant-cost industry and constant returns to scale (where the long-run average-cost curve is horizontal)?

7.   In the short run, explain what would happen to an industry's price and output if the demand for the product suddenly fell because of bad publicity.

8.   In Exhibit 1, the table shows fixed costs are $48. If fixed costs were raised to $60, how would the supply schedule be affected in the short run? How would the supply schedule be affected in the long run?

9.   Imagine that a firm faces the cost schedule given in Table A.
   a. Calculate the firm's profit or loss for each level of output when the price is $5.99, when the price is $6.01, and when the price is $10.01.
   b. How many units of output will the profit-

maximizing or loss-minimizing firm produce at those three prices?
   c. What is the firm's supply schedule?

TABLE A

Quantity, Q	Variable Cost, VC	Fixed Cost, FC	Total Cost, TC
0	$0	$5	$5
1	6	5	11
2	14	5	19
3	24	5	29
4	36	5	41

10.   You observe the (competitive) airline industry making economic losses. What do you expect to happen to ticket prices, to the quantity of airline passengers, and to the number of airline companies as time passes?

11.   You observe a highly profitable new industry producing a product of advanced technology (such as computers). What do you expect to happen to the price of the product, to profits, to the industry's output, and to the number of firms as time passes?

12.   Explain why, in the long run, the industry supply curve is perfectly horizontal in the case of a constant-cost industry.

13.   What is the key difference between a constant-cost industry and an increasing-cost industry?

14.   The long-run elasticity of supply for cucumbers is estimated to be 2.20. Is the cucumber industry a constant-cost industry? Explain.

15.   If dry cleaning is a constant-cost industry, what would you expect to happen to the price of dry cleaning in a particular town in both the short run and the long run as the size of the town increases?

Doing Economics

Consider the retail market for gasoline in your city. How closely does it approximate the textbook conditions for

perfect competition? Now go out and observe the price of regular unleaded gasoline at ten or more stations. As you record your price data, you may wish to note the location and chain name of each station, as well as any other particular distinguishing characteristics. In a perfectly competitive market, each seller charges the same price. Do your data support the hypothesis that the local gasoline market is perfectly competitive? How would you explain any price variation that you may have observed? Do you think that sellers in this market face perfectly elastic demand curves? Do you think that they make economic profits?

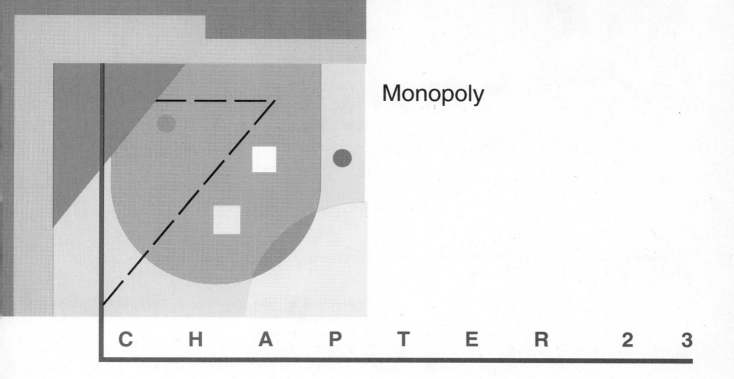

Monopoly

CHAPTER FOCUS The word "monopoly" evokes the image of evil capitalists oppressing downtrodden consumers with high prices. Monopoly brings to mind oil-rich countries forcing high prices on consumers in both rich and poor countries, of greedy pharmaceutical firms treading on the poor and the sick with outrageous drug prices, and of cable-TV companies with ever-increasing monthly charges.

Economists, heeding the early warnings of Adam Smith in 1776, emphasize the dangers of monopoly. A monopoly raises prices, restricts output, and reduces economic efficiency. The invisible hand works best when competition is present. It does not work effectively when markets are monopolized.

Monopolies can arise for a number of reasons. They can be dictated by technology: One firm produces output much more efficiently than two or more firms. Surprisingly, a major source of monopoly is government. Governments, through licenses, franchises, and other means, can create monopoly markets. In fact, much of the activity of lobbyists at the local, state, and federal levels devoted to receiving monopoly rights to produce and sell some output.

After studying this chapter, you will be able to:

- Discuss the conditions giving rise to monopoly.
- Calculate marginal revenue for a monopolist
- See how the monopolist maximizes profit.
- Understand that a profit-maximizing monopoly cannot be efficient from a social standpoint.

CHARACTERISTICS OF MONOPOLY

Literally, *monopoly* means "single seller." The definition of monopoly focuses on the conditions necessary for there to be only one producer in the market and on the control over price which that one producer has.

Definition of Monopoly

A **pure monopoly** has the following characteristics.

A **pure monopoly** exists
1. when there is one seller in the market for some good or service that has no close substitutes,
2. when the seller has considerable control over price, and
3. when barriers to entry protect the seller from competition.

Like perfect competition, examples of monopoly in this pure form are rare, but the theory of pure monopoly does shed light on the behavior of firms that approximate the conditions of pure monopoly. Many firms possess at least a little bit of monopoly power. For example, a corner at a particularly busy intersection may be the best spot in town for a service station, and only one firm can occupy that spot. For purposes of clarity our discussion will focus on firms with a great deal of monopoly power.

Limitations on Monopoly Power

"Pure" monopoly is hard to find in the real world for several reasons. First, substitutes of some kind exist for almost all products. National magazines and TV news substitute for local newspapers; stainless steel and copper substitute for aluminum; aluminum foil substitutes for cellophane; foreign imports substitute for domestically produced goods. A pure monopoly requires that there be no good substitutes, but where does one draw the line between good and poor substitutes? Modern technology is good at creating new products to substitute for a monopoly product.

Second, a sole supplier in a particular market may not act like a pure monopolist if it fears that rival firms may enter the market. If the monopolist's economic profits become too high, rivals may find ways to overcome existing barriers to entry. In other words, there is the competition from *potential* substitutes.

Joan Robinson (1903–1983)

Joan Robinson, born in England in 1903, was the daughter of Major General Sir Frederick Maurice and Helen Marsh. She married the economist E. A. G. Robinson in 1926 and began a long teaching career at Cambridge University in the same decade. Her most important work, *The Economics of Imperfect Competition,* was published in 1933. In that masterpiece she completed the Marshallian tradition by examining the detailed consequences of monopoly and monopolistic competition for the pricing of both goods and factors. She was one of the first economists to point to the advantages of price discrimination. She argued: "It may happen, for instance, that a railway would not be built, or a country doctor would not set up in practice, if discrimination were forbidden."

While in her seventies, she traveled for one month in central Africa. The economist Luigi Pasinetti remarked that it was amazing how she endured ". . . living in most primitive conditions with raw food, lack of facilities and exposure to harsh tropical weather, day and night."

Joan Robinson contributed to many areas of economics—international trade, macroeconomics, Marxian economics, the theory of wages, and economic growth. She was perhaps the greatest economist to deserve—but not receive—the Nobel Prize before she died.

Barriers to Entry

If new firms could freely enter the market, there would be no monopoly. In cases where a single firm is earning an economic profit, additional firms would enter, thereby destroying the monopoly. To exist as a monopoly, the existing monopoly must be protected in some manner from the entry of new firms into the market.

The basic source of any monopoly power is the presence of *barriers to entry*. A barrier to entry is anything that gives the existing firm an advantage over new firms that might seek to enter the market. Five factors tend to give existing firms advantages over new entrants. They are:

1. economies of scale,
2. patents,
3. exclusive ownership of raw materials,
4. public franchises, and
5. licensing.

Economies of Scale. New firms enter markets at smaller levels of output than established firms. If the industry is characterized by economies of scale, the average costs of the new firm will be higher than the average costs of an established firm. The lower average costs of large established firms (the result of economies of scale) protects them from the entry of new firms. The established firm can offer goods to the market at a lower price due to its lower production costs. A *natural monopoly* illustrates the case when the cost advantages of established firms are extreme. A natural monopoly occurs when economies of scale are so large that there is room for only one firm in the industry. Competition is either unworkable or highly inefficient. Examples of possible natural monopolies are the local public utilities that deliver telephone services, gas services, water services, and electricity.

Patents. American *patent* laws allow an inventor the exclusive right to use the invention for a period of seventeen years. During that period, the patent prohibits others from using the invention; the patent holder is protected from competition. The IBM Corporation's patents on tabulating equipment, the Xerox Corporation's patents on copying equipment, the United Shoe Machinery Company's patents on shoemaking machinery, and Smith Kline's patent on the drug Tagamet are examples of this type of entry barrier. The Bell System (now AT&T) achieved a monopoly in the nineteenth century when Alexander Graham Bell was granted a patent just hours before a rival inventor. Even if rival firms wish to enter the market, they are not legally allowed to do so. The patent-holding firm has a legal monopoly to the product as long as the patent remains in effect.

Exclusive Ownership of Raw Materials. Established companies may be protected from the entry of new firms by their control of critical inputs or raw materials. The International Nickel Company of Canada used to own virtually all the world's nickel reserves; virtually all the sales of the world's diamond mines are under the control of the DeBeers Company of South Africa.

Public Franchises. State, local and federal governments grant to individuals or organizations exclusive *franchises* to be the sole operator in a particular business. Competitors are legally prohibited from entering the market. The U. S. Postal Service is a classic example of a public franchise. According to its franchise, only the U. S. Postal Service has the right to deliver and pick up postage from patrons' postal boxes. Along tollways, the state grants exclusive franchises to operate restaurants and service stations; duty-free shops in airports and at international borders are also franchise operations. Most public utilities operate under state or local franchises.

Licensing. Entry into an industry or profession may be regulated by government agencies and by autonomous professional organizations. The Federal Communications Commission licenses radio and television stations and controls entry into the lucrative broadcasting industry. Most countries license airlines and, thus, limit entry into the industry. Every state regulates attorneys, nurses, teachers, physicians, and real-estate agents.

HOW MONOPOLISTS MAXIMIZE PROFITS

The most fundamental difference between monopoly and perfect competition is that the competitive firm must accept whatever price the market dictates. The perfectly competitive firm is literally a *price taker,* while the monopolist is a **price maker**. The monopolist has its own market demand curve. Thus, the monopolist has the problem of searching the demand curve for the profit-maximizing price. Such price-making behavior is not restricted to just *pure* monopolies. Even the local grocery store has some control over price and must determine the right price.

> A **price maker** is a firm with the ability to control to some degree the price of the good or service it sells.

Exhibit 1 illustrates the difference between price takers and price makers. The demand curve facing the price taker, panel (a), is perfectly elastic because the price is dictated by the market and because more units can be sold without lowering the

EXHIBIT 1   Price making Versus Price Taking

a. The Price Taker

b. The Price Maker

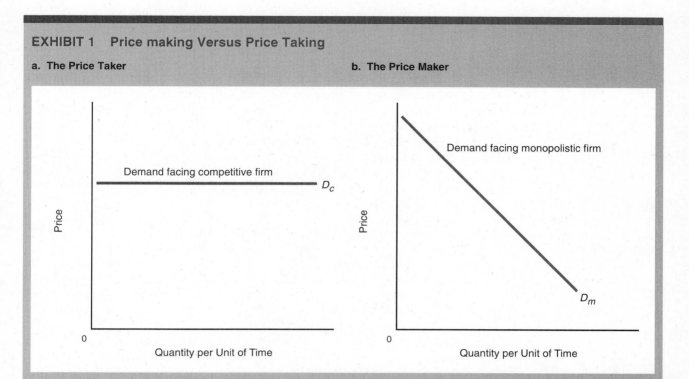

In panel (a), the demand curve D_c facing the competitive firm is perfectly horizontal, meaning that the firm can sell additional units without lowering its price. The price taker can sell all it wants at the going market price. In panel (b), the demand curve D_m facing the monopolistic firm is downward-sloping.

price. In contrast, the price-making firm, shown in panel (b), must lower its price on all units sold in order to sell more.

Price and Marginal Revenue

In the previous chapter we defined **marginal revenue** as the extra revenue generated by a unit increase in output. To a perfectly competitive, price-taking firm, the price of the good in the market measures the marginal revenue to the firm. To the monopolist, or price maker, price no longer measures marginal revenue. Let's consider why this is so.

> Marginal revenue *(MR)* is the increase in revenue divided by the increase in output caused by the change in price; in other words, it is the additional revenue raised per unit increase in quantity sold.

The monopolist, unlike the price taker, faces a negatively sloped demand curve. This means that the monopolist *must lower price in order to sell more output.* The perfectly competitive firm can sell all it wants at the market price. It need not have a lower price to sell more. Take the case of the monopolist who wishes to produce more output. To sell that extra output, the monopolist must lower price on all units sold. The effect on the monopolist's revenue from producing more output is uncertain. By selling more units of output, the monopolist's revenue expands, but having to sell at a lower price contracts revenue. Marginal revenue tells which effect dominates.

Marginal revenue tells what happens to revenue when output is changed by a small amount. Equivalently, marginal revenue tells what happens to revenue when price is changed by a small amount. Marginal revenue is the ratio of the change in revenue divided by the change in output brought about by the change in price.

The fact that price makers must lower the price to sell additional units of output means that marginal revenue must be less than price. When a price maker sells one more unit, the extra revenue generated equals the (new) price of the extra unit minus the loss in revenue from having to reduce the price on output that was previously sold at a higher price. In other words, price exceeds marginal revenue because a new but larger output "spoils the market" for the old output level that was previously sold at a higher price.

For a price maker, price is greater than marginal revenue: $P > MR$.

For example, suppose a price maker faces a demand schedule in which one unit per week can be sold if the price is $19; two units can be sold if the price is $17. The total revenue is the number of units multiplied by the price per unit for that quantity. When the number of units sold is 1, revenue is $19 (= $19 × 1); when the number of units sold is 2, revenue is $34(= $17 × 2). Marginal revenue is the extra revenue raised by increasing output by one unit. Therefore, the change in revenue can be calculated by comparing revenues at each output level. The marginal revenue of a change from one to two units is $34 − $19 = $15.

This example illustrates why price is greater than marginal revenue for the price maker. The price of the second unit ($17) is greater than the marginal revenue for the second unit ($15). To sell the second unit, the firm must lower price on both the first and second units from $19 to $17. The firm gains $17 in revenue on the sale of the second unit but loses $2 on the sale of the first unit. Hence, the marginal revenue of the second unit is $17 − $2 = $15. In effect, selling one more unit spoiled the market on the first unit because the price falls.

Marginal revenue per additional unit sold is measured by taking the ratio of the change in revenue to the change in total units sold brought about by the change in price. It is not necessary to change the number of units sold by only one unit, as in the above example. To illustrate, imagine that a producer of chocolates can sell 500 boxes at $10 per box and 600 boxes at $9 per box. At a price of $10, the firm's revenue would be $5,000; at a price of $9, the firm's revenue is $5,400. The change in revenue is $400 and the change in quantity sold is 100. Thus, the marginal revenue is $MR = \$400/100 = \$4$. Again, notice that the marginal revenue of $4 is less than the new $9 price.

Monopoly Equilibrium in the Short Run

Consider now the profit-maximizing strategy of a pure monopolist. We will study the case of the short run, where the monopolist has fixed plant and equipment. The key to monopoly is that each firm has its own demand curve and that to sell more of its product the price must be lowered. To the monopolist, the law of demand means that it cannot have both higher prices *and* a higher output. The monopolist faces a tradeoff between higher prices or higher output. (See Example 1.)

The previous chapter gave a general rule for the profit-maximizing firm—be it a price taker or a price maker. This rule gives the optimal strategy for any firm:

The price-making firm should lower price as long as the marginal revenue of the extra output sold exceeds the marginal cost of production.

Any firm should undertake those actions that raise revenues more than costs. If producing an extra unit adds more to revenues than to costs, the firm's profits are raised (or losses reduced).

Exhibit 2 shows the profit-maximizing strategy of a monopolist. The cost figures are the same as those studied in Exhibit 3 in the chapter on "Costs and

EXAMPLE 1

What Price for a Cancer Cure?

Ever since studies by the National Cancer Institute concluded that taxol, a substance that comes from the Pacific yew tree, provides an effective treatment for ovarian and lung cancer, cancer patients have waited for its appearance on the market. Up until November 1992, taxol was available only on an experimental basis from the National Cancer Institute.

In November 1992, taxol was approved for release on the open market. The drug company with the monopoly right to market taxol decided to sell taxol at a monthly cost of $300 to users. Although there was a public outcry about the high price of taxol, many desperate patients, who saw in it a chance for cure, would have been willing to pay much more for treatment.

How did the drug company settle on the $300 per month price? Just as in the case of other products, the company had to consider the tradeoff between higher prices and a smaller number of units sold. A $1,000-per-month price would have discouraged too many users, who understand its experimental nature. Monopolists price their product so as to achieve a maximum profit. In the case of taxol, the marginal cost of producing more taxol is very high because of the limited supply of Pacific yews. The profit-maximizing monopolist will restrict sales to that level at which the marginal revenue from more sales just equals the marginal costs of producing more output.

Even a monopolist producing an essential product does not charge the highest possible price. If the price is too high, too few units are sold and profits will not be maximized.

Productivity." The new information is the demand curve, shown as the downward-sloping D curve in panel (b) and in columns 1 and 2 of panel (a) in Exhibit 2. Nothing is demanded at a price of $46. When the price is $41, one unit is demanded. To sell two units, the price must be lowered to $36, and so forth. Column 3 shows the revenue produced at each level of output ($P \times Q$), and column 4 shows marginal revenue at each output level. In panel (b), MR is the **marginal revenue curve**. It shows that for any output level price P exceeds MR.

> The **marginal revenue curve** shows how much marginal revenue is at each level of output.

The marginal revenue values in column 4 of Exhibit 2a are positioned vertically between the rows corresponding to the relevant output levels. Each number that appears in color in column 4 is the marginal revenue when output increases by 2 units. For example, the MR for the output level 3 is determined by raising output from 2 units to 4 units. Increasing the output from 2 units to 4 units raises revenue from $72 to $104. The increase in revenue is $32. Since marginal revenue is the increase in revenue divided by the increase in output, MR is $16 (= $32/2).

Exhibit 2's cost figures are just the ATC and MC studied in previous chapters. Like the marginal-revenue values in Exhibit 2a's column 4, the marginal-cost values in column 7 are shown in between the relevant output levels. Again, each number in color represents the marginal cost of increasing output by 2 units (one above and one below the given output level).

EXHIBIT 2 Monopoly Equilibrium

a. Cost and Revenue Schedules

Output (units), Profit = Q (1)	Price or Average Revenue, P = AR (2)	Total Revenue, TR = P × Q (3) = (1) × (2)	Marginal Revenue, MR (4)	Average Total Cost, ATC (5)	Total Cost, TC (6)	Marginal Cost, MC (7)	Profit = TR − TC, (8) = (3) − (6)
0	$46	$ 0		∞	$ 48		−$48
			41			20	
1	41	41	36	$68	68	15	−27
			31			10	
2	36	72	26	39	78	8	−6
			21			6	
3	31	93	16	28	84	5	9
			11			4	
4	26	104	6	22	88	6	16
			1			8	
5	21	105	−4	19.2	96	10	9
			−9			12	
6	16	96	−14	18	108	16	−12
			−19			20	
7	11	77	−24	18.3	128	26	−41
			−29			32	
8	6	48		20	160		−112

b. Monopoly Profit

The table in panel (a) shows the demand and marginal-revenue schedules of a price maker. The demand schedule is given in the first two columns. Because all customers are charged in the same price, price and average revenue are the same. Revenue—in column 3—equals P × Q. Marginal revenue is the increase in total revenue brought about by increasing output by 1 unit. Panel (b) shows the same data in graphical form. The downward-sloping demand curve is D and the marginal revenue curve is MR. The monopolist's profit is maximized by producing 4 units of output, where profit equals $16, and the monopolist charges a price equal to $26. A lower or higher price brings smaller profits.

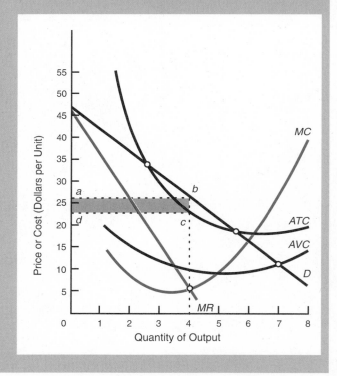

The monopolist has an incentive to lower price and expand output when marginal revenue exceeds marginal cost. Suppose our monopolist is charging $41—the highest price possible without losing all customers. At $P = \$41$, the firm is losing money because $P < ATC$. The firm's losses are $-\$27$. If the firm lowers its price to $36, its revenue increases by $31, and its cost increases by only $10. By lowering the price, the firm cuts its losses to $-\$6$. A price of $36 is better for the monopolist than a price of $41.

The $36 price is still not the "best" price for the monopolist. It pays the firm to continue to lower the price. When it lowers the price to sell 3 units, the firm's MR exceeds MC. The firm finally maximizes its profit by lowering the price to $P = \$26$ and producing exactly 4 units of output. At this point, $MC = MR = \$6$. To expand output any further lowers profit because costs rise by more than revenue. The firm's maximum profit is $16, which is achieved by charging a price of $26 and selling 4 units of output.

To maximize profit, the monopolist selects that output at which marginal revenue and marginal cost are equal. In Exhibit 2b, the MR and MC curves intersect at a point below the demand curve (because for a monopolist MR is less than P). To determine the price that maximizes profit, simply draw a vertical line through the intersection of MR and MC until it meets the demand curve. The vertical line drawn at 4 units of output meets the demand curve at $P = \$26$—the profit-maximizing price. Profit per unit of output is measured by the distance bc between the price and average total cost. Total profit is shown by the shaded rectangle $abcd$, which is the amount of output multiplied by the profit per unit.

The Loss-Minimizing Monopolist

In the short run, the monopolist need not make a profit. Exhibit 3 shows a case in which at the price where $MC = MR$ the monopolist is making a loss. With the given demand and marginal revenue curves, the firm's loss-minimizing price and output are $P = \$23$ and $Q = 3$ units, respectively. The firm's $ATC = \$28$ at that output, and thus is losing $5 per unit produced. It pays the firm to produce 3 units instead of 0 units because it is more than covering its variable costs (AVC is less than P at that point).

Being a monopoly does not guarantee automatic economic profits. Every patent issued by the U.S. patent office is a monopoly, but only a handful of those patents issued are actually used because price is less than average cost for most patentholders. Monopolies can incur losses just like competitive firms. The major distinction is that monopoly profits have a tendency to persist over time, while the above-normal profits of competitive firms are squeezed out by the entry of new firms.

Monopoly Profits in the Long Run

When there is competition in an industry, the distinction between the short run and the long run is critical. In the short run, the number of firms in the industry is fixed; in the long run, new firms can enter the industry or old firms can exit in response to economic profits or losses. The long-run entry and exit of firms ensures that economic profits will be squeezed out of perfectly competitive industries.

In the case of the monopolist, the long-run/short-run distinction is not as important because barriers to entry prevent new firms from entering the industry and squeezing out monopoly profits. There is no automatic tendency for monopoly profits to be eliminated by the *entry of new firms*.

Monopolies maximize short-run profits, or they minimize short-run losses, by producing where $MC = MR$. The monopoly price is not the highest price possible, but it exceeds the marginal cost of production.

EXHIBIT 3   A Loss-Minimizing Monopolist

The monopolist is minimizing losses by producing where *MC* = *MR* at *Q* = 3 units because at that point *P* > *AVC*. Its losses are equal to the rectangle *abcd*.

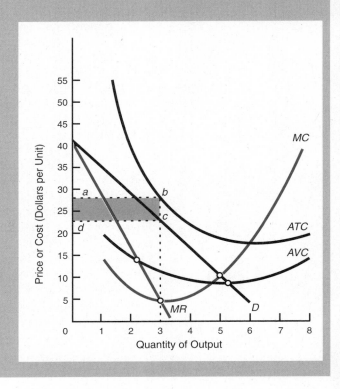

Unlike competitive profits, monopoly profits can persist for long periods of time.

In the real world, it is difficult to find pure monopolies because of actual or potential substitutes and because absolute barriers to entry are rarely present. Exceptional monopoly profits have historically promoted the development of closer substitutes for the monopolist's product. The railroads' monopoly over freight transportation was eventually broken by the development of trucking and air freight; AT&T's monopoly over long-distance telephone service was broken by the advent of microwave transmission.

Although monopoly profits will not automatically be driven down to the normal return, there is a tendency for high monopoly profits to promote the development of substitutes in the very long run. (See Example 2.)

Price Discrimination

Thus far this chapter has dealt with price makers who charge the same price to all buyers. This is not necessarily the case. Customers often pay different prices for the same product. Movie prices are often lower for senior citizens; doctors and lawyers often charge wealthy clients more than poor clients; airlines charge business travelers higher fares by requiring advance ticket purchases and minimum stays for discounts. All of these situations are examples of **price discrimination**.

Price discrimination exists when the same product or service is sold at different prices to different buyers.

EXAMPLE 2

Intel's Microprocessor Monopoly

Intel Corporation's 80386 microprocessor is the chip of choice for IBM and IBM-compatible computers. Microprocessors are fingernail-sized wafers of silicon containing circuitry that functions as a personal computer's brain. Intel's virtual monopoly of the microprocessing industry stems from its Microcode patent, the strength of its brand-name identification (the 80386 name), and its reputation for technological innovation. Advances in processing speed and reductions in the cost of Intel's microprocessors have resulted in a steep drop in personal computer prices over the past decade.

Intel's monopoly is facing challenges on several fronts. First, Advanced Micro Devices has used reverse engineering to develop an 80386 clone with different circuity that mimics the 80386. Second, Advanced Micro has received permission to call its reverse-engineered microprocessor the 80386. Third, Intel has been charged with antitrust violations by companies seeking to develop their own microprocessors. Intel has responded to these challenges with an attempt to maintain its monopoly by producing better chips. Its new microprocessor will run 51 percent faster and cost 34 percent less than previous versions.

This example illustrates the constant challenges faced by firms in monopoly positions. The most effective way to preserve a monopoly is to continually innovate and produce better products than potential competitors.

Not all monopolists can engage in price discrimination. They can do so only if a number of conditions are met. These conditions are:

1. The seller must exercise some control over the price (price discrimination is possible only for price makers).
2. The seller must be able to distinguish easily among different types of customers.
3. It must be impossible for one buyer to resell the product to other buyers.

If the firm is not a price maker, it cannot control its price. The seller who cannot distinguish between customers will not know which buyers should be charged the lower price. The electric company meters electricity usage and can readily distinguish high-volume from low-volume users; doctors and lawyers can often identify wealthy clients on the basis of appearance, home address, and stated profession. By placing advance-purchase and minimum-stay requirements on tickets, airlines can create conditions that many business travelers cannot meet. If one buyer can sell to another, low-price buyers can sell to high-price buyers, and no one will be willing to pay the high price. For example, poor clients cannot resell legal and medical services to the wealthy; industrial users of electricity cannot sell their electricity to households; airline tickets with a one-week-minimum-stay requirement cannot be sold to someone departing on a two-day business trip. (See Example 3.)

If the above conditions are met, the seller can divide the market into distinct groups. A profit-maximizing seller will then charge prices according to the price elasticity of demand of each group. A low price elasticity means the buyer is less sensitive to price than a buyer with a relatively high price elasticity. If residential users of electricity have a more elastic demand for electricity than industrial users, it pays the electric company to charge a higher price to the less price-sensitive industrial users. If business travelers have a lower price elasticity of demand, the airlines will charge them higher prices.

EXAMPLE 3

Price Discrimination: Manufacturer's Coupons

Grocery shoppers are familiar with manufacturer's coupons that arrive through the mail or can be clipped out of the daily newspaper. Economic theory explains why some manufacturers offer coupons and others do not. In effect, the holder of the coupon is entitled to buy the product at a lower price than others. If Nabisco places a coupon offering 50 cents off one of their cereals in the daily newspaper, this means that you can buy the cereal at a lower price than other shoppers. Manufacturer's coupons are a form of price discrimination. The coupon issuer reasons as follows: Anyone taking the trouble to cut out the coupon has a higher elasticity of demand than other shoppers. Without the 50 cents off, many shoppers would not buy the cereal. The 50-cent price reduction, therefore, brings about a substantial increase in quantity purchased from careful shoppers. Shoppers not taking the trouble to clip out the coupon have a lower price elasticity of demand. Their purchases are not strongly affected by the 50-cent reduction. We have seen that price discrimination is possible only when the manufacturer has price-making power, when high-price-elasticity customers can be identified, and when low-price buyers cannot resell the product. Manufacturer's coupons follow this pattern. Typically, manufacturers in highly concentrated markets (with only a few sellers), such as cereal or soap manufacturers, offer coupons. Such manufacturers exercise significant market power. Requiring coupons to obtain the lower price allows manufacturers to differentiate high-elasticity from low-elasticity customers. Although low-price buyers could theoretically sell to high-price buyers, the price difference usually is not big enough to cause this to happen.

> When price discrimination is possible, the higher is the price elasticity of demand, the lower will be the price charged.

To see how price discrimination raises profits and why the price varies with demand elasticity, take the case of an electric utility that charges the same price in both residential and industrial markets. Assume the demand of residential users is more price elastic than is the demand of industrial users. Why is this monopolist not gaining the maximum profit possible?

Recall that marginal revenue is less than price because it is necessary to cut the price on all units to sell additional output. The more elastic is demand, the smaller the cut in price necessary to stimulate a unit increase in quantity demanded. Thus, at the same price, the electric company's marginal revenue from selling another unit to residential customers would exceed its marginal revenue from selling another unit to industrial customers. Accordingly, it would pay the firm to shift output from industrial users to residential users by raising the industrial price and lowering the residential price. The process of raising the price to the users with a low price elasticity of demand and lowering price to users with a high price elasticity of demand would continue until the marginal revenue the firm earns in each market is the same.

MONOPOLY AND EFFICIENCY

Most economists believe that competition is more efficient than monopoly. Let us first see why competition is efficient.

The Case of Perfect Competition

The chapter on perfect competition demonstrated that perfectly competitive markets produce output at minimum average cost in the long run. It did not point out another property of perfect competition that leads to an efficient outcome: Market equilibrium in perfectly competitive markets brings about the right balance between consumer utility and the costs of production.

Perfect competition forces firms to produce where price equals marginal cost. The price consumers pay measures the *marginal benefit* they receive from consuming another unit. Marginal cost measures the *opportunity cost society pays to produce another unit of the good*. When price equals marginal cost, there is **economic efficiency** because consumers are buying what they want at the minimum cost to society. When the economy is efficient, the resources of society are being used in such a way that the total economic pie is as large as possible. When efficiency prevails, to give one person a larger slice of the economic pie means someone else must get a smaller slice. When the economy is inefficient, a larger pie can be produced and everyone gets a larger piece.

> **Economic efficiency** is present when society's resources are so organized that it is impossible to make everyone better off by *any* reallocation of resources; in other words, making one person better off must be at the expense of someone else.

Monopoly and Contrived Scarcity

The basic argument against monopoly is that monopolies maximize profit by restricting output to the scale where price exceeds marginal cost. Remember that monopolies maximize profit where $MR = MC$, but $P > MR$. Therefore, price will exceed marginal cost at that output which maximizes monopoly profit. Perfectly competitive industries, on the other hand, produce that quantity of output at which $P = MC$. This means that if everything else is equal, perfectly competitive industries tend to produce more output and sell at a lower price than monopolists. Monopoly restricts output to obtain a profit-maximizing price. By restricting output —or *contriving scarcity*—monopolists produce less output than is socially optimal.

We compare the monopoly outcome with the perfect competition outcome in Exhibit 4. We consider an industry in which a single monopoly producer can produce output at exactly the same average cost as a large number of perfectly competitive firms (there are no economies of scale; average costs are the same for all levels of output). Average cost and marginal cost are the same: $AC = MC$. Marginal cost ($= AC$) is a constant \$4 per unit.

If the industry were organized as a monopoly, it would produce 300 units of output because at that output level MR equals MC. Both equal \$4. The monopoly would sell the 300 units at the monopoly price of \$7. Monopoly profits are represented by the color shaded area, which equals \$900.

If the industry were perfectly competitive, free entry would squeeze out any economic profits. Free entry would cause output to expand to 600 units, at which point price (\$4) would equal marginal cost (\$4) and economic profits would disappear (the price of \$4 equals average cost).

Monopolies are *inefficient* because they restrict output so as to be able to sell at a price greater than marginal cost. Why is $P > MC$ an inefficient outcome? We consider only the case where there are no externalities (Chapter 4), so that private and social values or costs coincide. Price measures marginal benefit to consumers, and marginal cost measures marginal cost to society; therefore, when $P > MC$, society gains by producing more of the monopolized good. A monopolized good is characterized by **contrived scarcity** because too little is produced. The economy

The direct comparison of monopoly and perfect competition demonstrates that, under identical cost conditions, a monopoly produces less output and charges a higher price than a perfectly competitive industry. The monopoly restricts output and sells at a price that is greater than marginal cost. The perfectly competitive industry does not restrict output and sells at a price equal to marginal cost.

EXHIBIT 4　Monopoly and Competition Compared

This industry has constant returns to scale where $AC = MC = \$4$ for all levels of output. If the industry were perfectly competitive, price would be $4 and output would be 600 units. If this industry were a single-firm monopoly, price would be $7 and output would be 300 units, with a monopoly profit of $900 (= $3 × 300). Monopoly profit is the grey area. The monopolist creates profits by the contrived scarcity of 300 units (the monopolist produces 300 units less than the competitive industry). The loss from contrived scarcity is the white area.

would be better off—more efficient in the sense of making it possible to give more to everyone—if more of the monopolized good were produced. This can be demonstrated in Exhibit 4 where the monopoly firm sells its 300 units of output at a price of $7—the $7 price is $3 greater than the marginal cost of $4. Society values an extra unit of output at $7, while it costs only $4 to produce an extra unit of output. Price greater than marginal cost signals a social opportunity. If $P > MC$, there is a social payoff to producing more of the good. Remember that marginal cost is the opportunity cost at the margin—what is being given up elsewhere. To say that price exceeds marginal cost is to say that the resources used in the production of this particular good have a higher marginal benefit to society than those resources have elsewhere because marginal costs measure opportunity costs.

> **Contrived scarcity** is the production of less than the economically efficient quantity of a good by a monopoly.

When $P > MC$, one more unit of output adds more to social welfare than to social costs, and it is possible make everyone better off by producing more of the monopolized good (and less of other goods). Exhibit 4 even shows how to measure the net gains to removing the inefficiency of contrived scarcity. When contrived scarcity is removed (by converting the industry to perfect competition), the social gain exceeds the monopolist's loss of profit. Since consumers gain more than the monopolist loses, it is possible to make everyone better off by taxing consumers and redistributing the proceeds to the monopolist.

Monopoly-Profit-Seeking Behavior

Monopoly is inefficient because output is restricted. The costs of monopoly can be far more severe, however. Monopolies are not costlessly granted to certain individuals or companies. *People seek monopoly power.* Let us reconsider Exhibit 4. Instead of considering a move from the monopoly output to the competitive output, think about the reverse. If the industry were perfectly competitive, the price/quantity combination would be $4/600 units, or point *c*. If someone could turn this industry into a monopoly, that person could gain the potential monopoly profit of $900 (grey color area). People would be willing to spend real resources—or engage in **monopoly-profit-seeking behavior**—to turn the industry into a monopoly and acquire the monopoly profit.

> **Monopoly-profit-seeking behavior** is the activity of anyone trying to achieve or maintain a monopoly in order to gain the monopoly profits.

A prime example of monopoly-profit-seeking behavior would be lobbying. Monopolies can be achieved and maintained through government charters, franchises, and regulation. There are more than 10,000 registered lobbyists in Washington, D.C. The offices they occupy, the secretarial services they employ, and their own labor could be used elsewhere in a world of scarcity. A prominent case is the lobbying in Congress by American automobile manufacturers for protection from foreign imports.

Monopoly-profit-seeking behavior can lead to substantial social losses. To limit such behavior, it would be necessary to lessen substantially the possibility of "buying" monopoly through the manipulation of government. This is easier said than done.

Monopoly and Innovation

The discussion of monopoly so far has emphasized its negative features. Monopolies contrive scarcity. They cause resources to be wasted as people attempt to gain monopoly power. In terms of the production-possibilities frontier discussed in Chapter 1, monopolies cause the economy to operate inside the frontier. Chapter 1 also emphasized that technological progress causes the production-possibilities frontier to shift outward. If monopolies do a better job of creating technological advances, this advantage may compensate for monopoly's disadvantages.

Economists have long debated whether monopoly (or big business) or competition is better suited to creating new technology. *Monopoly* and *big business* are not the same; but more often than not, monopolies (or companies that possess considerable monopoly power) are giant concerns. Giant corporations like AT&T, Du Pont, and IBM maintain enormous, privately financed laboratories and employ thousands of scientists. Indeed, Nobel Prizes for the discovery of the laser, superconductors, and the transistor were awarded to scientists employed by giant corporations.

The ability of large companies to finance research and product development has convinced economists such as Joseph Schumpeter and John Kenneth Galbraith that big businesses are more likely to come up with significant scientific inventions than competitive businesses. Big corporations with profits protected by barriers to entry can devote more of their resources to research and development (R&D). Both Schumpeter and Galbraith argue that the most significant innovations of the industrial era can be traced to giant concerns, not to small competitive firms.

Studies of major innovations fail to answer conclusively the question of monopoly and innovation. The evidence shows that both small, competitive firms and giant concerns with considerable market power have produced major innovations. A study of the case histories of 61 important twentieth-century inventions found that less than one-third were discovered in large industrial laboratories. A

Should Cable TV Be a Monopoly?

At first glance, it appears that cable TV must be a monopoly. To have more than one cable-TV company in a community would require building separate underground cables to homes. If each company had to have its own underground cables, the costs of delivering cable service likely would be raised so much that consumers would pay lower prices if there were only one cable-TV company in town.

Studies by a number of economists show that communities served by more than one cable-TV company pay lower rates. The competition for customers between rival companies gives lower rates to customers, who have a choice, despite the higher cost of parallel underground cables. Why is it that competition yields lower cable-TV rates? First, competition forces cable-TV companies to hold their costs down so that they can offer their service at competitive rates. Second, when local communities grant cable-TV companies a local monopoly, they often require that the cable-TV company offer 100 channels, public-access channels, and talk-back systems, all of which raise costs above what a competitive system would have required. Third, cable-TV companies have to spend considerable sums on lobbying state and local government to receive the monopoly right to operate. This money spent on monopoly rent-seeking raises the cost to the consumer.

It is a matter of public policy to decide what is the better market structure for cable TV. The local government can decide to franchise only one cable-TV company for the entire community. Alternatively, local government can operate on an open-access basis, whereby more than one company is allowed to compete for cable customers. Experience to date suggests that customers are better off with competition.

Despite the obvious benefits of competition, most local cable-TV service is provided by monopoly suppliers. The result has been that cable-TV rates have risen much more rapidly than other prices, causing a backlash of consumer resentment. The U.S. Congress in 1992 passed legislation giving regulatory agencies at the state and local level the power to set the rates for cable-TV services, just as they set electricity rates and rates for local telephone service.

It is doubtful that government regulation will result in lower prices and better service for consumers. Public policy has passed up an opportunity for competition, which would have benefited consumers.

little more than one-half were the product of academic investigators or of individuals working independently of any research organization.[1] F. M. Scherer summarizes the evidence and its bearing on public policy:

> No single firm size is uniquely conducive to technological progress. There is room for firms of all sizes. What we want, therefore, may be a diversity of sizes, each with its own special advantages and disadvantages.[2]

Diversity can be important to technological innovation. A small firm might discover a new product or process, but a large firm may be needed to put the invention on the shelf for the consumer. Basic ideas may come from small firms or even individuals, but a large laboratory may be needed to develop the idea so it can be put to practical use.

---

[1] John Jewkes, David Sawers, and Richard Stillerman, *The Sources of Invention* (New York: St. Martin's Press, 1959), pp. 71–85.
[2] F.M. Scherer, *Industrial Market Structure and Economic Performance,* 2nd ed. (Boston: Houghton Mifflin, 1980), p. 418.

Chapter Summary

The most important point to learn from this chapter is: Compared to perfect competition, monopolists restrict output and raise product prices above marginal costs of production.

1. A pure monopoly exists when there is one seller producing a product that has no close substitutes. Barriers to entry keep out competitors. The monopolist is a price maker and has considerable control over price. Pure monopoly is rare in the real world because of substitutes and because of the absence of absolute barriers to entry, especially in the long run. Sources of monopoly are: economies of scale, patents, ownership of critical raw materials, public franchises, and collusion.

2. Price makers face downward-sloping demand curves; they must lower their price in order to sell more. For price makers, price will exceed marginal revenue. When marginal revenue is positive, demand is elastic; when marginal revenue is negative, demand is inelastic.

3. Monopolists maximize profits by producing that output quantity at which marginal revenue and marginal cost are equal or by charging that price at which $MR = MC$. Once the monopolist has chosen the optimal output, the market will dictate the price, and vice versa.

4. Price makers can raise their profits through price discrimination. Buyers with inelastic demand will pay higher prices than those with elastic demand.

5. In perfect competition, economic efficiency is present because society's resources are so organized that it is impossible to make at least one person better off by any reallocation of resources without harming someone else. Efficiency prevails where price equals marginal cost. Monopoly is inefficient because price exceeds marginal cost and monopoly-profit-seeking behavior absorbs resources.

6. Schumpeter and Galbraith argue that large business firms or large concentrations of monopoly power are conducive to technological progress. Studies of major innovations show that diversity of industrial organization is required for innovation.

Key Terms

pure monopoly (p.456)
price maker (p.458)
marginal revenue (p.459)
marginal revenue curve (p.461)

price discrimination (p.464)
economic efficiency (p.467)
contrived scarcity (p.467)
monopoly-profit-seeking behavior (p.469)

Questions and Problems

1. The ABC corporation can sell 5 widgets at a price of $20 each and 10 widgets at a price of $12. What is its marginal revenue per additional unit sold?

2. The XYZ corporation can sell 100 plastic oranges at a price of $2 and 300 at a price of $1 What is its marginal revenue per additional unit sold?

3. Explain why a price maker can choose either its profit-maximizing output level or its profit-maximizing price. Why is it that when one choice is made, the firm has no choice about the other?

4. A monopolist produces 100 units of output, and the price elasticity of demand at this point on the demand curve is 0.5. What advice would you give the monopolist? From this information, what can you say about marginal revenue?

5. A price maker produces output at a constant marginal cost of $5 and has no fixed costs. The demand curve facing the price maker is indicated in Table A.
   a. Determine the price maker's profit-maximizing output, price, and profit.

b. Show that by producing more or less output, the firm would decrease its profit.

c. Explain what happens to marginal revenue when output is raised from 15 to 20 units.

TABLE A

Price (dollars)	Quantity Demanded (units)
12	0
10	5
8	10
6	15
4	20

6. A food concession in a sports stadium makes an economic profit of $100,000 in the first year of operation. Explain what will happen to profits in subsequent years

a. if the concessionaire is granted an exclusive franchise to stadium concessions, and

b. if potential competitors have the freedom to set up concession stands in the stadium.

In the latter case, can the concessionaire do anything to protect long-run profits?

7. Prices of movie tickets and tickets to sports events and concerts are typically lower for children than for adults. Explain why, using the theory of price discrimination.

8. Assume a monopoly is making an economic profit. The monopoly is sold to the highest bidder. Would the new owner make an economic profit? Why or why not?

9. Explain why marginal revenue is less than price for a price maker.

10. A natural water fountain is discovered in the middle of a city. The demand schedule for the drinking water is shown in Table B. There is no cost of production.

TABLE B

Price (cents per drink)	Quantity Demanded (drinks per day)
6	0
5	10
4	20
3	30
2	40
1	50
0	60

a. Draw the demand curve.

b. Calculate marginal revenue for each level of output.

c. How would the city maximize its revenues from the water fountain?

11. Restate the reason why $P = MC$ is the condition for economic efficiency.

12. Why do economists say that monopolists contrive scarcity?

13. Explain why monopolists produce too little output from the standpoint of economic efficiency.

14. What does the evidence indicate about the relationship between the size of business firms and technological progress? Is technological innovation a "monopoly" of large business enterprises?

15. What is the difference between monopoly-profit-seeking losses and the losses that result when the monopolist produces at marginal revenue = marginal cost?

16. Why is production at an output level where marginal cost = marginal revenue socially inefficient for monopolies but socially efficient under perfect competition?

17. The marginal cost of production for a hypothetical drug is $2 per dozen. The demand schedule for the drug is shown in Table C

a. Calculate the marginal revenue by centering a 2-unit increase in output at each output level (for example, at the output level 2, consider the marginal revenue going from one unit of output to 3 units of output).

b. What is the monopoly price for the drug?

c. Calculate monopoly profit.

d. How does the monopoly output compare to the perfectly competitive output?

TABLE C

Price (dollars per dozen)	Quantity (dozens)
10	0
9	1
8	2
7	3
6	4
5	5
4	6
3	7

Doing Economics

A monopoly is a situation in which consumers have no good alternative to consuming a particular product or service. Is this situation faced by students at your college in selecting courses, owing to restrictive graduation requirements? Are there particular departments or individual professors who have monopoly power with respect to student choices? What are the incentives for faculty in such courses? How do these incentives differ from those in courses for which many substitutes exist? Are these differences in incentives reflected in the style and popularity of the "monopoly" courses?

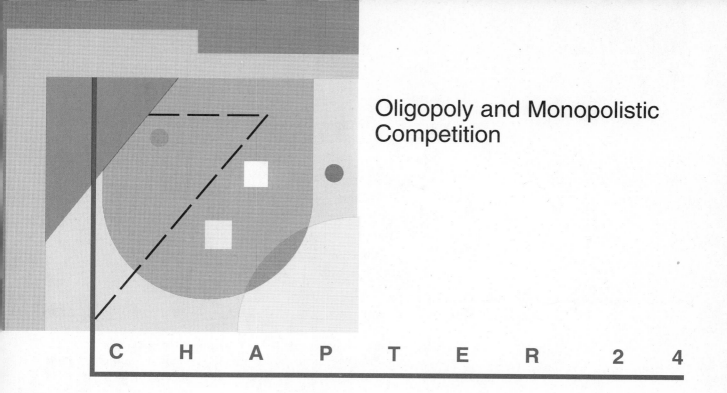

Oligopoly and Monopolistic Competition

CHAPTER 24

CHAPTER FOCUS   Most of the output of the U.S. economy is produced by firms that are somewhere between perfect competition and monopoly. These firms range from household names like Exxon, Ford Motors, Proctor and Gamble, Burger King, and Alcoa to the corner grocery store or the neighborhood dry cleaners. All of these firms can select their own prices, but they all have to worry about competition. In markets where competitive pressures are intense, a small increase in price may cause a precipitous decline in market share. Even when immediate competitive pressures are not intense, firms must worry about the long-term effects of price increases on their market position.

This chapter is about how firms that are neither perfectly competitive nor monopolistic deal with these competitive pressures. There is no single approach. Some producers band together to behave as a monopoly; others work out through custom and practice procedures for coexistence; yet others get involved in competitive pricing wars. Some firms adopt complex pricing strategies to see how their competitors will react.

When the number of producers is small, the conduct of business becomes like a game of strategy. To survive in the marketplace, managers must be sure that they play the competitive game as well as or better than their competitors.

After studying this chapter, you will be able to:

- Understand how monopolistic competition differs from monopoly and perfect competition in the short run and the long run.
- See the difference between nonprice and price competition.
- Learn how concentration is measured for different industries.
- Understand how the prisoners' dilemma game explains oligopoly behavior.
- Explain the kinked-demand curve model of oligopoly.
- Describe the different ways oligopolists can collude.
- Name the economic obstacles to collusion.

MONOPOLISTIC COMPETITION

Recall from the monopoly chapter that the monopolist's price depends on the monopolist's output. Firms that can affect prices by changing output are *price makers*. Price-making firms are not necessarily monopolists. In fact, few price makers are monopolies. Price makers can be anything from a pure monopoly to a firm closely resembling a perfect competitor. The characteristic common to all price makers is the downward-sloping demand schedule they face. To sell more of their product, they must lower their price.

Characteristics of Monopolistic Competition

Usually some basis exists for distinguishing between the goods and services produced by different sellers. These distinctions may be based on the physical attributes of the product (hamburgers at one restaurant are different in some respects from hamburgers at other restaurants), on location (one gas station may be more conveniently located than another), on the type of service offered (one dry cleaner offers two-hour service, another offers one-day service), and even on imagined differences (one type of aspirin is perceived as "better" than another). The point is that there are usually differences—real or imagined—among products. Sellers of these different products have some monopoly power over the customers who prefer their product. How much monopoly power they have depends on the strength of this preference.

In **monopolistic competition**, the degree of control over price is quite limited because of the large number of firms and the existence of close substitutes.

> **Monopolistic competition** is an industry in which:
> 1. the number of sellers is large enough so that each seller acts independently of the other;
> 2. the product is differentiated from seller to seller;
> 3. there is free entry into and exit from the industry;
> 4. sellers are price makers (although to a very limited degree).

With a large number of sellers, each seller presumes that its decisions have no discernible effect on the rest of the market. The many other sellers would not be expected to react to the actions of any single seller. Monopolistic competitors hence make their decisions independently—without expecting to affect the decisions of others. Monopolistic competitors are price makers because of product

GALLERY OF ECONOMISTS

Edward Hastings Chamberlin (1899–1967)

Edward Chamberlin, the father of modern industrial organization, was born in La Conner, Washington. He received his Ph.D. from Harvard University in 1927 and a full professorship from that institution ten years later.

Throughout his career, Chamberlin viewed the real world as a mixture of monopoly and perfect competition. His Ph.D. thesis, published in 1933 as *Theory of Monopolistic Competition,* continued through eight editions. In it Chamberlin attempted to convince readers that the polar concepts of monopoly and perfect competition were inadequate to describe the real world. He stimulated economists' interests in oligopoly, advertising, product differentiation, and economies of scale. Along with Joan Robinson, he is credited with discovering the theory of monopolistic competition. In the 1960s, his theory of monopolistic competition came under heavy attack from economists such as George Stigler. Not only has Chamberlin's theory survived the attack, it has been given new life by modern economists.

differentiation. Differences in products (by physical traits, location, type of service, or imagined differences) give the seller some limited control over price. The seller who raises price will not lose all customers (as would the perfect competitor); some loyal customers will have a strong enough preference to accept the higher price.

Profit Maximization in the Short Run

The chapters on perfect competition and monopoly explained how firms maximize profits in competitive and monopolistic markets. The key difference between monopolistic competition and perfect competition is that the product is differentiated from firm to firm. Firms find it advantageous to differentiate their product because it allows them some measure of control over the price. Take the hypothetical firm of Jolley's Turkey Farm. In the beginning, Jolley's Turkey Farm is just like any of the thousands of other turkey farms. It is a small fraction of the total turkey market, and its turkeys are undifferentiated—buyers cannot distinguish Jolley Farm turkeys from any other turkey. In other words, we begin with Jolley operating in a perfectly competitive market. Exhibit 1a begins with Jolley Farm selling turkeys for 18 cents per pound and producing at the minimum point on its *ATC* curve. Jolley Farm's demand curve is perfectly elastic (horizontal) at the 18 cents market price. Jolley Farm is in long-run equilibrium, earning a zero economic profit. This outcome is identical to the long-run equilibrium of perfect competition described in the chapter on perfect competition.

After careful consideration, Jolley Farms management decides to differentiate their turkeys from other turkeys by spending a few cents per turkey to add a plastic thermometer that pops out when the turkey is done. With this unique feature, Jolley Farm starts advertising a "great tasting Jolley Farm turkey that you can't cook wrong." The advertising campaign is successful: people start looking for Jolley Farm turkeys in their supermarkets. Because of the thermometer, they are prepared to pay slightly more.

Exhibit 1b shows the consequences of product differentiation for the demand for Jolley Farm turkeys. As a monopolistically competitive firm selling a differentiated product, Jolley Farm now faces a downward-sloping demand curve. The firm's marginal-revenue curve lies below its demand curve, just as a monopolist's

Product differentiation is the key difference between monopolistic competition and perfect competition.

a. Before Product Differentiation

b. After Product Differentiation

c. Demand Curve After Long-Run Adjustments

Panel (a) shows Jolley's Turkey Farm in long-run competitive equilibrium earning zero profits. Through product differentiation, Jolley's Turkey Farm succeeds in shifting its demand curve to *D* in panel (b). Jolley's Turkey Farm now can make an economic profit by setting the price at 40 cents, where marginal revenue equals marginal costs. This economic profit will encourage new firms to enter and rivals to differentiate their products. Panel (c) shows Jolley's demand curve after long-run adjustments have taken place. Rival firms introduce their own product-differentiating devices, and Jolley's demand curve shifts to the right and becomes more elastic. In long-run equilibrium, Jolley's demand curve must be tangent to the *ATC* curve. The firm charges a price that just equals average total cost, yet marginal revenue equals marginal cost, and output falls short of the most efficient level.

does. Profits are maximized where MC equals MR. Jolley Farm maximizes its profit at the price of 40 cents per pound and makes a substantial economic profit of *abcd*. Product differentiation has raised Jolley Farm's profit, but Jolley will have trouble keeping this profit in the long run.

Monopolistic Competition in the Long Run

In the long run, monopoly and monopolistic competition are strikingly different. Barriers to entry protect the monopolist from new competitors. If a monopoly earns substantial profits, new firms will not automatically enter to squeeze out those profits. Monopolistic competition, however, shares with perfect competition the characteristic of *freedom of entry*. Free entry means that if a monopolistic competitor earns economic profits in the short run, new firms can (and will) enter the market, eventually driving these profits down to zero.

Return to the example of Jolley Farm. Other turkey farmers have noticed Jolley's success. Now they begin to differentiate their products. Some copy Jolley Farm's pop-up thermometer, others add new features: One firm adds a self-basting feature, another stresses that it produces turkeys without artificial chemicals, and others use other product-differentiating devices. Jolley Farm's demand curve now shifts to the left (demand drops) because some of Jolley's customers are attracted to some other brand. Jolley Farm's demand curve also becomes more elastic as the number of very close substitutes (brand-name turkeys) on the market increases.

In the long run, new firms can enter monopolistically competitive markets. Each new entrant will reduce the demand facing Jolley Farm. As in the case of perfect competition, the entry of rival brands ends when economic profits have been driven down to zero.

The long run equilibrium of a monopolistically competitive firm is shown in Exhibit 1c. In the long run, new firms will enter until economic profits are driven down to zero. At zero profits, Jolley Farm's demand curve D must be tangent to its ATC curve. In the long run, Jolley Farm's profits will equal zero where the price is approximately 27 cents per pound and output is 3,000 turkeys per year. Since profits are maximized at the price of 27 cents, it must be that at the output of 3,000 units marginal revenue equals marginal cost (the condition required for profit maximization).

The level of output at which Jolley Farm's average total cost is minimized is 6,000 units (at that output level, $MC = ATC$). Jolley Farm's optimal production capacity is 6,000 units. Yet Jolley Farm produces only 3,000 units—only one-half of optimal capacity. Jolley Farm produces below optimal capacity because of product differentiation. As long as the monopolistic competitive firm faces a downward-sloping demand curve, its long-run equilibrium output falls below optimal capacity. There is *excess capacity,* making monopolistic competition appear less efficient than perfect competition. Excess capacity is the price we must pay for the variety introduced by product differentiation.

Product differentiation yields only short-run profits. Entry of new firms and product differentiation of established firms eliminate economic profits in the long run.

Monopolistic competition is characterized by excess capacity in the long run.

Advertising, Brand Names, and Product Differentiation

The entry of new firms and the loss of economic profits are facts of life for monopolistic competitors. Monopolistic competitors, by definition, produce goods and services that are different. If they can use **nonprice competition** to make their product different from their competitors, customer loyalty will be stronger. The stronger is this customer loyalty, the smaller will be the loss of customers as new firms enter and the less elastic will be the demand for their product.

> Nonprice competition is the attempt to attract customers through improvements in product quality or service that shift the firm's demand curve to the right.

Monopolistically competitive firms use advertising and brand names as sources of nonprice competition. They clearly identify their product with a brand name (such as "Jolley Turkey Farm"), and they use advertising to convince customers that their brand is better than competitive brands. In fact, nonprice competition—successfully applied—yields short-run profits for the firm and can delay profit loss. Once loyal customers are convinced that Jolley Farm turkeys are easier to prepare (are more nutritious, more lean, and so on), they will continue to be willing to purchase Jolley Farm turkeys at the same price despite the existence of close substitutes. When advertising creates strong brand loyalty, the entry of new firms does not increase the price elasticity of demand as much.

Nonprice competition yields both long-run and transitory profits. Profits on some brand-name products, like Bayer aspirin or Borden's condensed milk, have persisted for a long time. Advertising and brand names have successfully differentiated these products from substitutes, despite relative freedom of entry. Even though all aspirin and condensed milk are basically the same, many consumers are convinced that these particular brands are better. In other cases, nonprice competition yields only transitory profits. Advertising cannot always convince consumers that one particular product is indeed better (that California oranges are better than other oranges, for example). Also, in many cases competitors can duplicate the means of product differentiation. If the gas-station owner differentiates the product by staying open all night or by offering a free car wash, then competitors can do the same. Any gains from product differentiation are then temporary.

Advertising brand names are sources of nonprice competition.

OLIGOPOLY

The industries that make headlines fall somewhere between monopoly and monopolistic competition. The Fords, the IBMs, and the General Foods compete with a relatively small number of rivals. They are aware of their rivals' actions, and they must consider their rivals' responses before making their pricing and output decisions. These industries share certain characteristics.

An **oligopoly** is an industry that is dominated by a few relatively large firms.

> An oligopoly is an industry characterized by:
> 1. moderate to high barriers to entry,
> 2. a relatively small number of firms in the industry,
> 3. recognized mutual interdependence, and
> 4. price making (firms are able to exercise varying degrees of control over price).

There is diversity among oligopolies. Some have high barriers to entry; others have more moderate barriers. The degree of control over price varies. Some oligopolies produce a homogeneous product (aluminum); others produce a heterogeneous product (automobiles). The common denominator is mutual interdependence. How oligopolies deal with mutual interdependence is the subject of most of this chapter.

Mutual interdependence is the common denominator of oligopoly.

DETERMINANTS OF CONCENTRATION

An oligopoly is an industry in which there are a relatively small number of firms. In some oligopolistic industries, there are only two or three firms that completely dominate industry sales. In other oligopolistic industries, there are ten to fifteen firms that share the market fairly evenly. Within oligopoly, there is great diversity as to the number of firms and the dominance by key firms.

Barriers to Entry Revisited

Whenever there are a relatively few firms in a profitable industry, there probably are barriers to entry. With free entry (as perfect competition and monopolistic competition show), profits entice new entrants, and the number of firms increases. The last chapter discussed *barriers to entry* in the context of monopoly. For a monopoly, the entry barriers could be such factors as economies of scale, patents, the exclusive ownership of raw materials, public franchises, and licenses. The same factors are at work in oligopoly, except that the entry barriers must be low enough to allow at least two firms to remain in the industry. In the case of monopoly, entry barriers are stronger because there is only one firm in the industry. In oligopoly, there is an additional barrier to entry—product differentiation. Monopolists, as sole producers, do not need to worry about differentiating their product. Oligopolists, however, face rival firms. For them, product differentiation can be an important source of profits.

Barriers to entry explain the relatively few firms in oligopoly industry.

Experts on industrial organization have attempted to classify industries according to the strength of barriers to entry. They have concluded that industries such as distilled liquors, newspapers, drugs, automobiles, and heavy electrical equipment have high barriers to entry. Clothing, printing, cement, and footwear have low barriers to entry. Industries with high barriers are likely to be populated by a relatively small number of oligopolistic producers. Industries with low entry barriers are likely to be populated by a relatively larger number of producers. As the following discussion shows, the relative number of firms influences the way firms react to mutual interdependence.

Measuring Concentration

There is no magic formula for measuring the extent of oligopoly. A statistical tool economists use to gauge oligopoly is the **concentration ratio**.

> An *x*-firm **concentration ratio** is the percentage of industry sales (or output, or labor force, or assets) accounted for by the *x* largest firms.

The 4-firm sales concentration ratio, for example, is the percentage of industry sales accounted for by the four largest firms in the industry. Exhibit 2 shows concentration ratios for U.S. industrial concerns. Concentration ratios are an imperfect guide to the extent of oligopoly for four reasons.

First, concentration ratios do not reflect competition from foreign producers or from substitute products at home. The 4-firm concentration ratio of the U.S. automobile industry is 90 percent—a figure that fails to measure the competition of foreign imports. The 4-firm concentration ratio in metal cans (54 percent) does not reflect the competition from stainless steel and plastic.

EXHIBIT 2   Concentration Ratios

Industry	4-Firm Concentration Ratio (percent)	Number of Firms
Motor vehicles and car bodies	90	352
Cereal and breakfast foods	87	33
Photographic equipment	72	717
Tires and inner tubes	69	114
Aircraft	72	137
Metal cans	54	161
Soaps and other detergents	65	683
Cookies and crackers	58	316
Semiconductors	40	755
Farm machinery	45	1,516
Blast furnaces and steel mills	44	271
Toilet preparations	32	648
Hardware	32	1,127
Gray iron foundries	30	692
Men's footwear	26	110
Petroleum refining	32	200
Women's footwear	50	123
Periodicals	18	3,759
Motor homes	56	144
Paper mills	33	122
Pharmaceutical preparations	22	640
Canned fruits and vegetables	29	462
Nonwoven fabrics	9	91
Men's and boy's suits	34	285
Radio and TV equipment	37	572
Corrugated and solid fiber boxes	26	952
Sawmills	15	5,252
Wood household furniture	20	2,771
Nuts and bolts	16	834
Valves and pipe fittings	20	372
Women's dresses	6	5,398
Ready-mix concrete	8	3,749

SOURCE: U.S. Department of Commerce, "Concentration Ratios In Manufacturing", *1987 Census of Manufacturers*, MC87-S-6.

Second, concentration ratios may not measure concentration in the relevant market. The 4-firm concentration ratio in the concrete business is only 8 percent, but it is nearly 100 percent in some local markets.

Third, many markets, such as newspapers, cement, and real estate, are local or regional. Concentration ratios for percentages of national sales are misleading in such markets. A local or regional firm may dominate its relevant market, but the national concentration ratio may not reflect this fact.

Fourth, concentration ratios do not measure *potential* competition. They do not indicate those industries in which new firms can overcome existing barriers to entry. One airline may account for 90 percent of the flights between two cities, but the number of *potential* entrants into this market may be large.

Although concentration ratios can be misleading, they can—if used with care—provide insights into how concentrated an industry is. Combined with additional information, such as the amount of foreign competition, and applied to meaningful market definitions, concentration ratios indicate which industries are indeed populated by a relatively small number of firms. Oligopoly theory explains why this makes a difference. It shows that oligopolies with two to three dominant producers behave differently from those with eight to ten producers.

Concentration ratios are a statistical tool for measuring the extent of oligopoly.

OLIGOPOLY THEORY

When oligopoly firms are interdependent, the marginal revenue resulting from a price change depends on how rival firms respond to the price change.

Oligopoly theory is more complicated than perfect competition, pure monopoly, or monopolistic competition because there is no one theory of oligopoly. In either perfect competition or monopoly, the firm need only equate marginal cost and marginal revenue. In the case of oligopoly, things are not that simple. Because of mutual interdependence, the marginal revenue an oligopolist gains from changing price depends on the actions and reactions of rival firms. If these reactions cannot be predicted, the oligopolist will not know the marginal revenue of a pricing action.

Mutual Interdependence

An oligopolistic industry was defined as one with a "relatively small" number of firms. What is meant by "relatively small"? There are a relatively small number of firms in an industry when each firm must consider the reactions of rival firms. One firm must consider how a rival firm will respond to its actions and vice versa. When firms in an industry must consider the responses of rival firms, the industry is characterized by **mutual interdependence**.

> **Mutual interdependence** is characteristic of an industry in which the actions of one affect other firms in the industry and in which these interrelationships are recognized.

Mutual interdependence is the most important feature of oligopoly. In making decisions concerning prices, quantities, and qualities of output, mutually interdependent firms must consider the reactions of rival firms. In some oligopolistic industries, the pattern of reaction may be easy to anticipate by all participants; it may be dictated by custom or agreement. In other industries, the reactions of rival firms may be unpredictable, and participants use strategy to outguess and outmaneuver their rivals.

The Prisoners' Dilemma

Oligopolists must use strategic behavior to outguess their rivals if they are to earn large profits. One way to understand oligopolistic industries is to study the strategies that people use in strategic games. Oligopoly is like a game where there are two or more players, each trying to figure out what the other players will do. *Game theory* is the study of the strategies people follow when players receive different rewards or payoffs depending on the strategies or "plays" of all the players.

The **prisoners' dilemma game** analyzes a situation much like that often faced by oligopolistic producers. It explains why some oligopolists cooperate with rivals while others try to outmaneuver them. In the game, two bank robbers have been apprehended by the police; they are being interrogated in separate rooms. If both talk, both go to prison for five years. If one talks and the other remains quiet, the one who talks is set free while the silent bank robber receives a 20-year jail sentence. If neither talks, both get only a year for carrying a concealed weapon. Each prisoner is in a dilemma. Each knows that by keeping quiet both can get off with a light one-year sentence. But each suspect has an incentive to talk—each can get off free if he or she confesses while the other keeps quiet. Game theory

Tit-for-Tat and the Prisoners' Dilemma

Robert Axelrod has studied how best to play the prisoners' dilemma game, particularly when it is repeated over and over so that players can learn from experience. Axelrod invited 14 authorities on the game to compete in a prisoners' dilemma tournament. Each contestant was required to submit a strategy for the following game: For each of the 200 rounds of the game, each player's strategy should give either a C (cooperate) or D (don't cooperate—defect) response. If both players produced a C, then each received 3 points. If both produced a D, then each received 1 point. If one offered a D while the other offered a C, the defecting player got 5 points and the cooperating player 0 points. The winning program was the shortest program of all—called Tit-for-Tat by its author, Anatol Rapoport. The Tit-for-Tat strategy is very simple: Offer a C on the first move, and then do whatever your opponent did on the previous move. As long as your opponent cooperates, you cooperate too. If your opponent defects, you punish by defecting on the next move. The Tit-for-Tat program amassed the highest number of points in the first tournament and beat out 62 entrants from six countries in Axelrod's second tournament. The simplest winning strategy achieved its victory by being cooperative. Game theorists are studying whether or not people naturally employ cooperative behavior in real-life business "games" that are played frequently.

SOURCE: William F. Allman, "Nice Guys Finish First," *Science* 84 (October 1984): pp. 25–32.

concludes that both will confess even though they would both be better off if both kept silent. (See Example 1.)

> A **prisoners' dilemma game** is a game with two players in which both players benefit from cooperating, but in which each player has an incentive to cheat on the agreement.

The Oligopolist's Dilemma

The prisoners' dilemma is much like the oligopolist's dilemma: cooperate with rivals or act independently. In both cases, the consequence of one "player's" decision depends on the decision of another "player". Suppose Firm A and Firm B each sell a differentiated product. Suppose also that when the two products have equal prices, both firms enjoy exactly the same profit. If one charges a slightly lower price than the other, however, that firm will make larger profits.

Exhibit 3 shows a set of outcomes. Each firm has the option of choosing a price of either $20 or $19. Firm A's price choices are shown down the left side; Firm B's price choice are shown along the top. The *profits* earned by Firm A and Firm B are determined by the prices the two firms choose. Firm A's profit payoffs are shown in the lower-left corner of each box (in grey); Firm B's profit payoffs are shown in the upper-right corner of each box (in color). When both charge $20, both earn $2,500; when both charge $19, both earn $1,500. When one charges $20 and the other charges $19, the lower-priced firm earns $3,000 while the higher-priced firm earns only $1,000.

The two oligopolists are like the two prisoners. One stands to gain a high profit (at the expense of the other) by selecting the lower price while the rival selects the

EXHIBIT 3   Profit Payoffs to a Two-Firm Oliogopoly

Each square (cell) shows the profits that each firm would earn when various combinations of prices are charged by the two firms. Firm A's profits are shown in grey in the lower left-hand corner of each cell, and Firm B' s profits are shown in color in the upper right-hand corner of each cell. For example, if A charges $19 and B charges $20, A would earn a profit of $3,000 and B would earn $1,000. This exhibit illustrates the oliogopolist's dilemma: If both charge low prices ($19), they both earn an intermediate-level profit ($1,500). If both agree to charge a high price ($20), they both earn a high profit ($2,500). However, if one cheats on the agreement and charges a lower price ($19 versus $20), the cheater earns a very high profit ($3,000) while the noncheater earns a low profit ($1,000)

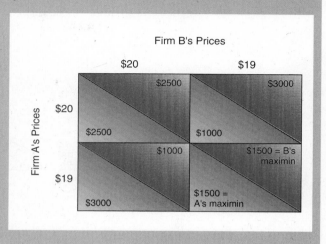

higher price. Both stand to earn a decent profit if both select the lower price. If both select the higher price, they each earn a substantial profit. Yet, like the prisoners in isolated cells, each oligopolist must make a pricing decision not knowing what the other firm will do.

What would each firm consider as it makes its pricing decision? Each might reason: "My rival probably won't risk charging the higher $20 price for fear that I would select the lower $19 price. Therefore, my rival will select the lower $19 price. If I select the higher $20 price, my rival will get the larger share of profit ($3,000 versus my $1,000). I therefore decide to select the lower $19 price." If each firm reasons the same and decides to select the lower price, the two firms are in equilibrium. They have correctly anticipated each other's actions and they have chosen the appropriate strategy. If each believes the other will charge $19, each should charge $19. When both actually charge $19, each has guessed correctly, and each is able to employ the best strategy for the situation in which the *other* charges $19.

In this situation, A and B would both decide to select prices of $19 and pocket a profit of $1,500 each. They are, however, aware that if both charged $20, they could each earn a profit of $2,500. If A and B played this game repeatedly over a fairly long period of time, it is likely that A and B would realize that they are both better off charging higher prices. They might learn to cooperate and choose the strategy (a $20 price) that maximizes joint profits. There is another way they could settle immediately on a $20 price: They could simply agree that both would charge the higher price.

Oligopolist firms must make decisions not knowing what other firms will do. They will select the correct strategy if they correctly anticipate the strategy of their rivals.

Kinked Demand

The prisoner's dilemma shows that oligopolists must try to anticipate the actions of rival firms. If they anticipate properly, they will have adopted their best strategy. If they anticipate incorrectly, they will have to revise their strategy. The behavior of an oligopoly can take many forms. One of the simplest ways oligopolistic firms might anticipate the behavior of their rivals is illustrated by the **kinked-demand curve**. Subsequent sections show other ways.

In an oligopolistic industry characterized by kinked demand, firms match price reductions but ignore their rivals' price increases. Suppose Ford's rivals tend to match Ford's price *cuts* but hold their prices when Ford raises its price. Ford would face a more elastic demand for price increases than it would for price reductions. Price hikes would cost Ford substantial business; price cuts would be matched by General Motors, Chrysler, and Toyota so that Ford's demand would not increase at their expense. The demand curve would have a "kink" in it at the current price as shown in Exhibit 4.

> A **kinked-demand curve** results when rival firms match a firm's price decreases but don't match the firm's price increases.

Exhibit 4 shows an oligopoly firm facing a kinked-demand curve. The current price charged by this firm is $12. Because rival firms do not follow price increases but do match price cuts, the firm's demand curve, *D*, is more elastic above the $12 price than below the $12 price. Thus, the firm's demand curve has a kink at the current price. Because of the kink, the *MR* curve drops sharply at the price of $12. Marginal revenue is $7 at a price just above $12 and only $2 at a price just below $12. Because the marginal-revenue curve has a vertical segment (*feg*) just below the demand kink, there is a *range* of *MR* values associated with the $12 price. The oligopolist maximizes profits at the price of $12 if the *MC* curve intersects the *MR* curve anywhere in the vertical segment *feg*.

The kink in the demand curve means that if the firm's *MC* curve shifted up or down within the range *f* to *g*, *MR* would still equal *MC* at the current price! The firm would not change its output and price. Moreover, there could even be slight changes in demand without altering the profit-maximizing price.

The kinked-demand model says that in industries in which rivals match price reductions but ignore price increases, prices should remain relatively stable. They should not change with every change in market demand and in marginal cost as in perfectly competitive industries.

A kinked-demand curve results when rivals ignore price increases but match price reductions. When the demand curve is kinked, prices should be relatively stable.

EXHIBIT 4   The Kinked-Demand Curve

This firm's rivals follow price reductions but not price increases. For prices below the current $12 price, the demand curve, *D*, is less elastic than it is for prices above $12. The marginal-revenue curve, *MR*, drops sharply from *f* to *g*. The *MC* curve can shift up or down (as long as it remains within this vertical portion of the *MR* curve) without changing the firm's price or output decisions.

Oligopoly Coordination

The kinked-demand model of oligopoly assumes there is no overt coordination among firms. Each firm knows that price increases will not be followed but that price reductions will be, and firms make their pricing decisions on this basis. The prisoners' dilemma, however, showed that there are substantial gains through coordination. If the two prisoners could agree beforehand not to confess, they would both get off lightly. If both oligopolists in Exhibit 3 agree to charge the higher price, they can both earn higher profits. These examples show that oligopolists can benefit from coordination.

Oligopoly coordination takes a variety of forms. Oligopolists can *collude* on pricing and output decisions. They can enter into formal agreements either in secret (if such agreements are against the law) or in the open (in cases where such agreements are legal and even sanctioned by government). Coordination can take on looser forms when it is based upon custom, habit, or informal agreement. The effectiveness of coordination varies from oligopoly to oligopoly. In some cases, coordination is rigidly enforced; in other cases, it is loosely enforced and tends to break down.

Cartel Agreements. The most direct way for an oligopoly to coordinate pricing and output policy is to enter a **cartel** agreement, binding on all parties, to set the prices or market shares of each producer. If successful, such agreements allow the oligopolistic firms to earn monopoly profits for the industry as a whole.

> A **cartel** is an arrangement that allows the participating firms to coordinate their output and pricing decisions to earn monopoly profits.

Exhibit 5 shows an oligopolistic industry consisting of three identical firms (with the same costs and producing the same product). Barriers to entry are so high that the three firms need not worry about attracting new entrants should profits be high. The three identical firms agree to each share one-third of the market and to charge the same monopoly price. The industry demand curve is D. Firm A's demand and marginal-revenue curves (which are the same as those of Firms B and C) are shown as D_A and MR_A. Because all three firms are part of a cartel agreement to share the market equally, Firm A's demand curve is D_A, $(= \frac{1}{3} \times D)$. The monopoly price is determined by drawing the MR_A curve corresponding to D_A and locating its intersection with the MC curve. Firm A would maximize its profit by producing 100 units at a price of $50 per unit (point a). The other two firms also charge $50 and produce 100 units each. Industry output is 300 $(= 3 \times 100)$.

Firm A is strongly tempted to cheat. The two rival firms are selling 200 units at the price of $50. Firm A could charge $49.50 and sell slightly more than its third. As long as its secret sales remain small and don't drive down the cartel price, $49.50 is now essentially the cheating firm's marginal revenue. The marginal revenue of $49.50 clearly exceeds marginal cost ($20) to each firm. Hence, substantial gains accrue to the firm that breaks the cartel agreement. Firms B and C are subject to the same temptation. Cheating on the agreement has its long-run costs. When the other firms detect cheating, they will break the agreement. Price warfare could erupt, and economic profit would be driven down. (See Example 2.)

Greed both creates and destroys cartels. Cartels offer their members a share of monopoly profits as long as every member adheres to the cartel agreement. Each cartel member, however, can gain by cheating on the agreement if the others do not cheat. Cartel members are like the two prisoners of the prisoners' dilemma. If one cheats and the other does not, the cheater wins. If both cheat, they both lose.

EXHIBIT 5   Collusive Oligopoly

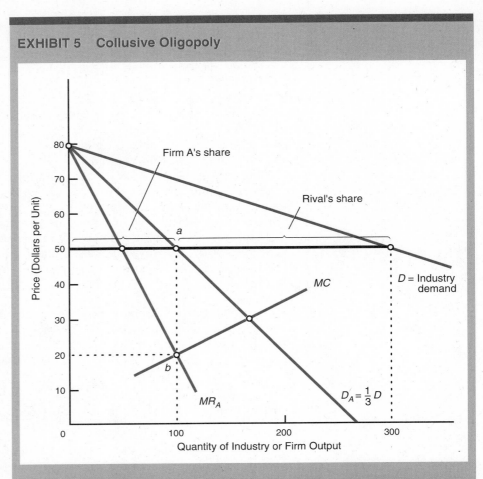

Curve *D* represents the industry demand curve. The industry consists of three oliogopolistic firms who agree to share the market equally and charge the same price. D_A is the demand schedule of Firm A; it is one-third of the industry demand schedule. MR_A is the marginal-revenue curve of Firm A. Firm A maximizes profits by producing that output at which *MC* equals *MR*, or 100 units at $50 per units (point *a*). Firm A is tempted to cheat on the agreement because if it lowers price a little, it gains sales from its two rivals. As long as A's lower price exceeds A's marginal cost, Firm A's profits will increase. If all three firms cheat, however, a competitive bidding war should break out, and they could end up earning virtually no economic profits.

The desire to earn monopoly profits causes interdependent firms to form cartels. Interdependent firms can get an even larger share by cheating on the cartel agreement. This explains why cartels are unstable.

If both do not cheat, they are better off than if both cheat, but each one constantly is tempted to cheat.

Cartels are unstable because it is difficult to enforce cartel agreements. Very few cartels succeed over the long run. Most, like the ill-fated sugar, cocoa, tin, and coffee cartels, either disappear quickly or have no noticeable effect on prices.

There are numerous examples of cartel agreements on pricing. The Organization of Petroleum Exporting Countries (OPEC) meets regularly, with full coverage by the world's press, to attempt to set the price of crude oil. The International Air Transport Association (IATA) also meets openly with the blessing of the member country governments to set air fares for travel between countries.

With some minor exceptions, formal price-setting agreements violate U. S. law, but a number of price-conspiracy cases have come to light. While formal secret agreements continue, there are other less risky ways to coordinate prices. These methods are discussed in the next sections.

EXAMPLE 2

Yakutia Diamonds Threaten the DeBeers Cartel

The DeBeers Company, founded by Cecil Rhodes in 1871 in the diamond fields of South Africa, has proven to be the world's most lasting and effective cartel. DeBeers has controlled world diamond prices since the 1930s through its Central Selling Organization (CSO). The CSO is DeBeers' marketing arm, through which virtually all the world's diamonds are sold. Although only 15 percent of today's world diamond production originates in South Africa, the CSO has purchasing pacts with the world's major diamond producers (such as the former Soviet Union, Zaire and other African nations, and Australia). DeBeers prevents its *buyers* from cheating by inviting only a select group to its London sales every five weeks. Buyers must accept the cartel price or risk not being invited to subsequent sales. DeBeers also prevents cheating by diamond *producers* by offering faithful members stable contracts, stable prices, and financial security. Third, DeBeers has ways to punish disloyal members. When Zaire attempted to leave the cartel in 1981, DeBeers flooded diamond markets with low-quality diamonds similar to those from Zaire to drive their price down.

The collapse of the former Soviet Union poses the most serious threat to the DeBeers cartel in recent history. Under the Soviet regime, a top-secret government agency cooperated with DeBeers to market Russian raw diamonds produced almost exclusively in remote Yakutia—the population-poor but resource-rich Russian republic located in the polar north.

In the confusion that accompanied Moscow's central power collapse and Yakutia's growing control over its diamond resources, Yakutia mine operators began to sell their diamonds, which could potentially account for more than 20 percent of the world market, to buyers other than DeBeers. In high-level negotiations with Russian and Yakutian officials, DeBeers sought to convince the new Russian and Yakutian authorities that all Yakutia diamonds should be marketed through DeBeers. If DeBeers fails to achieve agreement, its long-time monopoly over world diamond sales would end.

Informal Agreements. Informal agreements can also be used to coordinate pricing and output decisions. The most notable case of informal agreement was that of the so-called Gary Dinners of the early twentieth century. Mr. Gary, president of U. S. Steel Corporation, would invite steel-company executives representing more than 90 percent of the industry to dinner and urge them to cooperate in holding prices. Gary dinners and their like confirm Adam Smith's perception that "people of the same trade seldom meet together, even for merriment and diversion, but the conversation ends in a conspiracy against the public, or in some contrivance to raise prices."

Price Leadership. A more subtle method of collusion occurs when a recognized **price leader** sets industry prices. When a price leader sets prices, there is no kinked-demand curve because rival firms follow the price leader's price decreases and price increases. The price leader keeps a sharp eye on market demand and costs that are common to all firms.

> A **price leader** is a firm whose price changes are consistently imitated by other firms in the industry.

Examples of price leadership are plentiful. In the ready-to-eat breakfast-cereal industry, whose "big three" corporations are Kellogg's, Post, and General Mills,

Kellogg's is the price leader for most product lines while General Mills and Post lead for their own best product lines.

Conscious Parallelism.   The most subtle form of collusion is **conscious parallelism**. Conscious parallelism occurs when oligopoly firms behave in the same way even though they have not agreed to act in a parallel manner. Examples would be the submitting of identical bids or switching to high season rates at the same time of year without any formal agreement to do so.

> **Conscious parallelism** is the coordination of actions of producers without formal or even informal agreements. All firms use their understanding of the industry to make their own decisions and anticipate the behavior of rival firms.

Conscious parallelism is explained by the use of *focal points* to set prices. A focal point is an obvious benchmark by which prices or output could be coordinated without an explicit agreement. Oligopolist firms are intimately acquainted with the way things work in their own industries. Business practices followed in the industry are well-known. The focal points may be certain standardized business practices—such as common percentage markups, the use of round numbers, the charging of prices like $4.95, and policies like "splitting the difference" or charging high season rates at the same time each year. As long as each oligopolist understands these standard practices, it can anticipate how rival firms will behave. If all firms in the oligopolistic industry use standard focal points, they will behave in a parallel fashion, even without formal agreements.

Oligopolies can coordinate their actions without formal agreements through price leadership and conscious parallelism.

Obstacles to Collusion

Despite the considerable gains from cooperation, oligopolists often do not cooperate. They cheat on cartels. They suddenly abandon focal points. The price leader raises prices and other firms don't follow. Some industries are characterized by cooperative behavior. Others are characterized by cheating and breaking of formal or informal agreements. The chances for effective and lasting collusion decrease when there are:

1. many sellers,
2. low entry barriers,
3. product heterogeneity,
4. high rates of innovation,
5. high fixed costs, and
6. difficulty of detecting cheating.

Many Sellers.   The more firms there are in the industry, the more difficult it is to agree on common prices. When there are two sellers, there is only one communication link: when there are three sellers, there are three different information links: A must agree with B, B must agree with C, and C and A must agree. When there are 10 sellers, there are 45 ways information must flow! The number of information channels increases at a faster rate than the number of sellers increases. It becomes far more difficult to coordinate collusive actions as the number of colluders grows.

Low Entry Barriers.   If it is easy for new firms to enter an industry, existing firms may not find it worthwhile to enter into cumbersome agreements to raise prices. Effective collusion would only bring in new firms. High prices create profitable opportunities for new firms. There would be no lasting benefits to the original firms that worked out the pricing agreement. Higher prices would simply encourage new firms—who are not parties to the agreement—to enter, and this entry would continue until prices were driven back down to where a normal return was earned.

Product Heterogeneity.

The more differentiated the product is from firm to firm, the more difficult it is for the industry to achieve coordination or collusion. Reaching an agreement creates both costs and benefits. It is costlier to reach an agreement if the product is not homogeneous. Because steel is homogeneous, an agreement on prices and market shares between large steel producers may be fairly easy to conclude. But an agreement between McDonnell Douglas and Boeing over the relative prices of MD-11s and Boeing 747's may be quite difficult because of product differences and complexity. An agreement between the producers of high-quality goods and low-quality goods may break down because of disagreement over quality differences. It would be difficult for a fast-food chain like McDonald's to enter into a pricing agreement with a full-service restaurant chain like Red Lobster because of the difficulty of agreeing on the proper relative price.

High Rates of Innovation.

If there is a high rate of innovation in an industry, collusive agreements will be more difficult to reach. The costs of reaching an agreement are higher when the industry is constantly turning out new products and developing new techniques. For example, it would be difficult for Eastman Kodak and Polaroid to reach an agreement because of rapid technological change in the camera and instant-development industry. The same would be true of the personal-computer market—characterized by virtually monthly advances in technology.

High Fixed Costs.

The higher fixed costs are relative to total costs, the more likely is cheating on the pricing agreements. As long as the price covers average variable costs, there is something left over to pay fixed costs. By granting a secret price concession, a firm may gain much in the short run if marginal costs are very low. Thus, the benefits to secret price reductions are increased by high fixed costs.

Detecting Cheating.

If it is easy to cheat without being detected, firms will tend to break a collusive agreement. It is easier to cheat on price agreements when actual prices charged by one party cannot be known with certainty by the other parties to the agreement. For example, barbers often agree to charge uniform prices within a city because the prices of haircuts must be posted. Rival barbers can easily detect barbers who undercut the agreed-upon price. When the terms of price negotiations are not revealed (as in the cases of long-term oil-delivery contracts or purchases of commercial aircraft by the airlines), it is easier to cheat on pricing agreements. When the cartel lacks an effective punishment for cheaters, enforcing discipline is difficult.

OLIGOPOLY AND EFFICIENCY

The previous chapter described positive features of perfect competition and negative features of monopoly. In their extreme form—the cartel—oligopolies are basically monopolies, and they share the inefficiencies of monopolies. In its other extreme—an oligopoly with ten or so firms engaging in a bitter price war—it resembles perfect competition.

Economists have debated whether oligopolies that are dominated by one or

POLICY FOCUS

Predatory Pricing

The antitrust laws of the United States prohibit predatory pricing. Predatory pricing occurs when one firm deliberately lowers its prices for the purpose of driving rival firms out of business. These laws will be studied in the next chapter. Predatory pricing was allegedly used by John D. Rockefeller to create Standard Oil at the turn of the century.

Is predatory pricing a problem? A company that wishes to drive its rivals, who have the same costs, out of business must charge prices that the competitors cannot match. This would require pricing below average variable costs. Any price above average variable cost would leave the rival firm above its shutdown point, and the firm would continue to operate. Accordingly, the predator would have to incur extra losses to drive a rival firm out of the market. For predatory pricing to pay off, the increase in profits due to the rival's departure would have to more than offset the losses from predatory pricing. Unless barriers to entry are very high, the rival firm could either return after the price has been raised or a new firm (that may have bought the assets of the failed firm cheap) may enter the market with low average costs.

If the market is comprised of a low-cost producer and high-cost producers, government policy should not force the efficient producer to keep prices high enough to cover the higher average variable costs of rivals, even if it means their demise. If the management of one firm has done a better job at containing costs, it should be able to reap the rewards.

The most highly publicized case of possible predatory pricing was the decision by American Airlines in the spring of 1992 to cut its full-fare tickets by one-half. American Airlines, the financially strongest U.S. airline, was accused in formal complaints by Continental, TWA, and Northwest of using "predatory" prices that they could not match and survive.

An examination of American Airline's "predatory pricing" reveals that American Airlines continued to price above its average variable cost and that American's low fares were a consequence of the weak demand for air travel resulting from the 1990–91 recession.

If the weaker airlines cannot survive in a low-fare climate, it is because they made serious mistakes in the 1980s. Specifically, they all borrowed too much money for an expansion that never came and ended up with excessive interest costs.

In the fall of 1993, the courts ruled that American Airlines had not engaged in predatory pricing.

The rules against predatory pricing should not be used to protect companies that have raised their average costs due to poor business decisions.

Even if American Airlines were pursuing a policy of predatory pricing, it is doubtful that it would achieve the desired result. As the weaker airlines go into bankruptcy, new investors can buy their assets at bargain-basement prices and keep the airline operating at much lower average costs. These new low-cost airlines might even pose a serious threat to American Airlines.

SOURCE: "The Airline Mess," *Business Week*, July 6, 1992, pp. 50–55.

two giant firms are necessarily inefficient. Some believe there is little difference between such oligopolies and monopoly. Others believe that if superior performance gained this domination, the outcome is efficient.

The noted Austrian economist Joseph Schumpeter argued that technological progress—the moving force behind economic progress—often establishes some firms as dominant in their industry. This dominance, however, does not last. Through the process of "creative destruction," Schumpeter believed that new ideas and new technologies eventually replace the old. The dominant concerns of yesteryear—the Western Unions and the U.S. Steels—are inevitably replaced by new dominant concerns—the IBMs and the Microsofts. These new dominant firms will eventually be replaced. Creative destruction means that the monopoly power created by technological innovation will not last forever.

If one or two firms dominate an industry because they have played the game better than others (Schumpeter's "creative destruction"), are not high profits their just reward? This important issue will be discussed in the following chapter on antitrust policy.

Chapter Summary

The most important point to learn from this chapter is:
Most markets fall between the extremes of monopoly and perfect competition. There is no single model or explanation of oligopoly because of strategic behavior. For every possible strategy—price leadership, collusion, focal points—there is a different explanation for how the industry behaves.

1. Monopolistic competition prevails when there are many small firms producing a differentiated product and there is free entry. The number of firms is so large that the actions of one firm have no impact on other firms.

2. An oligopoly is an industry characterized by a small number of firms, barriers to entry, mutual interdependence, and price making. The number of firms is so small that the actions of one firm will not have a significant effect on other firms in the industry.

3. An industry's concentration ratio is the percentage of domestic sales accounted for by the top (four or eight) firms. It is an imperfect measure of oligopoly power.

4. The prisoners' dilemma game explains the dilemma of oligopolists. It is a game situation in which it pays both players to cooperate, but it also pays each to cheat provided the other cooperates. Oligopolists are often in the same situation. There are benefits to cooperation, but it pays to cheat if other oligopolists do not cheat.

5. Oligopolies can exercise varying degrees of control over price. Because of mutual interdependence, the oligopolist's demand curve cannot be defined until the reaction of rival firms is known. The demand curve can vary from the kinked-demand curve to the market sharing of a cartel. Methods of oligopoly coordination range from formal agreements (cartels) to informal arrangements, such as price leadership or conscious parallelism. Collusive agreements, if successful, allow the participating firms to earn monopoly profits. Because there are incentives to cheat on the cartel agreement, however, collusive agreements tend to be unstable.

6. Collusion is difficult when there are many sellers, low barriers to entry, heterogeneous products, high rates of innovation, high fixed costs, and easy price cheating.

Policy Focus: **Predatory pricing is best controlled by the incentives of firms to make a profit in a competitive environment.**

Key Terms

monopolistic competition (p. 474)
nonprice competition (p. 477)
oligopoly (p. 478)

concentration ratio (p. 479)
mutual interdependence (p. 481)
prisoners' dilemma game (p. 481)

kinked-demand curve (p. 483)
cartel (p. 485)

price leader (p. 487)
conscious parallelism (p. 488)

Questions and Problems

1. Consider the four-firm concentration ratio for motor vehicles shown in Exhibit 2. Is this figure an accurate measure of the extent of oligopoly? Explain.

2. What is the relationship between the small number of firms and mutual interdependence in oligopoly theory? Why was mutual interdependence not considered in the chapter on monopoly and monopolistic competition?

3. Firm ZYX is one of three equal-sized firms in the widget market. It currently charges $20 per widget and sells 1 million widgets per year. It is considering raising its price to $22 and needs some estimate of what will happen to its widget sales. Why would it be difficult to make such an estimate?

4. Firm ZYX and the two other widget manufacturers meet in secret and agree to charge a uniform price of $50 and share the market equally (each gets one-third of sales). At the price of $50, each firm's marginal cost is $10. What are the rewards to cheating on the agreement if ZYX does not get caught? What is likely to happen if all three try to cheat?

5. Try to apply the prisoners' dilemma game to advertising in highly concentrated oligopolies.

6. Why is nonprice competition encountered frequently in oligopolistic industries?

7. In which situation would oligopoly prices be more stable: when rival firms match both price increases and price reductions; or when rival firms match price reductions but not price increases?

8. How does oligopoly theory explain why there are so many different types of oligopoly behavior—collusion, nonprice competition, conscious parallelism, price leadership?

9. Mel and Alice own the only two diners in a small town. If they agree to serve small portions, they can make larger joint profits. Is this cartel agreement stable?

10. How is the prisoners' dilemma game similar to a cartel?

11. Consider an industry that consists of three equal-sized firms. Their marginal cost of production is $2.99 at each level of output. The industry demand schedule is given in Table A. Assume that the three firms divide the market equally.
    a. What is the demand schedule facing each firm?
    b. What will be the cartel price and quantity?
    c. What is the incentive for each firm to cheat on the agreement?

TABLE A

Price (dollars per unit)	Quantity Demanded (units)
15	3
12	6
9	9
6	12
3	15

Doing Economics

Airlines are often characterized as an oligopoly in the United States. Are there barriers to entry in the airline industry? Is the product homogeneous or differentiated? Do you think that airlines are mutually interdependent? What evidence can you use to support this? Look in the financial press or in a major financial publication to find a report of airline quarterly or annual profit or loss. Are airlines making economic profits? Pick a pair of cities (one near you) between which at least three airlines fly. Call the airlines' local or toll-free reservations numbers and inquire about coach-class fares, both unrestricted and with advance-purchase and overnight-stay restrictions. Do all the airlines quote the same price? Does it seem that there is significant price competition between airlines? (Be careful answering this.) What about nonprice competition? If you have seen airline commercials on television, do they advertise price or nonprice aspects of their service?

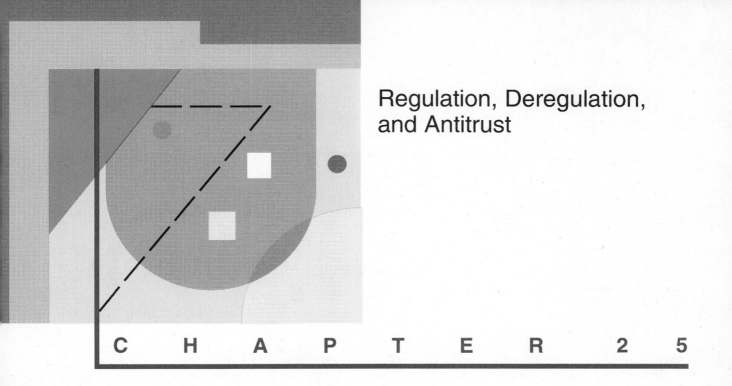

Regulation, Deregulation, and Antitrust

C H A P T E R   2 5

CHAPTER FOCUS

Government can protect citizens from monopoly. If a powerful monopoly is uncontrolled, it can charge its customers high, monopoly prices. Historical and contemporary examples of monopoly abuse of consumers abound: One need only think of the robber barons of the 19th century, charging farmers monopoly prices for rail transport and families high prices for kerosene and fuel oil, or of drug manufacturers charging sick people monopoly prices for medications produced under monopoly patents.

Public policy can provide protection against monopoly in a variety of ways: Government regulatory bodies can actually set the prices that monopolists are permitted to charge. Legislators can pass laws that prohibit certain types of market behavior or even prohibit monopoly outright. Oversight commissions can monitor potential abuses by monopolists.

The choice of appropriate public policy toward monopoly is sometimes difficult. Patents that grant pharmaceutical manufacturers monopolies may be necessary to promote research and development. If businesses are prohibited from aggressive competition, they may behave less forcefully in the marketplace. What should public policy do about monopolies that are won in a fair competitive struggle?

After studying this chapter, you will be able to:

- Describe the pricing formula of regulators and its problems.
- Explain how regulatory lag might raise the efficiency of regulated enterprises.
- Discuss the deregulation movement.
- List the legislation that makes up U.S. antitrust laws.
- Discuss the rule of reason.
- Explain why superior innovation creates problems in interpreting the Sherman Act.

REGULATION

One way to control monopoly power is to regulate monopoly prices and services. Such regulation is carried out by regulatory agencies of federal, state, and local government. Municipal and state governmental agencies regulate the rates of the local gas, electric, and phone company. Federal regulatory agencies regulate companies that serve national markets. Regulation at the state and local level is primarily directed at monopolies—the electric, gas, water, and telephone companies. However, state and local regulators also regulate businesses, such as taxicabs and barber services, that are potentially competitive. At the national level, federal regulatory commissions regulate a number of industries, some of which are potentially competitive. (See Exhibit 1.)

Some businesses are regulated for reasons that have nothing to do with monopoly power. Manufacturers of prescription drugs are regulated to ensure the safety and purity of their products. Manufacturers of automobiles are regulated to ensure that their cars meet emission and safety standards. Restaurants are regulated to ensure that they meet cleanliness standards. This chapter is not about such regulation. It is about regulation designed to control monopoly power.

The Scope of Regulation

It is difficult to estimate what proportion of the U.S. economy is regulated because most businesses are regulated in some way. On the one hand, regulated industries could include only those industries (such as communications, utilities, and insurance) in which rates and prices are controlled by government agencies. According to this criterion, as much as 10 percent of national output may be produced by regulated firms. If businesses that are government-supervised (such as the drug or meatpacking industries) are added, the regulated sector may be as high as one-fifth of national output.

Regulation of Prices

Monopolies abuse power by charging monopoly prices to earn monopoly profits. To protect the public from monopoly power, therefore, regulators must lower prices below the monopoly price. In addition to controlling prices, regulators issue licenses and franchises, and establish rules for product quality and safety. Their most important business, however, is to regulate monopoly prices.

Government uses **rate regulation** to control monopoly power.

George J. Stigler (1911–1992)

George Stigler was awarded the Nobel Prize in Economic Science in 1982 for his notable contributions to microeconomics and to industrial organization. Stigler grew up in Seattle, attended the University of Washington, and received his Ph.D. from the University of Chicago. At Chicago, Stigler studied under three prominent economists, Frank Knight, Henry Simons, and Jacob Viner, who taught him that "great reputation and high office deserve little respect in scientific work." Instead, Stigler learned to listen to the argument, look at the evidence, and ignore the position, degrees, and age of the speaker. After teaching at Iowa State University, the University of Minnesota, Columbia University, and a stint at the National Bureau of Economic Research, Stigler returned to the University of Chicago.

Stigler made scientific contributions in a number of areas of economics, ranging from the history of economic thought to microeconomics and to industrial organization. Stigler is best known for his pioneering contributions to the theory of the economics of information. He proposed that costly information explains why prices for seemingly identical products differ in the marketplace. Stigler's use of information costs to explain price dispersion is important to this chapter because economists had largely viewed price differences as the result of market power. In addition to theoretical work, Stigler pioneered empirical testing of theoretical propositions. Stigler's work on information economics was supported by his empirical observation that price dispersion is less for products that make up a significant portion of family expenditures.

Stigler's work on the economics of regulation is particularly relevant to this chapter. In his first paper on this subject, Stigler found that early state regulation of electrical utilities in the United States had a surprisingly weak effect on electricity prices. Stigler later sought to explain the weak effects of regulation by pointing out that regulators typically serve the interests of the regulated, shielding them from market forces.

> **Rate regulation** is government control of the prices (rates) that regulated enterprises are allowed to charge.

Regulators must decide what prices regulated firms can charge. They must use a reasonable pricing formula that is "fair" to both the regulated firm and to its customers.

The Regulatory Pricing Formula.   Consider how a government regulatory commission would go about setting the price (rate) for a regulated monopoly. If the firm were unregulated, it would charge the (monopoly) price that maximizes its profit. The regulatory commission's job to protect customers from monopoly pricing would require it to set the price below the monopoly price.

The regulatory commission must set "reasonable" prices. It cannot set a rate below operating costs plus a "fair" rate of return on invested capital. If regulators fail to allow regulated monopolies to earn a fair rate of return, the monopoly could appeal to the courts. In addition, regulators must allow a fair return on invested capital to attract further investment. If returns are too low, no new power plants or underground gas pipelines would be built. The requirement that rates must be reasonable has caused regulators to use a simple pricing formula: Price equals average operating cost plus a fair rate of return on invested capital.

Regulators set prices to cover operating costs plus a rate of return on capital.

EXHIBIT 1 Federal Regulatory Commissions

Commission	Established	Purpose
Interstate Commerce Commission	1887	Regulates railroads, interstate oil pipelines, and interstate motor and water carriers.
Federal Power Commission	1920	Regulates power projects and the interstate transmission of electricity and natural gas.
Federal Communications Commission	1934	Regulates interstate telephone and telegraph service and broadcasting.
Securities and Exchange Commission	1934	Regulates securities markets.
The Civil Aeronautics Board	1938	Supervised domestic and international aviation until its dissolution at the end of 1984.

This pricing formula creates two problems. First, regulated monopolies may lose their interest in combining resources efficiently to minimize costs. Second, the formula may encourage regulated monopolists to overinvest in capital. Let us consider each problem.

Inflated Costs. The pricing formula automatically passes increases in operating costs (whether justified or not) on to the consumer in the form of higher prices. If operating costs increase, so does the regulated price. The regulated firm need not be overly concerned with minimizing its production costs. Regulators typically do not have the information to determine whether reported costs are padded or legitimate. Regulators are reluctant to substitute their judgments on what costs are reasonable for those of management. (See Example 1.)

Overinvestment. The pricing formula calls for a fair rate of return on invested capital. If regulators determine that 10 percent is a fair rate of return, the regulated firm's profit cannot exceed 10 percent of its invested capital. If the company has $10 million worth of invested capital and the profit-rate ceiling is 10 percent, this company can earn a maximum profit of $1 million per year.

An unregulated company will add to its invested capital only if the resulting increase in profits justifies the investment cost. The regulated monopoly, however, can increase its profits merely by acquiring more capital. By investing an additional $5 million, the regulated company can now earn $1.5 million profit per year. Regulated firms have an incentive to acquire more capital than unregulated firms. This incentive leads to inefficiencies because regulated firms invest at the margin in projects with lower rates of return than those acceptable to unregulated firms.

Price regulation causes inflated costs and overinvestment in capital.

Regulatory Lag

Rate regulation appears to eliminate rewards to efficiency and innovation *if regulators raise rates immediately when operating costs rise.* In reality, rate increases are typically not granted on a timely basis. Regulated utilities must appeal to regulatory officials to raise rates, and red tape and foot dragging can create substantial delays. If rate increases are delayed while operating costs rise, the regulated firm will not earn its fair rate of return.

Regulatory lag pressures regulated monopolies to economize on costs. If

Chapter 25 Regulation, Deregulation, and Antitrust

EXAMPLE 1

Who Should Pay the Cost of Nuclear Power?

When capital capacity expands, short-run cost curves shift out. Once the investment has been undertaken, the industry operates on a new cost curve and cannot return to its original cost curve even if demand does not expand. In the case of electrical power, there is a substantial lag between the decision to build generating plants and their completion. Electrical utilities must make decisions based on the projected demand for electrical power ten years hence. Most nuclear power plants were planned during the late 1960s and early 1970s, when the demand for electricity was expanding rapidly. Electrical utilities started constructing nuclear power plants while anticipating steady increases in demand. With growing demand, the shifting out of the cost curve would mean that the industry could operate a lower average cost. In fact, the first nuclear power plants that came on stream did so in a period of expanding demand, and they proved quite profitable.

The energy crisis of the mid- and late 1970s had a profound impact on electricity demand. With rising energy prices, consumers cut back on energy usage, and the demand for electricity stopped growing. As new power plants came on stream, they could not be operated efficiently at the lower-than-anticipated demand levels of the late 1970s and early 1980s. The plants ordered more than a decade earlier were being finished at a time when no one wanted them.

The accompanying figure illustrates the economic problem of nuclear power. The figure shows an electrical utility that expected to be generating 600 megawatts of electricity in 1992. It therefore built a nuclear power plant to expand its capacity. The completion of the nuclear power plant shifts its cost curve from *ATC* to *ATC'*. *ATC'* yields a much lower cost for generating 600 megawatts than *ATC*. However, the 1992 demand for electricity is much less than expected. Only 400 megawatts are generated. The electrical utility (now located on *ATC'*) generates this lower-than-expected output at high cost.

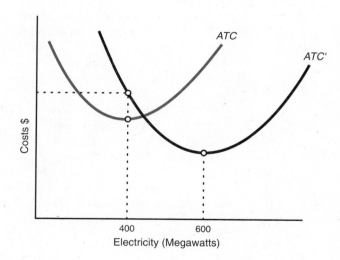

As a regulated industry, the rates of electrical utilities have traditionally been set to cover *ATC*. The fact that the electrical utilities that chose nuclear power were operating at higher costs than other electrical utilities raised a difficult issue for regulators: Should customers of the utility pay for the failure to choose the right *ATC* curve or should the company itself pay?

Regulators in California and in New England decided to make the utilities that chose nuclear power pay by not allowing them to charge customers prices high enough to recover their investment in nuclear power. The companies argued that this was unfair. If they had made a similar wrong decision that had not involved unpopular nuclear power, they would have been allowed to recover their investment. They were simply being penalized for the unpopularity of nuclear power.

operating costs rise and if years are required for the approval of higher rates, company earnings fall. By the time higher rates are granted, they are already outdated, and the incentive to hold down costs is still present. Regulatory lag is especially harmful to profits during inflationary periods when costs increase faster than rates.

Regulatory lag occurs when government regulators adjust rates some time after operating costs and invested capital have increased.

Regulatory lag reintroduces some incentives for regulated firms to use their resources efficiently, but it is only a partial (and very imperfect) solution to the fundamental problem: How can regulators encourage efficient operation when they are basically guaranteeing a fair rate of return?

The Effects of Regulation

To evaluate the effects of regulation, the rates, services, and costs that would have existed in the absence of regulation have to be compared to regulated rates. To compare actual regulated rates with unregulated rates, researchers have examined the history of U.S. utilities. Surprisingly, these studies show that the regulation of prices has made very little difference.

Why has regulation not had more of an impact on prices? First, the staffs of regulatory agencies are small and underpaid and cannot compete with the large and well-paid staffs of the regulated firms. Only the regulated firms know the details of the company's operation, and they can sidestep orders from the regulatory commission. Profits in excess of the fair rate of return can be concealed by creative accounting.

Second, the monopoly power of regulated monopolies may be exaggerated. If there are indeed effective substitutes (natural gas for electricity) or if industrial or commercial customers are prepared to move to another utility region if rates become excessive, then rate regulation does not make much difference.

Third, regulators tend to be loyal to the industry they regulate. Regulators often are closer to the companies they regulate than to the public they represent. Regulators are often recruited from the ranks of the regulated companies and often join the regulated companies upon leaving the regulatory agency. (See Example 2.)

DEREGULATION

Regulation is not limited to monopolies. There are numerous examples of regulation of potentially competitive industries. Examples of potentially competitive industries that are (or have been) regulated by federal agencies are radio and

EXAMPLE 2

Does Regulation Protect the Consumer or the Regulated Company?

City councils typically determine what taxicab companies will be allowed to operate in the city. State regulatory commissions determine what trucking companies can transport goods within the state and according to what rules. The rationale for government regulation in both cases is that someone must protect the public from dangerous unlicensed operators who operate according to their own rules. If taxi and trucking companies were free to make up their own rules and operate where they wished, the public interest might be harmed. During the 1992 election campaign, one candidate for a transportation regulatory commission spoke of the dread of sighting an unlicensed truck in one's rear-view mirror.

The consumer ultimately pays for regulation. In the case of taxicabs, the city will typically limit the number of taxicab operators. Licensed companies are usually those that have contributed to the campaigns of local public officials. New operators will not be allowed into the market on the grounds that they are unsafe. Only one taxicab company may be allowed to pick up passengers at the municipal airport. By limiting access to the market, the city council raises the price of the service.

State regulatory agencies limit the number of trucking companies allowed to operate within the state. Not only is the number limited, they are also required to follow complex and often arbitrary rules. For these reasons, it has proved cheaper for customers to ship materials across a state border to take advantage of cheaper interstate rates (such as from Houston to Dallas via Baton Rouge, Louisiana, rather than directly from Houston to Dallas).

Although the argument that regulation is required to protect public safety is persuasive, in reality, regulation often serves the economic interests of the companies being regulated.

television broadcasting, trucking, telecommunications, stock brokerage, passenger and freight airlines, railroads, and banking. In addition, state and local governments regulate numerous businesses that are potentially competitive, such as barbers, veterinarians, insurance, and taxicabs.

Economists tend to favor deregulation of potentially competitive businesses.

Most economists favor deregulation of industries that are potentially competitive. Deregulation advocates argue that it is better to let firms make decisions themselves—rather than bureaucrats—when the market is competitive. The public will likely get better service at lower cost.

Whenever regulation raises costs and prices, it creates social costs. Regulation cost between an estimated 0.7 percent and 1.8 percent of total national output in the late 1970s. If such percentages applied today, the costs of regulation would be $42 to $108 billion per year.[1]

Deregulation Legislation

In October 1978, President Jimmy Carter signed the Airline Deregulation Act, the first of the major deregulation acts. The Airline Deregulation Act allowed the airlines, rather than the Civil Aeronautics Board, to set fares and to select routes. Service to smaller communities was to continue for 10 years, financed by

[1] Robert E. Litan and William D. Nordhaus, *Reforming Federal Regulation* (New Haven: Yale University Press, 1983), p. 23.

government subsidy if necessary. The act phased out the Civil Aeronautics Board by the end of 1984. Other federal deregulation legislation followed. The Motor Carrier Act of 1980 curbed the Interstate Commerce Commission's control over interstate trucking. The Staggers Rail Act of October 1980 gave the railroads more flexibility in setting their own rates and allowed railroads to drop unprofitable routes. The Depository Institutions Deregulation and Monetary Control Act of 1980 eliminated interest-rate ceilings and allowed savings-and-loan associations to offer checking accounts. The Thrift Institutions Restructuring Act enabled savings-and-loan institutions to operate on a more equal footing with commercial banks. The 1982 Bus Deregulatory Reform Act allowed intercity bus lines to operate without applying for federal licenses in many circumstances.

Since 1972, the Federal Communications Commission has been gradually deregulating the television-broadcast industry by increasing the number of channels, removing barriers to direct satellite broadcasting, licensing new low-power television stations, and removing restrictions on cable television.

In 1975, the Securities and Exchange Commission made the brokerage fees charged by stockbrokers on the New York Stock Exchange freely negotiable. Prior to this, U.S. brokers were required to charge fixed commissions for stock transactions and were not allowed to compete on price. In the 1960s, the Federal Communications Commission began authorizing competitive long-distance telephone companies to build microwave networks. In a settlement with the Justice Department in 1982, rival long-distance companies gained access to the same connection to local telephone networks as did AT&T.

The Results of Deregulation

The early years of deregulation were anything but tranquil. Airline deregulation occurred during two costly recessions and a period of escalating fuel bills. Deregulation of trucking was fought by unions and by major trucking firms. Banking deregulation occurred during a period of soaring interest rates, bank failures, and an international debt crisis. Rival long-distance telephone companies did not gain equal access to local telephone exchanges until the mid-1980s.

Deregulation should be judged by its effects on prices, costs, and quality of service. Experience has shown that deregulation leads to lower prices for most but not all consumers. Air fares remained below what they would have been had regulation continued. Trucking rates fell. Stockbroker commissions on large trades fell. Bank customers enjoy more competitive rates on their savings. Long-distance phone rates are lower than under regulation. Firms previously protected by regulation lowered their costs, and these lower costs were passed on to their customers.

Deregulation has increased diversity of services, and has given consumers more choices. Customers have more trucking firms from which to choose. Airline customers can choose among a larger number of fares, destinations, and types of service. Banking customers can write checks on savings accounts. Television viewers have many more viewing channels. Long-distance customers can select among a number of long-distance companies offering different prices and services.

Deregulation has had both winners and losers. Customers in high-cost markets have had to pay more. Firms that could not meet competitive pressures have gone out of business or have been acquired by more successful firms. Employees have seen their earnings fall as firms have sought ways to lower their costs. Airline pilots, flight attendants, and baggage handlers would be earning more if there had been no deregulation. Bank profits would probably be higher if regulation had continued.

Deregulation has meant lower prices to most, but not all, consumers.

ANTITRUST LAW

Rather than regulating monopolies directly, the government can set the legal rules of the game through **antitrust legislation**.

> Antitrust legislation is legislation that controls market structure and conduct.

Antitrust law is made up of different pieces of legislation passed over the years and of court interpretations of these laws.

The Sherman Act of 1890

The Sherman Act of 1890 is the main piece of antitrust legislation.

The cornerstone of antitrust legislation is the Sherman Antitrust Act of 1890. The Sherman Act was enacted as a reaction to the public outrage against the monopoly abuses of the late nineteenth century in the railroad, steel, tobacco, and oil industries. People were convinced that too much monopoly power was bad, and Congress responded by passing the Sherman Act.

The Sherman Act contains two sections. Section 1 provides that

every contract, combination in the form of a trust or otherwise, or conspiracy, in restraint of trade or commerce among the several States, or with foreign nations, is hereby declared to be illegal.

Section 2 provides that

every person who shall monopolize, or attempt to monopolize, or combine or conspire with any other person or persons to monopolize any part of the trade or commerce among the several states, or with foreign nations, shall be guilty of a misdemeanor. . . .

Section 1 prohibits a particular type of market *conduct* (conspiring to restrain trade), while section 2 outlaws a particular market *structure* (monopoly). The vague language of section 2 has led to varying court interpretations over the years. Section 2 prohibits *monopolization*, not *monopolies*. Although the act of creating a monopoly is clearly prohibited, the legality of existing monopolies is unclear.

The Clayton Act and the Federal Trade Commission Act, 1914

The Sherman Act prohibited "acts in restraint of trade" but did not specify actual restrictive or monopolistic practices that were illegal. Moreover, the Sherman Act did not establish any agency (other than the existing Department of Justice) to enforce the provisions of the Sherman Act.

The Clayton Act of 1914 declared illegal the following four specific monopolistic practices if their "effect was to substantially lessen competition or tend to create a monopoly":

1. price discrimination (charging different prices to different customers for the same product),
2. exclusive dealing and tying contracts (requiring a buyer to agree not to purchase goods from competitors),
3. acquisition of competing companies, and
4. *interlocking directorates* (in which the directors of one company sit on the board of directors of another company in the same industry).

The Clayton Act gave private parties the right to sue for damages for injury to business or property as a result of violations of the antitrust laws, along with other penalties.

The Federal Trade Commission Act established the Federal Trade Commission (FTC). The FTC's role was to secure compliance with the ban on "unfair methods of competition" stated in the FTC Act. It was empowered to prosecute unfair competition and also to issue cease-and-desist orders to violators.

Other Antitrust Legislation

The Robinson-Patman Act of 1936 amended the anti–price-discrimination section of the Clayton Act. The basic purpose of the Robinson-Patman Act—which was passed during Depression times, when the rate of failure for small businesses was high—was to protect small businesses from the competition of the growing chain stores who were passing along discounts for large purchases to customers in the form of lower prices. Because the act sought to protect small businesses from the lower prices of large competitors, many authorities regard the Robinson-Patman Act as anticompetitive.

The Wheeler-Lea Act of 1938 extended the general ban on "unfair methods of competition" to include "unfair or deceptive" acts or practices. The FTC was empowered to deal with false and deceptive advertising and the sale of harmful products.

The Celler-Kefauver Act of 1950 broadened the Clayton Act's ban on corporate mergers by limiting mergers that occurred through the acquisition of one company's assets by another company. This antimerger provision applied if the acquisition served to lessen competition substantially or to create a monopoly.

Exhibit 2 provides a brief summary of antitrust legislation.

Interpretation of the Sherman Act

American antitrust policy is decided in the courts as well as in Congress. The Sherman Antitrust Act, the mainstay of antitrust legislation, left unresolved a basic issue: Do antitrust laws prohibit only market *conduct* that leads to monopoly, or is monopoly by the fact of its existence a violation of antitrust law?

The "Rule of Reason."   In early court rulings, the courts interpreted the Sherman Act as outlawing specific market *practices* in restraint of trade (mergers, price fixing, price slashing to drive out competition), not the existence of monopoly in and of itself. This interpretation became known as the **rule of reason**.

> The **rule of reason** stated that monopolies were in violation of the Sherman Act only if they engaged in unfair or illegal business practices. Being a monopoly in and of itself was not considered a violation of the Sherman Act.

The early landmark tests of the Sherman Act were the Standard Oil and American Tobacco Company cases, both tried in 1911. In both cases, the court ruled that these companies should be broken up into smaller companies (many of the major oil companies of today are spinoffs of Standard Oil). Both Standard Oil and American Tobacco accounted for more than 90 percent of output in their respective industries. The court's ruling, however, was not based on their 90 percent market share. The court ruled that Standard Oil and American Tobacco

EXHIBIT 2 Antitrust Laws of the United States

Acts	Enacted	Purpose
Sherman Act	1890	Prohibits business behavior that limits competition and attempts to monopolize.
Clayton Act	1914	Specifies illegal business practices that restrict competition.
Federal Trade Commission Act	1914	Established Federal Trade Commission to prosecute unfair competition and issue cease-and-desist orders.
Robinson-Patman Act	1936	Protected small businesses from growing competition of chain stores.
Wheeler-Lea Act	1938	Banned unfair or deceptive methods of competition.
Celler-Kefauver Act	1950	Broadened ban on corporate mergers.

The rule of reason declared that monopolies that did not use unfair business practices were not in violation of the Sherman Act.

violated the Sherman Act because they had both engaged in unreasonable business practices, not because they were in fact monopolies.

The implication of the Standard Oil and American Tobacco rulings was that if a monopoly does not engage in unfair business practices, it is not in violation of the Sherman Act.

Alcoa. The rule of reason prevailed until the Aluminum Company of America (Alcoa) case of 1945. The courts ruled that Alcoa was in violation of the Sherman Act because it controlled more than 90 percent of the aluminum-ingot market in the United States. Although Alcoa was also accused of using unfair pricing (setting ingot prices too high relative to aluminum sheet prices), the courts ruled that Alcoa was in violation of the Sherman Act because of its 90-percent market share.

The rule of reason said that companies that used unfair business practices that would ultimately lead to monopoly were in violation of the Sherman Act, while companies that were already monopolies, if they were well behaved, did not violate the Sherman Act. The Alcoa case appeared to reject this interpretation. In its place a *structure test* was applied in which size was the determining factor. Actual monopolization, not the attempt to monopolize, was Alcoa's offense.

Definition of Market. The Alcoa decision raised a fundamental issue: If the existence of monopoly is itself a violation of the Sherman Act, how is the market to be defined? Alcoa controlled 90 percent of the virgin aluminum-ingot market in 1945, but it had to compete in the scrap ingot market and to face competition from stainless steel, lead, nickel, tin, zinc, copper, and imported aluminum. In the 1945 Alcoa decision, aluminum substitutes were not included in Alcoa's market.

Subsequent court cases established a broader interpretation of what constitutes a market. The Du Pont cellophane case of 1956 established that the market should be defined to include products that are "reasonably interchangeable" with cellophane (such as aluminum foil, waxed paper, or vegetable parchment). The IBM case (which was dismissed in 1982) again used a broad interpretation of the market. Although IBM dominated the mainframe computer market in the early 1980s, its shares of other computer markets were relatively small: 20 percent of the minicomputer market, 18 percent of the word-processor market, and less than 5 percent of the telecommunications and computer-services markets.

Superior Innovation The Alcoa case raised concern that the Sherman Act would be used to punish businesses that had gained a dominant position through superior innovation and risk-taking. What about businesses that had gained a dominant position by fairly outcompeting rivals? Subsequent court cases have established the principle that firms that have fairly gained dominant positions in their markets have not violated the Sherman Act. In 1972, a smaller competitor charged that Eastman Kodak's method of introducing its pocket-sized instamatic camera gave Kodak an unfair advantage over other film processors. The court ruled in favor of Eastman Kodak, concluding that Kodak had earned certain advantages as a result of "reaping the competitive rewards attributable to efficient size." The principle that superior firms should not be punished for success was upheld in subsequent court rulings.

The Alcoa ruling required the courts to define the market and how to deal superior innovation.

MERGERS

One business firm can gain monopoly power by merging with another. If one company acquires another company, the new and larger company will likely have more market power than the two single firms. Antitrust legislation—directed against the creation of monopoly power—must therefore determine what types of mergers are to be permitted.

The Clayton Act of 1914 and the Celler-Kefauver Act of 1950 prohibit the acquisition of one company by another if this action reduces competition. The test for whether a merger is to be allowed is therefore whether the merger creates "monopoly power." There is no simple way to determine by how much a merger lessens competition. Federal agencies that deal with mergers have had to make this judgment.

There are three types of mergers. Mergers may be a **horizontal merger**, a **vertical merger**, or a **conglomerate merger**.

The three types of mergers are horizontal, vertical, or conglomerate mergers.

A **horizontal merger** is a merger of two firms in the same line of business (such as an insurance company merging with another insurance company or a shoe manufacturer merging with another shoe manufacturer).

A **vertical merger** is a merger of two firms that are part of the same materials, production, or distribution network (such as a personal-computer manufacturer merging with a retail computer-distribution chain or a machinery manufacturer merging with a machinery-parts supplier).

A **conglomerate merger** occurs when one company takes over another company in a different line of business.

The courts (especially since 1950) have adopted a virtual prohibition of horizontal mergers between two companies if both have substantial market shares. Exceptions are allowed when one firm takes over another firm that is on the verge of bankruptcy. For example, Jones & Laughlin Industries and Youngstown Steel were allowed to merge in 1978 to form the third largest steel producer. The approval of a multitude of airline mergers in the 1980's was motivated by the desire to keep these insolvent airlines in business.

Vertical mergers violate the Clayton Act if a buyer merges with a supplier, thereby restricting supplies to rivals, or if the merger results in a transfer of significant market power. On these grounds, Du Pont (a major supplier of automotive fabrics and finishes) was required to sell its 23 percent of General

EXAMPLE 3

Coke, Pepsi, Dr. Pepper, and Seven-Up

In early 1986, Coca-Cola announced its intention to acquire Dr. Pepper and Pepsi announced its intention to purchase Seven-Up. At the time, Coke and Pepsi accounted for two-thirds of the carbonated-drink market, while Dr. Pepper and Seven-Up accounted for another 11 percent.

In July 1986, a federal district court ruled against the two mergers. The purchases by Coke and Pepsi of their smaller rivals would not be allowed. The court ruling hinged on the following economic arguments. First, the courts ruled that the carbonated-drink market is distinct from the beverage market (fruit juices, coffee, tea, and other beverages). Coke and Pepsi accounted for a much smaller percentage of the beverage market, but combined they accounted for $2 out of every $3 of sales of carbonated drinks. Second, the courts ruled that Coke and Pepsi possessed significant market power. They were able to raise prices in specific sales regions without the loss of a significant number of customers. Third, the courts ruled that there were significant barriers to entry into the carbonated drink market. If the mergers were allowed, it was unlikely that new companies could and would enter the market. Although smaller companies could economically manufacture carbonated-drink concentrate, the advertising cost of launching a new product was in the range of $50 million. Another barrier to entry for a new drink is that vending machines have only a limited number of buttons—only four to six different brands can be accommodated. A final barrier to entry is that bottlers must operate at an economical scale of operations. The concentrate can be produced economically by small manufacturers, but bottling requires at least a 10 percent market share before profits can be achieved.

SOURCE: Lawrence J. White, "Application of the Merger Guidelines: The Proposed Merger of Coca-Cola and Dr Pepper," John Kwoka and Lawrence White (eds.), *The Antitrust Revolution* (Glenview, Ill.: Scott, Foresman and Company, 1989, pp. 46-79.

Motors stock in 1957 because Du Pont's influence over GM gave it a competitive advantage over other automotive suppliers. For similar reasons, Brown Shoe Company was not allowed in 1962 to acquire Kinney (a large shoe-retailing chain). The ban on vertical mergers between moviemakers and movie theaters was eased in 1986 in response to technological change in the entertainment industry. (See Example 3 for another example.)

The major exception to the prohibition of mergers among large companies is the conglomerate merger because it does not involve merger of competing companies. U.S. Steel was permitted to acquire Marathon Oil and Du Pont was allowed to acquire Conoco because the merging companies operated in different markets.

Conglomerate mergers have led to a substantial increase in the share of corporate assets controlled by the largest U.S. corporations over the past 30 years. The 451 largest corporations controlled 50 percent of corporate assets in 1960; by 1990, they controlled approximately 75 percent of corporate assets.

The pace of mergers in the United States has been uneven over the years (see Exhibit 3). In part, this pattern reflects the fact that antimerger legislation has changed over the years, as has the rigorous enforcement of antimerger legislation. It has been especially difficult to stop conglomerate mergers because the government has to prove that the proposed merger will actually reduce competition. When two companies in different lines of business merge, it is extremely difficult to prove that the merger will lessen competition.

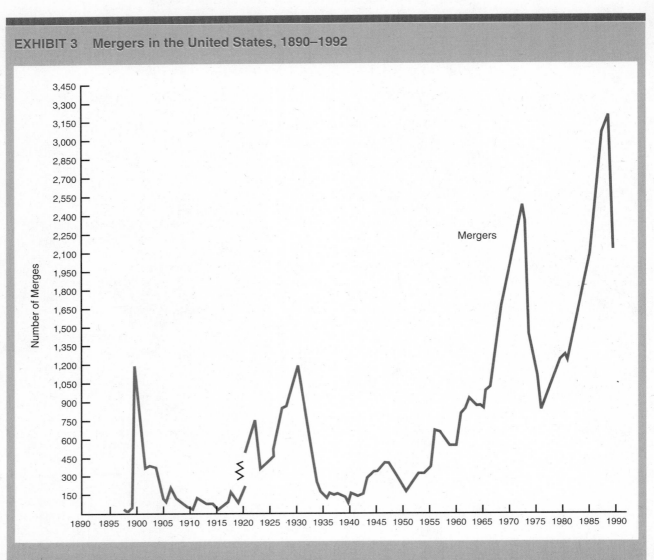

EXHIBIT 3   Mergers in the United States, 1890–1992

Number of Merges (y-axis): 150, 300, 450, 600, 750, 900, 1,050, 1,200, 1,350, 1,500, 1,650, 1,800, 1,950, 2,100, 2,250, 2,400, 2,550, 2,700, 2,850, 3,000, 3,150, 3,300, 3,450

Mergers

(x-axis): 1890, 1895, 1900, 1905, 1910, 1915, 1920, 1925, 1930, 1935, 1940, 1945, 1950, 1955, 1960, 1965, 1970, 1975, 1980, 1985, 1990

SOURCE: The National Bureau of Economic Research and the Federal Trade Commission, *Mergers and Acquisitions* updated data courtesy of W. T. Grimm and Company.

DO WE NEED ANTITRUST LAWS?

A number of economists argue that the costs of antitrust laws outweigh the benefits to consumers. Antitrust battles force corporations to spend billions of dollars on legal expenses, and litigation can stretch over decades. The IBM case, for example, lasted 13 years before its dismissal, cost the government more than $12 million, and cost IBM even more.

Some experts argue that the growth in international trade has largely antiquated antitrust laws, which were passed in the early part of this century. Major U.S. corporations that account for substantial shares of U.S. production must now compete with foreign companies. Modern technology is able to develop substitutes for the products that monopolists sell, and substitutes threaten all monopolies with

Should We Reregulate Airlines and Banking?

Deregulation began in earnest in the United States in 1978 and was hailed as the major achievement of the Carter and Reagan presidencies. The deregulation laws of the late 1970s and 1980s are discussed in this chapter.

Has deregulation been a success or failure? Critics of deregulation point to two industries, airlines and banking, as proof that deregulation has failed and should be reversed.

We maintain that regulation has been healthy for the U.S. economy, should not be reversed, and should be expanded into new areas such as intrastate trucking.

The Airline Deregulation Act of 1978 gave the airlines the freedom to set their own fares and pick their own routes. Prior to this act, the Civil Aeronautics Board awarded routes and set rates. The consequence was that consumers paid high prices and pilots and flight attendants received high salaries. In the years that followed, the number of airlines expanded to include new airlines such as Air California, People Express, Midway, and many others. A number of commuter airlines were established to serve smaller communities.

The 1980s and early 1990s were difficult for the airlines. The deep recession of 1980–81 and the rise in fuel prices associated with the Iran-Iraq war cut deeply into airline profits. Terrorism reduced the revenues of U.S. carriers with international routes, and the recession of 1990–91 again destroyed airline profits. In this newly competitive environment, weak airlines either failed or were taken over by stronger airlines. By the early 1990s, the U.S. airline industry had been reduced to three strong carriers with a number of weak airlines fighting for survival.

How can we argue that deregulation was good for the airline industry in light of this history? Deregulation has been good for airline customers. Prior to deregulation, flying was reserved for the wealthy and for business travelers on expense accounts. Since deregulation, flying has become accessible to virtually all. Airlines fares today are about 40 percent what they would have been without deregulation. Today the airlines offer more variety in terms of types of fares, connections, and services than before deregulation. The airlines have had to improve their productivity in the new competitive environment. Labor productivity in commercial aviation has risen more rapidly than productivity in other branches.

Many people blame the Depository Institutions Deregulation and Monetary Control Act of 1980 for the banking crises and failures that occurred subsequent to deregulation. This act reduced the legal distinction between banks and savings-and-loans institutions and allowed financial institutions to select their own investment activities and interest rates. Prior to this reform, savings-and-loans institutions were restricted primarily to making real-estate loans and could not issue checking accounts.

The root causes of the banking crises of the 1980s and 1990s were not deregulation but other factors. First, savings-and-loans associations, which were forced to make primarily real-estate loans under strict banking regulation, were caught with unprofitable loans in the 1970s as interest rates rose and real-estate values fell. Second, government bank-insurance programs encouraged banks to make risky loans knowing that their customers were insured by government bank-insurance programs. Third, the government felt that it could not afford to let big banks fail, no matter how badly managed, for fear that such failures would threaten the stability of the banking system.

What would happen if the airlines and banks were to be reregulated? First, customers would be denied the benefits of competition. Airlines could again pass cost increases along to consumers and airline ticket prices would rise. Banks again would have to follow strict rules concerning loans and investments. Second, government agencies would either directly or indirectly manage the nation's airlines and banking system. Some government agency would determine what airlines could fly where and at what prices. Another agency would tell banks what activities they could engage in and what interest rates they could charge.

Reregulation would raise prices to consumers, deprive them of diversity and quality, and lower productivity. There is no evidence that government regulators can do a better job running airlines or banks than can private management. In fact, many of the current problems of the airlines and banks can be traced to improper government policies (such as requiring savings-and-loan institutions to invest in real estate and poorly devised deposit insurance programs).

potential competition if their monopoly profits are too high. Finally, monopolies may indeed be the result of superior innovation and better management. To break up efficient companies may reduce rather than increase efficiency. Punishing successful companies could signal that aggressive innovation will be punished rather than rewarded.

The next chapter deals with agriculture, an industry that illustrates many of the principles of supply, demand, and competitive markets.

Chapter Summary

The most important point to learn from this chapter is:
There is no simple way for government to control monopoly power in the public interest. Price regulation leads to inefficiencies and antitrust legislation can punish superior competition.

1. Regulation of monopolies aims at preventing monopoly profits while allowing the monopoly to operate profitably and efficiently. Regulated monopolies are normally allowed to charge a price that covers operating costs plus a "fair" rate of return on invested capital. This pricing formula encourages inefficiency because higher costs can be passed on to the consumer and higher investment will automatically yield higher profits. Regulatory lag provides some incentive to minimize costs.

2. Deregulation frees competitive industries from government supervision. There has been a substantial move to deregulation since 1978.

3. Antitrust legislation seeks to control market structure and market conduct by setting legal rules for business. The Sherman Act outlaws actions that restrain trade and outlaws the act of monopolization. The Clayton Act specifies particular business practices that illegally restrain trade. The Federal Trade Commission Act established the Federal Trade Commission and banned unfair methods of competition. The Celler-Kefauver Act toughened the antimerger provisions of the Clayton Act. The "rule of reason" that only unreasonable restraint of trade violates the Sherman Act was applied by the courts until 1945. The rule of reason apparently was overturned in 1945 with the Alcoa decision when the courts ruled that size alone is a violation of the Sherman Act. In subsequent cases, the courts have ruled that monopolies created by superior technological achievement do not violate the Sherman Act.

4. The law prohibits mergers between firms in the same industry if both have substantial market shares. Exceptions are allowed when one firm takes over another that is on the verge of bankruptcy. Conglomerate mergers are usually not opposed because they do not involve mergers of competing companies.

Policy Focus: **A return to regulation of airlines and of banking would raise prices to consumers and lower efficiency.**

Key Terms

rate regulation (p. 494)
regulatory lag (p. 496)
antitrust legislation(p. 501)
rule of reason (p. 502)

horizontal merger (p. 504)
vertical merger (p. 504)
conglomerate merger (p. 504)

Questions and Problems

1. Explain why regulation of potentially competitive industries is not consistent with the objectives of regulation.

2. Explain why the Alcoa case of 1945 caused the definition of what constitutes the relevant market to become critical to antitrust cases.

3. You are the president of a regulated monopoly. You know that the regulators will allow you to set rates to cover operating costs plus a "fair" rate of return on invested capital. How would you behave? Would you behave differently if you were not regulated?

4. One explanation why regulating utilities has not made much difference in utility rates is that utilities face competition. How can a monopoly like an electrical power utility face competition and still be a monopoly?

5. You operate a regulated monopoly that sells in both a competitive and a monopolistic market. How would your company's price and output decisions differ in the two markets? What steps might you take to improve your position in the competitive market?

6. Deregulation of the television-broadcasting industry has been opposed by the three major networks. How would deregulation affect their profits?

7. Explain the contradiction raised by the rule of reason.

8. Why would innovative and risk-taking firms such as Boeing and Eastman Kodak oppose the Alcoa decision?

9. Explain why the government is more likely to approve a conglomerate merger, even of two giant firms, than a horizontal merger.

10. "Several ill-informed people have suggested doing away with our antitrust laws. To do so would return us to the robber barons of the nineteenth century." Evaluate this statement.

11. Would regulatory lag tend to raise or lower economic efficiency? Why?

12. Identify the following according to the type of merger:
   a. A merger of General Motors and Chrysler.
   b. A merger of Prudential Insurance with McDonalds.
   c. A merger of Hyatt Hotels and American Airlines.
   d. A merger of U.S. Foods with Safeway Stores.
   e. A merger of U.S. Steel with Ford Motor Company.
   f. A merger of B. F. Goodrich with General Motors.

Doing Economics

Consider the dormitory food service for your campus. How well does it satisfy the conditions listed in the text for a monopoly? What kinds of barriers to entry protect its position? Do you think it earns economic profits? Why or why not? Describe the demand situation faced by the food-service provider once it has won your school's contract and once the number of students subscribing to the board plan is determined. How are the provider's costs related to the quality of the food it serves? What incentives does it have in terms of food quality? If possible, examine a copy of the contract between the school and the food service or interview the college official in charge of food service. In what ways do the terms of the contract constitute "regulation?"

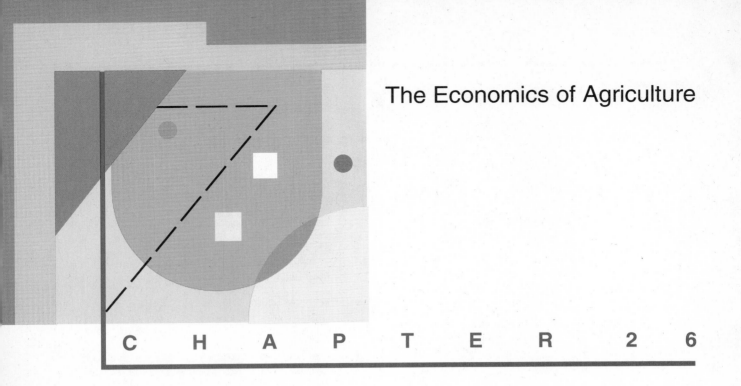

The Economics of Agriculture

C H A P T E R   2 6

CHAPTER FOCUS   The Great Depression of the 1930s focused attention on farming. In just three years (1929 to 1932), farm income fell to one-third of its previous level. The collapse of farm income was due to the collapse of farm prices. In 1932, farmers received less than half of what they had received in 1929 for their products.

The U.S. Congress and President Franklin Roosevelt responded to collapsing farm incomes by introducing programs aimed at stabilizing farm prices and farm incomes. In the early 1930s, it was widely accepted that farming exemplified the American life-style. Most nonfarming families still had friends and relatives in farming, and they could easily sympathize with the plight of farmers. Low prices were viewed as the culprit. So farm programs to raise farm prices were put in place in the 1930s. The Agricultural Adjustment Act of 1933 established the principle that farmers were entitled to higher prices (because agricultural prices had fallen more than other prices) and that it was the government's responsibility to support agricultural prices if they threatened to fall too low in private markets.

The American "farm problem" really consists of two problems. The first is the variability of farm prices, which causes farm incomes to fluctuate. The second is the long-run decline in farm prices relative to nonfarm prices. The second problem means that market forces hold the increase in farm incomes below the increase in incomes in nonfarm occupations.

This second problem has reduced the attractiveness of farming as a business and as a source of employment. The numbers of farms and the amount of farm employment have been shrinking for more than a half-century.

Public policy has tried to come to grips with the farm problem in an effort to halt the perceived decline of the farm sector of the U.S. economy.

After studying this chapter, you will be able to:

■ Explain why farm prices are more variable than other prices and why they have declined relative to nonfarm prices.

■ Know the consequences of price fluctuations and falling relative prices for American farmers.

■ Discuss the ways farm prices and farm incomes can be raised by government policy.

■ Understand the role of futures markets in allowing farmers to cope with uncertainty.

THE BUSINESS OF FARMING

Facts and Figures

Farming is a $100 billion business that accounts for about 2 percent of total output produced by the U.S. economy. In 1992, 3 million people worked on the 2 million American farms. The median farm family income was about $30,000. Eighty-seven percent of American farms were owned by individuals or families, 10 percent were owned by partnerships, and only 3 percent were owned by corporations. Although the rise of corporate farming has been widely publicized, American farming is still primarily a family business. Even though corporate farms account for only 3 percent of all farms, they account for 24 percent of the value of farm products. Corporate farms are much larger than family farms.

Farming and Competition

The American farm industry comprises about 2 million firms producing products such as wheat, corn, turkeys, chicken, livestock, and soybeans. Although corporate farms are much larger on average than family farms, they are still too small to dictate the prices of farm products. In other words, farms are price takers in product markets.

The individual farm faces a perfectly elastic demand curve. It is a price taker in product markets.

In perfectly competitive markets, the market demand curve is downward sloping, while the demand curve facing the individual firm is horizontal. As a price taker, the farm controls only one decision: How much output to produce? Based on market prices, the farmer must decide how much corn, cotton, or wheat to plant, or how many pounds of chickens, pigs, turkeys, and hogs to raise.

In the chapter on perfect competition we saw how a perfectly competitive firm would make these decisions. The farmer, as a perfectly competitive producer, produces that quantity at which price and marginal cost are equal. By equating price and marginal cost, the farmer maximizes profit. If prices do not cover variable costs, the farmer should temporarily shut down operations. If prices continue to not cover average variable costs in the long run, the farmer would have to leave farming.

Each farm follows the price equals marginal cost rule; therefore, the market supply curve for a particular farm product is the sum of the marginal cost curves of the thousands of farms that make up this particular market. The market supply curve is positively sloped. The market demand curve for a particular farm product is negatively sloped, and the equilibrium price is that price that equates quantity supplied and quantity demanded.

Ernst Engel (1821–1896)

Ernst Engel, a German statistician known for the discovery of the Engel curve and Engel's law, was born in Dresden. Engel's work with a French sociologist interested him in household budget surveys—a subject that would play an important role in his later work. Engel served as the director of the Prussian statistical bureau in Berlin, a post he resigned in opposition to Bismarck's protectionist policies. In 1885, he was among the founders of the International Statistical Institute.

Engel's study of the family budgets that he collected in various European countries convinced him that there was a strong negative association between the share of household expenditures on food and family income. This relationship is one of the first functional relationships ever established in economics, and it is this empirical proposition that has come to be known as Engel's law.

Engel's law is relevant to farming because it says that the income inelasticity of the demand for food products is less than unity. Demand is income inelastic when the demand for the product rises at a slower rate than income. If demand rises slower than income, the share of the product in total expenditures will fall. Engel's law explains why the share of resources devoted to agriculture falls with economic development and why farm prices have not kept pace with nonfarm prices.

TRENDS IN FARM PRICES AND FARM INCOMES

The incomes of owners of firms in the industry are affected by the prices their products receive. Farm products have inelastic price elasticities of demand. If the price falls by 10 percent, the quantity demanded of farm products will rise by far less than 10 percent. Demand for farm products is inelastic, for several reasons. First, food is a necessity. Second, in an aggregate sense, there are no substitutes for food. Third, any particular food item makes up a small portion of a family's total expenditures, and this reduces one's incentive to be price conscious. With inelastic demand, agricultural prices are positively related to total revenue or gross income. Thus, earnings in agriculture are positively related to agricultural prices. When prices rise, earnings from farming rise. When prices fall, earnings from farming fall. (See Example 1.)

The demand for farm products is inelastic. Agricultural income and farm prices are positively related.

Agricultural prices behave differently from manufacturing or service prices. It is these differences in price patterns that contribute to the farm problem. Most agricultural prices fluctuate more than nonfarm prices and agricultural prices have declined relative to other prices in the long run.

Farm Prices Fluctuate More Than Other Prices

Exhibit 1a plots the prices of some major farm products along with the prices of selected manufactured products. The difference between the two series is the much greater variability of farm product prices.

The variability of farm prices reflects itself in the variability of farm income. Farm income and farm prices are plotted in Exhibit 1b, which shows that the ups-and-downs of farm income follow the ups-and-downs of farm prices, as one would expect with inelastic demand. The lesser variability of manufacturing prices is a consequence of more elastic demand and the more stable supply conditions in manufacturing.

EXAMPLE 1

Price Elasticities of Demand in Agriculture

This chapter emphasizes the relatively low price elasticities of demand for agricultural products. The following chart gives estimates of the price elasticities of demand for various farm products along with some price elasticities for nonfarm products. Notice that the price elasticities of demand for farm products tend to be less than unity (although there are some exceptions). The price elasticities of demand for manufactured goods or services tend to be greater than for farm products.

Price Elasticities of Demand

Agricultural Products		Nonagricultural Products	
Milk	0.14	Automobiles	1.35
Eggs	0.23	Beer	1.13
Potatoes	0.30	Housing	1.00
Chicken	1.20	Alcohol	0.92
Lettuce	0.30	Tires	0.86
		Recreation equipment	0.88
		Tobacco products	0.46
		China and glassware	1.55

SOURCES: Hendrick S. Houthakker and Lester D. Taylor, *Consumer Demand in the United States: Analyses and Projections* (Cambridge, Mass.: Harvard University Press, pp. 166–67); Heinz Kohler, *Intermediate Microeconomics,* 2nd ed. (Glenview, Ill.: Scott, Foresman, 1983); George E. Brandow, "Interrelations Among Demands For Farm Products and Implications of Control of Market Supply," *Pennsylvania Agricultural Experimental Station Bulletin 680,* 1961, Table 1; Ralph T. Byrnes and Gerald W. Stone, *Microeconomics,* 3rd ed. (Glenview, Ill.: Scott, Foresman, 1987), pp. 105, 108.

The data on farm prices and farm income underscore the risks associated with farming. Farmers are unable to control farm prices because they act as price takers in competitive markets. Many of their costs are for nonfarm products such as machinery and chemical fertilizers which are more stable than farm prices, resulting in a cost-price squeeze. Farm profits are squeezed by falling output prices and rising input prices. When farm prices decline, farm profits and income tend to fall. If farm prices fall substantially, farmers find that their revenues do not cover their variable costs, and they must shut down.

Exhibit 2 uses supply, demand, and price elasticity to explain the greater variability of farm prices. The greater variability is deeply rooted in the nature of the supply and demand for farm products. The market demand curves for agricultural products tend to be relatively price inelastic, for the reasons noted above. On the supply side, agriculture is also different from manufacturing or services. Unlike manufacturing, the supply of agricultural products is subject to weather conditions. When temperatures are right and the amount of rainfall is right, harvests are abundant—the supply curve shifts to the right. When it is either too hot or too cold or too dry or too damp, the supply curve shifts to the left.

Exhibit 2 explains the effects on agricultural prices of the combination of an inelastic demand curve and a shifting supply curve. With an inelastic demand curve, relatively small increases in supply cause substantial drops in price. Relatively small decreases in supply cause substantial increases in price.

Shifting supply curves along inelastic demand curves are an important reason for volatile farm prices. There are even more reasons why farm prices are so

The shifting supply curve of agricultural products due to weather conditions causes movements up and down the inelastic demand curve for agricultural products, resulting in considerable variability in price.

EXHIBIT 1 Farm Prices and Farm Income

a. The Greater Variability of Farm Prices

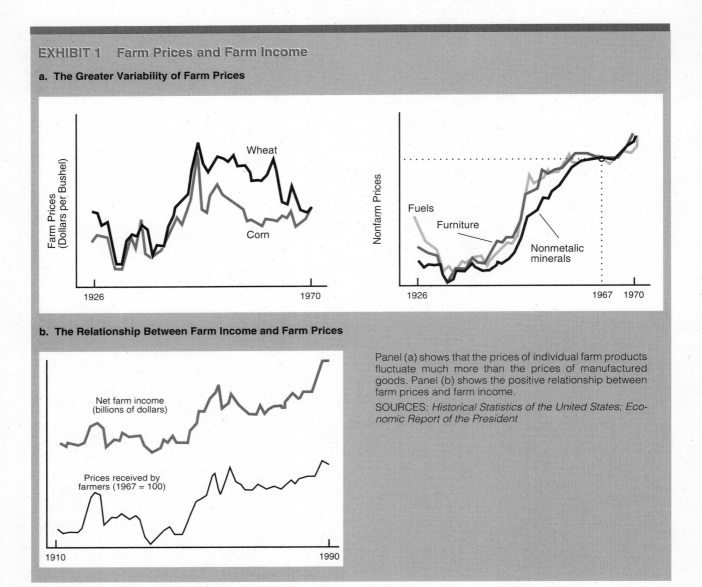

b. The Relationship Between Farm Income and Farm Prices

Panel (a) shows that the prices of individual farm products fluctuate much more than the prices of manufactured goods. Panel (b) shows the positive relationship between farm prices and farm income.

SOURCES: *Historical Statistics of the United States; Economic Report of the President*

volatile. Because of the time lag between planting and selling, farmers do not know what prices their crops will bring at market time. Farmers can mistakenly expect a high price and plant too much of one crop. Many farm products, like fruits and vegetables, are highly perishable. They must be sold before they spoil, even if prices are temporarily low.

Declining Relative Prices

Exhibit 3 plots long-term trends in farm and nonfarm prices. This exhibit shows that the *relative price* of farm products has declined over the long term. The relative price of farm products is measured as the ratio of prices which farmers receive to the prices which farmers pay. Exhibit 3 shows that not only is farming subject to greater price variability, it is also subject to a long-term decline in relative farm prices.

Supply, demand, and income elasticity explain the long-term decline in

EXHIBIT 2   Why Farm Prices Fluctuate

The demand curve for farm products is inelastic. We begin with the supply curve for "normal" weather conditions, S, which yields an equilibrium price of P. The supply curve under bad weather conditions, S', yields a much higher price, P', as the supply curve moves up the inelastic demand curve. The supply curve for good weather conditions, S'', yields a much lower price, P'', as the supply curve moves down the inelastic demand curve.

EXHIBIT 3   Trends in Agricultural and Nonagricultural Prices, 1910–1991

These data show that agricultural prices have risen less rapidly than nonagricultural prices over the long run.

SOURCES: *Historical Statistics of the United States; Economic Report of the President*

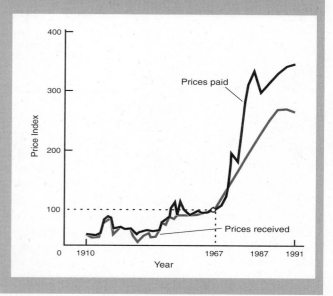

relative farm prices. In order to explain changes in prices over time, one must examine the factors that cause supply and demand curves to shift systematically over time.

Shifts in Supply.   Weather factors cause only short-run changes in supply. Technological improvements do, however, cause long-run increases in supply.

Technological improvements reduce the marginal costs of producing a given level of output and hence shift the supply curve to the right. If agricultural and nonagricultural firms experience equal rates of technological progress, then technological improvements would not explain the decline in the relative price of agricultural products (because both supply curves shift at the same rate). If, however, technological progress in agriculture is more rapid, then more rapid technological advances in agriculture explain at least part of the decline in relative agricultural prices. In fact, farm productivity has risen about 25 percent faster than nonfarm productivity since 1929, and the more rapid rise of productivity would depress farm prices relative to nonfarm prices.

The U.S. government has made substantial investments in agricultural technology through the Agricultural Experimental Stations located at land grant universities and through the U.S. Department of Agriculture. The government's Cooperative Extension Service has worked to disseminate technology information to farmers and to rural residents. No similar federal program exists for manufacturing. One need only think of the advances in hybrid seeds, biotechnology, and growth hormones to understand the rapid technological advances in agriculture.

The frequent complaints about farm crises shift attention from the fact the American agriculture is (along with Canada) the most productive in the world. (See Example 2.)

Shifts in Demand.   The decline in relative agricultural prices is also explained by shifts in demand. A long record of statistical research has confirmed that the demand for agricultural products is income inelastic. (See discussion of Engel's law in Gallery of Economists.) Income inelasticity means that when incomes rise by 1 percent, the demand for the income-inelastic product rises by less than 1 percent. Services and manufactured goods tend to be either unitary elastic or elastic, meaning that the demands for these goods rise at the same rate or faster than income.

The inelastic income elasticity of farm products means that as incomes grow over time, the demand curve for farm products will shift out relatively little because we do not eat much more. Farm-product demand curves shift out less than the demand curves for nonfarm products. The largest part of the increase in demand for farm products results from increases in population rather than from increases in income.

Shifts in Supply and Demand Together.   The supply curve of agricultural products has shifted out more to the right than the supply curve of nonagricultural products, owing to the more rapid technological progress of agriculture. The demand curve for agricultural products shifts less to the right than the demand curve for nonagricultural products as income rises. Exhibit 4 shows the effect of the shifts on agricultural and nonagricultural prices. Over the long run, the prices of agricultural products rise less rapidly than the prices of nonagricultural products, resulting in real price declines for agricultural products.

Agricultural prices have fallen relative to other prices because of rapid increases in farm productivity and income inelasticity of farm products.

THE DECLINING SHARE OF AGRICULTURE

The relative shift of labor resources out of agriculture over the past century has been substantial. In 1880, three out of four U.S. residents lived in rural areas. A century later, only one in five lived in rural areas. The shift of labor force was even more dramatic. In 1880 one in five American workers was employed in agriculture. A century later only one in one hundred was employed in agriculture.

EXAMPLE 2

How Productive Are American Farms?

The focus on the problems of American farming have diverted attention from its enormous success. American farms are the most productive in the world, along with Canadian farms. American farmers produce the surpluses that have been used to feed not only American families but families the world over. The success of American agriculture is explained by its rapid technological progress. American farmers now apply biotechnology and genetic engineering to raise the output of dairy and meat products, use the most sophisticated forms of chemical fertilizers, and use the research of the massive American farm research establishments located in land grant universities.

The accompanying table shows that the average American farm worker produces more than double the most productive European farmer, 15 times the Russian farmer, and 80 times the Chinese farmer.

Total Grain Production per Agricultural Worker, 1990

Country	Grain Production (millions of metric tons)
United States	84
France	41
Germany	25
Italy	9
Russia	7
Poland	5
Japan	3
China	1

Source: Handbook of Economic Statistics, 1990, Tables 23 and 99. Grains includes the major grains plus rice.

Economics teaches that factors must be paid their opportunity costs. As agricultural prices fall relative to nonagricultural prices, more and more people discover that agricultural employment does not pay them their opportunity costs. Accordingly, families move from farms to cities. They leave family farms or their jobs as hired hands on farms and find employment in nonagricultural occupations.

With declining real prices, only innovative farmers using technological advances and the most efficient production practices can lower costs faster than real prices fall. These farmers continue to earn profits and stay in farming without assistance. It is because of these highly efficient farms that only a small percentage of the labor force is required to feed the population and export farm goods to the rest of the world.

THE AGRICULTURAL CRISIS OF THE 1980s

The focus of this chapter has been the long-run economic forces that have shaped American agriculture. The 1980s was a period of "crisis" for American agriculture that concentrated even more attention on the farm problem.

The transformation of American agriculture actually began at the beginning of the 1970s, when the world turned to the U.S. to sell its large stocks of grains and

EXHIBIT 4   Why Agricultural Prices Have Risen Less Rapidly Than Nonagricultural Prices

a. Agricultural Prices

b. Nonagricultural Prices

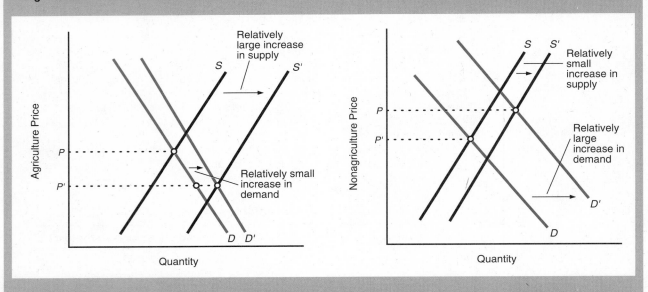

In both panels (a) and (b), the demand curve shifts to the right (demand increases) as income rises. But the demand curve for agricultural products shifts less than the demand curve for nonagricultural products. Because of more rapid technological progress in agriculture, the supply curve of agriculture shifts more to the right than the supply curve of nonagricultural products. The result is that nonagricultural prices rise more rapidly than agricultural prices over the long run.

oilseeds. In 1970, weather for raising crops had been poor worldwide, and only the U.S. had sufficient stocks of agricultural products to prevent hunger and political unrest. New customers for American farm products included the Soviet Union, which concluded large grain purchase agreements with the United States. Corn exports more than doubled from 1970 to 1972, driving the price of corn up from $1.08 per bushel in 1971 to $3.02 in 1974. As these figures show, the explosion of world purchases of American farm products caused farm prices to soar.

These events made farming a profitable business. This new situation caused two developments that continued to affect agriculture throughout the 1980s. First, U.S. farmers and the U.S. government became convinced that the expanding world market would continue to raise the demand for U.S. farm products. President Gerald Ford encouraged farmers to plant "fencerow to fencerow," and American farmers responded by borrowing to buy or rent more land and equipment. Second, the rise in market prices made it easy for the federal government to raise support prices because the high market prices made these moves initially costless.

The 1980s saw American farming expecting a further growth in world demand. This would raise farm prices even more and cause the immense investments in equipment and land made in the 1970s to pay off. Instead of rising farm prices, the 1980s was a period of generally falling farm prices. The decline in farm prices had a number of causes. First, the 1980s saw resumption of the downward course of farm prices. Second, the 1980s saw the rapid growth of agricultural output in other parts of the globe. Soviet grain harvests improved, and countries like India and even Saudi Arabia became relatively self-sufficient in certain agricultural commodities.

As farm prices fell, farm profits fell. Farmers who had borrowed heavily could no longer pay their costs of production and meet their interest and principal payments. Farm loans that had been secured by farm land were no longer covered because of a sharp drop in farm land prices. The net income of farmers fell, and a substantial percentage of American farmers operated at a loss and went out of business.

Major suppliers of agricultural inputs, such as International Harvester, went out of business after sustaining large losses, and a large number of rural banks folded. Price supports were lowered in an effort to reduce the need to purchase surplus agricultural products. Excess supply became so great that in 1983 the government paid farmers for not planting grain and cotton. Despite these efforts, harvests continued to be plentiful, and farm surpluses continued to build up. The cost of farm programs escalated as the federal government attempted to correct the problems in its programs while sustaining the income level of the agricultural sector.

The drought in the summer of 1988 was yet another disaster to befall farmers. It added to the growing number of farm bankruptcies and to the already declining number of farms. The number of farms shrank from almost 4 million in 1960 to 2 million by the end of the 1980s.

SPECULATION AND FUTURES MARKETS

Government farm programs (discussed below) aim to reduce the instability of farm incomes associated with fluctuating farm prices. It should be noted that private market forces also deal with the problem of variability of farm prices. Special private markets in which agricultural products are bought and sold now for delivery at a future date allow farmers to reduce the risks of price fluctuations.

Speculators affect the prices of commodities like wheat, corn, and pork bellies.

> **Speculators** buy and sell for the purpose of profiting from price fluctuations.

The business of speculation in commodities like wheat, corn, and pork bellies is so highly specialized that markets have developed that separate the business of storing commodities from the business of speculation. The grain speculator need not worry about what the purchased grain looks like, where it is stored, and how much to take out of storage.

Speculators can buy and sell commodities in a **futures market**.

> A **futures market** is one where a buyer and seller agree now on the price of a commodity to be delivered at some specified date in the future.

In the type of market most people know best there is an actual outlay of cash (or the arrangement of credit) for the immediate delivery of a good. The market in which a good is purchased today for immediate delivery is called a **spot (cash) market**.

Most of the goods consumers buy and sell are transacted in spot markets. In the grocery store, consumers pay now for goods that are delivered now. Stocks, foreign exchange, gold, and commodities like wheat, pork bellies, lumber, and copper are traded in organized exchanges. The organized markets in which commodities are traded are called *commodities markets*. In commodities markets, contracts can be made now for payment and delivery now.

In futures markets, prices are set now for products to be delivered in the future. In spot markets, prices are set for goods that are delivered at the time of the transaction.

Futures markets work quite differently from spot markets. *Futures contacts* are bought and sold in futures markets. In a futures contract, the terms (the price and the quantity) of a future transaction are set today. The buyer of a futures contract contracts today to purchase a specified quantity of a good (say, wheat) at a specified price at some specified date in the future. Both delivery and payment are to be made in *in the future*. The seller of a futures contract is obliged to deliver the specified quantity of the good at the specified price at the specified future date. The seller of a futures contract does not even have to own the commodity at the time of the sale.

For example, on January 1, the spot price of wheat is $3 per bushel. This means that buyers can buy wheat for immediate delivery at $3 per bushel. On the same day, the futures price of July wheat is $3.40. This means that buyers and sellers can enter into a contract on January 1 to buy wheat to be delivered in July at $3.40. The fact that wheat to be delivered seven months hence sells for more than wheat now means that speculators believe that wheat prices will rise over the next seven months.

Consider the farmer and the futures market. One substantial risk to the farmer is that prices will fall unexpectedly between the time the farmer plants and the time the farmer markets output. The farmer must decide what crops to plant without knowing what farm prices will be at harvest time. The existence of a futures market reduces uncertainty. If the farmer's crop will be harvested and sold six months hence, the farmer can contract to sell that output for delivery six months hence in the futures market.

Farmers can use futures markets to reduce the risks of price fluctuations.

Take the example of a farmer who plants a crop in April to be harvested in October. The spot price of the crop is $8 per bushel in April, but the futures price for October delivery is $9. The farmer can sell the crop for October delivery at $9 per bushel. If the spot price in October is $10 per bushel, the farmer has lost because the farmer has already sold at $9 per bushel. If the spot price in October is $7 per bushel, the farmer has gained. In either case, the farmer has been able to reduce the risks of price fluctuations by being able to sell in futures markets. Without futures markets, the farmer would have to bet on getting a favorable spot price at the time of actual delivery.

GOVERNMENT FARM PROGRAMS

Price Supports

Government farm programs use price supports to raise agricultural prices above the prices that would prevail in competitive markets. Exhibit 5 shows how price support programs work. The government sets a *support price* of wheat, for example. The price is called a support price because the government stands ready

EXHIBIT 5   How Government Farm Price Supports Work

The price *P* is the price that would be in effect in the absence of a government price support program. It is the equilibrium price. If, however, the government is willing to purchase any wheat not purchased by private buyers at a support price *P'*, and if this support price is above the equilibrium price, then the government must buy the surplus (the difference between the quantity supplied and the quantity demanded at the support price). By being willing to buy at the support price, the government ensures that the price will not fall below the support price.

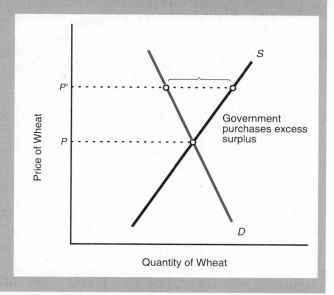

to purchase any wheat that is not purchased by private wheat buyers at this price. If the support price is above the private market price, then the government must buy the *excess supply, or surplus* of wheat. The government can accumulate this wheat to be sold when the support price is below the market price or to give wheat to needy countries through its foreign-aid program.

Who benefits and who loses from price supports? The farmer able to sell at higher prices benefits. The business that sells inputs to farmers also benefits as the demand for their goods and services increases. The consumer of farm products loses because the support program raises farm prices and hence food prices. The loss to consumers is a hidden loss. The consumer is not necessarily aware of what food prices would have been without the support program. Tax-payers pay for the program directly through higher taxes.

Direct Payments to Farmers

An alternative to price supports, incorporated in farm programs in 1973, is direct government payments to farmers. The magnitude of the direct payments, called *deficiency payments*, depends on the difference between the market price and a *target price* established by the government. For example, if the target price is $5 per bushel but the agricultural product is selling for $4 per bushel, the farmer receives $1 per bushel as a direct payment from the government. This is a simplified, but reasonably accurate portrayal of how a deficiency payment works. (See Exhibit 6.)

Direct deficiency payments do not increase the price paid by consumers. It puts the entire burden of the higher price on taxpayers. Some of the benefits are passed through to the suppliers of agricultural inputs, who are able to sell larger quantities of farm machinery, chemical fertilizers, and land to farmers at higher prices.

EXHIBIT 6   Direct Payments to Farmers With Target Prices

The government sets the target price, and farmers supply output *a* on the supply curve. With a supply of *ca* units, private markets will set a price of *cb* to clear the market. Farmers receive a direct payment of *ba* for each unit of output, for a total direct payment equal to *ab* × *Oc*.

Supply Control Programs

A third approach to raising farm prices is to reduce the supply of agricultural products. Because farmers operate in a competitive industry, it is not possible for them to form cartels to regulate output. If, however, government programs were to cause farmers generally to limit output, then agricultural prices would rise. Remember, with inelastic demand, a reduction in supply pushes up prices considerably.

American farm policy includes programs that provide economic incentives to farmers to restrict their sown acreage. Crop farmers are required to *set aside* a certain portion of land to qualify for the government program. Payments are made to farmers who put part of their land into soil conservation uses rather than planting them in crops.

The number of farms has continued to shrink despite government programs to prop up the American farmer. American farming remains the most productive in the world. (See Example 2.) The major policy issue is whether government intervention should continue or whether farm prices and farm incomes should be set by the marketplace, as are other prices and incomes.

A number of sectors of the economy have experienced declining relative prices, such as personal computers, natural gas, and long-distance telephone service, but they have not been protected from market forces by the government. In fact, most economists would argue that market forces have made them more healthy while making the consumer better off. The most innovative firms survive, and technological advances are passed on to the public in the form of higher quality products and lower prices. American farming, like personal computers and long-distance telephone service, has experienced rapid technological growth. The elimination of government supports would mean that marginal farms would not survive, just as marginal computer manufacturers do not survive when

Is It Up to Government to Solve the Farm Problem?

Although American farming is the most productive in the world, the government has intervened heavily in the business of farming since the 1930s. The perception has been that the government must act decisively to prevent the collapse of the American farm. The decline in the number of farms, the failure of farm prices to keep pace with other prices, and the massive failure of farms in the 1980s are cited to justify government farm programs.

The government has created a complex system of price supports, direct payments, and supply controls to aid the farmer. The goal of these policies has been to keep agricultural prices from falling too much relative to other prices. In this way, it was felt, the family farm would be preserved and American farming would remain healthy.

computer prices drop. The public policy question is whether the loss of marginal farms justifies expensive farm programs that cost both taxpayers and consumers dearly.

Chapter Summary

The most important point to learn from this chapter is: Agriculture is a perfectly competitive industry that has inelastic demand curves, unstable supply curves, and low income elasticities. These factors cause agricultural prices to be unstable and to fall relative to other prices over the long run.

1. Farming is a competitive business dominated by the small firm—the family farm. The farm acts as a price taker in product markets.

2. The farm problem is caused by fluctuations in farm prices as a result of shifting supply and inelastic demand, and by the long-term decline in farm prices relative to other prices. The long-term relative price decline has been caused by rapid technological progress, a price-inelastic demand, and an income-inelastic demand.

3. Futures markets allow farmers to reduce their risks by being able to enter into contracts now for future delivery of crops.

4. The 1970s was a period of rising world demand for American farm products. Farm prices rose, and farming was profitable. Increased world production drove prices down in the 1980s, causing farm profits to fall, and the number of farms to decline.

Policy Focus: **We must decide whether American farming, unlike other branches, requires special protection from market forces.**

Key Terms

speculators (p. 519)
futures markets (p. 519)

spot (cash) market (p. 519)

Questions and Problems

1. The demand curve facing a particular farm is perfectly elastic. This means that that farm can sell all it wants at the market price. Why do not farms supply an infinite amount if they can sell all they want at the prevailing price?

2. The government sets a price support for butter at $1.00 per pound. Explain what will happen to government purchases if the price established without government purchases is $1.00. If it is $1.20?

3. Explain the role of the income elasticity and the price elasticity of demand in accounting for the farm problem.

4. Why do farmers not form their organization of wheat-growing producers to control the amount of wheat produced?

5. Why does the text call price supports a hidden payment to farmers?

6. If productivity is rising rapidly in agriculture, what will be the effect of acreage restrictions? Would acreage restrictions be more likely to raise prices if there were no technological progress?

7. Using supply and demand curves, explain what would happen to wheat prices if Japanese laws protecting Japanese wheat farmers were abolished.

8. The chapter asserts that futures markets help farmers cope with risks. Explain why this is so.

9. Explain who pays for supply control programs, price support programs, and direct payments to farmers.

10. What are the differences between spot and futures markets?

Doing Economics

Most agricultural products have strong seasonal production cycles. For example, look at the monthly data on production and consumption of a major agricultural product such as cotton (listed under Textile Products) or rice (listed under Food and Kindred Products) in the blue-colored pages of a recent issue of the *Survey of Current Business,* a publication of the U.S. Department of Commerce that is available either in the government documents or general periodicals section of most libraries.

What is the seasonal pattern in production? Do you think the demand for these products moves very much over the seasons of the year? What do the data on consumption (or shipments of processed product) and exports say about the seasonal pattern of consumption? What seasonal pattern of price change would you predict? What is the actual seasonal pattern of prices? How do you explain this difference? Does the behavior of "stocks" (inventories) give you a clue?

Factor Markets

P A R T S I X

CHAPTER 27
Factor Markets

CHAPTER 28
Labor Markets

CHAPTER 29
Labor Unions

CHAPTER 30
Interest, Rent, and Profit

CHAPTER 31
Income Distribution and Poverty

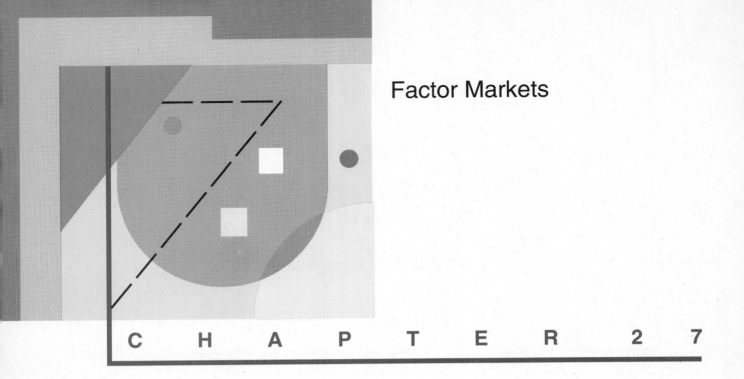

Factor Markets

CHAPTER 27

CHAPTER FOCUS   Although few of us own and operate businesses, most of us supply factors to businesses. If we have a job, we provide our physical and intellectual skills to our employers. If we own stocks, bonds, or certificates of deposits, we provide businesses with capital (credit) that they can use to expand and modernize their businesses. We may even own a tractor, truck, or Roto-Rooter that we lease out directly to businesses to use as capital. If we own farmland that has been leased to a farmer or a corner lot on which a gas station is located, we have supplied the land necessary to operate these businesses.

Almost everyone works at a job at some time in life. We therefore have a lot of practical experience with labor markets. In fact, about 75 percent of all income is earned as labor income. Earnings from capital are less significant, while earnings from the ownership of land are, at an economywide scale, relatively small.

This chapter focuses on factor markets in general. The following chapters will describe specific factor markets such as those for labor, capital, and land.

After studying this chapter, you will be able to:

- Calculate the marginal contribution of a factor to a firm's revenue.
- See the difference between price makers and price takers in the factor markets.
- Explain the profit-maximizing rule in the factor market.
- Understand the least-cost rule for hiring inputs.
- Describe how the functional distribution of income is determined.

THE CIRCULAR FLOW DIAGRAM

The circular flow diagram introduced in Chapter 2 shows the connecting link between product markets and factor markets. Exhibit 1 shows that firms produce goods and demand factors, but that households demand goods and supply factors. Households and firms meet in two distinct markets: the market for goods and the market for factors.

This is a highly simplified picture. In the real world, firms also demand factors from other firms. The Ford Motor Company buys tires from B. F. Goodrich and computer services from International Business Machines. General Mills buys wheat from farmers or grain elevators. However, the principles that govern the firm's purchases of labor or capital from households are identical to those that determine its purchases of inputs that are produced by other firms.

Firms hire inputs for the same reason they produce outputs: it is profitable. Similarly, households demand the output of firms for the same reason they supply factors: it adds to their utility. The circular flow diagram shows that everything takes place simultaneously.

THE TWO FACES OF THE FIRM

The firm shows two faces to the outside world. One face is that of a *seller of the goods and services it produces* in product markets. As a seller, the firm can be either a price taker or a price maker (as described in an earlier chapter). The other face is that of a *buyer of inputs* in factor markets. A firm can produce no output without factor inputs. In a factor market, the firm can again be either a price taker or a price maker.

Price Making and Price Taking in the Factor Market

The definitions of a **price taker** and **price maker** in factor markets are analogous to the definitions of price takers and price makers in product markets.

> A **price taker** in a factor market is a buyer of an input whose purchases are not large enough to affect the price of the input. The price-taking firm must accept the market price as given.

GALLERY OF ECONOMISTS

John Bates Clark (1847–1938)

John Bates Clark was born in Providence, Rhode Island, in 1847. His discovery of the marginal productivity theory of factor payments made him the first world-famous American economist. His book, *The Distribution of Wealth* (1899), argued that each factor of production—land, labor, and capital—is paid the value of its marginal product. Clark argued that unions had no effect on marginal productivity and, therefore, no impact on wages. He believed in compulsory arbitration of labor disputes, and that wages should be set at the level prevailing in comparable employments.

Clark taught at Carleton, Smith, and Amherst colleges and finished his career at Columbia University. His superb command of language once prompted one of his critics to complain that his literary skills gave him an unfair advantage. The American Economics Association honors him every year by bestowing the John Bates Clark medal to the best economist under the age of forty.

EXHIBIT 1   The Circular Flow of Economic Activity

The circular flow diagram shows that firms operate simultaneously in the product market and in the factor market. The upper half of the circular flow shows the flows of products and purchases between the business and household sectors. The bottom half shows the flows of factors from households to business firms and the payment of factor income from business firms to households for the factors of production.

Exhibit 2 shows the four possible market conditions the firm may face in its role as either a seller of products or a buyer of factor inputs and in its role as either a price taker or a price maker:

1. The firm may be a price taker in both the product and factor markets—panels (a) and (b).
2. The firm may be a price maker in both the product and factor markets—panels (c) and (d).
3. The firm may be a price taker in the product market and a price maker in the factor market—panels (a) and (d).
4. The firm may be a price maker in the product market and a price taker in the factor market—panels (b) and (c).

There is no necessary link between the amount of competition a firm faces on one side of the market and the amount it faces on the other side. A monopolist may purchase its land, labor, and capital inputs as a price taker. A perfectly competitive firm may be a price maker in the factor market. Although there are numerous exceptions, in the most likely scenario the firm will face more competition on the input (factor) side than on the output (product) side. In selling its products, the firm faces competition from other firms that produce either the same product or a product that serves as a substitute for the goods it produces. As demonstrated in previous chapters, such competition may be limited. The picture is different in factor markets. Factors, unless highly specialized, can typically be used by different firms and by different industries. Essentially all firms compete with one another for skilled and unskilled labor; they all compete with one another for capital and for land. The firm, therefore, faces competition for inputs not only from those firms with which it competes in the product market but also from firms in entirely different industries. Oil companies, universities, law offices, and retailers all compete for skilled secretaries. Restaurants, motels, gas stations, retailers, and home builders all compete for land in major cities.

As with most generalizations, there are exceptions to the rule that firms face more competition on the input side than the output side. A textile mill located in a small, isolated town may face little competition from other employers when hiring local labor, while its sales on the output side may be in a perfectly (or near perfectly) competitive product market. Certain skilled people—professional athletes, for example—are so specialized that they are suited for employment in only one industry. The employer is, therefore, likely to be a price maker in this factor market. Certain types of capital—such as oil-drilling rigs—are suited to only one use, unlike trucks, lathes, and computers. Firms purchasing such specialized equipment are more likely to be price makers.

When the firm has the power to influence the price at which it purchases inputs, the firm has **monopsony** power.

A firm will usually face more competition from other firms when hiring inputs than when selling outputs.

Like pure monopoly, pure monopsony is rare. Few firms are the sole buyer of a factor of production. Even if the isolated textile mill—which appears to have a

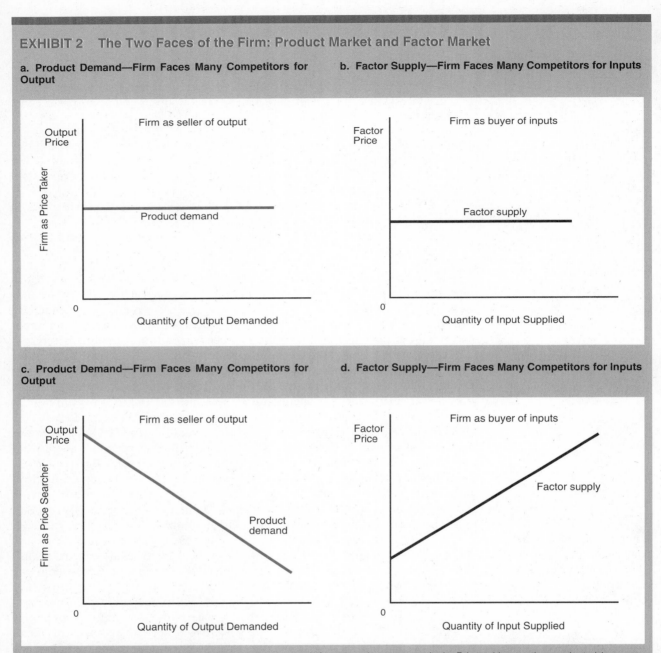

EXHIBIT 2   The Two Faces of the Firm: Product Market and Factor Market

a. Product Demand—Firm Faces Many Competitors for Output

Firm as seller of output

Output Price

Firm as Price Taker

Product demand

0   Quantity of Output Demanded

b. Factor Supply—Firm Faces Many Competitors for Inputs

Firm as buyer of inputs

Factor Price

Factor supply

0   Quantity of Input Supplied

c. Product Demand—Firm Faces Many Competitors for Output

Firm as seller of output

Output Price

Firm as Price Searcher

Product demand

0   Quantity of Output Demanded

d. Factor Supply—Firm Faces Many Competitors for Inputs

Firm as buyer of inputs

Factor Price

Factor supply

0   Quantity of Input Supplied

Panels (a) and (b) show a price-taking firm in the product and factor markets, respectively. Price taking on the product side means that the firm can sell all it wants at the existing market price (demand is perfectly elastic). Price taking in the factor market means that the firm can hire all the factors it wants at the prevailing factor price (factor supply is perfectly elastic). Panels (c) and (d) show price making in the product and factor markets, respectively. Price making on the product side means that the firm faces a downward-sloping product demand curve. To sell more, it must lower its price. Price making on the factor side means that the firm faces an upward-sloping factor supply curve. To hire more factor inputs, the firm must pay a higher factor price.

monopsony over the local labor market as the sole major employer in town—offers wages that are too low, people may move to other cities, or outside firms might be attracted into the market by the prospect of cheap labor. This textile mill faces competition from factories located in other cities (in the case where people move) and also from new firms entering the local labor market.

Marginal Factor Cost

The concepts of marginal revenue and marginal cost play a decisive role in the theory of product markets described in the preceding chapters. Profit-maximizing firms produce that level of output at which marginal revenue and marginal costs are equal. If they follow the $MC = MR$ rule, they will maximize profits or minimize losses. In the theory of factor markets, there are concepts analogous to marginal cost and marginal benefit that are applicable to the input side of the firm. Inputs have costs and benefits to the firm, just as production has costs and benefits to the firm. In making its input decisions, the most important cost the firm must consider is the additional cost of hiring one more unit of an input, or **marginal factor cost (MFC)**. As with other marginal measures, it is calculated by dividing the increase in costs by the increase in the amount of the factor in question.

> Marginal factor cost *(MFC)* is the extra cost to the firm per unit increase in the amount of the factor; it is the increase in costs divided by the increase in the amount of the factor.

The price of a factor of production is the wage (in the case of labor) or the rental (in the case of capital or land) that the firm must pay to hire or use the factor. Recall that, in the product market, price exceeds marginal revenue if the firm is a price maker but that price equals marginal revenue when the firm is a price taker. Being a price taker means that the buyer is too small a part of the market to affect the factor's price.

In the factor market, if the firm is a price taker, marginal factor cost is simply the factor's market price. The firm can hire one more unit of the factor (or more than one unit) at the going market price. The firm's actions have no effect on the input's price.

If the firm is a price maker in the factor market, the firm's marginal factor cost will exceed the market price of the factor. As a price maker, the firm is a large enough portion of the particular factor market so that it cannot buy more of the factor without driving up its market price. To use one more unit of the input per period, the firm must pay the same higher price for all units that it would need to pay for the last unit hired. In other words, the extra unit of the factor will cost the firm not only its market price but also the higher price paid on units hired at a cheaper price.

For example, Exhibit 3 shows that because Firm A is a price taker, it can rent as much farmland as it wants at the market price of $500 per acre. It currently rents 100 acres. For this firm, the price of the input and the marginal factor cost are equal. Firm B is a price maker that currently rents 1,000 acres at $500 per acre, but B would have to pay $500.10 to rent 1,001 acres. The marginal factor cost of Firm A is the market price of $500. The marginal factor cost of Firm B is the price of the 1,001st acre ($500.10) plus the $100 extra ($0.10 $\times$ 1,000) it must pay for the original 1,000 acres. Thus, the marginal factor cost of Firm B at an input level of 1,000 acres is $600.10, which is higher than the factor price ($500). Thus, B's *MFC* curve lies everywhere above the factor's supply curve. Monopsony is important because the additional cost of hiring a factor exceeds its price.

As noted earlier, price taking is more likely in factor markets than is price making (monopsony). The remainder of this chapter will examine the behavior of firms that are price takers in factor markets—firms in which marginal factor cost and factor price are the same. The next chapter will study the role of monopsony in the labor market.

For price makers in factor markets, marginal factor cost is greater than the factor prices; for price takers in factor markets, marginal factor cost equals factor price.

EXHIBIT 3 Competition Versus Monopsony in the Market for Inputs

a. Firm A

b. Firm B

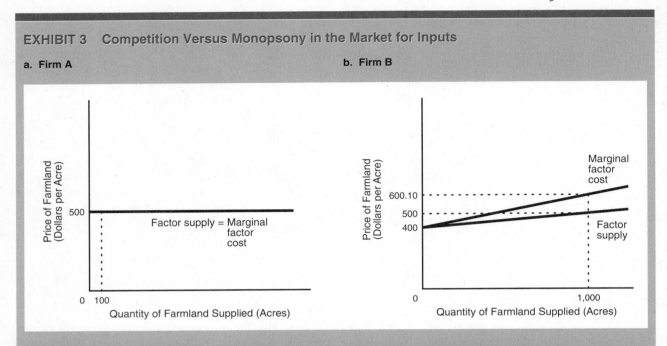

Panel (a) shows a price-taking firm that can hire all the inputs it wants at the going market price. The horizontal supply curve facing the firm is its marginal-factor cost curve. Panel (b) shows a price-making firm on the factor side that must pay higher input prices to get larger quantities of the input. To use more input per period requires a higher price for all quantities of the input; therefore, the extra cost of hiring one more unit of input is the price plus the increase in the cost of using the old input quantity. Thus, the *MFC* curve lies above the factor's supply curve.

THE FIRM'S DEMAND FOR FACTORS OF PRODUCTION

The firm's demand for a factor input depends on the input's physical productivity and on the demand for the good the factor is being used to produce.

The chapter on "Costs and Productivity" defined the production function as showing the relationship between output and inputs. Recall that we define a factor's *marginal physical product (MPP)* as the increase in output divided by the increase in the amount of the factor, holding all other factors constant.

All production functions exhibit the *law of diminishing returns*. As explained earlier, the law states that as ever larger quantities of a variable factor are combined with fixed amounts of the firm's other factors, the marginal physical product of the variable factor will eventually decline.

Derived Demand

Consumers buy products because they yield consumer satisfaction. The firm buys factors of production for a different reason. Inputs are purchased because they produce goods and services that create revenue for the firm. No matter how productive the input is in producing output, that input will not be demanded unless it produces an output that commands a positive price in the marketplace. The garment industry buys sewing machines because they help to produce suits, shirts, and dresses that consumers will buy. Automobile workers are hired because they help produce automobiles that people will buy. Wheat land is rented because it

EXAMPLE 1

Derived Demand: Air Travel, and Aircraft Leases

This chapter teaches that the demand for factors of production is a derived demand. The demand for the factor depends on the demand for the product that the factor assists in producing. A clear case in point has been the worldwide slowdown in passenger air travel that characterized the early and mid-1990s. The U.S. recession and its spread to Europe caused a sharp cutback in the volume of air travel and exerted downward pressure on ticket prices.

Air travel is produced by combining labor (pilots, flight attendants, mechanics) and capital (aircraft). If the demand for the product (air travel) falls, there should be a comparable decline in the demand for these two factors of production. Accordingly, the decline in pilot, flight attendant, and mechanics wages and in aircraft prices and lease rates should mirror declines in passenger air travel.

True to form, wages and salaries in commercial aviation have fallen dramatically behind wages in other industries in the early 1990s. Even more hard-hit have been the prices of new and used aircraft. A Boeing 737 that would have leased for $100,000 per month in 1990 leased for $40,000 per month in late 1992.

yields wheat that people will consume. If the most productive tailor in the world made only three-armed shirts, the demand for the tailor's services would be zero because the demand for three-armed shirts is zero. The demand for workers, the demand for wheat land, and the demand for tailors are all examples of **derived demand**. (See Example 1.)

> The demand for a factor of production is a **derived demand** because it results (is derived) from the demand for the goods and services the factor of production helps produce.

The principle of derived demand is essential to understanding the workings of factor markets. If consumers reduce their demand for lettuce, the demand for workers employed in lettuce growing, the demand for farmland used for lettuce, and even the demand for water used in farm irrigation would also fall. When demand for automobiles falls, there is unemployment in Detroit. When world demand for Boeing commercial aircraft grows, there is rising employment in Seattle and Wichita (the cities where Boeing is located). In short, the nature of the market for the good itself will be reflected in the derived demand for the factors used to produce it.

Joint Determination of Factor Demand

Another elementary but important fact about the demand for factors of production is that the production of a good generally requires the cooperation of different factors of production. Farm workers can produce no corn without land; corn land without farm labor is useless. Both corn land and farm workers require farm implements (ranging from hand tools to sophisticated farm machinery) to produce corn.

The farm worker's marginal physical product will be less if the cooperating factor is one square yard of farmland rather than one acre. The farm worker's

In general, the marginal physical product of any factor of production depends on the quantity and quality of the cooperating factors of production.

EXHIBIT 4 Marginal Revenue Product

Labor (workers), L (1)	Units of Output, Q (2)	Price P (3)	Total Revenue, TR (4) = (2) × (3)	Marginal Revenue Product, MRP (5) = (6) × (7) = Δ(4) ÷ Δ(1)	Marginal Revenue, MR (6) = Δ(4) ÷ Δ(2)	Units of Marginal Physical Product, MPP (7) = Δ(2)
0	0	$24	$ 0			
				$95	$19	5
1	5	19	95			
				40	10	4
2	9	15	135			
				9	3	3
3	12	12	144			

Columns 1 and 2 give the production function (the amount of output produced by 0, 1, 2, and 3 units of labor input). Columns 2 and 3 give the demand schedule facing the firm. Marginal revenue product (MRP) is calculated by taking the increase in total revenue associated with one-unit increases in the labor input. It can also be calculated by multiplying MR times MPP. Marginal revenue in column 6 is calculated by dividing the increase in revenue in column 5 by the difference between rows in column 2. Marginal physical product in column 7 is the increase in output for every unit increase in the factor, or the difference between rows in column 2.

marginal physical product will be higher on one acre of fertile Iowa land than on one acre of rocky New England land. The marginal physical product of the farm worker will be higher when working with modern heavy farm machinery than with hand implements. The interdependence of the marginal physical products of land, labor, and capital makes the problem of factor pricing in a market setting difficult to analyze.

Marginal Revenue Product

The demand for a factor of production—land, labor, or capital—is a derived demand. The factor is valuable because the firm sells the output on the product market. Thus, the dollar value of an extra worker, an extra unit of land, or an extra machine is that factor's **marginal revenue product (MRP)**—or the revenue from selling the marginal physical product (MPP) that the factor produces.

> The **marginal revenue product (MRP)** of any factor of production is the extra revenue generated per unit increase in the amount of the factor.

There are two ways to calculate a factor's marginal revenue product. Both methods yield the same value.

Method 1. Calculate marginal revenue product by simply changing the quantity of the factor and observing the change in revenue. According to this direct method, marginal revenue product is the change in total revenue (TR) divided by the change (increase or decrease) in the factor.

$$MRP = \frac{\Delta TR}{\Delta \text{Factor}}$$

Exhibit 4 demonstrates this method. The different quantities of labor the firm employs are given in column 1, and the resulting output is given in column 2.

Columns 1 and 2, therefore, represent the production function. Column 3 shows the market prices that clear the market for the various output levels produced. This firm is a price maker in the product market because the price falls with higher output levels. The firm's total revenue (price times quantity of output) is given in column 4. Because marginal revenue product, in column 5, is the difference between the revenues generated at consecutive levels of labor input, it is recorded between the rows corresponding to the input levels. The revenue generated when one worker is employed is $95; the revenue when two workers are employed is $135. The marginal revenue product is, therefore, $135 − $95 = $40. In other words, the firm's total revenue would increase by $40 if the firm hired a second worker.

Method 2.   The marginal physical product (*MPP*) is the increase in output associated with a one-unit increase in the factor but does not indicate the dollar value of this extra output. Marginal revenue (*MR*) indicates the increase in revenue associated with an increase in output of one unit. By multiplying *MR* and *MPP* we indirectly obtain the marginal revenue product. Therefore:

$$MRP = MR \times MPP.$$

The marginal revenue product of a factor can be calculated directly by determining the increase in revenue at different input levels or indirectly by multiplying marginal physical product times marginal revenue.

That this formula works for the price maker is shown in Exhibit 4. Because the firm increases its output from 5 to 9 units as a consequence of adding a second unit of labor, marginal physical product equals 4 units. The 4 extra units of output add $40 to revenue, or $10 per extra unit ($40/4); therefore, the marginal revenue is $10. Using the formula, $MRP = MR \times MPP$, one can calculate that marginal revenue product equals 10×4, or $40. Thus, the indirect method of calculating marginal revenue product yields the same answer as the direct method. The marginal revenue product in column 5 is just the product of *MR* in column 6 and *MPP* in column 7.

PROFIT MAXIMIZATION

In the product market, the firm maximizes profit by producing that output at which marginal revenue and marginal cost are equal. The firm also is guided by profit maximization in the factor market. Profit-maximizing decisions in the product market are also profit-maximizing decisions in the factor market because deciding on the quantity of inputs determines the level of output.

The *MRP = MFC* Rule

To understand how firms choose the profit-maximizing level of factor inputs, consider the case of a firm deciding how much unskilled labor to hire. *The firm will hire one more unit of unskilled labor if the extra revenue (the extra benefit) the firm derives from the sale of the output produced by the extra unit exceeds the marginal factor cost of the extra unit of unskilled labor.* As long as the extra benefit of a decision is larger than the extra cost, the firm's profits must increase. Recall that if the firm is a price taker, marginal factor cost will be the market wage. As in any other economic activity, a firm will hire inputs to the point where marginal benefits equal marginal costs.

The firm will continue to hire inputs as long as their marginal revenue product (*MRP*) exceeds their marginal factor cost (*MFC*). Since in this chapter we are

EXHIBIT 5   Firm Equilibrium: The Hiring of Factor Inputs

The firm's derived demand for Factor A is the marginal-revenue-product curve. The supply schedule of Factor A as seen by the firm is perfectly horizontal at the market price of $14. Equilibrium (e) will be reached at a price of $14 and a quantity of 110 units of Factor A. At this point, marginal revenue product equals marginal factor costs.

assuming that the firm is a price taker in the factor market, the market prices of the inputs the firm uses (wage rates, rental rates, interest rates) are the marginal factor costs of these inputs. The marginal benefit of an additional unit of factor input is its marginal revenue product. As long as the marginal revenue product exceeds the price of the input, it pays the firm to hire the factor. If the marginal revenue product of Factor A is $40 and its price is $30, it pays the firm to hire the factor. By hiring an additional unit of the factor, the firm increases its profit by $10 (= $MRP - MFC$).

The Demand Curve for a Factor

Exhibit 5 shows the marginal-revenue-product curve of Factor A. The MRP curve is downward sloping because the greater the amount of Factor A used, the lower will be its marginal physical product (because of the law of diminishing returns). Also, if the firm is a price maker in the product market, higher levels of output mean a lower marginal revenue. Thus, as the quantity of Factor A increases, both marginal physical product and marginal revenue tend to decline, so that MRP (which is $MR \times MPP$) declines. The firm will hire Factor A until its price equals marginal revenue product.

The *MRP* curve is the firm's demand curve for a factor because the firm hires that factor quantity at which the price of the factor equals the marginal revenue product of the factor.

In Exhibit 5, the supply curve of Factor A to the firm is horizontal at the market price of $14. The price-taking firm in the factor market can hire all it wants at $14. If the firm hired only 60 units of Factor A (point *a*), it would not maximize its profit: at 60 units, A's MRP equals $22 and A's MFC equals $14. The firm's incentive to hire additional factors continues as long as MRP exceeds $14. Thus, the firm will continue to hire to the point where MRP and MFC are equal, which occurs at 110 units of Factor A (point *e*). The firm will be in equilibrium (earning a maximum profit or minimizing its losses) when each factor is employed up to the point where marginal factor cost (which equals the price of the factor when the input market is competitive) equals the marginal revenue product of the factor. Since the firm adjusts its factor use to the point where the price of the factor equals the marginal revenue product, the firm's demand curve for a factor is the MRP curve or schedule.

In the product market, the rule of profit maximization is $MC = MR$. In the factor market, the rule becomes $MRP = MFC$ for each factor. These rules are logically the same. They are just different sides of the same coin. If the firm is maximizing profit, then it must be that marginal cost equals marginal revenue and marginal revenue product equals marginal factor cost. The rules are different ways of looking at the same process.

COST MINIMIZATION

The rules of profit maximization explain the behavior of firms in the factor market. These rules predict that firms will employ that level and combination of inputs that maximizes their profit. In the product market, firms produce that level of output (and charge the associated price) that maximizes their profit.

Because profit is revenue minus costs, to maximize profit it is necessary to minimize the cost of producing a given quantity of output. We have explained how a firm selects the optimal level of *one* factor input. But firms produce output with cooperating factors. How will they know when they are combining *all* their inputs in a least-cost fashion?

Most important to the firm is the effectiveness of labor and capital compared to their costs. Assume a worker can pick 20 pounds of pecans per hour. If the worker is paid $4 an hour, this means that each additional dollar spent on labor yields 5 pounds of pecans (= 20/$4). A pecan-picking machine may have an (MPP) of 100 pounds of pecans per hour and cost $10 an hour. A dollar spent on the machine yields 10 pounds of pecans (= 100/$10) per dollar. Thus, the machine would be more cost-effective than the worker. The firm could produce pecans more cheaply by substituting pecan-picking machines for workers. To determine the cheapest method to produce pecans, or any good or service, the firm will look at the marginal physical product *per dollar of cost*. The rational firm will minimize costs when the effectiveness of each factor is the same per dollar of cost. As the firm substitutes machines for labor, the law of diminishing returns will lower the MPP of machines and raise the MPP of workers until, at the margin, the effectiveness per dollar is equalized. (See Example 2.)

The marginal physical product *per dollar* of a factor is its marginal physical product divided by its price. The price-taking firm takes both the wage rate for labor (W) and the rental rate on capital (R) as given. As the above example shows, if the marginal physical product per dollar of labor is smaller than the marginal physical product per dollar of capital, the firm is not combining inputs in a least-cost fashion. It can produce the same output at lower cost by substituting capital for labor until:

According to the least-cost rule, the firm is producing at minimum cost only if the marginal physical products per dollar of the various factors are equal.

$$\frac{MPP_L}{W} = \frac{MPP_K}{R},$$

where MPP_K is the marginal physical product of capital.

THE MARGINAL-PRODUCTIVITY THEORY OF INCOME DISTRIBUTION

Economists distinguish between the **functional distribution of income** and the **personal distribution of income**. Both are determined in the factor markets.

EXAMPLE 2

Paying for Merchandise

The sensitivity of factor demand to factor prices is nowhere more evident than in comparisons between countries. Compare a department store in the United States, where clerical wages are $1,000 to $1,500 per month, to one in the Philippines, where clerical wages are $50 per month. In an upscale U.S. department store the clerk that helps you find the merchandise is often the one that takes your money or credit card. An upscale department store in the Phillipines, on the other hand, will have an army of clerks just to check you out. There may be five or six clerks at each of many check-out stands. One clerk will enter your purchase on the cash register, another might verify your credit card, a third will verify the correctness of your bill, and perhaps another will wrap your merchandise!

The **functional distribution of income** is the distribution of income among the four broad classes of productive factors—land, labor, capital, and entrepreneurship.

The **personal distribution of income** is the distribution of income among households, or how much income one family earns from the factors of production it owns relative to other families.

The profit-maximizing and least-cost rules resolve the *how* problem in economics. They show how firms go about combining inputs to produce output. These same rules also resolve the *for whom* problem.

Factors of production, unless they are highly specialized (such as 7-foot-tall basketball players), are demanded by many firms and by many industries. For example, the market demand for truck drivers will come from a wide cross section of American industry: the steel industry, retailers, the moving industry, and the local florist will all have a derived demand for truck drivers. The demand for urban land will also come from a broad cross section of American industry: heavy industry requires land for plant sites; motel chains require land for motels; home builders require land for subdivisions. Similarly, the demand for capital goods will come from a cross section of American industry.

How the price (wage) of truck drivers is determined is shown in Exhibit 6. The truck drivers' wage rate reflects two forces: the derived demand for truck drivers as represented by their marginal revenue product and the supply of truck drivers. At equilibrium, the market wage will equate quantity supplied and quantity demanded, and the wage will equal the marginal revenue product. In other words, truck drivers will be paid their marginal revenue product. The same is true of the other factors of production. According to the **marginal-productivity theory of income distribution**, skilled labor and unskilled labor will each be paid its marginal revenue product. Capital will be paid its marginal revenue product. Land will be paid its marginal revenue product.

According to the **marginal-productivity theory of income distribution**, the functional distribution of income between land, labor, and capital is determined by the relative marginal revenue products of the different factors of production. The price of each factor will equal the marginal revenue product of that factor.

The market supply curve of truck drivers is upward-sloping, which indicates that individuals are prepared to work more hours as truck drivers at high wages than at low wages. The market demand curve is derived from the marginal-revenue-product curve of truck drivers across several industries. Equilibrium is achieved at point *e*, where the quantity supplied of truck drivers equals the quantity demanded. At the equilibrium wage of $15, there are 10,000 labor hours used in the various industries using truck drivers.

Marginal Productivity and Factor Incomes

The marginal-productivity theory of income distribution suggests that a productive factor is usually paid its marginal revenue product. The marginal revenue product of one factor depends on the quantity and quality of cooperating factors. Two textile workers, one in the United States and the other in India, may be equally skilled and diligent, but one works with a $50 sewing machine while the other works with a $100,000 advanced knitting machine. The New England farmer may be just as skilled as the Kansas farmer but may have a low *MRP* because of the low quality of the land. Marginal revenue product also depends on the supplies of factors. The supply of residential land is limited in Hawaii but abundant in Iowa. The equilibrium *MRP* of land is, therefore, higher in Hawaii. If women are limited to employment in only a few professions, they will *overcrowd* these professions and drive down the *MRP* and, thus, wages. Finally, marginal revenue product, as stated earlier, depends on the demand for the product being produced. If product demand falls, so will the factor's *MRP*.

The marginal-productivity theory states that each factor of production will be paid its marginal revenue product. If the world is sufficiently competitive, the theory suggests that each factor of production will be paid its marginal physical product in value terms. When the firm is a price taker in the product market, $MR = P$ and, therefore, $MRP = P \times MPP$. Thus, for example, the wage rate $W = P \times MPP$. Each factor is then paid the dollar equivalent of its marginal physical product.

This chapter discussed how factor markets work, but each factor market—the labor market, the capital market, and the market for land—has its unique features. In the labor market, the supply of labor is determined by how individuals choose among market work, work in the home, and leisure. These are choices not faced by the owners of capital and land. Moreover, the labor market is affected by the organization of workers into unions and by the effect of education and training on labor's marginal physical product. In the capital market, intertemporal choices are

The marginal-productivity theory of income distribution states that a competitively determined factor price reflects the factor's marginal revenue product. Marginal revenue product is the result of (1) the relative supplies of the different factors, (2) the quantity and quality of cooperating factors, and (3) the market demands for the goods the factors produce.

Should Factors Be Paid Their Market Value or Their "Comparable Worth?"

This chapter explains the general principles of price determination in factor markets. The following three chapters look at price determination in labor, land, and capital markets. Over time, social critics have argued that prices determined in factor markets can be "unfair" or that they may not reflect the "true value" of the factor. Why should professional baseball players earn more than college professors or even the president of the United States? Why should credit-card companies receive 18 percent interest from credit-card holders? Why should high-fashion models, who are fortunate to have perfect complexions and figures, earn $5,000 per hour, while a hard-working office manager earns $10 per hour?

In most cases, the market determines the price paid the factor of production, be it judged as reflecting the true worth of the factor or not. Public policy has correctly been wary about interfering in the market process and dictating a different price.

Public policy has played a role in making sure that employees have a right to "equal pay for equal work." This principle has been applied to cases in which women earn less than men even though they perform exactly the same work as men. The principle of equal pay for equal work is well established in law and in practice.

A more difficult policy issue is whether people should be guaranteed equal pay for "comparable" work. Compare the pay of female guards in women's prisons with that of male guards in men's prisons. Typically, male guards have received more than female guards, yet the work is "comparable." Should some government agency step in and dictate that male and female guards earn the same pay?

Courts in Oregon and Washington have dictated that employers must pay workers with comparable jobs the same pay. In Washington, a committee assigns points to each job on the basis of knowledge and skills, mental demands, accountability, and working conditions. The committee awarded nurses the highest evaluation, well above computer systems analysts. Clerical supervisors were rated above chemists, and electricians were rated below beginning secretarial workers. In all of the above cases, the labor market had assigned different relative wages than the comparable worth commission.

Which verdict should be followed—the verdict of the market or that of a comparable-worth rating commission? We would argue that the market is a more reliable guide. First, there is doubt that experts will be able to find and agree on rational formulas for determining comparable worth. Second, if people are paid the "comparable worth wage," surpluses will develop in professions that have been assigned comparable worths above the market wage. Too many people will wish to work in secretarial positions and too few as electricians. Third, if wages are based on comparable worth rather than on market conditions, the "law of unintended" consequences will cause some employers to replace women with men in occupations such as coaching.

We would argue that the costs of using a comparable wage system outweigh its benefits.

---

involved: buyers of capital can receive the benefits of capital over a long period of time; suppliers of capital must choose between consumption today and more consumption tomorrow. The market for land is characterized by the relative fixity of the supply of land.

The next three chapters will examine each factor market in detail, but these discussions will build upon the general theoretical framework established in this chapter.

The most important point to learn from this chapter is:
In a market economy the problem of distributing the national output among cooperating factors is solved by profit-maximizing firms paying each factor its marginal revenue product.

1. Firms operate in two markets: the product (output) market and the factor (input) market. Firms sell their output in the product market, and they buy inputs to produce output in the factor market. The *what* problem is solved in the product market. The *how* and *for whom* problems are solved in the factor market. Marginal factor cost (*MFC*) is the extra cost of hiring one more unit of the factor of production. A price-making firm in the factor market will have a marginal factor cost that is greater than price. A price taker in the input market will have a marginal factor cost equal to the price of the input.

2. The firm's demand for a factor of production will depend upon the demand for the product being produced and upon the factor's productivity. The marginal physical product (*MPP*) of a factor of production is the increase in output that results from increasing the factor by one unit, other things equal. The demand for a factor of production is a derived demand because it depends on the demand for the goods and services the factor helps produce. Production requires the cooperation of the factors of production. The marginal physical product of one factor will depend on the quantity and quality of cooperating factors. Marginal revenue product (*MRP*) is the increase in revenue brought about by hiring one more unit of the factor of production.

3. Profit-maximizing firms will observe the following rule in factor markets: factors of production will be hired to the point where *MFC* = *MRP*. The *MFC* = *MRP* rule in the factor market is equivalent to the *MR* = *MC* rule in the product market. If firms are perfectly competitive in the factor market, they will hire the various factors of production to the point where the *MRP* of each factor equals its price.

4. The least-cost rule for firms is to hire factors of production so that *MPP* per dollar of one factor equals the *MPP* per dollar of any other factor.

5. The marginal-productivity theory of income distribution explains the functional distribution of income (among the four classes of production factors) and the personal distribution of income (among households).

Policy Focus: **The costs of replacing market wages by comparable worth formulas exceed the benefits.**

Key Terms

price taker (p. 527)
price maker (p. 527)
monopsony (p. 529)
marginal factor cost (*MFC*) (p. 531)
derived demand (p. 533)

marginal revenue product (*MRP*) (p. 534)
functional distribution of income (p. 537)
personal distribution of income (p. 537)
marginal-productivity theory of income distribution (p. 538)

Questions and Problems

1. The *MPP* of a 100th worker is 33 units of output. The marginal revenue of the firm for the corresponding level of output is $2, the price of the product is $3, and the wage rate is $99.

a. Is the firm maximizing its profit?

b. What would the wage rate have to be for 100 workers to maximize profit?

2. Explain how workers in Country X could earn $10 per hour while workers in the same industry in Country Y earn only $0.50 per hour. Do the higher wages in Country X mean that workers in this country work harder than those in Country Y?

3. The last unit of land rented by a farmer costs $100 and increases output by 1,000 bushels. The last unit of capital costs $1,000 to rent and increases output by 20,000 bushels. Is this farmer minimizing costs? If not, what should he or she do?

4. In Soviet industry, capital grew about 10 times as fast as labor. What would you expect to happen to the marginal physical product of capital?

5. Workers are paid $20 per hour; the price of the output is $2. What is the best estimate of the marginal physical product of labor? (Hint: use the profit-maximizing rule.)

6. A manufacturing plant in a small town accounts for 85 percent of employment in the town. The plant receives a large contract and decides to expand its work force by 40 percent. What will be the relationship between marginal factor cost and the wage rate in this case? Construct a graph to illustrate your answer.

7. One type of equipment—such as specialized oil-drilling equipment—can be used only in one particular industry. Another type—such as general-purpose lathes—can be used in a wide variety of industries. How would the amount of competition differ for these two types of equipment?

8. Complete Table A by filling in columns 4 and 5.
a. Is the firm maker or a price taker in the product market?
b. If the wage rate is $55, how many units of labor should the firm hire?

TABLE A

Labor (number of workers, L (1)	Units of Output, Q (2)	Price, P (3)	Units of Marginal Physical Product, MPP (4)	Marginal Revenue Product, MRP (5)
0	0	$8		
1	10	8		
2	17	8		
3	23	8		
4	28	8		

9. Assume that the marginal physical product (MPP) of a first worker is 20 units of output, that the MPP of a second worker is 30 units, that the MPP of a third worker is 20 units, and that the MPP of a fourth worker is 15 units. If four workers are hired, how many units of output are produced?

10. An additional engineer costs a firm $50,000 per year; an additional lathe operator costs $20,000 per year. Do you have enough information to determine which worker the firm should hire? If not, what information do you need?

Doing Economics

On most campuses, student labor is used for many tasks, from filing in offices to food-service assistance to helping in academic laboratories. Much of this labor is provided under federal work-study programs as part of students' financial-aid package. Under the work-study program, educational institutions pay only a small part (currently 20 percent) of the cost of student employees, with federal funds making up the rest. How would this affect the demand by campus employers for work-study vs. regular student employees? What sort of equilibrium do you predict if students eligible for work-study are as productive as those who are not? (Remember that the college's hourly cost of work-study labor is below the minimum wage.) How are the results different if work-study students on average have lower productivity than other students? Now try to find out from your college's administration or from a personal survey of campus workers what fraction of student workers are supported on work-study and what kinds of jobs are typically staffed with work-study students and what jobs are performed by other student employees. Do your results accord with your predictions?

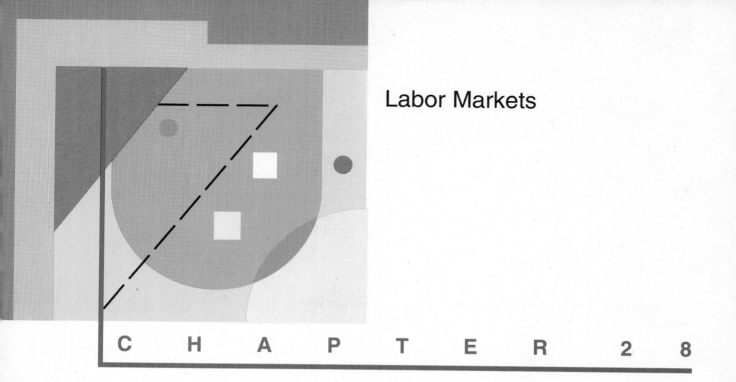

Labor Markets

C H A P T E R   2 8

CHAPTER FOCUS

Some 75 cents out of each dollar is earned as wages and salaries. The remaining 25 cents is for dividends, profits, rents, etc. Except for the relatively few who live on dividends, profits, and rents, our economic livelihoods depend on what we earn in the labor market. Individuals who work hard at high-paying jobs do well, in contrast to those who lack marketable skills and who must work at minimum wages.

More than 110 million people work in the American labor force. They earn an average hourly wage of over $10. A skilled surgeon earns $5,000 per hour, a corporate lawyer earns $200, a management consultant $125, an automotive worker $25, and a fast-food employee $4.25. Why do some people command high wages while others command low wages? What determines the overall level of wages in the economy?

After studying this chapter, you will be able to:

- Understand how labor differs from other factors of production.
- Explain why wages would differ even if people were all identical.
- Explain why wages would differ even if all jobs were the same.
- Describe the principal/agent problem and how it fosters incentive payments.
- Use the backward-bending supply curve to explain why the average workweek is shorter.
- Understand why more women have entered the work force.

HOW LABOR DIFFERS FROM OTHER FACTORS

The preceding chapter explained how factor markets work and gave general rules that apply to land, labor, and capital inputs. The labor market differs from other factor markets because of the human element. Four features of labor make it different from the other factors of production:

1. A person cannot be bought like an acre of land or a piece of equipment; slavery is against the law. Land and capital assets can be bought and sold. Employers cannot "buy" labor. Employers and workers enter into contracts that specify the time period of employment and the conditions of employment.
2. If land and machines are not put to productive use, they stand idle, and the owners do not normally benefit. When people do not work in the labor market, they can spend time in work in the home or in leisure.
3. Unlike land and capital, people have preferences regarding the type of work and the location of the work. A drilling rig doesn't care whether it is placed in permafrost or in a tropical climate. Farm land does not care whether it is planted in wheat or cotton. People do care where they work and under what conditions they work.
4. People live in families in which there is often specialization. One family member may have a strong attachment to the labor market (as the major breadwinner), another may specialize in work in the home. Some family members may cross over regularly between work in the home and work in the labor force.

WAGES AND INCENTIVE PAYMENTS

Wages are the payments people receive for working. Wages may be paid on an hourly, daily, or monthly basis. Payment on a monthly basis of a specified amount (that does not vary with the number of hours worked) is typically called a salary. Some wages are based on how many units of output are produced per unit of time (hour, month, year)—called piece rates. In addition to their wages and salaries, workers can also receive incentive payments in the form of bonuses and premiums.

Nominal wages differ from *real* wages. The dollar wages received by workers

Gary Becker (1930–   )

Economists have been accused of being imperialists because they apply economics to other disciplines, like education, sociology, law, home economics, and demography. The most prominent "economic imperialist" is Gary Becker, professor of economics at the University of Chicago.

Becker made his mark by applying the cost/benefit logic of economics to education, discrimination, social behavior, fertility, and marriage. In his doctoral dissertation, Becker wrote that pay differentials between white and black workers could be explained by a taste for discrimination by both employers and employees. Becker's demonstration that people invest in education just as businesses invest in capital served as a starting point for the field of human capital in economics. Becker suggested in an article published in 1968 that crime can be analyzed just like other occupations, and that people become criminals depending upon the expected benefits of crime and its costs in terms of the likelihood of arrest and punishment. Becker's writings demonstrate that people respond to price effects and income effects in their social interactions as well as in their economic interactions. Economic considerations enter into the selection of marital partners, the decision on how many children to have, and even into questions of religion and suicide. By applying economic logic to family decision making, Becker has been able to provide clearer explanations for the increase in the percentage of working women and for declining fertility. Becker's writings have been controversial among economists and other social scientists because they have expanded economics into new areas that had previously been regarded as outside the realm of economics. Becker's work was honored with the 1992 Nobel prize in economics.

are their nominal wages. However, the purchasing power of dollar wages differs from region to region, and it changes as the general price level changes. Real wages are nominal wages adjusted for differences in the prices of the things people buy. For example, in 1969, the average manufacturing worker's nominal wage was $3.19 an hour. In 1992, the average manufacturing worker's nominal wage was almost four times higher at about $12 per hour. But over the same period, consumer prices also increased by nearly three times. Real wages scarcely changed over this period, although nominal wages rose by a factor of almost four. To understand trends in real wages it is also important to include fringe benefits, such as pensions and medical insurance. From 1973 to 1992 real manufacturing wages appeared to fall. But when fringe benefits are included, total real wages paid in manufacturing actually rose.

Workers normally base their labor force decisions on real wages, not on nominal wages. What counts is what the nominal wage will buy. If nominal wages are two times higher in Alaska but prices are three times higher, people would not move to Alaska for the higher nominal wages. If prices and nominal wages change at the same rate, there has been no change in real wages, and we would expect no changes in the number of hours people wish to work.

Why are some workers paid incentive wages in the form of bonuses, prizes, and premiums? Employees often have personal objectives that are different from the firm's objectives. One employee's objective may be to maximize the amount of income earned on a particular job. Another employee may wish to minimize job stress and exertion without being fired. As long as the employer and employee have different objectives, a **principal/agent problem** exists.

People base their labor force decisions on real wages.

Wages and Incentive Payments

EXAMPLE 1

First-Class Fares for Coach: The Principal/Agent Problem

Business travel costs corporations billions of dollars per year, and it is in the company's interest to hold down travel expenditures. If corporation employees shared this goal, they would seek out the most economical airline tickets on their own, and the corporation need not worry. The airlines, however, realize that a principal/agent problem exists with regard to airline travel. They therefore offer first-class seats to business travelers who purchase full-fare coach tickets (often at twice the expense of economy tickets). They offer free travel to business travelers who accumulate miles on that airline's frequent-flier program. Employees book more expensive flights just to take advantage of the frequent-flier program.

The travel departments of major corporations claim that this principal/agent problem costs corporations millions of dollars per year. Corporations, however, are not in a position to eliminate these abuses because it costs too much to monitor employee travel.

> A **principal/agent problem** exists between the firm and any of its employees when the firm (as the principal) and the employee (as the agent) have different goals and objectives for the employee's behavior.

Incentive pay systems seek to deal with principal/agent problems between employee and employer.

The employer cannot constantly monitor each employee's performance under normal conditions. Employers must motivate workers to act spontaneously in the firm's interests. To prevent assembly-line workers from shirking responsibility, the firm may pay them bonuses for exceeding production norms or goals. Professional athletes may receive performance-based incentive contracts. A baseball player may receive a bonus for every extra-base hit over 50 in a season. A company may give its employees an annual bonus if the company exceeds a profit goal it set for itself. All these bonus and incentive schemes are designed to improve the work performance of the agent (the worker) without raising the monitoring costs of the principal (the employer).

It is not easy to design incentive-pay systems that eliminate the principal/agent problem entirely. Assembly-line workers may achieve their bonuses by increasing the quantity of output while reducing the quality of their work. Professional baseball players may lose games by attempting to get extra-base hits when a sacrifice fly is required. The more specific is the incentive target, the more likely the employee is to achieve the target by sacrificing some other worthwhile outcome (such as sacrificing quality for quantity). The more general the incentive target—such as a bonus based on company profits—the less likely the employee is to believe that his or her actions affect the outcome. (See Example 1.)

THE DEMAND FOR LABOR

Wage rates are determined in labor markets by supply and demand. Labor exists in all sorts and sizes. People are different. They have different skills, training, and temperaments. Jobs are different. To learn about product prices, we must begin by studying a single product, such as oranges. The same is true of wages. We must begin by studying the wage determination of a specific type of worker. In the next sections, we look at how computer programmer wage rates are determined by the forces of supply and demand.

The Firm's Demand for Labor

How does a firm decide how much labor of a single type to hire at different wage rates? According to the preceding chapter, profit-maximizing firms hire factors up to the point where the marginal factor cost (*MFC*) equals its marginal revenue product (*MRP*).

Exhibit 1 applies the rule to the labor market for computer programmers. Together, the graph and data show a firm that is perfectly competitive in the computer-programmer market (it must take the market wage rate as given), and therefore its marginal factor cost is equal to the market wage rate. This firm can hire all the labor it wants at the prevailing market wage rate. Its labor-supply schedule is a horizontal line (perfectly elastic) at the market wage.

The firm shown in Exhibit 1 happens to be a price taker in the product market as well as in the factor market. Its marginal revenue product equals its product price, *P*, times labor's marginal physical product (*MPP*). The profit-maximizing firm will demand the quantity of labor at which $W = MRP$. The *MRP* of the

---

EXHIBIT 1   The Firm's Demand for Computer Programmers

a. Graph of Demand for Computer Programmers

Marginal revenue product (*MRP*) = demand for labor

b. Table of Demand for Computer Programmers

Labor Input (hours) (1)	Quantity of Output (lines programmed) (2)	Marginal Physical Product (lines), MPP (3)	Marginal Revenue Product, MRP = P × MPP (4)
0	0		
		20	$40
1	20		
		14	28
2	34		
		12	24
3	46		
		8	16
4	54		
		6	12
5	60		
		4	8
6	64		
		2	4
7	65		

The graph uses the data in panel (b). The labor demand curve shows the marginal revenue product of different quantities of labor hours. This firm is competitive in both the labor market and the product market. The price of the output is $2 per unit. The firm uses 4 programmer hours when the wage rate is $16 per hour (where the marginal revenue product is equal to the market wage). If the market wage rate rises to $28 per hour, the firm would employ only 2 programmer hours because the marginal revenue product of the second hour equals $28. Columns 1 and 2 of panel (b) show the amounts of output that are associated with various amounts of labor input for this firm. Columns 3 and 4 give the marginal physical product and marginal revenue product for each level of input. Since the price of the output is $2 per program line, *MRP* = $2 × *MRP*. Both columns 2 and 3 show that under these circumstances, the law of diminishing returns applies to the labor input. Panel (a) graphs the data from columns 1 and 4.

---

second programmer hour is $28; therefore, the firm will demand 2 programmer hours. If the market wage falls to $16 per hour, the firm would react by hiring more programmer hours. As the firm increases employment, *MRP* will fall because of the law of diminishing returns. The firm will continue to increase labor until the last hour's *MRP* just equals the market wage of $16. At a $16 wage, the firm would use 4 programmer hours because the *MRP* of the fourth hour is $16.

The quantity of labor demanded varies inversely with the wage rate, which can be seen by comparing columns 1 and 4 in Exhibit 1b or by observing the downward-sloping shape of the demand curve. The demand curve is nothing more than the marginal-revenue-product curve. At each wage, that quantity of labor is demanded at which $W = MRP$. More labor will be hired at lower wages than at higher wages, *ceteris paribus*.

The Market Demand for Labor

Earlier chapters explained that the market demand curve is constructed from individual demand curves. Exhibit 1 showed the demand curve for computer programmers of a single firm. The market demand curve for computer programmers is the summation of all the demand curves of firms that hire computer programmers. If there are 400 firms demanding computer programmers, the market demand for computer programmers is the summation of the demands of all 400 firms that purchase labor of that type. The market demand curve shows how the total quantity of labor demanded varies as the wage changes.

The market demand curve for labor of a particular type—computer programmers—is given in Exhibit 2. This market demand curve shows the quantities of computer programmer hours that are demanded by all 400 employers of that type of labor at different wage rates. Because the labor-demand curves of individual firms are negatively sloped, the market demand curve will be negatively sloped as well.

EXHIBIT 2   The Market Demand for Computer Programmers

The market labor demand curve for programmers shows the number of programmer hours that would be demanded by all firms that hire programmers at different wage rates. Because the demand curves of each firm are negatively sloped, the market labor demand curve is also negatively sloped.

THE LABOR SUPPLY CURVE

Employers must pay workers a wage that is at least equal to the opportunity cost of the next best alternative that the worker sacrifices in accepting that employment.

The market demand curve for labor of a single type explains only one side of the labor market. The market labor supply curve explains the other side of the market. The wage rate for labor of that type is determined by both supply and demand.

The amount of labor supplied depends on the wage rate, *ceteris paribus*. Workers, in choosing where to work, compare the wage they can earn in one occupation with their opportunity cost (the wage they could receive from employment in the next best occupation). The higher is the wage offered for labor of that type, the greater will be the number of workers who offer their services.

The employer who fails to pay workers their opportunity costs will have no workers because they would all take the next best alternative, which then becomes their best alternative.

Exhibit 3 is a market supply curve that shows the number of hours computer programmers are willing to work at different wage rates. The supply curve is positively sloped because at higher wages, computer-programming employment becomes more attractive relative to employment in other occupations. Computer programmers will, therefore, shift hours from other occupations for which they are qualified (engineering, accounting, math) into programming work. The market labor-supply curve is the summation of the individual labor-supply curves of computer programmers.

LABOR-MARKET EQUILIBRIUM

Wage rates are determined in labor markets by the interaction of supply and demand. The market demand curve for labor of a single type is negatively sloped;

EXHIBIT 3   The Market Supply of Computer Programmers

This market labor supply curve shows the number of hours programmers are willing to work at different wage rates, all other things remaining the same. The labor supply curve is positively sloped because at higher wages, programmer employment is more attractive relative to other types of employment.

EXHIBIT 4   Equilibrium in the Market for Computer Programmers

The market supply of programmers (from Exhibit 3) and the market demand for programmers (from Exhibit 2) are brought together in this figure. The equilibrium wage rate is $16 per hour. At the $16 wage, the quantity demanded (1,600 hours) equals the quantity supplied. At wage rates above $16, there is a surplus (quantity supplied exceeds quantity demanded); at wage rates below $16, there is a shortage of labor (quantity demanded exceeds quantity supplied)

the market supply curve of labor of a single type is positively sloped. The labor market coordinates the activities of firms and workers by setting an equilibrium wage rate.

The market supply and demand curves for computer programmers given in Exhibits 2 and 3 are brought together in Exhibit 4. The wage rate of $16 equates the quantity of programmer hours supplied with the quantity of programmer hours demanded, or 1,600 hours. At any other wage, the quantity demanded will not equal the quantity supplied.

In a competitive labor market, wage rates adjust until they equal the equilibrium wage rate. If there is a **labor surplus**, some workers willing to work at the prevailing wage will be without jobs. At the wage rate of $25 there are more workers willing to work than the quantity demanded by firms, and the market wage would fall. If there is a **labor shortage**, some firms wishing to hire workers at the prevailing wage rate will go away empty-handed. In Exhibit 4, at the wage rate of $10 the quantity of labor demanded exceeds the quantity of labor supplied, and the wage rate would rise.

> A labor surplus occurs when the number of workers willing to work at the prevailing wage rate exceeds the number firms wish to employ at that wage rate.

> A labor shortage occurs when the number of workers firms wish to hire at the prevailing wage rate exceeds the number willing to work at that wage rate.

Not all wages are permitted to adjust to surpluses or shortages due to regulations, trade groups, and certification. In Exhibit 4, if a law were passed making it illegal for the employers of computer programmers to pay less than $25 per hour, there would be a surplus of computer programmers. A number of

At any wage other than the equilibrium wage, there will be a labor surplus or shortage.

computer programmers, who are prepared to work at $25 per hour, would be without work. A number of states and the federal government have minimum-wage laws that require that qualifying employees not be paid less than a specified minimum wage.

Shifts in Labor Supply and Demand

Unless something happens to prevent it, the market wage is that wage which equates the quantity of labor demanded with the quantity of labor supplied. In this regard, labor markets are just like product markets. The price of labor will settle at that wage that equates quantity demanded with quantity supplied. The price of labor—the wage—will remain fixed at this rate until the labor demand curve shifts or the labor supply curve shifts. Changes in labor supply and demand change wage rates. If any of the factors capable of shifting a demand or supply curve were to change, the equilibrium would be disrupted and a new wage rate would be established. The factors that cause labor demand and supply curves to shift are discussed below, along with their effects on the wage rate.

Factors Causing Shifts in Labor Demand and Supply Curves

Shifts in the Demand. Factors other than wages affect the demand for a particular type of labor. If one of these factors changes, the demand curve for labor will shift. The demand for labor of a particular type increases (the demand curve shifts to the right), *ceteris paribus*, when:

1. the demand for the final product produced using that type of labor increases. If the demand for the final product increases, there will be an increase in that product's price. This price increase will raise the marginal revenue product of labor, shifting the demand curve to the right.
2. the price of a substitute factor of production increases. Substitute factors are those that can be substituted for the type of labor in question in the process of production. Automated equipment may be substituted for bank tellers; sophisticated word-processing equipment may be substituted for secretaries; skilled labor may be substituted for unskilled labor. If the prices of substitute factors increase, firms will increase their demand for labor of that type.
3. the price of a complementary factor of production decreases. Complementary factors are those that are used in combination with the factor in question. Materials, such as steel, aluminum, and plastics, are used in combination with labor to make automobiles, for example. If the prices of these materials fall the demand for labor will rise.
4. the productivity (marginal physical product) of labor increases. When the marginal physical product of labor rises (when labor productivity increases), the marginal revenue product of (and, therefore, the demand for) labor rises.

The demand for labor changes when the prices of substitute or complementary factors change, when product prices change, and when labor productivity changes.

Exhibit 5, panels (a) and (b), shows the effects of increases and decreases in the demand for labor. If demand increases, *ceteris paribus*, the wage rate rises. If demand falls *ceteris paribus*, the wage rate falls.

Shifts in Supply. The supply of labor to a particular occupation increases when:

1. the wages that can be earned in related occupations fall. The wages paid in other occupations affect the supply of labor to a particular occupation. If

EXHIBIT 5 Effects of Changes in Labor Supply and Demand on Wages

a. Effects of Changes in Labor Demand

b. Effect of Changes in Labor Productivity

c. Effect of Change in Price of Substitute Factor

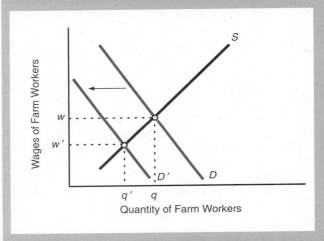

Panel (a) shows that a fall in the price of oil reduces the demand for oil workers—their wages drop. Panel (b) shows that an increase in the labor productivity of auto workers raises the demand for automobile workers—their wages rise. Panel (c) shows that a fall in the price of farm machinery reduces the demand for farm workers—their wages fall. Panel (d) shows that the wage rate of truck drivers falls from S to S' as wages of taxi drivers increase. Panel (e) shows that new bullet-proof vests and headgear make police work less dangerous, increasing the supply of police officers—the wage rates of police officers fall.

d. Effects of Changes in Labor Supply

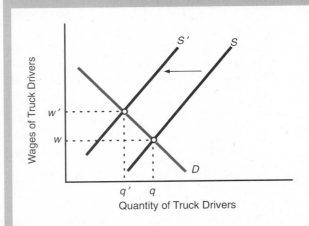

e. Effect of Change in Job Conditions

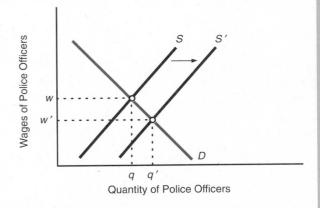

Chapter 28   Labor Markets

The supply of labor to a particular occupation is affected by wages in other occupations and by the conditions of work in that occupation.

the wages of mathematicians fall, the supply curve of computer programmers should shift to the right. More people will find computer programming as the occupation that pays them their opportunity cost.

2. the conditions of work in that occupation improve. Other things remaining the same, people prefer to avoid heavy, unpleasant, or dangerous work in harsh climates. A decrease in the unpleasantness or danger associated with a particular job will increase the supply of labor to that industry. If, for example, new filters are discovered that make working in an asbestos plant perfectly safe, the supply of labor to the asbestos industry would increase.

Exhibit 5, panels (c) and (d), gives examples of shifts in the labor supply curve and the resulting impact on wages. Increases in labor supply reduce the wage rate, and decreases in supply raise the wage rate.

WAGE STRUCTURE

The preceding explanation of wage rates for labor of a specific type did not explain why some people earn more than others or why some occupations command a higher wage than others. These wage differences occur, very simply, because *people are different* and because *jobs are different*. If all people were the same and if all jobs were the same, then everyone would earn the same wage in competitive labor markets. People don't earn the same wage. Some earn $2 million per year; others earn $5 per hour. The following discussion explains the structure of wages.

Compensating Wage Differentials

Underground coal miners are paid more than workers in manufacturing industries. For example, in the United States underground coal miners are paid more than 50 percent more than the average wage in nonagricultural industries.

Why are coal miners paid more than most other production workers? Coal mining does not require highly specialized skills or training; the skills that most manufacturing workers possess could readily be used in underground coal mining. The reason for the wage difference is the difference in the nature of the job.

The general desirability of a job can shift the labor supply curve. People prefer to avoid dirty, monotonous, and dangerous jobs, other things equal. Coal mining is a dangerous profession with a high fatality and disability rate.

Exhibit 6 shows the effect of differences in the danger of the occupation on relative wages. For simplicity, the demand curve for coal miners is assumed to be identical to the demand curve for textile workers. The labor supply curves are quite different. The position of the coal miners' supply curve (higher than the textile workers' supply curve) reflects the fact that workers prefer, *ceteris paribus*, less dangerous employment. To get an equivalent supply of coal miners, coal-mine employers must offer higher wages than textile employers. The higher wages paid to attract workers to dangerous and unpleasant occupations are called **compensating wage differentials**.

> Compensating wage differentials are the higher rewards that are required to induce people to enter occupations that have undesirable job characteristics.

Compensating wage differentials explain why welders on the Alaskan pipeline have to be paid so much (to compensate for the harsh climate and higher living

EXHIBIT 6   Wages in Coal Mining and Textiles

The demand curve for coal miners is drawn to be identical to the demand curve for textile workers. Wages are higher for coal miners because the quantity supplied of coal miners is less than the quantity supplied of textile workers.

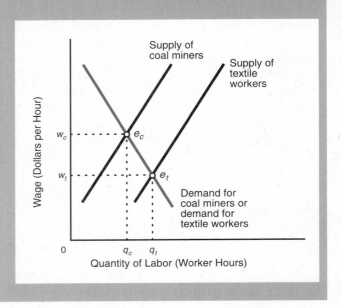

Compensating wage differentials are needed to induce people to enter unpleasant or dangerous occupations.

costs) or why sanitation workers are usually better paid than clerical workers (to compensate for the unpleasantness and social stigma). They also explain, in part, the decline in U.S. real wages since 1973. When fringe benefits are counted, total real wages have increased.

Numerous studies confirm that compensating wage differentials are indeed paid to offset undesirable job characteristics. Although individuals do differ a great deal (some enjoy heavy outdoor work and would detest office work; others enjoy work in the office but hate being outdoors), almost everyone wishes to avoid injury and disease. Wages are positively associated with the risk of being killed or seriously injured on the job. (See Example 2.)

Noncompeting Groups

Differences among people are a second source of differences in wages. Both jobs *and* people are different. Some individuals are qualified by mental and physical skills and training for a wide variety of occupations. Others are qualified for only a few occupations. Only a limited number of people have the peculiar abilities to become brain surgeons, trial lawyers, or theoretical physicists. Surgeons must have extremely sensitive and sure hands; trial lawyers must be articulate and be able to think quickly; theoretical physicists must have an enormous analytical aptitude. The number of individuals qualified to be professional athletes is limited to those possessing the necessary physical attributes. On the other hand, the number of individuals who are qualified to be stock clerks, management trainees, factory workers, and so on is much greater.

People are different for two basic reasons: first, people are born with different mental and physical abilities; second, people acquire different skills and talents through experience and training. Because of these differences, only certain groups of people qualify to fill certain jobs. Only women with slim figures and perfect complexions can become high-fashion models. Only people with good analytical

EXAMPLE 2

Compensating Wage Differentials: Land Mine Disposal in Kuwait

After the end of the Gulf War, a costly cleanup campaign was begun in Kuwait. Literally hundreds of thousands of land mines had been laid by the Iraqi forces to slow the advance of the Allied forces. These land mines had to be cleared.

The Kuwaiti government awarded contracts to American, British, and French firms to bring in specialists to remove the land mines. These firms had to pay technicians $80,000 to $100,000 per year, tax free, and all transportation and living expenses, to work at mine removal. Supervisors were paid even more. Mine disposal requires little advanced training for the technicians, who would have earned only a small fraction of this pay if they had worked in their next best alternative. The extra pay was a compensating wage differential paid to compensate workers for the danger of the job. In the course of the mine disposal work, more than a dozen technicians were killed.

skills can become mathematicians and physicists. Only individuals with superior athletic ability can become professional athletes. Because of these differences, people divide into **noncompeting groups** in the labor market.

> **Noncompeting groups** are groups of people who are differentiated by natural ability and abilities acquired through education, training, and experience to the extent that one group does not compete with another for jobs.

Because people are different, the labor force is divided into noncompeting groups.

Differences among people restrict movement among occupations. If the earnings of professional athletes or physicians were to double overnight, people lacking the necessary physical attributes and training would not be able to enter these two professions to compete for jobs.

LEISURE AND HOUSEHOLD PRODUCTION

Individuals do have options other than work in the labor force. These other options affect the total supply of labor to the economy. Individuals must choose among work in the labor force, **household production**, and **leisure**.

> **Household production** is work in the home and includes child care, meal preparation, and cleaning.

> **Leisure** is time spent in any activity other than work in the labor force or work in the home.

What determines how an individual allocates his or her time among these three activities? Opportunity costs explain how individuals decide how much time to devote to labor-force work, to leisure, and to work in the household.

Backward-Bending Labor Supply

The opportunity cost of leisure is the income (or household production) that must be given up to enjoy leisure. The opportunity cost of leisure, therefore, rises when the price of market work rises. As real wages rise over time, we would expect the quantity of market work that each person performs to increase. This has not happened. Real wages at the end of the 1980s were five times real wages 75 years earlier, but average hours worked have fallen. Why have people responded to rising real wages by working fewer hours? The backward-bending labor supply curve explains this phenomenon.

Exhibit 7 shows a labor supply curve relating wages and hours worked per person. It is drawn to be *backward-bending*—it has a section with a negative slope. The chapter on "Demand and Utility" identified two effects of a price change on the consumption of goods: the *income effect* (the impact of the change in real income that results from a price change) and the *substitution effect* (the substitution of cheaper goods for more expensive goods that results from a price change).

The increase in wages also results in income and substitution effects. In effect, the wage is the "price" of leisure. The increase in wages raises the relative price of leisure and motivates individuals to substitute other things—in this case, market work—for leisure, thereby discouraging leisure. Also, the increase in wages increases income (an income effect), making more income available to purchase leisure. Typically, as income rises, more consumption of a good occurs—if the good is a *normal good* (a good the demand for which increases as income rises). If the substitution effect of a wage increase discourages leisure, and the income effect of a wage increase encourages leisure, what then will be the overall effect on leisure of the wage increase? The overall effect depends on which effect is stronger, the substitution effect or the income effect.

In Exhibit 7, the labor supply curve is upward-sloping until a wage of $10 per

> **If the income effect of higher wages dominates the substitution effect, the labor supply curve will be backward bending.**

EXHIBIT 7 The Backward-Bending Labor-Supply Curve

When the wage is only $2 per hour and hours worked are only 15 hours per week, a dollar increase in wages adds up to only an additional $15 per week; the income effect is weak. When wages are $4 per hour and hours worked are 25 per week, a dollar increase in wages is like an extra $25 per week; the income effect is stronger. When wages are $10 per hour and 45 hours are worked per week, the income effect is even stronger. The income effect begins to dominate the substitution effect after wages reach $10 per hour. Further increases in wages cause hours worked per person to actually decline, as shown by the backward-bending section of the labor supply curve.

Technology, Employment, and Wages

Workers have an ambivalent attitude toward technology. They fear that advances in technology will deprive them of their jobs and livelihoods. The Communist philosopher Karl Marx warned that new technologies would displace workers by machines, creating a vast army of unemployed workers. A famous English movie of the 1950s showed English textile workers trying to foil the introduction of a more durable synthetic textile. Does new technology cost jobs? Is it a mistake for governments to promote research and development?

Public policy in the United States has been geared toward the production and creation of new technology. Government agricultural research has helped make American farming the most productive in the world. The National Science Foundation and other government agencies use government funds to promote new technologies, such as the supercomputer and supercollider. The private sector spends even more on research and development. Do these public and private investments in technology mean fewer jobs and lower wages?

This chapter teaches that the demand for labor depends on its productivity. If a new technology in computer technology makes the computer assembler twice as productive as before, the demand for computer assemblers will increase. Labor-saving techniques raise labor productivity; employers are now prepared to hire more workers at the same wage as before. As the demand for computer assemblers increases, more will be hired at a higher equilibrium wage.

If technology advances drive down wages, we would see a negative relationship between labor productivity and real wages. The accompanying table shows a clear positive relationship between labor productivity and real hourly wages. During periods of rapid advances in labor productivity, real wages also rise rapidly. During periods of slow labor productivity growth, wage growth is also slow.

What is the net outcome of higher technology? Real wages are higher; the national income of the country is higher. What about employment? High technology does not create unemployment, but it does have a side effect on employment. As real wages rise, people choose to take more of their time in leisure. The average workweek falls with rising affluence. This is the backward-bending labor supply curve discussed in this chapter.

	Average Annual Growth Rates Output per hour	Real Wages per hour
1960–69	2.7	2.7
1970–79	1.3	1.1
1980–86	1.3	.7
1987–90	0	−.3

Source: *Economic Report of the President.*

hour is reached. Below $10 the substitution effect of higher wages dominates the income effect of higher wages. At wage rates above $10, the quantity of labor supplied falls as the wage rate increases because the income effect dominates the substitution effect. Above $10, the labor supply curve bends backward.

Over the long run, mechanization has raised labor productivity, which translates into higher real wages. Higher real earnings enable people to opt for more leisure and fewer hours worked. Mechanization has enabled people to have more leisure while still earning high incomes.

Opportunity Costs and Household Production

One of the most striking changes in the U. S. labor force has been the substantial increase in the number of women working in it. At the turn of the century, only one in five women worked in the labor force. By the early 1990s, more than 50 percent of women worked in the labor force. A number of reasons account for the dramatic rise in women's numbers in the labor force: changing social roles, high divorce rates and one-parent families, more part-time jobs, and antidiscrimination legislation.

Opportunity costs provide another plausible explanation. Whether people work in the labor force or in household production depends in part on the value of their household production relative to the wage they could earn in market employment. If work in the home (child care, cleaning, food preparation) is worth, say, $10 per hour, and the market wage a woman could earn in the labor market is $8 per hour, she would not enter the labor force. The opportunity cost of labor-force work—household production—exceeds the market wage. If, however, the market wages of women rise more rapidly than the value of household production, then one would expect women to enter the labor force. For more women, market wages exceed the value of home production.

The real wages of women have risen substantially since the 1940s. With rising real wages, more and more women have found that market work yields returns greater than the value of home production, and they have entered the labor force.

This chapter examined how labor markets work. The next chapter will look at the effect of labor unions on the labor market.

Chapter Summary

The most important point to learn from this chapter is:
Wage rates are determined by supply and demand like any other price. People earn different wages because jobs are different and people are different.

1. Labor markets operate like other factor markets, but labor is different because workers desire leisure and because workers have preferences concerning different jobs. Labor cannot be bought and sold like the other factors of production. A labor market brings buyers and sellers of labor services together. Employers use incentive-pay schemes to deal with the principal/agent problem.

2. If firms are price takers, they hire labor to the point where $W = MRP$. The firm's MRP schedule is its labor demand schedule. The labor demand curve will be negatively sloped both for firms and for the market. The labor demand curve will shift if the demand for the firm's final product changes, if the price of either substitute factors or complementary factors changes, or if the productivity of labor changes.

3. The labor supply curve for a particular occupation will be positively sloped because workers must be paid their opportunity costs. The labor supply curve will shift if job conditions or wages in other industries change.

4. The equilibrium wage rate is that wage at which the quantity demanded of labor of a single type equals the quantity supplied. A shortage exists when the quantity demanded exceeds the quantity supplied at that wage. A surplus exists when the quantity supplied exceeds the quantity demanded at that wage. A new equilibrium wage/quantity combination will result when either the market supply or market demand curve shifts.

5. People are paid more who work in jobs that have undesirable characteristics. Noncompeting groups are workers with different abilities who do not compete for the same jobs. Wage differences are explained by job differences and differences among people.

6. When wage rates in general rise, the opportunity cost of leisure increases, as does income. Whether or not the aggregate labor supply curve will be backward-bending depends on the relative strengths of the income and substitution effects. Whether people work in household production or in the market labor force depends on the value of time in the home compared to the market wage.

Policy Focus: **Improvements in technology raise labor productivity, increase the demand for labor, and raise wages.**

Key Terms

principal/agent problem (p. 545)
labor surplus (p. 550)
labor shortage (p. 550)
compensating wage differentials (p. 553)

noncompeting groups (p. 555)
household production (p. 555)
leisure (p. 555)

Questions and Problems

1. Suppose between 1990 and the year 2000 wages increase from $10 an hour to $20 an hour. If the prices of the goods workers buy more than double, what would happen to real wages?

2. Explain why labor's special features cause the labor market to work differently from the other factor markets.

3. A price-taking firm in both its product and factor markets is currently employing 25 workers. The 25th worker's marginal revenue product is $300 per week, and the worker's wage is $200 per week. Is this firm maximizing its profits? If not, what would you advise the company to do?

4. There is a close positive association between labor productivity and wages. Using the theory presented in this chapter, explain this relationship.

5. State law in New Jersey requires that employees in licensed gambling casinos be residents of New Jersey for a specified period of time. What effect does this legislation have on the demand for casino employees in New Jersey?

6. During recessions and periods of falling wages, the number of volunteers for the all-volunteer army rises. Explain why this supply of labor rises.

7. Explain why a worker in India earns much less than a worker in West Germany.

8. "If all jobs were the same, everyone would earn the same wage." Evaluate this statement.

9. "If all people were the same, everyone would earn the same wage." Evaluate this statement.

10. You are a surgeon earning $200,000 per year. When the demand for your services increases, the charge for each operation increases by 25 percent. What effect will this increase have on the number of operations you perform?

11. Rank each of the following jobs according to the difficulty of devising an incentive-pay system that is compatible with the firm's overall objectives. Explain your ranking.
   a. Janitorial work performed at night in an office building.
   b. Assembly-line work in a washing-machine factory.
   c. Traveling sales work.
   d. The creation of hand-carved figures for a crafts company.
   e. Professional basketball playing.

12. Referring to Exhibit 1b, explain what would happen to the wage of computer programmers if the number of program lines produced per hour were to double for each level of labor input. Explain what would happen if the price of the product fell to $1.

13. Draw hypothetical labor supply and labor demand curves for truck drivers. Shift the curves to show what happens when:
   a. truck driving becomes more safe.
   b. truck drivers become more efficient.
   c. truck drivers must be licensed by a state agency.
   d. the earnings of surgeons increase.
   e. the earnings of moving-equipment operators fall.

14. What is a simple economic explanation for the shorter average U.S. workweek?

Doing Economics

This project explores wage differentials among student employees on your campus. Take a survey of student employees. Find students who work for at least ten different campus employers and ask them about their wage, how long they have worked at that job, what kind of work they do, the conditions in which they work, and the training or educational background required for the job. Can you explain the wage differentials you observe based on the factors discussed in this chapter? How important do specific skills or training seem to be? How important is experience? Are working conditions important at all?

employee negotiating individually with the employer concerning wages, fringe benefits, and work conditions, the union represents all members in negotiations or discussions with employers. Unions may bargain collectively about a number of issues, ranging from wage rates, vacation pay, and group health insurance to job-security provisions, lay-off rules, and safety conditions.

DECLINE OF UNIONISM

In the United States, there are fewer than 18 million union members; fewer than one in five people in the labor force belong to unions (see Exhibit 1). In the 1930s, union members accounted for between 6 and 7 percent of the labor force. This percentage rose in the late 1930s and 1940s and peaked at 25 percent in the mid-1950s. Since then, the share of union members has fallen steadily to under 17 percent in 1992.

Union membership as a percentage of employment has declined in recent years, for several reasons. In 1990, 22 percent of male workers and 15 percent of female workers belonged to unions. The percentage of women in the labor force has been rapidly increasing, and women have tended historically not to join unions. The share of white-collar workers in total employment has been rising as well; white-collar employees also tend not to join unions. Exhibit 2 shows that higher percentages of blue-collar workers than white-collar workers belong to unions. The shift in employment to services (which is only 7 percent unionized) has also reduced unionization. Moreover, there has been a well-publicized shift in popula-

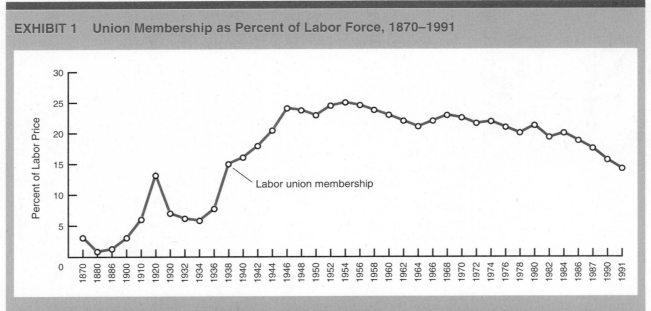

EXHIBIT 1　Union Membership as Percent of Labor Force, 1870–1991

Fewer than one in five people in the labor force in the United States belong to a union. Union membership rose from 6.7 percent in the 1930s to a peak of 25 percent in the 1950s before declining to recent levels.

SOURCES: *Statistical Abstract of the United States; Handbook of Labor Statistics; Historical Statistics of the United States, Colonial Times to 1970*, 1976, part I

The share of union members of the labor force has been falling because of the rising labor force shares of women and of white-collar employment.

tion from the northeastern and midwestern states to the southern and southwestern states, which are the states where union membership has been weakest.

The rapid unionization of public employees after 1964 has kept the percentage of union members from falling even more. In 1964, only 8 percent of state- and local-government employees belonged to unions. By 1992, the proportion had risen to 43 percent. The rise in public-sector unionism, while significant, has not been sufficient to stem the fall in the share of union members in total employment. Unionism in the United States is less well developed than in other industrialized economies. (See Example 1.)

HISTORY OF UNIONISM

Unions were not a powerful force in American life until the late 1930s, although the first national conventions of labor unions met as early as 1869 to lobby for restrictions on Chinese immigration. Union membership expanded rapidly after 1886 when the traditional craft unions banded together in the American Federation of Labor (AFL) under the leadership of Samuel Gompers, the "father of the American labor movement." Gompers made a lasting imprint on the American labor-union movement through his espousal of a nonpolitical, nonsocialist approach to unionism. Gompers believed that unions should be organized by craft and should not include unskilled workers.

Unskilled and semiskilled workers joined the Knights of Labor (organized in 1869), which experienced phenomenal growth in the early 1880s. Unlike the AFL, the Knights of Labor was committed as much or more to political goals as to wage increases. When violence in Chicago's Haymarket Square in May of 1886

EXHIBIT 2 Characteristics of Union Members: U.S. Labor Force

Category	Percent in Union	Median Weekly Earnings	
		Union Workers (dollars)	Nonunion Workers (dollars)
Total Work Force	18.6	494	372
16–24 years	7.4	335	252
25–34 years	16.5	473	378
35–44 years	23.6	518	438
45–54 years	25.5	523	431
55–64 years	24.4	504	401
65 years and over	10.7	470	306
Men	21.8	524	430
Women	14.9	416	312
White	17.7	503	384
Men	21.2	537	452
Women	13.7	423	317
Black	25.4	423	290
Men	28.0	470	305
Women	22.9	390	276
Hispanic	16.8	417	276
Men	18.5	451	291
Women	14.5	368	255
Full-time workers	20.9	494	372
Managerial and professional specialty	15.2	581	584
Technical, sales, and administrative support	12.1	431	346
Service occupations	15.1	406	226
Precision production, craft, and repair	28.2	568	405
Operators, fabricators, and laborers	29.0	448	287
Farming, forestry, and fishing	4.6	379	239
Private nonagricultural wage and salary workers	13.7	485	368
Mining	19.7	572	561
Construction	22.6	634	393
Manufacturing	23.1	458	400
Transportation and public utilities	34.1	561	458
Wholesale and retail trade, total	7.0	402	298
Finance, insurance, and real estate	3.1	399	407
Services	7.0	402	352
Government	43.6	506	419

Source: U.S. Bureau of Labor Statistics, *Employment and Earnings,* annual. The above data are for 1990.

stiffened employer resistance to the Knights of Labor and turned public opinion against organized labor, the Knights of Labor suffered a fatal collapse.

One reason for the difficulty in organizing the American labor force into unions is the unfavorable political climate that prevailed until the 1930s. Antitrust laws (the Sherman Antitrust Act of 1890) were applied against "monopolistic" labor unions; companies used private police forces, threats, and intimidation to prevent labor unions from forming. It was not until 1932 that the government adopted a conscious policy favoring the free organization of unions. Prior to 1932, management was often able to obtain court orders that prohibited union activity, and employers were allowed to require new employees to sign "yellow dog" contracts, in which the employee had to agree not to join a union as a condition of employment.

Industrial unionism (which suffered a severe setback with the collapse of the Knights of Labor) made a comeback in the 1930s under the leadership of John L. Lewis. The failure of the AFL to organize unskilled and semiskilled workers in

EXAMPLE 1

Labor Unions in International Perspective

There are significant differences between the labor union movements in the United States and in Europe. Although associations of journeymen existed in the form of medieval guilds, labor unions were not organized in Europe until the nineteenth century. The United Kingdom reversed earlier antiunion acts when it passed the Trade Union Act of 1871, which guaranteed legal recognition for labor unions. On the Continent, unions were organized on industrial rather than craft lines, and they engaged in more partisan political activity. In Germany, for example, unions were responsible for much social legislation prior to World War I.

In Europe today, labor organizations tend to be either constituted as or affiliated with political parties, usually from the left wing. In England, the labor unions joined forces with the socialists to form the Labour Party in 1893. In Sweden, there is a close alliance between the two major labor unions and the Social Democratic Party. In Italy, Belgium, and the Netherlands, rival Christian and socialist trade union movements are present. Unlike its European counterparts, the American labor movement has avoided forming a political party, remaining instead within the framework of the two-party system.

The United States is one of the least unionized industrial economies. Between 65 percent and 90 percent of workers in Scandinavian countries are unionized. The proportions for Germany, Japan, and the United Kingdom hover around one-third. The United States resembles France, Switzerland, Hong Kong, and Taiwan, where unionization rates are 20 percent or less.

The industrialized countries have developed many types of labor unions. In Germany, unions are organized on an industry basis and are grouped into federations. Collective bargaining usually takes place at industrywide levels, and compulsory arbitration is often used to settle disputes. German enterprise laws require that union representatives sit on management boards in large companies. The German labor movement plays a prominent role in the German Social Democratic Party.

Sweden is dominated by a highly disciplined and comprehensive labor movement. Virtually all blue-collar workers belong to the Confederation of Trade Unions, and white-collar workers belong to one of two other unions. As close allies of the Social Democratic Party, Swedish unions have developed profit-sharing plans and have pushed for social welfare policies to equalize the distribution of income.

The Japanese economy is characterized by company unionism. Each company has its own union that cuts across all craft and class boundaries. Japanese union presidents are key workers who are often promoted to the ranks of management. Japanese unions typically foster cooperation between management and workers and commonly adopt a management perspective. The founding slogan of the Nissan Company labor union is "Those who truly love their union, love their company."

UNION MEMBERS AS A PERCENTAGE OF THE LABOR FORCE

Country	Percentage	Country	Percentage
Israel	90%	Canada	31%
Sweden	90	Netherlands	29
Finland	80	Japan	29
Belgium	70	France	20
Norway	66	Switzerland	20
Denmark	65	Taiwan	18
Austria	62	Singapore	17
Italy	42	Hong Kong	15
United Kingdom	37	United States	14
Ireland	36	South Korea	10
Germany	34		

Source: *The World Factbook 1990.*

assembly-line production caused conflicts within the AFL organization. As a consequence, the Congress of Industrial Organizations (CIO) was formed in 1936 to organize workers on an industrial rather than a craft basis.

In 1955, the AFL and CIO merged to form the combined AFL–CIO. The AFL–CIO continues to try to bring major non-AFL–CIO unions back into the AFL–CIO. In 1985, the United Automobile Workers rejoined the AFL–CIO. In late 1987, the AFL–CIO scored a major victory when the nation's largest independent union—the Teamsters—joined the AFL–CIO.

UNION LEGISLATION

Until the passage of federal legislation in the 1930s, the courts ruled on union activities using common-law principles. Common law, however, presented the courts with difficult choices. On the one hand, it is a common-law principle that intentional harm to private property is illegal. Yet strikes, picketing, and boycotts are designed to place economic hardship on the private property of employers. On the other hand, the right of people to combine for mutual assistance was also accepted by common law. In the early nineteenth century, the courts typically held that union efforts to raise wages through strikes, picketing, and boycotts constituted criminal conspiracies. Under such rulings, union leaders were criminally prosecuted and sued for damages. The basic legality of trade unionism was not settled until 1842 when the Supreme Court of Massachusetts ruled that union legality depended on union objectives. Unions in themselves were not illegal. Following the 1842 ruling, peaceful strikes for improved wages, hours, or working conditions were generally accepted as legal, while violent strikes or sympathy strikes to aid workers in other industries were not accepted by the courts.

In the 1880s, employers began using court *injunctions* to prevent strikes, pickets, and boycotts. The injunction was originally designed to prevent threatened damage to property under conditions when regular court processes would be too slow. Employers could go to sympathetic judges when threatened with strikes to obtain a restraining order which could close down a picket line or head off a strike within a matter of hours. The use of injunctions was eventually broadened to safeguarding businesses' "justifiable expectation of profit." The liberal use of injunctions in the late nineteenth and early twentieth centuries made it very difficult for unions to strike a company without being restrained by an injunction. The company only needed to claim that the strike threatened damage to the employer's property. In the early twentieth century, court rulings further weakened unions by upholding "yellow dog" contracts. In effect, the courts ruled that employers could legally require a nonunion pledge as a legitimate condition for employment. A further problem for unions was the uncertainty about whether the restraint-of-trade provisions of the 1890 Sherman Act were meant to apply to union activities.

Two pro-union laws passed during the Great Depression paved the way for the growth of the organized labor movement in the 1930s and 1940s. The Norris-LaGuardia Act of 1932 declared that a worker "has full freedom of association, self-organization, and designation of representatives of his own choosing, to negotiate the terms and conditions of his employment . . . " and that workers should be "free from the interference, restraint, or coercion of employers" in the choice of union representatives. The Norris-LaGuardia Act restricted the use of court orders and injunctions to combat union organizing drives and strikes and prohibited "yellow dog" contracts, The National Labor Relations Act (the

Wagner Act) of 1935 defined specific unfair labor practices. Employers were required to bargain in good faith with unions representing a majority of employees, and it became illegal to interfere with employees' rights to organize into unions. The National Labor Relations Board (NLRB) was established and given the authority to investigate unfair labor practices. The NLRB was also authorized to conduct elections to determine which union the employees wanted, if any, to represent them.

The Norris-LaGuardia Act of 1932 and the Wagner Act of 1935 encouraged union growth in the 1930s and 1940s. Exhibit 1 makes it clear that until these laws were passed, labor unions were relatively insignificant in size. After World War II, unions lost some of their popular support. The Taft-Hartley and Landrum-Griffin acts were the result of anti-union sentiment. The Taft-Hartley Act of 1947 gave states the right to pass *right-to-work laws* that prohibited the requirement that union membership be a condition for employment. *Closed-shop agreements* that required firms to hire only union members were outlawed for firms engaged in interstate commerce. Major strikes that could disrupt the economy could be delayed by an 80-day cooling-off period if ordered by the president.

The Landrum-Griffin Act of 1959 was designed to protect the rights of union members and to increase union democracy. It included provisions for periodic reporting of union finances and for regulating union elections.

> The Norris-LaGuardia Act of 1932 and the Wagner Act of 1935 were pro-union laws that spurred the growth of labor unions.

UNION OBJECTIVES

What are the objectives of labor unions? Surprisingly, the answer to this question is not as obvious as it appears. Unions would like to obtain higher wages, better fringe benefits, and safer working conditions for their members. They would also like to prevent the unemployment of their members. Are the two objectives of higher wages and lower unemployment compatible—given the fact (demonstrated in the previous chapter) that the firm will hire more labor at low wages than at high wages, *ceteris paribus*?

Assume that two different unions—A and B—collectively bargain about wages with management. For simplicity, we assume that workers in each union are earning the same wage (w_c) and that employment is the same in both cases (at l_c). The demand curve for each union's labor force is shown in Exhibit 3. Demand curves for labor, just like demand curves for goods and services, can be either elastic or inelastic. The demand curve in the case of Union A is inelastic: moving from point c to point a in panel (a) means a large percentage increase in the wage (to w_a) compared to the percentage reduction in the quantity of labor demanded (from l_c to l_a). The demand is elastic in the case of Union B: moving from c to b in panel (b) means a small percentage increase in the wage compared to the percentage reduction in the quantity of labor demanded (from l_c to l_b).

The leadership of Union B is faced with a dilemma. If it pushes for wages higher than w_c—such as w_b—the number of jobs available to union members will decline from l_c to l_b. Jobs will be traded off for higher wages, and the rank and file of the union will likely be dissatisfied with the union leadership. This **wage/employment tradeoff** is less acute in the case of Union A because the same increase in wages loses fewer jobs (because of the difference in elasticity between A and B).

> Unions are faced with a wage/employment tradeoff when bargaining for higher wages.

EXHIBIT 3   The Tradeoff Between Wages and Employment

a. Inelastic Demand: Union A   **b. Elastic Demand: Union B**

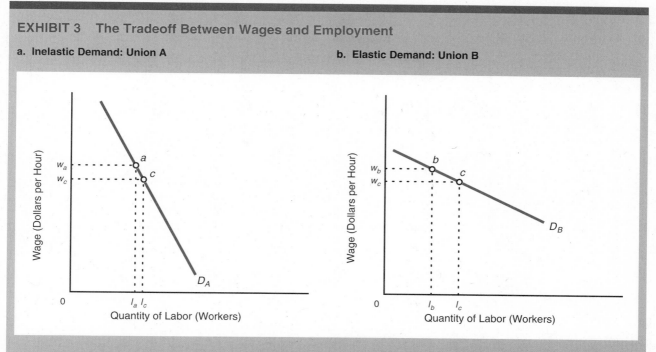

The demand curve for the members of Union A is relatively inelastic, while the demand curve for the members of Union B is relatively elastic. If both unions, in the collective-bargaining process, push for the same wage increases, more jobs will be lost by workers in Union B (where demand is elastic) than by workers in Union A.

> The **wage/employment tradeoff** confronts any labor union that faces a downward-sloping demand curve: higher wages means sacrificing the number of jobs; lower unemployment means sacrificing higher wages.

Example 2 provides an example of the tradeoff.

How Unions Deal with the Tradeoff

The wage/employment tradeoff explains why unions try to increase the demand for labor and to reduce the elasticity of demand for labor. If they succeed in increasing demand for labor, labor unions can obtain both higher wages and higher employment. By reducing the elasticity of demand for labor, unions can raise wages with a smaller cost in lost employment.

Unions attempt to increase the demand for union labor and lower its elasticity of demand in a variety of ways. Unions lobby for tariffs and quotas on competing foreign-produced products to increase the demand for the products produced by union workers. Unions conduct advertising campaigns telling the public to "look for the union label" or to "buy American." Unions have opposed relaxing immigration laws. Unions have traditionally supported raising the minimum wage—an act that makes unskilled labor more expensive relative to the more skilled workers that tend to belong to unions.

Unions have lobbied for minimum staffing requirements. The unions unsuccessfully lobbied for the MD-80 aircraft to be staffed by three cockpit personnel

Union Objectives

(two pilots and a flight engineer) rather than the two pilots that airline management wanted. Staffing requirements that call for the use of additional labor for jobs that have become redundant (such as fire stokers on diesel-powered locomotives) are called *featherbedding*. Unions may also bargain for rules that make it difficult or impossible to substitute other grades of labor for union labor. In construction, unions specify which jobs can be performed only by electricians and by no one else, and there are sanctions against builders who hire nonunion employees. Work rules are often a subject of negotiation along with wage rates when unions bargain with management.

Limitations of Labor Supply

Some unions seek to drive up the wage by limiting the supply of union labor. In these cases, the union controls who will be allowed to work in a particular occupation by means of certification and qualification requirements. In craft unions, the number of union members can be limited by long apprenticeships, by rules limiting entry into the union, by difficult qualifying exams, and by state licensing. In the process of limiting labor supply, the union screens out unqualified workers but may also exclude some qualified people who are prepared to work in that occupation.

Unions can raise wages by limiting the supply of labor.

Exhibit 4 shows the effect of limiting labor supply on wages. The decrease in supply (from S to S') moves the equilibrium wage/employment combination from e to e'; at e' wages are higher, but fewer jobs are available. When unions seek to control wages through limitations on the supply of union labor, it is especially important to prevent employers from substituting nonunion labor. For this reason, craft unions favor rigid certification requirements and rules prohibiting nonunion workers from performing certain tasks.

Collective Bargaining

Industrial unions that represent all the workers in a particular industry have a more difficult time limiting the supply of labor. Such unions can indeed affect overall

EXHIBIT 4   The Effect on Wages of Limiting Supply

By limiting entry into the profession, a craft union shifts the labor supply curve to the left (from S to S'), and the wage rate of union members is raised above what it would have been without the union.

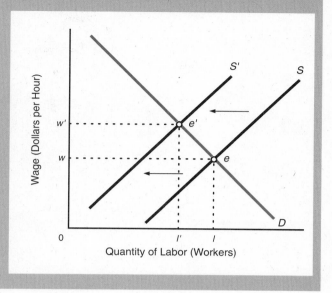

labor supply conditions by favoring restrictions on immigration, mandatory retirement, shorter workweeks, and laws against teenage employment. But they, unlike plumbers, electricians, and physicians, find it difficult to control the number of union members. Industrial unions, therefore, use **collective bargaining**, sometimes coupled with the threat of **strike**, to raise the wages of union members.

> **Collective bargaining** is the bargaining of unions as representatives of all union employees with management.

> A **strike** occurs when all union workers cease working until the employer agrees to specific union demands.

Industrial unions raise wages through collective bargaining with the threat of strike.

Collective bargaining gives workers a stronger voice than they would have if each worker bargained separately with management. The threat of strike is the union's strongest weapon in collective bargaining.

The effect of the collective-bargaining process (with threat of strike) is represented in Exhibit 5. The supply curve, S, represents the supply of labor to the industry *if each individual were to bargain separately with management*. When the union threatens to strike, the union is, in effect, telling management that: at wages less than w_c, no labor will be supplied; at the wage of w_c, management can hire as much labor as it wants up to l_c; as wages increase above w_c, management can hire ever-increasing amounts of labor beyond l_c. Thus, the new labor supply curve with the threat of a strike is shown by the heavy line that connects w_c, on the vertical axis with point c and then continues up the original supply curve above point c. Without the threat of strike, the supply curve would be the original curve S, and point e would be the equilibrium wage/employment combination. With the threat of a strike, the demand curve would meet the new supply curve at point a, and the firm would hire l_a workers at a wage of w_c.

Union Objectives

EXHIBIT 5   Collective Bargaining with the Threat of Strike

The supply curve, S, represents the labor supply if there were no union. The heavy blue supply curve that is S' to the left of point c and S above c is the supply curve with collective bargaining because no union labor will be supplied at a wage below w_c. Point e is the equilibrium wage/employment combination without collective bargaining or threat of a strike; point a is the equilibrium wage/employment combination with collective bargaining. The benefit to union members is that a higher wage is achieved (w_c is higher than w_e). The cost is that the number of jobs is reduced. Some union members who are willing to work at w_c are without jobs in the industry (the number represented by the difference between l_c and l_a is the number left without jobs).

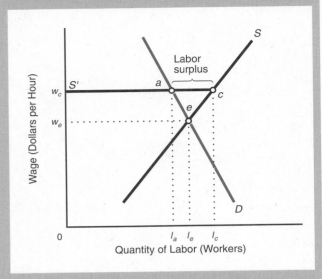

From the standpoint of union members, collective bargaining has its costs and benefits. The benefits are the higher wages that collective bargaining brings (w_c is higher than w_e). The costs are that some union members who are willing to work at the negotiated wage will not be employed. Although l_c workers are willing to work at w_c, only l_a workers will be hired. The unemployment effects of collective bargaining are softened by numerous rules within the union governing which members will be laid off first. Typically, union members who have *seniority* (have been in the union the longest time) are laid off last.

Collective Bargaining with Monopsony

If employers have monopsony power over their labor market, the tradeoff between higher wages and union employment does not hold. An employer has monopsony power if the employer accounts for a large enough portion of total hiring in that labor market to affect the market wage. The labor supply curve to a monopsonistic firm is not horizontal at the prevailing market wage because the employer cannot hire all the labor it wants at the market wage. Instead, to hire more labor, the monopsonistic firm will have to offer higher wages to all its employees.

Consider a monopsonist faced with the upward-sloping labor supply schedule given in Exhibit 6. The wage rate is not the marginal factor cost (MFC) in the case of the monopsonist. To hire one more unit of labor, the monopsonist must pay a higher wage not only to the new worker but also to workers previously hired. To hire the second worker, the monopsonist must pay a higher wage ($7 rather than the previous $5) to the first worker. The MFC of the second worker is, therefore, the wage paid the second worker ($7) plus the increase in the wage of the first worker ($2) for a total of $9. The MFC exceeds the wage in the case of the monopsonist.

The figure in Exhibit 6 shows the employment and wage rate offered by a monopsonist with and without collective bargaining. *Without collective bargaining,*

The marginal factor cost of the monopsonist is greater than the wage rate paid by the monopsonist because the monopsonist must raise the wage of all workers to increase employment.

EXHIBIT 6   Monopsony and Collective Bargaining

a. The Monopsonist's Marginal Factor Cost

Labor (workers), L (1)	Wage (dollars per hours), W (2)	Labor Cost (dollars) (3) = (1) × (2)	Marginal Factor Cost (dollars), MFC (4)
1	5	5	
			9
2	7	14	
			13
3	9	27	
			21
4	12	48	

b. Collective Bargaining: When *MFC* Exceeds the Wage

Because this industry is monopsonistic, *MFC* is greater than the wage at each quantity of labor. The monopsonist will hire that quantity at which *MFC* = *MRP* and pay the wage that corresponds to that labor quantity on the supply curve, or w_m. Without unions, *MFC* = *MRP* at point *e*; the monopsonist will hire l_m workers and pay the wage of w_m. If a union collectively bargains for a wage of w_u, the monopsonist's *MFC* curve shifts to *MFC'* because of the change in labor supply and becomes a horizontal line at w_u; *MFC'* will now equal *MRP* at point *u*. In this case, collective bargaining actually increased both wages (from w_m to w_u) and union employment (from l_m to l_u).

the monopsonist hires that quantity of labor at which *MFC* and *MRP* are equal (but will pay the wage corresponding to that quantity on the labor supply curve). The monopsonist hires l_m workers and pays a wage of w_m.

Since *MFC* exceeds the wage rate, the monopsonist will hire less labor than would be the case if the industry were competitive in the labor market and each firm treated the wage rate as its *MFC*. The competitive industry would operate at point *c*, where *S* (which equals the competitive firm's *MFC*) equals *MRP*. *Monopsony results in lower wages and fewer people being employed as compared to the case of the competitive employer.*

When facing a monopsonistic employer, collective bargaining can raise both employment and wages. If a union collectively bargains for a wage of w_u, the monopsonist's *MFC* curve becomes a horizontal line at w_u. Collective bargaining makes the supply of union labor perfectly elastic (horizontal) at the union wage. By demanding w_u the union makes this wage the *MFC* of the monopsonist. In this case, *MRP* = *MFC'* at point *u*, where the monopsonist hires l_u of labor.

There are no measures of the degree of monopsony in labor markets. Monopsony in factor markets is less likely than monopoly in product markets because virtually all employers compete among themselves for the factors of production. Although cases of monopsony can be found, the observed behavior of labor unions—the obvious efforts of unions to soften the wage/employment tradeoff—suggests that monopsony is not prevalent and that in most cases unions must trade off jobs for higher wages.

> Collective bargaining can raise both wages and union employment when the firm is a monopsonist.

THE EFFECT OF UNIONS ON WAGES

Unions can affect the wages of their members by limiting the supply of union labor, by increasing the demand for union labor through staffing requirements and programs to increase the demand for the product, and through collective bargaining. Considerable effort on the part of many labor economists has gone into estimating the extent to which unions have been able to raise the wages of their members relative to comparable nonunion workers.

Effect on Union Wages

Studies of the effect of unions on wages find that unions have indeed succeeded in raising the wages of their members above what those wages would have been without unions. In the mid-1990s, union members earned about one-third more per week than nonunion members. The effects of unions have varied among industries, over time and by gender and race as shown in Exhibit 7. From 1967 to 1975, the wage advantage of union members increased from around 12 percent to a near 17 percent advantage. Studies show that, historically, craft unions in construction and transportation have achieved the largest relative wage effects (20–25 percent). Industrial unions have had a smaller relative wage effect (10–15 percent). In competitive industries such as textiles and apparel, unions have had the smallest impact on relative wages. Whatever the case, union members earn more on average than nonunion workers.

Unions have succeeded in raising the wages of their members above nonunion wages.

Effect on Nonunion Wages

It is more difficult to establish the effect of unions on the general level of wages or on the wages of nonunion workers. Theory suggests that unions could either depress or increase the wage rates of nonunion workers.

Exhibit 1 showed that less than one U.S. worker in five is a union member. The economy's labor force is made up of both unionized and nonunionized sectors, with the nonunionized sector numerically dominant. If unions bargain for substantial increases in the union wage and trade off jobs for large wage increases, unemployed union members can "spill over" into the nonunion sector. The young union members with low seniority are the ones most likely laid off in the unionized

---

EXHIBIT 7   Union Wage Advantages

	Percentage Union Wage Effect			Percentage Unionized		
	1967	1973	1975	1967	1973	1975
All workers	11.6	14.8	16.8	23	26	25
White males	9.6	15.5	16.3	31	33	31
Black males	21.5	22.5	22.5	32	37	37
White females	14.4	12.7	16.6	12	14	14
Black females	5.6	13.2	17.1	13	22	22

SOURCE: Orley Ashenfelter, "Union Relative Wage Effects: New Evidence and a Survey of Their Implications for Wage Inflation," in *Econometric Contributions to Public Policy*, eds. R. Stone and W. Peterson (New York: St. Martin's, 1979), Tables 2.1 and 2.2.

Are Unions "Good" or "Bad" for Efficiency?

Public policy plays a major role in determining the overall level of health of unionism. Until the passage of pro-union federal legislation in the 1930s, unions played a relatively small role. President Ronald Reagan's decision to fire striking air-traffic controllers in August 1981 dealt a severe blow to the American labor movement.

To determine what stance public policy should take toward unions, it is important to determine the effect of unions on economic efficiency.

Do Unions Decrease Efficiency?

The traditional view is that unions have a negative effect on productivity. The reasons for this view include the following:

1. Unions bargain for staffing requirements *(featherbedding)* that prevent employers from using labor and capital in the most efficient manner. If union rules prevent carpenters from turning a screw on any electrical fixture, for example, the economy will operate below its potential.
2. Union strikes disrupt output and cause the economy to produce below its production potential. Strikes in major industries, like steel and rail transportation, can disrupt other sectors of the economy and cause losses of real output.
3. If workers of comparable quality are paid different wages because one belongs to a union and the other is in nonunion employment, the economy loses potential output. In both the unionized and nonunionized sectors, workers will be employed to the point where their wage equals their *MRP*, but the *MRP*s of union workers will be higher than those of comparable nonunion workers. The economy could have increased its output by reallocating workers from the nonunionized sector (where *MRP* is lower) into the union sector (where *MRP* is higher).

Do Unions Increase Efficiency?

A new breed of economists maintain that unions actually improve productivity. Unions improve productivity by acting as a *collective voice* for union members. Without unions, if workers are dissatisfied with their employer, their only recourse is to quit and seek another job. When workers "vote with their feet" to punish bad employers, the resulting job turnover costs the economy lost output. With high turnover, employees must learn new jobs and spend time in often lengthy job searches.

Unions can have a positive effect on productivity in three ways. First, when worker grievances are handled by the union, workers need not leave the firm in order to bring about an improvement in their work conditions. If fewer workers quit—because the union gives them a voice for their protests or complaints—the firm can reduce its hiring and training costs, and the work groups will function more smoothly. Workers with a voice are more willing to train in skills that are useful in only that industry. Second, senior workers (who are most important politically in the union organization) are more likely to provide informal training and assistance in enterprises where unions give them a voice. When the union provides a channel of communication between workers and management, the improved flow of information can increase the efficiency of the enterprise. Third, a well-established seniority system tends to reduce friction between junior and senior workers.

The empirical evidence suggest the following effects of unions on productivity. First, there is strong evidence that the presence of unions causes a dramatic reduction in employee turnover (see Exhibit 8). Although the quit rates of young workers (who happen to be the first laid off in unions) are only slightly reduced by unionization, other workers' quit rates are reduced by the presence of unions from 34

EXHIBIT 8 Unions, Turnover, and Productivity

a. Effect of Unions on Quit Rates

Sample	Percentage by which Quits Are Reduced by Unionism
All workers, 1968–78	45
All workers, 1973–75	86
Men 48–62 in 1969	107
Men 17–27 in 1969	11
Manufacturing workers	34–48

Source: Richard Freeman and James Medoff, "The Two Faces of Unionism," *The Public Interest* 57 (Fall 1979): p. 79.

b. Effect of Unions on Productivity in U.S. Industries

Industry	Percentage Increase in Output per Worker Due to Unions
Manufacturing, 1972	20–25
Wooden furniture, 1972	15
Cement, 1953–76	6–8
Underground coal, 1965	25–30
Underground coal, 1975	(−20)–(−25)
Construction, 1972	29–38
Construction, office buildings, 1973–74	30
Construction, retail stores and shopping centers, 1976–78	51

Sources: Richard Freeman and James Medoff, "The Two Faces of Unionism," *The Public Interest* 57 (Fall 1979): p. 80; Kim Clark, "The Impact of Unionization on Productivity: A Case Study," *Industrial and Labor Relations Review* (July 1980): pp. 451–69; and Ronald Ehrenberg and Robert Smith, *Modern Labor Economics*, 4th ed. (New York: HarperCollins, 1991), p. 483.

to 107 percent. Second, empirical studies find that productivity is generally higher in industries with higher rates of unionization.

The final chapter remains to be written on this issue. If unions do indeed promote efficiency, a more supportive public policy towards unions could be called for.

Higher wages in the unionized sector can depress the wages of nonunion workers by causing unemployed union members to spill over into nonunion employment.

sector when there is a tradeoff between higher wages and fewer jobs. When they seek employment in the nonunionized sector, the labor supply curve in the nonunionized sector shifts to the right (increases), and wages in the nonunionized sector are bid down.

On the other hand, unions could possibly raise wages in the nonunionized sector in two ways. First, employers of nonunion workers may fear that if they do not match union wage increases, pressure will build among their workers to form a union. Second, when a unionized worker is laid off, there is a possibility that that worker will not spill over into the nonunionized sector but will wait until he or she is recalled to a job in the union sector. The unemployed union member is least likely to "spill over" when there is a substantial wage differential between the nonunion and union job, when the likelihood of recall is high, and when unemployment benefits are generous. If unemployed union workers do not spill over into nonunionized jobs, the downward pressure on nonunion wages would be removed.

The empirical evidence on the question of union effects on nonunion wages is not decisive, but it does suggest that unions depress wages in nonunionized jobs. In cities where the percent of unionized workers is high the wages of nonunion workers are lower than in other cities where there is less unionization.

This chapter continued the discussion of labor markets begun in the preceding chapter by examining how unions affect wages and economic efficiency. The next chapter will turn to the nonlabor factors of production: land, capital, and entrepreneurship.

**The most important point to learn from this chapter is:
Unionized workers face a tradeoff between higher wages and fewer
jobs. In collective bargaining, unions must balance this tradeoff in their
bargaining strategy.**

1. A union is a collective organization of workers and employees whose objective is to
   improve the work conditions of its members. A craft union represents workers of a
   particular occupation. An industrial union represents workers of a particular industry.
   Currently less than 20 percent of the labor force belongs to unions—a decline from
   the high of 25 percent in the 1950s. The declining percentage is due to the rise of
   white-collar employment, the rising share of women in the work force, and the shift of
   industry to the South and Southwest. The most substantial gains in union
   membership have been in public employment.

2. During the nineteenth century, the courts used common-law rulings and injunctions
   to limit union activity. The formation of unions was aided by pro-labor legislation
   beginning with the Norris-LaGuardia Act of 1932, which facilitated union-organizing
   drives. The National Labor Relations Act of 1935 made it illegal for employers to
   interfere with the rights of employees to organize. The Taft-Hartley Act of 1947
   reacted against the pro-union legislation of the 1930s.

3. Unions must weigh the advantages of higher wages against the disadvantages of
   less union employment. Unions respond to the tradeoff between jobs and
   employment by increasing the demand for union labor and by promoting measures
   to reduce the elasticity of demand for union labor. In collective bargaining, the
   union's most potent weapon is the strike threat. If the employer is a monopsonist,
   the wage/employment tradeoff does not exist.

4. Unions are able to raise the wages of union members relative to comparable
   nonunion members. The amount wages are raised varies by industry and by union.
   Unions can have both a positive and a negative effect on nonunion wages. When
   unions raise wages in the union sector, the workers who are laid off spill over
   into the nonunion sector, and the increase in labor supply lowers nonunion wages.
   However, when unions raise wages in the union sector, nonunion employers
   may raise wages because they fear the formation of a union if they do not raise
   wages.

   Policy Focus: **Public policy can either promote or retard the
   development of unions. It is therefore important to understand the
   effect of unions on productivity. There are two views on the effect of
   unions on productivity. The traditional view maintains that unions
   adversely affect labor productivity. The new view argues that unions
   give workers a voice in the workplace and that this raises the labor
   productivity of union workers.**

Key Terms

labor union (p. 562)
craft union (p. 562)
industrial union (p. 562)
employee association (p. 562)

wage/employment tradeoff (p. 569)
collective bargaining (p. 571)
strike (p. 571)

Questions and Problems

1. The elasticity of demand for labor (the percentage change in quantity of labor demanded divided by the percentage change in the wage) is 1.5 in the widget industry and is 0.5 in the ratchet industry. Which industry would be easier to unionize? In which industry is the tradeoff between employment and higher wages more costly?

2. If you were the president of a major industrial union, what would your attitude be toward unlimited immigration? What would your attitude be toward the minimum-wage law? Explain.

3. Why do industrial unions not use the craft-union technique of restricting labor supply to raise union wages?

4. Explain why both the automobile unions and the management of the automobile industry favor import restrictions on imported cars.

5. Assume that you belong to a union of bank tellers. What would your attitude be toward automated bank tellers? Explain.

6. Explain why the impact of higher union wages on nonunion wages might depend on whether laid-off union members waited to be rehired as opposed to searching for jobs in nonunionized industries.

7. Which of the following policies would unions tend to favor? Explain your answer.
   a. Liberal immigration laws.
   b. Free trade.
   c. Reductions of quotas on foreign goods.
   d. A higher minimum wage.

8. If unions do succeed in raising productivity, what effect would this productivity increase have on the costs of production of unionized companies versus nonunionized companies?

9. Explain why common-law principles made it difficult for judges in the eighteenth and nineteenth centuries to rule on the legality of strikes.

10. Strikes have been called the strongest weapon available to industrial unions in collective bargaining. Explain how strikes can be used to change the labor-supply curve. What shape does the labor-supply curve have with and without the threat of strike?

11. If unions lower quit rates, why would productivity be expected to increase?

12. How is "featherbedding" used to raise union wages? What does "featherbedding" mean?

Doing Economics

Try to obtain an interview with a local union leader. Ask her what the objectives of her union are. How relatively important are high wages, improved benefits, expanded employment, dealing with grievances and working conditions, improved productivity, political action, and other union objectives? Does she view the union and the employer(s) as fundamentally in partnership or in conflict? What examples can she give of how the presence of the union enhances productivity through a more orderly operation of the workplace? Does she believe that pushing for higher wages or benefits necessarily reduces the amount of employment? Which of the arguments against unions presented in the text does she agree with and which ones does she dispute?

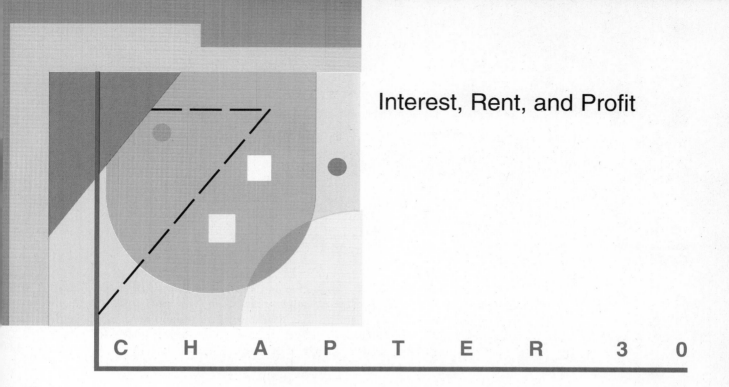

Interest, Rent, and Profit

C H A P T E R   3 0

CHAPTER FOCUS

This chapter is about the factors of production other than labor. They account for about 25 cents of every dollar earned by participants in the economy. These other factors—capital, land, and entrepreneurship—are less visible and less well understood, but they make essential contributions to economic well-being.

The average American manufacturing worker works with over $100,000 worth of manufacturing equipment. Through the process of past investment, American workers find themselves in a favorable position relative to workers in less-developed economies. The combination of labor with vast amounts of capital makes workers highly productive and makes it possible for them to earn relatively high wages. An American manufacturing worker working with primitive equipment would earn much less. What if this capital had not been accumulated?

What if no entrepreneur had been around to detect business opportunities? If farsighted persons, willing to take risks, had not foreseen the profit opportunities in automobile manufacturing, personal computers, fast-food chains, or commercial jet manufacturing, there would be little capital, little employment, and low wages.

Some people possess or own unique resources. Some women have perfect complexions and become supermodels earning astronomical salaries; others have unique athletic skills; yet others are fortunate to own valuable real estate located in the center of prosperous cities. How and why should people be rewarded for possessing these unique resources?

After studying this chapter, you will be able to:

- Understand how interest rates are related to productivity and thrift.
- Discuss why interest rates differ between different people and different assets.
- Explain the function of economic rent.
- Identify the sources of economic profit.

CAPITAL AND INTEREST

Ultimately, the function of production is to provide for consumption. Capital goods such as trucks, conveyors, lathes, cranes, and computers are ultimately useful only because they enable us to consume more goods and services. Cars and shirts and milk are produced indirectly by first producing capital goods. Indirect or roundabout production is typically more productive than direct production. Capital goods enlist the mechanical, electrical, and chemical powers of nature to expand the production possibilities of society far beyond what otherwise could be accomplished by unaided human hands or minds. Productivity is raised when a net is used instead of bare hands to catch fish. Productivity is raised when workers use an automated assembly line rather than hand tools to assemble cars.

Capital and Saving

Saving is necessary for a society to invest in capital goods. Resources must be diverted from producing consumption goods to producing capital goods. When people save, they buy stocks and bonds or deposit their funds in bank accounts. While some of these funds are used to finance consumption expenditures, the rest are channeled into investments in new buildings, plants, and machinery.

Interest is the price paid for borrowed funds or credit. Because capital is productive, a dollar invested today in capital goods yields more than a dollar tomorrow. But people are impatient. To be convinced to save a dollar today, they must be rewarded with more than a dollar tomorrow. Business firms that wish to invest are willing to pay interest and savers demand that interest be paid. Interest coordinates the number of dollars that businesses want to invest with the number that people want to save.

> **Interest** is the price of credit. Interest is set where the amount businesses wish to invest is balanced with the amount people are prepared to save.

Credit Markets

Interest plays its coordinating role in credit markets. **Credit markets** bring suppliers of credit (savers) together with demanders of credit (businesses that wish to invest). Credit markets, also called *capital markets,* make possible the production of capital goods.

> **Credit markets** are markets for borrowing and lending funds.

Frank Knight (1885–1972)

Frank Knight was born on a farm in Illinois, the first of eleven children, two others of whom became economists. Knight attended a series of small colleges and then spent two years at the University of Tennessee before going to Cornell to study philosophy. He switched to economics a year later and wrote a dissertation that appeared in 1921 as his classic work, *Risk, Uncertainty, and Profit.* Knight taught at Cornell, Iowa, and the University of Chicago, where he spent the rest of his teaching career. He served as president of the American Economic Association in 1950. In addition to contributing to the theory of profits, Knight explained how the efficiency of markets depends on property rights to resources being clearly defined.

In *Risk, Uncertainty, and Profit,* Knight sought to explain why profits exist even in competitive markets. Knight argued that profits are a reward for risk and uncertainty. Although some risks can be calculated, Knight thought that certain risks cannot be reduced to objective measures. In a changing business environment with technological advances, certain business risks will be unknown because they are unprecedented. Entrepreneurs who take unprecedented risks are rewarded by positive profits even in competitive industries. Knight's major contribution to economics was to provide a satisfactory explanation of profits in a competitive environment.

Robinson Crusoe, living alone on a deserted island, had no need for credit markets. Crusoe would simply *save* (give up some present consumption) so he could *invest* (produce capital goods). When Crusoe took three days off from fishing to weave a net (a capital good), he was both saving and investing. Similarly, farmers both save and invest by taking time off from current production to drain a swamp or build a dam (that is, to produce capital goods).

In a modern economy, however, credit markets are required to bring savers and investors together. Unlike Crusoe or the farmer draining land, the saver and the investor are typically not the same. Financial assets—stocks, bonds, bank credit, and trade credit—are used to finance capital goods. Credit markets make possible the separation of the act of saving from the act of investing.

Credit markets allow specialization. Business firms specialize in knowing profitable investment opportunities. They know when to build a new plant, buy new equipment, or to set up an advanced research and development lab. Households specialize in saving. They usually do not have the information to use their saving to act on profitable investment opportunities. There is, therefore, a natural trade that can be set up between households and businesses. In credit markets, firms wishing to invest in capital goods borrow from households (and other businesses).

The Rate of Interest

The **interest rate** measures the cost of borrowing to acquire capital goods. It is usually expressed as an annual percentage rate. If $1,000 is borrowed on January 1 and $1,100 (the $1,000 borrowed plus $100 interest) is repaid on December 31 of that same year, the $100 interest represents a 10 percent rate of interest on an annual percentage basis. If the loan were for only six months, and $1,050 were repaid on June 30, the $50 interest still represents a 10 percent annual rate.

Capital and Interest

EXAMPLE 1

Interest Rates, Present Value, and Insulation

Home owners are bombarded by press advertising and solicitations exhorting them to insulate their homes. The main argument for such sales pitches is that the reduction in heating bills will more than compensate for the cost of the insulation.

Present value calculations provide a means of assessing whether a home owner should insulate or not. Take the simple case where the homeowner determines that insulation will save an extra $200 per year on heating costs. At an interest rate of 10%, the homeowner could earn $200 per year from a deposit of $2,000 in a savings account. At a 10% interest rate, if the insulation cost less than $2,000, its installation could be justified. If the insulation cost more than $2,000, the homeowner would be better off putting the money in a deposit account and using the interest to pay the higher heating bill.

In this example, the present value of the heating-bill savings of $200 per year equals $2,000. If the interest rate had been a lower 5%, the present value of savings would have been a higher $4,000. If insulation had cost less than $4,000, its use could be justified.

> The **interest rate** measures the yearly cost of borrowing as a percent of the amount loaned.

As a price of credit or borrowing, the interest rate shows the terms of trade between things today and things tomorrow. For example, consider a $12,600 car today and the same $12,600 car in one year (ignore inflation). An interest rate of 5 percent means that the car next year can be bought with only $12,000 of today's purchasing power. Put $12,000 in the bank, and it will grow to $12,600 in one year at an interest rate of 5 percent ($12,000 + $600 interest). Consider now a 10 percent interest rate. To buy the same $12,600 car in one year requires that a person put only $11,455 in the bank. The higher interest rate makes the future car cheaper relative to the present car. Similarly, a lower interest rate makes a future car more expensive relative to the present car. This is why analysts suppose that higher interest rates discourage present-day car sales. (See Example 1.)

Interest-Rate Determination

The interest rate is determined in credit markets by the supply and demand for credit. The total amount of credit (also called *loanable funds*) supplied to credit markets consists of the total amount of lending from all households, businesses, and governments or bank credit made available to borrowers in credit markets.

The Supply of Credit. For credit markets as a whole, the supply of funds made available to credit markets comes primarily from the net savings of businesses and households during that period. The supply curve in Exhibit 1 shows the quantity of funds savers are prepared to make available to lenders at each interest rate. This supply curve of credit is positively sloped because a larger quantity will be saved (made available to lenders) at high interest rates than at low interest rates, *ceteris paribus*.

EXHIBIT 1 Interest-Rate Determination in Credit Markets

The supply curve shows the quantity of credit offered by lenders at different interest rates; lenders will offer more at high interest rates. The demand curve shows the quantity of credit demanded by borrowers at different interest rates; less will be demanded at high interest rates. The credit market is in equilibrium at an interest rate of 9 percent, where the quantity demanded equals the quantity supplied.

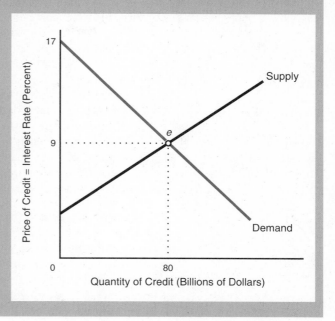

The Demand for Credit.   The demand for credit is made up principally of the demand for new investments in capital goods of businesses. Households also demand credit for automobile loans, consumer loans, and home mortgages, but this chapter will concentrate primarily on business investment.

What determines business demand for capital goods? New capital raises the output (and, therefore, the revenue) of the firm for a number of years because capital goods are in use for more than a single year. A machine will be used for 8 years on average, and a plant will be used for 35 years on average.

Business firms will want to invest in capital goods when the return on their investment exceeds the interest they could earn by placing those funds in the bank. Investment in new capital goods will be carried out until the **rate of return on capital** equals the rate of interest.

> The **rate of return on capital** measures the annual return of the capital investment as a percentage of the investment cost.

To see how interest rates affect the demand for credit by business firms, consider the hypothetical Ajax Sheet Metal Company. When the interest rate is exceptionally high, say 20 percent per year, Ajax may only be willing to borrow funds to replace essential but worn-out capital equipment (such as a machine for flattening the metal). At an interest rate of 15 percent, Ajax may consider adding robots to the manufacturing process. As interest rates fall further, to say 10 percent, Ajax might purchase more modern versions of its rolling machines. At an extremely low interest rate, such as 5 percent, Ajax might even double the size of its factory.

The law of diminishing returns applies to capital just as it applies to labor. Additional capital-investment projects will yield successively lower rates of return. In making their investment plans, businesses will consider a variety of investment projects. Successive projects bring lower and lower rates of return due to the law

Capital and Interest   583

The demand curve for credit is negatively sloped because at high interest rates there are fewer investment projects that have a rate of return equal to or greater than the interest rate.

The equilibrium interest rate equates the quantity of credit demanded with the quantity supplied.

of diminishing returns. As interest rates fall, the firm can carry out investment projects with lower rates of return.

The demand curve for credit in Exhibit 1 is downward-sloping. The demand curve reflects the rate of return on capital investment projects because business firms will be willing to add to their capital stock as long as the rate of return of investment projects exceeds the rate of interest. The demand curve shows the quantity of credit funds businesses are prepared to borrow for capital investments at each interest rate.

The Equilibrium Interest Rate.   Like any other price, the equilibrium (market) rate of interest established by the credit market is that rate at which the quantity of credit supplied equals the quantity demanded.

In Exhibit 1, when the interest rate is 9 percent, there are $80 billion worth of investment projects that yield a rate of return of 9 percent or above. Since the quantity of credit supplied equals the quantity demanded at that rate, the equilibrium rate of interest is 9 percent.

Productivity of Capital and Thrift.   The demand for credit reflects the basic productivity of capital. Firms demand funds for investment as long as rates of return are greater than or equal to the rate of interest. Anything that makes capital more productive will shift the demand curve to the right and cause the interest rate to rise. The supply curve of funds supplied to credit markets reflects the basic thriftiness of the population. Anything that causes the population to be more thrifty (that is, to save more at each interest rate) will shift the supply curve to the right and cause the interest rate to fall.

The impacts of productivity improvements and changes in thrift on interest rates are shown in Exhibit 2. If an important technological breakthrough raises the productivity of capital, the demand curve for credit would shift to the right and would drive up the interest rate, *ceteris paribus*, as in Exhibit 2, panel (a). If there were a change in tax laws to reward those families that save, the supply curve would shift right and lower the market rate of interest, *ceteris paribus*, as in Exhibit 2, panel (b).

The Structure of Interest Rates

Although the interest rate is the price of credit, this price is not the same for all borrowers. Some borrowers pay higher interest rates than others. Savings-and-loan associations may pay as little as 2 percent when they borrow from their depositors. Individuals who borrow from the savings-and-loan association may be charged interest rates of 8 percent for automobile and home-mortgage loans. The U.S. treasury may pay 3 percent to purchasers of its six-month treasury bill and 4 percent on a three-year treasury bond, while a near-bankrupt company must pay 21 percent on a six-month bank loan. *Different interest rates are paid on different financial assets.* Interest rates differ because of differences in the conditions of *risk, liquidity,* and *maturity* associated with a loan.

Risk.   Borrowers with high credit ratings pay lower interest rates than borrowers with low credit ratings. Lenders must be compensated for the extra risk associated with lending to borrowers with low credit ratings if they are to be competitive and earn a normal profit. If certain types of borrowers are known to be more likely not to repay a loan, that type of borrower will be charged a higher interest rate. The extra interest higher-risk borrowers are required to pay is called a *risk premium*.

Liquidity.   A financial asset that can be turned into cash quickly or with a small penalty is said to be *liquid*. People may be willing to hold savings accounts paying 5 percent interest when six-month certificates of deposits pay 10 percent simply

EXHIBIT 2 Interest Rates, Productivity, and Thrift

a. Increase in Productivity

b. Increase in Thriftiness

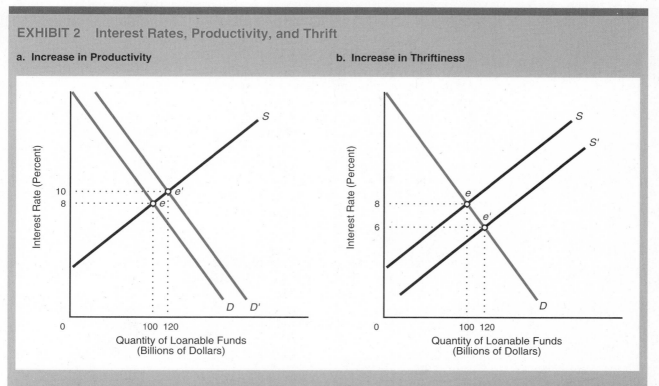

Panel (a) shows that an increase in the productivity of capital raises interest rates and panel (b) shows that an increase in thriftiness of the population lowers interest rates.

because the savings account can be turned into cash quickly and without penalty. The general rule is that interest rates will vary inversely with liquidity, *ceteris paribus*.

Maturity. Interest rates will also vary with the term of maturity. A corporation borrowing $1,000 for one year may pay a lower rate of interest than if it borrows the same $1,000 for two years. If the credit market expects the interest rate on one-year loans to be 6 percent during the first year and 12 percent during the second year of a two-year loan, the interest rate on a two-year loan will be 9 percent. If $1,000 were invested for one year at 6 percent, it would yield $1,060 in one year; if the $1,060 were then reinvested at 12 percent it would yield $1,180. On the other hand, if $1,000 were invested at 9 percent for two years, it would also yield $1,180 at the end of the second year. Thus, $1,000 invested at 6 percent for one year with the proceeds invested for one more year at 12 percent is the same thing as investing $1,000 for two years at 9 percent. Roughly speaking, the two-year interest rate (expressed as an annual rate) will be an average of the one-year interest rates the credit market anticipates over the two years.

RENT

The differentiating feature of land and other natural resources is their relative inelasticity of supply. Land and natural resources are nature's bounty, and the quantity supplied is not affected by the price received as a factor payment.

The rent on land is a relatively small proportion—about 2 or 3 percent—of the total of all payments to factors of production. Even though land rents account for such a small portion of factor payments, relative inelasticity of supply can characterize productive factors other than land and natural resources. Because other types of factor payments resemble land rents, the study of rents for land and natural resources is much more important than the small percentages of factor payments to land suggests.

"Rents" paid for apartments, cars, tools, or moving trucks should not be confused with *economic rents*. "Rental payments" for the temporary use of a particular piece of property owned by someone else can be returns to land, labor, or capital. Apartment rent is a payment both to land (for the land on which the apartment building sits) and to capital (for the structure itself). Thus, the common term *rent* is simply a price or rental rate rather than a payment to a specific factor of production.

Pure Economic Rent

Exhibit 3 shows the determination of the competitive price—called rent in the case of land—for a fixed amount of land. The supply curve is completely inelastic: more land is not forthcoming at higher prices. The demand curve is like any other demand curve. It is determined by the marginal revenue product of land (*MRP*). The competitive rent paid to land is that price which equates the fixed quantity supplied with the quantity demanded. As such, the equilibrium price rations the fixed supply of land among the various claimants for the land. Exhibit 3 shows the case of **pure economic rent**.

> A **pure economic rent** is the price paid to a productive factor that is completely inelastic in supply. Land is the classic example of such a factor.

The main economic role of pure economic rent is to assure that the factors of production that are fixed in supply are used in the highest and best use. Pure economic rent in a competitive market serves as a guide to efficient resource use by rationing the available supply to the most efficient use. In Exhibit 3, the same quantity of land would be supplied, no matter what the price per acre ($0, $900, $1,400), as shown by the vertical supply curve. The quantity demanded, however, does depend on the price. At a zero price, the quantity demanded would be very large. At that zero price, prime agricultural land might be demanded for use as a garbage dump or as a junkyard for old cars. A higher price of land will cut off the various demands for the land that have a low *MRP*.

If the price is too high, the land will not be fully used, and there will be an excess supply. If the price is too low, the land may not be put to its best use. Land rents that are below equilibrium can allow land to be put to uses that yield relatively low *MRP*s. Efficiency requires that the price be set where the quantity supplied equals the quantity demanded of land. Although pure economic rent does not affect the amount of the fixed factor supplied to the market, it does ensure that the fixed factor is put to its best use.

When something is perfectly inelastic in supply, the price does not affect the quantity supplied. Taxing a good, service, or factor of production often reduces supply. Such is not the case for land. Land can be taxed without affecting its supply. This feature has made land a favorite object to tax.

Notice that changes in pure economic rent are completely demand-determined. Supply and demand analysis teaches that movement from the equilibrium price must be caused either by a shift in the demand curve or a shift in the supply curve. In the case of land, the supply curve is fixed. Shifts in supply are not possible. The price of

The pure economic rent that is paid to a productive factor does not affect the quantity supplied because the supply is perfectly inelastic.

anything that is perfectly inelastic in supply must, therefore, be demand-determined. If the demand curve in Exhibit 3 shifts from D to D' due to technological advances in the use of the land or increases in the final demands for goods that the land is used to produce, competitive economic rents will be bid up.

Economic Rent and Other Factors of Production

Pure economic rents represent an extreme case of factor payment. At the other extreme is a payment to a factor that just equals its opportunity cost. A factor of production that is perfectly elastic in supply earns no economic rents because the factor is paid its *opportunity cost* (its earnings in its next best alternative use). For example, a small farmer must compete with other farmers and potential users of the land. If the farmer does not pay what the land could earn in its next best use, the land will be used elsewhere.

In between factors of production that are perfectly elastic in supply and those that are perfectly inelastic are numerous cases where factors of production earn some surplus return over their opportunity costs, or **economic rent**.

> **Economic rent** is the excess of the payment to the factor over its opportunity cost.

The major distinction between *economic rent* and *pure economic rent* is that a factor that earns pure economic rent has an opportunity cost of zero. A factor that earns economic rent has an opportunity cost that is positive but smaller than the payment to the factor.

The amount of economic rent earned by a factor depends on the perspective from which the factor is viewed. The corn land rented by an Iowa farmer does not earn economic rent—because the *individual* farmer is paying the land's opportu-

EXAMPLE 2

Babe Ruth and Economic Rents

The legendary baseball player, Babe Ruth, who played for the New York Yankees during the 1920s and early 1930s, was the highest-paid professional athlete of his day. Babe Ruth's remarkable batting skills helped him set batting records, many of which have yet to be surpassed. Babe Ruth's salary as a baseball player illustrates the concept of economic rent. Although Ruth earned more than the president of the United States, he would have been able to earn very little in his next best alternative. Ruth grew up in an orphanage and had little formal education. If he had not become a baseball player, he would have worked as a manual laborer. The difference between his actual salary and what Ruth would have earned outside baseball is the economic rent that Ruth earned. Babe Ruth often declared that he would play baseball for no salary; yet he was the highest-paid athlete of his day.

If Babe Ruth was willing to work for only a fraction of his baseball salary, would it not have been better to pay him, say, what he would have earned as a day laborer? The economic rent received by Babe Ruth ensured that he would be engaged in that activity that created the highest marginal product. If Babe Ruth had worked as a day laborer, millions of people would have been denied the entertainment and enjoyment gained from watching him play.

nity cost—but Iowa corn land *in general* does earn economic rent. In other words, *rents accrue to factor owners, not factor users.* The economic rent of John Smith as an engineer differs from the economic rent of John Smith as an engineer *for General Motors Corp.* Smith can earn $30,000 per year working for GM, $29,000 working for Ford, and $20,000 working in his best nonengineering job. Smith's economic rent as a GM engineer is $1,000 (the excess of his earnings over his opportunity cost); his economic rent as an engineer is $10,000 (the excess of his earnings as an engineer over his next best nonengineering alternative).

The prices paid to an attractive movie star, a late-night talk-show host, the winningest pitcher in major-league baseball, Iowa farm land, and offices in New York City surprisingly have much in common: a large fraction of the factor's income is economic rent. These factors receive payments in excess of their opportunity cost (their earnings in their next best alternative use). The factor payment assures that the factor is employed efficiently in its highest and best use. Paying one of the world's most talented tenors $50,000 per performance assures that he devotes himself to opera and not to working as a plumber. (See Example 2.)

Although people often resent individuals with inherited talents, rare skills, or good looks who earn substantial salaries, other factors as oil-drilling rigs, Iowa corn land, and high-speed computers earn similar rewards; namely, payments in excess of their opportunity costs. Although land rents account for only a small portion of total factor earnings, economic rents are paid to a wide variety of economic factors. Actors, professional athletes, musicians, surgeons, professors, television-repair persons, and even nobility can earn economic rents.

PROFITS

Economic profit is revenue above the firm's opportunity costs. Hence, it is the firm's economic rent.

Sources of Economic Profits

Firms have three basic sources of economic profits. The first source is the existence of barriers to entry in an industry or business. Such economic profits, called *monopoly profits,* are the basis of popular misgivings about profits. The second source of profits is provided by the dynamic and ever-changing nature of the economy. Such profits arise from the uncertain or risky nature of economic activity. The third source of economic profits is innovation. The individual (or group of individuals) who engages in risk taking and innovation is called an *entrepreneur.* For this reason, economic profits that are not the result of monopoly restrictions are often considered the reward to entrepreneurship.

Entry Restrictions.   As we have shown, monopolies can earn a profit rate in excess of normal profits. Moreover, unlike competitive profits, which are transitory in nature, monopoly profits can persist over a long period of time. In other words, under conditions of monopoly, businesses can earn revenues that exceed the opportunity costs of the factors they employ. In this sense, monopoly profits are like economic rents; for this reason, economists often refer to monopoly profits as *monopoly rents.* Monopoly profits can also be earned in a potentially competitive industry where entry is restricted by government licensing or franchising. If monopoly profits cannot be competed away by the entry of new firms, existing firms can enjoy monopoly rents.

Examples of monopoly profits due to entry restrictions are not hard to find. Cable-television franchises are granted by municipal authorities and by local governments. Once the franchise is granted, the cable-television company is protected by law from the entry of competitors. In many cities, taxicab drivers must be licensed, and entry into the business is controlled by the high cost of the license. Monopoly profits in the prescription-drug industry are protected by patents. Economies of scale also limit the entry of competitors into power generation, telecommunication services, and parcel deliveries.

Risk Taking.   If there were no entry restrictions, if people could predict the future perfectly, and if there were no costs for obtaining information about current market opportunities, there would be no economic profit. All businesses would earn normal profits. If an opportunity arose to earn economic profits, it would be anticipated and the free entry of new firms would serve to keep profits down to a normal return.

Unfortunately, no one can predict the future. Industry is unprepared for wars, changes in fashions and preferences, weather, and new inventions. Even with free entry, at any given time, some industries will earn economic profits and others will suffer negative economic profits. Unanticipated shifts in demand or costs cause economic profits to rise and fall. The majority of people wish to limit their exposure to the ups and downs of the economy; they want a steady income. Therefore, there must be rewards to those who are willing to risk the ups and downs of economic fortunes. Just as those who lend money to poor credit risks require risk premiums, so those who want to earn economic profits must be willing to bear risks.

Uncertainty turns the quest for profits into something resembling a game of chance in which there will be winners and losers even in the long run. All is not fair in love, war—and business. As in a game of chance, profits will average out to a normal return over all firms, but there will be a wide range of profit outcomes with a few big winners, a few big losers, and a larger number of intermediate winners and losers.

Economists have studied the relationship between the rate of profit and risk (as

Why Usury Laws Don't Necessarily Help the Poor

Earlier chapters discussed what happens when prices are not allowed to adjust to equilibrium. If wage rates are held above equilibrium, there will be unemployment of labor of that type. The same thing can happen in the case of interest rates. If interest rates are not allowed to adjust to their equilibrium rate, credit shortages or surpluses develop.

Usury laws place ceilings on interest rates charged by lenders. A particular state, for example, might pass a law stating that credit-card companies cannot charge more than 18 percent per annum or a law stating that no one can charge more than 15 percent interest. Such usury laws are in effect in many states and countries. Usury laws have considerable popular support because they claim to protect the poor from excessive interest rates charged by the rich. Insofar as the rich are the large lenders and the poor are the ones who borrow, usury laws are thought to redistribute wealth from the rich to the poor.

An interest-rate ceiling is said to be *effective* if the legislated rate is below the market interest rate that would have prevailed without the usury law. If the usury law sets the maximum interest rate at 20 percent, and the prevailing interest rate is 10 percent, then the ceiling is not effective (except in rare cases). If the ceiling is set at 15 percent and the market interest rate would have been 17 percent, the ceiling rate is effective.

If an interest-rate ceiling is effective, there will be an excess demand for loans. In the accompanying figure, an interest-rate ceiling of 7 percent creates a $50 billion shortage of loanable funds. Some people who wish to borrow at the ceiling rate cannot obtain loans. Lenders will be made worse off by the ceiling (at least those lenders that abide by the law) because they are able to lend fewer funds at lower interest rates. The borrowers who actually obtain financing at lower rates are made better off because they borrow at interest rates below market rates. Those shut out of the loan market lose the returns they could have gained if they had had funds for investment.

Interest-rate ceilings redistribute wealth from the unlucky (those who are unable to obtain financing at the ceiling rate) to the lucky (those who are able to get financing at the ceiling rate). Are the poor—whom the usury law is supposed to help—likely to be among the lucky few who obtain loans? When there is excess demand in credit

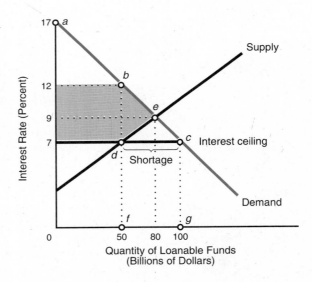

markets, lenders will engage in *credit rationing.* They approve loans to their best customers and to those who have the best credit ratings. The lucky few who obtain loans will be the rich. In fact, interest-rate ceilings typically force the poor to seek loans from disreputable lenders who are willing to disobey the usury law and lend at rates above the ceiling.

The policy conclusion: Usury laws or interest ceilings that are designed to help the poor often achieve the opposite result. It is better to let the market allocate scarce loanable funds. This is yet another example of the law of unintended consequences in economics.

measured by the variability of profits) and find (although there is some dispute on this matter) that profit rates are indeed higher in risky industries. Firms and industries that are subject to greater risk earn *risk premiums.* Entrepreneurs and stockholders earn higher average profits for bearing more risk than others.

Innovation. Blind luck cannot explain all economic profits. The economy is in a constant state of flux. New technologies are developing; consumer tastes are changing; new markets are being discovered. Resource availabilities are changing. To be an innovator requires ability, foresight, luck, and the willingness to bear risk.

Business history is replete with success stories of business geniuses—Henry Ford and the Model-T, Edwin Land and the Polaroid camera, Richard Sears and Alvah Roebuck and mass retailing, and Louis Marx and his children's toy empire. Ability and entrepreneurial genius explain the success of each of these companies. More was involved than a game of chance with an uncertain outcome. Yet even ability does not guarantee success. Many able people are trying to become the next Henry Ford or the next Sears or Roebuck, but few succeed.

The last three chapters surveyed how the economy determines wages, rents, interest, and profit—the payments to the productive factors of labor, land, capital, and entrepreneurship. The next chapter will turn from the functional distribution of income to the personal distribution of income and will address questions like: How equally or unequally is income distributed among persons? What has happened to the personal distribution of income? How does America's income distribution compare to that of other countries? What can be done about poverty?

Chapter Summary

**The most important points to learn from this chapter are:
Interest rates ration the scarce supply of loanable funds among all those who might demand credit. All factors may earn economic rent, if they earn more than their opportunity cost. Profit is a return to risk and uncertainty.**

1. Interest is payment for the use of capital. The supply of capital is the result of past saving and investment decisions. Interest rates are determined in credit markets, which make possible the specialization of savings and investment decisions. The structure of interest rates depends on risk, liquidity, and maturity. Interest rates are determined in the market for loanable funds by the demand and supply of credit.

2. Rent is payment for the use of land or natural resources. Pure economic rent is the payment to a factor of production that is completely inelastic in supply and is demand determined. Economic rent is the excess of the payment to a factor over its opportunity cost.

3. The sources of economic profits are: restrictions to entry into an industry, uncertainty, and entrepreneurship.

> *Policy Focus:* **Usury laws (interest-rate ceilings) designed to help the poor achieve the opposite result. They make it difficult if not impossible for the poor to obtain credit.**

Key Terms

interest (p. 580)
credit markets (p. 580)
interest rate (p. 581)

rate of return on capital (p. 583)
pure economic rent (p. 586)
economic rent (p. 587)

Questions and Problems

1. Explain what would happen to interest rates if the productivity of capital goods increased.

2. This chapter emphasized that the credit market is another example of specialization in economics. Explain how this specialization works and its effect on economic efficiency.

3. If you borrow $10,000 from the bank and repay the bank $12,000 in one year, what is the annual rate of interest?

4. A new business owner remarked: "The bank ripped me off, they charged me 15 percent interest while they charged my biggest competitor only 12 percent." What would you tell the business owner?

5. Explain what would happen to interest rates if the thriftiness of the population decreased.

6. A company has four investment projects that yield returns of 20 percent, 15 percent, 10 percent, and 5 percent. Explain how the company will decide which of these projects to carry out.

7. Distinguish between *pure economic rents* and *economic rents*.

8. "Pure economic rents play no useful role in the economy because the supply of the factor in question is fixed. The factor will be supplied no matter what rent is paid." Evaluate this statement.

9. Why should the profit rate be higher in businesses that are risky? How do we measure risk?

10. What would be the logic of taxing pure economic rents as opposed to taxing other kinds of factor incomes?

11. Identify the sources of economic profits earned:
   a. by steel companies after the government imposed restrictions on competitive steel imports from foreign countries.
   b. in the coal industry after the Organization of Petroleum Exporting Countries quadrupled the price of oil in 1974.
   c. by a firm that developed a surefire method of increasing gas mileage.

12. The demand schedule for a particular acre of land is given in Table A. How much is the economic rent in equilibrium?

Table A

Rent	Quantity
$1,000	1/4
900	1/2
800	3/4
700	1
600	1 1/2

Doing Economics

There are many different kinds of "loans" in our economy. Student loans, car loans, and home mortgages are common loans from financial institutions to consumers. Savings deposits and certificates of deposit are the reverse. Corporate bonds (long-term) and "commercial paper" (short-term) are loans from investors to corporations. Government securities reflect borrowing by the government from whoever buys them. Using both direct surveys of nearby financial institutions and published data on financial markets from a newspaper, collect information about the interest rates and characteristics of a wide variety of kinds of loans on a particular day. How much of the variation can you explain by differences in risk, liquidity, and maturity? (Be sure to consider whether each loan is guaranteed or insured by the government.) For homogeneous loans such as those to the government, are long-term interest rates higher or lower than short-term rates today? What does that imply about the market expectation of future short-term rates on these loans?

Income Distribution and Poverty

CHAPTER FOCUS   Philosophers have argued for centuries: What is a fair distribution of income? Should society allow extremes of wealth and poverty? Is it society's role to ensure that no poverty exists? Although there is agreement that extremes in wealth and poverty should be avoided, there is less agreement about what constitutes the "right" distribution of income.

In every organized society, the government has a role in determining the distribution of income. Through its power to tax and to redistribute goods like education, public medicine, and welfare payments, the government affects how income is distributed. What families earn in factor markets determines the distribution of income before government action. If the government taxes the rich much more than the poor and distributes goods primarily to the poor, the actual distribution of income can differ significantly from the factor-market distribution.

Although there is general agreement that poverty is bad and that societies should avoid extremes of wealth and poverty, there is a lack of agreement on the appropriate balance. If the government were to take too much away from the rich to give to the poor, there would be little incentive to become rich. There would be less risk taking, less sacrifice for training and education, and less hard work.

After studying this chapter, you will be able to:

- Understand the Lorenz curve and how it measures the distribution of income.
- Explain the natural law, utilitarian, and Rawls views of distributive justice.
- Know the sources of inequality of income distribution.
- Discuss how to measure poverty and trends in poverty.
- Describe the negative income tax.

MEASURING INCOME INEQUALITY

Some people earn high incomes; others earn low incomes. If one person earned all the income, this would clearly be the most unequal distribution of income possible. If everyone earned exactly the same income, this would be the most equal distribution of income possible. The Lorenz curve measures where the actual income distribution falls between these two extremes.

The **Lorenz curve** measures the degree of inequality in the distribution of income.

> The **Lorenz curve** shows the percentage of all income earned by households at successive income levels. The cumulative share of households (ranked from lowest to highest incomes) is plotted on the horizontal axis and the cumulative share of income earned by the cumulative percent of households is plotted on the vertical axis.

The Lorenz curve measures the distribution of income.

Lorenz curves are normally plotted in *quintiles*, or fifths. A household in the top fifth of the income distribution earns more than at least 80 percent of all households. A household in the bottom fifth earns less than at least 80 percent of all households.

Exhibit 1 gives the U.S. distribution of income in 1929, 1970, and 1991. The table in panel (a) shows the cumulative percentage of households and their cumulative share of income. In 1991, the bottom fifth of households accounted for 4.6 percent of all income. The cumulative share of income of the first two quintiles (the lowest fifth and the second fifth) was 15.4 percent—the bottom 40 percent of U.S. households accounted for 15.4 percent of all income. The top 20 percent earned 44.3 percent of all income. The Lorenz curve is plotted in panel (b) of the exhibit and shows exactly the same information as the table.

If all households earned exactly the same income, there would be perfect equality in the distribution of income. Perfect equality is shown by a 45-degree line drawn through the Lorenz curve. If income were equal, the bottom 20 percent of households would receive 20 percent of all income, the bottom 40 percent of households would receive 40 percent of all income, and so on.

If the 45-degree line shows a perfectly equal distribution of income, then the more bowed the Lorenz curve is from the 45-degree line, the more unequal is the distribution of income. Changes in the income distribution between two points in time can be seen in movements of the Lorenz curve. The less bowed the Lorenz curve becomes, the more equal the income distribution becomes. Lorenz curves for different countries show which countries have a more equal distribution of income. (See Example 1.)

John Stuart Mill (1806–1873)

John Stuart Mill was one of the most influential social philosophers of the nineteenth century. He was educated by his father, James Mill, the famous British philosopher, economist, and historian. He rose to a high position in the East India Company and during his years there contributed to various periodicals and discussion groups. Mill's first important book, *A System of Logic*, was published when he was thirty-seven. His most important work, *Principles of Political Economy*, appeared in 1848. Mill married Harriet Taylor, a widow, with whom he had been in love for twenty years. He worked with his wife, and through her influence became interested in women's rights, socialism, social reform, and humanitarianism. Mill served as a member of parliament in the 1860s, after which he retired to France. Mill's famous *Autobiography* appeared one year after his death.

In his *Principles of Political Economy*, Mill wrote that society could distribute income according to whatever rules it thinks best. Mill recognized that various schemes could be used to distribute income, and that it was up to society to select that system that it felt was best. If society chose a system of private property, Mill felt that society should first eliminate "initial inequities and injustice." Resources should be divided fairly among people, so that "all might start . . . on equal terms." Individuals should be compensated by society for "injuries of nature" and less robust members should be given compensation that would place them on par with others. Once this initial "fair" distribution of resources was made, however, it should not be interfered with. "Individuals would be left to their own exertions and to the ordinary chances, for making advantageous use of what has been assigned to them." By not interfering, society would be insured that people would have the incentives to use their resources to best advantage.

The U.S. distribution of income has become more equal over the past half-century.

The Lorenz curves for the United States in 1929, 1970, and 1991 tell us that the U.S. distribution of income is far from equal—a not surprising result. More important, they tell us that, over the past half-century, there has been a distinct trend toward more equality. The 1991 Lorenz curve lies *inside* the 1929 curve. Households in the top fifth accounted for 54.5 percent of all income in 1929 but for a smaller 44.3 percent in 1991. The top 5 percent accounted for 30 percent of all income in 1929 but for a much smaller 17.4 percent in 1991. The *middle class* (households in the third and fourth quintiles) increased its relative standing most over the past half-century: its share of income rose from 33.1 percent to 40.4 percent.

SOURCES OF INEQUALITY

Households earn different incomes for a variety of reasons. Household income consists of two basic types—income earned from labor and from **wealth**.

> **Wealth** is the value of assets that represent claims to land and capital resources. Such assets yield returns in the form of dividends, interest, rent, or capital gains.

Examples of income earned from wealth are land rents, dividends, and interest payments. Three out of every four dollars earned in the economy are earned from

EXHIBIT 1

a. The U.S. Distribution of Income, 1929, 1970, and 1991

Quintile of Households	1929		1970		1991	
	Share of Income (percent)	Cumulative Share of Income (percent)	Share of Income (percent)	Cumulative Share of Income (percent)	Share of Income (percent)	Cumulative Share of Income (percent)
Lowest fifth	3.9	3.9	5.5	5.5	4.6	4.6
Second fifth	8.6	12.5	12.2	17.7	10.8	15.4
Third fifth	13.8	26.3	17.6	35.3	16.6	32.0
Fourth fifth	19.3	45.6	23.8	59.1	23.8	55.8
Highest fifth	54.5	100.0	40.9	100.0	44.3	100.0
Top 5 percent	30.0		15.6		17.4	

b. Lorenz Curves of the U.S. Income Distribution, 1929, 1970, and 1991

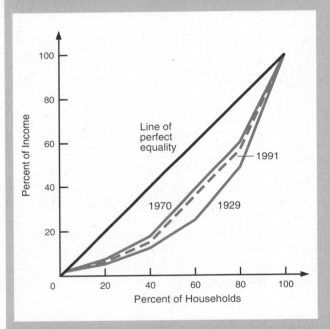

These Lorenz curves are drawn using the data in panel (a). The Lorenz curve measures the cumulative percentage of households (ranked from lowest to highest incomes) on the horizontal axis and the cumulative percentage of income earned by these households on the vertical axis. If all households earned the same income (perfect equality), the Lorenz curve would be a 45-degree line. The more the Lorenz curve is bowed away from the line of perfect equality, the greater is the inequality in the distribution of income. The 1929 and 1991 Lorenz curves show that for more than 50 years there has been a trend toward more equality in the U.S. distribution of income.

SOURCE: *Historical Statistics of the United States; Statistical Abstract of the United States*

Income is earned from labor and from wealth.

labor; therefore, the main income differences among households are due to different earnings from labor. However, earnings from wealth are more concentrated among a few households, and they contribute to the more extreme disparities between the rich and everyone else.

Differences in People and in Jobs

The chapter on labor markets emphasized that people earn different wages and salaries because jobs are different and people are different.

EXAMPLE 1

International Comparisons of Income Distribution

The accompanying figure shows the income distribution in four countries—Sweden, the United States, Hungary and Brazil. The figure illustrates two important facts about the distribution of income. First, income tends to be more unequally distributed in low-income countries than in rich countries. Brazil is representative of low-income countries, and it has an income distribution that is much more unequal than other countries. Second, demographic characteristics and government policy affect the distribution of income. Sweden has about the same average income as the United States, but Sweden's income distribution is more equal. Sweden's greater equality is explained by the greater homogeneity of the Swedish population and by the greater role of the Swedish state in redistributing income. Third, planned socialism equalizes income distribution. Although Hungary is relatively poor, its income is more equal.

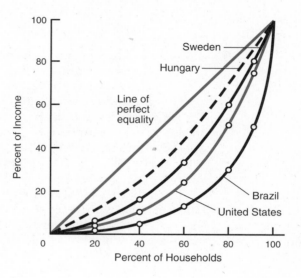

SOURCE: *The World Bank*

Compensating Differentials and Risk.   To encourage people to take unpleasant and dangerous jobs, *compensating wage differentials* must be paid. Sanitation workers earn more than bank clerks and often schoolteachers because of compensating wage differentials. Compensating wage differentials mean that some inequality is a consequence of occupational choice.

Uncertainty affects inequality. Different occupations involve different degrees of income risk. The wheat farmer, whose crops may be destroyed by blights and droughts, has a more uncertain income than the union employee with seniority. Individuals have differing attitudes towards risk. *Risk seekers* are more willing to incur risks than others, while *risk avoiders* are reluctant to take on risks. If society has only a small number of risk seekers, the distribution of income will be unequal. Some of those willing to incur risks will strike it rich and rise to the top income level. Other risk seekers will be less fortunate and fall to the bottom level. The vast majority—the risk avoiders—will be in the middle.

Ability and Human Capital. The chapter on labor markets emphasized that people divide into *noncompeting groups* in the labor market. Those who have the ability, talents, and skill to become doctors, lawyers, and physicists compete among themselves for such jobs. Those who have the athletic ability and determination compete among themselves for jobs as professional athletes. Those who have few skills compete among themselves for manual labor jobs. Even though one group earns substantially more than other groups, there is little crossing over from lower- to higher-paying groups.

Although natural ability accounts for some large earnings (such as for professional athletes and entertainers), they are not the most important source of income inequality. Mental and physical abilities are distributed much more evenly among the population than is income.

The skills, ability, and training we acquire through **human-capital investment** are much more important in explaining income unequality.

> **Human-capital investment** is the expenditure of resources on schooling, health, and training.

When individuals make human-capital investments, they acquire new skills and abilities that raise their productivity. They also enter into noncompeting groups. Only those persons who have invested in medical training and certification can compete for jobs as physicians.

Human-capital investments require the sacrifice of economic resources. Tuition must be paid; earnings must be sacrificed until a college degree is obtained; people must bear the personal and financial costs of moving to an area where jobs are more abundant. Human-capital investments also offer rewards. They qualify people for higher-paying and more satisfying jobs. Human-capital investment has its costs and benefits.

Income inequality due to human capital is partly the result of deliberate choice. Individuals choose between more money now (going to work after high school) and more money later (going to college and not earning money now). Individuals who place a high value on having money now are less likely to acquire human capital.

Income inequality due to human capital can be reduced by social policy. Some individuals are in a better position to pay for human-capital investment. If society bears the main cost of human-capital investment (in the form of subsidized public education), there will be less income inequality. Over the years (especially in the 1960s), various government programs have been used to increase the human capital of the poor and the young. These government programs (such as the Job Corps, Manpower Training and Development, and Neighborhood Youth Programs) all have been aimed at training disadvantaged persons to learn marketable skills.

> Differences in human capital are more important for explaining income inequality than are differences in natural ability.

Chance and Inheritance

Chance. Accidents and poor health can unexpectedly destroy one's earning capacity. Choosing to train for a profession (such as teaching English or modern languages) in which there is an unexpected decline in demand can lead to low earnings. Likewise, having the good fortune to train for a profession (such as petroleum engineering in the 1970s) in which there is an unexpected increase in demand can have a significant positive and unplanned effect on earnings. Luck determines whether individuals earn the economic rents discussed in the preceding

EXAMPLE 2

Chance, Luck, and Earnings: The Vietnam Draft Lottery

No one has been drafted into the armed forces since 1972. Congressional authority to conscript expired in July 1973, largely as a consequence of the unpopular drafts of the Vietnam War. There were five draft lotteries during the Vietnam War period. Birth dates were drawn by lottery, and men with birth dates drawn early were the first to be drafted.

Sufficient time has passed to allow economists to determine the effect of being drafted for Vietnam upon earnings after return to civilian life. Earnings information from the Social Security Administration show that white male veterans in the 1980s earned 15 percent less than comparable nonveterans. Vietnam veterans were earning about $4,000 less per year than nonveterans in the early 1990s.

Why did service in Vietnam reduce lifetime earnings? One explanation is that people who served in Vietnam lost about two years of experience in the civilian labor market. In addition, some employers may have systematically avoided hiring Vietnam veterans.

Although earnings statistics clearly show that Vietnam veterans earn less, they are less clear on the effects of service in World War II on earnings. In fact, many studies show the effect of World War II service to be positive or at least neutral on lifetime earnings.

SOURCE: Joshua Angrist, "Lifetime Earnings and the Vietnam Era Draft Lottery," *American Economic Review*, 80 (June 1990): pp. 313–36.

chapter. Having the good fortune to be in the right place at the right time can have a marked impact on relative income. (See Example 2.)

Chance and luck have short-term effects on income distribution. Spells of unemployment pass; the entrepreneur who has good luck in one period has bad luck in the next. The other factors (ability, human capital, and occupational differences) have longer-run effects.

Inheritance and Wealth. Income from wealth is distributed more unequally than income from labor. **Personal wealth** is held in the form of assets (stocks, bonds, real estate, precious metals) that represent ownership of capital and land resources.

> **Personal wealth** (or net worth) is the value of one's total assets minus one's liabilities.

Stocks pay dividends and capital gains. Interest is earned on bonds. Rental income is earned from real estate. In the late 1980s, the top 1 percent of wealth holders in the United States accounted for 37 percent of all wealth. The top 10 percent accounted for about 68 percent of all wealth. Wealth is distributed more unequally than income. The top 10 percent of families accounted for 68 percent of all wealth, while the top 10 percent of families earned 34 percent of all income (Exhibit 2).

Wealth can be created either by its current owner or by previous generations. One important cause of the unequal distribution of wealth is *inheritance*, or the passing of wealth from one generation to the next. Wealth passes from one

Wealth is distributed more unevenly than is income.

EXHIBIT 2 Distribution of Wealth in the United States

Population Segment	Share of Total Wealth (percent)	
	1963	1989
Top 0.5 percent	25	29
Top 1 percent	32	37
Top 10 percent	64	68

Sources: *Statistical Abstract of the United States*, 1981, 453; *Federal Reserve Bulletin, Survey of Consumer Finances*, 1992.

generation to the next because of several factors. First, the children of the wealthy, in addition to inheriting assets, typically receive better educations and training and develop important social contacts. Second, the children of the wealthy tend to marry wealthy spouses.

Discrimination

Discrimination occurs when qualified individuals are blocked from entering higher-paying jobs and occupations or when workers with equal skills and qualifications performing the same tasks are treated differently on the grounds of race, sex, or creed. Individuals who are denied equal access to education, training, and union membership will be limited in their career opportunities.

During the postwar period, the median income of nonwhite households has averaged about 60 percent that of white households. The postwar trend in the ratio of nonwhite to white incomes has been upward, beginning at 51 percent in 1947 and rising to an average of 61 percent in the mid-1970s. The economic downturns of the late 1970s and early 1980s caused a slight reversal of the upward movement, so that in 1991, the ratio of median nonwhite to white income was 56 percent.

Substantial differences also exist in the average incomes of males and females. Women who work full time have had an average income equal to slightly more than 60 percent of male incomes since the late 1950s. Although the ratio has improved since 1947, the female/male income difference remained almost constant until 1980, after which it jumped from 60 percent to 70 percent of men's earnings.

Studies of discrimination conclude that about one-half of observed differences in earnings can be attributed to objective factors like schooling, training, or years of experience. In fact, women have on average about as much education as men.

The fact that not all of the difference in earnings can be explained by factors such as schooling or labor market experience suggests the presence of discrimination in labor markets. Labor market discrimination does not normally assume the form of discriminating between two workers (of different race or sex) performing the same job. In fact, there are federal laws guaranteeing equal pay for equal work. More often discrimination occurs when nonwhites or women are channeled into occupations regarded as "suitable" for them. This channeling may be the result of the employee's own preferences (a woman may want to be a schoolteacher and nothing else) or employer discrimination (an employer may be unwilling to hire women for assembly-line work). As a consequence, these "suitable" professions—say, nursing and teaching for women or bus driving for black males—become *crowded*, and the relative earnings of these professions are driven down. (See Exhibit 3.)

Empirical studies of male/female earnings differences seek to determine how much of the 30 percent to 35 percent female earning gap is explained by "objective" factors such as less education or less experience. Empirical studies find that the gap is not satisfactorily explained by objective differences among men and women. Researchers agree that a major cause of the female earning gap is the concentration of women into low-paying professions.

One study of the personnel practices of 373 firms found that in 60 percent of them, men and women were perfectly segregated by job title. In other words, there was not a single job type in those establishments to which the employer assigned both sexes. Another study, based on wage surveys, found extensive segregation in white-collar job titles within firms, despite the availability of women for each job title. If a firm hired men for a particular job title, it hired no women for that title. Since salary is usually set by job title, such segregation allows employers to create different pay scales for men and women. Sometimes, however, the disparity is not so subtle. Research has demonstrated that even within narrowly defined occupations, for which it is relatively certain that the jobs have similar duties, men earn more than women (see table below).

Average Weekly Wages for Women and Men in Selected Narrowly Defined Occupations, 1985

Occupation	Women	Men
Secretaries	$278	$365
Stock and inventory clerks	265	326
Bookkeepers, accounting and auditing clerks	263	341
Expediters	257	413
Machinists	257	408
Bus drivers	257	404
General office clerks	255	323
Cost and rate clerks	254	483
Sales workers, furniture and home furnishings	252	307
Grinding, abrading, buffing machine operators	251	330
Production inspectors, checkers, examiners	249	406
Traffic, shipping and receiving clerks	247	305
Electrical and electronic equipment assemblers	243	284
Packaging and filling machine operators	234	286
Printing machine operators	225	363
Molding and casting machine operators	222	347
Painting and paint-spraying machine operators	218	313
Solderers and brazers	216	287
Photographic process machine operators	208	297
Butchers and meat cutters	204	326
Bakers	202	301
Truck drivers, light	200	281
Slicing and cutting machine operators	192	303
Hotel clerks	191	279
Sales workers, apparel	168	281

Note: These figures are estimates of medians of usual weekly earnings of employed wage and salary workers who usually work full-time. They are based on data collected by the Bureau of Labor Statistics, but the medians have been computed on a basis that differs slightly from the method used to produce the official BLS estimates. Moreover, BLS does not officially issue figures on wages for groups of less than 50,000, while some of the wages quoted in the table are for groups of size 19,000–50,000. Wage estimates included in the table have a standard error of estimate less than 10 percent.

SOURCE: Barbara Bergmann, "Does the Market for Women's Labor Need Fixing?" *Journal of Economic Perspectives* 3 (Winter 1989): pp. 43–60.

DISTRIBUTIVE JUSTICE

Philosophers have debated **distributive justice** for centuries.

Distributive justice is present when society's resources are distributed fairly among the members of society.

The first chapter explained the difference between normative economics (what ought to be) and positive economics (what is). Questions of distributive justice—is it fair to have extremes of wealth and poverty? What is a just distribution of income?—are matters of normative economics. Over the years, different philosophies have been formulated.

Natural Law

According to the natural-law philosophers of the seventeenth century, each individual has the right to the fruits of his or her labors. In terms of modern economic theory, this philosophy supports income distribution according to marginal productivity. When owners of the factors of production are paid their marginal-revenue product, factors that are more productive receive higher rewards. Their factors have contributed more to output; therefore, they deserve more income. Inequality is justified by the fact that some factors contribute more to output than others.

When income is distributed according to marginal productivities, the owners of factors of production are encouraged to raise the marginal productivity of their factors. Individuals are encouraged to invest in human capital; owners of capital are encouraged to save to acquire more capital; entrepreneurs are encouraged to assume risks. If factors of production were not paid in accordance with marginal productivity, there would be a tendency to reduce effort, to acquire less capital, and to take fewer risks. The end result would be that the economy would earn less income in total. (See Example 3.)

Most economists agree that there is a tradeoff between more equality and more income. If income were redistributed from those who possess high-priced factors of production to those less fortunate (by means of a high tax on the fortunate, for example), the efficiency of the economy would decline, and less income would be available for society as a whole. Redistributing income from the fortunate to the unfortunate is like transferring water from one barrel to another with a leaky bucket. In the process of making the transfer, water (income) is lost forever. If the leak is a slow one, then the costs to society of the redistribution are small. If the leak is large, then the losses of total income will be substantial. Society must decide whether the costs of greater equality are worth the price.

Critics of the natural-law philosophy point out that distribution according to productivity can be quite unfair. Some individuals will inherit factors with high productivities; others will be fortunate to be born with superb natural abilities; those who are lucky will receive high rewards.

Utilitarianism

Natural-law philosophy argues that inequality allows individuals to reap the fruits of their efforts and raises economic efficiency. The *utilitarian theory* argues, to the contrary, that an equal income distribution is better for society.

The law of diminishing marginal utility (studied in an earlier chapter) supplies the basic rationale for the utilitarian view of distributive justice. If people are basically alike, then the total utility of society will be greatest when income is distributed equally because everyone is subject to the law of diminishing marginal utility. If Jones were rich and Smith were poor, Jones would be getting much less utility from his last dollar than Smith. If income were shifted from Jones to Smith, Smith's utility would increase more than Jones' would decrease. Therefore, the

The natural law view of distributive justice is consistent with income distribution according to marginal productivity.

EXAMPLE 3

Christy Turlington: Fashion Model at $1.75 Million per Year

In 1991, 23-year-old high-fashion model Christy Turlington earned $1.75 million. Her 1992 earnings were twice this figure. Turlington is the face of Calvin Klein fragrances in the United States, and she represents Guerlaine in France. She represents on the side other cosmetic firms at $25,000 per day.

Asked by a major business magazine whether she wasn't embarrassed to earn so much, Turlington answered: "There's a tremendous amount of money made in fashion and cosmetics. When you think of my earnings as commission, it's not that ridiculous." Turlington went on to explain that no one would pay her $25,000 per day if she did not pull in enough business to more than cover the $25,000.

Rightly or wrongly, market economies pay the factors of production according to their contributions to revenues. The high earnings that anger many people are explained by the fact that that particular person adds a considerable amount to revenues.

SOURCE: James W. Michaels, "Should Anyone Earn $25,000 Per Day?" *Forbes*, May 25, 1992, p. 10.

In the utilitarian view, society's welfare is maximized when income is distributed equally.

decrease in inequality would increase the total utility of society. If indeed everyone is alike, then the total utility of society would be greatest when income is distributed perfectly equally among individuals.

The criticism of utilitarian theory is that people are indeed different. Some care little for money and worldly goods; others care a great deal. Therefore, it is not at all certain that the rich person gets less marginal utility from his or her last dollar than does the poor person. Critics also point out that it would be difficult to encourage effort and to persuade people to accumulate capital and take risks when income is evenly divided.

Rawlsian Equality

A different argument for equality has been proposed by philosopher John Rawls. Rawls maintains that a "fair" distribution of income is the distribution that people would want if they knew nothing in advance of their chances of being rich or poor. In reality, people start out in life with a pretty good idea of whether they will be rich or poor. If people did not know in advance whether they would be rich or poor, what type of income distribution would they prefer? According to Rawls, rational, self-interested individuals would act as risk avoiders. They would favor an equal distribution of income because they themselves might end up at the bottom of the ladder.

Because distributive justice is a matter of normative economics, there will be disagreement on what constitutes a fair distribution of income.

The policy implication of Rawls' notion of distributive justice is that government should step in to equalize the distribution of income. The government should push society toward that income distribution that people would favor if they did not know in advance who would be privileged and who would not be privileged. Without government action, an unequal distribution of income would prevail because the rich would not favor a change in the prevailing distribution of income. A change toward more equality could not take place voluntarily. It could only be accomplished by government.

GOVERNMENT POLICY AND INCOME DISTRIBUTION

People earn wages, rent, interest, and profit in factor markets. These earnings do not constitute the *final* distribution of income because government can redistribute income among households. If Jones earns $50,000 and Smith earns $10,000, and the government takes $20,000 from Jones and gives it to Smith, both end up with $30,000. Government alters the distribution of income through taxes and money transfers and through the distribution of valuable public services.

Exhibit 4 shows the effect of taxes and public services on the distribution of income. The Lorenz curve *before income and payroll taxes* is shown as curve *B*, and curve *A* shows the Lorenz curve *after taxes*. Income and payroll taxes equalize the distribution of income only slightly.

Household income consists of money income and **in-kind income**.

> **In-kind income** consists primarily of benefits—such as free public education, school-lunch programs, public housing, or food stamps—for which the recipient is not required to pay.

The Lorenz curve *C* shows the distribution of income *after taxes* and *after the distribution of in-kind income.* Comparison of Lorenz curves *A* and *C* indicates that the distribution of income becomes much more equal when all sources of income and in-kind benefits are included as income because the poor receive a larger share of public services than the rich.

Calculations of the effect of in-kind service are inexact. It is difficult to place an appropriate price tag on in-kind benefits. The recipient of a public service that costs $20 to produce (say, a vaccination in a public health clinic) may value that service at less than $20 or may even place a zero value on the service. Nevertheless,

---

EXHIBIT 4   The Effect of Income Taxes and Payroll Taxes and Benefits on the U.S. Distribution of Income

Income and payroll taxes have only a minor equalizing effect on the U.S. distribution of income, as shown by the difference between curve *A* (the distribution before taxes) and curve *B* (the distribution after taxes). The Lorenz curve *C* shows the distribution after both taxes and in-kind benefits are included. Comparing it with *A* shows that the inclusion of in-kind benefits makes the distribution of income more equal. The figures are for 1972.

SOURCE: Based on Edgar K. Browning, "The Trend Toward Equality in the Distribution of Net Income," *Southern Economic Journal* 43, 1 (July 1976): p. 914.

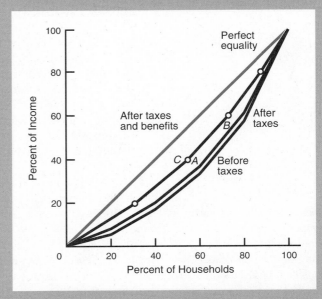

Public policy alters the distribution of income through the tax system and the distribution of in-kind income.

it is clear that the distribution of in-kind benefits to the poor has a more substantial impact on the distribution of income than taxes.

Each society must determine by how much government should alter the distribution of income.

POVERTY

The causes of poverty are the same as the causes of income inequality. The poor are poor because of their limited endowments of ability and skills, their limited amount of human capital, bad luck, discrimination, and (some might even argue) conscious choice. The poor are poor because their capacity to earn a "sufficient" income is, for some reason, impaired.

Defining poverty is not an easy task. Analysts will always disagree over what constitutes a poverty income. Some define poverty in terms of the amount of income necessary to provide a family of a certain size with the minimum essentials of food, clothing shelter, and education. This approach provides an **absolute poverty standard**.

> An **absolute poverty standard** establishes a specific income level for a household of a given size, below which the household is judged to be living in a state of poverty.

But is an absolute measure of poverty appropriate? Poverty can, after all, be relative. A person's sense of poverty depends on the incomes of others in the community. Thus, a person whose income is 10 percent of everyone else's may feel poor even if that income is above the level required to purchase the minimum essentials. Similarly, the American conception of poverty does not necessarily match that of other countries. The American poor would he considered wealthy in many Asian and African nations. Yet, they are still categorized as poor because they measure themselves against other Americans, not against the poor in other countries. A second approach to poverty, therefore, is a measurement in relative terms. A **relative poverty standard** might classify a household as poor if the household's income is, say, less than 25 percent of an average household's income.

Poverty can be measured either according to an absolute poverty standard or a relative poverty standard.

> A **relative poverty standard** defines the poor in terms of the income of others in some defined group.

If an absolute standard is used, increasing real living standards will push more and more families above the poverty line. According to a relative standard, poverty can be eliminated only by equalizing the distribution of income. If both the rich and the poor experience equal percentage increases in income, the poor will not have improved their relative position.

Trends in Poverty

Exhibit 5 shows the official statistics on the number of persons below poverty levels in the United States for the period 1959–1991. According to the absolute poverty standards of the U.S. government, the number of persons in households below the poverty level declined from 39.5 million to 34.1 million between 1959 and 1991.

EXHIBIT 5 Poverty in the United States

a. Persons Living in Households with Money Incomes Below Poverty Levels, 1959–1991

Year	Number of Persons Below Poverty Level (millions)	Percentage of Population	Poverty Income for Household of Four (dollars)
1959	39.5	22.4	2,973
1960	39.9	22.2	3,022
1965	33.2	17.3	3,223
1966	28.5	14.7	3,317
1968	25.4	12.8	3,553
1970	25.4	12.6	3,968
1972	24.5	11.9	4,275
1974	24.3	11.6	5,038
1976	25.0	11.8	5,815
1978	24.5	11.4	6,662
1979	25.3	11.6	7,412
1980	29.3	13.0	8,414
1981	31.8	14.0	9,287
1982	34.4	15.0	9,862
1983	35.3	15.2	10,178
1984	33.7	14.4	10,609
1985	33.1	14.0	10,989
1986	32.4	13.6	11,285
1987	32.2	13.4	11,611
1988	31.7	13.0	12,092
1989	31.5	12.8	12,675
1990	33.6	13.5	13,207
1991	34.1	14.1	13,682

Sources: *Economic Report of the President;* U.S. Bureau of the Census.

b. Characteristics of Poverty

Category	Percentage of Families Below Poverty Levels
Race	
White	17.8
Black	27.8
Hispanic	23.4
Size of family	
2 persons	8.2
3 persons	9.8
4 persons	10.1
5 persons	13.5
7 or more persons	32.3
Education of family head	
Less than 8 years	25.5
8 years	15.9
1–3 years high school	19.2
4 years high school	8.9
1 or more years college	3.6
Families headed by single mothers	45.0
Age of family head	
15–21 years	30.4
25–31 years	14.9
35–41 years	9.4
45–51 years	6.3
55–61 years	7.4
65 or more years	6.6
Did not work	23.4

Source: *Statistical Abstract of the United States.* These figures are for 1989.

Assistance According to Demonstrated Need or Negative Income Tax?

The Current Welfare System

The current welfare system is founded on the principle that public assistance should be granted primarily on the basis of need. For this purpose, the government has established a number of programs—such as Aid to Families with Dependent Children (AFDC), the food stamp program, public housing, and Medicaid—in which the amount of public assistance is based on family income. Welfare authorities determine what resources the family has (totaling the earnings of the family head, contributions from relatives, and so on) and grant public assistance on the basis of the perceived need. The greater the resources of the family, the less public assistance it receives. The welfare family is, therefore, discouraged from working because additional earnings—if detected by welfare authorities—will cause a reduction in public assistance. Proposals have been made to build better incentives into the existing system. In particular, it has been suggested that welfare recipients be permitted to keep a specified percentage of extra earnings without a reduction in existing public assistance.

Documenting needs and resources is costly, requiring an army of welfare workers to staff the program. Dollars that could have been devoted to public assistance are diverted into the bureaucratic costs of operating the system.

Exhibit 6 shows the effects of current government welfare programs. It shows that welfare programs more than halve the number of poverty households, although they are less successful in reducing poverty among black and hispanic families.

The Negative Income Tax

Economists have proposed that the current system be replaced by a **negative income tax**.

> A **negative income tax (NIT)** would supplement incomes by giving recipients who earn less than the *break-even income* an amount equal to a minimum acceptable income and subtracting a given percentage of each extra dollar the family earns on its own.

A negative income tax would work as outlined in Exhibit 7. First, the government would set a floor below which family incomes would not be allowed to fall. For purposes of illustration, Exhibit 7 sets this floor at $6,000 for a family of four. Second,

EXHIBIT 6   The Percentage of Persons Below Poverty Before and After Government Antipoverty Programs

Classification	All Households (percent)	White Households (percent)	Black Households (percent)	Hispanic Households (percent)
Income before taxes and cash payments	19.4	16.7	37.3	29.9
Income after cash payments	12.8	10.0	30.7	26.2
Income after cash and in-kind payments	8.9	6.9	21.2	19.4

Source: U.S. Bureau of the Census, *Current Population Reports.* The above data are for 1986.

EXHIBIT 7 The Negative Income Tax

a. Graph of Negative Income tax

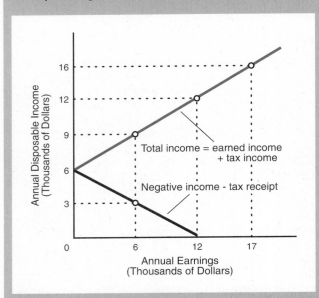

Total income = earned income + tax income

Negative income - tax receipt

b. Table of a Negative Income Tax

Earnings (dollars)	Amount of Negative Income Tax Received (dollars)	Total Disposal Income = Earned Income + Tax Receipt (dollars)
0	6,000	6,000
3,000	4,500	7,500
6,000	3,000	9,000
9,000	1,500	10,500
12,000	0	12,000

Panel (a) is based on the data in panel (b). It illustrates a hypothetical negative income tax with a negative tax rate of 50 percent and a $6,000 floor income. A family with $0 income would receive $6,000 in benefits. Any family that earned more than $0 would have their $6,000 benefits reduced by $0.50 for every dollar earned. A family earning $3,000 would receive $4,500 in addition to the $3,000 they earned. Up to an income of $12,000, families would still receive some benefits in addition to their income (benefits equal to $6,000 minus $0.50 times the amount of income earned). At an income of $12,000, families would receive no benefits in addition to their income.

the government would set a negative tax rate. In our example, this negative tax rate is 50 percent.

As Exhibit 7 shows, a family earning $0 would be guaranteed $6,000. If the family earned income, it would be allowed to keep 50% of its earnings until it reached a break-even level of earnings.

The negative income tax offers two advantages over the existing system. First, it preserves work incentives up to the break-even income level by allowing low-income families to keep a prescribed portion of earnings. Second, it promises to do away with the costly bureaucracy of the existing welfare system. Administration of the negative income tax would be carried out by the same authority—the Internal Revenue Service—that administers the current personal-income-tax system.

As a percent of the U.S. population, the figure declined from 22.4 percent to 14.1 percent. Progress has been uneven, however. Large percentage declines were experienced in the 1960s; subsequently, the number of people below the poverty level remained roughly the same through the 1970s, rose with the severe recessions of the early 1980s, declined with the recovery of the mid-1980s, and rose with the recession at the outset of the 1990s.

A long-run decline in poverty rates is to be expected in a world of rising living standards. Rising real output pulls up the poor along with the rich. Similarly, as the figures show, the incidence of poverty remains quite sensitive to general economic downturns.

Who Are the Poor?

Exhibit 5, panel (b), provides a statistical profile of poor families in the United States. The poor tend to be disproportionately black and of Hispanic origin. They tend to live in large families; the family head seems to have little education, to be young, and to be female. Over 40 percent of the American poor are children under the age of 18. The poor tend to concentrate in central cities and in rural areas. Contrary to popular myth, a majority are working poor. Similarly, only 64 percent of the poor receive some form of cash assistance from government antipoverty programs.

These figures suggest that for the majority of families, poverty results from a limited earning capacity. Employment *per se* does not pull them out of poverty. Only in poor families headed by females do a majority of household heads not hold jobs.

The official poverty income standard does not provide for an attractive standard of living. The 1991 poverty income standard of about $13,500 for a family of four allowed for $3.00 per person each day in food expenditures. A Gallup poll asking Americans what poverty income would be required to make ends meet yielded a figure 50 percent larger than the official poverty standard.

Even the most avid supporters of the existing welfare system recognize its deficiencies. It destroys work incentives, it breaks up homes, it fosters one-parent families, and it has created a massive bureaucracy that the poor have come to regard as their enemy.

The negative income tax promises to do away with the bureaucracy and restore, at least partially, work incentives. It is for these reasons that most economists favor the negative income tax over the current system.

Income-maintenance programs offer only a short-run solution to the poverty problem. The long-run solution of poverty requires an attack on the fundamental sources of poverty—limited human capital and discrimination—that are responsive to government action.

To provide a long-run solution to the problem of poverty, government policy should aim at eliminating job-market discrimination and race and sex discrimination in education. Moreover, government policy should encourage the children of the poor to invest in human-capital resources. The problem is how to devise a policy that does not defeat itself by reverse discrimination or by making the tradeoff between equity and efficiency too costly. The intended effects of legislation can often differ dramatically from the actual effects.

In the 1960s and 1970s, the government embarked on a series of training programs (called the "Great Society" programs in the 1960s) aimed at providing education and training for the children of the poor. Many of these programs have been abandoned in recent years, but they represented an important social effort to eliminate the root sources of poverty.

This chapter examined the causes of inequality in the distribution of income and directed attention to the role of government in the redistribution of income to the poor. The next chapter will focus on externalities.

Chapter Summary

**The most important point to learn from this chapter is:
The challenge to a society that wishes to have a more equal**

distribution of income is to redistribute income without substantially reducing the total amount of income.

1. The distribution of income among households is determined first in factor markets. Household income is the sum of the payments to the factors of production that the household owns. The government may change this distribution of income through taxes and the distribution of public services. The Lorenz curve measures inequality in the distribution of income. It shows the cumulative percent of all income earned by households at successive income levels. If the Lorenz curve is a straight 45-degree line, income is distributed perfectly equally. The more the Lorenz curve bows away from the 45-degree line, the more unequal is the distribution of income. The U.S. distribution of income has become more equal since 1929.

2. The sources of inequality are: different abilities, discrimination, occupational differences, different amounts of human-capital investment, chance and luck, and property inheritance.

3. The distribution of income is made more equal by taxes and especially by the distribution of in-kind services.

4. There are different views on what constitutes distributive justice. Natural-law theory calls for a distribution of income according to the marginal productivity of the resources owned by households. The utilitarian school believes an equal distribution of income maximizes total utility. John Rawls calls for a distribution of income that maximizes the utility of the least-fortunate members of society.

5. Poverty can be measured either in absolute or relative terms. The absolute measure is based on an estimate of the minimum income necessary to allow a household to buy the minimum essentials. The relative standard measures poverty in terms of the household's location in the income distribution. According to government absolute measures of poverty, the number of those living below the poverty line has declined substantially since the 1950s. If in-kind payments are included in income, slightly more than 8 percent of Americans are living below the poverty line. Poor Americans tend to be nonwhite, poorly educated, members of households headed by females, and either very young or very old.

Policy Focus: **The current welfare system requires a large bureaucracy and discourages work effort. A negative income tax would be simpler to implement and could be set up to encourage work effort. Income-maintenance programs are a short-run solution to the problem of poverty.**

Key Terms

Lorenz curve (p. 594)
wealth (p. 595)
human-capital investment (p. 598)
personal wealth (p. 599)
distributive justice (p. 601)

in-kind income (p. 604)
absolute poverty standard (p. 605)
relative poverty standard (p. 605)
negative income tax (NIT) (p. 607)

Questions and Problems

1. Identify the following statements as issues of normative or positive economics:
   a. It is not right to have 15 percent of the population living under conditions of poverty.
   b. If the income distribution is made more equal by redistributive taxes, there will be a tradeoff between equality and efficiency.

2. Draw a Lorenz curve for absolute equality. Draw a Lorenz curve for absolute inequality. Explain in words what the absolute-inequality Lorenz curve means.

3. "If all people were the same, the Lorenz curve would be a 45-degree line." Evaluate this statement.

4. "The fact that women earn on average seventy percent of what men earn proves beyond a shadow of a doubt that there is sex discrimination." Evaluate this statement.

5. There are two views of the causes of poverty. One view says that the poor are poor through no fault of their own. The other says that the poor are poor through choice. Give arguments for each position.

6. Does the "leaking bucket" analogy apply to Rawls' view of distributive justice as well as to the utilitarian view?

7. Contrast the utilitarian view of distributive justice with the Rawlsian view.

8. Explain why under a relative poverty standard poverty would be more difficult to eliminate.

9. Would the work incentives be greater with a 25 percent negative income tax (NIT) rate or a 50 percent NIT rate? Rework Exhibit 6 in the text to illustrate your answer.

10. Consider two hypothetical societies. One consists of 8 risk avoiders and 2 risk seekers. The other consists of 5 risk seekers and 5 risk avoiders. Which society would have a more equal distribution of income?

11. If society dictated that all blue-eyed males can only work as janitors, what would happen to the incomes of blue-eyed males?

12. Joe wants goods today; Bill is more willing to wait until tomorrow for goods. Which one would be more likely to invest in human capital?

13. The official U.S. poverty-income standard is adjusted upward each year to account for the general increase in prices. If a family's income just keeps up with the poverty income over the years, what is happening to its relative poverty position?

14. Explain why the market value of in-kind benefits provided to the poor may be a misleading measure of their impact on poverty.

15. Education is distributed among the population more equally than income. What does this tell us about education and inequality?

Doing Economics

Based on the sources of income differences discussed in the text, develop a list of possible reasons for income inequality (willingness to work, innate ability, level of education, luck, riskiness or unpleasantness of job, discrimination, etc.). Ask at least ten noneconomic students and at least ten people who are not students, faculty, or staff to rank the importance of these factors on a scale from 1 (not important) to 5 (very important). In addition, ask them whether they think that most income differences between people are "just" in an ethical sense. Which factors do students think are most important? Are their significant differences between the responses of students and nonstudents? Can you explain these?

Issues in Economics

P A R T   S E V E N

CHAPTER 32
Environmental Economics and
Market Failure

CHAPTER 33
Capitalism and Socialism

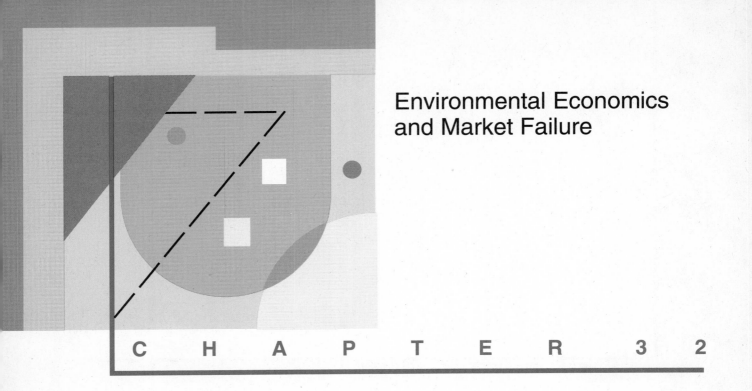

Environmental Economics and Market Failure

C H A P T E R 3 2

CHAPTER FOCUS   Everybody's business is frequently nobody's business. This chapter examines two types of market failure—externalities and public goods. Externalities are present when the person imposing costs on others (and society), does not have to weigh these costs in private cost/benefit calculations. Externalities include environmental pollution—the pollution of the air, the dumping of chemical wastes into rivers and the atmosphere, and the depletion of the ozone layer by the discharge of aerosol sprays.

People have strong views regarding the relationship between the economy and the environment. Many believe that news reports of oil spills, toxic waste dumping, and the killing of whales and dolphins indicate the failure of private economic decision-making. A more extreme conclusion, drawn from reports of global warming and a disappearing ozone layer, is that our lives or the lives of future generations are in danger. In both cases, people call for steps to be taken to preserve the environment. Perhaps it is necessary to return to a simpler life-style, with less production, fewer automobiles, and no aerosol spray cans.

Our knowledge is still insufficient to evaluate long-run environmental risks. Not knowing the risks, we must still select a course of action to ensure a reasonable environment for future generations.

After studying this chapter, you will be able to:

- Define externalities.
- Define the social optimum.
- List the three approaches to internalizing externalities.
- Determine optimal abatement expenditures.
- Differentiate between the regulatory approach and the incentive approach to environmental protection.

EXTERNALITIES AND MARKET FAILURE

When a factory dumps wastes into a lake, the people who use the lake for recreational purposes (swimming and boating) or economic production (fishing) will find that their level of satisfaction is directly reduced. The polluting factory does not pay a price for its dumping activities. Private markets do not necessarily penalize the factory for dumping waste. The waste-dumping factory may not be required to pay for the costs it imposes on the other parties. Pollution is an example of **market failure**.

> **Market failure** occurs when the price system fails to produce the quantity of a good that would be socially optimal.

Externalities are present whenever the actions of one agent have direct economic effects on other parties. Externalities represent one source of market failure, because they cause private parties (individuals and firms) to produce output levels that are different from the socially optimal level.

> **Externalities** exist when a producer or consumer does not bear the full marginal cost or enjoy the full marginal benefit of an economic action.

When externalities are present, market transactions between two parties have harmful or beneficial effects on third parties. The effects are *external to the price system and are not the outcome of mutual agreement* between all the interested parties.

Take the example of a factory that imposes external cleaning or health-care costs on the community by polluting its air or water. The unique feature of these costs is that they are not paid by the factory, but by economic agents external to the factory. These costs do not show up anywhere in the factory's accounting.

Externalities can benefit third parties as well. The person who pays for an education is not the only one who benefits from that education. Society benefits because education provides a common culture and language and encourages scientific progress.

External costs or external benefits cause **social costs** and **social benefits** to deviate from the private costs and benefits studied in earlier chapters. When externalities are present, private costs and benefits do not capture the full social costs or benefits of economic actions.

Ronald Harry Coase (1910–)

Ronald Coase founded the movement applying economics to the law. Born in England in 1910, he attended the London School of Economics and taught there from 1935 to 1951. Other teaching posts included the University of Buffalo (1951–1958), the University of Virginia (1958–1964), and finally the University of Chicago (1964–1982). He strongly believed that economics should always be discussed in the context of real-world problems. His famous contribution to economics, the paper, "The Problem of Social Cost," published in *Journal of Law and Economics* (October, 1960), is exceptional in modern economics because it uses no math. It is a fascinating blend of simple economics, real-world examples, and law.

Coase did not bow to conventional wisdom, and earned perhaps lasting fame by inspiring the Coase theorem. Before his work, economists followed A. C. Pigou (1877–1959), who argued that the party responsible for imposing external costs (such as polluters and smokers) should be the one restrained by government-imposed taxation. Coase challenged this view by showing that the damage could be dealt with more efficiently by the straightforward enforcement of property rights. He argued that as far as economic efficiency is concerned it does not make any difference whether the damaged party bribed the polluter or the polluter compensated the damaged party. In Coase's world, government action may only be needed if transaction costs are too high for private parties to carry out an agreement. To Coase government's main role is to enforce property rights, whether those rights belong to the polluting party or the damaged party.

Coase received the Nobel Prize in economics in 1991.

Social costs are the sum of private costs and external costs.

Social benefits are the sum of private benefits and external benefits.

Externalities are present when private costs or benefits deviate from social costs or benefits.

If there are no external costs or external benefits, private and social costs are the same and private and social benefits are the same. The polluting factory, however, imposes external costs on the community that do not enter into the factory's private costs. Hence, the factory's social cost exceeds its private cost by the amount of the external cost.

Externalities cause the economy to produce output levels either above or below the socially optimal levels. Private firms will produce "too much" of goods and services that are produced with significant external costs. Private firms will produce "too little" of goods and services that are produced with significant external benefits. The following discussion concerns social inefficiencies due to external costs.

If economic agents must pay for the costs imposed on others, they will take into account these costs in private cost/benefit calculations. In the late 1980s evidence accumulated that chlorofluorocarbons (CFBs), used in aerosol sprays such as deodorants, contribute to the depletion of the ozone layer that protects the earth from the sun's harmful ultraviolet rays. Only a handful of firms produce CFBs. In early 1988 the major producer ceased producing CFBs, largely to avoid the possibility of facing multi-billion dollar lawsuits.

An externality can be internalized in three ways:

1. by redefining property rights,
2. by making voluntary agreements, or
3. by taxing the party causing the externality.

Redefining Property Rights

A simple example of the effects of internalization would be the merger of two factories located on a river. Prior to the merger, the downstream factory has to pay water-purification costs because the upstream factory is polluting the water. After the merger, the external costs imposed on the downstream factory become *internal costs* to the merged firms. Pollution costs will now be considered in private cost/benefit calculations by both factories. The merging of two factories involved the redefining of **property rights**.

> **Property rights** specify who owns a resource and who has the right to use it.

When the two factories located on the same river merged, the owners of the downstream factory acquired property rights in the polluting factory. Poorly defined property rights are an important cause of externalities. When it is unclear to whom property rights belong—such as who owns the air people breathe, the fish in the seas, or the water of a river—externalities usually result.

If the property rights for a resource are held by the community, but each person has free access to the resource, the resource will likely be exploited and abused. Fishing businesses will overfish ocean waters; factories will overpollute the air.

If private property rights for the resource could be established, most externalities would disappear. If hunting land that had been commonly owned becomes privately owned, the private owner can charge hunters fees to hunt game on that land. The rational private owner would set fees high enough to prevent game from being depleted. The same principle could be applied more broadly. If one person in the community were somehow given ownership of the community's air, that person would have the legal right to charge the polluting factory for its use of the air. Every month, the polluting factory would get a bill from the owner of the community's air. If one country held the property rights to the ocean's fishing grounds, it could charge fishing businesses from all countries for their use of the ocean and could prevent the depletion of reserves of fish.

In many cases, it is not easy to eliminate externalities by changing property rights. When persons take private ownership of hunting land, it is relatively easy and inexpensive for them to erect fences, control access, and charge hunters appropriate fees. In other cases, it is difficult if not impossible to define and enforce private property rights.

Air pollution is an example of the problems caused by poorly defined property rights. The ownership rights to clean air are too poorly defined to allow an "owner" of clean air to sue polluters. Even if some entity could be assigned the ownership of air, the "owner" would have to know how much pollution each car or factory has emitted. The owner would then have to be in a position to collect a fee from each polluter equal to the marginal external cost, which the owner would have to be able to calculate. The amount of information the private "owner" of air would have to be able to collect to put appropriate private price tags on air is clearly excessive. A similar problem would face the person who had been assigned ownership of the ocean's fish. The difficulty of redefining private property rights in a meaningful way limits this approach to internalizing externalities.

Poorly defined property rights create externality problems.

Redefining property rights to internalize externalities is difficult because it is costly to define and enforce property rights.

Voluntary Agreements

Voluntary agreements between those that create the externality and affected third parties are a second means of internalizing externalities. The above example of a merger of two factories on a river illustrates how voluntary agreements internalize externalities. The two firms agreed to merge. Each firm had clear property rights to their own property, and the merger took place through the legal system. With well-defined property rights, voluntary agreements negotiated through the legal system can internalize external costs.

The proposition that voluntary agreements can handle some externality problems is called the *Coase theorem*, after Ronald H. Coase. (See Gallery of Economists.) Coase argued that external costs and benefits can be internalized by negotiations among affected parties. Coase gave the example of a rancher whose cattle occasionally stray onto a neighboring farm and damage the neighbor's crops. If the rancher were legally liable for the damage to the farmer, then private bargaining would result in a deal between the rancher and the farmer in which the farmer would be paid for the increased cost of growing crops imposed by the straying cattle. These extra costs would induce the rancher to reduce the size of the herd (or build better fences) and the potential externality would disappear.

Likewise, the externality could be internalized even if the rancher's cattle had the legal right to stray onto the farmer's land. The farmer in this case would make a deal in which the rancher would agree to reduce the size of the herd or build a fence in return for a cash payment from the farmer. Again, when a price tag is placed on the externality, it disappears. In either case, the same amounts of crops and cattle would be produced. The social effect is the same, but the income-distribution effects are quite different. In the first case, the rancher transfers income to the farmer. In the second case, the farmer transfers income to the rancher. The distribution of income depends on who has the property rights.

Whenever externalities are present, perfect competition does not lead to economic efficiency. The competitive firm produces too much output when it imposes external costs. The competitive firm produces that level of output at which marginal *private* costs and marginal *private* benefits are equal; it ignores the external costs of its actions. At the profit-maximizing level of output, marginal social costs *exceed* marginal social benefits. Society as a whole would be better off if the competitive firm reduced its output to the point where marginal social costs and marginal social benefits are equal. These propositions are illustrated in Exhibit 1, which shows the optimal level of output for a competitive firm when external costs are present.

> The Coase theorem says that externalities can be internalized by voluntary agreements.

> Externalities cause production to deviate from social efficiency.

INTERNALIZING EXTERNALITIES

If external costs are included in calculations of private gain, competitive economic decisions will push the economy to produce the social optimum of goods and services. **Internalization** occurs when private price tags are placed on externalities.

> **Internalization** is the process of putting private price tags on externalities.

Under what conditions can externalities be dealt with by means of voluntary agreements? The most important requirement is that the number of individuals involved in a voluntary agreement be small to keep bargaining costs down. The factory-merger example involved only two negotiating parties. If it had been

EXHIBIT 1 Perfect Competition with External Costs

When external costs are present, competitive firms produce too much output. They produce at the output level where marginal private costs equal price, not where marginal social costs equal price.

necessary to merge not two but four factories located on the river, the agreement would have been more difficult to reach. If bargaining costs were high, the other downstream factories would have an incentive to sit on the sidelines and hope that the other downstream factories would arrange the reduction in pollution by the upstream factories.

Government Action

Governments can internalize externalities by imposing corrective taxes. Exhibit 1 demonstrates that competitive firms produce "too much" output when external costs are present. By considering only private marginal cost, the firm is led to produce at an output level above the social optimum.

Governments have the power to levy taxes on the production of goods and services, and these taxes become part of the private costs of the firm. If a tax equal to marginal external cost could be placed on the firms that cause external costs, the externality would be internalized. The firm would consider not only the private marginal cost but also the external marginal cost (which is paid in the form of a tax).

Exhibit 2 shows how this tax would be structured. Consider a competitive cotton farm; the pesticides it uses harm the environment. Thus, the marginal social cost, MSC, exceeds the firm's MC. Without government action, the firm will produce q_2 units where $MC = P$. The optimal level of output is only q_1 units. If a government follows the optimal policy, it would impose a tax of ab units in Exhibit 2. The firm must now take into account the costs imposed on others and will, accordingly, reduce production to the efficient level where marginal social costs equal marginal social benefits.

Government can internalize externalities by imposing a tax equal to the marginal external cost.

The use of taxes to internalize externalities is especially appropriate when private bargaining costs are high and voluntary agreements cannot be reached. When the government steps in with corrective taxes, the government in effect takes on the bargaining costs of the private parties. If the externality affects many people, it is cheaper to use collective or government action to internalize the externality. If

EXHIBIT 2   Internalizing Externalities with a Tax

A tax of *ab* per unit will cause the firm to produce where *MSC* = *P* instead of *MC* = *P*.

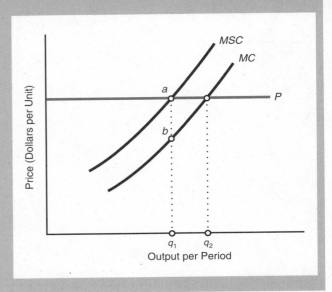

external costs are imposed on thousands of individuals, voluntary agreement among the affected parties is unlikely.

Externalities do not automatically require government action. Some externalities can be dealt with on a private basis through voluntary agreements among affected parties. In fact, in some cases private markets come up with inventive solutions to externalities. Other externalities impose costs that are too low to warrant government action. Both government action to correct externalities and externalities themselves can impose costs on individuals. Both the market mechanism and government action have advantages and disadvantages. There are, therefore, few hard-and-fast rules on whether the government or the market should solve the problem.

PUBLIC GOODS

One of the most important functions of government is to provide **public goods**. Competitive markets will fail to supply or will undersupply public goods because they are unprofitable. Thus, public goods and services are provided by the government. Goods and services such as public schools, public parks, public roads and bridges, national defense, police protection, or public health services are generally made available to the public at no explicit charge and are financed by taxes (although in some instances governments charge for government services, as in the case of postage or admission fees to public parks).

> **Public goods** are goods or services with the following qualities:
> 1. the provision of the public good to one person also gives the good to everyone in the same neighborhood; and
> 2. no one in the neighborhood can be excluded from enjoying the benefits of the good or service.

Nonrivalry

If a dam is built that protects a particular geographic area from flooding, everyone who lives in the protected area benefits. Moreover, the fact that one person's house is protected by the dam does not reduce any other house's protection. Residents of the area are not *rivals* for flood protection. Similarly, viewers of television programs are not rivals. One person can view a program without affecting another viewer's enjoyment.

If the government builds an antimissile system that substantially reduces the likelihood of nuclear attack by a foreign nation, everyone in the protected geographical area benefits. The protection of one person's life and property does not reduce the protection enjoyed by others.

Public goods can be contrasted with ordinary private goods such as food and drink, cars, houses, shoes, dresses, and medical services. Different consumers are indeed "rivals" for private goods. A hamburger eaten by one person cannot be eaten by someone else; a house occupied by one family cannot be occupied by another.

Some goods can have public or private characteristics depending on the circumstances. For example, one person can enjoy an uncrowded movie without reducing another person's consumption, but a crowded movie or sporting event is like a private good because each additional spectator displaces another possible spectator. The problem of rationing the available supply of most private goods is solved by charging prices; those who consume the good place a higher value on it than those who do not consume the good.

Nonexclusion

The second characteristic of public goods is that people cannot be excluded from using them once they are provided. Excluding people from using the good (once it has been produced) is too costly. National defense and flood control are cases in point. Once a missile system has been put in place, it is not possible to exclude anyone in the protected area from being protected. Once a flood-control dam has been built, it is not possible to exclude homeowners in the protected area from benefiting.

In the case of private goods, it is easy to exclude people (who do not pay for the good) from using the good. The grocery store will not allow you to take out groceries that have not been paid for (and it has security personnel to back this up). The gas-station attendant will not pump gas for nonpayers.

It should be noted that goods can have both private- and public-good characteristics. Nonrival goods such as cable television or an uncrowded movie are provided as private goods because nonpayers can be excluded quite simply. In order to be a public good, the good must possess both characteristics of public goods. An uncrowded movie theater sells tickets on the private market—even though one person attending the movie does not prevent another person from enjoying the movie—because nonpayers can easily be prevented from viewing a movie.

Public goods are characterized by nonrivalry and nonexclusion.

Free Riders

A public good can be provided privately only if beneficiaries finance it with voluntary contributions. Since those who benefit from the good cannot be excluded from its use whether or not they are paying for it, people need not contribute. In the case of public goods, there will be a strong temptation not to pay. A person who enjoys the benefits of a good without paying is a **free rider**.

> A **free rider** is anyone who enjoys the benefits of a good or service without paying the cost.

When some of the beneficiaries act as free riders, the private revenues voluntarily contributed to pay for a public good will be less than the social benefits the good generates—in which case, the good will not be produced at all or will be underproduced by the private market. Public television is a case in point. Noncontributors cannot be prevented from viewing public-television programming. Despite frequent public appeals against free riding, few public television stations are self-supporting. Instead, they require government assistance to survive.

Free riding makes it difficult for private markets to provide public goods.

The free-rider problem confounds the production of public goods. Voluntary agreements will work if free riding is not excessive. Voluntary cooperation is more likely the smaller the group, the more often collective decisions are made, and the greater the gain from adopting cooperative behavior.

Examples of cooperative behavior abound. Some people make voluntary contributions to civic clubs for extra police protection; volunteers work to improve the community; private roads are built that connect several families to public roads. But if the group is large, if collective decisions are made infrequently, and if the individual gains little by cooperating, free riding will be more prevalent.

Example 1 classifies a number of goods as private or public goods.

EXTERNALITIES AND ENVIRONMENT

Externalities are present whenever social costs or benefits differ from private costs or benefits. When one firm imposes external costs on a second firm, when one neighbor's rundown house disrupts the enjoyment of the neighborhood by other home owners, you have an externality. Environmental pollution is a particularly important form of externality because it imposes external costs broadly on the community. Environmental pollution is a form of externality that is typically hard to deal with by redefining property rights and voluntary agreements. Property rights to the atmosphere, rivers, lakes, and oceans are difficult to define, and the number of people affected is large, making it difficult to negotiate agreements. Hence, in the area of environmental pollution government looms large.

Optimal Abatement

Modern production and consumption patterns impose significant **waste-disposal costs** on society. When firms produce goods and services, wastes in the form of air pollutants, toxic chemicals, solid wastes, and noise are created. Wastes are also created by modern consumption; we as consumers produce wastes (automobile exhausts, noise, solid wastes). Wastes must be disposed of either in the ground, in water, or in the air. (Someday, they may be disposed of in outer space.)

> **Waste-disposal costs** are the costs of disposing of the residual materials generated by production and consumption.

EXAMPLE 1

Classifying Selected Goods as Private Goods or Public Goods

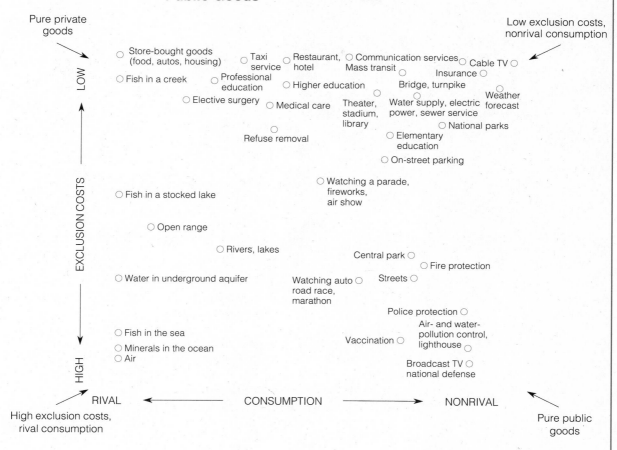

Pure private goods, in the upper left corner, are characterized by low exclusion costs (free riders can be excluded easily) and by rival consumption. Pure public goods, in the lower right corner, are characterized by high exclusion costs (free riding can't be prevented) and by nonrival consumption (one person's consumption of a good does not detract from another's consumption of it). Goods in the other two corners meet only one of the two characteristics of a public good. In the lower left corner, goods are characterized by high exclusion costs but rival consumption. In the upper right corner, goods are characterized by nonrival consumption but low exclusion costs.

SOURCE: E. S. Savas, *Privatizing the Public Sector* (Chatham, NJ: Chatham House Publishers, Inc., 1982), p. 34.

Waste-disposal costs are real opportunity costs. If public or private resources are devoted to pollution prevention (scrubbers on smokestacks, for example), these resources are not available for other uses. If individuals purchase unpolluted water to avoid drinking health-damaging polluted water, they also incur opportunity costs. If the health of individuals in the community deteriorates because of

EXHIBIT 3   Optimal Pollution Abatement

This figure shows how the optimal amount of pollution abatement is determined. The marginal-social-benefit curve is downward-sloping (people place a higher value on the first units of abatement). The marginal social cost of pollution abatement is assumed constant. The optimal amount of abatement is quantity *a* (where marginal social costs equal marginal social benefits). Point *b*, the total prohibition of pollution, is not optimal because the marginal social benefit (zero) is less than the marginal social cost.

pollution from toxic-waste dumps, there are costs to the individual and community, be they explicit cash outlays or less visible opportunity costs.

Modern societies produce vast quantities of wastes, and each society must decide how much of its resources to devote to pollution abatement. Cost/benefit analysis provides, at least in principle, a practical guideline. Exhibit 3 shows the marginal social costs and marginal social benefits of different quantities of resources devoted to pollution abatement—in this case, the number of gallons of water purified through filtration procedures. For simplicity, we let the marginal social cost of each successive unit of abatement be constant. Marginal social benefits decline with more abatement because society values the first units of abatement more highly than subsequent units.

As Exhibit 3 shows, a choice must be made among the different amounts of pollution abatement. At one extreme, absolutely no resources are devoted to abatement. At the other extreme, resources are devoted to abatement to the point where additional expenditures on abatement yield no further marginal social benefit. The optimal level of abatement occurs when the marginal social cost of an extra unit of abatement equals the marginal social benefit. If additional abatement exceeds this optimal level, the extra benefits to society fall short of the extra opportunity costs to society.

Exhibit 3 demonstrates why society should not aim for the total elimination of pollution. To totally eliminate pollution, society would have to devote scarce resources to pollution abatement until the marginal social benefits are driven down to zero. The last dollar spent on pollution abatement yields zero benefits but has a positive marginal cost to society. The last dollar uses up scarce resources that could have been devoted to producing other things; yet it yields no marginal benefit to society.

The theoretical standard for evaluating pollution-abatement programs used in Exhibit 3 has a number of practical problems. First, it is very difficult to know the exact costs and benefits of various pollution-abatement activities. Some costs and benefits occur only over time. Measuring the full costs even at one point in time is

Regulation or Markets to Protect the Environment?

Throughout the world, societies rely on government action to deal with pollution. In the United States, a number of state, local, and federal agencies are involved in pollution control. The most important federal agency is the Environmental Protection Agency (EPA), which, since 1970, has been charged with regulating pollution activities, acting through the states and through its own authority. The EPA derives its authority through a number of congressional acts (the Clean Air Act, the Water Pollution Control Act, the National Environmental Policy Act, the Toxic Substances Control Act, and many other environmental acts).

The Regulatory Approach

To enforce federal environmental laws, the EPA usually follows a *regulatory approach*. The EPA specifies what each individual waste discharger must do with respect to air, water, and noise pollution. The EPA sets ceilings on the amounts of pollutants that can be discharged and requires that the discharger meet these ceilings by a specified date using the best practical (or best available) pollution-control technology. The EPA issues permits to each pollution source, and the permit specifies how much of each pollutant can be discharged and a time schedule for pollution reduction.

Aside from enforcing its directives, the most basic problem facing the EPA is to decide how much pollution to allow. Environmental laws are not always specific. Cost/benefit analysis shows that the absolute prohibition of pollution discharges is not a reasonable social goal. This policy would cause all pollution-abatement activities to be carried out to levels where marginal social costs far outweigh marginal social benefits. The resource costs to society of this action would be prohibitive.

Devising direct controls that lead to optimal abatement policies is difficult. The EPA sets discharge limits without reference to the marginal costs and benefits of its actions. Yet there is a growing realization that environmental policies (which are already costly) require a balancing of costs and benefits. For this reason, the EPA has experimented with economic-incentive-based environmental policies.

Market Solutions

Exhibit 2 demonstrated that governments could internalize externalities by imposing per-unit taxes or charges equal to marginal external costs. This principle applies to optimal pollution abatement. The government could impose fees—called *effluent charges*—for the discharge of pollutants that equal the marginal external cost of the pollutant. Such effluent charges would cause the polluting firm to consider the external costs of pollution in its private economic calculations. Establishing optimal effluent charges is difficult because estimating the marginal external costs of each pollution-discharge activity is difficult.

The EPA has experimented with a number of "market solutions." In one program, firms or groups of firms are allowed to create pollution-abatement programs (which they presumably do at the least cost to themselves) subject to a total-emissions limit assigned to the plant or region. If several firms are involved, they are allowed to trade pollution rights among themselves and even to buy and sell rights to pollute. Another EPA program permits new pollution sources to operate if they are able to obtain an offset (a reduction in pollution discharges) from existing firms. (See Example 2.)

The basic notion behind these incentive schemes is that the costs of pollution abatement will be reduced if dischargers are allowed to make their own decisions. Firms that can reduce discharges cheaply will buy pollution rights from firms that can only reduce emissions expensively. Even if the end result is not an optimal balance of costs and benefits, at least the costs of pollution control will be reduced under such programs.

The market solution ensures that pollution abatement occur at a lower cost of society's resources. Hence, it is preferable to the regulatory approach.

EXAMPLE 2

Trading Pollution Rights

In December 1990, in an unprecedented arrangement, Metallized Paper Corporation of America bought pollution rights from USX's Clairton Works and from Papercraft Corporation in Allegheny County, Pennsylvania. Metallized Paper paid USX $75,000 for the right to emit 75 tons of pollution per year, purchased 32 tons from Papercraft, and received an additional 500-ton donation from USX. This sale of pollution rights was legal under the Federal Clean Air Act. Both USX and Papercraft Corporation possessed rights to emit a certain number of tons of pollutants into the environment up to a limit determined by the Environmental Protection Agency. By selling these rights, both agreed to cut back on their pollution emissions by the number of tons sold.

The sale was sanctioned by county and state officials, who had spent two years persuading Metallized Paper to locate in Allegheny County. Various environmental groups protested the sale because the company's plant would emit chemicals, known as volatile organic compounds, that contribute to the formation of ozone. State officials, however, defended their action on the grounds that the overall amount of pollution would not increase. Rights to pollute were merely traded from companies that could reduce their emissions cheaply to one that required significant expenditures to limit pollution.

SOURCE: "Trading of Pollution Rights Draws Fire," *Christian Science Monitor*, December 4, 1990.

difficult because of the large number of people and things that are affected to varying degrees. Second, waste-disposal problems involve complicated physical, biological, and chemical interactions with the total environment. A particular abatement procedure increasing water purity may shift discharges to the atmosphere. Third, there are income-distribution effects associated with pollution abatement. Someone in society must pay for pollution abatement. Who should receive the benefits and who should bear the costs of pollution abatement? Should private firms pay? Should only affected individuals pay? Should the general public pay?

Chapter Summary

The most important point to learn from this chapter is: Externalities may justify government action if private parties have difficulties placing price tags on external costs and benefits; the appropriate policy response for the government is to create a market for externalities either with taxes, subsidies, or privately priced permits.

1. Market failure occurs when the price system fails to produce the socially optimal quantity of a good. Two examples of market failure are externalities and public goods. Externalities occur when marginal social costs (or benefits) do not equal marginal private costs (or benefits). Social efficiency requires that marginal social benefits and marginal social costs be equal, but private market participants equate marginal private benefits with marginal private costs. Externalities can be

internalized by redefining property rights, by making voluntary agreements, or by taxing or subsidizing the externality generator.

2. Pure public goods have two characteristics: First, the consumption of the good by one user does not reduce its consumption by others (nonrival consumption). Second, no one can in practice be prevented from using the good (nonexclusion).

3. Waste disposal costs arise because modern production and consumption require disposing of residual wastes such as air pollutants, toxic chemicals, and solid wastes. Pollution problems cannot easily be solved by redefining property rights or by voluntary agreement; government intervention is typically required.

Policy Focus: **Policymakers must decide between a regulatory approach or a market approach to dealing with pollution. The market approach appears better because it allows pollution abatement to occur at a lower cost of society's resources.**

Key Terms

market failure (p. 615)
externalities (p. 615)
social costs (p. 615)
social benefits (p. 615)
property rights (p. 617)

internalization (p. 618)
public goods (p. 620)
free rider (p. 622)
waste-disposal costs (p. 627)

Questions and Problems

1. Factory A produces 1,000 tons of sulfuric acid. It costs A $10,000 to produce 1,000 tons. As a consequence of producing 1,000 tons of sulfuric acid, people in the community must increase their medical payments by $5,000; they lose $4,000 in wages by being sick; their dry-cleaning bills increase by $1,000. What are the private and social costs of the 1,000 tons of sulfuric acid?

2. Explain how the external costs calculated in the previous example might be internalized. Will this internalization be handled differently when there are three people hurt by the factory compared to when 300,000 people are hurt? In which case is government action more likely?

3. Almost everybody thinks we need national defense. Why is it, therefore, difficult to get people to pay voluntarily their share of national defense costs? Why is there no problem in getting people to pay for shoes?

4. If new cost-efficient technologies were developed that reduced the marginal costs of pollution abatement, what would happen to the optimal level of pollution abatement?

5. Does the pollution-trading concept used in recent years by the EPA solve the problem of choosing the optimal level of pollution?

6. Explain why economists do not favor the total elimination of pollution. Why would it not be efficient to totally eliminate pollution from our environment?

7. Discuss the two characteristics of public goods.

8. In 1986, it was proposed that a worldwide tax be placed on aerosol sprays to protect the world's ozone layer. At what rate should the tax be set?

9. In which case would it be easier to establish property rights? First, Farmer Jones wishes to keep stray cattle off his farmland. Second, Farmer Jones wishes to prevent the commercial jets landing at a nearby airport from disturbing his egg-laying chickens. Third, Farmer Jones wishes to keep Farmer Smith from depleting the stock of fish in a lake they share.

10. The 15th Annual Report of Council on Environmental Quality quoted a group of scientists who stressed the need to measure environmental quality accurately:

"Although ecologists measure numerous variables as indicators of change, many measurements are based on inadequately tested assumptions, and most have relatively poor precision with limited potential for improvement. The lack of precision and occasional controversy over the validity of an approach have lessened the effectiveness of ecological inputs to decision making."[*]

What does this mean for the application of economics to controlling externalities?

---

[*]T. Tietenberg, *Environmental and Natural Resource Economics*, 2nd ed. (Glenview, Ill.: Scott, Foresman and Company, 1988).

Doing Economics

Does anyone living near you do something on a regular basis that bothers you? Analyze the situation using the economics of externalities. Are property rights clearly defined? Could you resolve the situation individually via a market? If you could, but have not done so, why not? What authoritarian or regulatory resolution could be imposed? How would the other person in this situation answer these questions?

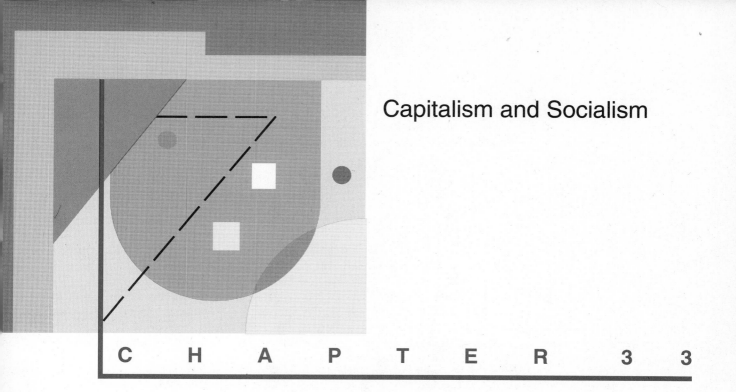

Capitalism and Socialism

C H A P T E R 3 3

CHAPTER FOCUS   The terms capitalism, socialism, and communism evoke emotional responses. From their early years on, people are taught that one "ism" is good and that another "ism" is bad. Cold and hot wars have been waged between countries that represent different "isms." The American economy is a capitalist economy. It uses primarily market forces to solve the economic problem of *what, how,* and *for whom.* Individuals—in their capacities as consumers and producers—solve the economic problem. Although the economic role of government appears to be large to most of us, in proportion to the huge size of the American economy, it is still smaller than in most other countries.

The collapse of the communist economic system in the Soviet Union and Eastern Europe is probably the most significant event of the twentieth century. The Soviet command economy established in the 1920s by Stalin as an alternative economic system failed in the late 1980s and early 1990s.

No former communist country has navigated the transition from communism back to capitalism. The major challenge of the current generation is to find ways to reestablish market economic systems in the former Communist world.

ECONOMIC SYSTEMS

Societies must find orderly ways of allocating resources. Each society uses an **economic system** to solve allocation problems and to maintain order.

> An **economic system** is the set of property rights, resource-allocation arrangements, and incentives that a society uses to solve the economic problem.

Economic systems are differentiated according to the specific institutions they establish for each of these three attributes.

Property rights, allocation, and incentive systems determine the economic system.

1. *Property Rights.* The factors of production may be owned primarily by society (or by a government that is supposed to represent society), by private individuals, or by a combination of the two. The person or body that holds property rights has the right to determine how the resource is used and to receive the income the resource generates.

2. *Allocation Arrangements.* Resources can be allocated by the price system or by government planners. In economic systems in which resources are allocated by price, individual firms decide what and how to produce; in systems in which allocation is determined by the government, officials give orders about production to enterprises. When the price system allocates resources, decision-making is *decentralized*. When planners make allocations, decision making is centralized.

3. *Incentive Systems.* An economic system must motivate its participants (workers, managers, entrepreneurs) to carry out their economic tasks. *Economic incentives* can be used to motivate people. Alternatively, *moral incentives* (medals, public praise) or even *threats* may induce individuals to produce.

The two major economic systems are **capitalism** and **socialism**.

> **Capitalism** is an economic system characterized by private ownership of the factors of production, market allocation of resources, and the use of economic incentives.

> **Socialism** is an economic system characterized by state ownership of the factors of production, the use of moral as well as economic incentives, resource allocation by economic plan, and centralized decision-making.

No real-world economy fits exactly into one of these two molds. In all economies, there is a mixture of private and public ownership, administrative and market allocation, economic and moral incentives, and centralized and decentralized decision-making. However, in most economies, the major traits of one particular economic system will dominate.

Property Rights

In a capitalist economy, **property rights** are taken for granted. It is assumed that goods (e.g., a quart of milk), services (e.g., a shoe shine), and assets (e.g., a piece of land or a share of stock) can be bought or sold.

GALLERY OF ECONOMISTS: Von Mises and Marx

Ludwig von Mises (1881–1973)

Ludwig von Mises was born in Lemberg, Austria, the son of a Viennese construction engineer. He received his doctorate in law and economics from the University of Vienna and then taught at the University of Vienna from 1913 to 1934. In response to the growing Nazi influence in Austria, Mises moved to Switzerland and then to New York University, where he taught until retirement.

Mises' many contributions to economic theory made him a prime proponent of the "Austrian" school of economics, along with his student, Nobel laureate Friederich von Hayek. Mises taught that economic behavior was best understood by logically analyzing the actions of individuals rather than by studying market equilibrium. Mises' interest in prices stemmed more from their role in providing economical information to participants in the economy rather than in their equilibrium properties.

Mises was an early critic of socialism. In his classic article "Economic Calculation in the Socialist Commonwealth," published in 1922, Mises anticipated most of the modern-day problems of the planned socialist economies. He argued that planned socialist economies would lack market exchange and would hence lack the vital information provided by the price system. Without relative prices, socialist managers would lack the information to make rational economic decisions. Moreover, lacking property rights, socialist managers would not behave in an economically rational manner, but would overdemand and waste scarce resources.

The problems predicted by Mises in 1922 appear to be the very ones that caused the failure of the Communist economic system.

Karl Marx (1818–1883)

Karl Marx remains the most prominent critic of capitalism. As a newspaper editor, his calls for radical reforms led to his suppression and flight to Paris in 1843. In 1847, Marx joined the Communist League, and in 1848 he wrote the famous *Communist Manifesto*, calling for a socialist revolution based on a united worker class. Exiled from the continent, Marx lived in poverty in London. He was plagued by chronic illnesses, and several of his children died. He worked as a correspondent for the *New York Times* and received a small pension from benefactors. In 1864 he formed the International Working Men's Association (The First International), an organization that promoted international socialism and socialist revolution. Marx's views on economics and revolution are summarized in his four-volume *Das Kapital*, three volumes of which were published after his death.

Although Marx was the prophet of socialism, he said remarkably little about socialism as an economic system. He did write that a transitional period would follow the overthrow of capitalism. During this phase, called socialism, scarcity would prevail, individuals would be paid according to their contribution to production, and a strong state (the dictatorship of the proletariat) would direct the economy. As the productive capacity of the economy grew, eventually a second stage of absolute abundance, called communism, would be reached. Class conflicts would disappear, people would work for pleasure, and distribution would be according to need.

Property rights are the rights of an owner to buy, sell, or use and exchange property (i.e., goods, services and assets).

Prevailing property rights are a key determinant of the nature of the economic system.

Property Rights in a Capitalist System. In a capitalist society, most property is owned by private individuals. Adam Smith argued that if individuals are allowed to own property and to pursue their own economic self-interest, an "invisible hand" will cause them to act in the public interest. By pursuing private profits, they will produce the goods and services that people want and will offer them at prices that are reasonable compared to costs of production.

Private owners of property are motivated by self-interest to obtain the best deal possible for themselves. The legal system protects private property from theft, damage, and unauthorized use and defines where property rights reside. This legal protection ensures that owners will reap the benefits of decisions that are in their self-interest and will suffer the consequences of decisions that are not in their self-interest.

Property Rights in a Socialist System. In a socialist society, most property is owned by the state, and the state has rights to use and exchange that property. Individual ownership of property has been limited to a few head of livestock, a private home in some circumstances, a private car, a TV, and so on.

Allocation Arrangements

Resources can be allocated either by market or by plan. Capitalism is characterized by market resource allocation. Socialism is characterized by resource allocation through government decree.

Market Allocation. Market allocation is the use of relative prices to determine what, how, and for whom to produce. Private ownership and market allocation are intertwined.

An owner of private property has the right to use the property to the owner's best advantage and to sell the property at the best price possible. The actions of the owners of private property will be guided by relative prices. For example, the farmer will look at the relative prices of corn and soybeans to decide how much of each crop to plant; the private owner of an oil refinery will use the relative prices of gasoline, fuel oils, and kerosene to determine how much of each petroleum product to refine. The private owner of labor (that is, the individual worker) will look at the relative wage rates in different occupations to help determine where to seek employment.

Allocation by Plan. In planned resource allocation systems, the decisions concerning what, how, and for whom to produce are made by the government. A central authority determines output targets and makes the basic investment decisions. Industrial ministries issue output targets to enterprises and tell them what materials to use. Although planners cannot decide exactly for whom the output is produced, they play a significant role in determining who will get the scarce automobiles, apartments, and vacations.

Incentive Systems

Any economic system must provide incentives for people to work hard and to take economic risks.

Incentives in a Capitalist System. A capitalist system uses economic incentives to motivate employees. Higher salaries, bonuses, and stock options are rewards for tasks that are well done. Entrepreneurs are rewarded by having the value of their businesses grow.

Incentives in a Socialist System. A socialist system relies more heavily on moral incentives, although no economic system can afford to rely on moral incentives alone. In socialist systems, there is greater emphasis on "working for the good of society." Medals, honorary positions, and other noneconomic incentives are used to motivate workers.

THE RISE AND FALL OF COMMUNIST SOCIALISM

Marx predicted that socialism inevitably would replace capitalism because of worker exploitation and class struggle.

Karl Marx was the prophet of state ownership and government resource allocation. In Marx's judgment, economies based on private ownership and market allocation would ultimately collapse to be replaced by a new type of economy. Marx argued that Adam Smith's system was unfair to workers, who were exploited by the factory owners, and that capitalism was unstable. The exploited workers, living near subsistence, would be unable to buy goods spewed out by the prolific factories; the factory owners would increase their exploitation of workers; and large-scale economic crises would result. Eventually, the workers of the world would unite against the factory owners in a revolutionary movement that would demand a new economy based on social ownership and government command.

Marx argued that this new economy would prove superior to Adam Smith's "invisible hand." Workers would prosper, income would be fairly distributed, and work would cease to be a chore. Everyone would relish working for the public good. Scarcity would disappear; the economic problem would cease to exist.

Two historic events appeared to lend credence to Marx's predictions: the Russian Revolution in 1917 and the Great Depression. During much of the nineteenth century Russia was a hotbed of anarchistic ideas. Vladimir Lenin and then Joseph Stalin used an oppressive one-party dictatorship to eliminate private ownership and to destroy market allocation. Government planners and ministry officials replaced market allocation. Rigid labor codes dictated hours of work and pay. The price system ceased to play a real role in the economy. Prices were set arbitrarily by government officials.

During the Great Depression (starting in England and Europe in the mid-1920s and spreading to the United States with the stock market crash of 1929), aggregate output plummeted and unemployment soared. The Great Depression appeared to substantiate Marx's claim that Adam Smith's system was unstable. Workers began to look to the radical alternatives proposed by Marx, while politicians looked for solutions to preserve the existing order.

The Soviet propaganda machine provided a vivid contrast to the despair of the Great Depression. Smiling workers were shown enthusiastically building the world's largest hydroelectric dam; cheerful farmers were shown bringing in bumper crops. Soviet statisticians published reports of astonishing successes both in industry and in agriculture.

As the world divided into political blocs at the end of World War II, the Soviet system was installed in Eastern Europe and China. The one-party propaganda systems of these countries immediately began to herald astonishing economic successes. In 1957 the Soviet launching of the first manned space vehicle, *Sputnik*, added considerable weight to Nikita Khrushchev's threat to outperform the West economically.

Thirty years later, it was evident that Khrushchev's faith in socialism had been misplaced. Living standards in the Soviet Union and Eastern Europe had fallen to a small fraction of their potential. (See Exhibit 1.) Consumers were no longer content to stand in long lines for shoddy products. The technology gap between the capitalist and socialist countries had become enormous. Growth rates, which

EXHIBIT 1   Relative Efficiency: The Former Soviet Union and USA

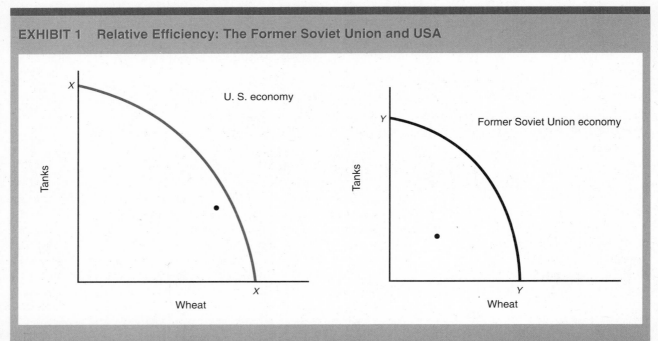

It is impossible to determine just how close an economy is to operating on its production-possibilities frontier (*PPF*). Most evidence suggests, however, that the economy of the former Soviet Union operates well below its *PPF*, while the U. S. economy operates close to its *PPF*. (Note: The U.S. economy has been drawn to have a larger resource base owing to its more advanced technology.)

had been acceptable in the 1950s and 1960s, declined steadily in the 1970s and 1980s. (See Example 1.)

In 1985 Mikhail Gorbachev, dissatisfied with the socialist system, announced his intent to restructure the Soviet economy. The economic, political, and social reforms that Gorbachev initiated permitted Eastern Europe to emerge from Soviet dominance. Democratic forces in those countries overthrew the communist political system and enacted their own dramatic economic and political reforms, which culminated with the dismantling of the Berlin Wall and the subsequent unification of Germany. The failed coup of Soviet hard-liners in August 1991 triggered the disintegration of the Soviet Union into independent countries. Almost without exception, these new countries vowed to replace their socialist economies with a market system. Only a few countries, such as Cuba, North Korea, and China, had leaders in favor of keeping the socialist system.

REASONS FOR FAILURE

The Communist economic system failed for a number of reasons.

Incentives and Information

For an economy to operate on its *PPF*, its participants must be properly motivated and informed. If they lack motivation or information, they will be unable to use their resources to best advantage. The failure of the administrative-command economy can be traced to motivation and information problems.

EXAMPLE 1

Soviet Productivity and the Origins of Perestroika

Long-term observers of the Soviet economy were caught off guard in March 1985 when Mikhail Gorbachev announced his intent to radically reform the Soviet economy. Press censorship was reduced; a free press emerged; the people were allowed to elect a parliament and then directly elect the presidents of the various republics and mayors of major cities. Although Gorbachev was undoubtedly unaware of the consequences of his actions (the August 1991 coup, and the collapse of the Communist Party, and the end of the Soviet Union), he set into motion a process that could not be reversed. Why was Gorbachev willing to take such a dramatic and bold step in 1985?

The Soviet leadership had always been concerned about economic performance, which was broadly measured by productivity. Productivity growth is indicated by expansion of the production-possibilities frontier (*PPF*) and is measured by comparing the growth of factor inputs with the growth of output. If output has grown by 10 percent and inputs have grown by 3 percent, productivity has grown by 7 percent.

The accompanying table shows the dismal record of Soviet productivity growth from 1966 to 1985. In 1976 Soviet output began to grow less rapidly than factor inputs. From 1976 to 1980, output grew at an annual rate of 2.2 percent while factor inputs grew at 3.9 percent annually. In effect, the Soviet *PPF* was shrinking.

Gorbachev referred to the period from 1970 to 1985 as the "period of stagnation." The productivity growth during this period indicated there was a drastic need for restructuring. An economy that produces far below its *PPF* cannot survive.

Soviet Productivity Growth (annual rates of growth)

Years	Output	Factor Inputs	Productivity
1966–70	6.0	5.6	0.4
1971–75	5.3	5.0	0.3
1976–80	2.2	3.9	−1.7
1981–85	1.9	3.0	−1.1

Source: *Handbook of Economic Statistics*, 1990, p. 66.

The Incentive of Property. In a capitalist economy, the private owners of capital seek out the best profit opportunities for their capital and economize on their use of resources. If they need to hire a professional staff of managers, they can devise a reward system that encourages efficient use of resources. In an administrative-command economy, capital is owned by the state—by everyone and hence by no one. If no one owns the capital resources, there is no incentive for the state enterprise manager to innovate or increase productivity.

Managerial Rewards. In administrative-command economies, rewards must be determined according to objective standards. The manager must be rewarded on the basis of how well he or she meets the enterprise "plan." Because the plan is made up of a large number of tasks—how much to produce, what assortments, what costs, that new equipment, and so on—planners must focus on one or two measurable targets. Usually those are targets that are important to the planners themselves, such as the volume of output. Enterprise managers, therefore, have typically been rewarded on the basis of how close they come to fulfilling the state's output targets.

Basing managerial rewards on output leads to two important incentive problems. First, managers can more easily fulfill output targets by sacrificing quality or assortment. The shoe manufacturer will mass produce only one type of shoe style because the enterprise has been told to produce 10,000 pairs of shoes per month. The construction firm will rely on gravity in place of mortar, thereby producing apartments that collapse during earthquakes. The oil-well-drilling company, instructed to drill 10 wells per month, will select easy drilling terrain even though it will yield no oil.

Second, enterprise managers will also be tempted to conceal capacity from their superiors. The managers' lives are easy when their output targets can be fulfilled using 60 percent of the enterprise's capacity. Hence the manager will try to persuade superiors that the enterprise can only produce a maximum of 10,000 pairs of shoes per month instead of the 15,000 pairs it can realistically produce. The manager knows that if the enterprise overfulfills the plan (and reveals its true capacity), it may gain temporary bonuses, but the enterprise will be subject to more ambitious plan targets in the future.

Information Problems.   The price system provides invaluable information on opportunity costs. In market economies, such costs are the basis for resource allocation decisions. When the price system indicates that a previously used material has become too expensive relative to new materials, the manufacturer will seek out substitutions. A shoe manufacturer will switch from one shoe fashion to another when the old brand can only be sold at a substantial discount.

The administrative-command economy does not use the price system to make allocation decisions. If there is "too little" of one resource, its relative price does not rise. Rather, an administration official calls users of the resource to make sure they use less.

The early critics of socialism argued that the lack of information on opportunity costs would prove fatal. Without markets to determine relative prices, no one in the economy knows what things are worth. If the manager does not know whether aluminum, composite plastics, or ceramics are "cheap," that manager cannot make a rational decision on what material to use. If the manager does not know what goods buyers want (as reflected in a high price), the manager cannot produce those goods.

Moreover, planners do not have as much information about local production conditions as managers do. The enterprise managers may even gain by concealing information from their superiors or by providing them with false information. Therefore, planned socialism often operates on the basis of inadequate or even false information.

Inherent Shortage.   The planned socialist economies are plagued with shortages: people stand in line for goods; enterprise managers cannot find the materials they need. Although it may appear that these shortages are a result of planners ordering incorrectly, such shortages may be inherent in these economies.

The Hungarian economist Janos Kornai has argued that the administrative-command economy automatically generates shortages because enterprises lack the incentive to use resources economically. Enterprises are judged on their ability to produce outputs, not on their ability to make a profit. Planners, reluctant to let their enterprises fail even when they are losing money, do not hesitate to use subsidies to bail them out. This lack of budget discipline, which Kornai calls "soft budget constraint," leaves enterprises unrestrained in their demands for resources. This drive to stockpile resources causes all goods to be in short supply. Everyone is chasing resources, but few succeed in getting what they want.

How Can the West Best Help Russia's Transition?

It is clear that the Western world has a great stake in the success of the Russian transition to a market economic system. A successful transition will bring economic and political stability to an intensely troubled region in which thousands of nuclear warheads aimed at Western targets are still located. Moreover, a successful transition will make the reemergence of the Communist Party even more unlikely. The amount of money the West could save from the permanent end of the Cold War is minuscule compared to the amount of assistance needed by Russia for its transition.

How, then, should the West go about helping Russia and the other republics of the former Soviet Union? In order to create a market economy in Russia, a number of events must occur. Prices have to be determined by markets and not by administrative decrees; property rights have to be assigned; the legal framework for a market economy has to be established; and enterprises must be allowed to make their own decisions, even if that means going bankrupt.

The Russian transition must overcome immense obstacles. It must establish a market economy during a period of severe disruptions. An economy geared to producing for defense and heavy industry must shift to the production of consumer goods. Many large factories cannot survive in a competitive environment; they must be allowed to go under. Existing channels of supply based on administrative means must be replaced by normal market relations.

The West must combine financial and technical assistance to help with this difficult transition. Technical assistance is required to permit the Russians to create the institutions of a market economy, such as a legal framework and a normal banking and currency system. Financial assistance must be aimed not at propping up the old system (for example, keeping uneconomical factories afloat) but at investing in enterprises that can survive in a competitive environment.

Although the temptation may be strong to provide financial assistance to ease the transition, the West must be wary in giving assistance that simply allows the Russians to delay the transition to a market economy. For example, if Western financial assistance is used primarily to preserve unprofitable industries or to hold prices at artificially low levels, the West will simply have succeeded in delaying reform, not in assisting reform.

Transition to a Market Economy

Restructuring the administrative-command economy will not be easy. There is no precedent for dismantling a socialist economy.

Immense economic and political problems must be solved if the transition to a market economy is to be successful. The administrative-command economy created large enterprises and whole industries that have been operated inefficiently and that have produced products that no one wants. These enterprises cannot survive in a market environment, yet a large proportion of the work force is employed in such industries. For example, Russian enterprises that produce low-quality, reinforced concrete will not survive in a market economy; however, the demise of such enterprises has a high price in terms of jobs, with such industries employing more than 100,000 workers.

Defining property rights is another problem that must be solved before the transition to a market economy can be made. In the administrative-command economy, the slogan was, "Property belongs to everyone and hence to no one." A market economy cannot operate under this assumption. Property rights must be defined, but it will be an extremely difficult economic and political task. How it is done determines who will be rich and who will be poor.

Market economies developed their economic laws, customs, and institutions over centuries. The administrative-command economies have operated for over 60 years without laws and institutions that are supportive of market allocation. To make the transition, new laws must be put in place and modern economic institutions (such as a modern banking system) must be established. These things will not be accomplished quickly.

The transition alternatives are shock therapy and a go-slow approach.

In those countries such as Poland that have opted for a quick transition from socialism to capitalism—a shock therapy treatment—the costs of transition have been high. Inflation has soared, output has fallen, and unemployment has risen. There is evidence, however, from the Polish experience with shock therapy that inflation stabilizes rather quickly and that stores fill up with goods. The major problem has been dealing with inefficient state enterprises that account for most of the employment. It is considered too costly to close them down. Countries that have opted for a slow transition, such as the Soviet Union prior to the August 1991 coup, faced growing stagnation as they were caught in a no-man's-land between planned socialism and market resource allocation. Inflationary pressures grew, output stagnated, consumers and workers became more disenchanted, and corruption grew.

Chapter Summary

The main point of this chapter is:
Fatal internal flaws have forced the leadership of the former Soviet Union to abandon the communist economic system and to attempt the transition to a market economy.

1. Economic systems are characterized by property-rights arrangements, resource-allocation methods, and incentive systems. Capitalism is characterized by private property rights, market allocation, and economic incentives. Socialism is characterized by public ownership, government allocation, and moral incentives.

2. Marx argued that capitalism had fatal flaws and that a new and superior type of economy, called socialism, would inevitably replace it.

3. The inefficiencies of the Soviet economy related to property and incentive problems, a faulty system of managerial rewards, and information problems. The administrative-command economy also appeared to generate shortages.

4. The inefficiency of the socialist economy has prompted a search for ways to transform it into a market economy. No one knows the best way to convert an administrative-command economy into a market economy.

Policy Focus: **The west must provide financial and technical assistance for the transition in such a manner as to create market institutions. Assistance should not be used to prop up the old system and delay reform.**

Key Terms

economic system (p. 630)
capitalism (p. 630)

socialism (p. 630)
property rights (p. 630)

Questions and Problems

1. Imagine first that you are the owner of a small business, and then, in contrast, that you are the manager of a state-owned enterprise. Would you behave differently in these two situations? Why?

2. You are the manager of a state-owned factory that produces light bulbs. You are judged on the basis of how close you come to fulfilling the state's target for light bulb production. Explain how you might ensure that you can fulfill your light bulb production quota.

3. Explain why the Soviet economy operated well below its potential as defined by its resource base.

4. Economists argue that property rights and incentives are closely related. Explain why this relationship exists.

5. In socialist economies, a common complaint is: "Everyone owns capital and no one owns capital." Explain what this means and how this might affect economic activity.

6. Consider how the lack of price information in the administrative-command economy may complicate economic decision making.

7. Explain why a lack of budget discipline at the enterprise level can lead to persistent shortages in the administrative-command economy.

8. Explain how capitalism differs from socialism in terms of the four characteristics of an economic system.

Doing Economics

In some ways, the internal operation of most colleges and universities resembles a socialist economy. Resources are allocated centrally; broad decisions about what products are offered are made by centralized committees; prices are controlled (and usually uniform across courses) without regard to scarcity; production targets of individual departments are set by the central authority. In what ways are the problems that caused the demise of modern socialist economies present in institutions of higher education? Are there any market signals that are used to guide decision-making? How would a "capitalist" university work? Do you think that resource allocation would be better or worse? Would students be better off or worse off? How about faculty?

absolute advantage is possessed by a country in the production of a good if it uses fewer resources to produce a unit of the good than any other country (16).

absolute poverty standard establishes a specific income level for a given-sized household below which the household is judged to be living in a state of poverty (31).

accounting cost see **explicit cost**.

activist policy is one that selects monetary- and fiscal-policy actions on the basis of perceived economic conditions and that changes as economic conditions change (14).

AD see **aggregate demand (AD)**.

adaptive expectations are expectations of the future that people form from past experience and only gradually modify as experience unfolds (13).

advantage see **absolute advantage, law of comparative advantage**.

AE see **aggregate expenditures**.

agent is a party that acts for, on behalf of, or as a representative of a principal (20).

aggregate demand (AD) is a schedule that shows the aggregate quantities of real goods and services demanded at different price levels, holding all other factors constant (7).

aggregate expenditures (AE) are a schedule that shows the relationship between the desired amount of total spending $(C+I+G+X-M)$ and income (8).

aggregate supply (AS) is a schedule of various quantities of goods and services businesses are prepared to supply at different price levels (7); see also **short-run aggregate supply (SRAS)**.

antitrust legislation is the legislation that controls market structure and conduct (25).

AS as **aggregate supply (AS)**.

assets are anything of any value that is owned (11).

auction market is a market in which the market price is renegotiated on a regular basis (14).

automatic stabilizers are government-spending or taxation actions that take place without any deliberate government control and that tend automatically to dampen the business cycle (9).

autonomous changes in taxes and government spending are changes in tax rates or government spending that are independent of changes in income (9).

average cost see **long-run average cost (LRAC)**.

average fixed cost (AFC) is fixed cost divided by output:
$$AFC = FC \div Q \qquad (21).$$

average total cost (ATC) is total cost divided by output, or the sum of average variable cost and average fixed cost:
$$ATC = TC \div Q = AVC + AFC \qquad (21).$$

average variable cost (AVC) is variable cost divided by output:
$$AVC = VC \div Q \qquad (21).$$

balance of payments is a summary record of a country's economic transactions with foreign residents over a year or any other period (17).

balance sheet summarizes the current financial position of a firm by comparing the firm's *assets* and *liabilities* (11).

bank money is a deposit in checking accounts (10).

bankrupt the condition of a corporation that cannot pay its bills or its interest obligations (20A).

bargaining see **collective bargaining**.

basket see **currency basket**.

behavior see **monopoly-profit-seeking behavior, opportunistic behavior**.

benefits see **social benefits**.

bonds are obligations that bind the corporation to pay a fixed sum of money (the principal) at maturity and also to pay a fixed sum of money annually until the maturity date. This fixed annual payment is called *interest*, or the *coupon payment* (20A).

budget line is all the combinations of goods the consumer is able to buy given a certain income and set prices. The budget line shows the consumption possibilities available to the consumer (19A).

business cycle is the pattern of upward and downward movements in the general level of real business activity (5).

capital good see **rate of return on capital**.

capitalism is an economic system characterized by private ownership of the factors of production, market allocation of resources, the use of economic incentives, and decentralized decision making (1,33).

capitalist society is characterized by private ownership of property and by market allocation of resources (3).

capital productivity measures output per unit of capital input (15).

cartel is an arrangement that allows the participating firms to operate the industry as a shared monopoly. In effect, the participating firms coordinate their output and pricing decisions to yield that industry price and output combination that would have prevailed had this industry been a pure monopoly with each firm as a branch of one giant firm **(24)**.

cash leakage occurs when a recipient of a check converts it into cash rather than depositing it in a checking account. This cash remains in circulation outside of the banking system **(11)**.

cash market see **spot (cash) market**.

ceteris paribus is an assumption that considers the effects of change in one factor assuming that all other relevant factors remain the same **(1)**.

changes see **autonomous changes**.

check is a directive to the check writer's bank to pay lawful money to the bearer of the check **(10)**.

circular-flow diagram summarizes the flows of goods and services from producers to households and the flows of the factors of production from households to business firms **(2)**.

circulation see **velocity of circulation**.

clearing price see **equilibrium (market-clearing) price**.

collective bargaining is the process whereby the union bargains with management as the representative of all union employees **(29)**.

commercial banks are banks that have been chartered either by a state agency or by the U.S. Treasury's Comptroller of the Currency to make loans and receive deposits **(11)**.

commodity money is money whose value as a commodity is as great as its value as money **(10)**.

comparative advantage see **law of comparative advantage**.

compensating wage differentials are the higher rewards (wages or fringe benefits) that must be paid workers to compensate them for undesirable job characteristics **(28)**.

competition see **nonprice competition, perfect competition**.

competitive market see **perfectly competitive market**.

complements are two goods related in such a way that the demand for one rises of the price of the other falls (or the demand for one falls if the price of the other rises) **(3)**.

concentration ratio is the percentage of industry sales (or output, or labor force, or assets) accounted for by the x largest firms **(24)**.

conglomerate merger occurs when one company takes over another company in a different line of business **(25)**.

conscious parallelism is the process through which the actions of producers can be coordinated within certain ranges without formal or even informal agreements. All oligopolists use their understanding of the industry to make their own decisions and may anticipate the behavior of other oligopolists **(24)**.

constant-cost industry is relatively small and, hence, can expand or contract without significantly affecting the terms at which factors of production used in the industry are purchased. The long-run industry supply curve for a constant-cost industry is horizontal **(22)**.

constant-monetary-growth rule is that the money supply should increase at a fixed percentage each year **(12)**.

constant returns to scale are present when a given percent change in inputs results in the same percent change in output **(21)**.

consumer equilibrium occurs when the consumer has spent all income and marginal utilities per dollar are equal on each good purchased $(MU_A/P_A = MU_B/P_B)$. At this point, the consumer is not inclined to change purchases unless some other factor (such as prices, income, or preferences) changes **(19)**.

consumption/income schedule shows the amount of desired consumption at different levels of national income or output **(8)**.

contractionary fiscal policy lowers aggregate demand by lowering autonomous government spending or by autonomously raising taxes **(9)**.

contrived scarcity is the production of less than the economically efficient quantity of a good by a monopoly **(23)**.

corporation is a form of business enterprise that is owned by a number of stockholders. The corporation has the legal status of a fictional individual and is authorized by law to act as a single person. The stockholders elect a board of directors that appoints the management of the corporation, usually headed by a president. Management is charged with the actual operation of the corporation **(20)**.

cost see **average variable cost (AVC), average total cost (ATC), average fixed cost (AFC), explicit cost, implicit cost, information cost, long-run average cost (LRAC), opportunity cost, transaction cost**.

cost industry see **constant-cost industry, increasing-cost industry**.

costs see **fixed costs (FC), social costs, transaction cost, variable costs (VC), waste-disposal costs**.

craft union is a union that represents workers of a single occupation **(29)**.

credit markets are markets for borrowing and lending funds **(30)**.

cross-piece elasticity of demand (E_{xy}) is the percentage change in demand of the first product (x) divided by the percentage change in the price of the related product (y) **(18)**.

crowding out occurs when an increase in government spending causes a reduction in investment spending due to higher interest rates or a reduction in consumption. Spending due to substitutions of public for private spending **(9)**.

currency basket is simply a bundle of currencies such as 2 French francs, 1 German mark, 400 Japanese yen. The dollar, on the average, depreciates if this currency basket becomes more expensive and appreciates if this currency basket becomes less expensive **(17)**.

cycle see **business cycle**.

cyclical deficit is that part of the deficit that is caused by movements in the business cycle **(9)**.

cyclical unemployment is unemployment associated with general downturns in the economy **(5)**.

deficit see **cyclical deficit, full-employment deficit, structural deficit, trade deficit**.

deflation is a general decline in prices **(5)**.

deflationary gap exists if the equilibrium level of output falls short of the natural level of output **(7)**.

demand see **aggregate demand (AD), law of demand**.

demand curve or **schedule** for a good shows the various quantities demanded at different prices, holding other factors constant, over a specified time period **(3)**; see also **kinked-demand curve, market-demand curve**.

demanded see **quantity demanded**.

demand-side inflation occurs when the amount of money purchasers of goods and services want to spend increases more rapidly than the supply of such goods and services, resulting in the bidding up of prices (5); occurs when aggregate demand increases and pulls prices up (13).

demographic transition is the process by which countries change from rapid population growth to slow population growth as they modernize (15).

dependent variable is the variable that changes as a result of a change in the value of another variable (1A).

deposit multiplier is the ratio of the change in total deposits to the change in reserves (11).

depreciation is the value of the existing capital stock that has been consumed or used up in the process of producing output. Depreciation includes not only the physical wear and tear on capital goods but also the loss of value resulting from the obsolescence of old capital (6).

derived demand is the demand for a factor of production that results (is derived) from the demand for the goods and services a factor of production helps produce (27).

diagram see **circular-flow diagram, scatter diagram**.

differentials see **compensating wage differentials**.

dilemma see **prisoners' dilemma game**.

diminishing marginal rate of substitution see **law of diminishing marginal rate of substitution**.

diminishing returns see **law of diminishing returns**.

direct relationship see **positive relationship**.

discretionary fiscal policy is a government spending and taxation action that has been deliberately taken to achieve specified macroeconomic goals (9).

discrimination see **price discrimination**.

diseconomies of scale are present when a given percentage change in inputs leads to a smaller percentage change in output (21).

disposal costs see **waste-disposal costs**.

dissaving—total saving is negative—occurs in an economy when consumption spending exceeds disposable income. The economy is either increasing its indebtedness or financing consumption by drawing down its savings (8).

distortion see **growth distortion, inflation distortion**.

distribution of income see **functional distribution of income, personal distribution of income**.

distributive justice is present when society's resources are distributed fairly among the members of society (31).

earnings (P/E) ratio see **price/earnings (P/E) ratio**.

earnings per share (EPS) is the annual profit of the corporation divided by the number of shares outstanding (20A).

economic efficiency is present when society's resources are so organized that it is impossible to make everyone better off by *any* reallocation of resources; in other words, making one person better off must be at the expense of someone else (23).

economic growth is an increase from one period to the next in real GDP; an increase from one period to the next in real GDP per capita, which is real GDP divided by the country's population (15).

economic problem is how to allocate scarce resources among competing ends (2).

economic profits are the excess of revenues over total opportunity costs (21).

economic rent is the excess of the payment to the factor over its opportunity cost (30); see also **pure economic rent**.

economics is the study of how a society chooses to use its limited resources (land, labor, and capital goods) to produce, exchange, and consume goods and services; the study of how *scarce resources* are *allocated* among *competing ends* (1); see also **positive economics**.

economic system is the set of organizational arrangements and institutions that are established to solve the economic problem (1,33).

economies of scale are present in the production process when large output volumes can be produced at a lower cost per unit than small output volumes (2); are present when a given percentage change in input leads to a larger percentage change in output (21).

effect see **income effect, interest-rate effect, real-balance effect, substitution effect**.

effectiveness lag is the time it takes the change in the money supply to affect the economy (12).

efficiency results when no resources are unemployed and when no resources are misallocated (1).

efficient stock market hypothesis states that stock prices are determined by the information currently available on the present and future earnings of corporations. Changes in stock prices are due to changes in the information available on present and future earnings of corporations (20A).

elastic demand see **perfectly elastic demand**.

elasticity of demand see **cross-price elasticity of demand (E_{xy}), income elasticity of demand (E_i), price elasticity of demand (E_d)**.

elasticity of supply see **price elasticity of supply (E_s)**.

elastic supply see **perfectly elastic supply**.

employee association is an organization that represents employees in a particular profession (29).

employment trade-off see **wage/employment trade-off**.

entitlement program requires the federal government to pay benefits to any person or unit of government that meets the eligibility requirements stated in the entitlement legislation (9).

equilibrium (market-clearing) price of a good or service is that price at which the amount people are prepared to buy equals the amount offered for sale (2); the price at which the quantity demanded by consumers equals the quantity supplied by producers (3).

excess reserves are reserves in excess of required reserves. Excess reserves equal total reserves minus required reserves (11).

exchange see **foreign exchange**.

exchange rate see **floating exchange rate, fixed exchange rate**.

exhaustive expenditures are government purchases of goods and services that divert real economic resources from the private sector, making them no longer available for private use (4).

expansion see **multiple-deposit expansion**.

expansionary fiscal policy increases aggregate demand by raising autonomous government spending and or by autonomously lowering taxes (9).

expectations see **adaptive expectations, rational expectations**.

expenditures see **aggregate expenditures (AE)**.

explicit cost (also called an *accounting cost*) is incurred when an actual payment is made (21).

export promotion occurs when a country encourages exports by subsidizing the production of goods for export (15).

export restraint see **voluntary export restraint**.

extensive growth is economic growth that results from the expansion of factor inputs (15).

externalities are present when private parties do not bear the full marginal cost or enjoy the full marginal benefit of an economic action. A part of the costs (or benefits) is borne by third parties (4).

factor productivity increases when more output is produced per unit of factor input (15).

factors of production are the resources used to produce goods and services; they can be divided into three categories—land, labor, and capital (1).

fiat money is money whose value or cost as a commodity is less than its value as money (10).

final goods are goods that are not used up in the production of other goods in the current period (6).

financial intermediaries borrow funds from one group of economic agents (people or firms with savings) and lend to other agents (11).

fiscal policies see **discretionary fiscal policy**.

fiscal policy is the deliberate control of government spending and taxation to pursue macroeconomic goals (9); see also **contractionary fiscal policy, expansionary fiscal policy**.

fixed cost see **average fixed cost (AFC)**.

fixed costs (FC) are those costs that do not vary with output (21).

fixed exchange rate is an exchange rate that is set by government decree or intervention within a small range of variation (17).

fixed investment is the addition of new plants, equipment, commercial buildings, and residential structures (6).

floating exchange rate is an exchange rate that is freely determined by the interaction of supply and demand (17).

flow diagram see **circular-flow diagram**.

foreign exchange is the national currency of another country that is needed to carry out international transactions. Normally, foreign exchange consists of bank deposits denominated in the foreign currency but may sometimes consist of foreign paper money when foreign travel is involved (17).

free rider is anyone who enjoys the benefits of a good or service without paying the cost (32).

free trade is international trade unimpeded by artificial barriers, such as tariffs (import taxes) or import quotas (16).

frictional unemployment is the unemployment associated with the changing of jobs in a dynamic economy (5).

frontier see **production-possibilities frontier**.

full-employment deficit or **surplus** is what the government budget surplus or deficit would have been had the economy been operating at the natural level of real GDP (full employment) (9).

functional distribution of income is the distribution of income among the four broad classes of productive factors—land, labor, capital, and entrepreneurship (27).

futures market is one where a buyer and seller agree now on the price of a commodity to be delivered at some specified date in the future (26).

gap see **deflationary gap, GDP gap, inflationary gap**.

GNI see **gross national income**.

GDP see **nominal GDP, real GDP**.

GDP gap is the difference between current GDP and *potential GDP* (the output the economy would conceivably have produced at full employment) and is a measure of social costs of unemployed resources (14).

"GDP in constant dollars" see **real GDP**.

"GDP in current dollars" see **nominal GDP**.

goods see **inferior goods, normal goods, public goods**.

government debt is the cumulated sum of outstanding IOUs that the government unit owes it creditors (4).

government deficit is an excess of government outlays over government revenues (4,9).

government surplus is an excess of government revenues over government outlays (4,9).

Gresham's Law states that *bad money drives out good*. When depreciated, mutilated, or debased currency is circulated along with money of high value, the good money will disappear from circulation; only the bad money will remain in circulation (10).

gross domestic income (GDI) is the sum of all factor incomes. Because GDP equals GDI, GDP can also be calculated by adding together all income earned from labor, land, capital, and entrepreneurship in the course of one year's time (6).

gross domestic product (GDP) is the market value of all final goods and services produced by an economy in one year's time (6).

groups see **noncompeting groups**.

growth see **economic growth, extensive growth, intensive growth**.

growth distortion is the measurement of changes in a variable over time that does not reflect the concurrent change in other relevant variables with which the variable should be compared, such as population size (1A).

growth rule see **constant-monetary-growth rule**.

horizontal merger is a merger of two firms in the same line of business (such as an insurance company merging with another insurance company or a shoe manufacturer merging with another shoe manufacturer (25).

household production is work in the home, including such activities as meal preparation, do-it-yourself repair, child rearing, and cleaning (28).

human capital investment is the expenditure of resources on schooling, health, and training (31).

human-resource policy is the use of government training programs, unemployment services, and unemployment-insurance programs to lower the natural rate of unemployment over the long run (13).

immediate run is a period of time so short that the quantity supplied cannot be changed at all. In the immediate run—sometimes called the *momentary period* or *market period*—supply curves are perfectly inelastic (18).

implicit cost is incurred when an alternative is sacrificed but no actual payment appears to be made (21).

import quota is a quantitative limitation on the amount of imports of a specific product during a given period (16).

import substitution occurs when a country substitutes domestic production for imports by subsidizing domestic production through traffic, quotas, and other devices (15).

incidence of a tax is the actual distribution of the burden of tax payment (4).

income see **functional distribution of income, in-kind income, national income, personal income, personal disposable income, personal distribution of income**.

income accounting see **national-income accounting**.

income effect is the change in the quantity of X demanded that is attributable to the welfare change that accompanies the price change (19).

income elasticity of demand (E_i) is the percentage change in the demand for a product divided by the percentage change in income *holding all prices fixed* **(18)**.

income tax see **negative income tax *(NIT)***.

increasing-cost industry is one in which, when the industry expands, the factor prices of resources used in the industry are bid up. As the number of firms in the industry contracts, the prices of these factors fall. Hence, the long-run industry supply curve for an increasing-cost industry is upward-sloping **(22)**.

independent variable is the variable that causes the change in the value of the dependent variable **(1A)**.

index see **stock-price index**.

indifference curve shows all the alternative combinations of two goods that yield the same total satisfaction to a particular consumer and among which the consumer is indifferent **(19A)**.

industrial union is a union that represents employees of an industry or a firm regardless of their specific occupation **(29)**.

industry see **constant-cost industry, increasing-cost industry**.

industry-supply curve see **long-run industry-supply curve**.

inelastic demand see **perfectly inelastic demand**.

inelastic supply see **perfectly inelastic supply**.

inferior goods are those for which demand falls as income increases, holding all prices constant **(3)**.

inflation is a general increase in prices **(5)**; see also **demand-side inflation, supply-side inflation**.

inflationary gap exists if the equilibrium level of output exceeds the natural level of output **(7)**.

inflation distortion is the measurement of the dollar value of a variable over time without adjustment for the inflation rate over that period **(1A)**.

information cost is the cost of acquiring information on prices, product qualities, and product performance **(2)**.

in-kind income consists primarily of benefits—such as free public education, school-lunch programs, public housing, or food stamps—for which the recipient is not required to pay **(31)**.

instruments see **policy instruments**.

intensive growth is growth that results from increases in output per unit of factor input **(15)**.

interest is the price of credit. Interest is set where the amount businesses wish to invest is balanced with the amount people are prepared to save **(30)**.

interest rate measures the yearly cost of borrowing as a percent of the amount loaned **(30)**.

interest-rate effect occurs when desired investment increases as price-level changes alter credit conditions for a given nominal money supply. When the price level rises, interest rates rise and discourage investment spending; when the price level falls, interest rates fall and encourage investment spending **(7)**.

interest-rate target is a rate of interest that the Fed seeks to achieve through monetary policy **(12)**.

intermediaries buy in order to sell again or simply to bring together a buyer and a seller **(20)**.

intermediate goods are goods that are completely used up in the production of another good. The value of the intermediate products is reflected in the price of the final goods **(6)**.

internalization is the process of putting private price tags on externalities **(32)**.

inventory investment is the increase (or decrease) in the

value of the stocks of inventories that businesses have on hand **(8)**.

inverse relationship see **negative (or inverse) relationship**.

investment see **fixed investment, inventory investment, unintended investment**.

investment-demand curve shows the amount of investment desired at different interest rates **(8)**.

Keynesian equilibrium is attained at that output at which desired investment equals desired saving **(8)**.

kinked-demand curve results when other firms match a firm's price decreases but don't match the firm's price increases **(24)**.

labor force equals the number of employed plus the number unemployed **(5)**.

labor productivity measures output per unit (usually per hour) of labor input **(15)**.

labor shortage occurs when the number of workers firms wish to hire at the prevailing wage rate exceeds the number willing to work at that wage rate **(28)**.

labor surplus occurs when the number of workers willing to work at the prevailing wage rate exceeds the number firms wish to employ at that wage rate **(28)**.

labor union is a collective organization of workers and employees whose objective is to improve conditions of pay and work **(29)**.

lag see **effectiveness lag, recognition lag, regulatory lag**.

laissez-faire means a hands-off government policy toward the economy. Government intervention in macroeconomic affairs should be strictly limited **(7)**.

law of comparative advantage states that it is better for people to specialize in those activities in which their advantages over other people are greatest or in which their disadvantages compared to others are the smallest **(2)**; the law of comparative advantage states that people or countries specialize in those activities in which they have the greatest advantage or the least disadvantage compared to other people or countries **(16)**.

law of demand states that there is a negative (or inverse) relationship between the price of a good and the quantity demanded, holding other factors constant **(3)**.

law of diminishing marginal rate of substitution is that as more of one good (A) is consumed, the amount of the other good (B) that the consumer is willing to sacrifice for one more unit of good A declines **(19A)**.

law of diminishing marginal utility states that as more of a good or service is consumed during any given time period, its marginal utility declines, holding the consumption of everything else constant **(19)**.

law of diminishing returns states that as ever larger quantities of a variable factor are combined with fixed amounts of the firm's other factors, the marginal physical product of the variable factor will eventually decline **(21)**.

law of increasing costs states that as more of a particular commodity is produced, its opportunity cost per unit will increase **(2)**.

law of scarcity states that the wants of every society exceed its ability to satisfy those wants **(1)**.

leader see **price leader**.

leakage see **cash leakage**.

leisure is time spent in any activity other than work in the labor force or work in the home **(6)**.

less developed country *(LDC)* is a country that has yet to reach a reasonably high level of economic development **(15)**.

level of economic development of a country is measured by its per capita GDP, its industrial structure, its population dynamics, and the health and education of the population (15).

liabilities are anything owed to other economic agents (11).

line see **budget line**.

liquidity-preference theory states that the opportunity cost of holding money—a completely liquid asset—is the interest sacrificed, and the interest rate is determined by the supply of and demand for money (12).

long run is a period of time long enough for new firms to enter the market, for old firms to disappear, and for existing plants to be expanded. In the long run, firms have more flexibility in adjusting to price changes (18); a period of time long enough to vary all inputs (21).

long-run average cost (LRAC) consists of the minimum average cost for each level of output when all factor inputs are variable and when factor prices and the state of technology are fixed (21).

long-run industry-supply curve shows the quantities that the industry is prepared to supply at different prices *after* the entry or exit of firms is completed (22).

Lorenz curve shows the percentage of all income earned by households at successive income levels. The cumulative share of households (ranked from lowest to highest incomes) is plotted on the horizontal axis of the Lorenz curve, and the cumulative share of income earned by the cumulative percent of households is plotted on the vertical axis (31).

luxuries are those products that have an income elasticity of demand greater than 1 (18).

M1 is the sum of currency (paper money and coins), demand deposits at commercial banks held by the nonbanking public, travelers' checks, and other checkable deposits like NOW (negotiable order of withdrawal) accounts and ATS (automatic transfer services) accounts (10).

M2 equals M1 *plus* savings and small time deposits plus money-market mutual-fund shares plus other highly liquid assets (10).

macroeconomic equilibrium see **short-run macroeconomic equilibrium**.

macroeconomics is the study of the economy in the large. Rather than dealing with individual markets and individual consumers and producers, macroeconomics examines the economy as a whole (1).

marginal analysis aids decision making by examining the consequences of making relatively small changes from the current state of affairs (4).

marginal cost (MC) is the addition to total cost (or equivalently to variable cost) of producing one more unit of output:

$$MC = \frac{\Delta TC}{\Delta Q} = \frac{\Delta VC}{\Delta Q} \qquad (21).$$

marginal factor cost (MFC) is the extra cost to the firm of using one more unit of a factor of production (27).

marginal physical product (MPP) of a factor of production is the increase in output per period that results from increasing the factor by one unit, holding all other inputs and the level of technology fixed (21).

marginal-productivity theory of income distribution states that the functional distribution of income between land, labor, and capital is determined by the relative marginal revenue product of that factor (27).

marginal propensity to consume (MPC) is the change in desired consumption *(C)* per $1 change in income *(Y)* of $1: $MPC = \Delta C / \Delta Y$ (8).

marginal propensity to save (MPS) is the change in desired saving *(S)* per $1 change in income *(Y)* of $1: $MPS = \Delta S / \Delta Y$ (8).

marginal rate of substitution (MRS) is how much of one good a person is just willing to give up to acquire one unit of another (19A); see also **law of diminishing marginal rate of substitution**.

marginal revenue (MR) is the increase in total revenue *(TR)* that results from each one-unit increase in the amount of output:

$$MC = \frac{\Delta TR}{\Delta Q}$$

(22); the additional revenue raised per unit increase in quantity sold (23).

marginal revenue curve shows how much marginal revenue is at each level of output (23).

marginal revenue product (MRP) of any factor of production is the extra revenue generated by increasing the factor by one unit (27).

marginal utility (MU) of any good or service is the increase in utility that a consumer experiences when consumption of that good or service (and that good or service alone) is increased by one unit. In general,

$$MU = \frac{\Delta TU}{\Delta Q},$$

where *TU* is total utility and *Q* is the quantity of the good (19).

marginal utility per dollar is the ratio *MU/P* and indicates the increase in utility from another dollar spent on the good (19).

market is an established arrangement by which buyers and sellers come together to exchange particular goods or services (3); see also **auction market, futures market, perfectly competitive market, spot (cash) market**.

market-clearing price see **equilibrium price**.

market-demand curve is the demand curve of all persons participating in the market for that particular product (3); the total quantities demanded by all consumers in the market at each price. It is the horizontal summation of all individual demand curves in that market (19).

market failure occurs when the price system fails to produce the quantity of a good that would be socially optimal (32).

market operations see **open-market operations**.

market period see **immediate run**.

markets see **credit markets**.

market test is the process that ensures that goods and services in the private sector yield a benefit equal to or greater than their cost (4).

material balance planning is a system of resource allocation in which centralized planning controls the output levels of the most important industrial commodities (18).

maximization see **profit maximization**.

maximization rule see **profit-maximization rule**.

mercantilist fallacy is that exporting is better than importing (17).

merger see **conglomerate merger, horizontal merger, vertical merger**.

microeconomics studies the economic decision making of firms and individuals in markets; it is the study of the economy of the small (1).

midpoints formula for determining the elasticity of demand *(E_d)* for a given segment of the demand curve is:

$$E_d = \frac{\text{Percent Change in Quantity Demanded}}{\text{Percent Change in Price}}$$
$$= \frac{\dfrac{\text{Change in Quantity Demanded}}{\text{Average of Two Quantities}}}{\div \dfrac{\text{Change in Price}}{\text{Average of Two Prices}}} \qquad \textbf{(18)}.$$

momentary period see **immediate run**.

monetarism is the doctrine that monetary policy should follow a constant-money-growth rule **(12)**.

monetarists advocate a policy of constant monetary growth, such as 3 percent growth in the money supply per year **(14)**.

monetary-aggregate target is a particular money supply or growth rate of the money supply that the Fed seeks to achieve through monetary policy **(12)**.

monetary base is the sum of reserves on deposit at the Fed, all vault cash, and the currency in circulation **(11)**.

monetary policy is the deliberate control of the money supply and, in some cases, credit conditions for the purpose of achieving macroeconomic goals, such as a certain level of unemployment or inflation **(9,12)**.

monetization of debt is the creation of demand-deposit liabilities in the process of making bank loans **(11)**.

money is anything that is widely accepted in exchange for goods and services **(2)**.

money multiplier the ratio of the money supply, M, to the monetary base, H. If k is the ratio of currency in circulation to deposits, and r is the reserve/deposit ratio, the money multiplier is

$$M/H = \frac{1+k}{r+k} \qquad \textbf{(12)}.$$

money price is a price expressed in monetary units (such as dollars, francs, etc.) **(2)**.

money supply of a country is the sum of all commodity money, fiat money, and bank money held by the nonbanking public as of a given date **(10)**.

monopolistic competition has four characteristics:
1. the number of sellers is large enough so that each seller acts independently of the other;
2. the product is differentiated from seller to seller;
3. there is free entry into and exit from the industry;
4. sellers are price makers **(24)**.

monopoly see **pure monopoly**.

monopoly-profit-seeking behavior is the activity of anyone trying to achieve or maintain a monopoly in order to gain the monopoly profits **(23)**.

monopsony is a market in which buyers can affect the price of the product by altering the quantities they purchase. A *pure monopsony* is a market with only one buyer **(27)**.

multiple-deposit expansion of the money supply occurs when an increase in reserves causes an expansion of the money supply that is greater than the reserve increase **(11)**.

multiplier *($\Delta Y/\Delta I$)* is the ratio of the change in output to the shift in the *AE* curve (due to an independent change in investment, government spending, exports, or imports) **(7)**; see also **deposit multiplier, money multiplier**.

mutual interdependence is a characteristic of an industry in which the actions of one firm will affect other firms in the industry and in which these interrelationships will be recognized **(24)**.

national debt is (approximately) the sum of outstanding federal government IOUs upon which interest and principal payments must be made **(9)**.

national income equals net national product minus indirect business taxes. National income equals the sum of all factor payments made to the factors of production in the economy **(6)**; see also **gross domestic income (GDI)**.

national-income accounting is the study of methods of measuring the aggregate output and aggregate income of an economy **(6)**.

national product see **gross domestic product (GDP), net national product (NDP)**.

natural level of output is the real GDP that the economy produces when its actual unemployment rate equals the natural rate of unemployment **(7)**.

natural rate of unemployment is that unemployment rate at which there is an approximate balance between the number of unfilled jobs and the number of qualified job seekers. Modern macroeconomists consider the natural rate of unemployment to be full employment **(5)**.

necessities are those products that have an income elasticity of demand less than 1 **(18)**.

negative income tax *(NIT)* would supplement incomes by giving recipients who earn less than the *break-even income* an amount equal to a minimum acceptable income and subtracting a given percentage of each extra dollar the family earns on its own **(31)**.

negative (or inverse) relationship exists between two variables if an increase in the value of one variable is associated with a *reduction* in the value of the other variable **(1A)**.

net national product (NDP) equals GDP minus depreciation **(6)**.

net output, or **value added**, of a firm is the value of its output minus the value of its purchases from other firms. Accordingly, the **net output**, or **value added**, of an industry is the output of that industry minus its purchases from other industries **(6)**.

net worth see **wealth**.

NIT see **negative income tax**.

NDP see **net national product (NDP)**.

nominal GDP (or "GDP in current dollars") is the value of final goods and services for a given year in that year's prevailing market prices **(6)**.

nominal interest rate is the cost of borrowing expressed as an annual percentage rate unadjusted for the effects of inflation **(13)**.

nonactivist policy is one that is independent of prevailing economic conditions and that is held steady when economic conditions change **(14)**.

noncompeting groups are groups of people who are differentiated by natural ability and abilities acquired through education, training, and experience to the extent that one group does not compete with another for jobs **(28)**.

nonprice competition is the attempt to attract customers through improvements in product quality or service that shift the firm's demand curve to the right **(24)**.

normal profit requires zero economic profit or accounting profit equal to a normal competitive return on the resources used in the firm **(22)**.

normative economics is the study of *what ought to be* in the economy **(1)**.

oligopoly is an industry characterized by a recognized mutual interdependence, moderate to high barriers to entry, a relatively small number of firms in the industry, and price making (firms are able to exercise varying degrees of control over price) **(24)**.

open-market operations are purchases and sales of federal-government securities by the Fed (as directed by the Federal Open Market Committee) **(11)**.

opportunist behavior occurs when the agent is able to formally fulfill a contract while engaging in behavior that is not in the interests of the principal **(20)**.

opportunity cost of a particular action is the loss of the next best alternative **(1)**; the value of the next best forgone alternative **(21)**.

output see **net output**.

parallelism see **conscious parallelism**.

parity see **purchasing-power parity (PPP)**.

partnership is a business enterprise that is owned by two or more people (called partners), who make all the business decisions, who share the profits of the business, and who bear the financial responsibility for any losses **(20)**.

payments see **balance of payments, transfer payments**.

P/E ratio see **price/earnings (P/E) ratio**.

perfect competition is true of an industry in which
1. there is a large number of buyers and sellers in the market.
2. each buyer and seller has perfect information about prices and product.
3. the product being sold is homogeneous; that is, it is not possible (or even worthwhile) to distinguish the product of one firm from that of other firms.
4. there are no barriers to entry into or exit from the market; there is freedom of entry and exit.
5. all firms are price takers: no single seller is large enough to exert any control over the product price, so each seller accepts the market price as given **(22)**.

perfectly competitive market has the following characteristics:
1. The product's price is uniform throughout the market.
2. Buyers and sellers have perfect information about price and the product's quality.
3. There are a large number of buyers and sellers.
4. No single buyer or seller purchases or sells enough to change the price **(3)**.

perfectly elastic demand is illustrated by a horizontal demand curve, in which case quantity demanded is most responsive to price **(18)**.

perfectly elastic supply is demonstrated by a horizontal supply curve; quantity supplied is most responsive to price **(18)**.

perfectly inelastic demand is illustrated by a vertical demand curve, in which case quantity demanded is least responsive to price **(18)**.

perfectly inelastic supply is demonstrated by a vertical supply curve; quantity supplied is least responsive to price **(18)**.

personal disposable income equals personal income minus income-tax payments **(6)**.

personal distribution of income is the distribution of income among households, or how much income one family earns from the factors of production it owns relative to other families **(27)**.

personal income equals national income
1. *minus* retained corporate profits, corporate income taxes, and social-insurance contributions
2. *plus* transfer payments and consumer interest payments and net government interest payments **(6)**.

personal saving equals personal disposable income minus personal-consumption expenditures **(6)**.

personal wealth (or net worth) is the value of one's total assets minus one's liabilities **(31)**.

Phillips curve shows the relationship between unemployment and inflation and seems to reveal that a reduction in the rate of unemployment requires an increase in the rate of wage (or price) inflation **(13)**; see also **short-run Phillips curve**.

policy instruments are variables, such as the size of the money supply, the amount of government spending, or the structure of the tax code, that affect output, employment, and prices **(14)**.

positive economics is the study of *what is* in the economy **(1)**.

positive (or direct) relationship exists between two variables if an increase in the value of one variable is associated with an *increase* in the value of the other variable **(1A)**.

possibilities see **production-possibilities frontier (PPF)**.

poverty standard see **absolute poverty standard, relative poverty standard**.

PPF see **production-possibilities frontier (PPF)**.

preferences are a person's evaluations of goods and services independent of budget and price considerations **(19)**.

preference theory see **liquidity-preference theory**.

present value (PV) of money to be received in the future is the most anyone would pay today in order to receive the money in the future. The present value is sometimes called the *discounted value* because it is smaller than the amount to be received in the future **(20A)**.

price see **equilibrium price, money price, relative price**.

price discrimination exists when the same product or service is sold at different prices to different buyers **(23)**.

price/earnings (P/E) ratio is the stock price divided by the earnings per share **(20A)**.

price elasticity of demand (E_d) is the percentage change in the quantity demanded divided by the percentage change in price **(18)**; see also **cross-price elasticity of demand (E_{xy})**.

price elasticity of supply (E_s) is defined as the percentage change in the quantity supplied divided by the percentage change in price **(18)**.

price index shows the current year's cost of a particular market basket as a percentage of the cost of the same market basket in some base year **(18)**.

price leader is a firm whose price changes are consistently imitated by other firms in the industry **(24)**.

price maker is a firm with the ability to control to some degree the price of the good or service it sells **(23)**; in a factor market is a buyer of inputs whose purchases are large enough to affect the price of the input **(27)**.

price system coordinates economic decisions by allowing people with property rights to resources to trade freely, buying and selling at whatever relative prices emerge in the market-place **(2)**.

price taker is a seller that does not have the ability to control the price of the good it sells **(22)**; in a factor market a buyer of an input whose purchases are not large enough to affect the price of the input. The price-taking firm must accept the market price as given **(28)**.

prime interest rate is the base, or reference, rate on which banks decide to price their loans. It may be regarded as the base cost of commercial bank credit **(18)**.

principal is a party that has controlling authority and that engages an agent to act subject to the principal's control and instruction **(20)**.

principal/agent problem exists between the firm and any of its employees when the firm (as a principal) and the employee (as an agent) have different goals and objectives for the employee's behavior **(28)**.

principle of substitution states that practically no good is irreplaceable in meeting *demand* (the amount of a good people are prepared to buy). Users are able to substitute one product for another to satisfy demand **(2)**.

prisoners' dilemma game is a game with 2 players in which both players benefit from cooperating, but in which each player has an incentive to cheat on the agreement **(24)**.

private saving is the sum of the personal saving of individuals and of business savings (in the form of retained profits and depreciation accounts) **(6)**.

problem see **economic problem, principal/agent problem**.

product see **gross national product (GDP), net national product (NNP)**.

production see **factors of production**.

production-possibilities frontier *(PPF)* shows the combinations of goods that can be produced when the factors of production are utilized to their full potential. It reveals the economic choices open to society **(1)**.

productivity see **capital productivity, labor productivity, total-factor productivity**.

profit see **normal profit**.

profit maximization is the search by firms for the product quality, output, and price that give the firm the highest possible profits **(20)**.

profit-maximization rule is that a firm will maximize profits by producing that level of output at which marginal revenue *(MR)* equals marginal cost *(MC)* (This rule applies to all firms, be they perfectly competitive or monopolistic.) **(22)**.

profits see **economic profits**.

progressive tax is one where the higher the income, the larger the percentage of income paid as taxes **(4)**.

property rights are the rights of an owner to use and exchange property **(2)**.

proportional tax is one where each taxpaying unit pays the same percentage of income as taxes **(4)**.

proprietorship see **sole proprietorship**.

public goods have two properties:
1. no one can be excluded from using the good once it is provided; and
2. the use of the good by one person does not detract from the use by another person (that is, consumption is nonrival) **(4,32)**.

purchasing-power parity *(PPP)* exists between two currencies when changes in the exchange rate reflect only relative changes in the price levels of the two countries **(17)**.

pure economic rent is the price paid to a productive factor that is completely inelastic in supply. Land is the classic example of such a factor **(30)**.

pure monopoly exists
1. when there is one seller in the market for some good or service that has no close substitutes,
2. when the seller has considerable control over price, and
3. when barriers to entry protect the seller from competition **(23)**.

quantity demanded is the amount of a good or service consumers are prepared to buy at a given price (during a specified time period), holding other factors constant **(3)**.

quantity supplied of a good or service is the amount of the good or service offered for sale at a given price, holding other factors constant **(3)**.

quota see **import quota**.

rate see **interest rate, law of diminishing marginal rate of substitution, real interest rate**.

rate effect see **interest-rate effect**.

rate of return on capital measures the annual return of the capital investment as a percentage of the investment cost **(30)**.

rate of unemployment see **natural rate of unemployment**.

rate regulation is government control of the prices (rates) that regulated enterprises are allowed to charge **(25)**.

ratio see **concentration ratio, price/earnings *(P/E)* ratio**.

rational expectations are expectations that people form by using all available information and by relying not only on past experience but also on their predictions about the effects of present and future policy actions **(13)**.

rational expectations economists maintains that anticipated monetary and fiscal policies cannot stabilize the economy **(14)**.

real-balance effect occurs when desired consumption at each income level changes as price-level changes alter the purchasing power of assets, including money balances. Price increases reduce purchasing power and reduce desired consumption at each income level; price declines raise purchasing power and raise desired consumption at each income level **(7)**.

real GDP (or "GDP in constant dollars") measures the volume of *real* goods and services by removing the effects of rising prices on nominal GDP **(15)**.

real interest rate is the nominal interest rate minus the anticipated rate of inflation **(13)**.

recognition lag is the time it takes the Fed to decide to change the supply of money in response to a change in economic conditions **(12)**.

regressive tax is one where the higher the income, the smaller the percentage of income paid as taxes **(4)**.

regulatory lag occurs when government regulators adjust rates some time after operating costs and the rate base have increased **(25)**.

relationship see **direct relationship, negative (or inverse) relationship, positive relationship**.

relative price is price expressed in terms of other commodities **(2)**.

relative poverty standard defines the poor in terms of the income of others **(31)**.

rent see **economic rent, pure economic rent**.

required-reserve ratio is the amount of reserves required for each dollar of deposits **(11)**.

requirements see **reserve requirements**.

reserve requirements are rules that state the amount of reserves a bank must keep on hand to back bank deposits **(11)**.

reserves are the funds that the bank uses to satisfy the cash demands of its customers **(11)**; see also **excess reserves**.

resource policy see **human-resource policy**.

restraint see **voluntary export restraint**.

returns see **law of diminishing returns**.

returns to scale see **constant returns to scale**.

rider see **free rider**.

right see **special drawing right (SDR)**.

rights see **property rights**.

rule see **least-cost rule, profit-maximization rule, shutdown rule**.

rule of reason stated that monopolies were in violation of the Sherman Act if they engaged in unfair or illegal business practices. Being a monopoly in and of itself was not considered a violation of the Sherman Act according to this rule **(25)**.

run see **immediate run, long run, short run**.

saving/income schedule shows the desired amount of saving at different levels of national income or output **(8)**.

Say's Law states that *desired* aggregate expenditures can never depart from *actual* aggregate expenditures. Whatever output is produced will be demanded **(8)**.

scale see **constant returns to scale, diseconomies of scale, economies of scale**.

scarcity exists when the goods and services that people want exceeds the ability of the economy to produce those goods and services **(1)**; see also **contrived scarcity**.

scatter diagram consists of a number of separate points, each of which plots the value of one variable (measured along the horizontal axis) against a value of another variable (measured along the vertical axis) for a specific time interval **(1A)**.

share see **earnings per share** *(EPS)*.

shock see **supply shock**.

shortage results if at the current price the quantity demanded exceeds the quantity supplied; the price is too low to equate the quantity demanded with the quantity supplied **(3)**; see also **labor shortage**.

short run is a period of time long enough for existing firms to produce more goods but not long enough for existing firms to expand their capacity or for new firms to enter the market. Thus, output can be varied but only within the limits of existing plant capacity **(18)**; a period of time so short that the existing plant and equipment cannot be varied; such inputs are fixed in supply. Additional output can be produced only by expanding the variable inputs of labor and raw materials **(21)**.

short-run aggregate supply *(SRAS)* is a schedule of the quantities of real output the economy is prepared to supply at different price levels, holding the expected price level and other factors constant **(7)**.

short-run macroeconomic equilibrium occurs at that price level at which aggregate quantity demanded and short-run aggregate quantity supplied are equal **(7)**.

short-run Phillips curve, like the original Phillips curve, shows a negative relationship between inflation and unemployment. In the short run, less inflation means more unemployment **(13)**.

shutdown rule is: If the firm's revenues at all output levels are less than variable costs, it minimizes its losses by shutting down. If there is at least one output level at which revenues exceed variable costs, the firm should not shut down **(22)**.

slope of a straight line is the ratio of the rise (or fall) in Y (measured on the vertical axis) over the run in X (measured on the horizontal axis) **(1A)**.

social benefits are private benefits plus external benefits **(32)**.

social costs are private costs plus external costs **(32)**.

social efficiency occurs when the economy produces all those goods and services whose marginal social benefits equal their marginal social costs **(32)**.

socialism is an economic system in which land and capital are owned by the state and the use of these resources is determined by the state **(1)**.

sole proprietorship is a form of business that is owned by one individual who makes all the business decisions, receives the profits that the business earns, and bears the financial responsibility for losses **(20)**.

speculators are those who buy or sell in the hope of *profiting* from market fluctuations **(26)**.

special drawing right (SDR) is essentially an international money that can be exchanged between monetary authorities **(17)**.

spiral see **wage/price spiral**.

spot (cash) market is an arrangement where buyers and sellers agree now about payment and delivery of the product now **(26)**.

stabilizers see **automatic stabilizers**.

stagflation is the combination of high unemployment rates and high inflation over a period of time **(5,13)**.

standard see **absolute poverty standard, relative poverty standard**.

stock each share of stock represents the ownership of $1/n$ percent of the corporation, where n is the number of shares outstanding. Owners of shares can vote on corporate matters and receive dividends proportional to their share holdings **(20A)**.

stock exchange is a market in which shares of stock of corporations are bought and sold and in which the prices of shares of stock are determined **(20A)**.

stock-price index (such as the Dow Jones Industrial Average, the Standard & Poors Index, and the New York Stock Exchange Index) measures the general movements of stock prices **(20A)**.

strike occurs when all unionized employees cease to work until management agrees to specific union demands **(29)**.

structural deficit is that part of the deficit that would occur if there were no business cycle and the economy were operating at the natural level of real GDP **(9)**.

structural unemployment is the unemployment that results from the long-run decline of certain industries. Industries may decline because of rising costs, changes in consumer preferences, or technological advances that make the industry's product obsolete **(5)**.

substitutes are two goods for which the demand for one rises when the price of the other rises (or if the demand for one falls when the price of the other falls) **(3)**.

substitution see **import substitution, law of diminishing marginal rate of substitution, principle of substitution**.

substitution effect is the change in quantity of X demanded that occurs when the price of X changes and the consumer is compensated to keep utility or welfare constant **(19)**.

supply of a good or service is the amount that firms are prepared to sell under specified circumstances during a specified time period **(4)**; see also **aggregate supply** *(AS)*, **money supply, short-run aggregate supply** *(SRAS)*.

supply curve or **schedule** of a particular good or service shows the various quantities supplied at different prices, holding other factors constant, during a particular time period **(3)**; see also **long-run industry-supply curve**.

supply shock occurs when the short-run aggregate supply curve shifts **(7)**.

supply-side inflation (or *cost-push inflation*) occurs when increases in prices of inputs caused by reductions in their supply generally cause fewer goods and services to be offered at prevailing prices, resulting in the bidding up of their prices **(5)**; occurs when aggregate supply declines and pushes prices up **(13)**.

surplus results if at the current price the quantity supplied exceeds the quantity demanded; the price is too high to equate the quantity demanded with quantity supplied **(3)**; see also **full-employment surplus, government surplus, labor surplus**.

surplus value is the value of any labor over and above the amount of labor the worker would have to provide to meet subsistence needs **(18,33)**.

taker see **price taker**.

tangent is a straight line that touches the curve at only one point **(1A)**.

target see **interest-rate target**.

tariff is a tax levied on imports **(16)**.

tax see **incidence of a tax, progressive tax, proportional tax, regressive tax**.

terms of trade is the rate at which two products can be exchanged for each other between countries **(16)**.

total costs *(TC)* are fixed costs plus variable costs: $TC = VC + FC$ **(21)**; see also **average total cost (ATC)**.

total-factor productivity measures output per unit of combined labor and capital input **(15)**.

total revenue *(TR)* of sellers in a market is equal to the price of the commodity times the quantity sold: $TR = P \times Q$ **(18)**.

total revenue test is:
1. If price and total revenue move in different directions, $E_d > 1$ *(demand is elastic)*.
2. If price and total revenue move in the same direction, $E_d < 1$ *(demand is inelastic)*.
3. If total revenue does not change when price changes, $E_d = 1$ *(demand is unitary elastic)* **(18)**.

total utility is the amount of satisfaction (utility) obtained from consuming a particular quantity of a good or service. It is the sum of the marginal utilities of each successive unit of consumption **(19)**.

trade see **free trade**.

trade deficit is an excess of import over exports **(9)**.

trade-off see **wage/employment trade-off**.

transaction cost is the cost associated with bringing together buyers and sellers **(2)**.

transfer payments transfer income from one individual or organization to another **(4,6)**.

transition see **demographic transition**.

unemployment rate is defined as the number unemployed divided by the number in the labor force **(5)**.

unintended investment is the difference between desired saving and desired investments at each level of income **(8)**.

union see **craft union, industrial union, labor union**.

utility is the satisfaction that a person enjoys from consuming goods and services **(19)**; see also **law of diminishing marginal utility, total utility**.

value see **present value (PV)**.

value added see **net output**.

variable see **dependent variable, independent variable**.

variable costs *(VC)* are those that do vary with output **(21)**; see also **average variable cost (AVC)**.

velocity of circulation is the number of times the average dollar is spent on final goods and services in one year's time **(10)**.

vertical merger is a merger of two firms that are part of the same materials, production, or distribution network (such as a personal-computer manufacturer merging with a retail computer-distribution chain or a machinery manufacturer merging with a machinery-parts supplier) **(25)**.

voluntary export restraint is an agreement between two governments in which the exporting country voluntarily limits the export of a certain product to the importing country **(16)**.

wage differentials see **compensating wage differentials**.

wage/employment trade-off confronts any labor union that faces a downward-sloping demand curve: higher wages can be obtained only by sacrificing the number of jobs; lower unemployment can be obtained only by sacrificing higher wages **(29)**.

wage/price spiral is the phenomenon of higher prices pushing wages higher and then higher wages pushing prices higher, or vice versa. This spiral is sustained when the monetary authorities ratify the resulting supply-side inflation **(13)**.

waste-disposal costs are the costs of disposing of the wastes created by economic activity **(32)**.

wealth (or net worth) is the value of one's total assets minus one's liabilities **(31)**.

PHOTO CREDITS

Unless otherwise acknowledged, all photographs are the property of Scott, Foresman.

48—The Granger Collection, New York; 72—Courtesy James M. Buchanan; 92—BBC Hulton/The Bettmann Archive; 113—Courtesy Harvard University; 134—B.J. Harris, Oxford; 152—UPI/Bettmann; 176—Courtesy Franco Modigliani; 197—AP/Wide World; 212—Courtesy University of California Press; 232—Courtesy Stanford University; 250—Culver Pictures; 270—Courtesy Robert E. Lucas; 307—New York Public Library, Astor, Lenox and Tilden Foundations; 328—Courtesy University of Chicago; 346—The MIT Museum; 364—BBC Hulton/The Bettmann Archive; 389—AP/Wide World; 415—The Granger Collection, New York; 435—Bibliotheque Cantonale et Universitaire Lausanne; 457—Ramsey and Muspratt, Ltd.; 475—AP/Wide World; 495—Courtesy George Stigler; 512—Staatsbibliothek, Berlin; 528—The Granger Collection, New York; 545—Donald Rocker; 563—Courtesy Duke University; 581—UPI/Bettmann; 595—Brown Brothers; 616—Courtesy Ronald H. Coase; 631—UPI/Bettmann.

INDEX

Page numbers in italics indicate exhibits.

Ability and human capital, in income distribution, 598
Ability-to-pay principle, in taxation, 77, 87
Absolute advantage, 39
Absolute poverty standard, 605, *606*, 609, 610
Accountability of Federal Reserve System, 243
Activist policy(ies), 283
    case for, 274–277
    common ground with nonactivist policy, 281
    to control business cycle, 168
    costs of lost output and, 274–275
    counterproductive effects of, *276–277*, 278–279
    difficulty of devising, 278
    versus nonactivism, 275, *276–277*, 277
    rational expectations theory and, 280
    to stabilize business cycle, 269
Actual budget deficit, 182
AD (*see* Aggregate demand)
Adaptive expectations, inflation and, 253
Administrative-command economy, 635–636
Advertising, 478
    by unions, 569
AFC (*see* Average fixed cost)
AFDC (Aid to Families with Dependent Children), 607
AFL (American Federation of Labor), 564–565
AFL-CIO, 567
Agents, 394
    opportunistic behavior of, 396–397
    principal/agent problem, 401, 545–546
Aggregate demand (AD), 132–136, *133*
    activism versus nonactivism and, 270–271, *271*
    conditions of, *135*, 135–136
    effect of money on, 235, *236*
    foreign trade effect and, 134
    increase in, 185
    interest-rate effect and, 133
    in quantity theory, 205–206
    real-balance effect and, 132–133
    shifts in, 140, *140*
Aggregate demand curve, 132, *133*, 146
    in quantity theory, 206
    slope of, *133*, 134–135

Aggregate expenditure(s), desired, 161, *162*
    realization of, *162*, 162–163
Aggregate-expenditure curve, 169
    shifts in, 165
Aggregate supply (AS), 136–138
    activism versus nonactivism and, 270–271, *271*
    aggregate demand and, 131–147
    increase in, 185
    in quantity theory, 205–206
    Say's law and, 151
    in short run, 136–138, *138*
    wage rigidities and, 136
Aggregate-supply curve, in classical macroeconomics, 150, *151*
Agricultural Adjustment Act of 1933, 510
Agricultural economies, growth model for, 295–298
Agricultural Experimental Stations, 516
Agricultural price fluctuations, 512–514, *514, 515*
Agricultural speculation, futures markets and, 519–520
Agriculture, 510–523
    business of farming, 511
    crisis of the 1980s, 517–519
    declining share of, 516–517
    fluctuations in prices, 523
    government programs, 520–523, *521*
    inelastic demand for products, 512
    long-term relative decline in prices, 523
    price inelasticities of demand in, 513
    productivity of American farms, 517
    speculation and futures markets, 519–520
    supply shocks from, 141
    trends in prices and incomes, 512–516
    See also Government farm programs
Aid to Families with Dependent Children (AFDC), 607
Air pollution, 617
Airline deregulation, 507
Airline Deregulation Act of 1978, 499–500, 507
Alcoa case of 1945, Sherman Antitrust Act and, 503
Allegheny County, Pennsylvania, sale of pollution rights in, 626

Allman, William F., 482
Allocation, 15
    of resources, 30–31
    systems for, 4
Allocation arrangements, 630
    in capitalist system, 632
    in socialist system, 632
American Airlines predatory pricing case, 490
American Federation of Labor (AFL), 564–565
American Stock Exchange (ASE), 408
American Tobacco Company case, Sherman Antitrust Act and, 502
Ando, Albert, 176
Angrist, Joshua, 599
Announcement effect, 232
Annual percentage rate (*see* Interest rate)
Antitrust legislation, 408, 501–504, *503*
    Clayton Act of 1914, 501–502, *503*
    Federal Trade Commission Act of 1914, 502, *503*
    Robinson-Patman Act of 1936, 502, *503*
    Sherman Antitrust Act of 1890, 501, *503*
        interpretation of, 502–504
    unnecessary, 506, 508
Appreciation, 330
Arab oil embargo, 66–67
Area of rectangle, 27, *27*, 28
Arithmetic growth rate in food production, 296
Arrow, Kenneth J., 134
AS (*see* Aggregate supply)
ASE (American Stock Exchange), 408
Ashenfelter, Orley, 574
Assets, 201, 213
    money value of, consumption expenditures and, 160
ATC (*see* Average total cost)
Auction markets, 275
Autobiography (Mill), 595
Automatic stabilizers, 176, 177, 192
    discretionary policy and, 175–178
Autonomous changes in tax rates and expenditures, 177
AVC (*see* Average variable cost)
Average cost, marginal cost and, 422–423
Average fixed cost (AFC), 422–423, *439*, 440
Average/marginal rules, 417, *418*

Average total cost (ATC), 423, 431, 438, *439*
Average values, 417, *418*
Average variable cost (AVC), 422–425, *424*, 431, 438, *439*
marginal cost and, 425, *425*
Axelrod, Robert, 482

Backward-bending labor-supply curve, *556*, 556–557, 559
Balance in labor market, 96
Balance of payments, 333–334, *335*
domestic money supplies and, 332
exchange rates and, 341
international capital movements and, 333–336
Balance sheets of commercial banks, 212–213, *214*
Balanced budget, 179, 191
in nonactivist policy, 269–270
Balanced budget amendment, 86, 191
Balanced-budget rule
inability to respond to recession, 275, 277
skepticism about ability to implement, 282
Bank(s)
failures of, 216
Federal Reserve System limitation of borrowing, 232
regulation by Federal Reserve System, 215
Bank money, 201, 208
Banking, deregulation of, 507–508
Banking Act of 1933, 215
Banking Act of 1935, 215
Bankruptcy, 406
Barriers to entry
cartels and, 485
by monopolies, 457–458
in oligopoly, 478
Barter, 41, 124
Barter economy, 196, 197
Becker, Gary, 63, 545
Benefit principle, in taxation, 75–77
Benefits, exhaustion of, 422
Benefits principle in taxation, 87
Bergmann, Barbara, 601
Berle, Adolf A., 389
Berlin Wall, 634
Birth rate in less developed countries, 299
"Black Monday," 411
Blanchard, Olivier, 109
Blinder, Alan, 263
Board of Governors (Federal Reserve System), 214, 217, 243
Bond(s), 233, 404
Bond-market rally, 234
Bond prices, 406–407
relationship to interest rates, 233–234, 412
Braeutigam, Ronald, 430
Brand names, 478
Brandow, George E., 356, 513
Brazil, income distribution in, 597
Bretton Woods system, 337–338, 341
fall of, 338–339
Brookings Institution study of export restraints, 317
Browning, Edgar K., *79*, 604
Buchanan, James, 72, 191
Budget deficit, 192
Budget line, 379–380, *380*, 385

Bureau of Labor Statistics, 91
Bus Deregulatory Reform Act of 1982, 500
Bush, George, 80, 128, 174
Business cycle(s), 83, 105–107, *107*, 109
contribution of inflation to, 102
controlling, 168
monetarism and, 244
phases of, 105, *106*
swings in, activist policy and, *276–277*, 278–279
Business downturns, unemployment and, 94
Business firms, 387–401
forms of organization of, 389–393, *390–391*
goals of, 388–389
Byrnes, Ralph T., 513

Campaign contributions, limiting, 86
Capital, 591
credit markets and, 580–581
financial, 6
limited access of sole proprietor, 390–391
formation in less developed countries, 299–300
interest and, 580–585
rate determination, 582–584
rate structure, 584–585
raising, 404–412
bond prices, 406–407
by corporations, 393
efficient stock market hypothesis, 410–411
present value, 404–406
stock markets and, 407–410
requirements for, in bank regulation, 215
saving and, 580
Capital markets [*see* Credit market(s)]
Capital productivity, 292
Capitalism, 4, 629–638
allocation arrangements in, 632
incentive systems in, 632
property rights in, 632
Capitalism and Freedom (Friedman), 232
Cartel(s), 491
cheating on agreements, 485–486
in oligopoly, 485–486, *486*
Cash leakage, 220
Celler-Kefauver Act of 1950, 502, *503*
Ceteris paribus, 8, 10, *11*, 16
Chamberlin, Edward Hastings, 475
Chance, income inequality and, 598–600
Vietnam draft lottery, 599
Change in demand, 60, *61*, 67
Change in quantity demanded, 60, *61*, 67
Change in quantity supplied, 60, *61*, 67
Change in supply, 60, *61*, 62, 67
"Channeling", income inequality and, 600, *601*
Checks, 201
Choice, scarcity and, 3–4
CIO (Congress of Industrial Organizations), 567
Circular-flow diagram, 30, *31*, 44, 112, 113, *114*
of product and factor markets, 527, *528*
Civil Aeronautics Board, 499, 500, 507
Civil War, hyperinflation during, 207
Clark, John Bates, 528
Clark, Kim, 576

Classic Motor Carriages (economies of scale), 429
Classical economics, 149
Classical growth model
for agricultural economies, 295–298
diminishing returns in, 295–296, *297*
for less developed countries
capital-formation problems in, 299–300
population pressures in, 298–299
poverty in, 298
technological backwardness and, 300
Malthusian population laws and, 296
stationary state of, 296–298, *297*
Classical macroeconomics
laissez-faire policy in, 152–153
Say's law, 150–152, *151, 153*
Classical model, self-liquidation of high unemployment in, 156
Classical quantity theorists, 233
Classical quantity theory of money (*see* Quantity theory)
Clayton Act of 1914, 501–502, *503*
vertical mergers and, 504–505
Clean Air Act, 625, 626
Clinton, Bill, 80, 128, 174
Closed-shop agreements, 568
Coal Question, The (Jevons), 364
Coase, Ronald Harry, 616, 618
Coase theorem, 618
Coins, 200
Collected Papers of Franco Modigliani (Modigliani), 176
Collective bargaining, 562–563, 570–572, *572*, 577
with monopsony, 572–573, *573*
with threat of strike, 571, *572*
Collective voice, unions as, 575
Collusion
obstacles to, 488–489
in oligopoly, 485
Collusive agreements, 491
Commercial banking, Federal Reserve System and, 210–228
Commercial banks, 211–213, 228
balance sheets of, 212–213, *214*
combined balance sheet of, *214*
profits of, 212
Commodities markets, 520
Commodity money, 199–200, 208
Commodity stabilization programs, 303
Common law, unions and, 567
Communist Manifesto (Marx), 631
Communist socialism
living standards of, 633–634, *634*
reasons for failure of, 634–638
incentives and information, 634–636
transition to market economy, 637–638
rise and fall of, 633–634, *634*
Comparable worth, 540
Comparative advantage
law of, 39–40
of U.S. in new products and processes, 315
Compensating wage differentials
example of (land mine disposal in Kuwait), 555
risk and, 597
wage structure and, 553–554, *554*
Competition, 48
in agriculture, 511

in factor markets, 529
  foreign trade effect and, 134
  photo-processing example of, 451
  world trade and, 436
Competitive devaluations, 337
Competitiveness, U.S. trade deficit and, 337
Complement(s), 52
Complementary factors of production, shifts in labor demand and, 551, 552
Complete crowding out, 184
Comptroller of the Currency, 215
Computers, denationalization of money and, 227
Concentration ratios, 479–480, 491
  in oligopoly, 479–480, 480
  problems with, 479–480
Conditions of work, shifts in labor supply and, 552, 553
Conglomerate mergers, 504, 505
Congress of Industrial Organizations (CIO), 567
Congressional Budget Office, 188
Conscious parallelism, in oligopoly, 488
Constant-cost industries, 452
  long-run industry supply curve in, 447, 449, 450
Constant returns to scale, 428, 431
Constitutional constraints, 72
Consumer(s), gain from lower prices, 318, 318
Consumer equilibrium, 368, 368–369, 380–381, 381
  effect of income change on, 382, 382
  effect of price change on, 382–385, 383, 384
Consumer goods, U.S. imports of, 307
Consumer preferences
  budget line and, 379–380, 380
  demand and, 363–365
  indifference-curve theory and, 377–380, 378
  law of diminishing marginal rate of substitution and, 377–379, 378, 379
Consumer Price Index (CPI), 98, 109
Consumer price sensitivity, 344
Consumer satisfaction, 372
  maximizing, 380–381, 385
  maximum, 366, 367
Consumption
  aggregate demand curve and, 134
  expectations and, 159–160
  income and, 166
  in income/expenditure model, 156–158, 157
Consumption/income schedule, 157, 158, 159
Contract(s), 394, 396–397
  information costs and, 394, 396
  in labor market, 544
  opportunistic behavior and, 396–397
Contract-type labor markets, 137
Contractionary fiscal policy(ies), 178, 182
Contractionary monetary policy, decrease in money supply and, 236, 237
Contrived scarcity, monopoly and, 467–468, 468
Cooperative Extension Service, 516
Coordination, in oligopoly, 483, 485–487
  cartel agreements, 485–486, 486
  conscious parallelism, 488
  informal agreements, 487

price leadership, 487–488
Corporate abuse of shareholders' interests, 399
Corporate bonds, 201
Corporate charter, 392
Corporate finance
  financial markets and, 403–412
  raising capital, 404–411
Corporation(s), 392–393, 395, 396, 400
Corporation and Private Property, The (Berle and Means), 389
Cost(s)
  minimization in factor markets, 537
  of production
    changes in level of output and, 425, 425
    supply shocks in, 139, 140
  productivity and, 413–431
  of protection in international trade, 321
  of supplying government services, 116
Cost/benefit analysis
  applied to government spending, 87
  of pollution abatement, 624, 624
Cost curves, 417–426, 423–426, 424, 425
  fixed and variable costs, 419
  law of diminishing returns and, 420–422, 421
  marginal and average costs and, 422–423
  shifts in, 426, 427
  in short run, 423–426, 424, 425
  long run and, 418–419
Council of Economic Advisors, 273
CPI (Consumer Price Index), 98, 109
Craft unions, 562
"Creative destruction," 38
Credit
  demand for, 583, 583–584
    equilibrium interest rate and, 583, 584
    productivity of capital and thrift, 584, 585
  supply of, 582, 583
Credit demand, deficits and, 190
Credit market(s), 580–581
  deficits and, 190
  need for, 581
  specialization and, 581
Credit rationing, 590–591
Crime, "market" for, 64
Cross-price elasticity, 359
Cross-price elasticity of demand, 353
Crowding out, effective fiscal policy and, 183–184
Curvilinear relationships, slope and, 23–25, 24, 25
Cyclical deficit, 181
Cyclical unemployment, 94, 109

Danger of job, compensating wage differentials and, 553–554, 554
Darby, Michael, 295
Darwin, Charles, 287
Das Kapital (Marx), 631
Data, displaying in graphs, 20, 21
DeBeers Company, Yakutia diamonds and, 487
Debt, money and, 219–220, 220
Decision-making, decentralization of, 630
Deductions, 80
Deficiency payments in agriculture, 521
Deficit(s)
  fiscal policy and, 177–181

inflation and, 189, 189–190
  interest rates and, 190, 191
  reduction of
    opposition to, 191
    problems of, 190–191
Definition of market, Sherman Antitrust Act and, 503
Deflation, 97, 109
Deflationary gaps, 143, 147, 175, 245
  automatic removal of, 144, 144, 146
  eliminating by discretionary fiscal policy, 178, 179
  inflationary gaps and, 140–142, 142
  monetary policy and, 236, 236–238, 237
Deflationary pressures, during Great Depression, 332
Degree of responsiveness, in price elasticity of demand, 345
DeLong, J. Bradford, 282
Demand, 49–54, 372
  consumer preferences and, 363–365
  demand curve and, 49–51, 51
  law of, 49
    marginal utility and, 365–371, 367, 368
  rational consumer behavior and, 363
  shifting, relative agricultural prices and, 516
  shifts in demand curve, 51–54
  utility and, 362–374
Demand curve, 49–51, 51, 67, 358, 359
  expectations and, 53–54, 54
  for factors, 536, 536–537
  of foreign exchange, 341
  income and, 42
  marginal utility and, 370
  negatively sloped in monopoly, 459–460
  perfect elasticity of, in perfect competition, 437
  perfectly elastic/perfectly inelastic, 350, 351
  potential buyers and, 53
  preferences and, 52–53
  prices of related goods and, 42
  shifts in, 51–54
    example of, 53
  slope of, 383
Demand deposit(s)
  in banks, 201
  creating, 218–224
Demand-deposit liabilities, 219
Demand equation in quantity theory, 206
Demand for labor, 546–548
  of firm, 547, 547–548
  of market, 547, 547, 548
Demand schedule, 49–50
Demand-side economics, 169
  view of tax cuts, 185
Demand-side inflation, 99–100, 248–249, 249, 265
Democratic political processes, spending and, 74
Demographic transition, 298
Denationalization of money, 227
Denison, Edward, 293
Department of Commerce, GDP estimates of, 116, 128
Department of Justice, 501
Department of the Treasury, 273
Deposit insurance, 213, 215
Deposit multiplier, 218, 221, 222, 224

Depository Institutions Deregulation and Monetary Control Act of 1980, 500, 507
Depreciation, 117, 330
Depression, 105
    See also Great Depression
Deregulation, 408, 498–500
    legislation for, 499–500
    of natural gas prices, 430
    results of, 400
Derived demand
    in air travel and aircraft leases, 533
    in factor market, 532–533
    for factors of production, 538, *539*
Desirability of job, compensating wage differentials and, 553–554, *554*
Desired aggregate expenditures, 161, *162*
    realization of, *162*, 162–163
Desired investment, 152, *153*
Desired-reserve ratio, 223
Desired saving, 152, *153*
Determinants of concentration
    barriers to entry, 479
    measuring concentration and, 479–480, *480*
    in oligopolies, 479–480
Diamond/water paradox, 366
Direct crowding out, 184
Direct foreign assistance to less developed countries, 301–303
Direct relationship (*see* Positive relationship)
Direct support payments in agriculture, 521, *522*
Discount rate, 228
    changes in, 226
    of Federal Reserve System, 217
    as instrument of monetary policy, 231–232
Discouraged workers, 93
Discretionary fiscal policy, 177–178, 192
    automatic stabilizers and, 175–178
    eliminating deflationary gap by, 178, *179*
    eliminating inflationary gap by, 178, *179*
    full-employment deficit and, 181–182
Discretionary government spending, 272
Discretionary monetary policy, 177
    to control business cycle, 168
    self-correcting mechanism and, 237, *237*
Discretionary tax cuts, 185
Discrimination, income inequality and, 600
Diseconomies of scale, 428–429, 431
    economies of scale and, 427–428, *428*
Disequilibrium, adjustment of economy to, 163
Disposable income, GDP and, 120–123, *122*
Dissaving, 124, 159, 179
    national debt and, 184
Distribution of income, 37, 610
    changes in, Ricardian model of international trade and, 313–314
Distribution of Wealth, The (Clark), 528
Distributive justice, 601–603, 610
    natural law and, 602
    Rawlsian equality and, 603
    utilitarianism and, 602–603
Diversity
    among oligopolies, 478
    technical innovation and, 470

Dividends, 406, 407
Dollar votes, 37
Domestic-content rules, as nontariff barriers, 317
Domestic money supplies, balance of payments and, 332
Double coincidence of wants, in barter economy, 196
Dow Jones Industrials Index, 410
Downward-sloping curve, 19
DuPont cellophane case of 1956, Sherman Antitrust Act and, 503

Eastman Kodak case of 1972, Sherman Antitrust Act and, 504
Economic activity, circular flow of, 30, *31*
Economic "bads," 129
    omitted from GDP, 126–128
Economic behavior, effect of taxes on, 74
"Economic Calculation in the Socialist Commonwealth" (Mises), 631
Economic Consequences of the Peace (Keynes), 92
Economic development, 286–303
    lack of, 289–290, *290*
    level of, 289
Economic efficiency, 467, 471
    perfect competition and, 618
Economic growth, 287–289
    extensive and intensive, 291, *292*
    increasing rates of, 288
    of industrialized world, 290–295
    labor and, *293*, 294–295, *295*
    role of productivity in, 291–292, *293*
"Economic imperialists," 545
Economic incentives, 630
Economic policymaking, 273
Economic problem, 30–31
Economic profits, 416–417, 592
    sources of, 589, 591
Economic rents, 586, 592
    accrual to factor owners, 588
    distinguished from pure economic rents, 587–588
    other factors of production and, 587–588
Economic systems, 4–5, 630–633
    allocation arrangements in, 632
    incentive systems in, 632–633
    property rights in, 630–632
Economies of scale, 39, 427–428, 431
    Classic Motor Carriages example, 429
    diseconomies of scale and, 427–428, *428*
Economy
    effect of money supply on, 203
    efficiency of, natural-law philosophy and, 602
    measuring performance of, 111
E_d (*see* Price elasticity(ies) of demand)
Effectiveness lag, 242–243
    in fiscal policy, 183
Efficiency, *8*, 9–10
    international trade and, 310
    monopoly and, 466–470
        contrived scarcity, 467–468, *468*
        innovation, 469–470
        perfect competition and, 466–467
        profit-seeking behavior, 468–469
    oligopoly and, 489–491
    unions and, 575–576, *576*
        evidence for decrease, 575
        evidence for increase, 575–576, *576*

Efficient production, 449
Efficient resource use, pure economic rent and, 586, 587
Efficient scale of operation, 449
Efficient stock market hypothesis, 410–411, 412
Ehrinberg, Ronald, 576
E_i (Income elasticity of demand), 352–353, 359
Elastic demand, *347*, 348
Elasticity of demand and supply, 344–360
Elasticity of demand curve, slope and, *347*, 349–350
Elements of Pure Economics, The (Walras), 435
Employee associations, 562
Employee travel, as principal/agent problem, 546
Employment, 92
    full, 95–96
Employment Act of 1946, 91, 109
Energy crisis of 1970s
    floating exchange rates and, 340–341
    impact on demand for electricity, 497
    as supply shock, 141
Energy prices as example of supply-side inflation, 101
Engel, Ernst, 512
Engineering complexity, long run and, 419
Entitlement programs, 176
Entrepreneurs, 388, 452, 589
Entry
    barriers to
        of monopolies, 457–458
        obstacles to collusion and, 488–489
        in oligopoly, 478
    freedom of, 477, 479
Entry and exit, in perfect competition, 446–448, *447*, 452
Entry restrictions
    in bank regulation, 215
    as source of economic profits, 589
Environmental economics, market failure and, 614–627
Environmental pollution
    as externality, 622–624, 626
    optional abatement of, 622–624, *624*, 626
Environmental protection
    market solutions to, *620*, 625
    regulatory approach to, 625
Environmental Protection Agency (EPA), 625, 626
Equation of exchange in quantity theory, 204
Equilibrium, 36
    in factor markets, 536
    oligopolistic pricing and, 483
    of supply and demand, *51*, 55, 58–60, *59*
Equilibrium expenditures, 160–165
Equilibrium output, *162*, 163–164
    changes in, 138–140
Equilibrium price, 36, 58, 62, *63*, 359
    adjustment time and, 357
    changes in, 60–63, 138–140
Equilibrium price/quantity combination, 67
Equilibrium quantities, adjustment time and, 357
Equilibrium rate of interest, 234, *235*
Equilibrium wage rate, 558
Ericson, E. W., 356
E_s (*see* Price elasticity(ies) of supply)

Essay on the Principle of Population (Malthus), 287, 296
European Monetary System, 328
  similarity to Bretton Woods system, 339
Excess capacity, 477
Exchange, specialization and, 37–39
Exchange rate(s)
  fixed, 340
  flexible, 340
  market forces affecting, 330–331
  for U.S. dollar, 238
Exemptions, 80
Exhaustive expenditures, 71
Exhaustive government expenditures, 86
Expansionary fiscal policy, 178, 182
Expansionary monetary policy, increase in money supply and, *236, 237*
Expectations
  consumption and, 159–160
  demand curve and, 53–54, *54*
  shifts in supply curve and, 57, *57*
Expenditures, reallocating, 369–370
Explicit cost, 414–415
Export promotion, 301, 303
Exports as cost of imports, 334, *335*
Extensive growth, 291, 292, 294
External debt, 188–189
  internal debt and, 187–191
Externalities, 81–82, 614, 626–627
  environment and, 622–624, 626
    optimal abatement, 622–624, *624, 626*
  internalizing, 618–620
    by government action, *619,* 619–620, *620*
  market failure and, 615–618
    redefining property rights, 617
    voluntary agreements, 618, *619*

Factor income(s), 121
  marginal-productivity theory and, 537–540, *539*
  receipts from foreigners, GNP and, 121
Factor inputs, productivity and, 303
Factor markets, 526–541, *541*
  circular flow diagram of, 527, *528*
  cost minimization in, 537
  demand for factors of production, 532–535
    derived, 532–533
    joint determination of, 533–534
    marginal revenue product and, *534,* 534–535
  firm and, 527, 529–531
    marginal factor cost, 531, *532*
    price making and price taking, 527, 529–530, *530*
  marginal-productivity theory and, 537–540, *539*
    factor incomes and, 539–540
  profit maximization in, 535–537
    demand curve for factor and, *536,* 536–537
    MRP=MFC rule, 535–536
Factor payments, 129
  explicit and implicit, 415
Factor productivity, 291
Factors of production, 6, 113
  firm's demand for, 532–535
    derived, 532–533
    joint determination of, 533–534
    marginal revenue product and, *534,* 534–353

interest, rent and profit, 579–592
Fairness in taxation, 75, 87
  ability-to-pay principle and, 77
  benefit principle and, 75–77
Fallacy of composition, 222
Falling costs, shift in aggregate supply curve and, 146
Falling prices, aggregate demand and, 132
Falling wages, shift in aggregate supply curve and, 146
Farming (*see* Agriculture)
Favorable supply shocks, 139
FC (*see* Fixed costs)
FDIC (*see* Federal Deposit Insurance Corporation)
Featherbedding, 570, 575
Federal Communications Commission, 500
Federal deficit, defined, 184
Federal Deposit Insurance Corporate Improvement Act of 1991, 216
Federal Deposit Insurance Corporation (FDIC), 215, 216, 223, 228
Federal Open Market Committee (FOMC), 217, 224
  policy directive of, 241
Federal Reserve Act of 1913, 214, 243
Federal Reserve Notes, 200, 201
Federal Reserve System, 200, 201, 214–218, 223, 228, 273
  bank regulation by, 215
  borrowing from, 217
  commercial banking and, 210–228
  Federal Open Market Committee (FOMC) of, 217, 224, 241
  functions of, 214
  monetary base and, 217–218, *218*
  policy of, 224–226, 231–233, 272
    changes in discount rate, 226
    changes in reserve requirements, 226
    open-market operations, 224–226
    recent, 240
  reserve requirements of, 215–216
  structure of, 214–215
Federal Savings and Loan Insurance Corporation (FSLIC), 215
Federal Trade Commission, 502
Federal Trade Commission Act of 1914, 502, *503*
Fiat money, 200–201, 208
Final expenditures, GDP and, *114,* 116–118
Final goods, 113
Finance Committee (Senate), 273
Financial capital (*see* Capital, financial)
Financial intermediaries, 211, 227
Financial markets, corporate finance and, 403–412
Fine-tuning, of discretionary policy, 281
Fiscal policy, 192, 240
  as activist policy instrument, 271, 272
  automatic stabilizers versus discretionary policy, 175–178
  deficits and, 178–181
  effectiveness of, 183–187
  expansionary, 178, 182
  full-employment deficit and, 181–182, *182*
  goals of, 175
  national debt and, 174–193
Fisher, Irving, 197, 203, 204
Fixed costs (FC), variable costs and, 419
Fixed exchange rates, 328

gold standard and, 331–332, *332*
Fixed investment, 117
Fixed monetary rule in nonactivist policy, 269
Fixed prices in Keynesian model, 155
Floating exchange-rate(s), 328–330, *329, 331*
  system of, 341
Flows of money expenditures, 30
Focal points, in conscious parallelism, 488
FOMC (Federal Open Market Committee), 217, 224
  policy directive of, 241
Food production, arithmetic rate of growth, 296
Food stamp program, 607
Ford, Gerald, 518
Ford, Henry, 452, 591
Foreign exchange, 327
Foreign-exchange market, 327–328
Foreign-exchange rates, 327–328
  demand curve and, *329,* 329–330
  supply and, 330, *331*
Foreign saving, as source of investment finance, 125
Foreign trade effect on aggregate demand, 134
Formal agreements in oligopoly, 485
Foundations of Economic Analysis (Samuelson), 346
"Free ride," 82
Free riders
  public goods and, 621–622
  public TV example of, 622
Free trade, 315, 323
Freedom of entry, 477, 479
Freeman, Richard, 576
Frictional unemployment, 94, 109
Friedman, Milton, 152, 183, 191, 232, 244, 258, 269, 278, 279
Fringe benefits, 137
FSLIC (Federal Savings and Loan Insurance Corporation), 215
Full employment, 95–96, 109, 141
  balanced budgets and, 191
  as norm in classical theory, 151
Full-employment budget, 192
Full-employment deficit, 181–182, *182*
Full-employment model, classical, 169
Full-employment surplus, 181
Full-employment target, as national economic goal, 274
Functional distribution of income, 537–538
Furness, William III, 198
Futures contacts, 520
Futures markets, 519, 523

Gains from international trade, 313–314, *314*
Galbraith, John Kenneth, 469, 471
Gallup Poll on fear of inflation, 103
Game theory, 481
Gasoline tax, price elasticities and, *358,* 358–359
GATT (General Agreement on Tariffs and Trade), 325
GDI (*see* Gross domestic income)
GDP (*see* Gross domestic product)
GDP deflator (*see* Consumer Price Index)
Gender, income inequality and, 600, *601*
General Agreement on Tariffs and Trade (GATT), 322–324

General Theory of Employment, Interest, and Money, The (Keynes), 92, 134, 155
General wage cuts, inflexibility of labor market and, 155
Geometric rate of population growth, 296
Germany
  Great Depression in, 156
  labor unions in, 566
Glass-Steagall Act of 1933, 215
GNP (*see* Gross national product)
GNP deflator, 109
Gold, as commodity money, 199
Gold standard
  breakdown of, international, 336–337
  ending of, 201
  equilibrating mechanism of, 332
  fixed exchange rates and, 331–332, *332*
Gompers, Samuel, 564
Goods, 115
  price elasticity of demand and, 351
Gorbachev, Mikhail, 634, 635
Gordon, Robert, 143
Gould, David, 302
Government, 70–87
  action of, 81–83, 87
    to internalize externalities, *619*, 619–620, *620*
    bureaucracy as growth-reducing factor, 302
  debt of, 78–79
  dissaving by, 125
  evaluating resource allocation of, 83–84
  facts and trends in finance, 179–181, *180*
  income distribution and, 593, *604*, 604–605, *605*
  intervention by, 145
  monetary policies of, 135
  procurement practices of, as nontariff barriers, 317
  programs of
    for need-based assistance, 607, *607*
    reducing income inequality by, 598
  purchases of goods and services, 116–117
  resource allocation by
    market test and, 83–84
    rationality of public choices and, 84, *85*
  saving as source of investment finance, 125
  spending by, 71–74
    federal, state, and local, 74, *75*
    size of government and, 72–74, *73*
    types of, 71, *73*
  spending of, 71–74
  surpluses and deficits, 78–79, 81, *81*
  taxes and, 74–78, *76*
Government bonds, 201
Government budgets, 192
Government debt, 87
Government deficit, 87, 179
  surplus and, 78–79, 81, *81*
Government farm programs, 520–523, *521*
  direct payments, 521, *522*
  price supports, 520–521, *521*
  supply control programs, 522–523
  See also Agriculture
Government securities, 217
Government services, spending and, 74
Government surplus
  deficit and, 78–79, 81, *81*

defined, 179
Gradualism, 262–264, *264*
  for lowering inflation rate, 266
Graphs, 18–28
  areas of rectangles in, 27, *27*, 28
  understanding slope in, 21–27
  value of, 19–21, 28
Great Britain
  Great Depression in, 156
  labor unions in, 566
Great Depression, 105, 143, 145, 169, 322, 324–325, 510
  deflationary pressures during, 332
  images from, 154
  impact on public attitudes, 153–154
  Keynesian revolution and, 155
  policy blunders causing, 279
  predictions of Karl Marx and, 633
  sluggishness of self-correcting mechanism and, 274–275
"Great Society" programs, 609
"Greenmail," 399
Greenspan, Alan, 230, 243
Gresham, Sir Thomas, 200
Gresham's law, 200
Griffin, James, 141
Groshen, Erica L., 137
Gross domestic income (GDI), 118
Gross domestic product (GDP), 111–129, 128
  calculating, 129
  in constant dollars, 120, *121*
  in current dollars, 120, *121*
  disposable income and, 120–123, *122*
  in international perspective, 127
  national-income accounting and, 112–115
  omissions from, 124, 126–128
  savings and investment and, 123–124
  as sum of final expenditures, *114*, 116–118
  as sum of incomes, *114*, 118, *119*
  as sum of output or income, 115–120
Gross domestic product (GDP) per capita, international
  perspective and, 127
Gross national product (GNP), 120–121, 129
  gap in, 274
Growth-enhancing factors, 302
Growth-neutral factors, 302
Growth-reducing factors, 302

Hayek, Friedrich A. von, 42, 43, 227, 631
Haymarket Square labor riot, 564–565
Hicks, John R., 134
High fixed costs, as obstacle to collusion, 489
Hitler, Adolf, 156
Hoover, Herbert, 322
Horizontal mergers, 504
House Banking, Finance, and Urban Affairs Committee, 273
House Education and Labor Committee, 273
House Ways and Means Committee, 273
Household production, leisure and, 555–558
Houthakker, Hendrick S., 356, 513
Hubbard, R. Glenn, 430
Human capital, 6
  in income distribution, 598

Human-capital investment, 598
Human-resource policies
  for lowering unemployment, 266
  natural rate of unemployment and, 264
Hume, David, 203, 287, 334
Hungary, income distribution in, 597
Hyperinflation, 91, 97, 207, 249

IATA (International Air Transport Association), 486
IBM case (1982), Sherman Antitrust Act and, 503
Icahn, Carl, 397
Illegal activities, omitted from GDP, 126
IMF (*see* International Monetary Fund)
Immediate run, elasticity of supply in, 354–355, *355*
Implementation lag in fiscal policy, 183
Implicit cost, 414–415
Import licenses, 316
Import quotas, 316, 324
Import substitution, 300–301, 303
Impounding, 272
In-kind income, 604–605
Incentive(s), Communist socialism and, 634–636
Incentive systems, 630, 638
  in capitalist system, 632
  for limiting opportunistic behavior, 397
  in socialist system, 633
Incentive wages, 545–546
Incidence of a tax, 77
Income, 192
  agricultural, trends in, 512–516
  allocating, *368*, 368–369
  change in, consumer equilibrium and, 382, *382*, 385
  consumption and, 166
    in income/expenditure model, 156–158, *157*
  demand curve and, 52
  distribution of, 37
  inequality of
    measuring, 594–595, *596*
    sources of, 595–600
  redistribution by inflation, 101–102, 105
  saving and, *157*, 159
Income distribution
  distribution of population and, 289, *290*
  government policy and, *604*, 604–605, *605*
  international comparisons of, 597
  poverty and, 593–610
  shown by Lorenz curve, 594–595, *596*
Income effect, 370, 371, 385
  in backward-bending labor-supply curve, *556*, 556
  on consumer equilibrium, 383, *384*, 385
Income elasticities, 356, 357
Income elasticity of demand (E_i), 352–353, 359
Income/expenditure model (*see* Keynesian income/expenditure model)
Income tax, history of, 80
Increasing cost(s), law of, *8*, 8–9
Increasing-cost industries, 452
  long-run industry supply curve in, 449–451, *450*
Independence of Federal Reserve System, 243–244, *245*
Independent decisions of monopolistic competitors, 474–475

Independent monetary authority, case for, 282
Indifference curve(s), 377, 378–379, *379*
  properties of, 379
Indifference-curve analysis, 385
  marginal-utility theory and, 381
Indifference-curve equilibrium rule, 381
Indifference-curve theory, 376–385
  consumer equilibrium and, 380–381, *381*
  consumer preferences and, 377–380, *378*
  effect of income change, 382, *382*
  effect of price change, 382–385, *383, 384*
Indirect business taxes, 122
Industrial policy for United states, 452
Industrial revolution, 286, 290–291
  technological revolution and, 291
Industrial unions, 562
Industrialized world, sustained economic growth of, 290–295
  extensive and intensive, 291, *292*
  labor productivity and, *293*, 294–295, *295*
  role of productivity in, 291–292, *293*
Industry equilibrium, short-run, *439, 441, 443*, 445, *445*
Industry supply curve
  as horizontal summation, 444
  profit-maximizing firm and, 442, 444, *444*
Inefficiency(ies)
  appearance of, in monopolistic competition, 477
  inflation and, 102
  of monopolies, 467–468
    restricted output and, 468–469
  transition to market economy and, 638
Inelastic demand, 348
Inelasticity of supply, of land and natural resources, 585
Inequality, 83
Inequality of income
  chance and inheritance, 598–600
    luck, 598–599
    wealth and inheritance, 599–600, *600*
  differences in people and jobs, 596–598
    ability and human capital, 598
    compensating differentials and risk, 597
  discrimination and, 600
  fashion model example of, 603
  sources of, 595–600, 610
Inferior goods, 52
Inflated costs, price regulation and, 496
Inflation, 33, 96–102, 109, 139, 248–254
  cases of, supply-side, 250–251
  contracts and, 101
  deficits and, *189*, 189–190
  defined, 97
  demand-side and supply-side, 248–249, *249*
  expected, 137
  fear of, 101–102
  government policy toward, 103
  how expectations are formed, 253–254
  inevitability of, 252
  interest rates and, 251–253
  measuring, 98
  monetary growth and, 249–250, *251*
  trends in, 98–99, *99–100*
  types of, 99–101
  unemployment, stagflation and, 247–266
  wage/price spiral in, 254, *255*

Inflation rates, 109
  floating exchange rates and, 330
  interest rates and, 265
  lowered, independent monetary authority and, 282
Inflationary cyclical upturns, balanced budgets and, 191
Inflationary expectations, 253–254
  lowering, 261–262
  Phillips curve and, 259, *260*
Inflationary gaps, 143, 147, 175, 245
  automatic removal of, *144*, 146
  deflationary gaps and, 140–142, *142*
  eliminating by discretionary fiscal policy, 178, *179*
  monetary policy and, *236*, 236–238, *237*
Inflationary pressures, in balanced labor market, 96
Information, 400–401
  equilibrium price and, 60
  incentives and, failure of Communist socialism and, 634–636
Information costs, 396–397
  contracts and, 394, 396
  transaction costs and, 41–43
Information specialists, 400
Inheritance, income inequality and, 598–600
Injunctions, by employers against strikes, 567
Innovation
  monopoly and, 469–470
  as obstacle to collusion, 489
  as source of economic profits, 591
Input costs, fixity in, 137
Intensive growth, 291, 292, 294
Interest, 580, 591
Interest and Prices (Wicksell), 212
Interest rate(s), 405–406, 581–582
  consumption and, 160
  deficits and, 190, *191*
  determination of, 582–584
  effectiveness of ceiling on, 490–591
  Federal Reserve System control of, 235, *235*
  inflation and, 251–253
  international capital movements and, 335
  inverse relationship to bond prices, 233–234
  present value calculations and, 582
  relationship to bond prices, 412
  relative, exchange rates and, 330–331
  structure of, 584–585
    liquidity and, 584–585
    maturity and, 585
    risk and, 584
Interest-rate effect, on aggregate demand, 133
Interest-rate targets, 238–239, 245
Intermediaries, 394, 396–397
  information business and, 398–400
  role of, 398–400
  value of, 400
Intermediate goods, 113, 115
Internal debt, 187–188
  external debt and, 187–191
Internal Revenue Service, 126, 608
Internalization of externalities, 618–620
International Air Transport Association (IATA), 486

International capital movements, 334–335
  balance of payments and, 333–336
  reasons for, 335
International gold standard, breakdown of, 336–337
International Monetary Fund (IMF), 337–338
  Jamaican agreements and, 339–341
International monetary mechanisms, 327–332
  fixed exchange rates and gold standard, 331–332, *333*
  floating exchange rates, 328–330, *329, 331*
  market forces affecting, 330–331
  foreign-exchange market, 327–328
International monetary system, 326–341
  balance of payments in, 333–334, *335*
  evolution of, 336–341
  international capital movements in, 334–335
  mechanisms in (*see* International monetary mechanisms)
  U.S. trade deficit in, *335*, 336
International perspective of labor unions, 566
International Statistical Institute, 512
International trade
  benefits of, 323
  gains from, 313–314, *314*
  law of comparative advantage in, 40, 307–313, *310*
  obsolescence of antitrust laws and, 506, 508
  protection and, 305–325
    case against, 318–321
    protectionism, 314–315
    trade barriers, 315–317
  reasons for, 306
  United States in, 306–307
  trade policies, 321–324, *322*
International Working Men's Association, 631
Inventory investment, 164
Inverse relationship (*see* Negative relationship)
Investment, 129
  changes in, aggregate expenditure curve and, 165
  in classical theory, 151–152, *153*
  expenditures for, 117
  inventory, 117
  saving and, 123–124, *162*, 163–164
  sources of finance, 125
Invisible hand, 29, 35–36, 44
  example of, 38
  limits of, 43
Involuntary unemployment, social and private costs of, 95
Irrationality of stock market, 410–411
Island of Yap (stone money), 198
Isolated State with Respect to Agricultural and Political Economy, The (Thunen), 415

Jamaican agreements of International Monetary Fund, 339–341
Japan, labor unions in, 566
Jevons, William Stanley, 364
Jewkes, John, 470
Job Corps, 598
Job preferences, 93

Job search, 95
Johnson, Harry G., 328
Johnson, William R., *79*
Joint determination of factor demand, 533–534
Journal of Law and Economics, 616
Journal of Political Economy, 270

Kelley, Allen C., 302
Kendrick, John W., *293*
Kennedy, John F., 152
Kennedy Round (of multilateral trade negotiations), 323
Keynes, John Maynard, 15, 83, 92, 134, 145, 149, 155, 156, 158, 163–165, 168, 169, 212, 233, 257, 274
Keynes, John Neville, 92
Keynesian economists, modern, activist policy of, 274–277
Keynesian equilibrium, 163–165
Keynesian income-expenditure model, 149–160, 169
Keynesian income/expenditure model
    approach to, *151,* 155–160
    consumption, income, and saving in, 156–158, *157*
    for determining real output, *151,* 155–160
    equilibrium expenditures in, 160–165
    factors affecting consumption in, 159–160
    marginal propensities in, *157,* 158–159
    multipliers in, 165–167, *166, 167*
Keynesian macroeconomics, transition to, 153–155
    fixed prices in, 155
    Great Depression and, 153–155
Keynesian monetary policy, 245
    bond prices and interest rates in, 233–234
    effect of money on aggregate demand in, 235, *236*
    money and interest rates in, 234–235
Keynesian revolution, Great Depression and, 155
Khazzoom, J. D., 356
Khrushchev, Nikita, 633
Kinked demand, 483–484, *484*
Kinked-demand curve, 483–484, *484,* 491
Kinnear, Jim, 397
Knight, Frank, 495, 581
Knights of Labor, 564–565
Kohler, Heinz, 513
Kornai, Janos, 636
Kuznets, Simon, 113

Labor
    costs of, 538
    demand for, 546–548
        shifts in, 551, *552*
    differentiated from other factors, 544
    productivity of, 292, *293,* 294–295, *295*
    shortage of, 550
    supply limited by unions, 570, *571*
    surplus of, 550
Labor-demand curve, 558
    market demand curve and, 548, *548*
Labor force
    defined, 93
    persons not in, 92–93
    shifting, in agriculture, 516–517
    women in, 558

Labor market(s), 539, 543–559, 558
    in classical macroeconomics, 150
    demand in, 546–548
    equilibrium in, *548–550, 549*–553
    inflexibility of, 155
    leisure, household production and, 555–558
    supply curve in, 549, *549*
    wage structure in, 553–555
    wages and incentive payments in, 544–546
Labor market classifications, 91–93
Labor-market equilibrium, *548–550, 549*–553
    shifts in labor supply and demand and, 551
        factors causing, 551–553
Labor market search, 95, *95*
Labor supply, shifts in, 551, *552,* 553
Labor supply curve, 549, *549,* 558
Labor unions, 561–577
    decline of, 563–564, *564, 565*
    defined, 562–563
    effect on wages, 574, 576
    efficiency and, 575–576, *576*
    history of, 564–565, 567
    in international perspective, 566
    objectives of, 568–573, *569*
    union legislation and, *564,* 567–568
    See also specific unions; Union(s); Unionism
Lags
    activist policy and, 278
    in fiscal policy, 183
    problem of, 242–243
Laissez-faire macroeconomic policy, 145
    in classical theory, 152–153
    in Great Depression, 154
Land, Edwin, 591
Landrum Griffin Act of 1959, 568
Law of comparative advantage, 39–40, 307–313, *310,* 323
    case against protection and, 318
    in international trade, *310,* 312–313
    self-sufficiency and, 310–312
Law of demand, 49, 67, 362, *369,* 369–370, 383
    example of, 40
    marginal utility and, 365–371, *367, 368*
    profit-maximizing strategy of monopolist and, 460–461, *462*
Law of diminishing marginal rate of substitution, consumer preferences and, 377–379, *378, 379*
Law of diminishing marginal utility, 365, 372, 374, 602–603
Law of diminishing returns, 296, *297,* 420–422, *421, 424,* 430, 532
    rate of return on capital and, 583–584
Law of downward sloping demand, 50
Law of increasing costs, *8,* 8–9
Law of scarcity, 3–4
Layard, Richard, 109
LDCs (*see* Less developed countries)
Least-cost rule, 537, 541
Legal system, property rights and, 34, 632
Leisure
    household production and, 555–558
    labor market and, 544
    value of, omitted from GDP, 126
Lender of last resort, Federal Reserve System as, 232

Lenin, Vladimir I., 207, 633
Less developed countries (LDCs), 124, 126, 289
    classical growth model and, 295–298
    explanation for poverty in, 295–303
    external assistance for, 301–303
    literacy and life expectancy in, 300
    poverty in, 303
        sources of, 298–300
    progress in, 300, *301*
    trade policies in, 300–301
Level of economic development, 289
Level of output, costs of production and, 425, *425*
Lewis, H. Gregg, 564
Lewis, John L., 565
Liabilities, 213
Licensing, 458
Life-styles, modern economic growth and, 291
Limited liability, of corporations, 393, 404
Linear relationships, *21–23,* 23
Liquidity, structure of interest rates and, 584–585
Liquidity-preference curve, 234, *235*
Liquidity-preference theory (Keynesian), 234–235
Litan, Robert E., 499
Living standards
    of Communist socialism, 633–634, *634*
    determining, 101
    inflation and, 101
Lloyds of London, unlimited liability and, 394
Loanable funds (*see* Credit)
Lobbying
    as monopoly-profit-seeking behavior, 469
    by unions, 569
Logrolling, 72, 73, 322
    example of, 85
Long run, 146–147, 355, *355,* 357
    critical distinction from short run, 463
    monopolistic competition in, *476,* 477
    monopoly profits in, 463–464
    in perfect competition, 451–452
    variability of all costs in, 419
    variable costs in, 430
Long-run average cost (LRAC), 426–427, *427*
Long-run average-cost (LRAC) curve, 431
Long-run cost(s), 426–429
    constant returns to scale and, 428
    diseconomies of scale and, 428–429
    economies of scale and, 427–428
    long-run cost curve and, 426–427, *427*
    shifts in cost curves, 426, *427*
Long-run cost curve, 426–427, *427*
Long-run equilibrium, 143–144, 146
    efficient production in, 449
    efficient scale of operation in, 449
    macroeconomic, 143–144, 146
    of monopolistically competitive firm, *476,* 477
Long-run industry supply curve, *447, 448,* 449–451
    constant-cost industries and, *447,* 449, *450*
    increasing-cost industries, 449–451, *450*
Long-run solution to poverty problem, 608–609

Long-run supply
  economic profit and resources in, 446
  entry and exit of firms and, 446–448
  long-run equilibrium and, *447, 448,* 448–449
  long-run industry supply curve and, *447, 448,* 449–451
  in perfect competition, 446–451
Long-term trends in unemployment, 96, *97*
Lorenz curve, 610
  income inequality and, 594–595, *596*
Loss-minimizing firm
  losses per unit of output in, 442
  short-run supply curve and, 440, *441,* 442
Loss-minimizing monopolist, 463, *464*
Low average cost, in long-run equilibrium, 449
Low entry barriers, as obstacle to collusion, 488–489
Lower employment, monopsony and, 573
Lower wages, monopsony and, 573
LRAC (Long-run average cost), 426–427, *427*
Lucas, Robert, 270, 278
Luxuries, elasticity of demand and, 352

Macroeconomic aggregates, 12, 131–147
Macroeconomic equilibrium, 140
  long-run, 143–144, 146
Macroeconomic goals
  budgets and, 191
  matching policies to, 272–274
Macroeconomic instability, 83
Macroeconomic policy
  fiscal and monetary policies as tools, 240
  laissez-faire, 145
Macroeconomics, 12, 16, 90, 108
  classical, 150–153
  microeconomics and, 11–12
  new theories of, stagflation and, 104, *104*
  two views of, 150, *151*
Maddison, Angus, 288
Majority-rule voting, 87
  public expenditure and, *85,* 84
Malthus, Thomas R., 287, 295, 296, 303
Managed exchange rates, 340
Management of corporations, 393
Management skills, diseconomies of scale and, 429
Manager of Domestic Operations, 241
Managerial allocation, 400
Managerial rewards, 635–636
Manpower Training and Development, 598
Marginal analysis, 83–84
Marginal benefit, in perfect competition, 467
Marginal cost (MC), 422, 431, 438
  average cost and, 422–423
  economic decisions based on, 423
Marginal-cost curve, 444
Marginal-cost figures, 424, *424, 425*
Marginal factor cost (MFC), 531, *532,* 541, 547, 572
Marginal physical product (MPP), 420–422, *421,* 430, 532, 541, 547–548
  per dollar of cost in factor markets, 537
  shrimp-boat example of, 420–422, *421*

Marginal productivity
  factor incomes and, 539–540
  natural-law philosophy and, 602
Marginal-productivity theory, 541
  of income distribution, 537–540, *539*
Marginal propensity to consume (MPC), 169
  in income/expenditure model, *157,* 158–159
  multiplier and, 166, *167*
Marginal propensity to save (MPS), 169
  in income/expenditure model, *157,* 158–159
Marginal rate of substitution (MRS), 377
Marginal revenue (MR)
  for perfectly competitive firms, 438
  price and, 459–460
Marginal revenue curve, 461
Marginal revenue product (MRP), *534,* 534–535, 541, 547–548
  direct method of calculation, *534,* 534–535
  indirect method of calculation, *534,* 535
Marginal utility (MU), 364, 372
  diminishing, 365
  examples of, 370
  law of demand and, 365–371, *367, 368*
  per dollar, *367,* 367–368
Marginal utility schedule, 365, *367*
Marginal-utility theory, indifference-curve analysis and, 381
Marginal values, 417, *418*
Market(s), 47–49
  equilibrium and, 59–60
  perfectly competitive, 48–49
  product and factor, conditions in, 529, *530*
  types of, 47
Market allocation, 400
Market basket, in measuring inflation, 98
Market-clearing price (*see* Equilibrium price)
Market demand, 371–372, *372*
  for factors of production, 538, *539*
Market-demand curve, 50, 371–372, *372, 374*
Market economy, Russian transition to, 637–638
Market equilibrium, short-run, *439, 441, 443, 445, 445*
Market failure, 626–627
  environmental economics and, 614–627
  externalities and, 615–618
    redefining property rights, 617
    voluntary agreements, 618, *619*
Market price/quantity combination, 58
Market solutions to environmental protection, *620, 625*
Market supply curve (*see* Industry supply curve)
Market test, government resource allocation and, 83–84
Marriage, "market" for, 63–64
Marsh, Helen, 457
Marsh, Maj. Gen. Sir Frederick Maurice, 457
Marshall, Alfred, 48, 203, 204, 212, 346
Marx, Karl, 557, 631, 633, 638
Marx, Louis, 591
Maskus, Keith E., 321
Maturity, structure of interest rates and, 585

Maximum satisfaction, 366, *367*
Maximum value of relationship, 24, 28
MC (*see* Marginal cost)
Means, Gardner, 389
Measure of economic welfare, 127
Mechanization, labor productivity and, 557
Medicaid, 607
Medical care, "free lunch" in, 14
Medicare benefits, national debt and, 188
Medium of exchange, money as, 195–197, 208
Medoff, James, 576
Menger, Carl, 364
Mercantilist fallacy, 334
Mergers, 408
  in carbonated beverage market, 404
  legislation regarding, 504–505, *506*
Metallized Paper Corporation, purchase of pollution rights, 626
MFC (*see* Marginal factor cost)
Michaels, James W., 603
Microeconomics, 11, 16
  macroeconomics and, 11–12
Middle class, 595, *596*
Midpoints formula, for calculating price elasticity of demand, 346–348, *347*
Military spending, 73
Mill, James, 287, 595
Mill, John Stuart, 305, 595
Miller, Merton, 176
Millsaps, S. W., 356
Minimum average cost, in perfectly competitive industries, 450–451
Minimum staffing requirements, union support of, 569–570
Minimum value of relationship, 24, 28
Minimum wage, union support of, 569
Minimum-wage laws, inflexibility of labor market and, 155
Ministry for Industry and Trade (MITI) in Japan, 452
Mises, Ludwig von, 631
Mistakes, diseconomies of scale and, 429
Mitchell, B. R., 156
MITI (Ministry for Industry and Trade), 452
Models
  classical, 165
  classical growth, for agricultural economies, 295–298
  full-employment, 169
  Keynesian income/expenditure, 149–160, 169
    multipliers in, 165–167, *166, 167*
  of production-possibilities factor, 7–10, *8*
Modern Keynesian economists, 283
Modernization, 298, 299
Modigliani, Franco, 176, 183
M1 money supply, 201
Monetarism, 230, 244
Monetarists, 277, 278
Monetary-aggregate targets, 238–239, 245
Monetary base, 217–218, *218*
Monetary Control Act of 1980, 215–217, 223
Monetary growth targets, emphasis on, by Federal Reserve System, 281–282
Monetary History of the United States, A (Friedman and Schwartz), 232
Monetary phenomena, protracted inflation, 250

Monetary policy, 175, 192, 230–245
  as activist policy instrument, 271, 272
  complexities of, 238–240
  deflationary and inflationary gaps and, 236, 236–238, 237
  Federal Reserve System and, 243–244
  instruments of, 231–233
  Keynesian, 233–235
  problems of, 240–243
Monetary reform, 207
Monetary restraint in lowering inflation rate, 266
Monetary sector, real sector and, 205
Monetizing debt, 228
  creating money by, 219
Money, 41
  created by banks, 218–224
  debt and, 219–220, 220
  effect on aggregate demand, 235, 236
  functions of, 196–199
    as medium of exchange, 196–197
    as store of value, 198–199
    as unit of value, 197–198
  prices and, 195–208
  as social invention, 197
  supply of (see Money supply)
  types of, 199–201
Money market funds, 201
Money multiplier, 218, 224, 241–242
Money prices, relative prices and, 32–33
Money savings, purchasing power of, 160
Money supply, 135
  changes in, 204–205
  controlling, 228
  definitions of, 201–203, 203
  expansion of, 222–224
    cash leakages and, 223
    excess reserves and, 223–224
  link with real GNP, 233
  problems of controlling, 240–241
  stock market crashes and, 223
Monitoring systems, for limiting opportunistic behavior, 397
Monopolistic competition, 434, 474–478, 491
  characteristics of, 474–475
  in long run, 476, 477
  nonprice competition of, 477–478
  oligopoly and, 473–491
  profit maximization in short run and, 475, 476, 477
  turkey farm example of, 475, 476, 477–478
Monopoly(ies), 81, 434, 455–471
  cable TV as, 470
  characteristics of, 456–458
    barriers to entry, 457–458
    definition of, 456
    limitations on power of, 456
  efficiency and, 466–470
  in microprocessors by Intel Corporation, 465
  profit maximizing and, 458–466, 459
  protection against, 493–508
  regulation of, 408
Monopoly-profit-seeking behavior, 468–469
  lobbying as, 469
Monopoly profits, 589
Monopoly rents, 589
Monopsony, 529–531
  collective bargaining with, 572–573, 573

Moonlighting activities, 126
Moral-hazard problem, 398
Moral incentives, 630
Motor Carrier Act of 1980, 500
Movement along consumption/income curve, 160, 161
MPC (see Marginal propensity to consume)
MPP (see Marginal physical product)
MPS (see Marginal propensity to save)
MR (see Marginal revenue)
MRP (see Marginal revenue product)
MRS (Marginal rate of substitution), 377
M2 money supply, 201
MU (see Marginal utility)
Multiple contraction of deposits, 225
Multiple-deposit creation, 220, 220–221, 221
Multiple-deposit expansion, 221, 221
  open-market purchases and, 225
Multiplier(s), 165–167, 166, 167, 169
  marginal propensity to consume and, 166, 167
  real-world, 168
Multiyear money contracts, in anticipation of inflation, 101
Muth, J. F., 270
Mutual interdependence
  of oligopolies, 478
  in oligopoly theory, 481

National Cancer Institute, 461
National debt, 192
  burden of, 185–187, 186
    on different generations, 188
  fiscal policy and, 174–193
    effectiveness of, 184–187
  as percentage of GDP, 185, 186
  trends in, 184–185, 186
National defense, as public good, 82
National Environmental Policy Act, 625
National income, 122
National-income accounting, 112–115, 128, 151
  circular flow of, 112
  example of, 112–113, 114, 115
  gross domestic product and, 115
National Labor Relations Act of 1935 (Wagner Act), 567–568, 577
National Labor Relations Board (NLRB), 568
Natural Gas Policy Act of 1978, 430
Natural gas prices, 430
Natural-law philosophers, 602
Natural-law philosophy, 610
  in distributive justice, 602
Natural level of output, 142
Natural monopoly, 457
Natural rate of unemployment, 96, 109, 141, 181, 256
  targeting, activist policy and, 278
Necessities, elasticity of demand and, 352
Negative income tax (NIT), 607, 607–609, 608
  advantages of, 608
Negative productivity growth in 1970s, 293, 294–295
Negative relationship
  shown in scatter diagram, 26, 26
  between variables, 19, 27–28
Negative slope of aggregate demand curve, 132, 133

Negotiable orders of withdrawal (NOW) accounts, 201
Neighborhood Youth Programs, 598
Nerlove, M., 356
Net costs imposed by tariffs, 319–320, 320
Net exports
  aggregate demand curve and, 134–135
  of goods and services, 117
Net national product (NNP), 121–122, 129
Net output, 118
New Classical Economics (Lucas), 270
New Deal Program, as cause of Great Depression, 279
New York Stock Exchange Index, 410
New York Stock Exchange (NYSE), 408
"News", exchange rates and, 331
Nickell, Stephen, 109
NIT (see Negative income tax)
Nixon, Richard, 201, 263, 339
NLRB (National Labor Relations Board), 568
NNP (Net national product), 121–122, 129
Nominal GDP, 120, 121, 129
Nominal interest rates, 252–253
Nominal quantity, value of money and, 206–207
Nominal supply of money, Great Depression and, 279
Nominal wages, 544–545
Nonactivist policy, 283
  common ground with activist policy, 281
  to stabilize business cycle, 269–270
Noncompeting groups, 559, 598
  wage structure and, 554–555
Nonexclusion, as characteristic of public goods, 621
Nonmarketed goods and services, omitted from GDP, 124, 126
Nonprice competition, in monopolistic competition, 477
Nonrivalry, as characteristic of public goods, 621
Nontariff barriers to trade, 317
Nonunion wages, effect of unions on, 576, 577
Nonunionized sectors of labor market, 137
Nordhaus, William D., 499
Normal goods, 52, 556
Normal profit, 446
Normative economics, 13–14, 16
  positive economics and, 12–14
  tax systems and, 78
Norris-LaGuardia Act of 1932, 567–568, 577
NOW (Negotiable orders of withdrawal accounts), 201
Nuclear power
  economic problem of, 497
  paying costs of, 497–498
NYSE (New York Stock Exchange), 408

Obstacles to collusion, 488–489, 491
  detecting cheating, 489
  high fixed costs, 489
  high rates of innovation, 489
  low entry barriers, 488–489
  many sellers, 488
  product heterogeneity, 489
Office of Management and Budget, 273
Oligopoly, 434, 478–480, 491
  characteristics of, 478

determinants of concentration in, 479–480
  barriers to entry, 479
  measuring, 479–480, *480*
efficiency and, 489–491
kinked-demand curve and, 483–484, *484*
monopolistic competition and, 473–491
Oligopoly theory, 481–489
  coordination in, *483*, 485–487
  kinked demand in, 483–484, *484*
  mutual interdependence in, 481
  obstacles to collusion, 488–489
  oligopolist's dilemma and, 482–483, *483*
  prisoners' dilemma and, 481–482
OPEC (Organization of Petroleum Exporting Countries), 486
Open-market operations, 217, 245
  of Federal Reserve System, 224–226
    purchases, *225*, 225–226
    sales, 224–225, *225*
  as instrument of monetary policy, 231
Opportunistic behavior of agents, 396–397
Opportunity costs, 5–6, 15, 414–417
  average/marginal rules, 417, *418*
  economic profits and, 416–417
  economic rent and, 587
  example of, 5
  explicit and implicit, 414–415
  of household production, 558
  in international trade, 310, 311, 312
  of job search, 95
  for labor, 549
  of large families in less developed countries, 299
  of leisure, 555–557, 559
  natural gas prices and, 430
  pilot salaries and, 416
  as sum of explicit and implicit costs, 415–416
  waste-disposal costs as, 623–624
Optimal output, 471
Organization of businesses, types of, 389–393, *390–391*
Organization of Petroleum Exporting Countries (OPEC), 486
Overinvestment, price regulation and, 496

PACs (*see* Political Action Committees)
Paper currency, 200
Papercraft Corporation, sale of pollution rights, 626
Partnership, 391–392, 400
Pasinetti, Luigi, 457
Patents, 458, 463
Peak phase of business cycle, 105, *106*
Pechman, Joseph, *79*
Per-capita incomes in free-trade countries, 323
Percentage changes in quantity or price, 345
Perestroika, origins of, 635
Perfect competition, 433–452
  cases of, 440–442
  characteristics of, 434–437
    conditions for, 435–436
    industry and firm, 436–437, *437*
  economic efficiency and, effect of externalities on, 618
  entry of firms into, 446–447, *447*
  exit of firms from, 447–448, *448*

industry market models and, 434
long-run supply in, 446–451
short-run supply curve in, 437–445
Perfect equality in income distribution, shown by Lorenz curve, 594–595, *596*
Perfect equality of distribution, 610
Perfectly competitive markets, 48–49, 67, 451
Perfectly elastic demand, 350, *351*
Perfectly elastic demand curve in agriculture, 511
Perfectly elastic supply, 353–354, *354*
Perfectly inelastic demand, 350, *351*
Perfectly inelastic supply, 354, *354*
Permanent income, effectiveness of fiscal policy and, 183
Permissible activities, restriction in bank regulation, 215
Perot, H. Ross, 86, 174, 358, 393
Perpetual income stream, 406
Perpetuity formula, 406, 409
Personal consumption expenditures, GDP and, 116
Personal income, 122
  disposable, 122–123
  distribution of, 537–538
Personal income tax, 80
Personal saving, 123
Personal wealth, 599–600, *600*
Phelps, Edmund S., 258
Philips, L., 356
Phillips, A. W., 250
Phillips curve, 258, *259*
  short-run, 258–260, *260*
    upward shifts of, *260*, 260–261
  swirling pattern in, 258, *259*
Physical capital, 6
Physical flows, 30
Pigou, A. C., 150, 616
"Poison pills," 399
Policy blunders, Great Depression and, 279
Policy choices, 261–264
  business cycle and, 283
  gradualism, 262–264, *264*
  human-resource policies, 264
  implications of value of money, 207
  lowering inflationary expectations, 261–262
  unemployment costs of lowering inflation, 262, *264*
Policy goals, fiscal, 175
Policy instruments
  of activism, 271–274
  to deal with business cycle, 283
Political Action Committees (PACs), 86
Political Economy Club, 92, 287
Pollution abatement
  choice of amounts of, 624, *624*
  complete, 624, *624*
  evaluation standard for programs, *624*, 624–625
Pollution rights, buying and selling, 626
Population
  distribution of, distribution of income and, 289, *290*
  growth of
    geometric rate of, 296
    as growth-neutral factor, 302
    slower rate in industrialized countries, 291

shifts in, decline of unionism and, 563–564
Population pressures in LDCs, classical growth model and, 298–299
Positive economics, 12–13, 16
Positive relationship between variables, 19, 27–28
Potential buyers, demand curve and, 53
Potential competition
  deregulation and, 499
  for oligopolies, 480
Potential substitutes, monopolies and, 456
Poverty, 605–609
  causes of, 604
  income distribution and, 593–610
  in less developed countries, 303
  sources of, 298–300
  official income standard, 609
  statistical profile of, 609
  trends in, 605, *606*, 609
PPF (*see* Production-possibilities frontier)
Predatory pricing, 490
Preferences, 363, 365, *367*, 372
  consumer
    budget line and, 379–380, *380*
    demand and, 363–365
    indifference-curve theory and, 377–380, *378*
    law of diminishing marginal rate of substitution and, 377–379, *378, 379*
  demand curve and, 52–53
  in jobs, 93, 544
  in labor market, 544
  product, 331
    exchange rates and, 331
Present value (PV)
  bonds and, 404–406
  stock prices as, 409
Present-value calculations, interest rate and, 582
Present-value formula, 405–406, 411
Price(s)
  agricultural
    decline in 1980s, 518–519
    declining relative, 514–516, *515*
    fluctuations in, 512–514, *514, 515*
    trends in, 512–516
  changes in
    effect on consumer equilibrium, 382–385, *383, 384*
    price elasticity of demand and, 351
  decreases in
    aggregate supply increase and, 185
    due to deregulation, 500
  goods allocated by, 373–374
  increases in
    aggregate demand increase and, 185
    revenue from, 349
  money and, 195–208
  regulation of, 494–496
    inflated costs and, 496
    lags in, 496, 498
    overinvestment and, 496
    regulatory pricing formula for, 495–496. *See also* Price control
  shifts in supply curve and, 56
  stability in oligopoly, 474
  unanticipated decline in, 138
  See also Relative prices
Price control, 48, 491
  in perfect competition, 436

Price discrimination, 471
    conditions for, 465
    manufacturer's coupons, 466
    by monopolies, 464–466
Price/earnings (PE) ratio, 409–410, 412
Price elasticity(ies) of demand (E_d), 345–
    352, 356–357
    calculating, 345–348, *347*
    demand curves in, 350, *351*
    determinants of, 350–352
    elastic and inelastic demand, *347*, 348–
    349
    elasticity and slope, *347*, 349–350
    profit maximizing and, 465
Price elasticity(ies) of supply (E_s), 353–
    357, 356, 357, 359
    supply curves in, 353–354, *354*
    in three time periods, 354–355, *355*, 357
Price index, in measuring inflation, 98
Price inelasticities of demand in agriculture,
    513
Price leadership in oligopoly, 487–488
Price levels
    consumption and, 160
    relative, exchange rate and, 330
Price makers, 458, 471, 474
    in factor markets, 527, 531
Price making, in factor market, 527, 529–
    530, *530*
Price supports in agriculture, 520–521,
    521
Price system, 29–44
    calculating relative prices, 33
    circular flow of economic activity in, 30,
    31
    as coordinating mechanism, 35–36
    defined, 36
    economic problem and, 30–31
    information costs in, 41–43
    operation of, 36–37
    principle of substitution in, 34
    property rights and, 34–35
    relative prices and money prices in, 32–
    33
    specialization and, 37–41
    transaction costs in, 41–43
Price takers, 434, 437, 451, 458, 523, 558
    in factor markets, 527, 531
    farmers as, 511, 513
Price taking, in factor market, 527, 529–
    530, *530*
Pricing formula, 495–496
Principal(s), 394
    principal/agent problem, 401, 545–546
Principal/agent problem, 401
    employee travel and, 546
    in labor, 545–546
Principle of substitution, 34, 37, 44
    decline of IBM and, 35
Principle of unintended consequences, 13
Principles of Economics (Marshall), 48
Principles of Political Economy and Taxation
    (Ricardo), 307
Principles of Political Economy (Mill), 595
Prisoners' dilemma game, 491
    oligopoly theory and, 481–482
    tit-for-tat and, 482
Private demand, aggregate demand curve
    and, 135
Private saving, 123–124
    as source of investment finance, 125
Privatization, 43

"Problem of Social Cost, The" (Coase),
    616
Producers, gain from higher prices, *318*,
    318–319
Product differentiation
    consequences of, 475, *476*, 477
    in monopolistic competition, 474–475
Product heterogeneity, as obstacle to col-
    lusion, 489
Product market, 541
Product preferences, exchange rates and,
    331
Production-possibilities factor, 7
Production-possibilities frontier (PPF), 7–
    10, *8*, 15, 634, *634*, 635
    of America in international trade, 310–
    311, *311*
    of Europe in international trade, *311*,
    311–312
    example of, 9
Productivity
    comparative advantage and, 39–40
    economies of scale and, 39
    factor inputs and, 303
    growth, development and, 286–303
    international trade and, 39–40
    measures of, 292
    role in American economic growth, 291–
    292, *293*
    shifts in labor demand and, 551, *552*
    as source of growth, 292
    Soviet, origins of perestroika and, 635
    specialization and, 39–40
Profit(s), 588–589, 591
    of commercial banks, 212
    of corporations, 393
    economic, sources of, 589, 591
    nonprice competition and, 478
    in perfect competition, 438
Profit-maximization rule, 438
Profit maximizing, 388–389, 400, 471
    factor markets and, 535–537
      demand curve and, *536*, 536–537
      MRP=MFC rule, 535–536
    monopolies and, 458–466, *459*
      equilibrium in short run, 460–461,
      462, 463
      loss-minimizing monopolist, 463, *464*
      price and marginal revenue, 459–460
      by price discrimination, 464–466
      profits in long run, 463–464
Profit-maximizing firms, 541
Profit-seeking behavior of monopolies,
    468–469
Profitability of agriculture, past, 517–519
Profitable firm, short-run supply curve and,
    439, 440
Program for Monetary Stability, A (Fried-
    man), 232
Progressive taxes, 77, 78
Property
    in administrative-command economy,
    635
    in capitalist economy, 635
Property rights, 34–35, 44, 630
    in capitalist system, 632
    redefining in internalization, 617
    in socialist system, 632
    transition to market economy and, 637–
    638
Proportional taxes, 77
Prospectus, 407

Prosperity, deficit and, 181
Protection, case against, 318–321
    costs of, *318*, 318–319, *319*, 324
    explanation for tariffs, 320–321
    net costs of tariffs and, 319–320, *320*
    ratio of annual costs to benefits, 321
Protectionism, 314–315
Protracted inflation (*see* Sustained inflation)
Public Choice (Buchanan), 72
Public choice economics, 84, *85*
Public debt as percentage of GDP, *186*, 187
Public franchises, 458
Public goods, 82, 620–622, 626–627
    free riders and, 621–622
    nonexclusion, 621
    nonrivalry, 621
Public-health improvements, in less de-
    veloped countries, 299
Public housing, 607
Public policy
    comparable worth and, 540
    health of unionism and, 575
    to prevent corporate abuse, 399
    technology and, 557
Public saving, 124
Purchasing Power of Money, The (Fisher),
    197
Purchasing power parity rates, 127
Pure economic rents, 586–587, *587*, 591
    demand-determined changes in, 586–
    587
    distinguished from economic rents, 587–
    588
    marginal revenue product (MRP) of land
    and, 586
Pure monopoly(ies), 456, 471
    rarity of, 464
Pure private goods, 623
Pure public goods, 623, 627
PV (Present value), 406–409

Quantity demanded, 49
Quantity of output, in perfectly competitive
    industries, 451
Quantity supplied, 54
Quantity theory, 208
    aggregate supply and aggregate demand
    in, 205–207, *206*
    monetary growth and, 249–250
    of money, 203–204
Quintiles, Lorenz curve plotted in, 594

Race, income inequality and, 600
Rapoport, Anatol, 482
Rate of return on capital, 583
Rate regulation, 494–495
Rational consumer behavior, 363
    income and substitution effects and, 371
    indifference curves and, 381
Rational expectations, 270
    gradualist policy and, 263–264
    inflation and, 253–254
Rational expectations economists, 277, 278
Rational expectations theory, activist policy
    and, 280
Rationing, equilibrium price and, 59–60
Raw materials, 302, 458
Rawls, John, 603, 610
Rawlsian equality in distributive justice, 603
Reagan, Ronald, 80, 174, 243, 575
Real-balance effect, 146
    on aggregate demand, 132–133

Real GDP, 120, *121*
  declining, deficit and, 181
  economic growth and, 287–289
  less than full employment and, 155
Real GDP per capita
  economic growth and, 287–289
  as indicator of economic development, 289
Real GNP, 303
Real GNP per capita, 303
Real interest rates, 252, 253
Real-output determination, 161
Real sector, monetary sector and, 205
Real wages, 544–545
  purchasing power of, 545
  of women, 558
Recession, anticipating, activist policy and, 278
Recession phase of business cycle, 105, *106*
Reciprocal Trade Agreements Act of 1934, 322
Recognition lag, 242
  in fiscal policy, 183
Recovery stage, of business cycle, 105, *106*
Rectangles, areas of, 27, *27*, 28
Redistribution of income by inflation, 101–102, 105
Regressive taxes, 77, 78
Regulation
  in economic interests of regulated companies, 499
  effects of, 498
  lags in, 496, 498
  of monopoly power, 494–498, *496*
  of prices, 494–496
    effects of, 498
  scope of, 494
Regulatory approach to environmental protection, 625
Regulatory lag in price regulation, 496, 498
Related goods, prices of, demand curve and, 52
"Relationship Between Unemployment and Rate of Change of Money Wage Rates in the United Kingdom, 1861–1957, The" (Phillips), 250
Relationships
  maximum and minimum values of, 24, 28
  showing in graphs, 20, *21*
Relative poverty standard, 605, 610
Relative prices, 44
  agricultural
    declining, 514–516, *515*
    shifts in demand, 516
    shifts in supply, 515–516
    shifts in supply and demand, 516, *518*
  buying and selling decisions and, 33
  calculating, 33
  money and, 198
  money prices and, 32–33
  substitution and, 34
  See also Price(s)
Relative productivity changes, exchange rates and, 330
Rent, 585–588, 591
  economic
    Babe Ruth example, 588
    other factors of production and, 587–588

monopoly, 589
  pure economic, 586–587, *587*
"Reopener clauses," 137
Required-reserve ratio, 216
Reserve components, 213
Reserve requirement(s)
  changes in, 226
  doubled, Great Depression and, 279
  of Federal Reserve System, 215–216
Reserve-requirement policy as instrument of monetary policy, 232–233
Resource(s)
  allocation of, 30–31
    by government, 83–84
    stock prices and, 411
  of business firms, 388
  economic profit and, in perfect competition, 446
Resource allocation methods, 638
Restriction of interest payments, in bank regulation, 215
Revenue(s)
  from higher prices, 349
  marginal, 438, 459–460
  tax, 190
  total, 348, 349
Rhodes, Cecil, 487
Ricardo, David, 150, 287, 295, 303, 307–309
Right-to-work laws, 568
Rising prices, aggregate demand and, 132
Risk
  compensating differentials and, 597
  structure of interest rates and, 584
Risk, Uncertainty, and Profit (Knight), 581
Risk avoiders, 597, 603
Risk seekers, 597
Risk taking, 589, 591
Riskiness, control in bank regulation, 215
Rival firms, fears of, by monopolies, 456, 463
Robinson, E. A. G., 457
Robinson, Joan, 457, 475
Robinson-Patman Act of 1936, 502, *503*
Rockefeller, John D., 490
Roebuck, Alvah, 591
Romer, Paul, 288
Roosevelt, Franklin D., 201, 279, 389, 510
Rousseau, Jean-Jacques, 287
Rule of reason, 502–504
Russian Revolution (1917), 633

Samuelson, Paul A., 346
Sargent, Thomas, 270
Savas, E. S., 623
Saving(s), 129
  in classical theory, 151–152, *153*
  consumption and, in income/expenditure model, 156–158, *157*
  income and, *157*, 159
  increases in, deficits and, 190
  investment and, 123–124, *162*, 163–164
  as leakages of income, 166–167, *167*
Saving/income schedule, *157*, 158, 169
Savings accounts, 211
Sawers, David, 470
Say, Jean Baptiste, 150
Say's law, 150–152, *151*, *153*, 163, 169
Scarcity, 15
  allocation and, 4
  choice and, 3–4
  law of, 3–4

Scatter diagrams, slope of, *26*, 26–27
Scherer, F. M., 470
Schumpeter, Joseph, 38, 469, 472, 490
Schwartz, Anna, 232
Sears, Richard, 591
Securities and Exchange Commission, 399, 500
Security, international capital movements and, 335
Self-correcting mechanism, 143–144, 146, 147
  demand management and, 270–271, *271*
  dependability of, 145
  discretionary monetary policy and, 237, *237*
Self-interest, 32, 363
  property rights and, 632
Self-sufficiency
  in America, *310*, 310–312, *311*
  in Europe, *311*, 311–312
  international trade and, 310–312
Sellers, shifts in supply curve and, 56–57
Senate Appropriations Committee, 273
Service(s), 115
  increased due to deregulation, 500
Service employment, decline of unionism and, 563
Sherman Antitrust Act of 1890, 501, *503*, 565
  interpretation of, 502–504
Shift(s)
  in aggregate demand, 140, *140*
  in aggregate-expenditure curve, 165
  in aggregate supply curve, 139, *140*, 146
  in agricultural labor force, 516–517
  in consumption/income curve, 160, *161*
  in cost curves, 426, *427*
  in demand curve, 51–54
  in graphs, 21, *21*, 22
  in labor supply and demand, 551–553, *552*
  in short-run Phillips curve, *260*, 260–261
  in supply and demand, relative agricultural prices and, 515–516, *518*
  in supply curve, 56–57, *57*
Shmenner, Roger W., 429
Short run, 143, 146–147
  control of money supply in, 242
  cost curves in, 417–426
  critical distinction from long run, 463
  elasticity of supply in, 355, *355*
  fixed costs in, 430
  fixed GDP in, 205
  long run and, 418–419
  monopoly equilibrium in, 460–461, *462*, 463
  in perfect competition, 451
Short-run aggregate supply (SRAS), 136–138, *138*
Short-run aggregate supply (SRAS) curve, 147
  shifts in, 146
Short-run equilibrium, short-run supply curve and, *439*, *441*, *443*, 445, *445*
Short-run macroeconomic equilibrium, 138, *139*, 147
  supply shocks and, 139, *140*
Short-run Phillips curve, 259–260, *260*, 266
  upward shifts of, *260*, 260–261
Short-run solution to poverty problem, 608

Short-run supply curve
    maximizing profit and, 437–438, *439*,
        440
    in perfect competition, 437–445
    short-run equilibrium and, *439, 441, 443,
        445, 445*
Shortage, 58
    in labor market, 558
Shrimp-boat example of law of diminishing
        returns, 420–422, *421*
Shutdown case, short-run supply curve
        and, 442, *443*
Shutdown rule, 442
Silver as commodity money, 199
Simons, Henry, 495
Simplified model of trade, 309–310, *310*
Single markets, 47
Slope, 21–27
    of aggregate demand curve, 132, *133*
    curvilinear relationships and, 23–25, *24,
        25*
    of demand curve, 383
        elasticity and, *347,* 349–350
        negative in monopoly, 459–460
    of market-demand curve, 371
    of scatter diagrams, *26,* 26–27
    of straight lines, 21–23, *21–23,* 28
Slow monetary growth, lowering infla-
        tionary expectations by, 262
Smith, Adam, 29, 32, 35–36, 38, 44, 72,
        203, 306, 307, 334, 366, 433, 455,
        487, 632, 633
Smith, B. A., 356
Smith, Robert, 576
Smoot-Hawley Tariff Act of 1930, 321,
        324–325
Social benefits, 615
Social costs, 615
Social goals
    personal income tax and, 80
    taxes and, 75
Social opportunity, price greater than mar-
        ginal cost and, 468
Social overhead capital, 299–300
Social policy, reducing income inequality
        by, 598
Social Security
    national debt and, 188
    as transfer payment, 71
Social Security Administration, 599
Social-welfare programs, spending and, 74
Socialism, 4, 5, 638
    allocation arrangements in, 632
    capitalism and, 629–638
    incentive systems in, 633
    property rights in, 632
"Soft budget constraint," 636
Soil conservation programs, 522
Sole proprietorship, 389–391, 400
Sources of poverty, in less developed coun-
        tries, 298–300
Soviet economy, inefficiencies of, 638
Spann, R. M., 356
Special interest(s), logrolling and, 85
Special-interest(s), 84
    international trade protection and, 324
Special-interest legislation, balanced budg-
        ets and, 191
Specialization, 37–41, 44
    credit markets and, 581
    exchange and, 37–39
    international trade and, 306, 313

in labor market, 544
    money and, 41
    productivity and, 39–40
    trade and, gains by, 324
Speculation
    agricultural, futures markets and, 519–
        520
    fall of Bretton Woods system and, 338–
        339
Speculators, 519
Spot (cash) market, 519–520
Sputnik, 633
SRAS (Short-run aggregate supply), 136–
        138, *138*
Stabilization policy, 268–283
    activism as choice of U.S. policymakers,
        281–282
    case for activism, 274–277
    case for nonactivism, 277–280
    instruments and activism, 271–274
    options, 269–271
    reduction in differences, 280–281
Stagflation, *97, 99–100,* 102, 104, *104,* 109,
        247, 257–261, 266
    inflation, unemployment and, 247–266
    new Phillips curve in, 258–260, *260*
    Phillips curve and, 258, *259*
        breakdown of, 258, *259*
    short-run Phillips curve in
        understanding, *259,* 261
        upward shifts of, *260,* 260–261
Staggers Rail Act of 1980, 500
Stalin, Joseph, 629, 633
Standard Oil Case, Sherman Antitrust Act
        and, 502
Stationary state, 303
    of economic growth, 295, 296–298, *297*
Steele, Henry, 141
"Sticky" money wages, 155, 169
Stigler, George J., 3, 475, 495
Stillerman, Richard, 470
Stock, 392, 407, 412
Stock exchanges, 407–408, 412
Stock indexes, 410, 412
Stock issues, 407
Stock market(s), 407–411
    irrationality of, 410–411
Stock market crashes, money supply and,
        223
Stock of money (money supply), 200
Stock price(s), *408,* 408–409
    determining, *408,* 409
    as present values, 409
    price/earnings ratios and, 409–410
Stock-price indexes, 410
Stock variable, money supply as, 201
Stockholders, 392
Stone, Gerald W., 513
Stone money (Island of Yap), 198
Store of value, money as, 198–199, 208
Straight lines, slope of, 21–23, *21–23,* 28
Strategic behavior of oligopolists, 481
Strikes, 572, 575
    for lower wages, wage/employment
        tradeoff and, 570
Structural deficit, 181
Structural unemployment, 94–95, 109
Studies in Business-Cycle Theory (Lucas),
        270
Subsistence wages in stationary state, 296
Substitute(s), 52, 344
    monopolistic competition and, 477

potential, monopolies and, 456
    price elasticity of demand and, 351
    promotion of, high monopoly profits and,
        464
Substitute factors of production, labor de-
        mand and, 551, *552*
Substitution effect, *369,* 370, 371, 385
    in backward-bending labor-supply curve,
        556, 556–557
    on consumer equilibrium, 383–384, *384*
Substitution principle, 34
Sugar bill as example of logrolling, 85
Summers, Lawrence, 109, 282
Superior innovation, Sherman Antitrust
        Act and, 503–504
Supply, 54–57
    of factors of production, 538, *539*
    shifting, relative agricultural prices and,
        515–516
    shifts in supply curve and, 56–57
    supply curve and, *55,* 55–56
Supply and demand, 46–67
    changes in equilibrium price and, 60–63
    effects of change in, 62, *63*
    equilibrium of, *51, 55,* 58–60, *59*
    example of interference with, 66–67
    markets and, 47–49
    shifting, agricultural prices and, 516, *518*
    simultaneous changes in, 63, *65*
    unconventional uses of, 63–64, 67
Supply control programs, in agriculture,
        522–523
Supply curve, *55,* 55–56, 67, *358,* 359
    of foreign exchange, 341
    shifts in, 56–57
Supply schedule, 55
Supply shocks, 254
    energy crisis (1974) as, 141
    shifts in aggregate supply curve and, 139,
        140
Supply-side economics, 185
    view of tax cuts, 185
Supply-side inflation, 100–101, 248–249,
        249, 265
    cases of, 250–251
Support price, 520
Surplus, 58
    in labor market, 558
Sustained deficits, 191
Sustained growth, 303
Sustained inflation, monetary growth and,
        249–250, *251*
Sweden
    income distribution in, 597
    labor unions in, 566
Sweeney, James L., 356
System of Logic, A (Mill), 595

Taft-Hartley Act of 1947, 568, 577
Tangent, 24
Target price in agriculture, 521
Tariffs, 315–316, 324
    explanation for, 320–321
Tax(es), 74–78, *76*
    incidence of, 77
    to internalize externalities, *619,* 619–620,
        620
    progressive and regressive, 77–78, *79*
Tax incentives, as growth-enhancing fac-
        tor, 302
Tax increases, Great Depression and, 279
Tax policy, fiscal policy and, 272

Tax reform(s), 80
Tax Reform Act of 1986, 80
Tax revenues, deficit reduction and, 190
Tax system, as automatic stabilizer, 177
Taxation, consumption and, 160
Taxol (cancer treatment), monopoly and, 461
Taylor, Harriet, 595
Taylor, Lester D., 356, 513
T-bills (treasury bills), 233
TC (Total costs), 419
Teamsters in AFL-CIO, 567
Technical standards, as nontariff barriers, 317
Technological innovation, 471
  backwardness in LDCs and, 300
  importance of diversity to, 470
  increased rate of economic growth and, 288
  shifts in supply curve and, 56
  shifts in supply in agriculture and, 516
Temporary tax increases, effects of, 183
Terkel, Studs, 154
Terms of trade, 312–313
Texaco, acquisition of Getty Oil, 397
Textiles, voluntary export restraints in, 317
Theory(ies)
  classical quantity theory of money, 203–204, 208
    aggregate demand and supply in, 205–206
    monetary growth and, 249–250
  indifference-curve, 376–385
  liquidity-preference (Keynesian), 234–235
  marginal productivity, 541
    of income distribution, 537–540, 539
  marginal-utility, 381
  oligopoly, 481–489
  rational expectations, 280
  utilitarian, 602, 610
Theory of Interest, The (Fisher), 197
Theory of Monopolistic Competition (Chamberlin), 475
Theory of Moral Sentiments, The, (Smith), 32
Theory of Political Economy, The (Jevons), 364
Theory of the Consumption Function, A (Friedman), 232
Thrift, consumption and, 160
Thrift institutions, 211–212
Thrift Institutions Restructuring Act, 500
Thunen, Johann Heinrich von, 415
Time deposits, 201
Tobacco money in colonial Virginia, 200
Tobin, James, 152, 250, 593
Tokyo Round (of multilateral trade negotiations), 323–324
Total costs (TC), 419
Total factor productivity, 292
Total revenue, price elasticities of demand and, 348
Total-revenue test, 349
Total utility, 365
Toxic Substances Control Act, 625
Trade, simplified model of (Ricardo), 309–310, 310
Trade-agreements program, GATT and, 322–324
Trade and Tariff Act of 1984, 324
Trade barriers, 315–317, 324

import quotas, 316
nontariff, 317
tariffs, 315–316
voluntary export restraints, 316–317
Trade deficit of United States, 335, 336
Trade Expansion Act of 1962, 323
Trade policies
  benefits to less developed countries, 300–301
  of United States, 321–324, 322
Trade Reform Act of 1974, 323
Trade Union Act of 1871 (United Kingdom), 566
Transaction costs, 44
  example of, 42
  information costs and, 41–43
Transfer payments, 71, 86, 117
Treasury bills (T-bills), 233
Tregarthen, Timothy, 5, 116
Trough phase, of business cycle, 105, 106
Turlington, Christy, 603

Unanticipated inflation, in rational expectations theory, 280
Uncertainty
  economic profit and, 589
  inequality and, 597
  reducing, futures markets and, 520
Uncontrollable outlays, deficit reduction and, 190
Unemployed people, 255
Unemployment, 91–96, 255–257, 265–266
  composition of labor force and, 256, 257
  defined, 92
  full employment and, 95–96
  inflation, stagflation and, 247–266
  inflationary expectations and, 262
  labor market classifications and, 91–93
  labor market search and, 95, 95
  long-run rise in, 256, 256–257
  matching people to jobs and, 255
  methods of dealing with, 109
  multiple earners and, 256
  rate of, 93
  self-liquidation of, in classical model, 156
  trends in, 96, 97
  types of, 93–95
  unemployment insurance and, 256–257
Unemployment compensation, as automatic stabilizer, 177
Unemployment insurance, inflexibility of labor market and, 155
Unemployment rate(s), 93, 109, 145, 255
Unintended consequences
  money and, 242
  principle of, 13
Unintended disinvestment, 164
Unintended investment, 164
Union(s), 562, 577
  objectives of, 568–573, 569
    collective bargaining and, 570–572, 572
    dealing with wage/employment trade-off, 569–570
    limitation of labor supply, 570, 571
    monopsony and, 572–573, 573
  See also specific unions; Labor unions; Unionism
Union contracts, inflexibility of labor market and, 155
Union legislation, 564, 567–568

Unionism
  decline of, 563–564, 564, 565
  history of, 564–565, 567
  industrial, 565, 567
  See also specific unions; Labor unions; Union(s)
Unionism and Relative Wages in the United States (Lewis), 564
Unit of value, money as, 197–198, 208
Unitary elastic demand, 348–349
United Automobile Workers in AFL-CIO, 567
United States
  comparative advantage in new products and processes, 315
  Great Depression in, 156
  income distribution in, 597
    shown by Lorenz curve, 594–595, 596
  labor unions in, 566
  payments deficit of, Bretton Woods system and, 338
  trade deficit of, 335, 336
  in world trade, 306–307
    imports and exports, 307, 308, 309
    volume of trade, 306, 308
United States Constitution, Sixteenth Amendment to, 80
United States Department of Agriculture, 516
United States government, policy toward inflation, 103
United States payments deficit, Bretton Woods system and, 338
United States Steel Corporation, Gary Dinners of, 487
Unlimited liability
  Lloyds of London and, 394
  of partners, 392
  in sole proprietorship, 390–391
Unstable monetary growth, business cycle fluctuations and, 277, 279
Upward-sloping curve, 19
Uruguay Round (of multilateral trade negotiations), 324
Usury laws, 590–591
USX Clairton Works, sale of pollution rights, 626
Utilitarian theory, 602, 610
Utilitarianism in distributive justice, 602–603
Utility, 364, 372
  demand and, 362–374
  marginal, 364, 365
  total, 365

Value
  of a good, 377–378
  of intermediaries, 400
  of leisure, omitted from GDP, 126
Value added, 118
  example of, 113, 114
Value and Capital (Hicks), 134
Variable costs (VC), fixed costs and, 419
Vault cash, 213
VC (variable costs), 419
Velocity of circulation in quantity theory, 204
Vertical mergers, Clayton Act of 1914 and, 504–505
Vietnam War, income inequality and, 599
Viner, Jacob, 495
Volcker, Paul T., 239

Volume of stock transactions, 408
Voluntariness, of unemployment, 93
Voluntary agreements
    in internalization, 618–619, *619*
    taxes as alternative to, 619–620
Voluntary export restraints, 316–317, 324
Vote trading, 72, 73

Wage(s)
    compensating differentials in, 559
    effect of unions on, 574, 576
        nonunion, 574, *574*
        union, *564*, 574, 576
    flexibility of, 137
    incentive payments and, in labor market,
        544–546
    rigidities in, aggregate supply and,
        136
    shifts in labor supply and, 551, *552*,
        553
Wage contracts in anticipation of inflation,
    101–102
Wage/employment tradeoff, 568, 577
    unions and, 569–570

strike for lower wages in, 570
Wage/price controls, 262
    for lowering inflation rate, 266
    of Nixon, 263
Wage/price inflexibilities, 275
Wage/price spiral, 254, *255*
Wage structure, 553–555
    compensating wage differentials, 553–
        554, *554*
    noncompeting groups and, 554–555
Wagner Act (National Labor Relations Act
    of 1935), 567–568, 577
Wallace, Alfred Russell, 287
Walras, Leon, 364, 435
Waste-disposal costs, 622–624, *624*, 626,
    627
Water Pollution Control Act, 625
Wealth, 595–596
    accumulating, 198–199
    consumption and, 160
Wealth of Nations (Smith), 32, 36, 307, 366,
    433
Welfare programs
    as automatic stabilizer, 177

privatization of, 43
Wheeler-Lea Act of 1938, 502, *503*
White, Lawrence J., 404
White-collar workers, decline of unionism
    and, 563
White House staff, 273
Wicksell, Johan Gustav Knut, 212
Women
    decline of unionism and, 563
    in labor force, 558
    real wages of, 558
World Bank, 292
World economy(ies)
    business cycles and, 106, *107*
    interrelation of, 106, *107*
World inflation rates, 251
World trade, competition and, 436
Wyrick, Thomas, 423

Yakutia diamonds, DeBeers Company and,
    487

Zero growth rate in stationary state, 296
Zero inflation, 265